Diplomatic Studies in
Latin and Greek Documents
from the Carolingian Age

Also by Luitpold Wallach

Berthold of Zwiefalten's Chronicle, reconstructed and edited
Alcuin and Charlemagne: Studies in Carolingian History and Literature
Liberty and Letters: The Thoughts of Leopold Zunz
*The Classical Tradition: Literary and Historical Studies in Honor of
Harry Caplan*, editor

Diplomatic Studies in Latin and Greek Documents from the Carolingian Age

LUITPOLD WALLACH

University of Illinois at Urbana

Cornell University Press

ITHACA AND LONDON

First published 1977 by Cornell University Press.
Published in the United Kingdom by Cornell University Press Ltd.,
2–4 Brook Street, London W1Y 1AA.

International Standard Book Number 0–8014–1019–3
Library of Congress Catalog Card Number 76–28027
Printed in the United States of America
*Librarians: Library of Congress cataloging information
appears on the last page of the book.*

To Barbara

uxori carissimae

Preface

Of the great events that confronted Charlemagne's rule during the last decade of the eighth century, the three most important, in addition to his incessant military campaigns, were certainly the controversy over the worship of images inaugurated by the decisions of the Council of II Nicaea, 787, the adoptionist Spanish heresy advocated by Felix of Urgel and Elipand of Toledo, and last but not least his recognition as emperor at Rome on Christmas Day of the year 800. Frankish reaction to these happenings has been one of the main interests in my studies in Carolingian historical documents.

Antiadoptionist documents, written by Alcuin for Charlemagne and the Frankish episcopate assembled at the Frankfurt Synod of 794, are dealt with in Chapter IX of my book *Alcuin and Charlemagne: Studies in Carolingian History and Literature*. The present volume deals with the two other actions, namely, the official Frankish rejection of the Byzantine image-worship through the *Libri Carolini*, written by Alcuin for Charlemagne, and the latter's recognition as emperor. My studies in the last-named historical development led to my realization (Chapters XV–XVI) that the well-known oath of purgation ascribed by historians for centuries to Pope Leo III is a forgery from the middle of the ninth century that is somehow tied up with the *Pseudo-Isidorian Decretals*, and that moreover Leo III was never tried by the Roman Synod held during the month of December in the year 800. Thus, the most significant single historical event in the medieval political development of Western Europe, the "coronation" of Charlemagne as emperor and Leo III's participation in it, appears in a new light that is closer to historical truth. My interest in the *Libri Carolini*, the most important literary product of the Carolingian Renaissance, has produced the collection of studies (Chapters I–XIV) which may be looked upon as prolegomena to the critical edition of Charlemagne's *Libri Carolini* that has occupied me largely during the past decade. The results of this preoccupation are not only the second and the third parts of this volume, but also Part One, since Hadrian I's *Synodica* of 785 (*JE* 2448) is one of the basic sources of the Caroline Books. The exposure in Part Three of the fiction of Theodulph of Orléans' alleged authorship of the *Libri Carolini* was a concomitant and necessary task.

I am indebted to the following for permission to reproduce some of my earlier pertinent studies:

The editors of *Traditio* and H. G. Fletcher of Fordham University Press for Chapter I, "The Greek and Latin Versions of II Nicaea and the *Synodica* of Hadrian I (*JE* 2448)," *Traditio* 22, 1966, and for Chapter XV, "The Genuine and the Forged Oath of Pope Leo III," *Traditio* 11, 1955;

The President and Fellows of Harvard College and Harvard University Press for Chapter XVI, "The Roman Synod of December 800 and the Alleged Trial of Leo III," *Harvard Theological Review* 49, 1956, and for Chapter V, first published under the title "Ambrosii verba retro versa e translatione Graeca," *Harvard Theological Review* 65, 1972;

Professor Sesto Prete and the publisher Bernard M. Rosenthal, Inc., for Part Two, Introduction, and Chapter III, the partial reproduction of "The Unknown Author of the *Libri Carolini*: Patristic Exegesis, Mozarabic Antiphons, and the *Vetus Latina*," in *Didascaliae: Studies in Honor of Anselm M. (Cardinal) Albareda* (New York, 1961);

Cornell University Press for Chapter IV, "The *Libri Carolini* and Patristics, Latin and Greek: Prolegomena to a Critical Edition," in *The Classical Tradition: Literary and Historical Studies in Honor of Harry Caplan* (Ithaca, N.Y., 1966);

Dr. R. W. Fuchs of the Anton Hiersemann Verlag, Stuttgart, Germany, and Professors Friedrich Prinz, Franz-Josef Schmale, Ferdinand Seibt, the editors of *Die Geschichte in der Gesellschaft: Festschrift für Karl Bosl zum 65. Geburtstag* (Stuttgart, 1974), for

Chapter II, "The Testimonia of Image-Worship in Hadrian I's *Synodica* of 785 (*JE* 2448)," for Chapter VII, "*Actus Silvestri, Libri Carolini*, and the *Constantine Donation*," and for the section Q of Chapter IV, subtitled "Hadrian I's *Synodica JE* 2449 and the *Quinisextum*, c. 82'';

Professor Horst Fuhrmann, President of the Monumenta Germaniae Historica (Munich, Germany), and Dr. Gottwald of the Böhlau Verlag, Köln am Rhein, for Chapter VI, the English original of the German translation of "Ambrosiaster und die *Libri Carolini*," in *Deutsches Archiv für Erforschung des Mittelalters* 29, 1973.

I am furthermore indebted to the Bibliothèque Nationale and to the Bibliothèque de l'Arsenal (both at Paris), as well as to the Biblioteca Apostolica Vaticana at Rome, for providing me with microfilms and photostats of Latin and Greek manuscripts, and for permission to use them in my studies (see Chapters IV, V, IX). The Biblioteca Apostolica Vaticana granted permission to reproduce folia from *Vaticanus Latinus 7207* and Vaticanus Ottobonianus Graecus 85, and in 1969 provided me upon request with a photographed copy of the *Vaticanus Latinus 7207*. The condition of this manuscript's fol. 158 (see Chapter VIII n. 6) was verified for me through the good offices of the Vaticana's Prefect, Professor Alfonso Stickler, S.D.B., who generously supplied me with good copies of the folium. The Universitätsbibliothek Würzburg (Germany) through its director, Dr. H. Thurn, renewed the permission to publish the facsimiles for Chapter XV.

Part Three and the Chapters VIII–XIV are published here for the first time, also the sections E 1, F 1, and R of Chapter IV. Chapter XVI originally appeared in the *Harvard Theological Review* 49, 1956, and is offered in a materially enlarged version.

Changes and minor and larger additions occur in all previously published chapters.

The work has been brought to publication with the generous assistance of a subvention from the Research Board of the Graduate College of the University of Illinois at Urbana.

An appointment as Associate in the Center for Advanced Study at the University of Illinois at Urbana during the academic year 1969/70 was of great help to my studies.

I am greatly indebted to friends and colleagues: to Professor James Hutton, Cornell University, Ithaca, New York, and to

Professor Joseph Trahern, Jr., University of Illinois at Urbana, for their critical reading of the manuscript and for some valuable suggestions which they have contributed; to Professor Heinrich von Fichtenau, Universität Wien, Austria, and Direktor of the Institut für österreichische Geschichtsforschung, for information communicated to me through letters (see Chapters XIII and XVI); to Professor Don M. Randel, Cornell University, for discussing with me Mozarabic antiphonaries and manuscripts (see Chapters XI and XII); to Professor Gerald M. Browne, University of Illinois at Urbana, for the coreading of the galleys. My thanks are extended to the staff of Cornell University Press for the care accorded to a complex book manuscript.

The volume is dedicated to my wife, Dr. Barbara P. Wallach, my research assistant during the academic year 1973/74, not only because I wish to thank her for dedicating her first book to me, but also because she realizes that she has to share me and my time with Clio.

LUITPOLD WALLACH

Urbana, Illinois
October 1976

Contents

Plates

(following page 208)

PART ONE

Pope Hadrian I's *Synodica* of 785 to the Byzantine Emperors and the Controversy on the Images in the Frankish Kingdom and in the West

Hadrian I's *Synodica* of 785 (*JE* 2448),* addressed to the Byzantine Emperors Irene and her son Constantine VI, which encouraged the rulers in their planned restoration of image-worship, is one of the most important official Latin documents of the eighth century.[1] In the East, it became in 787 the basis of the discussions at the Seventh Ecumenical Council (II Nicaea), which restored the worship of images in Byzantium. In the West, the Franks and Charlemagne based their rejection of image-worship and of II Nicaea on certain sections of the *Synodica* which were critically discussed in the Frankish *Capitulare adversus Synodum* of ca. 788–89, as well as in Hadrian I's refutation of this lost capitulary, whose

---

* See in general Harry Bresslau, *Handbuch der Urkundenlehre für Deutschland und Italien* I (2nd ed. Leipzig, 1912), II (1915–31); A. de Boüard, *Manuel de diplomatique française et pontificale* I: *Diplomatique générale* (Paris, 1929); A. Giry, *Manuel de diplomatique* (2nd ed. Paris, 1925); C. Paoli et G. C. Bascapè. *Diplomatica* (Firenze, 1942); G. Tessier, *Diplomatique royale française* (Paris, 1962); also Rudolf von Heckel, "Der Ursprung des päpstlichen Registerwesens," *Archiv für Urkundenforschung* 1 (1908), and Peter Classen, "Kaiserreskript und Königsurkunde," *Archiv für Diplomatik* 1 (1955), 84–87.

[1] Ed. J. D. Mansi, *Sacrorum Conciliorum Nova et Amplissima Collectio* XII (Florence, 1767), 1055–76D; C. Baronius, *Annales Ecclesiastici* 13, ed. A. Theiner (Barri-Ducis, 1868), 171a–178b; partly in J. P. Migne, *PL* 96.1215C–1234C; A. Gaudenzi, "La Vita Adriani Papae," *Bulletino dell' Istituto Italiano* 36 (1916), 297–310, an insert from Anastasius Bibliothecarius' translation of the Greek *Acta* of II Nicaea, as correctly surmised by Th. R. von Sickel, "Die Vita Hadriani Nonantulana und die Diurnus-Handschrift V," *Neues Archiv* 18 (1893), 109.

text is cited extensively in the chapter headings of the so-called *Hadrianum* (*JE* 2483) of ca. 791.[2] Greek and Latin testimonia invoked in *JE* 2448 in favor of image-worship are rebuked in Charlemagne's *Libri Carolini*,[3] the official Frankish protest against II Nicaea. Finally, numerous fragments of the *Synodica*'s text, especially from its catena of patristic testimonia, were inserted into the *Libellus Synodalis* of the Paris Synod of 825.[4]

The textual transmission of *JE* 2448—whose size is that of a small treatise[5]—is inseparably tied up with the transmission of the Greek *Acta* of II Nicaea and its Latin versions, of which the first (about 788), the so-called *First Latin Nicaenum*, originated at Rome upon the request of Hadrian I, while a second Latin version, of 873, was dedicated by Anastasius Bibliothecarius to John VIII. Discrepancies between the abridged Greek version of *JE* 2448 inserted into the Greek proceedings of II Nicaea, *actio* II, and the fuller Latin version of the *Synodica* as offered in Anastasius' Latin translation of the synodal acts, have led to the mistaken assumption[6] that the Bibliothecarius' transmission actually preserves the original text of *JE* 2448 intact. But as I shall show,[7] the assumption is not borne out by the available evidence, notwithstanding the fact that Anastasius indeed supplies a long section of *JE* 2448 which is missing in the Greek translation of the document. The complex textual history of Hadrian's *Synodica* of 785 can be understood only if the Latin original of *JE* 2448 and its shortened, and otherwise adulterated, Greek version are investigated in the context of their common transmission in the Greek and Latin versions of the Acts of II Nicaea. This approach obviously depends on the procedure followed by the ancient ecumenical councils when dealing with official Latin documents, secular and ecclesiastical, that were inserted into the Greek record of their proceedings.

[2] See the edition of the *Hadrianum* by Karl Hampe in *MGH, Epistolae* 5 (Karolini Aevi 3; Berlin, 1899), 5–57.

[3] Cf. Chapters II and IV.

[4] Ed. A. Werminghoff, *MGH, Concilia* 2.2. (Aevi Karolini 1.2; Hannover and Leipzig, 1908), 473–551, including the *Epitome*.

[5] See n. 1 above.

[6] Cf., e.g., Levison and Ostrogorsky, as cited in Chapter I n. 23, and G. Ostrogorsky, *Geschichte des byzantinischen Staates* (2nd ed. München, 1952), 149 n. 1.

[7] See Chapter IV, section II. I call the reader's attention to the fact that throughout the present volume the *cauda* of the *e caudatum* in Latin quotations *often* is either omitted or transcribed as *ae*. As a rule, punctuation and accentuation in Greek texts quoted from eighteenth- and nineteenth-century editions have been preserved.

CHAPTER I

The Greek and Latin Versions of II Nicaea, 787, and the *Synodica* of Hadrian I (*JE* 2448)

It was an established custom of synodal procedure to insert original Latin documents together with their Greek translations into the official acts of ecumenical councils, after original and translation had been read to, and endorsed by, the synodal assembly. This bilingual character of synodal *acta* is further evinced by the fact that Latin subscriptions of Roman participants in ecumenical councils survive in Greek codices, because Roman ecclesiastics used to write their approbations in Latin. Most of this evidence of the bilingual nature of synodal procedure has disappeared in Mansi's edition of conciliar acts. Some traces of the procedure are, however, still noticeable in manuscripts of the acts of earlier councils, as Eduard Schwartz has shown.[1]

In 564–566, the Roman deacon Rusticus found at Constantinople a Greek codex of the Acts of the Council of Chalcedon (451) which contained some of the Latin documents included in the Greek synodal protocols, also the Latin interventions (*interlocutiones*) of the Roman legates in attendance, and even the Latin address (*allocutio*) of Emperor Marcian delivered in *actio* VI of October 25, 451.[2]

---

[1] "Zweisprachigkeit in den Konzilsakten," *Philologus* 88 (1933), 245–53; also *Der sechste nicaenische Kanon auf der Synode von Chalkedon.* Sb. Akad. Berlin (1930), 614–16; see furthermore H. Steinacker, "Die römische Kirche und die griechischen Sprachkenntnisse des Frühmittelalters," *MIOEG* 62 (1954), 28–66.

[2] See Eduard Schwartz, *Acta conciliorum oecumenicorum* [= *ACO*] II.3.3 (Berlin-Leipzig, 1937), p. xviii, with a list of all the relevant *adnotationes Rustici*, from *ACO* II.3.1 (1935), 40.16 (first intervention of the legates) to II.3.2 (1936), 409.10ff. (the imperial allocution); also Schwartz, *Aus den Akten des Konzils von Chalkedon*, Abh. Akad. München 32.2 (1925), 13ff.

The *Collectio Atheniensis*, saec. XIII, of the Acts of the Ecumenical Council of Ephesus (431) preserves in the Greek synodal records
a Latin document and its Greek translation, as well as some Latin
subscriptions to the Acts by certain Roman participants. The
Latin letter of one Flavius Dionysius, *magister utriusque militiae per
orientem*, addressed to the *consularis* Theodorus of the Province of
Cyprus, was read during a session of the synod. The reading of the
Latin original was immediately followed by the public reading of
its ἑρμηνεία.[3] The technique observed by the synodal meeting is
rather simple. One Reginos presents the Latin *epistola* to the assembly, which then decides that it be read publicly. Thereupon the
Latin document, πρόσταγμα, and then its ἑρμηνεία, are recited
before the assembly, and original and translation are both inserted
into the synodal record, which reads as follows:[4]

Ῥηγῖνος ἐπίσκοπος εἶπεν · Ἐπειδὴ καὶ πρόσταγμα ἐπιφερόμεθα τοῦ . . . .
Διονυσίου γραφὲν πρὸς τὸν λαμπρότατον ἄρχοντα τῆς ἐπαρχίας, ἀξιῶ
γενέσθαι αὐτοῦ τὴν ἀνάγνωσιν.

   Ἡ ἁγία σύνοδος εἶπεν · Ἀναγινωσκέσθω καὶ τὸ τοῦ μεγαλοπρεπε-
στάτου Διονυσίου πρόσταγμα.
FLAVIUS DIONYSIUS, etc. [pp. 119.30–120.10: *the Latin epistola*]. Ἑρμηνεία
[p. 120. 11–31: *the Greek translation of the Latin epistola*].

The *Collectio Vaticana* of the *Acta* of Ephesus (431) contains the
following discussion concerning the insertion of a Latin document
into the Greek synodal acts.[5] Philip, one of the legates, submitted
a Latin *epistola* of Pope Celestine to the assembly and asked that
it be read into the synodal record (. . . τῆι ἁγίαι συνόδωι ἀναγνωσθῆναι
κελεύσατε καὶ τοῖς ἐκκλησιαστικοῖς ὑπομνήμασιν ἐνταγῆναι). The Latin
letter is then read publicly by the notary Siricius (νοτάριος τῆς ἁγίας
καθολικῆς ἐκκλησίας πόλεως Ῥωμαίων ἀνέγνω).

After this reading (καὶ μετὰ τὸ ἀναγνωσθῆναι Ῥωμαϊστὶ), Juvenal of
Jerusalem suggests that the Latin document be inserted into the

---

[3] Schwartz, *ACO* I.1.7 (Berlin-Leipzig, (1929), 119f.; see the Latin *subscriptiones*
interspersed among the Greek signatures of the synodal proceedings, *ibid.* 111–117,
passim.
   [4] *Ibid.* 119.25–120.31.
   [5] Schwartz, *ACO* I.1.3 (1927), 53.31–54.24. In 866, Nicholas I referred to this
discussion, *epist.* 90: " . . . ita ut . . . ipsa epistola cum competenti honore Latine
primitus et postea in Graecam dictionem sine ullo fuco falsitatis iam translata sit
coram synodo lecta" (ed. E. Perels, *MGH, Epistolae* 6 [Karolini Aevi 4; Berlin,
1925], 492.39–493.4).

Greek acts (γράμματα... ἔχοντα ἐμφερέσθω τοῖς πραττομένοις). Thereupon the assembly requests that the letter be returned and translated into Greek, and the translation be read to the assembly (πάντες οἱ εὐλαβέστατοι ἐπίσκοποι ᾔτησαν ἑρμηνευθῆναι τὴν ἐπιστολὴν καὶ ἀναγνωσθῆναι).

The procedure followed at II Nicaea in 787 with regard to the public reading of Hadrian's *Synodica JE* 2448 is identical with that employed at Ephesus in 431.

During the first session of the synod, the letter (*sacra*) of the Emperors Constantine VI and Irene addressed to the assembly of II Nicaea is read (Mansi XII.1002D–1007B; Dölger, *Reg.* 346).[6] Toward the end of this document the arrival of *JE* 2448 at the court is mentioned: two papal legates had brought it to Constantinople. The *sacra* orders the public reading of the *synodica* in accordance with synodal custom (Mansi XII.1007B: κατὰ τὸν συνοδικὸν θεσμὸν εἰς ἐπήκοον πάντων ἀναγνωσθῆναι.) Its recital is put on the agenda of *actio* II, and the imperial official *a secretis* Leontius (Mansi XII.1054DE) reminds the assembly of the earlier reference to the document in the imperial *sacra*. He then asks for the synod's instruction concerning the Latin original of *JE* 2448 (Mansi XII.1054D–1055A):

1. Λεόντιος ὁ εὐκλεέστατος βασιλικὸς ἀσηκρῆτις εἶπε · μέμνηται ἡ... σύνοδος, ὡς .. γράμματα ἀνεγνώσθησαν τῶν, .. βασιλέων ἡμῶν, ἐν οἷς ἐνεφέρετο μνήμη τῶν συνοδικῶς ἀποσταλέντων γραμμάτων παρὰ τοῦ.... πάπα τῆς πρεσβυτέρας Ῥώμης ...
2. Ἡ ἁγία σύνοδος εἶπεν · ἀναγνωσθήτωσαν οἱ λίβελλοι τοῦ... πάπα Ἀδριανοῦ τῆς πρεσβυτέρας Ῥώμης.
3. Καὶ ἀνέγνω Νικηφόρος ὁ εὐκλεέστατος βασιλικὸς ἀσηκρῆτις.
4. Ἑρμηνεία γραμμάτων Ῥωμαϊκῶν Ἀδριανοῦ τοῦ ἁγιωτάτου πάπα τῆς πρεσβυτέρας Ῥώμης.

Upon the motion of the imperial secretary Leontius, the synodal assembly endorses the public reading of the Latin original and its Greek translation. Nicephorus, the other imperial official *a secretis*,[7] first reads the Latin original of Hadrian's *Synodica*. This is plainly stated in the Greek synodal *Acta* (above section 3); afterward the

---

[6] Franz Dölger, *Regesten der Kaiserurkunden des oströmischen Reiches: I. Teil: Regesten von 565–1025* (München-Berlin, 1924).

[7] The later patriarch; see P. J. Alexander, *The Patriarch Nicephorus of Constantinople* (Oxford, 1958), 6of.

Byzantine translation of *JE* 2448 is read (above section 4). Although the Greek Acts preserve here the original synodal custom of reading first the Latin document and then its Greek translation, Anastasius Bibliothecarius in his translation of the Greek synodal Acts omitted the reading of the Latin original of *JE* 2448, and translated the Greek sections 3 and 4, cited above, as follows (Mansi XII.1056A):

Et legit Nicephorus inclytus et regius a secretiis interpretationem literarum latinarum Hadriani papae Romani.

What has been said of the public reading of Hadrian's Latin *Synodica* applies also—*mutatis mutandis*—to the reading, in the Latin original and in its Greek translation, of the letter sent about the same time by Hadrian I to the Patriarch Tarasius of Constantinople (*JE* 2449) on the occasion of Tarasius' announcement of his election to the patriarchate.

Following the Greek version of the *Synodica JE* 2448, the Greek Acts of II Nicaea record a brief discussion by the assembly testifying to its authenticity (Mansi XII.1075D–1078A). Then Cosmas, deacon, notary, and *cubuclesius* on the patriarch's staff, reports that a letter, γράμματα (*JE* 2449), had been sent by Hadrian I to Tarasius, "our ecumenical patriarch," and the assembly asks that it be read publicly (Mansi XII.1078B). The aforementioned Cosmas then reads the Latin original of *JE* 2449 (Κοσμᾶς ὁ προειρημένος . . . ἀνέγνω) and afterward the Greek translation of the document. The mention of the reading of the Latin original is again omitted by Anastasius in his Latin translation, which conveys the mistaken impression that only the Greek version of *JE* 2449 was read publicly.

There is sufficient evidence available to prove that the original Greek Acts of II Nicaea contained in *actio* II also the Latin originals of JE 2448 and 2449, and not only the Greek versions of these *synodicae*. To be sure, this synodal procedure has not escaped the attention of historians. Erich Caspar[8] once incidentally referred to a sentence in the *Libri Carolini* drawn "aus der ursprünglichen,

---

[8] *Das Papsttum unter fränkischer Herrschaft* (Darmstadt, 1956), 54 n. 47. Caspar's posthumously edited studies, first published in *Zeitschrift für Kirchengeschichte* 54 (1935), contain a number of confusing references to the *Hadrianum* (*JE* 2483) and Hadrian I's *Synodica* 2448 which are mistakenly interchanged: instead of *JE* 2448 read 2483 on p. 78 nn. 110 and 111, p. 79 n. 116; instead of *JE* 2483 read 2448 on p. 83 n. 130, p. 84 n. 132; also, p. 84 n. 131 has *JE* 2448 in mind, but cites the text of 2483 which was never included in the Acts of II Nicaea; on p. 86 read 692 instead of 612.

den griechischen Akten [that is, of II Nicaea] beigegebenen lateinischen Version [of *JE* 2448].'' And the bilingual character of the synodal Acts of 787 was pointed out by Wolfram von den Steinen,[9] when he called attention to the fact that the two papal legates at II Nicaea subscribed the ὑπομνήματα in Latin. The record of the fourth session preserves a Ἑρμηνεία ὑπογραφῆς Ῥωμαίων, an *Interpretatio subscriptionis Romanorum* (Mansi XIII.133A–C). This indicates that the two legates subscribed in Latin and that their Latin statements of approval were then translated into Greek. The later version of the Acts of II Nicaea (printed in Mansi XIII.624C–D) reads "Petrus . . . subscripsit Romane, cuius haec est interpretatio," and thus retranslates into Latin the Greek rendering of the original Latin signatures of the legates. More evidence for the insertion of Latin original documents into the Greek Acts of II Nicaea is supplied, on the one hand, by some letters of Nicholas I and John VIII, and, on the other, by Anastasius Bibliothecarius himself—both as the dictator of some of the letters of Nicholas I issued after 862, and as the translator of the Greek Acts of II Nicaea and the Eighth Ecumenical Council (IV Constantinople, 869–870). A trace of the bilingual character of synodal *Acta* survives in the printed text of the last-mentioned synod in Mansi XVI.316A: a *libellus* is read before the assembly at first in Latin and then in the Greek translation, . . . καὶ ἀνεγνώσθη πρῶτον μὲν Ῥωμαϊστὶ εἶτα δὲ καὶ Ἑλληνιστὶ ἔχων οὕτως . . .

At Rome, in the papal *scrinium*, and at Constantinople, in the imperial chancellery and in the library of the patriarchate, complete copies of the Latin text of *JE* 2448 and its Greek version were available, both inserted into the Greek Acts of II Nicaea. This is vouched for by certain papal letters sent from Rome to Byzantium.

In 860, Nicholas I addressed to the Byzantine Emperor Michael III a letter (*epistola* 82) taking issue with the deposition of the Patriarch Ignatius of Constantinople and the rapid enthronement of the layman Photius on the patriarchal see. He refers to the precedent of the layman Tarasius, who had been criticized by Hadrian I in *JE* 2448, "cuius textum si scire vultis, in concilio [II Nicaea, 787] quod eius tempore in supradicta urbe [Constantinople] celebratum est, invenire potestis."[10] Nicholas and the

---

[9] "Entstehungsgeschichte der Libri Carolini," *Quellen und Forschungen aus Italienischen Archiven und Bibliotheken* 21 (1929–30), 24.

[10] Ed. E. Perels, *MGH, Epistolae* 6.436.

draftsman of the letter thus call the emperor's attention to that part of the Latin *Synodica JE* 2448 which, according to Anastasius' testimony, is missing in the Greek version that appears in a Byzantine codex of the Acts of II Nicaea (see at note 16 below) and had been used by Anastasius for his own translation. The text of *JE* 2448 was accessible at Rome to Nicholas, and the draftsman of *epistola* 82 (1) in the copy of the *Synodica* kept in the papal *scrinium*, (2) in the transmission of the original Greek Acts of II Nicaea, and (3) in the *First Latin Nicaenum*, produced in 788 upon the request of Hadrian I. This is also proved by Anastasius' reference to the *First Latin Nicaenum* in the Preface of his own Latin version of the Greek Acts of II Nicaea, which he dedicated in 873 to John VIII.[11]

In 862, Nicholas I in his *epistola* 86 wrote to Photius, who had referred to Tarasius' case as a precedent for the election of a layman to the patriarchate of Constantinople (" . . . De Tarasii siquidem promotione qui similiter ex laicali coetu ad patriarchatus extimplo [= extemplo] culmen promotus est, quam et vos quasi auctoritatem vestrae defensionis assumere vultis . . . "). Nicholas tells Photius that if he would carefully scrutinize the Acts of II Nicaea, he should find Hadrian's decision concerning Tarasius ("si sanctam quae apud vos tempore . . . Hadriani celebrata est synodum diligentius scrutati fueritis atque attentius intenderitis, invenietis quid in ea idem . . . decreverit . . . Dicit enim . . . "). The paraphrase that follows in Nicholas' letter employs terms which occur in *JE* 2448 (*consecrationi assensum*; *enormiter*) and in *JE* 2449 (*inordinate*);[12] thus also this letter of Nicholas I presupposes that at Constantinople the original and unabridged Latin texts of both *synodicae* were available, being included in both the Greek and Latin versions of the Acts of II Nicaea.

A third letter by Nicholas I, addressed to the Byzantine Emperor Michael III in 865 (*epist.* 88),[13] again deals with the deposition of the Patriarch Ignatius and the raising of a layman to the patriarchate. Once more the pope advises the Byzantines to consult II Nicaea and, more specifically, Hadrian's *Synodica JE* 2448—if it

[11] Ed. E. Perels and G. Laehr, *MGH, Epistolae* 7 (Karolini Aevi 5; Berlin, 1928), 416.
[12] *MGH, Epistolae* 6.448–449.
[13] *MGH, Epistolae* 6.457, and cf. 458.

has not been falsified by the *Graeci*, as the emperor is told rather bluntly. This strongly suggests that *JE* 2448 had been mutilated and falsified at Constantinople in connection with the election in 858 of the layman Photius, and not in 787, as historians have hitherto assumed.[14] Nicholas states in *epistola* 88 that the Greeks

nostrum praesidium quaesierunt, sicut synodus sub Constantino et Herene facta indicat in cuius initio [in *actio* II], id est in epistola beatae memoriae praesulis Hadriani [*JE* 2448], quantum idem pontifex illam praesumptionem qua ex laicis quidam subito tonsorantur et in episcoporum numerum exacerbate prosiliunt, damnaverit, si diligenter inquisieritis profecto invenietis—*si tamen non falsata Graecorum more*, sed sicut a sede missa est apostolica penes ecclesiam Constantinopolitanorum hactenus perseverat…

The motive that led the Byzantines to falsify the text of *JE* 2448 is quite obvious: it was done to remove all evidence of Hadrian I's criticism of the election of the layman Tarasius to the see of Constantinople. Falsification by the Byzantines of papal letters was so well known at Rome that Nicholas I's *epistola* 88 closes with a deprecation of such practices: let him be cursed who in the process of translating the letter into Greek should change the text, or either omit from it or add to it, beyond the demands dictated by Greek style (" . . . ex ea quicquam mutaverit vel subtraxerit aut superaddiderit, praeter illud quod idioma Graecae dictionis exigit").[15] The three ways by which a Latin document might be falsified in its Greek version produced by the Byzantines are here described as changes made in the context, omissions from, or additions to, the original text. These are indeed the kinds of falsification suffered by *JE* 2448, as we shall see in the course of the present study.

The draftsman of *epistola* 88, whom Ernst Perels believed to be Anastasius Bibliothecarius, had indeed the complete Latin text of *JE* 2448 before his eyes when composing the letter. This is proved by his quotation (p. 457.16–17) of a section from the *Synodica* (Mansi XII.1073) which is missing in its Greek version in the Greek Acts of II Nicaea. He drew this quotation in all probability from the text of *JE* 2448 inserted in the *First Latin Nicaenum*, in which he also found the quotations (p. 458.22–25) from the *Divalia* sent by Constantine VI and Irene to Hadrian I (Mansi XII.985f.).

[14] See below, notes 23 and 24, and Dölger, cited in n. 36.
[15] See *MGH, Epistolae* 6.487.21; also *epist.* 91, p. 533, *epist.* 89, p. 488.9, *epist.* 90, p. 492.20–38, *epist.* 93, p. 541.36–40.

The connection of the abbreviated and mutilated version of
JE 2448 (Mansi XII.1055–72, and 1073–76) with the Photian
controversy should become obvious from the evidence submitted
below.

Anastasius Bibliothecarius' Latin translation of the Greek Acts
of the Seventh Ecumenical Council (II Nicaea) is based on a
Byzantine manuscript saec. IX, which offered *JE* 2448 in abbreviated and intentionally mutilated Greek and Latin versions
(Mansi XII.1055–72). The existence of such a manuscript falsified
by the Byzantines is expressely mentioned by him in the Preface to
his Latin translation of the Acts of the Eighth Ecumenical Council
(IV Constantinople, 869–870),[16] a work which he dedicated to
Hadrian II in 871. Anastasius saw the falsified versions of *JE* 2448
in all probability at Constantinople when attending the Council of
869–870. He wrote:

Porro in septimae synodi codice, quia saepe contra kanones Constan-
tinopoli ex neophytis antistites provehuntur et co tempore Tarasius ex
laicis patriarcha fuerat ordinatus, ita epistolam beatac recordationis papae
Hadriani existimant [*sc.* Graeci] transcribendam, ut nihil in ea ex his quae
ad praedictum praesulem vel contra neophytos idem sanctissimus pontifex
scripserat, vel *scriptum* vel *translatum Grece* repperiatur.

The Byzantine codex of the Greek Acts of II Nicaea which
Anastasius then had before his eyes originally contained the Latin
text of *JE* 2448 and its Greek translation, both complete versions,
unabridged. He therefore could say that in this codex of the Greek
Acts of 787 the Latin original (*scriptum*) of Hadrian's *Synodica* and
its Greek translation (*translatum Grece*) had been re-edited by the
Byzantines (*epistolam . . . existimant transcribendam*) in such a fashion
that nothing could be found in it (*repperiatur*) concerning Tarasius
and the neophytes; that is, the section of *JE* 2448, as printed in
Mansi XII.1073–76, was deleted in both versions. This proves
again that originally the Acts of II Nicaea contained in *actio* II
the Latin original of *JE* 2448 and its complete Greek translation.
The reason for the falsification of original *and* translation, presumably during the period of the Photian controversy was, as I
have indicated above, Hadrian I's earlier criticism (in 785) of the
uncanonical election of the layman Tarasius, the uncle of Photius,
as patriarch of Constantinople. The period during which *JE* 2448

[16] *MGH, Epistolae* 7.415.2–12.

would have been falsified in Byzantine codices of the Greek Acts
of II Nicaea probably begins with the election as patriarch in 858
of the layman Photius, professor at the University of Constantinople
and president of the imperial chancellery; Anastasius' *Constantinopolitanum* of 871 suggests the *terminus post quem non*.

Anastasius' words in the Preface, just cited, illustrate the statement in his Latin translation of the Greek Acts of II Nicaea concerning the mutilated versions of *JE* 2448 in the Byzantine codex
on which his translation rests. We read (Mansi XII.1073–74):

Ab hinc [1073A] usque ad finem huius epistolae (1076D) codex Graecus
non habet. Graeci namque, quia eodem tempore ex laicis fuerat Constan-
tinopoli patriarcha factus, ne publice ab Apostolica sede argui videretur,
et adversus eum tamquam reprehensione dignum, haereticis repugnandi
occasio praeberetur, ac per hoc synodi, cui intererat, utilitas excluderetur:
ea quae sive de non facienda laicorum promotione, sive de caeterarum
praesumptionum redargutionibus subsequuntur, in synodo hac nec recitari,
nec actis inseri passi sunt.

This statement hardly refers to the election of Tarasius and the
Seventh Ecumenical Council of 787. It fits much better the election
of the layman Photius as patriarch and the resulting controversy
between Rome and Constantinople that lasted from 858 until the
final recognition by John VIII in 879. This conclusion is supported
by additional evidence which will be discussed later.

Epistola 208, sent to Constantinople in August 879 by John VIII
after he had finally recognized Photius as patriarch, quotes the passage from the last section of *JE* 2448 (Mansi XII.1074D–1075B)—
omitted in falsified Byzantine MSS of the Acts of II Nicaea—
concerning the uncanonical election of the layman Tarasius as
patriarch.[17] This is the main passage in Hadrian's *Synodica* referred
to by Nicholas I in his *epistolae* 82 (of 860), 86 (862), and 88 (865)
when criticizing the election in 858 of the layman Photius as patriarch of Constantinople.

The presence of the complete, unabridged Greek translation of
JE 2448 in the Greek Acts of II Nicaea is presupposed also by a
tenth-century gloss to Nicholas I's *epistola* 86 found in the Vatican
MSS lat. 4965 (olim Capituli Veronensis) and lat. 5749 (olim S.

---

[17] See John VIII, *epist*. 208, ed. E. Caspar, *MGH, Epistolae* 7.176–181; the
section in the Tarasius passage, p. 178.22–37, is an unacknowledged quotation in
JE 2448 from Gregory the Great's *Registrum epistolarum* 9.215; see below, D, and
Chapter IV n. 96.

Columbani de Bobio) :[18]

Sciendum est quia quicquid Hadrianus papa tunc contra Tarasium scripsit apud Grecos in actis illius septime synodi non habetur. Quia enim ille de laicali catalogo subito est factus episcopus, quicquid reprehensionis in epistola repperit in synodicis actis *fautores* eius scribere minime pertulerunt, *sed hoc e codicibus eradentes* sub silentio contexerunt.

The gloss—whose author is Anastasius himself—states that the section in *JE* 2448 dealing with Tarasius (Mansi XII.1073–76) had been erased in the MSS (*hoc e codicibus eradentes*), by *fautores* of Tarasius, as the glossator believes. But the information on Byzantine conditions provided by Anastasius and the three epistles by Nicholas I, previously discussed, make it more plausible that the deletion of the section on Tarasius from the MSS of the Greek Acts of 787 was the work of the *fautores* of Photius, or—at the worst—of Photius himself.

A further argument for connecting the adulterated transmission of Hadrian I's *JE* 2448 with the Photian controversy can be found in the falsified Greek versions of the *epistolae* 207, 208, 209 (all of August 879) addressed by John VIII to the Emperor Basil and his sons, to the bishops of the Eastern patriarchates, and to the re-instated Photius himself. The Acts of the Photian Council of 879 contain these three letters in a "Versio graeca adulterata auctore Photio patriarcha," as Erich Caspar plainly says.[19] In *epistola* 209, Hadrian I is substituted for Hadrian II, *callide* according to Caspar (p. 185 n. 2), because Photius wanted to omit mention of the Eighth Ecumenical Council (IV Constantinople, 869–870) upon whose decision he had been deposed during the pontificate of Hadrian II.

It has become quite obvious in the course of the present investigation that the textual history of Hadrian's *Synodica JE* 2448 can be understood only if seen in the light of the transmission of the Greek and Latin versions of the synodal *Acta* of II Nicaea. An independent transmission of the *Synodica*'s Latin original outside the MSS of the Acts of 787 does not seem to be extant. The *Libellus Synodalis* of the Paris Synod of 825 quotes the patristic testimonia of image-worship in *JE* 2448, following the Latin original of the

---

[18] See Perels, *MGH, Epistolae* 6.448.31–35. Cf. now Claudio Leonardi, "Le glosse di Anastasio Bibliotecario," *Studi Medievali*, ser. III, 8 (1967), 176, where the identical gloss appears under no. 55; see also Daniel Stiernon, "Autour de Constantinople IV (869–870)," *Revue des études byzantines* 25 (1967), 155–188.

[19] *MGH, Epistolae* 7.166, 176, 181.

Synodica inserted in the *First Latin Nicaenum*. The text of *JE* 2448 inserted in the *Vita Hadriani Nonantulana*[20] is derived from the version in Anastasius' Latin translation of II Nicaea.

The diplomatic history of *JE* 2448 can now be surveyed from the *Synodica*'s first appearance in 785 to its version in Anastasius' Latin translation of the Acts of II Nicaea dedicated in 873 to John VIII. Taking into account the administrative procedure of depositing copies of official documents in the papal *scrinium* at Rome, in the imperial chancellery, and in the patriarchal library at Constantinople, as well as in Charlemagne's palatine archives of the royal chancellery, we arrive at the following copies of *JE* 2448 and the sundry versions of the Greek Acts of II Nicaea:

A (785): the Latin original of *JE* 2448 sent by Hadrian I to the Byzantine Emperors Constantine VI and Irene.

α (785): the copy of A deposited in the papal *scrinium* at Rome, used by the Roman translator (C) of the Greek Acts of II Nicaea (*β*), by Hadrian I in the *Hadrianum* (*JE* 2483), by Nicholas I and the *dictator* of his correspondence, and by Anastasius Bibliothecarius.

β (787): the Greek Acta of II Nicaea with the Latin original of A and its Byzantine translation in *actio* II.

β1: a codex of *β*, deposited in the patriarchal library at Constantinople.

β2: a codex of *β*, deposited in the imperial chancellery at Constantinople.

β3: a codex of *β*, brought to Rome by the two papal legates attending II Nicaea together with a *sacra* of Constantine VI and Irene, addressed to Hadrian I.

C (788): the first Latin translation of *β* on the basis of *β*3, the so-called *First Latin Nicaenum*, produced at Rome upon the order of Hadrian I;[21] it contained, in *actio* II, *JE* 2448 in the version of A (see above), probably as transmitted in *β*3, or as based upon a copy of *a* (see above).

C1 (788): a codex of C, deposited in the papal *scrinium*; this must have been the copy from which the draftsman of the *Hadrianum* (*JE* 2483) derived his citations of the *First Latin Nicaenum*; in all probability Anastasius (below: D) used the same codex for his translation.

C2 (788–789): a codex of C, sent by Hadrian I to Charlemagne, as Hincmar of Rheims reports (*PL* 126.360); this codex was kept in the

---

[20] Ed. A. Gaudenzi, *art. cit.* (see Part One, n. 1 above); *ibid.* pp. 296–297 see the *Divalia*, ed. Mansi XII.984–985.

[21] See *Liber Pontificalis*, ed. L. Duchesne (Paris, 1886–92; reprint: Paris, 1955), I, 512, and the comments by von den Steinen, *op. cit.* (n. 9 above), 11ff. I discount as a later concoction the report by Roger de Wendover (von den Steinen 12 n. 3) that Charlemagne had received the *Acta* of II Nicaea from Constantinople, and that he sent them to Alcuin in England, who wrote an *epistola* against them.

chancellery of the Frankish king, and was the source of the Frankish documents quoting II Nicaea: the *Capitulare adversus Synodum*, the *Libri Carolini*, and the *Libellus Synodalis* of the Paris Synod of 825.

β4x (ca.858–871): a codex of β with *falsified* Latin and Greek versions of *JE* 2448 which originated at a time between the election of Photius (858) as patriarch of Constantinople and Anastasius' dedication in 871 of his Latin translation of the *Constantinopolitanum* of 869–870 to Hadrian II.

D (873): Anastasius Bibliothecarius' Latin translation of β4x; C1 (above) and *a* (above) were available to him and were utilized for his own improved rendering.

The textual history of Hadrian I's *Synodica JE* 2448 can be viewed in the following stemma:

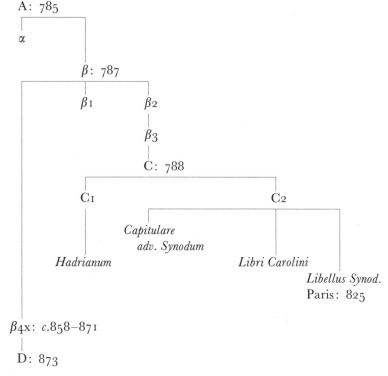

A: 785

α

β: 787

β1 β2

β3

C: 788

C1   C2

Capitulare
adv. Synodum

Hadrianum   *Libri Carolini*

Libellus Synod.
Paris: 825

β4x: *c.*858–871

D: 873

The Byzantine manuscript of the Greek Acts of II Nicaea used by Anastasius as the basis of his translation contained only mutilated and internally adulterated versions of *JE* 2448 (Mansi XII.1055–72). He therefore supplemented the shortened text of the *Synodica* from the genuine version in C1 and in *a*, both of which were available to him as *bibliothecarius* in the papal *scrinium*. The *Liber Pontificalis*[22] reports that the translation of the Greek *Acta* produced upon the request of Hadrian I was kept in *sacra bibliotheca*. Anastasius' version of *JE* 2448 is therefore occasionally in agreement with quotations from the *Synodica* occurring in documents earlier than his translation of 873. Nevertheless, his version does not always offer the genuine Latin wording of the original which had been inserted in 787 into the Greek Acts, and thereafter into the translation known as *First Latin Nicaenum* (C); for Anastasius frequently rewrote the genuine Latin text of *JE* 2448 on the basis of the Byzantine-Greek translation. To use the German diplomatic term, his Latin text of the *Synodica* is in spots *verunechtet*, that is, adultered. This means that the version of *JE* 2448 printed in Mansi (XII.1055–76) is not always identical with the original text, as Wilhelm Levison and Georg Ostrogorsky[23] believed. Fragments of the original Latin text survive, however, in the *Libri Carolini*, in the *Libellus Synodalis* of the Paris Synod of 825, and in the *Hadrianum*.

The assumption that Hadrian's *Synodica* of 785 addressed to Constantine VI and Irene had been abridged and otherwise mutilated in the imperial chancellery at Constantinople[24] before the document was read publicly in 787, in *actio* II of II Nicaea, is not at all substantiated by its textual history. Nor is there any other sufficient evidence that would point to the falsification of *JE* 2448 in 787. There was not any open quarrel at II Nicaea about the earlier uncanonical appointment in 784 by the Byzantine emperors of the layman Tarasius as patriarch of Constantinople. In 787, the mutilation of *JE* 2448 in the Greek synodal *Acta* of II Nicaea would hardly have served an immediate purpose. After all, Hadrian I, though criticizing severely the uncanonical election, nevertheless gave Tarasius credit for his iconophile attitude (*JE* 2449), and confirmed his appointment as patriarch. The synod ascertained the authenticity of *JE* 2448 and 2449 (Mansi XII.1075D–1078B), and Hadrian I's two papal legates asked the patriarch and the synod to accept and assent to the contents of the two *Synodicae*.

[22] See n. 21 above.

[23] Wilhelm Levison, *Aus Rheinischer und Fränkischer Frühzeit* (Düsseldorf, 1948), 434 n. 6, and Georg Ostrogorsky, "Rom und Byzanz im Kampf um die Bilderverehrung," *Seminarium Kondakovianum* 6 (1933), 75.

[24] A. Michel, "Die Kaisermacht in der Ostkirche," *Ostkirchliche Studien* 5 (1956), 2, charges the imperial chancellery with the adulterated version of *JE* 2448; cf. also M. Jugie, *Le schisme byzantin: Aperçu historique et doctrinal* (Paris, 1941), 85f.

The author of the *Vita* of Hadrian II in the *Liber Pontificalis*[31] was less reluctant and bluntly reported the Byzantine forgeries in the Acts of 869–870. The legates attending this council, he tells us, before putting their signatures under the synodal protocols, asked Anastasius, who happened to be at Constantinople at the time, to investigate the authenticity of the Greek synodal Acts ("ne quid Greca levitas falsum suatim congesserit"). Anastasius discovered that in an epistle by Hadrian II the encomium of the German emperor had been deleted ("omne quod ad laudem serenissimi nostri Caesaris . . . adiecerat, resecatum inveniunt").[32] Thereupon the legates declared that they would not subscribe to the synodal *actiones*, unless the text of the mutilated document were restored in full, and the original letter inserted into the *gesta* of the council.

To return to *JE* 2448: we may consider its falsification, in all probability, the product of the Photian controversy. The reading before a synod held in Constantinople in 861 of a falsified papal letter of Nicholas I addressed to Emperor Michael III[33] could have provided a pattern for the Byzantine falsification of *JE* 2448 in manuscripts of the Acts of II Nicaea. Historically, Hadrian's *Synodica JE* 2448 and his two legates attending II Nicaea in 787 did not provide a precedent for the deportment of Nicholas I's *missi*, Radoald of Porto and Zachary of Anagni in Constantinople.[34] Additional incentive to remove the criticism of Tarasius' election from *JE* 2448 in the synodal record of II Nicaea in Byzantine manuscripts could have resulted from the attempts made by Photius

[31] Ed. Duchesne, II, 181–183.

[32] *Ibid.* 181, and *MGH Epistolae* 7.411.11–13.

[33] Cf. *epist.* 86, *MGH, Epistolae* 6.451.15–16; also *epist.* 85 of 862, addressed to Emperor Michael III, *ibid.* 446.8–10. Compare also in the Acts of the Eighth Ecumenical Council (IV Constantinople), translated by Anastasius, Mansi XVI.331D–334E, the abridged text of *epist.* 82 by Nicholas I, addressed to Emperor Michael, *MGH, Epistolae* 6.433–439.

[34] On Radoald and Zachary see, for instance, *epist.* 82, *ibid.* 439.12ff. and *epist.* 84, *ibid.* 441.15ff. Francis Dvornik, *The Photian Schism: History and Legend* (Cambridge, 1948), 90, relies on Baronius' *Annales ecclesiastici*, and instead of referring to Mansi XII.1055–76, misinterprets the contents and the diplomatic nature of *JE* 2448. J. Haller, *Nikolaus I. und Pseudoisidor* (Stuttgart, 1936), 277ff., in my opinion also misjudges the intentions of Hadrian I. See furthermore F. Dölger in Dölger and A. M. Schneider, *Byzanz: Wissenschaftliche Forschungsberichte* 5 (ed. Karl Hönn; Bern, 1952), 134–138, *passim*; Dvornik, "The Patriarch Photios in the Light of Recent Research," *Berichte zum XI. Internationalen Byzantinischen Kongress* (München, 1953), Section III.2, pp. 1–56, and the *Koreferat* by P. Stephanou (pp. 17–26), challenging Dvornik's theories.

in 861, and again in 867, to ratify II Nicaea as the Seventh Ecumenical Council, an endeavor he renewed at his council of 879–880 after his long-contested election as patriarch had been confirmed by John VIII.[35]

It must also have been during this period, and not in 787, that some dogmatic changes discussed by Ostrogorsky[36] were made in the context of the Byzantine-Greek version. Other discrepancies between the original Latin and the Greek versions of the Greek patristic testimonia on image-worship in *JE* 2448 are certainly traceable to the Roman draftsman of the *Synodica* and not to the falsification of *JE* 2448 in Byzantine codices.

To sum up: The Latin documents and their Greek versions, which were mutilated and falsified in the Greek *Acta* of 787 and of 869–870 were differently treated by Anastasius in his translations of 873 and 871, respectively. The papal letters falsified in the synodal proceedings of IV Constantinople were not supplemented by Anastasius in his Latin translation of the Acts after their originals, accessible to him in the *scrinium* at Rome. The falsified version of *JE* 2448, however, which he encountered in a Byzantine codex of the Acts of II Nicaea was translated and supplemented by him after the original Latin version of the *Synodica*; this was available to him either in the copy kept at the *scrinium*, or else in the *First Latin Nicaenum* (see stemma, above), whose poor Latin translation of the Greek text he intended to replace by a more exact and readable Latin version. Anastasius' supplementation (Mansi XII.1073A–1076D) of *JE* 2448 deals with that part of the *Synodica* in which Hadrian claims ecclesiastical jurisdiction over Illyricum, Calabria, and Sicily,[37] all of which had in 732–733 come under the authority of the patriarchate of Constantinople.

As has been indicated above, the *Synodica JE* 2448 as inserted in Anastasius Bibliothecarius' Latin version of the Greek *Acta* of II Nicaea was *verunechtet* by him in a number of instances. But the authenticity of *JE* 2448 as a whole cannot be questioned. As a matter of fact, it is variously confirmed by the *Diktatvergleich* of its

[35] Cf. Cyril Mango, *The Homilies of Photius* (Cambridge, Mass., 1958), 303.

[36] *Loc. cit.* (n. 23 above) especially p. 77f.; and F. Dölger, *Byzanz und die europäische Staatenwelt* (Ettal, Bavaria, 1953), 103 n. 56 on suppression by Photius in papal documents of passages referring to the primacy of Rome.

[37] See Milton V. Anastos, "The Transfer of Illyricum, Calabria, and Sicily to the Jurisdiction of the Patriarchate of Constantinople," *Silloge Bizantina in onore di Silvio Giuseppe Mercati* (Studi Bizantini e Neoellenici 9; Rome, 1957), 14–31.

protocol, context, and eschatocol, which parallels in style and diction, throughout the entire long document as transmitted by Anastasius, the numerous letters issued by Hadrian I and his predecessors. These are mainly preserved in the *Codex Carolinus*,[38] that is, Charlemagne's edition (791) of the papal letters, from the time of Gregory III to that of Hadrian, addressed to Frankish rulers, from Charles Martel to Carloman and Charlemagne. Beyond this, we also observe other parallels in diction and style between *JE* 2448 and certain formulary letters of the *Liber Diurnus*.[39]

Some testimonia from the Greek catena of image-worship inserted in *JE* 2448 which are cited in the *Libri Carolini* and other Frankish documents have been dealt with and identified elsewhere.[40] Subsequently, we list six documentary sources, some of which are quoted in *JE* 2448 without indication of borrowing and hitherto have remained largely unknown: two quotations each from Byzantine imperial letters (*sacrae*), from papal decretals, and from the synodal acts of the *Concilium Lateranense* of 769.

A. Emperors Constantine VI and Irene, *Divalia sacra*, addressed to Hadrian I, quoted in *JE* 2448, Mansi XII.1056C:

De his quippe in ipsis venerandis iussionibus vestris referebatur *quae pridem facta sunt in* vestra *regali civitate propter venerabiles imagines, qualiter qui ante* vos *regnaverunt, eas destruxerint et in inhonestate atque injuria posuerint. Utinam non illis imputetur: Melius enim illis fuisset non mittere manus eorum in ecclesiam; et quia omnis populus qui est in orientalibus partibus erraverunt, et pro sua voluntate usi sunt illis, usquequo Deus erexit* vos *regnare qui in veritate quaeritis gloriam eius, et quae tradita sunt a sanctorum apostolorum et omnium simul sanctorum magisterio tenere.* Quas reserantes, et venerabiles imagines ad vestrum piissimum imperium laudabiliter exaratas reperientes. . . .

The Greek version of *JE* 2448, Mansi XII.1055C, reads as follows:

Περὶ δὲ τῶν ἐν τῇ εὐσεβεῖ ὑμῶν κελεύσει ἐμφερομένων τῶν πρώην γενομένων ἐν τῇ ὑμετέρᾳ βασιλίδι πόλει ἕνεκεν τῶν σεβασμίων εἰκόνων τὸ ὅπως οἱ προβεβασιλευκότες ὑμῶν κατέστρεψαν καὶ ἐν ἀτιμίᾳ καὶ ὕβρει κατέθηκαν ἑαυτοὺς καὶ αὐτάς. Εἴθε μὴ λογισθείη αὐτοῖς ἡ ἁμαρτία ἐκείνη ·

---

[38] Ed. Wilhelm Gundlach, *MGH, Epistolae* 3 (Merowingici et Karolini Aevi 1; Berlin, 1892), 469–657.

[39] *Liber diurnus Romanorum pontificum*, ed. Theodor von Sickel (Wien, 1884); cf. Hans Foerster, *Gesamtausgabe* (Bern, 1958).

[40] See especially Chapters II and IV.

κρεῖττον γὰρ ἦν αὐτοῖς μὴ ἐμβαλεῖν χεῖρας αὐτῶν εἰς τὴν Ἐκκλησίαν · ὅτι
πᾶς ὁ λαὸς ὁ ὢν ἐν τοῖς ἀνατολικοῖς μέρεσιν ἐπλανήθησαν καὶ ἐν τῇ ἰδίᾳ
βουλήσει ὡς ἔδοξεν ἑκάστῳ ἐχρήσαντο αὐταῖς, ἕως οὗ ὁ Θεὸς ἤγειρεν ὑμᾶς
βασιλεύειν τοὺς ἐν ἀληθείᾳ ζητοῦντας τὴν δόξαν αὐτοῦ καὶ τὰ παραδοθόντα
παρὰ τῶν ἁγίων ἀποστόλων καὶ πάντων διδασκάλων κρατεῖν καὶ τιμᾶν
τὰς σεβασμίας εἰκόνας, τὰς διὰ τῆς ἀνοίας τῶν αἱρετικῶν κατενεχθείσας.
Ἀρτίως δὲ διὰ τῆς εὐσεβοῦς ὑμῶν κελεύσεως εὑρόντες.

The *Divalia* (Dölger, *Reg.* 341) is extant only in the Latin translation, Mansi XII.984–85. The Byzantine translator of *JE* 2448
doubtless did not produce a translation of the Latin quotation. He
naturally cited from the copy of the original which must have been
accessible to him in the imperial chancellery at Constantinople.
The section from τῶν πρώην γενομένων to . . . καὶ πάντων διδασκάλων
κρατεῖν is the only surviving fragment of the original document.
The Latin quotation—in italics—of this fragment in *JE* 2448 offers
a literal translation; only the *pluralis maiestatis* of the *Divalia* was
changed by the draftsman of the *Synodica* from the first person
(*nostra*; *nos*: Mansi XII.984) to the second person. See above the
nonitalicized pronouns *vestra* (ὑμετέρα) and *vos* (ὑμῶν, ὑμᾶς).

There are additional though brief quotations of the *Divalia* in
JE 2448, some of them appearing in that part of the *Synodica* for
which the Greek translation is not preserved (Mansi XII.1073–76).
Compare, for example, *JE* 2448, Mansi XII.1073D "sicut in vestra
serenissima iussione exaratum est: *confundatur . . . adversus eam*"
= *Divalia*, 986B.

The *Divalia* is also cited in other documents: in the *Capitulare
adversus Synodum*, the *Libri Carolini*, and the *Hadrianum*. The quotations to be found in these documents naturally represent fragments
of the first Latin translation of the *Divalia* inserted into the *First
Latin Nicaenum*. Two excerpts from the Latin version of the *Divalia*,
985B "rogamus . . . ascendat huc," and 986AB "si enim non
potuerit . . . cum sillabis," were cited in 865 by Nicholas I in
epistola 88 to the Emperor Michael (*JE* 2796; *MGH, Epistolae*
6.458.21–25).

The Latin text of the *Divalia* belonged to the dossier of docu-
ments appended to the *First* and *Second Latin Nicaenum*. Though
Anastasius Bibliothecarius was in all likelihood the *dictator* of
Nicholas' *epistola* 88, I assume that the Latin *Divalia* appended to
Anastasius' translation of the *Nicaenum* is identical with the version
in the *First Latin Nicaenum*.

B. *Sacra* of Emperor Constantine IV Pogonatos, addressed to Pope
Donus in 678, quoted without indication of source in *JE* 2448,
Mansi XII.1073B:

pia *sacra* nobis dirigere vestra dignetur imperialis potestas, quia *non est apud*
vos *partis cuiuslibet favor* aut defensio, *sed aequalitatem utrisque partibus con-*
*serva*bitis, *nullatenus necessitatem facientes in quocumque capitulo eis qui a* nobis
diriguntur quoquomodo, sed et omni honore cum munificentia competenti et susceptione
dignos eos habebitis. et si quidem utrique convenerint, ecce bene; si autem minime
convenerint, iterum cum omni humanitate eos ad nos dirigere satagetis, quia . . .

The *sacra* of Constantine IV (Dölger, *Reg.* 242) informed Donus
of the imperial decision to convene the Sixth Ecumenical Council,
which was held in 680–681 at Constantinople. This document is
the counterpart to the *Divalia* of Constantine VI by which Hadrian I
was informed of the imperial decision that the Seventh Ecumenical
Council was to be called together. When Hadrian I writes to
Charlemagne in the *Hadrianum* (*MGH, Epistolae* 5.56.25) that II
Nicaea was convened upon his, that is the pope's, request, "Et sic
synodum istam secundum nostram ordinationem fecerunt," this is
contrary to historical precedent since all ecumenical councils met
upon the order of the Roman emperor.[41]

The draftsman of Hadrian's *Synodica JE* 2448, addressed to the
Byzantine Emperor Constantine VI, thus copied from an earlier
imperial *sacra* sent to Donus by Constantine IV. Only the *pluralis*
maiestatis of some verbs is changed by him to the second person
(*conservabimus, -bitis; habemus, -bitis; dirigemus, dirigere sategetis*).

The draftsman did not produce his own translation of the excerpt
from the Greek *sacra*, but used an already existing Latin version of
the document which he found in the Acts of the Sixth Ecumenical
Council. His version is identical with the translation in Mansi
XI.198E–199A.

The same excerpt from the *sacra* of Constantine IV was cited in
865 by Nicholas I in *epistola* 88, to the Emperor Michael. Ernst
Perels (*MGH, Epistolae* 6.458.13, n. 5) was the first to notice the
anonymous quotation from the *sacra* in *JE* 2448.

---

[41] On the exclusive prerogative of the Roman emperor to convene an ecumenical
council see E. Schwartz, *Gesammelte Schriften* IV (Berlin, 1960), 112, and F. X.
Funk, "Die Berufung der ökumenischen Synoden des Altertums," *Kirchenrechtliche*
Abhandlungen und Untersuchungen 1 (Paderborn, 1897), 49f., 55, 68f.

C. Gelasius I, *Ad episcopos Dardaniae* (*JK* 664), quoted without indication of source in *JE* 2448, Mansi XII.1074A:

Et *quem*admodum *beatus Petrus apostolus* per *Domini* prae*ceptum*[a] regens a*ecclesi*am, *nichilominus subsequens*[b] *et tenuit semper et retinet principatum. Quod* praeceptum *universalis* a*ecclesiae nullam magis oportet exsequi sedem quam primam quae unamquamque synodum et sua auctoritate confirmat et continuata moderatione custodit. Et valde mirati sumus quod* in vestris imperialibus iussis. . . .

[a] G p. 372 domini uoce perceptum ("praeceptum" in the abbreviated version of Pseudo-Isidore, *CSEL* 35, App. I, p. 778 ad lin. 8)
[b] G "ecclesia . . . subsequente"

The italics indicate the borrowing from the decretal *JK* 664: *Collectio Avellana*, no. 95, sections 10 and 1, ed. Otto Günther, *CSEL* 35 (1895), 372 and 369, "Valde mirati sumus quod" (= G):

10 (G 372.11–18) . . . confidimus quod nullus iam ueraciter Christianus ignoret uniuscuiusque synodi constitutum, quod uniuersalis ecclesiae probauit adsensus, nullam magis exsequi sedem prae ceteris oportere quam primam, quae et unamquamque synodum sua auctoritate confirmat et continuata moderatione custodit, pro suo scilicet principatu, quem beatus Petrus apostolus domini uoce perceptum, ecclesia nihilominus subsequente, et tenuit semper et retinet.

1 (G 369.1) Valde mirati sumus quod uestra dilectio.

The beginning of the same passage in *JK* 664 is quoted also in Hadrian's letter (787–792) addressed to Maginarius of St. Denis (*JE* 2491), ed. Hampe, *MGH, Epistolae* 5 no. 1, p. 3.21–4.3. The reference in *JE* 2491 to Constantinople following Rome, *in secundo ordine*, but preceding the patriarchates of Alexandria and Antioch, has a parallel in *JE* 2448, Mansi XII.1074B: "*In secundo enim ordine. . . .*" Nicholas I, *epistola* 88 (*JE* 2796; *MGH, Epistolae* 6.473.13f.) refers to *JK* 664 in a context similar to the one dealt with in *JE* 2448. The same Gelasius passage is furthermore cited by Nicholas I, *epistola* 79 (*JE* 2822; *ibid.* 422.10–15).

D. Gregory I, *Registrum* 9.215 (*JE* 1744), quoted without indication of source in *JE* 2448, Mansi XII.1075A–B:

Inc.: "*Et quod dicere pudet et grave tacere est*"; Des.: "*quippe qui non didicerint quod doceant. Unde canonica instituit censura, nequaquam ex laico ad sacerdotium repente transire.*"

See Gregory I, *Registrum Epistolarum* 9.215, ed. L. M. Hartmann, *MGH, Epistolae* 2 (Berlin, 1899), 202.17–26 ("et quod dicere . . . , quod doceant"), 34–35 . . . "nullum accipere nec quemquam *ex laico ad sacerdotium repente transire.*"

The principle of selection employed by the writer of *JE* 2448 is quite obvious. He was looking for an appropriate earlier papal letter asking rulers to convene a council: Gregory's letter is addressed to the Frankish Kings Theodoricus and Theodebertus, and urges them to convene a synod.

Anastasius' version (= A) of the excerpt shows a few minor deviations from Gregory's original (= G), of which I mention two:

> A: tacere est, qui regendi adhuc et docendi sunt, doctores;
> G: tacere est, regendi rectores et qui docendi sunt doctores.
> A: abstineant quippe qui; G: (p. 202.15) abstineant ne caeca honoris ambitio . . . , quippe qui.

I assume that the author of the *Libri Carolini*, reading in Hadrian's *Synodica* (1075A) of those who "ducatum animarum impudenter assumere," was reminded of Gregory, *Reg.* 9.218 (ed. Hartmann p. 207f.), and therefore quoted this letter in *LC* III.2[42] for in dealing with the *ducatus animarum*, it uses the same terminology as the *Synodica* in its excerpt from Gregory, *Reg.* 9.215.

Then, following the long quotation from Gregory, the *Libri Carolini* III.2 states: "dum superius memoratus Tarasius sacerdotale culmen, *ut* aiunt, *conscendit*, turbare potius quam gubernare dinoscitur plebes" (p. 110.3–5). The words "ut aiunt . . . plebes" are written in *Codex Vaticanus Latinus 7207 in loco raso*, and so represent the second redaction of the treatise. The contention that Tarasius preferred to disturb the people (ταράσσειν—turbare) rather than to guide them is a silent reference to *Libri Carolini* I.20 (p. 46.37–39), where the author of the treatise in a partly deleted section of the first redaction puns on the Greek "etymology" of Tarasius' name (*iuxta nominis sui ethimologiam*). This sarcastically conceived folketymology was available to him in all likelihood through some Greek-Latin or Latin-Greek glossary[43] where he possibly read

---

[42] *Libri Carolini sive Caroli Magni Capitulare de imaginibus*, ed. Hubert Bastgen (*MGH, Concilia 2, Supplementum* (Hannover-Leipzig, 1924), 109f.

[43] See *Glossae Latinograecae et Graecolatinae*, ed. Georg Goetz and Gotthold Gundermann (Corpus Glossariorum Latinorum 2; Leipzig, 1888), 149, and M. L. W. Laistner, *Philoxeni Glossarium* in *Glossaria Latina iussu Academiae Britannicae edita* 2 (Paris, 1926), 244b. Cf. P. J. Alexander, "The Iconoclastic Council of St. Sophia (815) and Its Definition (Horos)," *Dumbarton Oaks Papers* 7 (1953), 60, frg. 15.

ταϱάσσω—*turbo*, or *perturbat*—ταϱάσσει. The iconoclasts of 815 liked to misspell the name of Tarasius with two sigmas in order to belittle him through the association with *tarássein*. The author of the *Libri Carolini* probably had also in mind the passage of *JE* 2448 in which Hadrian I expressed his concern with respect to the election of the layman Tarasius (1074D: *nimis iterum conturbati ac conturbati sumus*), and then, using the words of Gregory the Great, says (1075A): "quales animarum duces esse possint qui *episcopatus culmen immatura cupiunt festinatione condescendere?*" Anastasius reads *condescendere*; Gregory, however, has *conscendere* (p. 202.23). Incidentally, this is also the reading ascribed to *JE* 2448 by the Carolingian corrector of the *Libri Carolini* with regard to Tarasius: "ut aiunt (= *JE* 2448) *conscendit*" (see above). *Conscendere* is, furthermore, the reading in the excerpt from *JE* 2448 inserted in *epistola* 208 of John VIII sent to Constantinople in 879, ed. Caspar, *MGH, Epistolae* 7.178, but otherwise the excerpt offers the same variants as given above for Anastasius' quotation from Gregory, *Reg.* 9.215. See also Chapter IV n. 96.

The origin of a correction in the context of the *Libri Carolini* III.2 now becomes quite clear. Gregory, *Reg.* 9.215, implicitly cited in *JE* 2448, reads at the end of the quotation (see above): ". . . nec quemquam *ex laico* ad sacerdotium *repente* transire." *LC* III.2 (p. 108.34–35) reads correspondingly: "(Tarasius) . . . *ex laico repente* ad episcopatum, *ut fertur, promotus*;" the words printed in italics are written *in loco raso* in *Codex Vaticanus Latinus 7207*, the autograph of the treatise. This means that the corrector of the *Libri Carolini* changed the text of the first redaction on the basis of the phrase he had read *-ut fertur-* in Gregory's epistles. The typically Gregorian phrase *ex laico repente* is repeatedly used in the two letters known in the present context to the author and corrector of the *Libri Carolini*, namely, *Registrum* 9.215 (p. 202.17, 34) and 9.218 (p. 207.29f.; 210.3).

E. Acts of the Lateran Council of 769, quoted without indication of source in *JE* 2448, Mansi XII.1064E–1065A:

(a) *Inc.* "*addendum est ad incredulorum satisfactionem*"; *Des.* "*et ab eorum doctrina nulla declinemus rationem.*"

This section appears in the *Hadrianum* 1.26 (*MGH, Epistolae* 5, p. 27.30–28.1) as a quotation from the Acts of the Lateran Council of 769 and the Roman Council of 731; see A. Werminghoff, *MGH, Concilia* 2.1 p. 91f. Von den Steinen[44] has shown that the excerpt from the *First Latin Nicaenum* cited in the *Capitulare adversus Synodum* and, as chapter heading, in the *Libri Carolini* I.18 (p. 42f.) as well as in the *Hadrianum* 1.26, renders a passage from that section of the *Synodica* which is derived from the synodal acts of 731 inserted in those of 769.[45]

(b) The "Chrysostomos" quotation in *JE* 2448 (Mansi XII. 1068C–D) occurred, according to the *Hadrianum* 2.13 (p. 47.10–17) "in praedecessoribus nostris sanctis pontificibus conciliis," that is, in the Acts of the Roman Council of 731 held under Gregory III, which in turn were incorporated into the Acts of the Lateran Council of 769 held under Stephen IV (III); cf. *MGH, Concilia* 2.1 (Aevi Karolini 1.1: Hannover-Leipzig, 1906), 92m. On the identification of this text with Severianus of Gabala see Chapter IV, M.

---

[44] *Op. cit.* (above n. 9) pp. 24, 61; also Hampe's note, *MGH, Epistolae* 5 *ad loc.* and p. 15, nn. 15, 16. The relationship between *JE* 2448 and the *Constitutum Constantini* is discussed in Chapter VII.

[45] The fragments of *JE* 2448 and 2449 cited in later collections of canon law are not included in the present study; their exact historical origin can now be assessed, I believe, on the basis of the present investigation. Cf. W. de Vries, "Die Struktur der Kirche gemäss dem II. Konzil von Nicäa (787)," *Orientalia Christiana Periodica* 33 (1967), 67. On the diplomatic methodology in the present chapter see the remarks by Heinrich Fichtenau in *MIOEG* 76 (1968), 469. Jean Darrouzès, "Listes épiscopales du Concile de Nicée (787)," *Revue des études byzantines* 33 (1975), 6 n. 4, refers to my interpretation of Anastasius' remark (*Tradito* 22, 1966, 111; above nn. 16–17), but neglects evidence for Byzantine falsifications of *JE* 2448 as indicated in the diplomatic sources. Unknown to Darrouzès, Anastasius himself is the author of the gloss in Nicholas I's *Epistola* 86 found in two MSS which expressly refer to Byzantine falsifications of *JE* 2448, as we know it now from Claudio Leonardi's publication cited above in note 18. The established custom of ecumenical synods concerning the insertion of Latin originals together with their Greek versions into the Greek synodal *Acta*, is not properly understood by Darrouzès, p. 61 n. 61, when he questions the opinion expressed by the present writer and by P. J. Alexander at note 7, above.

CHAPTER II

The Testimonia of Image-Worship
in Hadrian I's *Synodica*
of 785 (*JE* 2448)

The textual history of Hadrian I's *Synodica* of 785 (*JE* 2448), addressed to Constantine VI and his mother, Irene, shows the importance of the letter-treatise as a basic diplomatic source of some Carolingian and papal documents of the eighth and ninth centuries concerning image-worship.[1] The *Synodica* must have encouraged the Byzantine emperors in their rejection of iconoclasm, and, a few years later, in 787, also the synodal assembly of II Nicaea in their contemplated restoration of image-worship. The original Latin text of *JE* 2448 and its complete Greek translation were inserted into *actio* II of the *gesta* of the Seventh Ecumenical Council.[2] Two official Frankish state papers, the *Capitulare adversus Synodum* (II Nicaea, 787) and the *Libri Carolini*, question the concept of image-worship decreed by II Nicaea, and criticize severely not only the *Acta* of 787, but especially also biblical and patristic texts of *JE* 2448, which had been read into the synodal protocols. The *Capitulare* was sent by Charlemagne to Hadrian I, probably during 789–790, after a Latin translation (subsequently referred to as *Latin Nicaenum*) of the Greek *Acta* of 787, produced upon Hadrian's request in Rome (during 788), had arrived at the Frankish Court. The chapter headings of the *Capitulare* are preserved and critically discussed in Hadrian's answer to the *Capitulare*, that is, in the so-called *Hadrianum* (*JE* 2483) of about 791, addressed to Charlemagne.[3] The *Libri*

---

[1] See Part One and Chapter I.
[2] Cf. Chapter I n. 1.
[3] Ed. K. Hampe (*MGH, Epistolae* 5; Karolini Aevi 3; Berlin, 1899), 5–57.

Carolini, certainly the most important, and complex, literary and diplomatic product of the Carolingian age, constitutes the official Frankish protest against the Byzantine worship of images. This impressive work was probably composed upon Charlemagne's request during 791, and supplemented between 791 and 794, that is, between the arrival at the Frankish Court of the *Hadrianum* and the condemnation of image-worship by the national Frankish synod of Frankfurt in 794. The text of *JE* 2448 and its biblical, patristic, and diplomatic testimonia of image-worship are thus cited and discussed in sundry documents, namely, in the Greek *Acta* of II Nicaea and in their (now no longer extant) *First Latin Nicaenum*, the *Capitulare adversus Synodum*, the *Hadrianum*, and the *Libri Carolini*.[4] And most of the *Synodica*'s patristic testimonia have been inserted into the long catena of testimonia in the *Libellus Synodalis* of the Frankish synod of Paris, 825.[5] Recent investigation of the textual and diplomatic history of *JE* 2448 within the context of the Greek and Latin versions of the *Acta* of II Nicaea revealed certain Byzantine changes, if not falsifications and forgeries, in the *Synodica*'s original Latin text.[6] *JE* 2448 seems to survive only in the transmission of the second Latin translation of the Greek *Acta* of II Nicaea by Anastasius Bibliothecarius, dedicated by him to John VIII in 873.[7] Although Anastasius supplies a long section of *JE* 2448 missing in the Greek version of the *Synodica* which had been inserted into the Greek *gesta* of II Nicaea, his text of *JE* 2448 does not offer throughout the original Latin version. Its Greek and Latin testimonia of image-worship are often rewritten by Anastasius after the Byzantine translation of *JE* 2448 inserted into the Greek *Acta* of II Nicaea. The original Latin versions of those Greek and Latin testimonia, as well as other fragments of the no-longer-extant *First Latin Nicaenum*, are preserved in the *Capitulare adversus Synodum*, the *Hadrianum*, the *Libri Carolini*, and the *Libellus Synodalis* of the Paris Synod of 825.[8]

---

[4] On these writings see the beginning of Chapter III.

[5] Ed. A. Werminghoff: *MGH, Concilia* 2.2 (Aevi Karolini 1.2; Hannover, 1906), 473–551, including the *Epitome*.

[6] Cf. Chapter IV.

[7] See Anastasius Bibliothecarius' dedicatory letter, ed. E. Perels and G. Laehr (*MGH, Epistolae* 7; Karolini Aevi 5, 1928), 415–418, and his remarks on his translation of II Nicaea at the end of his letter of 871 addressed to Hadrian II (attached to his Latin version of the *Acta* of the Eighth Ecumenical Council).

[8] The adulteration of these testimonia is discussed in Chapter IV.

The following verifications of patristic and diplomatic testimonia (A–U) quoted in *JE* 2448 in support of image-worship may be considered as prolegomena to a future critical edition of *JE* 2448.[9] Some of these texts are discussed and identified in Chapter I and in Chapters III–VII; they are subsequently referred to by cross-references.

Diplomatic and Patristic Testimonia of *JE* 2448 (785), Inserted in the *Acta* of II Nicaea (787), Mansi XII.1055–1076.

A. *Divalia sacra* of Emperors Constantine VI and Irene, addressed to Pope Hadrian I in 784, quoted without indication of source in *JE* 2448 of 785: Mansi XII.1056C7 quae pridem facta sunt—D5 tenere.—Dölger: *Regesten* 341.[10] The Byzantine Greek version of *JE* 2448, inserted into *actio* II of the *Acta* of II Nicaea, 787, Mansi XII.1055C, preserves the original Greek text of this *sacra*, which otherwise is extant only in a Latin translation. Smaller passages of the *sacra*'s text are cited throughout *JE* 2448. See Chapter I, A.

B. *Actus Silvestri*, version A, quoted in *JE* 2448, Mansi XII.1057D–1060C. Lemma: Beato atque sanctissimo papa Silvestro testante, in ipsis enim exordiis Christianorum cum ad fidem converteretur pius imperator Constantinus,[11] sic legitur:

Inc.: Transacta die nocturno regi facto silentio,
Expl.: . . . quam istos promisisse suae saluti memorabat.

See *Actus Silvestri*, ed. B. Mombritius, *Sanctuarium seu Vitae Sanctorum* 2 (Paris, 1910), 511, 28–46, 511, 56–512, 5–18 (*passim*). The text of this testimonium is cited after the original Latin version of *JE* 2448 in the *Libellus synodalis* of the Paris Synod of 825 (*MGH*,

---

[9] B. Altaner, *Kleine patristische Schriften*, ed. G. Glockmann (*TU* 83, 1967), 406 n. 4, mistakenly states that Hadrian's patristic testimonia (in *JE* 2448 of 785) are "einfach aus der vom 2. Konzil von Nikaia (787) gebrauchten Testimoniensammlung übernommen und ins Lateinische übersetzt worden." This notion is untenable, not only chronologically, but also because (unknown to Altaner) the Latin original of Hadrian's *JE* 2448 and its Byzantine Greek translation had been inserted into the Greek synodal protocols of II Nicaea.

[10] F. Dölger, *Reg.*, 42.

[11] The *Hadrianum* I.53 (p. 39, 26–27) offers the same lemma "In ipsis enim exordiis cristianorum cum ad fidem converteretur imperator Constantinus," in connection with another reference to the *Actus Silvestri*.

Concilia 2; Aevi Karolini 1.2, 1908), 485, 6–23 (p. 536f. *Epitome*). Wilhelm Levison pointed out that *JE* 2448 renders the text of the unpublished version A of the *Actus Silvestri*. The presence of this text in *JE* 2448, in the *Constitutum Constantini*, in the *Libri Carolini*, and in the *Libellus Synodalis* of the Paris Synod of 825 is discussed and clarified in Chapter VII.

C. Gregory I, Epistle to Serenus of Marseilles, Mansi XII.1060D:

. . . atque in ecclesiis sanctorum sacrae figurae expressae atque depictae hactenus fuerunt, quatenus gentilitas paganorum, conspecta divinae scripturae depicta historia, ab idolorum cultura daemonum simulacris ad verum Christianitatis lumen atque amoris dei culturam verti deberet [see below], sicut et praecipuus pater atque idoneus praedicator beatus Gregorius huius apostolicae sedis praesul ait, *ut hi qui litteras nesciunt, saltem in parietibus videndo legant quae legere in codicibus non valent.* (Ob hoc quippe sancti probatissimi patres ipsas imagines atque picturas divinae scripturae et gesta sanctorum in ecclesiis depingi statuerunt), et cuncti orthodoxi atque Christianissimi imperatores, et omnes sacerdotes . . . .

This section contains a literal quotation (in italics) of Gregory I, *Registr.* IX.208 ed. L. M. Hartmann (*MGH, Epistolae* 2, 1899, 195). The section from *sicut—sacerdotes* reads in the Greek version of *JE* 2448 as follows (Mansi XII.1059C):

καθὼς ὁ ἅγιος Γρηγόριος ὁ διάδοχος τῶν ἀποστόλων ἐκήρυξε, τοῦ πάντας ἀνθρώπους ἀγραμματίστους καὶ μὴ δυναμένους ἀναγνῶναι, θεωρεῖν τὰς εὐαγγελικὰς ἱστορίας, [καὶ δι᾿ αὐτῶν ἀνάγεσθαι πρὸς δόξαν καὶ ἀνάμνησιν τῆς ἐνσάρκου οἰκονομίας τοῦ Κυρίου καὶ δεσπότου ἡμῶν Ἰησοῦ Χριστοῦ] καὶ πάντες οἱ ὀρθόδοξοι καὶ χριστιανικώτατοι βασιλεῖς σὺν πᾶσι τοῖς ἱερεῦσι . . .

Georg Ostrogorsky, "Rom und Byzanz im Kampf um die Bilder-verehrung," *Seminarium Kondakovianum* 6 (1933), 79f., points out the changes made on dogmatic grounds by the Byzantine translator in his translation of *JE* 2448. The sentence following the literal quotation from Gregory's Epistle, from (Ob hoc—statuerunt), is shortened and partly omitted in the translation, and the statement concerning ἔνσαρκος οἰκονομία, from καὶ δι᾿ to Χριστοῦ, is added.

A second letter by Gregory I, addressed to Serenus, the iconoclast of Marseilles, *Reg.* XI.10, *op. cit.*, p. 270.14, reiterated by and large Gregory's advice tendered in the first letter: "Nam quod legentibus scriptura, hoc idiotis praestat pictura cernentibus, quia in ipsa ignorantes vident, quod sequi debeant, in ipsa legunt qui litteras nesciunt."

Gregory's first letter to Serenus is cited in the *Libellus Synodalis* of 825 (p. 487.32), the second in the *Hadrianum* II.1 (p. 42f.) and in the *LC* II.23 (p. 82).

The Byzantine translator of *JE* 2448 in all likelihood produced an expanded translation of Gregory's statement not only for reasons of dogma, but also because he probably was unable to verify the quotation in a MS. Gregory's statement does not seem to be discussed in the *Acta* of II Nicaea which instead quote an Eastern authority for the theory that pictures are a substitute for the ignorant who cannot read, namely, Nilus Sinaita's Epistle to Olympiodorus (*PG* 79.577 D; Mansi XIII.36 C): ὅπως ἂν οἱ μὴ εἰδότες γράμματα, μηδὲ δυνάμενοι τὰς θείας ἀναγινώσκειν γραφὰς τῇ θεωρίᾳ τῆς ζωγραφίας μνήμην τε λαμβάνωσιν τῆς τῶν γνησίως τῷ ἀληθινῷ θεῷ δεδουλευκότων ἀνδραγαθίας . . . .

D. Augustine, untraced quotation, Mansi XII.1065C:

a. *Signatum est super nos lumen vultus tui, Domine* [Ps. 4.7]. Hinc et beatus Augustinus praecipuus pater et optimus doctor in suis admonitionum sermonibus ait: "Quid est imago dei nisi vultus dei, in quo signatus est populus dei?"

b. Greek version of *JE* 2448, Mansi XII.1066A:

Ἐσημειώθη ἐφ᾽ ἡμᾶς τὸ φῶς τοῦ προσώπου σου, Κύριε [Ps. 4.7].
Ὅθεν ὁ ἅγιος Αὐγουστῖνος ὁ μέγας διδάσκαλος ἐν ταῖς νουθεσίαις αὐτοῦ ἔφη·
Τί ἐστιν εἰκὼν Θεοῦ, εἰ μὴ πρόσωπον θεοῦ, ἐν ᾧ ἐσημειώθη ὁ λαὸς τοῦ θεοῦ;

This quotation is not recorded in the *Libellus Synodalis* of the Paris synod of 825, which lists many of the texts cited in *JE* 2448 and in the *First Latin Nicaenum* of II Nicaea. It is quoted and discussed in *Libri Carolini* I.23 (p. 50) and II.16 (p. 75), but not in the *Hadrianum*. And it is the only passage from Augustine to be found in the *Acta* of II Nicaea. The Byzantine translator of *JE* 2448 was unfamiliar with the source of the text, and therefore offered a literal translation. Nobody has been able to verify the presence of the passage in Augustine's works, not even B. Altaner, "Augustinus in der griechischen Kirche bis auf Photius," *Kleine patristische Schriften*, ed. G. Glockmann (*TU* 83, 1967), 94f.

E. Gregory of Nyssa, *De deitate filii et spiritus sancti et in Abraham*, Mansi XII.1065C–D (*PG* 46.572C). This text already appears as a testimonium of image-worship in John of Damascus, *De imaginibus, oratio*, *PG* 94.1269C, 1361C. On the interdependence of the Greek and Latin versions see Chapter IV, section I.

F. Gregory of Nyssa, *Commentarius in Canticum Canticorum*, Mansi XII.1065D; ed. H. Langerbeck (Leiden, 1960), 28.7–17; see Chapter IV, K.

G. Basil of Caesarea, apocryphal Epistle 360, addressed to Emperor Julian, Mansi XII.1065D:

a. *Inc.* Secundum id quod a Deo haereditate possidemus;
   Des. Ac ideo in omnibus ecclesiis nostris eorum designamus historiam.

b. The Greek version of *JE* 2448 reads as follows in Mansi XII. 1066C–D:

   Inc. Καθὼς ἐκληρονομήσαμεν ἐκ τοῦ θεοῦ τὴν ἡμετέραν ἄμεμπτον πίστιν;
   Des. ἀλλ᾽ ἐν πάσαις ταῖς ἐκκλησίαις ἡμῶν τὴν αὐτῶν ἀναστηλοῦμεν ἱστορίαν.

c. The original Latin version of the fragment in *JE* 2448 as quoted in *LS*, p. 511.4–12, reads:
   Inc. Secundum id quod divinitus datam haereditariam nobis;
   Des. Sed in omnibus ecclesiis nostris eorum designantes historiam.

d. The *Nicaenum, actio* IV, Mansi XIII.72E–73, cites the following Greek version:

   Inc. Κατὰ τὴν Θεόθεν ἐπικεκληρωμένην ἡμῖν ἀμώμητον πίστιν.
   Des. (b. Des.) . . . ἡμῶν τούτων ἀνιστορουμένων.

The version of the *Nicaenum* (d) was perhaps the original one, and it seems as if the Byzantine translator (b) was familiar with it when he translated *JE* 2448. Epistle 360 is not recorded by J. Bidez and F. Cumont: *Iuliani Imperatoris Epistolae* (Paris, 1922). Our transmission can be added to that listed by P. van den Ven, "Patristique," 348f., no. 18. A florilegium in Codex Paris gr. 1115, fol. 247v. lists the apocryphon with the *Nicaenum*'s *Incipit* (d); see Th. Schermann, *Die Geschichte der dogmatischen Florilegien* (*TU*, NF.

13.1, 1904), 76 no. 7c. P. F. De'Cavalieri, *Codices Graeci Chisiani et Borgiani* (Rome, 1927), MS 12 (R. IV.12), s. XIV, f. 46v, contains a version of Epist. 360, which is printed in *PG* 32.1100 in the version *d*, with an expanded *Desinit*.

H. Basil of Caesarea, *Sermo in XL martyres*, Mansi XII.1068A–B:

a. *Inc.* Nam et bellorum triumphos ac victorias et sermonum conscriptores;

  Des. Haec conscripta silens admonitio per demonstrationem demonstrat.

b. Greek version of *JE* 2448 in *Nicaenum*, Mansi XII.1066D:

  Inc. Ἐπεὶ καὶ πολέμων τρόπαια καὶ νίκας καὶ λογογράφοι πολλάκις;

  Des. ταῦτα γραφὴ σιωπῶσα διὰ μιμήσεως δείκνυσι.

The quotation in the *Libellus Synodalis* of 825 (p. 511.13) is identical with the text cited in *a*. The Greek version *b* corresponds with the original of Basil's *sermo*, *PG* 31.508D–509A, with the exception of the words τρόπαια καὶ νίκας (triumphos ac victorias) which are substituted for ἀνδραγαθήματα. But the redactor of *JE* 2448 does not quote *a* directly after Basil's treatise; he cites it in his collection of testimonia of image-worship because he had found it in the earlier collections appended to the collections by John of Damascus, *De imaginibus, oratio* I–III, *PG* 94.1265D, 1286A, 1312C, 1361A, 1401A. On the other hand, the Byzantine translator of *JE* 2448 did not produce a retranslation of *a* into Greek, because he obviously recognized the Greek original of the Latin quotation either directly in Basil's *sermo*, or—as I suspect—in one of John of Damascus' treatises.

The first part of the Basil text is cited in the *Greek Nicaenum*, Mansi XII.1014E, the second part in Mansi XIII.113CD, 300C; the *Incipit* of Basil's homily in Germanus of Constantinople's Epistle to Thomas of Claudiopolis, Mansi XIII.124C, ὅτι — εὐνοίας. The *Doctrina patrum de incarnatione verbi: Ein griechisches Florilegium aus der Wende des VII. und VIII. Jahrhunderts*, ed. F. Diekamp (Münster, 1907), 329, cites the same Basil text in a collection of patristic testimonia of image-worship.

I. Pseudo-Chrysostomos, *De parabola seminis*, Mansi XII.1068B–C, actually Severianus of Gabala, *De sigillis librorum*; see Chapter IV, L.

K. Pseudo-Chrysostomos, *Sermo in quinta feria paschae*, Mansi XII. 1068C–D, now identified with Severianus of Gabala; see Chapter IV, M.

L. Cyril of Alexandria, two fragments from Cyril's lost *Commentary on Matthew*, Mansi XII.1068D; see Chapter IV, O.

M. Athanasius of Alexandria, *De incarnatione verbi dei*, Mansi XII. 1068D–E; see Chapter IV, N.

N. Ambrosius, *De incarnationis dominicae sacramento*, Mansi XII. 1068E–1069A; see below Chapter V.

O. Epiphanius, *Panarion haer.* 65.8.10, Mansi XII.1069A:

a. Item sancti Epiphanii Constantiae Cypri: Numquid enim et imperator pro eo quod habet imaginem, duo sunt imperatores? Non sane; sed imperator unus est cum imagine.

b. The original text of this quotation in *JE* 2448 is preserved in *Libellus Synodalis* of the Paris Synod of 825, p. 511.34f.:

   Item sancti Epyphanii episcopi Constantiae Cypri: Etenim imperatores pro eo quod habent imagines, non duo sunt imperatores, sed imperator unus cum imagine.

c. The Greek original of text b is Epiphanius, *Panarion haer.* 65.8.10, ed. Karl Holl (*GCS, Epiphanius* III; Leipzig, 1933), 12:

   καὶ γὰρ καὶ οἱ βασιλεῖς οὐ διὰ τὸ ἔχειν εἰκόνα δύο εἰσὶ βασιλεῖς, ἀλλὰ βασιλεὺς εἷς σὺν τῇ εἰκόνι.

d. The Greek version of *JE* 2448 reads for a, Mansi XII.1067D:

   πάλιν τοῦ ἁγίου Ἐπιφανίου Κωνσταντίας τῆς Κύπρου·
   Μὴ γὰρ εἰ βασιλεὺς ἔχει εἰκόνα, δύο εἰσὶ βασιλεῖς; οὐμενοῦν.
   ὁ βασιλεὺς εἷς ἐστι καὶ μετὰ τῆς εἰκόνος.

K. Holl, *Die Schriften des Epiphanius gegen die Bilderverehrung*, in SB. Preuß. Akademie der Wiss. (1916), 828 n. 2, first traced this quotation. The version of the *Libellus Synodalis* of 825 is a literal translation of the original and renders the original text in *JE* 2448. Anastasius' version a seems to be an adaptation of b made by him after the Greek version d. It is obvious that the Byzantine translator of *JE* 2448 (d) did not know the original c, and for this reason he paraphrased b in his translation of *JE* 2448.

P. Stephen of Bostra, *De imaginibus sanctorum*, Mansi XII.1069A:

a. *Inc.* Quoniam omne opus quod sit in Dei nomine bonum est et sanctum.

   Des. Dignum enim est commemorari praepositorum nostrorum, et gratias referre deo (Mansi XII.1072B).

b. The original version of this quotation is preserved in *LS*, p. 511.36–512.30. Anastasius' text a offers by and large the same version which can be corrected in minor details after the text of the *Libellus Synodalis* of 825. E. J. Martin, *A History of the Iconoclastic Controversy* (London, 1930), 260, believes that the source of this text is unknown, and thus overlooks that he himself correctly lists as a source (p. 149):

c. John of Damascus, *De imaginibus*, *oratio* III, *PG* 94.1376B: Stephen of Bostra, *Contra Judaeos*, c. 4,

   Inc. Περὶ δὲ εἰκόνων θαρροῦμεν, ὅτι πᾶν ἔργον γινόμενον ἐν ὀνόματι θεοῦ, καλὸν καὶ ἅγιόν ἐστι.

The quotation of Stephen of Bostra in *JE* 2448 offers a fuller text of the same section from *Contra Judaeos*, c. 4, which is cited by John of Damascus. Yet John of Damascus nevertheless was the redactor's source for quoting Stephen of Bostra as an orthodox authority on image-worship. It is furthermore evident that the text of Stephen in the Greek version of *JE* 2448 is hardly a retranslation of the Latin version in the original of the *Synodica*. The Byzantine translator of *JE* 2448 seemingly quoted the original Greek version of Stephen, which must have been accessible to him at Constantinople. The parallels among the various Greek versions of Stephen's text in c, d, and e (below) support this assumption.

d. Compare the Greek version of *JE* 2448, Mansi XII.1067D:

   Inc. περὶ τῶν εἰκόνων τῶν ἁγίων ὁμολογοῦμεν, ὅτι πᾶν ἔργον τὸ γινόμενον ἐν ὀνόματι τοῦ Θεοῦ, ἀγαθὸν ἐστι καὶ ἅγιον.

   Des. Ἄξιον δέ ἐστι μνημονεύειν τῶν ἡγουμένων ἡμῶν, καὶ εὐχαριστίας προσφέρειν τῷ Θεῷ (1070D).

Compare furthermore the following passage in Stephen of Bostra's treatise as inserted by the Byzantine translator of *JE* 2448 in his translation of the *Synodica* (1), and as quoted by John of Damascus (2), with its Latin translation in the *Synodica*'s original as cited (3) in the *Libellus Synodalis* of 825:

1. Mansi XII.1070B:

   Ἡμεῖς δὲ πρὸς μνημόσυνον τῶν ἁγίων εἰκόνας ποιοῦμεν, ἤγουν Ἀβραὰμ, Μωσέως, Ἡλίου, Ἡσαίου, Ζαχαρίου, καὶ τῶν λοιπῶν προφητῶν, ἀποστόλων καὶ μαρτύρων ἁγίων τῶν διὰ τὸν Κύριον συντριβέντων, ἵνα πᾶς ὁ θεωρῶν αὐτοὺς ἐν εἰκόνι μιμνήσκηται αὐτῶν, καὶ δοξάζῃ τὸν Κύριον τὸν δοξάσαντα αὐτούς.

2. *PG* 94.1376B:

   Ἡμεῖς τὰς εἰκόνας τῶν ἁγίων εἰς μνήμην τῶν ἁγίων ἐποιήσαμεν, οἷον Ἀβραὰμ, καὶ Ἰσαὰκ, καὶ Ἰακὼβ, καὶ Μωϋσέως, καὶ Ἡλία, καὶ Ζαχαρίου, καὶ τῶν λοιπῶν προφητῶν καὶ ἁγίων μαρτύρων, τῶν δι' αὐτὸν ἀναιρεθέντων, ἵνα πᾶς ὁ ὁρῶν αὐτῶν τὰς εἰκόνας, μνημονεύῃ αὐτῶν, καὶ δοξάζῃ τὸν δοξάσαντα αὐτούς.

3. *LS*, p. 512.16–19:

   Nos autem ad memoriam sanctorum imagines facimus Abrahae, Moysi et Heliae, Isaiae et Zachariae et reliquorum prophetarum, apostolorum et martyrum sanctorum, qui propter Deum interempti sunt, ut omnis, qui videt eos in imagine, memoretur eorum et glorificet Deum, qui glorificavit eos.

e. The Greek version of our text in the *Nicaenum*'s transmission was unknown to J. M. Mercati when he published from the Ambrosianus graec. A 84, saec. XII or XIII, "*Stephani Bostreni nova de sacris imaginibus fragmenta e libro deperdito* κατὰ Ἰουδαίων," in: *Theologische Quartalschrift* 77 (1895), 653–658.[12] This fragment's *Incipit* is identical with the one cited by John of Damascus (above, c.). Its *Desinit* is almost identical with the closing words

---

[12] Mercati's study is reprinted in his *Opere minori* I (Studi e Testi 76; 1937). It is obvious that he did not publish an unknown text, but a later MS excerpt from the Greek *Acta* of II Nicaea which contained a Byzantine translation of *JE* 2448 and included the long fragment from Stephen of Bostra. G. B. Ladner, "The Concept of the Image in the Greek Fathers and the Byzantine Iconoclastic Controversy," *Dumbarton Oaks Papers* 7 (1953), 14f., fails to draw the final conclusions concerning the origin of the text published by Mercati.

of the fragment in the Greek version of *JE* 2448 (above, d):
Ἄξιον γάρ ἐστιν . . . ἡγουμένων (ἡ)μ(ῶ)ν καὶ εὐχαριστεῖν τῷ Θεῷ
(*om. με*). The text of the A(mbrosianus) parallels in content and
size the fragment's transmission in the *Synodica*. The N(*icaenum*)
probably represents a version of the text which is closer to the
lost original writing than is that of A. This is evident on the
basis of some identical readings in A and J(ohn of Damascus).
A few examples will be sufficient to illustrate this point:

AJ καλόν, N ἀγαθόν; AJ ἕτερον . . . ἕτερον, N ἄλλο . . . ἄλλο;
AJ ἀπόβλητος, N ἐκβεβλημένος; AJ ἀναιρεθέντων, N συντριβέντων;

On the other hand we find instances which show a close textual
proximity of N to AJ. Compare:

A: Καὶ εἰ γάρ ἐστιν ἡ τιμὴ τῆς εἰκόνος εἰ μὴ τιμὴ μόνον; καθὼς ἡμεῖς οἱ
ἁμαρτωλοὶ προσκυνοῦμεν ἀλλήλους κατὰ τιμὴν καὶ ἀγάπην. τὸν γὰρ
Θεὸν ἡμῶν ἄλλως προσκ(υνοῦ)μεν καὶ δοξάζομεν καὶ τρέμομεν.

J: Καὶ ἡ μὲν προσκύνησις τιμῆς ἐστι σύμβολον. καθὼς καὶ ἡμεῖς ἁμαρτωλοὶ προσκυνοῦμεν τὸν μὲν Θεὸν κατὰ τὴν Θεϊκὴν λατρείαν καὶ ἀξίαν
προσκύνησιν δοξάζομεν καὶ τρέμομεν.

N: Ποία γάρ ἐστιν ἡ τῆς προσκυνήσεως τιμή, εἰ μὴ μόνον καθὼς καὶ ἡμεῖς
οἱ ἁμαρτωλοὶ προσκυνοῦμεν καὶ ἀσπαζόμεθα ἀλλήλους κατὰ τιμὴν
καὶ ἀγάπησιν; Οὕτω γὰρ τὸν Κύριον ἡμῶν οὐκ ἄλλως προσκυνοῦμεν,
δοξάζοντες μέντοι καὶ τρέμομεν.

The comparison of this passage in the versions A, J, and N possibly
indicates that ἡ τιμὴ τῆς εἰκόνος in A represents the original wording
which, for iconodulic reasons, was expanded in N to read ἡ τῆς
προσκυνήσεως τιμή after the earlier J: καὶ ἡ προσκύνησις τιμῆς. Compare finally the text in A, edited by Mercati, p. 667f., with the
parallel versions cited above in d. 1 (N), d. 2 (J), and d. 3 (*LS*):

Ἡμεῖς οὖν εἰς ἀνάμνησιν τῶν ἁγίων τὰς εἰκόνας ποιοῦμεν Ἀβραὰμ καὶ
Μωσῆ,
Ἠλία καὶ Ἡσαίου, Ζαχαρίου καὶ τῶν λοιπῶν προφητῶν, ἀποστόλων καὶ
μαρτύρων ἁγίων τῶν διὰ Θεὸν ἀναιρεθέντων, ἵνα πᾶς ὁ ὁρῶν αὐτοὺς ἐν
εἰκόνι μνημον   αὐτὸν καὶ δοξάζῃ τὸν Θεὸν τὸν δοξάσαντα αὐτούς.

The reference to Stephen of Bostra in the Greek version of *JE*
2448 can be added to Ch. Baur, *Initia Patrum Graecorum* II (Studi
e Testi, 1955), 315 s. v. Further, codex Paris, B.N. gr. 1115, f.
263v, lists our text in a florilegium of testimonia according to
Th. Schermann, *Die Geschichte der dogmatischen Florilegien* (*TU* NF.

13.1; 1904), 78. O. Bardenhewer, *Geschichte der altkirchlichen Literatur* 5 (Freiburg, 1932), 47, mistakenly deduces from the fact that John of Damascus cites Stephen of Bostra, Κατὰ ᾿Ιουδαίων, κεφάλ. δ᾿, that the lost work was "Ein großes, mindestens vier *Bücher* umfassendes Werk." But John's mention of chapter IV allows for only one book of the lost work. The present treatment of the fragment from Stephen of Bostra's lost work can be added to the information listed by H. G. Beck, *Kirche und theologische Literatur im Byzantinischen Reich* (München, 1959), 447, on the basis of Mercati's study.

Q. Jerome of Jerusalem, fragment of Dialogue, Mansi XII.1072B:

a. De sermone beati Hieronymi presbyteri Hierosolymitani:
 Etenim sicut permisit Deus adorare omnem gentem manufacta, Judaeos autem tabulas quas dolavit Moyes, et duos cherubim aureos, sic et nobis Christianis donavit crucem et bonarum operationum imagines pingere et adorare, venerari, et demonstrare opus nostrum.

b. This quotation reads as follows in the Greek version of *JE* 2448, Mansi XII.1070E:

  ᾿Εκ τοῦ λόγου τοῦ μακαρίου ῾Ιερωνύμου πρεσβυτέρου ῾Ιεροσολύμων. Καὶ γὰρ ὡς συνεχώρησεν ὁ Θεὸς προσκυνεῖν πᾶν ἔθνος τὰ χειροποίητα, ᾿Ιουδαίοις δὲ τὰς πλάκας ἐκείνας εὐδόκησεν, ἃς ἐλατόμησεν ὁ Μωϋσῆς, καὶ τὰ δύο χερουβὶμ τὰ χρυσᾶ· οὕτω καὶ ἡμῖν τοῖς Χριστιανοῖς ἐδωρήσατο τὸν σταυρὸν καὶ τῶν ἀγαθῶν ἔργων τὰς εἰκόνας γράφειν καὶ προσκυνεῖν, καὶ δεῖξαι τὸ ἔργον ἡμῶν.

c. Some traces of the same quotation, if not its actual source, occur in John of Damascus, *De imaginibus, oratio* III, *PG* 94.1409B:

  ῾Ιερωνύμου πρεσβυτέρου ῾Ιεροσολύμων. Τῆς γραφῆς ὑμῶν μηδαμοῦ ἐπιτρεπούσης ἡμῖν προσκυνεῖν τὸν σταυρόν, τίνος χάριν λοιπὸν αὐτὸν προσκυνεῖτε; Εἴπατε ἡμῖν τοῖς ᾿Ιουδαίοις καὶ ῞Ελλησι, καὶ πᾶσι τοῖς ἐπερωτῶσιν ὑμᾶς ἔθνεσι. ᾿Απόκρισις. Διὰ τοῦτο . . . τάχα συνεχώρησεν ὁ Θεὸς παντὶ ἔθνει σεβομένῳ τὸν θεόν, πάντως προσκυνεῖν τι ἐπὶ τῆς γῆς, . . . ῞Ωσπερ οὖν ὁ ᾿Ιουδαῖος προσεκύνει τὴν κιβωτὸν τῆς διαθήκης, καὶ τὰ δύο Χερουβὶμ τὰ χωνευτὰ καὶ χρυσᾶ, καὶ τὰς δύο πλάκας, ἃς ἐλάξευσε Μωϋσῆς, . . . οὕτω καὶ οἱ Χριστιανοὶ . . .

John's quotation belongs to the fragments of a dialogue *inter Judaeum et Christianum* in περὶ ἁγίας τριάδος (*PG* 40.865C–D) of a Greek presbyter, Jerome of Jerusalem. The textual parallels in b and c seem to indicate that the Byzantine translator of *JE* 2448 hardly offered a retranslation of a; may he have quoted directly from Jerome's original? The florilegium in codex Paris, B.N. gr. 1115, f. 263r lists our testimonium τῆς γραφῆς (above, text c), and καὶ γὰρ ὡς συνεχώρησεν (above, b), that is the query in the dialogue as quoted by John of Damascus, and the answer as cited in the Greek translation of *JE* 2448 (b), which was also the source of the Latin version (a). We recall that the Paris codex was copied in 1276 from a manuscript perhaps written in 859.[13] *Libri Carolini* I.19 (p. 44.10–12) summarizes and quotes the Jerome text as follows: "Quod magis sit temeritatis dicere: 'Sicut Judaeis tamen tabulae et duo cherubim, sic nobis Christianis donata est crux et sanctorum imagines ad scribendum et adorandum.'"

The Greek version of Jerome (above b) is published also in *PG* 40.865–66D, n. 14, following Cod. reg. 2951, now Paris, B.N. gr. 1115 (see above); cf. H. Omont, *Inventaire des manuscrits grecs de la Bibl. Nat.* III, (Paris, 1886), 223.

The fragment from Jerome may be added to the texts dealt with by P. Batiffol.[14] Other fragments ascribed to this Jerome, who, according to Batiffol, wrote about the year 740, are probably cited in the patristic catena of Paris grec. Coislinianus 80, s. XI, ff. 91 and 282.[15] All the apologetic texts ascribed to Jerome of Jerusalem are in need of a renewed investigation.

R. *Sacra* of Emperor Constantine IV Pogonatos, addressed to Pope Donus, in 678, Mansi XII.1073B4–B14; see Chapter I, B.

S. Gelasius I, *Ad Episcopos Dardaniae* (JK 664), Mansi XII.1074A5–A13; see Chapter I, C.

T. Gregory I, *Registrum* 9.215 (*JE* 1744), addressed in 599 to the Frankish kings Theodericus and Theudebertus, Mansi XII.1075A–B; see Chapter I, D.

---

[13] R. Devreesse, *Introduction à l'étude des manuscrits grecs* (Paris, 1954), 54 n. 8, 93 n. 6.

[14] Batiffol, "Jérome de Jerusalem d'après un document inédit," *Revue des questions historiques* 39 (1886), 248–255.

[15] R. Devreesse, *Bibliothèque Nationale: Catalogue des manuscrits grecs II: Le Fonds Coislin* (1945), 71 and Index, p. 412 with additional references. The fragment from Jerome in *JE* 2448 may be added to others referred to by H. G. Beck, *Kirche und theologische Literatur im Byzantinischen Reich* (1959), 448.

U. *Acta* of the Lateran Council of 769, Mansi XII.1064E4–
1065A13; a text drawn from the *gesta* of the Roman Synod of 731,
which was inserted into the protocols of the council of 769, in the
same fashion as the testimonia K and L, above; see Chapter I, E.

A passage of the text is of special significance; it reads as follows:
"*Aenei serpentis inspectione credimus Israeliticum populum* a calamitate
injecta liberari, et Christi Domini nostri et *sanctorum effigies aspicientes*
atque venerantes *dubitamus salvari?*" (Mansi XII.1065A 6–10).
This text is the basis of a Frankish criticism voiced in the *Capitulare
adversus Synodum* and in the *Libri Carolini* I.18 (p. 42.42–43.3): "Sicut
Israheliticus populus serpentis enei inspectione servatus est, sic nos *sanctorum
effigies aspicientes* salvabimur." The *Hadrianum* I.26 (p. 27.29) identifies the origin of this text in "predictis sacris conciliis," that is, in
the *Acta* of the Roman Synod of 731 which were inserted into the
Acta of the Lateran Council of 769. The *Hadrianum's* reference
(p. 27.24) to the presence of the passage in the *Latin Nicaenum, in
actione quinta*, is mistaken; we must read "in actione secunda." Von
den Steinen's surmise (*QF* 21 [1929–30], 61) that *Libri Carolini*
I.18, is rather an original chapter of the first redaction of the
treatise than a later addition, and not supplemented on the basis
of *Hadrianum* I.26, is quite correct.

The testimonia in *JE* 2448 listed under A–U are superficially of
a most diversified origin. Some seem to be cited directly after their
respective sources, e.g., A, B, F, and G. Others are quoted at
second hand, either from some independent collection of patristic
testimonia or else from some catena of texts inserted into the *Acta*
of a council. Thus the testimonia E, H, I, K, N, P, and Q occur
among the χρήσεις of image-worship in John of Damascus, *De
imaginibus, oratio I–III*. Such a relationship can be proved for the
testimonium N, which represents the Latin version of a Greek
Ambrose text uniquely offered by John of Damascus. But other
testimonia of *JE* 2448 for which the collections of *De imaginibus*
contain parallel texts are not directly derived from these collections,
but indirectly, that is, they are drawn from the *Acta* of certain
councils which may have used the testimonia collected by John of
Damascus. This is surely true of the testimonia K and U.

The text of Pseudo-Chrysostomos, that is, Severianus of Gabala
(K), occurs, according to the *Hadrianum* II.13 (p. 47.11) "in praedecessoribus nostris sanctis pontificibus conciliis," in the *Acta*

of the Roman Synod of 731 which were inserted into the *Acta* of the Lateran Council of 769. In addition, the two testimonia from Cyril of Alexandria (L) are drawn from the *gesta* of the same Lateran council. Wolfram von den Steinen once assumed that "the quotations of *JE* 2448 are, for the most part based on texts cited in the acta of Stephen III's Lateran Council of 769."[16] The attitude toward images expressed by Gregory the Great in his Epistles was surely known to the assembly of 769, because the interpolated Epistle, *Registrum* IX.147 to Secundinus, was according to the *Hadrianum* I.12 (p. 20.3) cited in the synodal *Acta* of 769. It is therefore quite possible also that Gregory's *Epistles* to Serenus of Marseilles (testimonium C) and to the Frankish Kings Theodericus and Theodebertus (T) were cited in *JE* 2448, because they had been quoted already in the *Acta* of 769. Of other synodal *Acta* those of the Sixth Ecumenical Council of 680–681 were known to the draftsman in the papal *scrinium* who had a hand in the composition of *JE* 2448, for the Latin passage from the Greek sacra by Constantine IV Pogonatos, addressed to Pope Donus in 678 (above, R), is cited in *JE* 2448 in the same Latin version that we find in the Latin *Acta* of 680–681.

The Greek versions of the five testimonia G, K, N, P, and Q in the catena of the Byzantine translation of *JE* 2448 are to be found also in the florilegium of the codex Paris, B.N. grec. 1115, which was copied in 1276 from a manuscript written during the year 859.[17] Theodor Schermann refers to these five texts in a list of testimonia of image-worship cited in the codex, f. 250–283, all of which are excerpted from the Greek *Acta* of II Nicaea, 787. Many of these synodal testimonia also occur in the collections by John of Damascus. But Schermann overlooked the fact that others, and certainly those five testimonia (previously mentioned) are not culled directly from *De imaginibus*, but from the Greek translation of *JE* 2448 which had been inserted into the Greek *Acta* of II Nicaea.[18] We recall in addition that at least one testimonium (K) of the five referred to

---

[16] "Entstehungsgeschichte der Libri Carolini," *QF* 21 (1929–30), 28f., 50.

[17] Cf. Devreesse, *Introduction*; Theodor Schermann, *Die Geschichte der dogmatischen Florilegien vom V.–VIII. Jahrhundert* (*TU* NF. 13.1; 1904), 74–78, especially Schermann's testimonia nos. 1, 7c, 14, 16, 27, listed on pp. 75–78.

[18] It seems that Altaner's mistaken opinion, pointed out in n. 9 (above), concerning the patristic testimonia of *JE* 2448, is based on Schermann's thesis.

is cited in *JE* 2448 after its occurrence in the *Acta* of the Lateran
Council of 769. This means that the draftsman of *JE* 2448 in the
papal *scrinium* may already have used John of Damascus' collections,
unless most, if not all of the *Synodica*'s testimonia were drawn from
chains of testimonia contained in the no-longer-extant *gesta* of the
Lateran Council of 769.[19] To be sure, Paul van den Ven's rejection of the likelihood that the synodal assembly of II Nicaea in
787 actually utilized John of Damascus' collections of testimonia
of image-worship cannot be extended, as we saw, to those testimonia
in the patristic catena of *JE* 2448 (inserted into the synodal protocols of II Nicaea) which directly or indirectly depend on *De
imaginibus*.[20]

[19] See the fragments of the Lateran Council of 769 edited by A. Werminghoff
(*MGH, Conc.* 2.1; Aevi Karolini 1.1, 1904), 90ff.

[20] Cf. P. van den Ven, "La patristique et l'hagiographie au Concile de Nicée
de 787," *Byzantion* 25–27 (1955–57) 336, 360. Cf. below, Chapter IV, at the end
of section R.

PART TWO

Prolegomena to a Critical Edition
of the *Libri Carolini*

The authorship of the *Libri Carolini*,* the official Frankish protest against the worship of images decreed by the Seventh Ecumenical Council of II Nicaea in 787, constitutes a problem which has puzzled historians since the sixteenth century.[1] At the Frankfurt Synod of 794, Charlemagne and his clergy simultaneously condemned Spanish adoptionism and the Byzantine image-worship. The lost synodal *Acta* may have contained but a part of the collection of documents concerning the adoptionist controversy; two of these documents were written by Alcuin. The bulk of all the documents is considerable even though the undoubtedly long transcript of the Frankfurt synodal discussions is missing. None of them deals with image-worship, and yet special documents dealing with this problem must have been discussed by the assembly when it rejected and

---

* This Introduction to Part Two and Chapter III are reprinted, with some insertions and additions, from "The Unknown Author of the *Libri Carolini*: Patristic Exegesis, Mozarabic Antiphons, and the *Vetus Latina*," in *Didascaliae: Studies in Honor of Anselm M. Albareda*, ed. Sesto Prete (New York, 1961), 469–485; pp. 486–519 are dealt with in Chapter XI.

[1] The basic studies dealing with the *Libri Carolini* are by Wolfram von den Steinen (referred to below in n. 7) and Donatien de Bruyne (see Chapter III, n. 9). See also the present writer's *Alcuin and Charlemagne: Studies in Carolingian History and Literature* (Cornell Studies in Classical Philology, 32; Ithaca, N.Y., 1959), ch. IX, especially pp. 169–177: "Charlemagne's Libri Carolini and Alcuin," the revised version of a study first published in *Traditio* 9 (1953), 143–49.

condemned the Byzantine heresy. The rejection of II Nicaea is known only from the Frankfurt Capitulary of 794 which contains the final decisions of the synod and of a simultaneously held Frankish Diet.[2] But in accord with known and established procedures[3] we may assume that the question of the images was also discussed by the assembly on the basis of the then-existing special documents. These were read and discussed publicly, and the question was finally voted upon by the participants who were seated in the prescribed circular and hierarchical order according to ecclesiastical rank. A number of documents, in bulk much larger than those available for the controversy against adoptionism, was at the disposal of the synod for the discussion of image-worship. What were these documents?

First, besides the *Libri Carolini*, there were two documents basically connected with the genesis and composition of the *Libri Carolini*: the *Nicaenum*,[4] a Latin translation of the original Greek Acts of II Nicaea, and the *Hadrianum*,[5] a letter-treatise sent by Hadrian I to Charlemagne, dealing with the papal answers to numerous Frankish objections to the *Nicaenum*. I believe that in addition two other documents were consulted during these discussions—one the so-called *Codex Carolinus*,[6] a collection of the papal correspondence (from the time of Gregory III to that of Hadrian I) with Frankish rulers from Charles Martel to Carloman and Charlemagne, and officially edited under the name and upon the request of Charlemagne in 791; and the second, in all probability, the MS of the *Liber Pontificalis*,[7] apparently produced in 791 for the Frankish court.

[2] Ed. A. Werminghoff, *MGH*, *Conc.* 2 (Aevi Karolini 2; Hannover-Leipzig, 1906), 165.

[3] Cf. Chapter XVI, below.

[4] See Chapter III n. 2.

[5] Ed. Karl Hampe, *MGH*, *Epistolae* 5 (Karolini Aevi 3; Berlin, 1899), 5–58.

[6] Ed. Wilhelm Gundlach, *MGH*, *Epistolae* 3 (Merowingici et Karolini Aevi 1; Berlin, 1892), 469–657.

[7] Wolfram von den Steinen, "Entstehungsgeschichte der Libri Carolini," *QF* 21 (1929–30), 73; cf. von den Steinen, "Karl der Grosse und die Libri Carolini," *Neues Archiv* 49 (1930–32), 207–280; the reprint of this study appeared in 1931 (in the second issue of the journal's vol. 49), as the present writer knows from the copy of the reprint sent to him by Professor Wolfram von den Steinen in 1954.

The deliberative technique of synodal procedures in arriving at a decision in a controversy strongly suggests the use of these five documents during the discussions. There is, however, no evidence available that the synodal assembly actually endorsed the *Libri Carolini* by public vote, although it did vote for the condemnation of image-worship. But we can be quite certain that the Frankfurt Synod of 794 used for its discussions concerning image-worship the *LC*, the *Nicaenum*, and the *Hadrianum*, for the final decision of the synod, as formulated in the Frankish Capitulary of 794, c. 2, condemns the statement in the *Nicaenum*, *in actione tertia*, which proclaims the identity of the adoration of images and of the trinity,[8] a statement also discussed in the *Hadrianum* I.9 and in the *LC* III.17.

Since Alcuin has been recognized as the author of two antiadoptionist documents written for Charlemagne and his clergy—he acted for both as synodal adviser—we may easily see him as does Bastgen as the author of the *LC*. Though only a deacon, Alcuin was accepted upon the king's recommendation into the presence (*consortium*) of the Frankfurt Synod, in order to authorize his public participation in the discussions leading to the rejection of adoptionism and image-worship. Had Alcuin been solely the redactor of official documents at Frankfurt, this special act that gave him theological authority with the synod's episcopate would hardly have been necessary. While it is true that he never, in his numerous letters, biblical commentaries, or didactic writings, mentions the controversy about the images, nevertheless newly found textual and stylistic evidence in the two Frankfurt documents which he wrote for the king and the Frankish episcopate point to Alcuin as the author of the *LC*. Some important central topics that are discussed in those two antiadoptionist Frankfurt documents written in his personal style[9] also occur in the *LC*, whose final redaction naturally preceded the Frankfurt Synod of 794.

The anonymous activity of Alcuin in the service of Charlemagne was even broader than used to be assumed. It extends, as I have indicated, to Charlemagne's capitularies and widespread correspondence. Thus Alcuin's co-authorship of the *Admonitio generalis*

---

[8] Von den Steinen, *QF*, 84f.
[9] See Wallach, *Alcuin and Charlemagne*, pp. 171–173.

as well as of three of Charlemagne's personal letters has been established by Friedrich-Karl Scheibe.[10] The assumption of Alcuin's authorship of the *LC* is opposed by the persistently alleged, but never proved, authorship of the *LC* by Theodulph of Orléans. That it must be rejected will become clear after we have examined the very involved origin of the *Libri Carolini*. There is no evidence at all for Theodulph's authorship.

[10] "Alcuin und die *Admonitio Generalis*," *DA* 14 (1958), 221–229; "Alcuin und die Briefe Karls des Grossen," *ibid.* 15 (1959), 181–193; cf. also Scheibe, "Geschichtsbild, Zeitbewusstsein und Reformwille bei Alcuin," *Archiv für Kulturgeschichte* 41 (1959), 35–62. For Alcuin's position at Frankfurt see H. B. Meyer, "Zur Stellung Alkuins auf dem Frankfurter Konzil," *Zeitschrift für katholische Theologie* 81 (1959), 455–460. On Alcuin as the author and editor of official Carolingian documents see Wallach, *Alcuin and Charlemagne*, chapters IX–XI.

CHAPTER III

Origin and Composition
of the *Libri Carolini*

How did the *Libri Carolini* originate? Wolfram von den Steinen[1] answered this question in a famous study. The key to the *LC*'s origin is the understanding of the proper interrelationship of three documents, the *Nicaenum*, the *Capitulare adversus Synodum*, and the *Hadrianum*.

The *Nicaenum* is a poor Latin rendering of the Greek Acts of II Nicaea sent about 788 by Hadrian I to Charlemagne, who had not received an invitation by the Byzantine emperors to attend the Seventh Ecumenical Council.[2] Quotations from these now lost Latin acts occur in the *Capitulare adversus Synodum*, in the *Hadrianum*, and in the *LC*. A second Latin translation of the Greek Acts was produced by the librarian Anastasius during the rule of John VIII in 873.

The *Capitulare adversus Synodum*, sent by Charlemagne to Hadrian I at the beginning or the middle of 789, represents the first Frankish reaction against the *Nicaenum*. This *Capitulare* was neither a preliminary version of, nor an excerpt from, the later *LC*. Fragments of the lost *Capitulare* are preserved in the *Hadrianum* where it is cited *in extenso* in the chapter headings.

The *Hadrianum* is a letter-treatise sent by Hadrian I to Charlemagne, probably at the beginning of 791 in response to the Frankish

---

[1] See Part Two n. 7.

[2] The first Latin translation of the Greek Acts of II Nicaea was still in the papal archives during the time of John VIII (872–882), when it was replaced by a second translation undertaken before 873 by the librarian Anastasius; see Mansi XII–XIII; also *PL* 129; cf. n. 15, below.

Vatican codex: for *LC* III.14 compare Chapter VI, A; for *LC* III.25 see Chapter VI, D; for *LC* IV.7 cf. Chapter VI, F. The recognition that Ambrosiaster's *ad Romanos* is cited in the *LC* without any acknowledgment accounts for the restoration of a few erased words in *LC* I.1, as is verified in Chapter VI, I.

Bastgen's modern edition of the *LC* was in the press from 1912 until 1924.[8] It is based on the *Vaticanus*, which lacks the Preface, the table of contents of *LC* I, a part of *LC* I.1, and Book IV of the work. The missing parts are, however, preserved in the Paris codex of the Bibliothèque de L'Arsenal lat. 663, a copy of the *Vaticanus* when it was still unimpaired. See the description of the *Vaticanus* in Chapter VIII.

Bastgen, who believed that Alcuin was the author of the *LC*, lists the numerous biblical and patristic sources, and in the *apparatus criticus* the many textual corrections, deletions, and additions occurring in V. Soon after the completion of his edition it became clear that much work remained to be done on the text and in tracing sources of the *LC*. Relevant contributions were offered by Wolfram von den Steinen, who advocated the authorship of the Visigoth Theodulph of Orléans, and by Donatien de Bruyne,[9] who nullified Allgeier's attempt[10] to tie up alleged quotations from the Mozarabic (Visigothic) *Psalter* in the *LC* with Theodulph's never proved authorship. Donatien de Bruyne and von den Steinen listed new sources used in the *LC*, and also suggested numerous improvements on Bastgen's text recension. De Bruyne in addition successfully explained the reasons for certain corrections in the *LC* text written in V *in loco raso*, simultaneously restoring for many passages the erased text of the first *LC* redaction.

The intricacy of the philological problems connected with the critical treatment of the *LC* text may be illustrated in the following instances. The first (A) deals with the technique of the translator who rendered into Latin the scriptural quotations of the Greek Acts of II Nicaea, that is, quotations which are cited in the *Hadrianum*

---

[8] *Libri Carolini sive Caroli Magni Capitulare de Imaginibus. MGH, Legum Sectio III, Concilia 2, Supplementum* (Hannover-Leipzig, 1912–24).

[9] Donatien de Bruyne, "La composition des Libri Carolini," *Revue Bénédictine* 44 (1932), 227–234.

[10] A. Allgeier, "Psalmenzitate und die Frage nach der Herkunft der Libri Carolini," *Historisches Jahrbuch der Görresgesellschaft* 46 (1926), 333–353.

and in the *LC*. The second example (B) offers the restoration of the probably original text of an erased passage of the *LC*'s first redaction which was replaced in the autographum V by another text written *in loco raso*. In Sections C and D, the literary and philological complications encountered in dealing with the genesis and composition of a *LC* chapter are extensively illustrated.

A. The technique of translation employed by the Roman ecclesiastic who translated the Greek Acts of II Nicaea has been investigated by Wolfram von den Steinen. He believed that the anonymous translator faithfully rendered into Latin the numerous Greek Bible quotations of the *Nicaenum*. The translator is said to offer his very own translations of biblical quotations except in the case of the *Psalter* whose citations are derived—with one exception— from the *Psalterium Romanum*. Newly found evidence, however, now shows that the translator of the *Nicaenum* used existing translations not only for his citations from the *Psalter*, but also for his citations from other books. The use he made of Jerome's Old Latin translation of Gen. 47.31 is apparent in Section C, below. I treat here another instance dealing with the *Canticum Canticorum*.

The *Hadrianum* I.20 (Hampe, p. 24.15) and the *LC* II.10 (Bastgen, p. 70f.) offer *Cant.* 2.14 in the following version of the *Nicaenum*: "Ostende mihi faciem tuam et auditam fac mihi vocem tuam, quoniam vox tua suavis est et facies tua speciosa." Bastgen's marginal reference reads "cf. Cant. 2.14," but the reference should have been to "*Cant. 2.14" because in this passage we are dealing with the *Vetus Latina*.

The Latin translation of *Cant.* 2.14 follows verbatim the Greek Acts, as von den Steinen already saw; it is, however, by no means a new Latin rendering produced by the translator of the *Nicaenum*. The *Greek Nicaenum* cites the LXX of Cant. 2.14: δεῖξόν μοι τὴν ὄψιν σου καὶ ἀκούτισόν μοι τὴν φωνήν σου, ὅτι ἡ φωνή σου ἡδεῖα, καὶ ἡ ὄψις σου ὡραία (Mansi XIII.221A). The *Latin Nicaenum* offers a literal translation of the LXX and as such an *antiqua* whose version, as quoted in the *Hadrianum* I.20 and the *LC* II.10, appears not only in Epiphanius Scholasticus' Latin translation of Philo of Karpasia's Commentary on the *Canticum Cant.* (*PG* 40.71–74), but also in Jerome, *Adversus Jovinianum* I.30 (*PL* 23.252C), and in the Latin translation of Origen, *In Canticum Cant.* 3, in *Origenes Werke* 8, ed.

W. A. Baehrens (Leipzig, 1925), 228.21–23. See also D. de Bruyne, "Les anciennes versions Latines du Cantique des Cantiques," *Revue Bénédictine* 38 (1926), 412.

B. The patristic sources of *LC* III.3 have been discussed by Wolfram von den Steinen[11] and by the present writer.[12] The chapter deals with the final Frankish position concerning the much-discussed *filioque* of the creed. Following John of Damascus, *De fide orthodoxa* (*PG* 94.849), who was the first to say ἐκ πατρὸς δι' υἱοῦ ἐκπορευόμενον, the Patriarch Tarasius used the same formula in his profession of faith pronounced at II Nicaea in 787. The Frankish theologians in the *Capitulare adversus Synodum* rejected this *ex patre per filium procedentem* in Tarasius' symbolum, as we know from the *Hadrianum* (ed. Karl Hampe, ch. 1, p. 7). Accordingly *LC* III.3 maintains that Tarasius' formulation is contrary to the Nicene creed; and it is therefore proposed to read *ex patre et filio procedentem*. The relevant final discussion in the *LC* contains in *Vaticanus Latinus 7207*, fol. 124b–125a, a statement written *in loco raso*,[13] designated i–i in Bastgen's edition, p. 112.32–35. The importance of the subject matter makes one wonder what was the original reading in the first redaction of the *LC*. The section i–i reads as follows:

Filius[i] solus de patre est natus, ideo solus dicitur genitus. Spiritus sanctus solus de Patre et Filio procedit, ideo solus amborum nuncupatur Spiritus.[I] Procedit enim ex utroque non nascendo, ut alicuius filius dici possit.[i]

This text is preceded and followed by excerpts from Augustinus, *De trinitate: LC*, p. 112.30–32, Pater...valuerint...proferentium, is a literal quotation from XV.26.47, 110–111, ed. W. J. Mountain and Fr. Glorie (*CCL* 50A, 1968), 528 f. *LC*, p. 112.35–37, Diceretur... spiritus, is from the same passage, lines 115–118. The lines 111–115, connecting these two quotations, read:

Filius autem de Patre natus est, et Spiritus Sanctus de Patre principaliter, et ipse sine ullo temporis intervallo dante, communiter de utroque procedit.

---

[11] "Karl der Grosse und die Libri Carolini," *Neues Archiv* 49 (1932), 227–237; "Entstehungsgeschichte der Libri Carolini," *QF* 21 (1929–30), 63.

[12] See Wallach, *Alcuin and Charlemagne*, 169–175.

[13] See the facsimiles of *Vaticanus Latinus 7207*, fol. 124b and 125a, below Plates I–II, and in *Didascaliae* (cited in *Part Two*, n. *), inserted between pp. 512 and 513.

This statement seems to supply the text of the first redaction of the *LC* passage for which the section i–i was substituted in the *Vaticanus*. The substituted text, however, is not original with the author of the *LC*. Instead of following the authority of Augustine, the corrector evidently preferred that of Isidore of Seville, for the text portion i–I of the section i–i (see above) renders the formulation of the *filioque* in the simplified version offered in Isidore's *Etymologiae* VII.4.4:

Filius solus de Patre est natus, ideo solus dicitur genitus. Spiritus Sanctus solus de Patre et Filio procedit, ideo solus amborum nuncupatur Spiritus.[14]

The thoroughgoing Augustinian character of the discussion in *LC* III.3 is obvious also in the rest of the chapter: pp. 112.37–113.4 is a newly found quotation from the pseudo-Augustinian *Dialogus quaestionum LXV*, qu. 2, as is shown below in Chapter IV, item D, while *LC*, p. 113.18–20, Verum ... sufficiat, is derived—verbatim— from *De trin.* XV.27.48, 1–4 (Mountain and Glorie, 529).

It is of interest to the historian of dogmatics to find that the first redaction of *LC* III.3 offered for the highly involved *filioque* discussion is in all probability Augustine's basic statement.

C. The *LC* repeatedly states that the *Nicaenum* does not quote the Bible text in an authentic version. *LC* I.13 (p. 32f.) offers an instance of this type of Frankish criticism.

The *Nicaenum, in actione quarta*, refers to Gen. 47.31 in connection with προσκύνησις, the *adoratio* due to images. We remember that λατρεία, *servitium*, is due to God alone. The Greek *Acta* read as follows:

Εἰ δὲ ἐγκαλεῖς μοι, ὅτι ὡς θεὸν προσκυνῶ τὸ ξύλον τοῦ σταυροῦ, διὰ τί οὐκ ἐγκαλεῖς τῷ Ἰακὼβ προσκυνήσατι ἐπὶ τὸ ἄκρον τῆς ῥάβδου τοῦ Ἰωσήφ; ἀλλὰ πρόδηλον, ὅτι οὐ τὸ ξύλον ἰδὼν προσεκύνησεν; ἀλλὰ διὰ τοῦ ξύλου τὸν Ἰωσὴφ ὥσπερ καὶ ἡμεῖς διὰ τοῦ σταυροῦ τὸν Χριστόν.[15]

---

[14] Isidore of Seville, *Etymologiae sive Origines Libri XX*, ed. W. M. Lindsay (*SCBD*, 1911).

[15] See Mansi XIII.46; Anastasius' Latin translation of the Greek Acts (see also *PL* 129.294C) makes use of the first Latin translation, as can be deduced from the closeness with which it follows the fragment (of the first tr.) preserved by the *Hadrianum* and the *LC*.

This text was accessible to the Franks in the Latin translation of the *Nicaenum*, and was criticized in the *Capitulare adversus Synodum* sent by Charlemagne to Hadrian I, who replied to the Frankish objection in the *Hadrianum* I.24 (ed. Karl Hampe, p. 27) as follows:

De eo quod indocte et inordinate dicunt: "Si calumniaris me, quoniam ut Deum adoro lignum crucis, cur non calumniaris Iacob adorantem summitatem virge Ioseph? Sed manifestum est, quoniam non lignum videns adoravit, sed per lignum Ioseph, sicut et nos per crucem Christum."

The identical objection against the *Nicaenum* is voiced in *LC* I.13 (p. 32). Bastgen (also p. 7.7) seems to assume that the text from *Si calumniaris* to *virge Ioseph*, put by him within quotation marks, offers the statement of the *Nicaenum*, while the remainder constitutes the alleged Frankish criticism of the *Nicaenum*. However, the comparison of the chapter heading of *LC* I.13 with its Greek original indicates that the chapter heading renders the text of the *Nicaenum* verbatim, and that Bastgen's second quotation mark belongs after *Christum* and not after *Ioseph*.

The *LC* stresses its preference for Jerome's *Hebraica veritas* (pp. 32.29; 33.12) "cui potissimum *fides adhibenda est*." Neither Bastgen nor Freeman[16] noticed that throughout *LC* I.13, the author of the tractate has in mind Jerome's *Epistola ad Damasum* (which prefaces his Vulgate Gospels), and especially Jerome's plaintive note about the confused textual transmission of the MSS: Si enim Latinis exemplaribus *fides est adhibenda*, respondeant quibus: tot sunt paene quot codices. In addition, the *LC*'s suggestion (p. 33.22–28), *nova ... legis translatio quaeritur*, that a new version of the Scriptures be fashioned after the Septuagint, after Theodotion, Symmachus, Aquila, reflects Jerome's often-repeated statement in the *Epistola ad Damasum*, referred to in *LC* 1.6 (Bastgen, p. 21).

The objections raised in *LC* I.13 are mistaken on two counts. First, the text portion quoted from the Latin translation of the Greek *Acts* does not represent an original statement made during the synodal discussions. It occurs in a document read into the record upon the request of Hadrian I's two representatives (Mansi XIII.43A) who attended II Nicaea as papal observers. The criticism of *LC* I.13 is therefore directed against the text offered by the

[16] *Speculum* 32 (1957), 692f.; see my remarks in *Didascaliae*, p. 480.

papal representatives. And second, the fact that we are dealing with a criticism aimed at Hadrian I also becomes clear when we recall that Hadrian,[17] in his letter of 785 addressed to the Byzantine Emperor Constantine and his mother Irene (*JE* 2448), a letter which was read into the record of the synodal proceedings, *in actione secunda* (Mansi XII.1064B–C), had stated:

Nam idem ipse Jacob proprio demum arbitrio summitatem virgae filii sui Joseph (Gen. 47.31) deosculatus est, fidei dilectione hoc agens, sicut beatus Paulus in epistola ad Hebraeos (11.21) testatur: non virgae, sed tenenti eam honoris ac dilectionis exhibuit affectum.

In the final analysis, it is Hadrian's text of Gen. 47.31 that is criticized in the *LC*—unjustly to be sure, for the supposition of the *LC* that the *Nicaenum*'s version of Gen. 47.31 "adoravit (Israel) summitatem virgae (scil. of Joseph)" does not occur in Latin MSS is incorrect! Neither the author of the *LC* nor Bastgen recognized that the *Nicaenum* offers Gen. 47.31 in the Old Latin version cited by Jerome, *Hebr. quaest. in Gen.* (*PL* 23; Paris, 1883; col. 1053C–1054A):[18]

Et dixit ei, jura mihi, et juravit ei: et adoravit Israel contra summitatem virgae eius.

This is a literal translation of the LXX: εἶπεν δέ : Ὄμοσόν μοι. καὶ ὤμοσεν αὐτῷ. καὶ προσεκύνησεν Ἰσραὴλ ἐπὶ τὸ ἄκρον τῆς ῥάβδου αὐτοῦ.

Augustine, *Quaestiones in Heptateuchum* I.162, quoted by the *LC*, refers to the changed meaning of Gen. 47.31 which results from the marking of αὐτοῦ either with a smooth breathing (-eius, scil. Ioseph) or with a rough breathing (αὐτοῦ-ἑαυτοῦ—suae, scil. Israel-Jacob).

In the light of these findings, Hampe's reference in the *Hadrianum* (p. 27.4) to Hebr. 11.21, listed by Bastgen at *LC* I.13 (p. 32.28), is insufficient; Gen. 47.31 should have been listed too. The contents of Hebr. 11.21 render and refer to Gen. 48.15–16, that is, Israel-Jacob's benediction of the sons of Joseph; the contents do not refer

---

[17] Cf. Hadrian's synodal letter of October 26, 785,."Deus qui dixit," *JE* 2448, *Regesta Pontificum Romanorum*, ed. Ph. Jaffé (2nd ed. Leipzig, 1885), 299.

[18] See now *Vetus Latina* 2: *Genesis*, ed. Bonifatius Fischer (Freiburg i. Br., 1951–54), 488; Jerome, *Hebr. quaest. in Gen.*, in *CCL* 72 (Turnholt, 1959), 51, and on p. 41, the passage quoted in Section D, below.

to the oath of Joseph in Gen. 47.31, tendered to Israel, promising his future burial in the land of his ancestors. Notwithstanding this fact, Hebr. 11.21 quotes from Gen. 47.31, though it deals with the situation of Gen. 48.15–16.

The incorrect statement of the *LC* concerning the allegedly unknown origin of the *Nicaenum*'s version of Gen. 47.31 did not escape the compilers of the *Libellus Synodalis* of the Paris Synod of 825, c. 59, who were acquainted with some of the *LC*'s original sources. When writing their expert opinion on the worship of images, the compilers of this *Libellus* addressed to Louis the Pious inserted into the document some of the basic sources cited in the *LC*. Not infrequently they even restored the original text sequence of source materials that had become separated in the *LC*. Thus the quotation in *LC* I.13 (pp. 32.35–33.9) of Augustine's work, the last lines of which are cited in *LC* I.13 (p. 32.30–33), is rendered in the Paris *Libellus*, c. 59, in the proper sequence, because its authors verified the *LC* source in a MS of Augustine's *Quaestiones*, and then in the *Libellus* restored the original order of the text.[19] On a Jerome text cited in *LC* IV.27, which appears in its wider context in the same *Libellus*, see below Chapter VI, note 6.

D. *LC* I.10 (Bastgen, 30–31) discusses and rejects the statement of the *Nicaenum, in actione quarta,* concerning *mens videns deum,* νοῦς ὁρῶν θεόν, one of the etymologies of Jacob's second name Israel. Bastgen does not list the patristic source of this interpretation. Ann Freeman in *Speculum* 32 (1957), 695, assumes that in this instance the *LC*'s source is not Jerome but Eucherius of Lyons, and that Eucherius' work entitled *De nominibus Hebraicis* furnished the *LC* with the preferred etymology, *Israel = Princeps cum Deo.* But Eucherius never wrote a work by this title, nor is his etymology the *LC*'s source. He wrote *Instructiones,* ed. Carl Wotke (*CSEL* 31; Prag-Wien-Leipzig, 1894), which contains at the beginning of Book II a brief section entitled *De nominibus Hebraicis,* and—following Jerome's earlier etymology (see below)—reads: Israel, vir videns deum, sed melius princeps cum deo (p. 141).

LC I.10 lists these etymologies of Israel: a. Vir videns deum; b. Fortis cum deo; c. Princeps cum deo; d. Mens videns deum.

---

[19] Cf. *MGH, Conc.* 2 (Aevi Karolini 1.2; Hannover-Leipzig, 1908), 499f.

The etymology *c* is called *veracius*, while the *Nicaenum*'s *d* is rejected on the ground that it is *paene inusitatum*. The *LC*'s preference for *Israel-Princeps cum deo* follows the preference expressed by Jerome, and also adopts Jerome's doubts concerning *a* and *d*. The rarely occurring *d* is found, for instance, in Jerome's translation of Didymus of Alexandria, *De spiritu sancto* 44 (*PL* 23.148A), *Israel, id est, mens videns deum* (νοῦς ὁρῶν θεόν); also in Optatus of Mileve, ed. C. Ziwsa (*CSEL* 26; Prag-Wien-Leipzig, 1893), 66.6:

dubium non est populum credentium Israhel esse vocatùm, plebes singulas filias Israhel, id est, qui mente deum viderint et deo crediderint.

The *LC* adopts the interpretations of Jerome, *Hebr. quaestiones in Genesim* (*PL* 23):

Princeps cum deo, hoc est Israel (1038C); illud autem quod interpretatur Israel, vir videns deum, sive mens videns deum, omnium pene sermonum detritum, non tam vere quam violenter mihi interpretatum videtur (1039A).

This exegesis of Jacob's name Israel is based on the concept of ὅρασις θεοῦ, often advocated by Philo of Alexandria who etymologizes: Israel—ἀνὴρ ὁρῶν θεόν (Vir videns deum); see *De Abrahamo* 57, ed. Leopold Cohn, *Philonis Opera* IV (Berlin, 1902): προσονομάζεται γὰρ Ἑβραίων γλώττῃ τὸ ἔθνος Ἰσραήλ, ὅπερ ἑρμηνευθέν ἐστιν ὁρῶν θεόν; or *De confusione linguarum* 146, ed. Paul Wendland, *Philonis Opera* II (Berlin, 1897): ... καὶ ὁ κατ᾽ εἰκόνα ἄνθρωπος καὶ ὁ ὁρῶν, Ἰσραήλ, προσαγορεύεται. Philo's ἀνὴρ ὁρῶν θεόν renders the Hebrew folk-etymology of ישראל as איש רואה אל.

The Philonic etymologies of Israel were adopted by Latin patristic exegesis not only through Jerome's work but also through that of Origen and Eusebius of Caesarea.

Origenis in Evangelium Joannis 2.31 (25), ed. A. E. Brooke, I (Cambridge, 1896), 97.30 quotes the etymology Ἰσραὴλ ἀνὴρ ὁρῶν θεόν, in a fragment from a now lost Hellenistic-Jewish OT apocryphon, the Προσευχὴ Ἰωσήφ.[20] This definition of Israel in the "Prayer of Joseph" is derived from Philo, *De confusione linguarum* 146, cited above. And the same passage in Origen's commentary is borrowed

---

[20] A.-M. Denis, *Fragmenta Pseudepigraphorum quae supersunt Graeca* (Leiden, 1970), 61–62, s.v. *Oratio Joseph*; cf. also Edmund Stein, "Zur apokryphen Schrift *Gebet Josephs*," *Monatsschrift für Geschichte und Wissenschaft des Judentums* 81 (1937), 280–286.

by Eusebius, *Praeparatio Evangelica* VI.11.64, ed. Karl Mras, I.1 (Berlin, 1954), 356.22–24, while the identical passage from Philo is quoted—verbatim—in XI.15.2, ed. Mras, I.2 (Berlin, 1956), 36.9–10.

The basic structure of the *LC*'s general theme is determined, as we saw, by the numerous theses of its individual chapter headings that question certain specific points made in the synodal discussions of the *Nicaenum*.[21] These headings are dealt with in the *LC* with the help of a biblical exegesis that argues quite naturally within the bounds of a traditionally established patristic method. Thus the formulations and meanings of scriptual quotations in the *LC* are inseparably tied up with their context and cannot be discussed properly if entirely detached from their background. See Chapter XI, below.

---

[21] Stephen Gero, "The Libri Carolini and the Image Controversy," *Greek Ortho-dox Theological Review* 18 (1973), 22, misrepresents the origin of the *LC*, since he assumes that its author knew only a set of extracts from the *First Latin Nicaenum*, and not the *Acta* of II Nicaea as a whole.

CHAPTER IV

The *Libri Carolini* and Patristics, Latin and Greek

Although Hubert Bastgen's edition of the *Libri Carolini*, which appeared in 1924,[1] has been corrected in numerous details by Wolfram von den Steinen,[2] Donatien de Bruyne,[3] and the present writer,[4] Bastgen's recension still is a valuable contribution to a future, more critical edition. Since the autograph of the *LC*, *Codex Vaticanus Latinus 7207*, in some places possesses some of the characteristics of a palimpsest, the investigation of the literary sources used in the treatise leads not infrequently to deleted, erased readings of the first redaction. This is true not only of biblical quotations, but also of patristic texts cited in the *LC*, which hitherto have not been identified at all, or else have been incorrectly recorded by Bastgen. The variety of complicated philological and literary problems which confront us becomes obvious from the following treatment of newly found Latin and Greek patristic sources.

Latin Patristic Texts

A. Victorinus of Pettau, *Commentarii in Apocalipsin.*—*LC* III.6 (117.29–35) ascribes to *quidam doctorum* the interpretation of a *canticum novum*, which Bastgen regarded as a reference to Ps. 149.1, thus

---

[1] *Libri Carolini sive Caroli Magni Capitulare de Imaginibus* (*MGH*, Legun Sectio III: *Conc.* 2, Supplementum; Hannover, Leipzig, 1924).

[2] "Entstehungsgeschichte der Libri Carolini," *QF* 21 (1929–30), 1–93; "Karl der Grosse und die Libri Carolini," *Neues Archiv* 49 (1930–32), 207–280.

[3] Donatien de Bruyne, "La composition des Libri Carolini," *Revue Bénédictine* 44 (1932), 227–234.

[4] See the study published in *Didascaliae*, cited above in the Introduction to Part Two, *n.

overlooking that the *LC* clearly points to the New Testament as the basis of its exegesis. The reference is to *Apocalypse* 5.9 with its *canticum novum*. Dom de Bruyne[5] correctly surmised that *quidam doctorum*, written on an erasure, replaces a proper name which was removed because a corrector of the *LC* judged the citation to be apocryphal. The text cited is drawn from Victorinus of Pettau, *Commentarii in Apocalypsin*, recensio Hieronymiana 5.3 to *Apoc.* 5.8–9.[6] The repetition of *est* after the second, third, and fourth *novum* in the *LC* occurs also in MSS belonging to this commentary's recension of Jerome. The same recension of Victorinus' *Commentary* was known to Alcuin, who mentions it in the *Preface* to his own *Commentary on the Apocalypse* (*PL* 100.1087BC). Further, Beatus of Liébana, one of Alcuin's correspondents, inserted the same passage from Victorinus into his *Commentary*, which was composed about 786.[7] He omits, however, the text of the second and third *novum* (. . . surgere: *LC*.117.31–32), and for this very reason his work could not have been the *LC*'s source. The name of *Victorinus, Petavionensis episcopus*, was deleted from the first redaction of the *LC*, because the former's *opuscula* are labeled *apocrypha* in the *Decretum Gelasianum*,[8] a work which provided the author of the *LC* with a list of canonically approved writings.[9]

B. Augustine, *De magis Pharaonis.*—*LC* III.25 (155.38–156.12) reads: " . . . Augustinus a demonibus miracula fieri . . . his verbis testatur. Ait enim: *Non oportet moveri . . . permissu tamen divino pro meritis animarum sua cuique tribuuntur.*" Bastgen identifies this text

---

[5] "La composition des Libri Carolini," *Revue Bénédictine* 44 (1932), 233.

[6] *Victorini Episcopi Patavionensis Opera*, rec. Iohann Haussleiter (*CSEL* 49; Wien, Leipzig, 1916), 67, 4–9, and *app. crit.* to line 7.

[7] *Beati in Apocalypsin* III.17, ed. Henry A. Sanders (Papers and Monographs of the American Academy in Rome 7; Rome, 1930), 330, 3–5; also Haussleiter, *op. cit.*, 67, 6 *app. crit.* The same section of the text as is missing in Beatus is also missing in the corresponding passage in Apringius, *Tractatus in Apoc.*, ed. P. A. C. Vega (El Escorial, 1940), 5.

[8] *De libris recipiendis et non recipiendis*, ed. Ernst von Dobschütz, *Decretum Gelasianum* (*TU* 38, 4; Leipzig, 1912), 13, 56, 84, 316f., 198.

[9] Cf. *LC* I.6 (20): "nec aliorum *doctorum* nisi eorum qui a Gelasio" etc.; and Hubert Bastgen, "Das Bilderkapitular Karls d. Gr. (libri Carolini) und das sogenannte Decretum Gelasianum," *Neues Archiv* 41 (1917–19), 682–690; see also Victorinus in *PL, Supplementum* I (Paris, 1958), 131.

with *quaestio* IV, *De miraculis magicis*, of Pseudo-Augustine, *Liber XXI Sententiarum* (*PL* 40.726f.). But the *Sententiae* are of unknown origin and date and consist of excerpts from the writings of Augustine. The text of *De miraculis magicis* occurs already in Eugippius' excerpts from the works of Augustine[10] under the heading *De magis Pharaonis* with the *Incipit* "Non oportet moveri..." and the *Explicit* "...permisso tamen divinae providentiae, ut pro meritis animarum suarum cuique tribuantur." The comparison of the variants of the text in question which are found in the *LC*, in the pseudo-Augustinian writing, and in the excerpt transmitted by Eugippius shows that the *Sententiae* are not the source underlying the text in the *LC* because the *Sententiae*, *PL* 40.726, line 12, reads *mali homines magicis artibus*, whereas *LC*.156.7 offers in the first redaction, like Eugippius' older text, *malis artibus*, which was deleted in the *LC* by a Carolingian corrector, who substituted *magicis* for *malis* artibus.

The transmission of Eugippius, *De magis Pharaonis*, contains at the very end (1048.4–5) the sentence (not listed in the *LC*): "Quare ergo magi Pharaonis fecerunt quaedam miracula sicut Moses, famulus dei?" But this is the title of Augustinus, *De diversis quaestionibus 83*, *quaestio* 79 (*PL* 40.90), cited by Eugippius, and listed in Augustine's *Retractationes*.[11] The established importance of Eugippius[12] *ad textum Augustini emendandum* suggests that *quaestio* 79, as printed in *PL* 40.90, should be supplemented and that *De magis Pharaonis* actually forms the beginning of the *quaestio*. This suggestion has been made before (in *PL* 47.1225), but evidently fell into oblivion, or else was overlooked. There can be little doubt as to the genuine nature of the text in view of other excerpts from Augustine's writings in Eugippius' *Excerpta* dealing with the *magi Pharaonis*.

---

[10] Eugippius, *Excerpta ex operibus S. Augustini*, ed. Pius Knöll (*CSEL* 9.1; Wien, 1885), no. 330 par. 364, pp. 1047.13–1048.5. Knöll (p. 1134 n. 1) could not find this text in editions of Augustine; it is printed, however, by A.-B. Caillau and V. Saint-Yves in *PL* 47.1225A–B, and cited in the *Sententiae*, *PL* 40.726f.

[11] Ed. Pius Knöll (*CSEL* 36; Wien, Leipzig, 1902), 129, 7–8; cf. *ibid.*, Preface, p. x; and André Wilmart, in *Miscellanea Agostiniana* 2 (Rome, 1931), 178 no. 42.

[12] Cf. *Clavis Patrum Latinorum*, ed. Dekkers-Gaar (2nd ed.; Brugge, The Hague, 1961), 156 no. 676. See Eugippius, *Excerpta*, pp. 221, 366, especially 90, 21–95, 5: *De miraculis quae magicis artibus fiunt. Ex libro Trinitate* 3, 7, 12–9, 16 (*PL* 42.875ff.).; cf. also Joseph Martin, "Die Augustinusüberlieferung bei Eugippius," in *Miscellanea critica* 2: *Aus Anlass des 150 j. Bestehens ... B. G. Teubner*, ed. J. Irmscher (Leipzig, 1965), 228–244. See Chapter IX, K,e below.

C. Augustine, *De diversis quaestionibus 83, quaestio* 64.8.—Bastgen, *LC* IV.6 (186 n. 1), correctly states that the text in 186.16–18 from "*oraturos . . . doctorem*" is identical with Alcuin, *Comment, in Ioh.* II.7.18 (*PL* 100.796C), while Bede, *In Joan. Evang. Expositio* (*PL* 92.684C)—with whom Alcuin otherwise agrees in the exegesis of the story on the Samaritan woman (John 4.9ff.)—offers the same passage with some apparently unique variants (*adoraturos . . . doctorum*). These alleged textual agreements between the *LC* and Alcuin are listed by Bastgen because they seem to lend support to his thesis of Alcuin's authorship of the treatise. But the text in the *LC* which is identical with Alcuin's is neither by Alcuin nor by the author of the *LC*, but comes from Augustine, *De diversis quaestionibus 83*, quaestio 64.8 (*PL* 40.59, lines 13–16). This means that the occurrence of the identical texts results from the fact that Augustine's *quaestio* 64, *De muliere Samaritana* (*PL* 40.55–59, *passim*) is used by Bede, by Alcuin, and in the *LC*, in each case individually and independently. The *LC* (for example, III.27) and Alcuin frequently quote Augustine's *quaestiones*. An excerpt from *quaestio* 19 (*PL* 40.15), hitherto not acknowledged, is found, for instance, in Alcuin, *Epistula* 163 (ed. Ernst Dümmler, *MGH, Epistolae* 4 [Karolini Aevi 2]; Berlin, 1895, 263.34–264.6).

D. Pseudo-Augustine, *Dialogus quaestionum LXV.*—Dom de Bruyne[13] refers to a section in *LC* III.26 (160.36–161.11) dealing with a theory of three *genera* of *visiones* which are ascribed in the deleted first redaction to an unidentified writing of Augustine. Von den Steinen[14] thinks that a pseudo-Augustinian treatise which renders Augustine's thoughts on those *visiones* as described at great length in *De Genesi ad litteram*, Book 12, is perhaps the source here. Bastgen lists as source Book 12, c. 6f. without realizing that the section contains passages that are literally excerpted from Book 12, c. 24.[15] But the author of the *LC* does not cite Augustine's commentary directly. His source is the pseudo-Augustinian *Dialogus quaestionum LXV*, *quaestio* 63 (*PL* 40.751–52), *Quot sunt genera visionum*, which in its

---

[13] *Revue Bénédictine* 44 (1932), 233.

[14] *Neues Archiv* 49 (1931), 243 n. 1.

[15] *LC* 160 n. 2; he lists Alcuin, *Epist.* 135, *MGH, Epistolae* 4, ed. Ernst Dümmler (Berlin, 1895), 204, which consists of unidentified excerpts from *De Genesi ad litteram* 12, 9–11, ed. Joseph Zycha (*CSEL* 28; Prag, Wien, Leipzig, 1894), 391–393.

turn consists of citations drawn for the most part from *De Genesi ad litteram* 12, c. 24. This identification permits the reconstruction of a few words erased from the first redaction. After *igitur* (160.37), MS V has an erasure of four letters (160.43f.). In this case the first redaction probably substituted the word *genus* for the original *visio*, and accordingly read (in 160.37): Corporale igitur (genus) est. The deleted word after *potest* (161.6) is *statim*, according to *PL* 40.752, line 5. The words *ista* (161.5c), and *non* (161.7f.), both added above the line, do not belong to the original text, but were supplemented in order to clarify the text. The substitution of *soliditatem* (161.11) for the original *similitudinem* (*PL* 40.752, line 14) follows from the *LC*'s marginal reference to the *quinque genera visionum* of Macrobius,[16] who speaks in 1.5.9 of the *soliditas autem corporum.*

An anonymous citation from the *Dialogus quaestionum, quaestio* 2 (*PL* 40.734–35), occurs in the dogmatically important chapter on the procession of the Holy Spirit in *LC* III.3 (112.38–113.4). This section presents a pseudo-Augustinian version of Augustine, *De trinitate* XV.26.45 (*PL* 42.1092–93, *passim*); its discovery voids also in this detail the notion that Theodulf of Orléans was the author of the *LC*.[17] The citations of *quaestiones* cited in the *LC* moves the date of the *Dialogus* back at least to the eighth century. The deletion from the first redaction of the *LC* in MS V of the introductory words "ut ait scs Augustinus" (Bastgen, 160.36d) doubtless indicates that the corrector recognized in their pseudo-Augustinian formulation the well-known words of Augustine in *De trinitate.*

Though Bastgen repeatedly refers to Augustine, *De Genesi ad litteram*, the *LC* hardly offers a single citation directly drawn from it. *LC* IV.17 (205.36–38) "in tribus ventriculis cerebri," is indeed a quotation from the "Commentary on Genesis" 7.18 (*CSEL* 28, 215.6–10), drawn, however, second-hand from Isidore of Seville, *Differentiae* 2.17.51 (*PL* 83.78B).

E. Pseudo-Augustine, *Categoriae decem*, in the edition of Alcuin.— Bastgen's reference at *LC* I.1 (9 n. 2) to Augustine, *De Genesi ad*

---

[16] Macrobius, *Commentarii in somnium Scipionis* I.3, ed. Iacobus Willis (Leipzig, 1963), 8–12; cf. p. 16, 14. This reference may be added to Hubert Silvestre, "Note sur la survie de Macrobe au moyen âge," *Classica et Medievalia* 24 (1963), 170–180.

[17] See below Part Three, Introduction.

litteram 4.34, as the allegedly underlying source is not in point. This chapter contains excerpts from Themistius' commentary on Aristotle's *Categories*, whose Latin version, probably from the fifth century, was edited by Alcuin between 780 and 790 and dedicated to Charlemagne. *LC* I.1 (9.28–10.1) quotes in the name of *Augustinus* from this translation—which Alcuin ascribed to Augustine—the treatment of the post-praedicamentum *simul* (ἅμα). The italics in the following text indicate the borrowings from the *Categoriae decem*:[18]

"*Simul*" namque quaedam iuxta eos qui sagacissime logice archana scrutantur, *tribus modis dicuntur: tempore, natura et genere.*

Tempore, ut ait beatus Augustinus, *cum quaelibet simul existunt uno tempore vel apparent ita ut neutrum de duobus vel prius sit vel alterum consequatur, sed utrique ortus videatur esse communis;* secundum quem modum. . . .

Natura, cum quaedam *naturaliter simul sunt, nullum tamen eorum praeest alteri, ut, verbi gratia simplum et duplum ponamus, necesse simul esse naturaliter, sed neque duplum facit ut simplum sit neque simplum efficit duplum;* sed nec secundum hunc modum. . . .

Genere, quoties ex eodem genere manantia simul videntur esse natura, sed specie discernuntur, ut est animal. Nam et pedestre et aquatile animal dicitur, sed specie discernitur *nullumque alteri aliud prius est, sed simul omnia ab animali (id est ab uno genere) orta nascuntur.*

The *LC* not only cites the text of Alcuin's edition of the *Themistian Paraphrase* but also inserts these excerpts into its context under the same headings as does Alcuin in the corresponding section of his *Dialectica*, c. XI: "*Tribus modis aliquid simul* esse dicimus, aut *tempore,* aut *natura,* aut *genere.*"[19] The text of the *Them. Par.* incorporated by

---

[18] See the critical edition of Pseudo-Augustini, *Categoriae decem* (Anonymi Paraphrasis Themistiana) by Laurentius Minio-Paluello, *Aristoteles Latinus* I.1–5: *Categoriae vel Praedicamenta* (Bruges, Paris, 1961), 128–188. The quotation in *LC* I.1 can be added to the testimonia on p. 173; on p. 133 read correctly among the testimonia Alcuinus, *De dialectica* (*PL* CI, not C). On Alcuin's edition of the *Categoriae decem* see Minio-Paluello, *Praefatio*, LXXXVI–XCI; excerpts of the *Categoriae* in Alcuin's *Dialectica* in the Appendix II, 189–192. *LC* I.1 (p. 9.41) reads *aquatile,* and thus follows Alcuin, *De dialectica* XI, *PL* 101.964 Cl: "aliud pedestre, aliud volatile, aliud *aquatile*"; the latter term does not occur in the *Categoriae decem.*

[19] *PL* 101.964B9–12, not C9–12, as listed by Minio-Paluello (p. 173) among the testimonia where the three references to 964C should read B. The text of Alcuin, *De dialectica* (*PL* 101.964B–C), is partly inserted in *LC* I.1 (p. 9f.) in the heading *Genere.*

Alcuin in his *Dialectica* is listed in Minio-Paluello's edition among
the testimonia. The differences pointed out by Minio-Paluello
between the definition of *omonyma* in the *Categoriae decem*, paragraph
10, and in Alcuin's *Dialectica*, c. 3, clearly show that two of Alcuin's
changes made in the original also occur in *LC* IV.23 (219.1–2):
plerumque etiam *unum* nomen secundum *omonyma duas* vel plures *res*
significat.[20] The example of *homo pictus* and *homo verus* in paragraph
10 and in Alcuin's *Dialectica* (*PL* 101.955B) is used in order to
indicate the agreement in name, but not definition, of *omonyma-
aequivoca* according to Aristotle, *Categories* 1 a 1–4. It is repeatedly
employed in the *LC* when the author of the treatise refutes arguments made by his opponents in favor of image-worship. The
terminology in these discussions involving *homo pictus* and *homo verus*[21]
is identical with that of Boethius' translation of, and comments on,
Aristotle's *De aequivocis*.[22] Compare Boethius' corresponding version
with the relevant passages in the *LC*.

Alcuin's edition of the *Categoriae decem* has left other traces in the
LC. The discussion at 1.8 (p. 25), concerning the *differentiae* among
imago, *similitudo*, and *aequalitas*, is carried on with the help of the
category *relatio*, which is naturally also listed among the ten categories in *LC* III.27 (p. 162.19). The *Themistian Paraphrase* uses *ad-
aliquid* (πρός τι), mentioned, for instance, in the *LC*'s discussion
(3.18–24) of *imago* as *genus* and of *idolum* as its *species*: imago ad
aliquid, idolum ad seipsum dicatur (cf. I Cor. 10.19–20).

The dependence of the logical argument in *LC* I.8 on the treatment of the category *ad-aliquid* in the *Categoriae decem*, §§ 93–111,

[20] Cf. Minio-Paluello, xc.

[21] Cf. *LC* I.2 (13.35–40); I.9 (26.20–23); I.17 (42.18–25); IV.1 (173.35–43); see
Alcuin, *Epist.* 204 (above n. 15), p. 339.25 on *homo verus et pictus*, also *De dialectica*
c. 3, *PL* 101.955B1–2, and D12.

[22] See Boethius, *In categorias Aristotelis* I, *PL* 64.163B–166D; *homo vivens . . . homo
pictus*, 164A; *homo pictus . . . vivus*, 165A; *homo pictus . . . verus*, 166B; also the text
edited by Pierre Hadot, "Un fragment du commentaire perdu de Boèce sur les
catégories d'Aristote," *Archives d'histoire doctrinale et littéraire du Moyen Age* 34 (1959),
10; Boethius, *In Isagogen Prophyrii Commenta*, ed. prima I.7, ed. Georg Schepss and
Samuel Brandt (*CSEL* 48; Wien, Leipzig, 1906), 18.18 *homo marmoreus . . . vivus;*
ed. secunda III.7, p. 223.8 *homo pictus . . . verus*.

Cf. Boethius' translation of Aristotle's *Categories*, ed. Minio-Paluello, *op. cit.*, p. 5,
and the *ratio nominum aequivocorum* in the *LC*, pp. 13.30, 173.33.38.42, which agrees
in name only: *in solo tantumdem nomine communionem habet*; 173.38; or *communio
nominis*, 173.39; or *in nominis societate iunguntur*, 13.36f.; but not in definition: 13.37,
26.22, 173.39.

is obvious. The corresponding elements in both texts are printed in italics:

§ 110, ed. Minio-Paluello, 158:

Mihi vero . . . *magis et minus* haec categoria, *non* omnis quidem nec sola, videtur posse suscipere; simile *enim* cuilibet et *magis simile et minus simile possumus dicere.* Sed hoc non in omnibus, ut dixi, quae sunt ad- aliquid poterit inveniri; namque *nec magis pater nec minus pater dici potest,* nec minus filius aut magis filius, nec minus duplum aut magis duplum.

§ 104 (157.6):

Inest autem huic categoriae et soli et omni ut inter coniuncta duo, quae ex se pendeant, sit *alterna conversio* (*quae graece dicitur* ἀντιστροφή), et duplum enim simpli dicitur et simplum dupli, et servus domini et dominus servi.

LC 1.8, ed. Bastgen, 25.18–25:

Nam imagini proprium est, ut semper ab altero expressa sit, . . . et *imago magis vel minus non* sibi admittat, similitudo vero et acqua- litas admittant. Sicut *enim dicitur magis similis vel minus similis,* magis aequalis vel minus aequalis, *non sic dici potest magis imago vel minus imago.* Nam et *in conversione earum quae grece antistrofe dicitur,* subtilis quaedam repugnantia est. Quae omnia per- sequi longum est.

The *LC* cuts short its own disquisition of the "differentia imaginis et similitudinis sive aequalitatis" (25.3–4) by citing a larger section from *quaestio* 74 of Augustine, *De diversis quaestionibus 83* (*PL* 40.85f.), whose *Incipit* reads—*mutatis mutandis*—like the chapter heading (above) of *LC* I.8: "Imago et aequalitas et similitudo distinguenda sunt." The author of the *LC* could all the more resort to this method because the *Categoriae decem* was to him, as we saw previously, but another treatise by Augustine.

E1. The *Categoriae decem* and the *Libri Carolini* II c. 31.—A text in the *LC* II.31 (p. 102.15–27) which hitherto has not been properly understood is of decisive importance for Alcuin's actual authorship of the *LC*. This text is further connected on the one hand with Alcuin's recension of the *Categoriae decem,* which is also one of the basic sources of Alcuin's *Dialectica.* Bastgen once believed that the

LC offers in *LC* II.31 (p. 102.21–24) just an "enumeration" of the cardinal virtues, whereas it actually analyzes the Aristotelian cardinal virtues as a mean between two evils on the basis of the *Categoriae decem*, 160 (ed. Minio-Paluello, p. 171). Compare the following texts A, B, and C:

A. *LC* II.31 (p. 102.15–25):

(a) Quae *duo mala* cum alterutrum sibi *contraria* sint et a recto tramite remota,

(b) restat nobis, ut *viam regiam* secundum *Apostolum gradientes* [cf. Num. 21.22] *neque ad dexteram neque ad sinistram declinemus* [cf. Isa. 30.21], ut nec . . . diiudicemus nec . . . decernamus, sed *solum* Deum adorantes et eius sanctos venerantes . . . eas in ecclesia in ornamento et memoria rerum gestarum, si libet, habeamus, et

(a) cum *iustitia* hinc *severitatem*, illinc *adolationem* contempnentes,
cum *prudentia* hinc *versutiam*, illinc *hebitudinem* declinantes,
cum *temperantia* hinc *libidinem*, illinc *insensibilitatem* spernentes,
cum *fortitudine* hinc *timiditatem*, illinc *audaciam* abiicientes. . . .

B. *Pseudo-Augustini Categoriae decem*, 160, ed. L. Minio-Paluello, in *Aristoteles Latinus I. 1–5* (Bruges, Paris, 1961), 171:

(a) . . . Aliquoties autem *mala malis opponuntur*, quoties contrariorum media bona sunt, ut est indigentia et redundantia (quod Graeci ἔνδειαν καὶ ὑπερβολήν vocant); his enim duobus malis sibi oppositis mediocritas media reperitur.

(a) Hanc rationem Peripatetici secuti *virtutes medias esse dixerunt* ut *plus iusto* πλεονεξίαν, *minus iusto* μειονεξίαν dicerent: *inter quae mala mediam iustitiam locaverunt.*
Similiter inter versutiam hebetudinemque prudentiam posuerunt; inter libidinem insensibilitatemque (quod Graeci ἀναισθησίαν vocant) *temperantia constituta est;*
inter timiditatem et audaciam, fortitudo.
Ita occultum quoddam genus oppositorum repperit perscrutata ratio, ut interdum *mala malis* inveniantur esse *contraria.*

C. Alcuin, *De dialectica* c. XI (*PL* 101.963C–D):

(a) *Carolus.* Si aliquando *mala malis opponuntur?*—
Albinus. Etiam secundum philosophos qui *virtutes semper medias esse dixerunt,* et ex utraque parte habere vitia.

(b) Et hoc reor *Apostolum* significasse dum dicit: *Via regia nobis gradiendum* [cf. Num. 21.22], *neque ad dexteram, neque ad sinistram declinandam* [cf. Isa. 30.21]:

(a)   *ut plus justum et minus justum.—*
      Carolus. Quomodo plus justum?—
      Albinus. Plus justum [MSS *justo*] est *severitas*; *minus justo adulatio. Inter quae duo mala mediam justitiam locaverunt.*
      Similiter inter versutiam hebetudinemque prudentiam posuerunt;
      inter libidinem insensibilitatemque temperantia constituta est;
      inter timiditatem et audaciam fortitudo regnat.

The conclusions that may be drawn from the comparative analysis of the interrelationship between these three texts are quite revealing. It is obvious that Alcuin's *Dialectica* c. XI is based directly on the *Categoriae decem*, while the *LC* passage is closer to Alcuin's logical textbook than to the pseudo-Augustinian tract. This recognition is based on the following readings to be found in the three texts: the *LC* in A(a) reads *duo mala*, while Alcuin in C(a) reads *mala malis*, with the *Categoriae decem* in B(a); only the *LC* in A(a) and Alcuin in C(a) define *iustitia* as the mean between *severitas* and *adulatio*, while the *Categoriae decem* in B(a) defines it with the help of the Greek terms for *plus iusto* and *minus iusto*. Alcuin's interpretation of the Aristotelian definitions of the cardinal virtues as offered by him in his *Dialectica* certainly reappears in *LC* II.31. In addition, Alcuin in C(b) quotes an unknown *Apostolus* with references to biblical texts (Num. 21.22; Isa. 30.21) concerning the idea of the King's Highway, which appears in an identical form also in the *LC* in A(b), but not at all in B. Alcuin's *Apostolus* referred to in connection with the idea of the *Via Regia* constitutes a characteristic concept of Alcuin's thought, as I have shown in *Alcuin and Charlemagne* (see Index s.v. Via Regia). The concept occurs in at least ten *Epistles* of Alcuin, in three of his treatises, and, as we saw, in the *LC* II.31, cited above in A(b). In addition, it is found in the *LC*'s *Praefatio* (p. 5.28–6.1) in a formulation which is certainly parallel to the one contained in Alcuin's *Dialectica* in C(b) as well as in the *LC* II.31. Quite significantly, this *LC* passage is identical with the texts cited in A(b) and C(b) not only in their references to the King's Highway, but also as to its subject matter and wording: its text in the *LC, Praefatio*, p. 6.1–2, from *imagines* to *venerationem*, is identical with *LC* II.31, p. 102.19–20, from *solum* to *rerum gestarum.*

We have seen that the *Categoriae decem* is directly cited in *LC* I.1 and in I.8. *LC* II.31 shows the indirect influence of the *Categoriae decem* through the intermediary of Alcuin's *Dialectica*, a fact that could be verified also for *LC* IV.23 concerning its use of *omonyma*. All these relations established between Alcuin, the *LC*, and the *Themistian Paraphrase* represent important and decisive evidence for Alcuin's actual authorship of the *Libri Carolini*. Minio-Paluello's critical edition of the *Categoriae decem* records Alcuin's recension of the treatise. He further lists Alcuin's contribution to the textual transmission of the *Categoriae decem* provided by the extensive testimonia contained in Alcuin's *Dialectica*. Although he refers in the *apparatus criticus* on p. 171 to testimonia in *De dialectica* c. XI (*PL* 101.963D), he fails to list Alcuin's unique readings *severitas* and *adulatio* connected with *iustitia*, and repeated in the *LC* II.31. Nor does Minio-Paluello trace the actual basis of the Greek terms in the *Categoriae decem*, 160, and of the interpretation of the two *mala* with the respective cardinal virtues in the middle, namely, *iustitia, prudentia, temperantia*, and *fortitudo*, all of which certainly parallel the older and younger *Commentaria in Aristotelem Graeca*. This tradition is easily seen, for example, in Ammonius, *In Porphyrii Isagogen*, ed. Adolf Busse (*CAG* IV.3; Berlin, 1891), 67f., or in Philoponus, *In Aristotelis Categorias Comment.*, ed. A. Busse (*CAG* XIII; Berlin, 1898), 188, and elsewhere, for instance, in *Hippolyti Philosophumenon* 19.16, ed. Hermann Diels, *Doxographi Graeci* (ed. tertia; Berlin, 1958), 569. Alcuin's unique readings are cited also by Ermenrich of Ellwangen in his abstruse ninth-century letter-treatise addressed to Grimald of St. Gall: "... iustitiam ... obpugnat *severitas* et *adulatio*" (*MGH, Epistolae* 5 [Karolini Aevi 3; Berlin, 1899]), 542.14–15.

The logic taught with the help of Alcuin's *De dialectica*, which was compiled as a textbook for the teaching of *ars dialectica* in Frankish monastic schools, was necessarily of a plain kind involving the most elementary processes of thought. Alcuin's recension of the pseudo-Augustinian *Categoriae decem* (see above, Section E and note 18), some of Boethius' logical books, and Cicero's *Topica*, constitute the basic sources of Alcuin's primer of dialectics. A more advanced knowledge and application of formal logic is shown by him in the *Libri Carolini*. *LC* IV.23 employs Aristotle's complete logical square and other elements of ancient logic which are used throughout the four books of the work, as has been shown in our Sections E, E1, and F. But the frequent occurrences in the *LC* of categorical and hypothetical propositions and syllogisms are not mentioned in any history of ancient or medieval logic. They show the intellectual stature of the Anglo-Saxon from the British Isles in the service of the Frankish king whose philosophical mastery of Boethius' *Consolatio Philosophiae* for the understanding of the *artes liberales* has been investigated recently by Pierre Courcelle, "Les sources antiques du *Prologue* d'Alcuin sur les disciplines," *Philologus* 110 (1966), 293–305.[23]

Alcuin's familiarity with Boethius' propositional logic was first mentioned in my note "Alcuin on Sophistry," *Classical Philology* 50 (1955), 259–261, in the wake of Karl Dürr's important book on *The Propositional Logic of Boethius* (Studies in Logic and the Foundations of Mathematics; Amsterdam, 1951). Dürr repeated the opinion held by Martin Grabmann, *Bearbeitungen und Auslegungen der aristotelischen Logik aus der Zeit von Peter Abaelard bis Petrus Hispanus* (Abh. der Preuss. Akademie der Wiss., phil.-hist. Klasse; Berlin, 1937, No. 5), that Boethius' logical monographs were hardly known to the European West or used before the end of the eleventh century. To be sure, Alcuin's *De dialectica* is listed for the eighth century, by A. van de Vyver and by Grabmann, and also mentioned in a bibliography of logical texts by I. M. Bocheński, *A History of Formal Logic* (Notre Dame, Ind. 1961; tr. German edition *Formale Logik*, 1956). But the *Libri Carolini* from the last decade of the eighth century, which contains the most extensive documentation for the actual use of categorical and hypothetical propositions and syllogisms to be found between the age of Boethius and the end of the eleventh century, seems to be unknown to modern historians of formal logic. The present writer has investigated the syllogisms of the *LC* in the forthcoming study entitled *The Syllogisms of the Libri Carolini: Aristoteles Latinus and Alcuin.*

F. Boethius, *In Librum Aristotelis Peri Hermeneias, prima editio.*—The Latin Aristotle is presented in the *LC* not only by the *Categoriae*

---

[23] Cf. Pierre Courcelle, *La Consolation de Philosophie dans la tradition littéraire: Antécédents et postérité de Boèce* (Paris, 1967), 29–47.

decem (above, Sections E and E1), but naturally also by Boethius' commentary on Aristotle's *Peri Hermeneias* in the first edition and by Apuleius, *Peri Hermeneias*.[24] Here the *auctor* of the *LC* displays his training in dialectics, whose method and Boethian terminology he employs throughout the *LC* in order to reject image-worship not only on theological grounds, but also with the help of purely logical argumentation.[25] The teacher of dialectics who wrote the *LC* in IV.23 (217–221) quotes extensively from Boethius' simpler commentary on Aristotle's *De interpretatione* and from Apuleius. He clearly distinguishes between texts quoted from Boethius' translation of Aristotle—*in Periermeniis* (218.22), and those cited from the comments made by Boethius himself ("iuxta . . . Boethii explanationem," 218.26f.). The statement "Quod enim quis diligit et adorat, et quod adorat omnino et diligit" (217.8) from the Latin version of the Greek *Acta* of II Nicaea, which the author of the *LC* characterizes as a silly and worthless conclusion (*frivola et inani conclusione;* 219.41) in support of image-worship, is then disproved in various ways with the help of *ars dialectica*.

The originators of the statement in question, so the *LC* argues, do not realize the inequality of the terms *diligere* and *adorare*, which are hardly convertible: *hec duo vicissim minime posse circumverti* (219.43). To be sure, "Quod adorat quis et diligit" is true, but not the *circumversio*, "Quod diligit quis et adorat." The latter is logically untenable because the *proprietas* (220.4) of those two terms does not admit reciprocal (*mutuo*) convertibility.

The *LC* then gives some illustrations of categorical and hypothetical propositions in which the *proprium* is convertible, and a few others in which it is not. In this context the convertibility of the example from the synodal *Acta* is again repudiated.

---

[24] Boethius, *Commentarii in Librum Aristotelis ΠΕΡΙ ΕΡΜΗΝΕΙΑΣ*, prima editio, ed. Carl Meiser (Leipzig, 1877); secunda editio, ed. Carl Meiser (Leipzig, 1880); Apuleius, *Liber ΠΕΡΙ ΕΡΜΗΝΕΙΑΣ*, ed. Paul Thomas in *Apulei Opera* III (Leipzig, 1908), 176–194. The same corpus of three dialectical textbooks appears in MS Rome, Casa Madre dei Padri Maristi (without Library number), a codex connected with Leidrad of Lyons, which, according to Bernhard Bischoff, "Die Hofbibliothek Karls des Grossen," in *Karl der Grosse* II (Düsseldorf, 1965), 48, may well testify to the existence of such a corpus in Charlemagne's Court Library.

[25] The extensive use made of Boethius (see n. 24) in the *LC* remained unknown to J. Isaac, *Le Peri Hermeneias en Occident de Boèce à Saint Thomas* (Paris, 1953), 39, and to L. Minio-Paluello, *Aristoteles Latinus II.1–2* (Bruges, Paris, 1965), p. xlii.

As an illustration of convertible categorical propositions the author, following Apuleius, cites τὸ χρεματιστικόν of the Greek commentators of Aristotle,[26] an ἴδιον that is convertible: "Quod hinnibile est equus est, et quod equus est, hinnibile est" (220.5).

The illustration provided for the reversible hypothetical proposition is the equally old favorite of the commentators—τὸ γελαστικόν— often used in the commentaries of Boethius: "Si risibile est, consequens inevitabiliter est, ut homo sit, et si homo est, necessario risibile est" (220.11).

This instance of a convertible *proprium* is introduced in the *LC* with the remark "*Circumverti* namque possunt hec, *ut si quis dicat*," which seems to point to its source, namely, Boethius, *In categorias Aristotelis* I (*PL* 64.190B–C): "haec (scil. propria) autem solum converti possunt quae omni solique contingunt . . . ut risibile. Omnis enim homo risibilis est, et solum est animal homo quod rideat."[27]

The first of the examples of irreversible conditional propositions is introduced as follows: "*Circumverti* autem nequaquam possunt hec, *ut si quis dicat:* 'Si dies est lucet'[28] . . . or 'Si adorat, consequens est ut id quod adorat, diligat' (220.13, 16)." Convertibility, however, is not possible in these instances, "cum plura luceant nec tamen sint dies," while in the case of the statement from the synodal *Acta* of II Nicaea, which here is turned into a hypothetical proposition, one cannot say "Si diligit, adorat," because sometimes *dilectio* does not reach *adoratio* (220.21).

Thus the *LC* has proved that the passage from the synodal *Acta, in actione septima*, Mansi XIII.404E8–9,

ὃ γάρ τις φιλεῖ καὶ προσκυνεῖ
καὶ ὃ προσκυνεῖ πάντως καὶ φιλεῖ,

which is cited in the *LC* IV.23 (p. 217.7–8) after the *First Latin*

---

[26] See, for example, Porphyry, *Isagoge*, ed. Adolf Busse (*CAG;* Berlin, 1887), 149, s.v. γελαστικός; p. 173, s.v. χρεματιστικός.

[27] Cf. Boethius, *Introductio ad syllogismos categoricos, PL* 64.768C–D: "*ut si quis dicat,* homo risibilis est . . . verso ordine . . .* " etc., also col. 781A, and Martianus Capella IV. 398, ed. Adolf Dick (Leipzig, 1925); in addition Boethius, *De differentiis topicis* I, *PL* 64.1179A.

[28] See Boethius, *In Topicis Ciceronis Commentaria* IV, *PL* 64.1125C.

Nicaenum of ca. 788 as follows:

> Quod enim quis diligit et adorat
> et quod adorat omnino et diligit,

cannot be treated as if it were either a categorical or a hypothetical proposition that admits convertibility. The *LC* now proceeds to disprove the *circumversio* (220.23) of the same passage from the synodal *Acta*, with the help of four propositions with the universal determinants *omne* and *nihil*, and the particular determinant *quiddam*, using the method known in dialectics as *quadrata formula*.[29] In this instance Apuleius serves as one of the sources, and is expressly named and extensively quoted. Bastgen's references to Alcuin's *Dialectica* can now indicate only that the Saxon and the *LC* rely on the same sources, but used them independently. Bastgen does not verify the source underlying the *LC*'s application of the logical square (220.26–221.18)—Boethius' first edition of his commentary on Aristotle's *De interpretatione*, which is repeatedly and prominently cited at the very beginning of *LC* IV.23 (217f.).

The opening words without doubt reproduce Apuleius (in italics): "Sunt enim *quattuor propositiones inter se* quodammodo *affecte quas* philosophi *in quadrata formula specta*ndas scribere consueverunt" (220.24).[30] The entire treatment of categorical propositions in the *LC* nevertheless follows (220.27–221.18) Boethius verbatim. That this is indeed the case becomes at once clear from the fact that the *LC* names *contrarie* (220.29) the reciprocal relation between the first and second propositions, while Apuleius speaks of *incongrue*, and what Apuleius calls *subpares*, the *LC* names *subcontrarie* (220.30). The logical square, *Quadrata formula*, below, charts the *LC*'s treatment of four propositions (220.25–9), which the author of the treatise fashioned on the basis of Boethius' treatment.[31] The sources for

---

[29] Cf. Günther Patzig, *Die Aristotelische Syllogistik*, Abh. der Akad. der Wiss. in Göttingen, phil.-hist. Klasse: Dritte Folge, no. 42; 1959, 161f.

[30] See Apuleius (above n. 24), 179.17–19; also *LC* 220.32, *ducantur deinde* . . . *quedam linee angulares* due una *ab* . . . *ad* . . . *altera ab* . . . *ad* . . . , follow (in italics) Apuleius, 179.26–29, while *LC* 220.36f. "Et his ita inter se pugnantibus cum utreque, id est" renders Boethius (above n. 24), 80.15–17.

[31] Boethius (above n. 24), prima editio I.7, p. 83.27–89; see also secunda editio II.7, p. 146.28–154.24. Cf. *PL* 98.1238D.

the *LC* (221.1–18) are listed in the notes in order to indicate again dependence on Boethius.[32] The vowels *A* and *I* (from *a*ffirmo) and *E* and *O* (from n*e*g*o*) are added to the propositions of the square in order to abbreviate the subsequent discussion in the *LC* concerning the truth and the falsity of exclusion and inclusion in the relations of the propositions.

Quadrata formula, Libri Carolini IV. 23 (220f.)

The author of the *LC* properly states that *A* and *O* cannot both be true, *vere esse non possint* (220.38), nor can both be false. If one is true, the other is certainly false, or if one is false, we may infer that the other is true. For this reason, *A* and *O* are contradictories, opposed to each other: *inter se contrarie vel opposite* (220.36). And what has been stated of *A* and *O* also applies to *I* and *E*.

---

[32] *LC* 221.1–2, *superiores universales—falsae* = Boethius, p. 86.1–3; *LC* 221.4–5, *inferiores particulares—utreque vere* = B., p. 86.2–3; *LC* 221.15–17: "*Et rursus si* hec *negatio universalis:* . . . *falsa* est, hec *adfirmatio particularis:* . . . *vera* est, et si . . . "; Boethius, p. 86.10–13: "Et rursus, si universalis negatio particulari adfirmationi comparetur, reperiuntur oppositae, ut . . . semper enim una vera est, altera falsa." I add here the interesting *Lesefrucht* I found in *LC* IV.23 (p. 219.21): "O *acumen omni pistillo retunsius!*"—an anonymous quotation from Jerome, *Epist.* 69.4, ed. I. Hilberg, *CSEL* 54 (1910), 686.10–11.

A and *E* cannot both be true. If one should be true, the other would be false; but if one is false, nothing can be said concerning the truth of the other proposition: "duae superiores *omnino* sibi contrarie sunt" (220.29).

With regard to the relation of *A* and *I*, it is clear that if *A* is true, then *I* is true. But if *A* is false, no inference concerning the truth of *I* can be made. *A* is the superaltern proposition in relation to *I*, and the latter in relation to *A* is the subaltern proposition: "adfirmatio universalis sive particularis *subalternae*" (220.30). The same applies to *E* and *O*: "negatio universalis et particularis *subalternae* nihilominus dicantur" (220.31).

Finally, although *I* and *O* are reciprocals, and therefore do not exclude each other ("duae inferiores *subcontrariae*, sibi *mutuo* sunt," 220.30), if we infer that *quiddam* is not supposed to exclude *omne*, the truth of either (*I* and *O*) cannot be inferred from the other. And if one of them is false, the other is necessarily true.

The *subcontrarie* (220.30) *I* and *O* are also the contradictories of *A* and *E* (which cannot both be true; see above and 220.29), and therefore *I* and *O* cannot both be false. But because *A* and *E* can both be false, *duae superiores universales . . . falsae* (221.1–2), *I* and *O* can both be true, *duae inferiores particulares utreque vere* (221.4).

In connection with the critical analysis of *LC* IV.23 it is important to record the fact that the technical terminology employed in this chapter with regard to the convertibility of the *proprium* is *converso ordine, circumversio*, and *circumverti* (219.43; 220.10,11,13), while Boethius has *verso ordine, conversio, converti*. The same terminology as in the *LC* is found in Alcuin's *De dialectica*, c. 2 (*PL* 101.953D), *proprium circumverti* posse necesse est; *circumversio, converso ordine* (954A); c. 12, *De argumentis* (965D4,6) *circumverti possunt*; also in Alcuin's *Epistula* 163 (ed. Dümmler, p. 263.19). Obviously, *LC* and Alcuin use the same source, namely, Boethius; both have changed the technical terminology of Boethius, and this terminology concerning the *proprium* is identical in both cases. This fact is stressed here for future reference concerning the authorship of the *LC*, which can in part be determined on the basis of the elements of logic employed in the treatise.

The author of the *LC* often argues about theological questions with the help of syllogisms. The first modus of the categorical syllogism with *igitur*, the customary sign of inference, or the functor that takes two arguments and the conclusion, is used, for example, in *LC* I.17 (42.18–19):[33]

> Omne quod caret vita, caret sensu.
> Omne quod caret sensu, caret fide.
> Omne igitur quod caret vita, caret fide.

The quinquepartite syllogism consisting of the *propositio* and its *probatio*, the *assumptio* and its *probatio*, and the *conclusio*, is correctly analyzed by the author of the treatise in *LC* III.27 (162.29–31) in a text quoted from Augustine's *De diversis quaestionibus 83*, c. 20 (*PL* 40.15):

> Deus non alicubi est.
> Quod alicubi est enim continetur loco.
> Quod continetur loco, corpus est.
> Deus autem non est corpus.
> Non igitur alicubi est.

Finally, it is of interest that *LC* III.27 (162) takes up the problem whether, and to what degree, the ten Aristotelian *praedicamenta* can be related to God. In answer to these questions each of the categories is related to a quotation from the Old Testament and stands for a specific divine attribute. Quite significantly, the identical confrontation of some categories with biblical quotations appears a few years after the composition of the *LC* in Alcuin's *De fide s. trinitatis*,[34] dedicated to Charlemagne as emperor, that is, after the

---

[33] Cf. Tertullian, *De anima* 42 . . . quod enim dissolvitur . . . *sensu caret, et quod sensu caret*, nihil ad nos; see ed. J. H. Waszink (Amsterdam, 1947), 459f., and Quintilian, *Institutio oratoria* 5.14.12, for *sensu caret*.

[34] I.15: "Quomodo intelligendae sint locutiones praedicamentorum de Deo," *PL* 101.22–23. A stray piece, possibly of pseudo-Augustinian origin, entitled *De locutione divina*, *PL* 47.1255–56, contains a list of categories which are identified with the same OT passages as listed by Alcuin, and in part in the *LC*. See the material discussed by Alban Dold, *Das Sakramentar im Schabcodex M 12 Sup. der Bibliotheca Ambrosiana* (Texte und Arbeiten I, 43; Beuron, 1952), 37–39. Augustine, *De trin.* 5.1–2 is also found in *Le Liber Mozarabicus Sacramentorum*, ed. Marius Férotin (Paris, 1912), 1227, and cited by Georg Manz, *Ausdrucksformen der lateinischen Liturgiesprache* (Beuron, 1941), 150. On the use made by Augustine of the categories see Alfred Schindler, *Wort und Analogie in Augustins Trinitätslehre* (Hermeneutische Untersuchungen IV; Tübingen, 1965), 156f. Pierre Courcelle, *Les lettres grecques en Occident: De Macrobe à Cassiodore* (2nd ed.; Paris, 1948), 224f., n. 8, convincingly suggests as source the lost commentary on Aristotle's *Categories* by Marius Victorinus.

year 800. The model for the author of the *LC* and for Alcuin was
naturally Boethius, *De trinitate*, c. 4, "Quomodo Deus sit in prae-
dicamentis,"[35] and Augustine, *De trinitate* 5.1–2 and 8.9 (*PL* 42.912,
917).

F1. Hilarius of Poitiers, *Tractatus in LI Psalm.* and *De trinitate*.—
The categorical syllogism *Omne quod caret vita, caret sensu* in *LC* I.17
dealt with towards the end of the preceding section F, could have
drawn some inspiration from the incomplete syllogism employed by
Hilarius' treatment of Ps. 51.7 (*PL* 9.313A; ed. *CSEL* 22, 1891,
p. 102.1–3):

Quod vero *caret sensu* intelligentiae, caret et rationis instinctu;
quidquid autem caret rationis instinctu, caret et meditatione consilii.

The missing conclusion can be supplemented as follows:

‹Quod igitur caret sensu intelligentiae, caret et meditatione consilii›.

   The probability that the author of the *LC* was indeed familiar
with some writings by Hilary can be shown with certainty. Nobody
has noticed that Hilarius of Poitiers, *De trinitate* I.20 is quoted anonymously in the *Preface* to *LC* II, as is obvious from the comparison of
the following texts. Compare the italicized words in both passages:
De trinitate I.20 (*PL* 10.39A):

Ac primum ita *totius operis* modum temperavimus, ut aptissimus legentium
profectibus connexorum sibi *libellorum ordo* succederet. *Nihil* enim *incom-*
positum indigestumque placuit afferre: ne operis inordinata congeries rusticum quem-
dam tumultum perturbata vociferatione praeberet. Sed *quia* nullus per praerupta
consensus est, nisi substratis paulatim gradibus feratur gressus ad summa;
nos quoque *quaedam gradiendi* initia *ordinantes*, arduum hoc intelligentiae *iter*
clivo quasi molliore [cf. Quintilian, *Inst. orat.* 12,10,78] lenivimus non jam
gradibus incisum, sed planitie subrepente devexum, ut prope sine scanden-
tium sensu, euntium proficeret conscensus.

LC II, *Praefatio* (p. 61,10–17, Bastgen):

. . . Ideo igitur *per quendam gradiendi ordinem* huius nostrae disputationis
quibusdam *librorum* intercapedinibus distinximus gressum, ne indistincti
itineris tramitem inordinata prolixitas efficeret fastidiosum, *nec libuit* nobis

---

[35] Ed. Rudolf Peiper (Leipzig, 1871), 156.

quiddam *afferre* [the first f suprascript in V] *incompositum vel indigestum, ne operis inordinata congeries* lectori *perturbata vociferatione rusticum quendam preberet tumultum, quia* et *iter* carpentes congruis quibusdam temporibus spatiari non renuunt et agrorum, vinearum et etiam hortorum cultores per quasdam camporum intercapedines vel etiam per agrorum dimensiones limites statuere consueverunt.

Naturally, the "[ordo] huius nostrae disputationis" referred to in the *LC* is identical—rhetorically—with the "ordo disputationis" dealt with in Alcuin's *Rhetoric*, c. 37, ed. C. Halm (Leipzig, 1863), 544.13. And the work's "ordo librorum" takes some guidance concerning style and arrangement tendered by Hilary of Poitiers. Alcuin in his antiadoptionist letters and treatises quotes from Hilarius, *De trinitate*, very frequently, as will be shown in detail by the present writer in a forthcoming study entitled "The Falsification in a Hilary Codex of Charlemagne's Court Library."

It is finally not without interest to record the fact that the same passage in Hilarius, *De trinitate* I.20, which is anonymously cited in the *LC*, is in a similar fashion used in the *tractatus* 6, 9, and 10 of the writings ascribed to Priscillianus, ed. Georg Schepss, *CSEL* 18 (1889), 76, 91, 100 (repr. in Migne, *PL, Supplementum* II; Paris, 1960). There is, however, to be certain, no connection noticeable between the *LC* and the works of Priscillianus.

G. Augustine, *Principia dialecticae.*—In conjunction with a discussion involving *homo verus* and *homo pictus* created by the artist, *LC* I.2 (13.23–35) offers an example *secundum aequivocorum rationem*[36] in which various "res" occur that are joined by name but differ by definition. The *LC* reads as follows:

. . . et *si quis* secundum aequivocorum rationem homines dici posse adfirmet,

> ut: "Augustinus fuit *summus philosophus*,"
> et: "Augustinus *legendus est*,"
> et: "Augustinus *pictus in ecclesia stat*,"
> et: "Augustinus *illo loco sepultus est*,"

animadvertat haec omnia quamquam ab *uno fonte*, id est Augustino, processerint, hunc solum fuisse *verum* Augustinum, de quo dictum est *summus*

---

[36] See note 22, above.

philosophus, cetera vero aliud esse *codicem,* aliud *imaginem,* aliud *corpus sepultum.*

This elementary illustration of the Aristotelian *aequivoca* ("When things have only a name in common and the definition of being which corresponds to the name is different" . . .) is modeled on Augustine, *De dialectica liber,* c. X:[37]

itaque *si quis* ex me flagitet ut definiam quid sit *Tullius* . . . possum enim recte dicere: Tullius est nomen quo significatur homo, *summus* quidam *orator.* . . . [18.4] diversis enim notionibus dicimus:

> . . . *Tullius* inauratus *in Capitolio stat,*
> et *Tullius* totus tibi *legendus est,*
> et *Tullius* hoc *loco sepultus est.* . . .

Nam aequivoca . . . *uno* tamen *fonte* demanant; ut est illud quod Tullius et *homo* et *statua* et *codex* et *cadaver* intellegi potest. non possunt quidem ista una definitione concludi, sed tamen *unum* habent *fontem,* ipsum scilicet *verum* hominem, cuius et illa *statua* et illi *libri* et illud *cadaver* est.

Since the *LC* believes that Augustine was the author of the *Categoriae decem,* it is not surprising to see the use made of Augustine's treatise, mostly referred to as *Principia dialecticae,* and now commonly assumed to be genuine.[38]

H. A forged iconoclastic text of John Moschus, *Pratum spirituale.*— Numerous statements made during the sessions of II Nicaea are characterized in the *LC* as *neniae,* trifles or incongruities, or the like. One of these pearls which is ridiculed as *incomparabilis absurditas* and as *vesania multis vesaniis praeferenda* (168.39f.) is discussed in *LC*

---

[37] *S. Aurelii Augustini de dialectica liber,* rec. Wilheim Crecelius, in Jahresbericht über das Gymnasium zu Elberfeld (Elberfeld, 1857), 17.18; 18.4; 18.27–19.3. Cf. Alcuin, *De dialectica* c. 10 (*PL* 101.962D) Augustinus, magnus orator, etc.; also Isidore of Seville, *Etymologiae* II.26.11.

[38] Cf. Augustine, *Retractationes* 1.5, 6, p. 28.5–6: "de dialectica . . . sola principia remanserunt"; Jan Pinborg, "Das Sprachdenken der Stoa und Augustins Dialektik," *Classica et Medievalia* 23 (1962), 148–177, assumes that the fragment is genuine; so also Georg Pfligersdorffer in *Wiener Studien* 66 (1953), 136f. Karl Barwick, *Probleme der stoischen Sprachlehre und Rhetorik* (Abh. der saex. Akad. der Wiss. zu Leipzig, phil.-hist. Klasse 49, Heft 3; Berlin, 1957), 18–20, analyzes Augustine's c. 9–10 dealing with the *genus* of *ambiguitas* and its divisions, *univoca* and *aequivoca.* On Augustine's *Dialectica* see Ulrich Duchrow, *Sprachverständnis und Biblisches Hören bei Augustin* (Hermeneutische Untersuchungen 3; Tübingen 1965), 42–62, *passim.*

Nicaea. The first, who, like Hampe and Bastgen, referred, as it were, to Mansi XIII.194, was the unknown redactor of the *Hadrianum* in the papal *scrinium*. He incorrectly listed the occurrence of the text of his chapter heading I.14, *In actione quinta*, instead of correctly *In actione quarta* (= Mansi XIII.60–61).[43] Edward Gibbon (*The History of the Decline and Fall of the Roman Empire* 6, ed. William Smith [London, 1855], 164) misinterpreted the text cited in *actio* IV, because he did not realize that it is an iconoclastic forgery, which was subsequently—in *actio* V—officially rejected by the synodal assembly of II Nicaea, and corrected by Tarasius and some iconodules.

Greek Patristic Texts

The author of the *LC* cites on his own only one Greek patristic text that deals with an iconoclastic episode. This text in *LC* IV.25 (223f.) is an excerpt from Epiphanius of Salamis' *Epistle* of about the year 392, addressed to John of Jerusalem, whose Latin version is found in Jerome's *Epistula* 51.[44] Paul Maas[45] investigated Jerome's translation in the light of the Greek original as well as the transmission of Jerome's *Letter* in the *LC*. Other Latin versions of Greek

---

[43] *Ibid.*, p. 20, line 36. The tables compiled by von den Steinen (see above n. 2), p. 48f., can now be supplemented. On p. 48 read with *LC* III.31 and *Hadrianum* I.14: *actio* IV, Mansi XIII.62A; on p. 49 read correspondingly under *Hadrianum* I.14—*LC* III.31—*in actione quarta* (not *quinta*).

[44] Jérome Labourt, *St. Jérome: Lettres* 2 (Paris, 1951), seems to be unaware of the fact that the Greek original of this letter survives; see n. 45.

[45] Paul Maas, "Die ikonoklastische Episode in dem Brief des Epiphanios an Johannes," *Byzantinische Zeitschrift* 30 (1929–30), 279–286, reprinted in Paul Maas, *Kleine Schriften*, ed. Wolfgang Buchwald (München, 1973), 437–445. Maas, p. 438, properly recognized that Jerome's *Epistula* 51 is cited after the *LC* IV.25 by the *LS*, p. 498.7–20 (Epitome, pp. 547.38–548.12). For more on the interrelationship between the *LC* and the *LS* see above Chapter III, at the end of section C; below toward the end of Chapter V; and in Chapter VI n. 6. On the transmission of *Epistula* 51 see Bernard Lambert, *Bibliotheca Hieronymiana Manuscripta* IB (Instrumenta patristica IV; Steenbrugge, 1969), 595–597, and *Addenda, ibid.* IVA (1972), 115–116. See also the text in Paul J. Alexander, "The Iconoclastic Council of St. Sophia (815) and Its Definition (Horos)," *Dumbarton Oaks Papers* 7 (1953), frg. 30D, p. 65; also Josef Lebon, "Sur quelques fragments des lettres attribuées à Saint Epiphane de Salamine," *Miscellanea Giovanni Mercati* I (Studi e Testi 121; Rome, 1946), 145–174.

patristic texts in the *LC* represent the Latin translation of the Greek synodal *Acta* of II Nicaea, 787, produced by an unknown Roman ecclesiastic during 788 upon the request of Hadrian I, who sent a copy of this version to Charlemagne.[46] This copy was the one used by the actual author of the *LC*, not only for his chapter headings but frequently also for quotations inserted by him into the context of his exposition and refutation. Of special interest to us in the present investigation are the Latin versions of certain Greek patristic texts which, to be sure, were part of this Latin translation of the Greek *Acta* of II Nicaea (subsequently always referred to by the present writer as *Latin Nicaenum*), yet as such were not the product of the Roman translator, but represent already existing translations of Greek patristic texts that were inserted by the translator into his own rendering. The author of the *LC* found the Latin versions of those patristic texts with which we shall deal in two *synodicae* by Hadrian I from the year 785, one addressed to the Byzantine Emperors Irene and her son Constantine VI, referred to as *JE* 2448,[47] the other to the newly elected Patriarch Tarasius of Constantinople, cited as *JE* 2449.[48] Copies of both documents that had been deposited in the papal *scrinium* were for this very reason accessible at Rome during 788 to the Roman translator of the Greek *Acta* of II Nicaea, who naturally inserted their original Latin text into *actio* II of his version. The texts of *JE* 2448 and 2449 were furthermore available to that translator in the form of inserts in the synodal protocols of the Greek *Acta* of 787 which were made in accordance with an established diplomatic custom of ecumenical councils.[49] The copies of the two *synodicae* of 785 were certainly accessible to Anastasius Bibliothecarius, who in 873 dedicated to John VIII his own Latin translation of II Nicaea.[50] Anastasius' version is published in Mansi XII–XIII, while the *First Latin Nicaenum* of 788 now is lost, save for the excerpts preserved in the *LC*, the *Hadrianum* (*JE* 2483), and the *Libellus Synodalis* of the Paris Synod of 825, sent

---

[46] See von den Steinen, above n. 2, "Entstehungsgeschichte," 11–28; below n. 54.
[47] See above, Chapter I n. 1.
[48] Cf. below n. 90.
[49] See section Q, below.
[50] Ernst Perels, *Papst Nikolaus I. und Anastasius Bibliothecarius* (Berlin, 1920), 263 n. 4.

to Louis the Pious.[51] The actual status of the transmission of the two *synodicae* of 785 which supplied the author of the *LC* with the Latin versions of some texts of Greek patres, was not properly recognized by Bastgen,[52] who assumed that the Latin versions of those Greek patres cited in the *LC* are retranslations into Latin of their Greek versions in *actio* II of the Greek *Acta* of II Nicaea. Von den Steinen[53] was aware of these facts as just outlined, but did not publish the proof he had promised.[54]

Our investigation of the following Greek patristic texts cited in the *LC* in the Latin versions of Hadrian I's *synodicae JE* 2448 and 2449 endeavors to clarify the philological and historical problems of their transmission. The verification of these texts is important not only for the formation of a critical edition of the *LC*, but also historically, since the apologetic controversy between iconoclasts and iconodules was carried on with the help of such texts drawn from Greek patres. These texts can be understood only if their origin and their authenticity are known.

I. Gregory of Nyssa, *De deitate filii et spiritus et in Abraham.*—The testimonia in Hadrian I's *Synodica* of 785 (*JE* 2448) derived from

---

[51] Louis Duchesne, *Liber Pontificalis* I (reprint; Paris, 1955), 522 n. 121, believes that the *Latin Nicaenum* of II Nicaea, 787, survives only in the excerpts found in the *LC* and in the *Hadrianum* (*JE* 2483). To these can now be added the numerous fragments (also of the original Latin text of *JE* 2448) to be found in the *Libellus Synodalis* (*LS*) of the Paris Synod of 825, *MGH, Conc.* 2.2 (Aevi Karolini 1.2; Hannover, Leipzig, 1908), ed. Albert Werminghoff, 480–551. V. Grumel in *Dictionnaire de théologie catholique*, VII (Paris, 1922), 775, as well as Albert Siegmund, *Die Ueberlieferung der griechischen christlichen Literatur in der lateinischen Kirche* (München, Pasing, 1949), 175f., and Ann Freeman, *Speculum* 32 (1957), 666 n. 7, are unaware of the fact that fragments of the now lost *Latin Nicaenum* are also contained in the *Hadrianum* and in the *Libellus Synodalis*.

[52] See *LC* 74 n. a, 78d, 79d; 73 n. 4, 76 n. 3, 77 n. 6, 78 n. 1, and 79 n. 2.

[53] In *QF*, 21 (1929–30), 21, nn. 2 and 4; p. 30; see also n. 54, below.

[54] Von den Steinen, *Neues Archiv* 49 (1932), 245 nn. 2–3, clearly indicates that the *LC* offers the original Latin text of the Athanasius quotation in *JE* 2448, and that Anastasius Bibliothecarius rewrote the original Latin version in 2448 following the Greek translation of the Athanasius quotation in the Greek *Acta* of II Nicaea. He proved this point in an unpublished paper on "Hadrians Synodalbriefe von 785 (*JE* 2448/9)" which he mailed to me in the fall of 1960, after I had reported to him the results of my studies concerning the verification of the Greek patres in the *LC*. On the patristic authors dealt with in Sections N–R see Johannes Quasten, *Patrology* III (Utrecht and Antwerp, 1960), s.v.

two writings by Gregory of Nyssa are rejected in *LC* II.17 (76f.) as evidence of image-worship without being cited in the context. This sweeping repudiation of the Cappadocian as a qualified authority is based not only on the argument that his life and *praedicatio* are unknown to the author of the treatise; the two quotations from Gregory are judged unsuitable for the confirmation of such *res dubiae* as image-worship. Actually, the *LC*'s rejection is determined by the fact that its guide for dogmatically approved Greek *patres ecclesiae*, the *Decretum Gelasianum*,[55] does not even mention the name of Gregory of Nyssa.

The two quotations from Gregory are cited after *JE* 2448 in the *Libellus Synodalis* of the Paris Synod of 825, but Albert Werminghoff[56] does not identify them, while E. J. Martin[57] assumes that the two texts are not extant in the works of Gregory. G. B. Ladner[58] surmises that the first citation survives only in the wider context of the *Acta* of II Nicaea, and as testimonium in the collections by John of Damascus, *De imaginibus* (*PG* 94.1269C, 1361C). But Karl Hampe[59] verified the first quotation long ago, and so also recently did Paul van den Ven;[60] the present writer has found the second citation in Gregory's *Commentary on the Canticles* (see below, Section K).

Compare the original text of Gregory in its various transmissions of *JE* 2448:

A. Gregory of Nyssa, *De deitate filii et spiritus sancti*, *PG* 46.572C:

Εἶδον πολλάκις ἐπὶ γραφῆς εἰκόνα τοῦ πάθους, καὶ οὐκ ἀδακρυτὶ τὴν θέαν παρῆλθον, ἐναργῶς τῆς τέχνης ὑπ᾽ ὄψιν ἀγούσης τὴν ἱστορίαν.

---

[55] See nn. 8 and 9, above.

[56] *MGH, Conc.* 2 (Aevi Karolini 1.2; Hannover, Leipzig, 1908), 486, 538, 900.

[57] *A History of the Iconoclastic Controversy* (London, 1930), 138 n. 2, and 258.

[58] "The Concept of the Image in the Greek Fathers and the Byzantine Iconoclastic Controversy," *Dumbarton Oaks Papers* 7 (1953), 4; nor is the frequently cited testimonium identified by Paul J. Alexander, *The Patriarch Nicephorus of Constantinople* (Oxford, 1958), 257 n. 3. Gert Haendler, *Epochen karolingischer Theologie: Eine Untersuchung über die karolingischen Gutachten zum byzantinischen Bilderstreit* (Berlin, 1958), 114 n. 555, even doubts the authenticity of the text ascribed to Gregory of Nyssa.

[59] The editor of the *Hadrianum* (*JE* 2483), sent by Hadrian I to Charlemagne, *MGH, Epistolae* 5 (Karolini Aevi 3; Berlin, 1899), 33 n. 4.

[60] See above, n. 41, *Byzantion* 25–27 (1955–57), 352 no. 38. Ernst Kitzinger, "The Cult of Images in the Age before Iconoclasm," *Dumbarton Oaks Papers* 8 (1954), 137, refers to the same passage from Gregory in another context.

B. *JE* 2448 cited in *LS*, p. 513.22–24 (486.35–36):

Item beati Gregorii Niseni episcopi inter plura (cetera 486.35), ubi de Abraham sermonem instituit:

Vidi (inquit *add.* 486.36) [multoties] imaginem passionis et non sine lacrimis visionem transivi (praeterii 486.36) opus (opere 486.36) artis ad faciem deducens historiam, et cetera.

C. *Greek Nicaenum*, Mansi XII.1066B, in the Greek version of *JE* 2448:

Ἐν τῷ μεταξὺ ὁ ἅγιος Γρηγόριος ὁ Νύσσης ἐπίσκοπος περὶ τοῦ Ἀβραὰμ λόγον συνεστήσατο, λέγων:

Εἶδον πλειστάκις τὴν ἐπιγραφὴν τοῦ πάθους, καὶ οὐκ ἀδακρυτὶ παρῆλθον ἔργον τέχνης εἰς πρόσωπον προσαχθὲν ἱστορίας, καὶ τὰ λοιπά.

D. Anastasius' version of *JE* 2448, Mansi XII.1065C–D:

Interea et beatus Gregorius Nyssenus episcopus inter plura quae in sermone quem de Abraham instituit, ita dixit:

Vidi multoties conscriptionem imaginis passionis, et non sine lacrymis visionem praeterii, opere artis ad faciem afferentis historiam, et caetera.

It is evident that text B is the translation of A, and that C is the Byzantine version of B. D represents the version B, which was adapted by Anastasius Bibliothecarius to the Byzantine translation C.

The *Hadrianum* I.37 (33.9) refers "in eadem [that is, *quarta*] actione" to this testimonium, without citing the text, whose Greek original is indeed cited verbatim in the *Greek Nicaenum*, *actio* IV (Mansi XIII.12A). The author of the *Libellus Synodalis* of the Paris Synod of 825 (*LS*) inserted the testimonium in his collection after the first Latin rendering in Hadrian I's *Synodica* of 785 (*JE* 2448), which in turn had been inserted into the *Latin Nicaenum*, *actio* II. This translation seems to contain a faulty rendering of the Greek original of Gregory, and therefore ἐναργῶς τῆς τέχνης was misread either as ἔργον, or else the adverb was brought into connection with ἐνέργεια. We thus understand the mistranslation *opus artis* in the quotation from *JE* 2448 in *LS*, and the ἔργον τέχνης in the Latin *Synodica*'s translation in the *Greek Nicaenum*. The latter translated into Greek (εἰς πρόσωπον προσαχθέν) the first Latin translation (*ad faciem deducens*) of Gregory's original (ὑπ' ὄψιν ἀγούσης). Anastasius adapts the Latin version of *JE* 2448 after the *Synodica*'s version in the *Greek Nicaenum*, and consequently adds to his translation the word *conscriptionem* for ἐπιγραφήν. It is obvious that the Byzantine translator of *JE* 2448 was not familiar with the original Greek version of Gregory, and for this reason retranslated the Latin version in the *Synodica*.

K. Gregory of Nyssa, *Commentarius in Canticum Canticorum.*—Compare the various transmissions of the second Gregory quotation in *JE* 2448:

E. *Gregorii Nysseni Commentarius in Canticum Canticorum*, ed. Hermann Langerbeck (Leiden, 1960), 28.7–17 (*PG* 44.776A):

ὥσπερ δὲ κατὰ τὴν γραφικὴν ἐπιστήμην ὕλη μέν τις πάντως ἐστὶν ἐν διαφόροις βαφαῖς ἡ συμπληροῦσα τοῦ ζῴου τὴν μίμησιν, ὁ δὲ πρὸς τὴν εἰκόνα βλέπων τὴν ἐκ τῆς τέχνης διὰ τῶν χρωμάτων συμπληρωθεῖσαν οὐ ταῖς ἐπιχρωσθείσαις τῷ πίνακι βαφαῖς ἐμφιλοχωρεῖ τῷ θεάματι, ἀλλὰ πρὸς τὸ εἶδος βλέπει μόνον, ὃ διὰ τῶν χρωμάτων ὁ τεχνίτης ἀνέδειξεν.

F. *JE* 2448 cited in *LS*, 513.25–29: (cf. above, B.):

Item ipse in interpretatione in cantica canticorum: Sicut vero conscripta doctrina materia quaedam est, ita omnino in diversis tincturis, quae complent animantis imitationem. Qui vero imaginem conspicit ex eadem arte per colores completam tabulam, non tincturis praefert contemplationem, sed visionem depictam conspicit tantummodo, quam per colores magister demonstravit.

G. *Greek Nicaenum*, Mansi XII.1066B–C, Greek version of *JE* 2448:

καθὼς ἡ γεγραμμένη διδαχὴ λέγει·
Ὕλη τίς ἐστι παντελῶς ἐν διαφόροις βαφαῖς ἀναπληροῦσα τὴν τῆς ψυχῆς μίμησιν. Ὁ γὰρ πρὸς τὴν εἰκόνα θεωρῶν τὴν ἐκ τῆς τέχνης διὰ χρωμάτων ἀναπληρουμένην σανίδα, οὐκ ἐκ τῆς βαφῆς τὴν ὁμοιότητα φέρει, ἀλλὰ πρὸς τὴν θεωρίαν τοῦ πρωτοτύπου ἀνάγεται.

H. Anastasius' version of *JE* 2448, Mansi XII.1065D:

de interpretatione eius in cantica canticorum, sicut conscripta doctrina dicit: Materia quaedam est omnino in diversis tincturis, quae complet animantis imitationem. Qui enim ad imaginem conspicit ex eadem arte per colores completam tabulam, non tincturis praefert contemplationem, sed ad visionem depictam conspicit tantummodo, quam per colores magister demonstravit.

The Latin translation of Gregory's original text in *JE* 2448, as cited in the *Libellus Synodalis* of 825 (F), is by and large a literal one. The *Greek Nicaenum* plainly offers a retranslation of F. Compare the opening words in

E: ὥσπερ δὲ κατὰ τὴν γραφικὴν ἐπιστήμην;
F: Sicut vero conscripta doctrina;
G: καθὼς ἡ γεγραμμένη διδαχή.

In addition see τοῦ ζῴου (E)—*animantis* (F)—τῆς ψυχῆς (G); and correspondingly τῷ πίνακι—*tabulam*—σανίδα; ἐμφιλοχωρεῖ—*praefert*—τὴν ὁμοιότητα φέρει.

Anastasius' version H, which is based on F, is clearly adjusted to the Greek translation of F in the *Greek Nicaenum*. The Byzantine translator of *JE* 2448 was obviously not familiar with the *Greek* original of F and thus translated the Latin quotation into Greek.

L. Severianus of Gabala, *De sigillis librorum.*—*LC* II.19 expresses doubts concerning the authenticity of two passages cited in the name of John Chrysostom. The *Hadrianum* I.8[61] ascribes the first of those two texts to Severianus of Gabala, and in II.13 only parts of the second passage to Chrysostom. The *LC* saw what modern patristic studies have shown,[62] namely, the occurrence among the spuria of Chrysostom of original sermons delivered by his opponent Severian. Johannes Zellinger[63] identified the Severian text in *JE* 2448, while John of Damascus, *De imaginibus, oratio II*, whose collections of testimonia in all probability provided the official in the papal *scrinium*

---

[61] Ed. Karl Hampe, *MGH, Epistolae* 5 (Karolini Aevi 3; Berlin, 1899), 17.

[62] Cf. B. Marx, "Severiana unter den Spuria Chrysostomi bei Montfaucon-Migne," *Orientalia Christiana Periodica* 5 (1939), 281–361. Marx does not deal with the citations from Severianus in the *Hadrianum* I, cc. 21, 26.

[63] *Studien zu Severian von Gabala* (Münsterische Beiträge zur Theologie 8; Münster i. W., 1926), 36; Zellinger deals with the text cited in *JE* 2448, and ascribed to Chrysostom; the texts in the *Hadrianum* (not identified by Hampe), and the one in the *LC*, are not mentioned by him, nor the fact that John of Damascus ascribes (below, text A) it to Chrysostom. The texts cited in item L concerning the authorship of Severianus of Gabala can be added to J. A. de Aldama, *Repertorium Pseudochrysostomicum* (Paris, 1965), No. 246.

who composed the document with some of the testimonia of image-worship which he cited, ascribes Severian's text to Chrysostom.

Compare the various transmissions of the excerpt from Severian's homily (below, C1) in its Greek and Latin versions:

A. John of Damascus, *De imaginibus, oratio II, PG* 94.1313C:

a. Τοῦ ἁγίου Ἰωάννου τοῦ Χρυσοστόμου, ἐκ τῆς ἑρμηνείας τῆς παραβολῆς τοῦ σπόρου:
b. Ἔνδυμα βασιλικὸν ἐὰν ὑβρίσῃς, οὐ τὸν ἐνδεδυμένον ὑβρίζεις;
c. οὐκ οἶδας ὅτι, ἐὰν εἰκόνα βασιλέως ὑβρίσῃς, εἰς τὸ πρωτότυπον τῆς ἀξίας φέρεις τὴν ὕβριν;
d. οὐκ οἶδας ὅτι, ἐάν τις εἰκόνα τὴν ἀπὸ ξύλου καὶ ἀνδριάντος χαλκοῦ κατασύρῃ, οὐχ ὡς εἰς ἄψυχον ὕλην τολμήσας κρίνεται, ἀλλ' ὡς κατὰ βασιλέως κεχρημένος τῇ ὕβρει;
e. Εἰκόνα δὲ ὅλως βασιλέως φέρουσα, τὴν ἑαυτῆς ὕβριν εἰς βασιλέα ἀνάγει.

B. *JE* 2448 cited in *LS*, p. 510.32–37; in *LC* II.19, p. 78.15–19 (Nonne eum . . . deducit):

a. Item beati Iohannis Chrysostomi de parabola seminis:
b. Indumentum imperiale si iniuriaveris, nonne eum qui induitur (-etur *LC*) iniurias?
c. Nescis quia, si quis imaginem imperatoris iniuriat, ad cum ipsum imperatorem, principaliter dignitati eius adfert (affert *LC*) iniuriam?
d. Nescis quia, si quis imaginem ex ligno aut ex colore detrahit (-et *LC*), non sicut ad elementum sine anima ausus iudicatur, sed sicut adversus imperatorem dissegregatam (-ta *LC*)?
e. imaginem totidem imperatoris gestans, eius (ei *LC*) iniuriam ad imperatorem deducit?

C.1 Severianus of Gabala, *De sigillis librorum, PG* 63.544, lines 7–15:

a. (Montfaucon in *PG* 63.531, note *a*, lists as title of the homily in a Paris MS: . . . Χρυσόστομος εἰς τὰς σφραγῖδας.)
b. Ἔνδυμα βασιλικὸν ἐὰν ὑβρίσῃς, οὐ τὸν ἐνδεδυμένον ὑβρίζεις;
c. οὐκ οἶδας ὅτι, εἰ εἰκόνα βασιλέως τις ὑβρίσει, εἰς τὸ πρωτότυπον τῆς ἀξίας φέρει τὴν ὕβριν;
d. οὐκ οἶδας ὅτι, ἐάν τις εἰκόνα τὴν ἀπὸ ξύλου ἢ ἀνδριάντα χαλκοῦν κατασύρῃ, οὐχ ὡς εἰς ἄψυχον ὕλην τολμήσας οὕτω κρίνεται, ἀλλ' ὡς κατὰ βασιλέως χεῖρας ἐκτείνας ἀφανίζεται;

e.   Ὕλη ἄψυχος τοῦ βασιλέως εἰκόνα φέρουσα τὴν ἑαυτῆς ὕβριν εἰς βασιλέα ἀνάγει.

C.2 *Hadrianum* I.8, p. 17.13–19, *in actione tertia:*

a.   Item sancti Severiani episcopi Gavalensis de homilia in qua demonstravit scripturas per Dominum explanatas, et cetera:

b.   Vestem imperialem si iniuriaveris, numquid non qui eam induit iniurias?

c.   Nescis, quoniam si quis imaginem imperatoris iniuriaverit, in prime forme dignitatis adfert iniuria?

d.   Nescis, quoniam si quis imago quae a ligno detrahet, non sicut inanimata materia audens sic iudicatur, sed sicut qui adversum imperatorem manus extendens fedatur materia, sine anima imperatoris segregata ab imperatore?

e.   Imago enim omnino ferente, eius iniuria ad imperatorem adtingit, etc.

D.   *JE* 2448 in *Greek Nicaenum*, Mansi XII.1066E–1067A:

a.   Πάλιν δὲ ἐκ τοῦ λόγου τοῦ ἁγίου Ἰωάννου ἐπισκόπου Κωνσταντινουπόλεως τοῦ Χρυσοστόμου, τοῦ εἰς τὴν παραβολὴν τοῦ σπόρου.

b.   Ἔνδυμα βασιλικὸν ἐὰν ὑβρίσῃς, οὐχὶ τὸν ἐνδυόμενον αὐτὸν ὑβρίζεις;

c.   (. . . ὁμοίως δὲ ὁ Χρυσόστομος, Mansi XIII.325D, *actio* VI):
     οὐκ οἶδας, ὅτι ἐὰν εἰκόνα βασιλέως ὑβρίσῃς, εἰς τὸ πρωτότυπον τῆς ἀξίας φέρεις τὴν ὕβριν;

d.   (Mansi XII.1066E):
     οὐκ οἶδας, ὅτι ὅστις τὴν εἰκόνα τὴν ἐκ ξύλου καὶ χρωμάτων λοιδορεῖ, οὐχ ὡς πρὸς ἄψυχον τολμήσας κρίνεται, ἀλλὰ κατὰ τοῦ βασιλέως;

e.   δισσῶς γὰρ τῷ βασιλεῖ προσφέρει τὴν ὕβριν.

E.   Anastasius' version of *JE* 2448, Mansi XII.1068BC:

a.   Item beati Joannis archiepiscopi Constantinopolitani, qui et Chrysostomus, de parabola seminis:

b.   Indumentum imperiale si contumeliis affeceris, nonne ei qui induitur contumelias irrogas?

c.   Nescis quia, si quis imagini imperatoris injuriam infert, ad ipsum imperatorem, id est, ad ipsum principalem et ad eius dignitatem refert injuriam?

d.   Nescis quod, si quis imagini quae ex ligno et coloribus est male dicit, non judicatur veluti si contra inanimatum quiddam praesumptuose se gesserit, sed tamquam is qui contra imperatorem egerit?

e.   Dupliciter enim imperatori contumeliam infert.

The comparison of the preceding text in its various transmissions leads to numerous conclusions, philological, political, and diplomatic. It is obvious that the *LC* text (B) represents a quotation drawn from the original version of *JE* 2448 which was inserted in the *First Latin Nicaenum* by the Roman ecclesiastic who produced it. The beginning of the Chrysostomos text, which is missing in the *LC* transmission, is fully cited (see B, above) in the *Libellus Synodalis* of 825, which like the *LC* cited *JE* 2448.

The first οὐκ οἶδας is omitted from the Greek version of *JE* 2448 (Dc). The missing text appears, however, in the synodal *Acta* in another context. The Byzantine translator of the *Synodica* may have deemed it unsuitable for public recitation even in the presence of imperial commissars representing the Byzantine Majesties who attended only the last session of II Nicaea.[64]

Differences in the translation of the same Severian passage cited in the *Hadrianum* and in *JE* 2448 (*LC* and *LS*) are traceable to the context in which both documents originated. Severian (C1c and Dc), for instance, reads: "εἰς τὸ πρωτότυπον τῆς ἀξίας φέρει τὴν ὕβριν"; which is translated in *JE* 2448 of 785 (see B) as follows: " . . . , principaliter dignitati eius adfert [affert *LC*] iniuriam?" but in the later *Hadrianum* (*JE* 2483), of about 791, as follows: " . . . , in prime forme dignitatis adfert iniuria?"

The *Hadrianum*'s rendering becomes understandable if we recall that its chapter headings quote from the lost *Capitulare adversus Synodum*, which in turn cited the text of the *First Latin Nicaenum* sent by Hadrian I to Charlemagne. This means that the passage from Severian of Gabala in 2448 parallels the wording of the title quoted in the *Hadrianum* I.8 (17.6–8) from the *Capitulare adversus Synodum*: "Capitulo VIII. Contra eos qui dicunt quod imaginis honor in prima forma transit."

LC III.16 (136.28f.) and the *Libellus Synodalis* of the Paris Synod of 825 (*LS* 509.3f., 511.2f.) cite the Latin translation in the *Latin Nicaenum* of a much-cited statement by Basil of Caesarea, *De spiritu*

---

[64] R. Janin, "Rôle des commissaires impérieux Byzantines dans les Conciles," *Revue des études byzantines* 18 (1960), 105, mistakenly assumes that Irene and Constantine VI never attended a session of II Nicaea; they were present at the eighth session (Mansi XIII.416E), and both signed the *Horos* (definition) of II Nicaea.

sancto 18.45:[65] "ἡ τῆς εἰκόνος τιμὴ ἐπὶ τὸ πρωτότυπον διαβαίνει," cited, as indicated by the *Hadrianum*, in the *Acta* of II Nicaea, *actio tertia*, Mansi XII.1146A. Anastasius in his translation of the Greek *Acta*, published in Mansi, reads (*ibid.*, XII.1145A): "secundum Basilium Magnum, quod imaginis honor ad principalem transeat."

Although Basil's saying refers to the dogma of the trinity, and actually has nothing to do with image-worship, it is used throughout the *Acta* of II Nicaea as proof of the worship of images (for example, Mansi XIII.69D), and is repeatedly quoted in earlier documents which had been read into the synodal record of 787 (Mansi XIII.71C, 326D, 378E) by sundry speakers and readers. The *First Nicaenum*'s rendering of Basil's statement occurs, for instance, in the translation of the Epistle sent by Gregory II to Germanus of Constantinople (*JE* 2181) and inserted in the *Nicaenum*, in a fragment preserved in the *Libellus Synodalis* of 825.[66]

The second *Nescis* of *JE* 2448 (above, Bd) offers a clear example either of the initially poor Latin translation of the Greek original by the redactor of the *Synodica*, or else of the poor textual transmission of the document.

The text of Bd–e, and also the *Hadrianum*'s version C2d–e, from Severian of Gabala's homily (C1d–e), present difficulties which, however, become clarified in the light of the newly found source. We read in

C1d: . . . ἀλλ' ὡς κατὰ βασιλέως χεῖρας ἐκτείνας ἀφανίζεται;
    e: Ὕλη ἄψυχος τοῦ βασιλέως . . . .

The *Hadrianum*'s section must be read correspondingly as follows:

C2d: sed sicut qui adversum imperatorem manus extendens fedatur?
    e: Materia sine anima imperatoris segregata ab imperatore, imago enim.

The "segregata ab imperatore" appears like a gloss inserted in the context. On the basis of the adjusted Latin translation in C2d–e,

---

[65] Cf. Hermann Dörries, *De spiritu sancto: Der Beitrag des Basilius zum Abschluss des trinitarischen Dogmas*, Abh. der Akad. der Wiss. Göttingen phil.-hist. Klasse, Dritte Folge, no. 39 (1939), 145f.; F. X. Funk, "Ein angebliches Wort Basilius des Grossen über die Bilderverehrung," *Kirchenrechtliche Abhandlungen und Untersuchungen* 2 (Paderborn, 1899), 251–253.

[66] *MGH, Conc.* 2, 2 (Aevi Karolini 1, 2; Hannover, Leipzig, 1908), 509.3–4.

the parallel passage in *JE* 2448, cited in *LC* II.19, should read:

Bd: . . . , sed sicut adversus imperatorem?
 e: Dissegregatam imaginem . . . .

The corrupt Byzantine translation of *JE* 2448 (Dd) . . . , ἀλλὰ κατὰ τοῦ βασιλέως, corresponds to the proposed correction in Bd. And *Dissegregatam* in Be looks as if it were based on the possible gloss *segregata ab imperatore* in C2d (above).

The citation in *JE* 2448 of the Severian passage as a testimonium of image-worship is naturally traceable to its insertion as such in John of Damascus, *De imaginibus, oratio II* (above, A). That it was initially an incomplete Latin translation in Bd is confirmed by the Byzantine translation of *JE* 2448 in Dd: Bd did not translate into Latin κεχρημένος τῇ ὕβρει at the end of Ad, nor does Dd offer an equivalent for this text. The meaning of the entire testimonium should now be clear. The first *nescis* (Bc) questions whether the damage inflicted on an inanimate image of the Roman emperor injures the dignity of the imperial office. The second *nescis* (Bd) deliberates within the context of the first query whether the insult inflicted on a statue or a painted image is to be judged not as an insult inflicted on something inanimate, but as a damage or injury to the living emperor. The implication seems to be that the image cannot be separated from its original, or as the *LC* II.19 (78.33) puts it: "non imagini sed eidem imperatori iniuriam inrogare credatur."

The Byzantine translator of *JE* 2448 was obviously familiar with the Greek original (A) of the Latin version (B), and therefore did not offer in D a retranslation of B, but basically the genuine Greek original, though he took liberties with the text, as has been pointed out above, with regard to the closing words of Dd which he omitted. Also the first part of Be is not translated in De, or, to put it differently, the beginning of the Greek original in Ae (or C1e) is replaced by the summary (δισσῶς) of the two questions introduced by *nescis* (Bc–d).

Anastasius' version E of *JE* 2448 was plainly rewritten by him following the Greek translation of the document in the *Greek Ni-caenum*, although the Latin original was available to him. Two examples will suffice. He reads in Ed *contra inanimatum*, following the Byzantine translator's πρὸς ἄψυχον, instead of Bd *ad elementum sine anima*, the inept rendering of the original (Ad/C1d) εἰς ἄψυχον ὕλην.

M. Severianus of Gabala, εἰς τὸν νιπτῆρα.—Neither the first nor the second quotation[67] ascribed to Chrysostom in *LC* II.19 was identified by Bastgen. The Greek original of the passage is preserved, as we shall see, in *actio* IV of the *Greek Nicaenum* (Mansi XIII.68DE) as an excerpt from a homily εἰς τὸν νιπτῆρα. This conclusion concerning the original of the Latin versions (G and H) is supported by the presence of the section g (below) in John of Damascus, *De imaginibus, oratio III*, (*PG* 94.1408C), under the same Greek title. Additional support can be derived from the chapter headings of *LC* II.19 and the *Hadrianum* (G), which render the identical Frankish criticism of the *Acta* of II Nicaea, a criticism that is assigned, also in the *Hadrianum* II.13, to *actio* IV of the *Latin Nicaenum*. The various titles under which the fragment from the homily is cited in its Greek and Latin versions are puzzling at first sight, unless one recalls the identity of *quinta feria* and *coena Domini*.[68] *LC* and *LS* (in H, below) derive their texts from the Latin original of *JE* 2448 inserted in the *Latin Nicaenum*, and ascribe the text to a homily *in quinta feria Pasche* and *in coena Domini*, respectively; the *Greek Nicaenum* and John of Damascus cite the excerpt under the Greek title mentioned above, while Anastasius ascribes it to a homily *in lavationem quintae feriae*. The *Hadrianum* II.14 (47.31) quotes a fragment from Chrysostom's homily *in cena Domini*, which is derived

---

[67] Cf. *LC* II.19 (78 n. 1); it is not identified by Karl Hampe, *Hadrianum*, 47 n. 7, nor by Werminghoff, *MGH, Conc.* 2 (Aevi Karolini 1, 2; 1908), 92 n. 4, 510 n. 4, 903a. Paul van den Ven in *Byzantion* 25–27 (1955–7), 352 no. 40, says: "n'est pas identifiée." Our M remained unknown to Antoine Wenger, "Une homélie inédite de Sévérien de Gabala Sur le Lavement des Pieds," *Revue des études byzantines* 25 (1967), 219–234, who convincingly ascribes the sermon to Severianus. I have adopted this identification without changing anything in my original treatment, first published in *The Classical Tradition* (Ithaca, N.Y., 1966), 478–86. Additional transmissions of the homily continue to appear; see M. Aubineau, *Codices Chrysostomici Graeci* I (Paris, 1968), 290.

[68] See Amalarius, *Liber officialis* I, c. 12, 1 (Studi e Testi 139; Rome, 1948): "... in quinta feria quam vocamus caenam Domini. Lavantur pedes fratrum," etc.

from the homily *De proditione . . . et in sancta et magna feria quinta* (*PG* 49.379),[69] and John of Damascus, *De imaginibus, oratio II* (*PG* 94.1316A) includes the same text among his testimonia. But notwithstanding the identical titles of the sermons, our passage does not occur in *De proditione*, which is registered as a reading for Maundy Thursday, with the *Inc. ὀλίγα ἀνάγκη σήμερον* in various types of Byzantine service books described by Albert Ehrhard.[70] The same service books often list the homily *εἰς τὸν νιπτῆρα* as a *lectio* for various days of the Easter week, but most frequently as an alternate reading for Maundy Thursday. Its *Incipit* Ἔλεον Θεοῦ καὶ φιλανθρωπίαν is mentioned by Robert Devreesse[71] as an *ineditum*, and recorded in Migne, *PG* 64.1346D, but as a *spurium* not published. It is indeed the ultimate source of our Latin fragment whose Greek original is reproduced here on the basis of five MSS of the Vaticana. When examining the pertinent Greek MSS of the Bibliothèque Nationale at Paris, I found that Louis Petit, in a forgotten note,[72] identified the fragment cited in *actio* IV of the *Greek Nicaenum* in four codices: B.N. gr. 582 (s. XI), 771, 1170, 1554a (s. XIV). The importance of this identification for an understanding of the Latin versions in *JE* 2448, the *Hadrianum*, the *LC*, and the *Libellus Synodalis* of 825, was not recognized, and remained unknown to Bastgen.

Compare the following Latin and Greek versions of the pseudo-Chrysostomian homily with the original text:

---

[69] It is *Sermo* 10 with the *Incipit* "Pauca hodie necessarium est" in André Wilmart, "La collection des 38 homélies latines de Sainte Jean Chrysostome," *Journal of Theological Studies* 19 (1918), 313f. Listed by J. A. de Aldama (above n. 63) as No. 313.

[70] *Ueberlieferung und Bestand der hagiographischen und homiletischen Literatur der griechischen Kirche I* (*TU* 50; Leipzig, 1937), for example, 131, 602, and *passim*, also in 2 (*TU* 51; Leipzig, 1938). On the MSS used for the edition of the text below, see Vat. Ottob. gr. 14: I, 216 no. 114; Ottob. gr. 85: II, 15 no. 42; Vat. graec. 2013: II, 145 no. 25, 4; Vat. graec. 1255: II, 148 no. 15, 3; Vat. Pii II graec. 23: II, 154 no. 15. I wish to thank the Vatican Library for sending me photographs of certain pages in these five manuscripts, and for permission to publish the facsimile of Vat. Ottobon. gr. 85, fol. 197r.

[71] *Bibliothèque Nationale: Catalogue des Manuscrits Grecs II, Le Fonds Coislin* (Paris, 1945), 377, MS 193.

[72] "Un texte de Saint Jean Chrysostome sur les images," *Echos d'Orient* 11 (1908), 80–81; cf. n. 67, above.

F. Pseudo-Chrysostomos, *sermo* (Plate III)

a. εἰς τὸν νιπτῆρα, in Vaticanus Ottob. gr. 85, saec. IX, fol. 197r, Inc.
   Ἔλεον θεοῦ καὶ φιλανθρωπίαν:
b. Τὰ πάντα γὰρ ἐγένετο διὰ δόξαν μὲν αὐτοῦ, χρῆσιν δὲ ἡμετέραν·
b1. ἥλιος, ἵνα ἀνθρώπους μὲν καταλάμπῃ,
c. νεφέλαι εἰς τὴν τῶν ὄμβρων διακονίαν,
d. γῆ εἰς τὴν τῶν καρπῶν εὐθηνίαν
e. καὶ θάλαττα εἰς τὴν τῶν ἐμπόρων ἀφθονίαν·
f. πάντα λειτουργεῖ τῷ ἀνθρώπῳ, μᾶλλον δὲ τῇ εἰκόνι τοῦ δεσπότου.
g. Οὐδὲ γὰρ ὅταν βασιλικοὶ χαρακτῆρες καὶ εἰκόνες εἰς πόλιν εἰσφέρονται
   καὶ ὑπαντῶσιν ἄρχοντες καὶ δῆμοι μετ᾽ εὐφημίας καὶ φόβου, οὐ σανίδα
   τιμῶντες οὐ τὴν κηρόχυτον γραφὴν ἀλλὰ τὸν χαρακτῆρα τοῦ βασιλέως
   τιμῶντες·
h. οὕτω καὶ ἡ κτίσις οὐ τὸ γήϊνον σχῆμα τιμᾷ, ἀλλὰ τὸν οὐράνιον χαρακτῆρα αἰδεῖται.

MSS:
   A—Vaticanus Ottobon. graecus 14, f. 178r, saec. X;
   B—Vat. gr. 1255, f. 99r, s. X;
   C—Vat. gr. 2013, f. 91r, s. X;
   D—Vat. Pii II gr. 23, f. 50v, s. XI;
   M—Mansi XIII.67DE, in *Greek Nicaenum* of 787.

Apparatus criticus:

b. Τὰ, γὰρ *om.* M; γὰρ) μὲν C, *om.* γὰρ; γὰρ) μὲν γὰρ D; ἐγένετο)
   ἐγένοντο M; μὲν αὐτοῦ) *om.* M, Θεοῦ *instead.*
b1. ABCD, *om.* M; ἀνθρώπους) ἀνθρώποις CD; μὲν) *om.* BCD; καταλάμπῃ) -πει BD.
c. νεφέλαι) νεφέλη M; ν. δὲ A; τῶν) *om.* B.
d. καὶ γῆ) A; εὐθηνίαν) εὐθυνίαν B.
e. ABDM, *om.* C; καὶ) *om.* BDM; θάλαττα) θάλατται M.
f. πάντα λειτουργεῖ) π. σοι λ. AM; π. συλλ. B; π. συνλειτουργ(εῖ)
   C; π. συνλειτουργη D; ἀνθρώπῳ) ανω ABCD; δεσπότου) ACDM,
   Θυ = Θεοῦ B;
g. οὐδὲ γὰρ) οὐδὲ μὲν γὰρ D, ὥσπερ γὰρ M; ὅταν) ὅτε BM; εἰκόνες)
   εἰκόναις C; εἰσφέρονται) εἰς *supra lin.* C, φέρονται D; ὑπαντῶσιν)
   αὐταῖς *add.* M; μετ᾽) μετὰ D; εὐφημίας) εὐφροσύνης A; καὶ φόβου)
   om. M; σανίδα τιμῶντες) σ. τιμοντες B, σ. τιμῶσιν M; οὐ τὴν) ἢ
   τὴν AB, οὐδὲ τὴν M; κηρόχυτον) χείριστον CD; γραφὴν) τοῦτο
   ποιοῦσιν *add.* A; τιμῶντες) *om.* A–M.
h. οὕτω) οὗτος B; σχῆμα) σκεῦος AB; γήϊνον) γιηνον B.

G. *Hadrianum* II.13, p. 47, 11–17 [*In actione quarta*]:

a. Nam in praedecessoribus nostris sanctis pontificis conciliis sancti Iohannis Chrysostomi ita fertur sententiam inter cetera:

b.–e. (*desunt*)

f. Omnia tibi ministrant homini, magis autem imagini (Dei);

g. quia nec quando imperiales vultus et imagines in civitatem introibunt et obviant iudices et senatus, cum laude et honore (timore V), non tabulam honorantes, neque effuse cere scripturam, sed vultum imperatoris,

h. sic et mundus hominum non terrenam speciem honorantes, sed caelestem vultum venerentur etc.

H. *JE* 2448 cited in *LS*, p. 510.25–31; *LC* II.19, p. 78.19–26:

a. *LS*: Item Iohannis archiepiscopi Constantinopolitani, qui et Chrysostomi. Iohannis Chrysostomi in sermone coenae Domini:
    LC: Et iterum idem de eodem patre, sermone in quinta feria Pasche:

b. *LS* and *LC*: Omnia facta sunt propter gloriam Dei, usui autem (vero *LC*) nostro:

c. nubes ad imbrium ministerium,

d. terra (-m *LC*) ad frumenti (fructuum *LC*) abundantiam,

e. mare ad negotiandum copiose (mare navigantium *LC*);

f. absque invidia omnia famulantur homini, magis autem imagini Domini (Dei *LC*).

g. Neque enim quando imperiales (imperialis *LC*) vultus et imagines in civitates introducuntur et obviant iudices et plebes cum laudibus, non tabulam honorantes neque effusas ex aere figuras (effusae cerae scripturas *LC*), sed figuram imperatoris,

h. sic et creatura (-m *LC*) non terrenam speciem honorat, sed eandem (eadem *LC*) ipsam caelestem figuram reveretur.

I. *Greek Nicaenum*, Greek version of *JE* 2448, Mansi XII.1067A:

a. Καὶ πάλιν ἐκ τοῦ λόγου τοῦ αὐτοῦ πατρός, τοῦ εἰς ἁγίαν πέμπτην τῆς πασχαλίας·

b. πάντα ἐγένοντο εἰς δόξαν Θεοῦ, εἰς χρῆσιν δὲ ἡμετέραν·

c. νέφη πρὸς τὴν τοῦ ὑετοῦ διακονίαν,

d. ἡ γῆ πρὸς καρποφορίαν πλήθους,

e. θάλασσα τῶν πλεόντων ἄφθονος.

f. πάντα δουλεύουσι Θεῷ, μᾶλλον δὲ τῇ εἰκόνι τοῦ Θεοῦ.

g. οὐδὲ γὰρ ὅτε βασιλικοὶ χαρακτῆρες καὶ εἰκόνες ἐν ταῖς πόλεσιν εἰσφέρονται, καὶ ἀπαντῶσιν ἄρχοντες καὶ λαοὶ μετὰ ἐπαίνων, τὴν σανίδα τιμῶσιν, ἢ τὴν κηρόχυτον γραφὴν, ἀλλὰ τὴν ἱστορίαν τὴν βασιλικήν·

h. οὕτω καὶ ἡ κτίσις οὐ τὸ ἐπίγειον εἶδος τιμᾷ, ἀλλὰ τὴν οὐράνιον ἱστορίαν εὐλαβεῖται.

K. Anastasius' version of F (above), Mansi XIII.67DE:

a. Sancti patris nostri Joannis Chrysostomi sermo in lavationem quintae feriae.
b. Omnia facta sunt propter gloriam dei et usum nostrum.
c. Nubes ad imbrium ministerium,
d. terra ad fructuum abundantiam,
e. mare ad mercatorum copiam.
f. Omnia tibi ministrant, imo autem imagini Dei.
g. Nam quando imperiales characteres et imagines in civitatem introducuntur, obviam veniunt principes et vulgus cum laudatione, non tabulam honorantes, neque perfusam cera picturam, sed characterem imperatoris:
h. sic creatura non terrenum habitum, sed celestem figuram veneratur.

L. Anastasius' version of *JE* 2448, Mansi XII.1068CD:

a. Et iterum de sermone ejusdem Patris habito in quinta feria Pasche:
b, c, d, identical with K (above), b, c, d.
e. mare navigantibus absque invidia est:
f. omnia famulantur homini, magis autem imagini Dei;
g. neque enim quando imperiales vultus et imagines in civitates introducuntur, et obviant judices et plebes cum laudibus, tabulam honorant, vel supereffusam cera scripturam, sed figuram imperatoris.
h. Sic et creatura non terrenam speciem honorat, sed coelestem ipsam figuram reveretur.

The comparison of F with the Latin versions G, H, and K, proves that F is their ultimate, not immediate source. The omission of Fb1 in the three Latin versions and the substitution in Hb and Kb of *Dei* for αὐτοῦ in Fb indicate that the Latin versions depend on a common, second-hand Greek transmission and its Latin rendering which was present in some collection of χρήσεις or testimonia advocating image-worship. The Latin version G is indeed cited in the *Hadrianum* of about 791 on the basis of the *Acta* of the Lateran Council of 769, which included those of the Roman Synod of 731 and its collection of testimonia of image-worship.[73] The differences between the two Latin versions in G and H of the same Greek testimonium F become understandable if we assume that in 785 the redactor of *JE* 2448 either rewrote the testimonium following its Greek version, although the Latin version G in the *Acta* of the Synod of 769 was then accessible to him, or produced his own translation. A bilingual version[74] of the same testimonium at the disposal of Hadrian I's redactor of *JE* 2448 could explain the discrepancies and parallels in the versions G, H, and K;[75] these I shall discuss below.

We read in the original

Ff: πάντα λειτουργεῖ τῷ ἀνθρώπῳ, μᾶλλον δὲ τῇ εἰκόνι τοῦ δεσπότου,

and correspondingly in *JE* 2448, the *LC*, and the *Libellus Synodalis* of the Paris Synod of 825, in

Hf: *omnia famulantur homini, magis autem imagini* Domini (Dei *LC*).

The *Hadrianum*, quoting from the *Acta* of the Roman Council of 731, which had been inserted into the protocois of the Lateran Synod of 769, offers for the same Greek passage the translation

Gf: *Omnia tibi ministrant* homini, *magis autem imagini* (Dei).

---

[73] See the fragments of the *Concilium Romanum* of 769, ed. Albert Werminghoff, *MGH, Concilia* 2 (Aevi Karolini I, 1; Hannover, 1904), 92. The collection of testimonia of the Roman Synod of 731 is the source not only of the Chrysostom excerpt of the *Hadrianum* (above text G), but also of the testimonia of Cyril of Alexandria, dealt with below in Section O, according to Karl Hampe, *Neues Archiv* 21 (1895–96), 111, and *Hadrianum* I.36, p. 32, 24. The origin of all the Greek testimonia in *JE* 2448 is discussed in Chapter II.

[74] Such a bilingual document dealing with the question of image-worship was then available in the papal *scrinium*: the *Synodica* by Theodore of Jerusalem sent to Paul I, and presented by Constantine II "in Latino et Greco eloquio" to the Frankish King Pippin; see *Codex Carolinus*, ed. Wilhelm Gundlach, *MGH, Epistolae* 3 (Merowingici et Karolini Aevi 1; Berlin, 1892), 652f. In 769, Theodore's *Synodica* together with its collection of testimonia of image-worship was inserted into the acta of the Lateran Synod of 769; cf. Karl Hampe, "Hadrians I. Vertheidigung der zweiten nicaenischen Synode gegen die Angriffe Karls des Grossen," *Neues Archiv* 21 (1895–6), 111f.

[75] According to Theodor Schermann, *Die Geschichte der dogmatischen Florilegien vom V.–VIII. Jahrhundert* (*TU* NF. 13.1; Leipzig, 1904), 77 no. 16k, our pseudo-Chrysostomian fragment is found also in the catena of the codex Paris B.N. gr. 1115, which, according to Robert Devreesse, *Introduction à l'étude des manuscrits grecs* (Paris, 1954), 54 n. 8, was copied in 1276 from a Roman MS of 859.

Also the Latin version of F as preserved in *Actio* IV of II Nicaea in Anastasius' translation of the *Acta* of 787, reads:

Kf: *Omnia tibi ministrant,* imo *autem imagini Dei.*

The Latin versions of f in G and K presuppose the variant of the codex A of F, and of the original Greek text of the Chrysostom passage according to *Actio* IV of the *Greek Nicaenum* of 787, as listed under Ff, *apparatus criticus:* AM πάντα σοι λειτουργεῖ. It is clear that in this instance Anastasius Bibliothecarius hardly changes the Latin version of Kf, but basically renders the Latin translation of the fragment as he found it in all probability in the *First Latin Nicaenum, actio* IV.

Another variant of G that requires comment is found in

Gg: *cum laude et honore (timore* MS V), which is the correct version of
Fg: μετ᾽ εὐφημίας καὶ φόβου.

The Latin versions have *cum laudibus* (H, L) and *cum laudatione* (K); this proves that they did not read καὶ φόβου in their sources, which phrase is also missing in F as cited in *actio* IV of II Nicaea (see F *app. crit.* under M). But καὶ φόβου certainly represents the original wording in the MSS, since it is translated in Gg, and also cited in in the section Fg as listed by John of Damascus, *De imaginibus, oratio III, PG* 94.1408C.

There remains the Greek version I of *JE* 2448 in the *Greek Nicaenum.* A comparison with F clearly proves that I is a direct Byzantine translation of the Latin version H, and that the Byzantine translator did not know the Greek original F. The literalness of his mechanical method of translation is quite obvious at the very beginning and elsewhere in the text. Compare Hb: *omnia facta sunt,* which becomes in Ib: πάντα ἐγένοντο, with disregard of the most elementary rule requiring that a neuter plural subject should have its verb in the singular, as for example in the Greek original F: πάντα ἐγένετο. The same habit is apparent in If, when πάντα δουλεύουσι renders Hf, *omnia famulantur,* which is the Latin version of Ff: πάντα λειτουργεῖ.

The identification of the original Greek of the fragment from the homily enables us to suggest an emendation in the version cited in the *LC.*

The text of the *LC* version of He–f is somewhat corrupt. Bastgen
(78, 21–22) reads:

He: mare navigantium;
Hf: *absque invidia* omnia famulantur homini.

But Bastgen's semicolon in He belongs after *absque invidia* (Hf), whose
rightful place is at the end of He, in correspondence, on the one hand
with its Greek original Fe, ἀφθονίαν, and on the other with the version
of the *Nicaenum* in

Ie: Θάλασσα τῶν πλεόντων ἄφθονος.

The *Libellus Synodalis* of the Paris Synod of 825, whose authors or
compilers were familiar with *JE* 2448 and the *LC*, adopted the
wrong *LC* reading in Hf, *absque invidia*, which is correct in

He: mare ad negotiandum *copiose*.

The original Latin translator of He–f obviously confused the double
meaning of ἄφθονος, *plentiful* or *unenvied*.
   Anastasius Bibliothecarius accordingly translates in

Ke: mare ad mercatorum *copiam*, but in
Le: mare navigantibus *absque invidia* est.

Hf in the version of the *LC* and *LS* reads *homini*, . . . *domini* (Dei
LC), which parallels the Greek original Ff: ἀνθρώπῳ, . . . δεσπότου.
The *Nicaenum*'s corresponding translation of *JE* 2448 (If), Θεῷ . . .
Θεοῦ, is incorrect and probably the result of an improper reading of
some abbreviations in the Greek text. The two *nomina sacra* can be
explained. Θεῷ could be a reading of the abbreviation αωι (for
ἀνθρώπῳ) as θωι (θεῷ). In like manner δεσπότου was abbreviated
δου, and this abbreviation was then read as θου, standing for θεοῦ.
The use of the initial letter of a word plus its last two letters as a
method of abbreviation is not unknown.
   The *LC* in Hg parallels Fg, while the *Libellus Synodalis* reads *ex
aere figuras*, but *aere* is an obvious typographical error for *cere*. The
LC reading *effusae cerae scripturas* occurs in all versions of g: . . . τὴν
κηρόχυτον γραφήν (F; I), and the more literal version in G: *effuse cere
scripturam*. This technical term is found in Severianus of Gabala, *De
legislatore* (*PG* 56.407), in a passage often cited at II Nicaea, but
there always assigned to John Chrysostom, for example, Mansi

XIII.9A.[76] A translation of this passage is quoted after the *Latin Nicaenum* in the *Hadrianum* I.42 (34f.).

The basis of Anastasius' version L of *JE* 2448 is—as a comparison with H indicates—the original Latin text in the *Synodica*. He reads in Le like the *LC* quotation He, and like the Greek version of 2448 (Ie): "mare navigantibus absque invidia est," apparently not taking into account the double meaning of ἄφθονος previously mentioned. We observe what we have already recognized in other instances as his basic approach in dealing with some of the original Greek citations given in the Latin of *JE* 2448, namely, the occasional adaptation of the Latin text of the *Synodica*'s quotations to the corresponding Greek version in the *Greek Nicaenum*. That this adaptation represents a conscious method of Anastasius, can be seen, for example, in the following example:

1. The original text of Hg reads in the version of the *LC*: "non tabulam honor*antes neque* effusae cerae scriptur*as*."

2. The Greek version Ig of Hg reads: "τὴν σανίδα τιμῶσιν ἢ τὴν κηρόχυτον γραφήν."

3. And Anastasius' version Lg accordingly adapts text 1 to that of 2: "tabulam honor*ant vel* supereffusam cere scriptur*am*."

On the other hand, Anastasius' translation Kg of Fg retains the original negative *non* (like the transmission of the *LC* in Hg), and also honor*antes* for τιμῶσιν in Fg (Mansi XIII.67), which in Lg is rendered literally: honor*ant*.

N. Athanasius, *De incarnatione verbi dei.*—Athanasius of Alexandria is quoted in *LC* II.14. Bastgen refers to the fuller quotation in *JE* 2448, which is contained in the *Nicaenum, actio* II (Mansi XII.1068). The chapter heading of *LC* II.14 is identical with that of the *Capitulare adversus Synodum*, cited in the *Hadrianum* I.34, where also its occurrence in the *Acta* of II Nicaea is listed, namely, *in actione quarta*. The identity of the chapter headings and the reference to *actio* IV of the *Nicaenum* show that both documents used the First Latin translation of the Greek *Acta*. Athanasius is frequently cited as an authority (*actiones* III, IV, VI), but, as was to be expected,

---

[76] A sentence from this passage in Severianus of Gabala, *De legislatore*, is quoted in the *LC* in the name of Chrysostom, and also by John of Damascus, *De imaginibus*, *PG* 94.1313B, 1400C; see Paul van den Ven, *Byzantion* 25-7 (1955-7), 352 no. 39, and von den Steinen, "Entstehungsgeschichte" (above n. 2), 17 and n. 3. See below, item R, the critical treatment of this text.

the *LC* does not cite the same quotation from Athanasius' work as the one listed in the *Hadrianum* I.34 after *actio* IV, but quotes rather the Athanasius text from *JE* 2448 in *actio* II. This may be looked upon as the independent act of the actual author of the *LC* when refuting the validity of Athanasius as a patristic authority advocating the worship of images.

Compare the following texts of the quotation from Athanasius in its various transmissions:

A. Athanasius, *De incarnatione verbi dei*, ed. Robert Pierce Casey (Studies and Documents 14.2, ed. Kirsopp Lake and Carsten Höeg; London, 1946), 1 and 20 (*PG* 25.96 and 120C):

1. Αὐτάρκως ἐν τοῖς πρὸ τούτων ἐκ πολλῶν ὀλίγα διαλαβόντες.

14. Ὡς γὰρ τῆς γραφείσης ἐν ξύλῳ μορφῆς παραφανισθείσης ἐκ τῶν ἔξωθεν ῥύπων, πάλιν χρεία τοῦτον παραγενέσθαι, οὖ καὶ ἔστιν ἡ μορφή, ἵνα ἀνακαινισθῆναι ἡ εἰκὼν δυνηθῇ ἐν τῇ αὐτῇ ὕλῃ · διὰ γὰρ τὴν ἐκείνου γραφὴν^a καὶ αὐτὴ ἡ ὕλη ἐν ᾗ καὶ γέγραπται, οὐκ ἐκβάλλεται, ἀλλ᾽ ἐν αὐτῇ ἀνατυποῦται·
a μορφὴν Mt. Athos, MS Dochiariou 78.

B. *JE* 2448 cited in *LS*, p. 513.14f.:

Item sancti Athanasii episcopi Alexandrini de humanatione Domini,
(1.) cuius initium: Sufficienter quidem de his multis pauca sumentes intimavimus.
(14.) Et post: (*LC* II.14, 74.3–6; *LS*, p. 513.15–18)
Sicut ea quae scribitur in lignis, forma abolita exterioribus sordibus, iterum necesse est in (est in *om. LS*) idipsum (id ipsum *LS*) recuperari atque uniri his (ei *LS*), cuius est forma, ut innovari possit imago in eadem materia atque elemento. Per eius enim formam et ipsa materia, ubi et conscribitur, non deicitur, sed in ea ipsa configuratur.

C. *Greek Nicaenum*, Mansi XII.1067B–C, Greek version of *JE* 2448:

Πάλιν τοῦ ἁγίου Ἀθανασίου ἐπισκόπου Ἀλεξανδρείας περὶ τῆς ἐνανθρωπήσεως τοῦ Κυρίου,
1. οὖ ἡ ἀρχή· Ἱκανῶς μὲν ἐκ πολλῶν ὀλίγα λαβόντες ἐγράψαμεν.
14. Ἔπειτα· Καὶ αὐτὰ τὰ ἐν ξύλοις γραφόμενα, μορφῆς παρελθούσης ἐκ τοῦ ἔξω ῥύπου, πάλιν ἀναγκαῖον τὸν αὐτὸν ἀναλαβέσθαι καὶ ἐνῶσαι, οὗτινός ἐστιν ἡ μορφή, τοῦ ἀνακαινίσαι δυνηθῆναι εἰκόνα ἐν τῇ αὐτῇ ὕλῃ καὶ στοιχείῳ. Διὰ γὰρ τὴν αὐτοῦ μορφὴν καὶ ἡ ὕλη, ὅπου καὶ γράφεται, οὐ καταβάλλεται, ἀλλ᾽ ἐν αὐτῇ συνιστορεῖται.

D. Anastasius' version of *JE* 2448, Mansi XII.1068D–E:

Item sancti Athanasii episcopi Alexandrie de humanatione Domini,
(1.) cuius initium est: Sufficienter quidem de multis pauca sumentes
        intimavimus.
(14.) Et post: Et ipsa quae scribuntur in lignis, abolita forma per exteriores
        sordes, iterum idipsum necesse est in omnibus resumere et unire,
        cuius est forma, renovari possit imago in eadem materia et elemento.
        Per eandem enim formam et materia, ubi et conscribitur, non
        dejicitur, sed in ea ipsa configuratur, et cetera.

A comparison of the same Athanasius text in its various transmissions reveals the nature of the interdependence between the
Greek and Latin versions. The *LC* contains the version of the text
as it was originally cited in *JE* 2448, and not, as Bastgen evidently
assumed, a retranslation into Latin of the Greek version of the *Greek
Nicaenum* (C). The versions of the quotation from Athanasius as
quoted in the *LC* and the *Libellus Synodalis* of 825 are identical
(see B), but *LS* offers the entire text of the quotation in the original
version of *JE* 2448. The Byzantine translator[77] does not insert the
Greek original A into his translation of 2448, but his own translation
of B. We therefore read in paragraph 1 Ἱκανῶς instead of Αὐτάρκως
(*sufficienter*), and in paragraph 14 we do not read with A Ὡς γὰρ,
but Καὶ αὐτά. On the other hand we recognize that Anastasius
Bibliothecarius rewrites in spots the original Latin of *JE* 2448 on
the basis of the *Greek Nicaenum*, as is evident from the beginning of
his paragraph 14: *Et ipsa*, after the *Nicaenum*'s translation καὶ αὐτά.
This dependence of Anastasius' version on the *Greek Nicaenum* is
obvious throughout, though he does not produce an entirely new
Latin translation of the testimonium, whose last sentence renders
verbatim the original Latin version B. Generally speaking, we may
again say that Anastasius adapted the Latin version of the Athanasius quotation in the original *JE* 2448 to its version in the *Greek
Nicaenum*. In addition, Hadrian's *Synodica* seems to offer evidence
which supports the assumption that the original Greek Athanasius
quotation may have belonged to some collection of patristic testimonia which existed either in the form of a special Greek florilegium,

---

[77] The editor of Athanasius in *PG* 25.120C, n. 6, states that the Greek version
of *JE* 2448 in the *Acta* of II Nicaea offers a version of c. 14: "verbis paulum diversis quod *ex Latina lingua in Graecam versa* fuerint;" see also above, n. 54.

or else as χρήσεις of image-worship, to be found independently in
MSS collections or within the *acta* of some council. Both possibilities
suggest themselves because the text of Athanasius in its Latin and
Greek versions is introduced by a formula also used in Greek synodal *Acta* when testimonia of patristic authors are cited (see for
instance, Mansi XIII.55E, 57D, 8B, and often elsewhere).[78]

The formula in question consists of the author's name and station
in life, the title of his work, the latter's *Incipit* introduced by . . . ,
οὗ ἡ ἀρχή (*cuius initium est*), and finally the testimonium introduced
by the stereotyped phrase καὶ μετ᾽ ὀλίγα (*et post pauca*). If the quotation is farther removed from the *Incipit*, the introductory term is
καὶ μεϑ᾽ ἕτερα (*et post alia*). In accordance with this scheme we read
in the various versions of the quotation from Athanasius in *JE* 2448
(see B, C, D): *cuius initium* (*est*)——οὗ ἡ ἀρχή, and *Et post* (*alia*)—καὶ
μεϑ᾽ (ἕτερα). In this instance the *Greek Nicaenum* (C) contains a
retranslation into Greek of the Latin rendering (B) of the original
Athanasius quotation (A). The reason for this retranslation is to be
found in the fact that this quotation as such was unknown to the
Byzantine translator of *JE* 2448, who was, however, as will be
shown subsequently, familiar with certain Greek florilegia of patristic testimonia of image-worship. On the other hand, the redactor
of the *Synodica* in Hadrian I's *scrinium* could have found the Greek
text of the Athanasius quotation perhaps in an appendix to a Greek
florilegium, saec. VII–VIII, the so-called *Doctrina Patrum de incarnatione verbi*, c. 45, 7: ῾Ως γὰρ τῆς ἐγγραφείσης ἐν ξύλῳ . . . ἐν αὐτῇ
ἀνατυποῦται.[79] This testimonium is identical with the Greek source
(above, A) of the Latin quotation of Athanasius in *JE* 2448. It
seems that this testimonium is not cited anywhere else in the *Acta*
of II Nicaea except in the Greek version of the *Synodica*.[80]

---

[78] Cf. Devreesse, *Introduction à l'étude des manuscrits grecs*, 78 n. 7, p. 181.

[79] Franz Diekamp, *Doctrina Patrum de incarnatione verbi: Ein griechisches Florilegium
aus der Wende des VII. und VIII. Jahrhunderts* (Münster i. W., 1907), 327; the quotation appears in MS C, twelfth century, and could have been culled from *JE* 2448?

[80] Our Athanasius text can be added to those treated by Berthold Altaner,
"Altlateinische Uebersetzungen von Schriften des Athanasios von Alexandreia,"
Byzantinische Zeitschrift 41 (1941), 45–59, and Gustave Bardy, "Sur les anciennes
traductions latines de Saint Athanase," *Recherches de Science Religieuse* 34 (1947), 239–
242; it is not found in Georg Karo and Johannes Lietzmann, *Catenarum Graecarum
Catalogus*, Nachrichten von der Kgl. Gesellschaft der Wissenschaften zu Göttingen,
phil.-hist. Klasse, 1892.

In accordance with the formula of citation previously described, Athanasius, *De incarnatione verbi*, c. 1, is listed in Cod. Plut. IV23 of the Laurentiana, f.117r: Ἐκ τοῦ περὶ πίστεως λόγου, οὗ ἡ ἀρχὴ Αὐτάρκως . . . διαλαβόντες.[81]

O. Cyril of Alexandria, *Commentary on Matthew.*—The Greek original of the two quotations in *LC* II.20 from Cyril of Alexandria's *Commentary on Matthew* has not been traced as yet. The *Hadrianum* I.37 (33.5–8) refers to both passages without quoting them. The two testimonia in *JE* 2448 are to be added to the fragments of Cyril's lost *Commentary on Matthew*, collected by Joseph Reuss.[82] Compare the following versions of the two fragments in *JE* 2448 as cited in the *Libellus Synodalis* of the Paris Synod of 825 (*LS*) and in the *LC*, the text in the *Greek Nicaenum* (B), and the Latin version in Anastasius Bibliothecarius' translation of the *Acta* of II Nicaea:

A. Cyril of Alexandria, *Commentary on Matthew*:

JE 2448 cited in *LS*, p. 511.25–30, *LC* II.20, p. 79.22–23, 26–28:

Item beati Cyrilli Alexandrini episcopi in sermone (expositione *LC*) Matthei evangelistae:

Depingitur enim fides, quod in forma Dei existit (exsistit *LC*) verbum, sicut et nostrae vitae redemptione oblatus est Deo secundum nostram (nos *LC*) similitudinem indutus (*om. LC*; but see *LC* p. 79.34 similitudine indutus) et factus homo.

Et idem ipse post pauca (post pauca see *LC* p. 79.26): Imaginum nobis explent opus parabolae significantium virtutem, cuidam (cui *LC*), quomodo et oculorum adhiberi et palpatu manus afferri, in vestigiis mentibus inapparabiliter habens visionem.

B. *Greek Nicaenum*, Mansi XII.1067B, Greek version of *JE* 2448:

Ὁμοίως δὲ καὶ τοῦ μακαρίου Κυρίλλου ἐκ τῆς τὸ κατὰ Ματθαῖον ἅγιον Εὐαγγέλιον ἑρμηνείας προφέρομεν λέγοντες.

Ζωγραφεῖ γὰρ ἡ πίστις τὸν ἐν μορφῇ τοῦ Θεοῦ ὑπάρχοντα λόγον, ὡς καὶ ἡ τῆς ζωῆς ἡμῶν λύτρωσις προσηνέχθη τῷ Θεῷ, τὴν καθ' ἡμᾶς ὁμοίωσιν ὑποδὺς καὶ γενόμενος ἄνθρωπος.

---

[81] See Eduard Schwartz, *Der sog. Sermo maior de fide des Athanasius*, in SB. Bayerische Akad. der Wiss. (phil.-hist. Klasse München, 1924), 32.

[82] *Matthäus-Kommentare aus der griechischen Kirche* (*TU* 61, V. Reihe, Bd. 6; Berlin, 1957), 153–169; I believe that the *Acta* of the Sixth Ecumenical Council of Constantinople, 680, Mansi XI.412B–E, contain additional unknown fragments of the lost commentary.

Καὶ πάλιν ὁ αὐτὸς μετὰ μικρόν· Εἰκόνων ἡμῖν ἀποπληροῦσι χρείαν αἱ παραβολαί, τῶν σημαινομένων τὴν δύναμιν οἰονείπως καὶ ὀφθαλμῶν παραθέσει, καὶ ἀφῇ χειρὸς ὑποβάλλουσαι, καὶ τὰ ἐν ἰσχναῖς ἐννοίαις ἀφανῶς ἔχοντα τὴν θεωρίαν.

C. Anastasius' version of *JE* 2448, Mansi XII.1068D:

Similiter et beati Cyrilli ex interpretatione sancti evangelii secundum Matthaeum sermonem proferimus:

Depingit enim fides quod in forma dei existit verbum, sicut et nostrae vitae redemptio oblata est deo, secundum nos carne indutus et factus homo.

Et idem ipse post pauca:

Imaginum nobis explent opus parabolae, significantes virtutem, ac si oculorum adhibitione et palpatu manus suggerant etiam ea quae in exilibus cogitationibus invisibiliter habent contemplationem.

In the first quotation the reading *similitudinem indutus* is confirmed by the *Nicaenum's* ὁμοίωσιν ὑποδύς, a phrase changed by Anastasius to *secundum nos carne indutus*, as if he had in mind the *LC*'s comments (79.54): "... verbum nostrae carnis similitudine indutus et factus est homo." In the original *JE* 2448 the connecting link between the two quotations of Cyril reads: *Et idem ipse post pauca* (*LS* and Anastasius), and correspondingly in the Greek version of the *Nicaenum*: Καὶ πάλιν ὁ αὐτὸς μετὰ μικρόν. The meaningless *in vestigiis mentibus* at the end of the second quotation is a mistranslation which is well attested by the *LC* and the *LS*, and therefore constitutes an original reading in the context of *JE* 2448. It was perhaps caused by the translator of the original Cyril text who instead of ἰσχναῖς read ἴχνεσι, having in mind, as von den Steinen[83] once suggested, τὸ ἴχνος, the track; ἐν ἰσχναῖς ἐννοίαις in the *Nicaenum* in all probability renders the original Greek version, because the term ἔννοιαι with the qualifying ἰσχναί is a favorite expression of Cyril.[84] We read of

---

[83] *QF* 21 (1929–30), 19. Von den Steinen, in the MS mentioned above in n. 54, states that the Cyril texts in the *LC* cannot be the basis of the Greek version in the *Greek Nicaenum*: "Wie sollte ein Grieche darauf kommen, *in vestigiis mentibus* zu übersetzen: ἐν ἰσχναῖς ἐννοίαις?"

[84] Cf. Alexander Kerrigan, *St. Cyril of Alexandria: Interpreter of the Old Testament* (Rome, 1952), 84, 114; also Hubert du Manoir de Juaje, *Dogme et Spiritualité chez Saint Cyrille d'Alexandrie* (Paris, 1944), 132.

"subtle thoughts" in his *Commentary on Micah*,[85] . . . εἰς ἐννοίας ἰσχνάς; elsewhere he speaks of ἰσχνότεραι ἔννοιαι (*PG* 70.460B). Anastasius correctly translates the phrase with "ea quae in exilibus cogitationibus," and otherwise clearly adjusts the original Latin version in *JE* 2448 of Cyril's texts on the basis of the Greek translation of the *Synodica*, thus translating Ὁμοίως by *Similiter*. Needless to say, his Latin version C does not render the original Latin version of *JE* 2448, which is preserved, as we saw, in the *LC* and in the *Libellus Synodalis* of 825. The presence of the meaningless translation *in vestigiis mentibus* in *JE* 2448 of a typical Cyrillian phrase in the Greek version of the document leads me to believe that the Byzantine translator of the *Synodica* was familiar with the Greek original of Cyril's *Commentary on Matthew*, and therefore inserted the original text into his translation.

P. The *Quinisextum*, c. 82.—*LC* II.18 contains a quotation ascribed to the Sixth Ecumenical Council of Constantinople, 680–681. It is found, as the *LC* states, "in eadem nugarum adglomeratione," which in *actio* IV of the *Greek Nicaenum* presents the Patriarch Tarasius' refutation of the *Horos* (definition) of the Iconoclastic Synod of 754. The *Acta* of the Sixth Ecumenical Council are repeatedly cited at II Nicaea and likewise in the *Hadrianum*. But the *LC* quotation ascribed to this council is cited from the *Quinisextum*, c. 82, that is the Concilium in Trullo of 692, which decreed disciplinary canons for the Fifth (533) and Sixth Ecumenical Councils. For this reason the Council of 692 is called Πενθέκτη, *Quinisextum*. Although the *Acta* of the latter are recognized by the Eastern Church, Rome never officially sanctioned them. Nevertheless Constantine (708–715), a Syrian, and some of his successors have recognized certain decisions of the *Quinisextum*,[86] and in such instances judged them as belonging to the Sixth Ecumenical Council.

It cannot be questioned that the *LC* II.18 quotes c. 82 in the form appearing in the *Nicaenum's* first Latin translation, *actio* VI, because the *LC*'s chapter heading is identical with the same statement from the *Capitulare adversus Synodum*, which is also cited in the *Hadrianum*

---

[85] Philip Eduard Pusey, *Sancti patris Cyrilli archiepiscopi Alexandrini in XII Prophetas* I (Oxford, 1868), 605, 21; also 113 no. 7, and *PG* 72.624C.

[86] Willibald M. Plöchl, *Geschichte des Kirchenrechts* I (München, 1953), 134, 402.

I.35 with the reference: *In actione sexta*. This is one of the instances previously listed by von den Steinen as evidence for the fact that the *Hadrianum* and the *LC* use the same Latin translation of the *Greek Nicaenum*.[87] It cannot be assumed with regard to c. 82 that the *Hadrianum*'s version was determined by the text in the *Capitulare*, or that the *LC*'s version was determined by that of the *Hadrianum*, for the *LC* citation is fuller than that of the former. To these two hitherto known transmissions of the *Quinisextum*, c. 82, can be added another which has not been used as yet in this context. It occurs in the *Libellus Synodalis* of the Paris Synod of 825 (below, B), and offers a fuller version of the Latin translation than is cited in either the *LC* or the *Hadrianum*. Although *LS* texts not infrequently depend upon the *Hadrianum*, one must in this case assume that its version, which cites more of c. 82 than does the *Hadrianum*, is directly derived from the Latin translation of the *Nicaenum*, on the basis of which the compiler of the *LS* supplemented the *Hadrianum*'s incomplete citation of the *Quinisextum*. These conclusions follow from a comparison of the various versions of the *Quinisextum*, c. 82, listed under A and B:

A. *Quinisextum*, c. 82, cited in *Greek Nicaenum*, actio VI, Mansi XIII.220; (cf. also Mansi XIII.40E, 41A, and the original in Mansi XI.978A):

a. Ἔν τισι τῶν σεπτῶν εἰκόνων γραφαῖς ἀμνὸς δακτύλῳ τοῦ προδρόμου δεικνύμενος ἐγχαράττεται, ὃς εἰς τύπον παρελήφθη τῆς χάριτος, τὸν ἀληθινὸν ἡμῖν διὰ τοῦ νόμου προϋποφαίνων ἀμνὸν Χριστὸν τὸν θεὸν ἡμῶν ‹...› τὸν τοῦ αἴροντος τὴν ἁμαρτίαν τοῦ κόσμου.[a]

b. Κατὰ τὸν ἀνθρώπινον χαρακτῆρα καὶ ἐν ταῖς εἰκόσιν ἀπὸ τοῦ νῦν ἀντὶ τοῦ παλαιοῦ ἀμνοῦ ἀναστηλοῦσθαι ὁρίζομεν, δι' αὐτοῦ τὸ τῆς ταπεινώσεως ὕψος τοῦ θεοῦ λόγου κατανοοῦντες, καὶ πρὸς μνήμην τῆς ἐν σαρκὶ πολιτείας, τοῦ τε πάθους αὐτοῦ καὶ τοῦ σωτηρίου θανάτου χειραγωγούμενοι, καὶ τῆς ἐντεῦθεν γενομένης τῷ κόσμῳ ἀπολυτρώσεως.

B. *Quinisextum*, c. 82, in the First Latin translation of the *Nicaenum*, actio VI, quoted in: *Hadrianum* I.35 (32.9–12), *In actione sexta*;[b] *LC* II.18, p. 77.10–13; *LS*, p. 513.1–4, 5–8.

a. *Hadrianum:* In—gratie; *LC:* In—nostrum; *LS:*
   In quibusdam venerabilium imaginum (imaginis *LC*) picturis (picture *Hadr.*, *LC*) agnus digito praecursoris[c] monstratus designatur, qui (quod

---

[87] *QF* 21 (1929–30), 16f.—On the *Quinisextum* see also André Grabar, *L'Iconoclasme byzantin: Dossier archéologique* (Paris, 1957), 77–79.

LC) in signum relictus (so *Hadr.*, *LC, LS*) est gratiae (gratie *Hadr.*), verum nobis per legem praemonstrans agnum, Christum Deum (Dominum *LC*) nostrum, ‹. . .› qui abstulit peccata mundi.

b. *Hadrianum:* Secundum—decernimus; not in *LC*; *LS*:
Secundum humanam figuram et in imaginibus a nunc (so *Hadr.*; a om. *LS*) pro veteri agno retitulari decernimus, per ipsum humilitatis altitudinem Dei verbi considerantes et ad memoriam quae in carne actionis quique*ᵈ* passionis eius et salutiferae mortis manibus educati et quae abhinc facta est mundi redemptio, et cetera.

ᵃ Cf. John 1:29.
ᵇ *Hadrianum* II.19 (51.1–4) refers to, and quotes from I.35.
ᶜ John the Baptist declared himself to be the precursor of the Messiah; cf. John I.15, 23, 30; Luc. 3.16, and Tertullian, *Adv. Iudaeos* 9.25 (*CCL* 2; Turnholt, 1954): . . . et praecursorem Christi, Iohannem; *Adv. Marc.* 5.16.4; 4.33.8.
ᵈ Probably *quoque;* see Ab (above): καὶ πρὸς . . . , τοῦ τε.

The common source of the identical version (B) of the *Quinisextum* in the *Hadrianum*, the *LC*, and the *LS* is obvious also from the occurrence of the same mistranslation in each of the three documents: παρελήφθη is always rendered *relictus est*, instead of correctly *assumptus est*, the translation in Mansi XI.978A. Mansi XIII.219C and von den Steinen point out[88] that the translator mistakenly read παρελείφθη. The Roman ecclesiastic who translated the *Greek Nicaenum* thus mistranslated παρελήφθη as the aorist passive ἐλείφθη of λείπω, while it is in fact that of λαμβάνω (ἐλήφθη).

The comparison of Aa with Ba in the transmission of the *Libellus Synodalis* of 825 furthermore shows that c. 82 in the now lost *First Latin* Nicaenum was quoted in *LS* when its compiler supplemented the fragment of c. 82 which he found cited in the *Hadrianum*. The missing part of c. 82 in Ba is indicated by ‹ . . . › and paralleled in the same fashion in the Greek original (above, Aa). It will be noted that the author of the *LS* in his supplementation of the text of c. 82 goes beyond the text portion cited in the *LC*. As a matter of fact, he had before his eyes the entire translation of c. 82 as offered in the *First Latin Nicaenum*, since the clause at the end of Ba is followed in Aa immediately by the text of Bb (= Ab), which is supplemented in the *LS* beyond the section cited in the *Hadrianum*. The Latin version of the *Quinisextum*, c. 82, in Ba–b thus represents the translation of the Greek original in the *First Latin Nicaenum*. The same version

[88] See n. 87, above.

of c. 82 must have been employed for all other occurrences of the *capitulum* cited within the context of the *Nicaenum*: Mansi XII.1080, 1125; XIII.39, 219.

Tarasius cited c. 82 of the *Quinisextum* in his *Synodica* sent to Hadrian I (Grumel, *Reg.* 351),[89] who in his own *Synodica* addressed to Tarasius (*JE* 2449) quoted c. 82 in a Latin translation which was based on the Greek original in the patriarch's letter. The substance of Tarasius' lost *Synodica* is preserved in his *inthronistica* to the three Eastern patriarchs (Grumel, *Reg.* 352). Hadrian I's *JE* 2449 is inserted in the *Acta* of II Nicaea, *actio* II (Mansi XII.1077–1084), and requires a special investigation in relation to the present inquiry concerning the Latin version of c. 82 in the *First Latin Nicaenum*.

Q. Hadrian I's *JE* 2449 and the *Quinisextum*, c. 82.—The transmission of Hadrian I's *JE* 2449, addressed to Tarasius of Constantinople,[90] which confirms the receipt of the newly elected patriarch's *Synodica* (Grumel, *Reg.* 351), parallels by and large the manuscript transmission of *JE* 2448.

The *Greek Nicaenum* contains a Greek translation of *JE* 2449, Mansi XII.1077C–1084D. The *First Latin Nicaenum* hardly offered a retranslation into Latin of the *Nicaenum*'s Greek version of *JE* 2449, but, as in the case of *JE* 2448, and for the same reasons, contained the original Latin version of *JE* 2449. The latter must have been available to the Roman translator of the *First Latin Nicaenum* also in the form of a copy filed away in the papal *scrinium*. The question is whether this copy of the document is identical with the version inserted by Anastasius Bibliothecarius into his second Latin translation of the *Acta* of II Nicaea, edited in Mansi XII.1077C–1084D.

The date line of *JE* 2449 is missing, but it is generally assumed to be contemporary with *JE* 2448 of October 26, 785. This fact demands some evidence that the Latin version of the *Quinisextum*, c. 82, cited in *JE* 2449 after Tarasius' lost Greek *Synodica*, was identical with the Latin version of c. 82 in the *First Latin Nicaenum*, all the more because *Libri Carolini* II.18 itself states that its version

[89] Cf. V. Grumel, *Les Regestes des Actes du Patriarcat de Constantinople* I: *Les Actes des Patriarches*, Fasc. II: *Les Regestes de 715 à 1043* (Socii Assumptionistae Chalcedonenses; Chalcedon, 1936).

[90] Ed. Mansi XII.1077C–1084D; C. Baronius, *Annales Ecclesiastici* XIII, ed. Aug. Theiner, 1868, 178b–180a; *PL* 96, 1233D–1242; Jaffé, *Reg.* 2449.

of c. 82 is somewhat disfigured. Does this circumstance mean that the author of the *LC* was familiar with another version in Latin of the Greek original of c. 82? And that this version was the version of c. 82 inserted in Hadrian's original *JE* 2449?

Tarasius' *Synodica* of 785 (Grumel, *Reg.* 351) is not extant, but identical quotations from its context are preserved in two documents inserted in the Greek *Acta* of II Nicaea. Both documents cite c. 82 of the *Quinisextum* with the identical introductory words from Tarasius' *Synodica*. Hadrian's two representatives at Nicaea state on their own that Tarasius' *Synodica* sent to Hadrian resembled Tarasius' *Inthronistica* sent to the Eastern patriarchs (Mansi XII.1127A: τοιαῦτα γράμματα . . .).

Compare the following texts:

A.a.   Tarasius' *Inthronistica*, addressed to the Eastern patriarchs (Grumel, *Reg.* 352), Mansi XII.1123 E:

> τῆς δὲ αὐτῆς ἁγίας ἕκτης συνόδου μετὰ πάντων τῶν ἐνθέσμως καὶ θειωδῶς ἐκφωνηθέντων δογμάτων παρ᾽ αὐτῆς, καὶ τοὺς ἐκδοθέντας κανόνας ἀποδέχομαι, ἐν οἷς ἐμφέρεται (*Quinisextum*, c. 82, see preceding section P).

A.b.   The Byzantine translation of Hadrian's *Synodica* (*JE* 2449), addressed to Tarasius, Mansi XII.1079A:

> Ὅτι τὰ ὑπὸ τῆς αὐτῆς ἁγίας ἕκτης συνόδου δέχομαι μετὰ πάντων τῶν ἐνθέσμως καὶ θειωδῶς ἐκφωνηθέντων παρ᾽ αὐτῆς κανόνων, ἐν οἷς ἐμφέρεται (*Quinisextum*, c. 82);

B.a.   Anastasius' version of Tarasius' *Inthronistica*, Mansi XII.1124E:
Ipsius autem sanctae sextae synodi cum omnibus dogmatibus quae legaliter ac divinitus ab ea promulgata sunt, etiam depromptos canones recipio; in quibus refertur: (*Quinisextum*, c. 82);

B.b.   Anastasius' version of *JE* 2449, Mansi XII.1080A:

> Quia et easdem sanctas sex synodos[a] suscipio cum omnibus regulis quae iure ac divinitus ab ipsis promulgatae sunt: inter quas continetur: (*Quinisextum*, c. 82).

---

[a] On the contradictions between the Latin translation of Tarasius' introductory words and his quotation of c. 82 (see A.a, above) in *JE* 2449, and the Greek version in B.a (above), see below, toward the end of this section.

Anastasius' two versions B.a + b of Tarasius' introductory words
to his quotation of c. 82 show to what degree he followed the original.
After the colon follows in A.a + b the Greek text of c. 82, which is
indeed identical with the original version of the synod of 692 (Mansi
XI.977E–980A; partly cited in section P,—text A.a + b). It must
be stressed that the Byzantine translator of *JE* 2449 hardly retranslated Hadrian's Latin version of c. 82 into Byzantine Greek. Instead
we must assume that he inserted c. 82 into his Greek translation of
JE 2449 after the copy of the Greek original of Tarasius' *Synodica*
addressed to Hadrian I. This *Synodica* was naturally accessible to the
Byzantine translator in the Patriarchal Library at Constantinople.

The Latin version of c. 82 in *JE* 2449 of 785 poses a problem. Was
it identical with that of the *First Latin Nicaenum* (of ca. 788) quoted
in the *LC*, the *Hadrianum*, and the *Libellus Synodalis* of Paris 825,
or is it identical with the Latin version cited by Anastasius in his
second translation of the *Nicaenum*? Compare the Latin version of
c. 82 in the *First Latin Nicaenum* (above P, text B) with the following
Latin versions of c. 82 in Anastasius' *Nicaenum*:

C.1. Anastasius' version of c. 82 quoted in Tarasius' *Inthronistica* to the
Eastern patriarchs, Mansi XII.1125A–B:

C.2. Anastasius' version of c. 82 in *JE* 2449, Mansi XII.1080A–B:

    a. In quibusdam venerabilium imaginum picturis agnus digito prae-
cursoris exaratur[b] ostensus, qui in figura[c] praecessit gratiae, verum
nobis per legem demonstrans[d] agnum, Christum videlicet[e] Dominum
nostrum . . . qui tollit[f] peccata mundi.

   [b] exaratus ostenditur 2   [c] figuram praeteriit 2   [d] praeostendens 2   [e] *om.* 2
[f] tulit peccatum 2

b1. (Mansi XII.1125A:

. . . characterem agni dei nostri Christi qui tollit peccata mundi), secundum
humanitatem etiam in iconis ex hoc pro veteri agno definimus depingi:
per eum videlicet celsitudinem humilitatis Dei verba considerantes, et ad
memoriam conversationis quam in carne gessit, passionis quoque ac
salutaris mortis eius adducti atque redemptionis quae hinc est mundo
effecta.

b2. (Mansi XII.1080B:

. . . agni Christi Dei nostri qui tulit peccatum mundi), secundum humanitatem, characterem, et imaginem hominis, pro veteri agno depingi

definimus, per ipsum Dei verbi humilitatis celsitudinem considerantes, et ad memoriam in carne conversationis, tam scilicet passionem eius, quam salutarem mortem atque redemptionem quae hinc est mundo effecta, manu quoddammodo reducentes.

The version of the *Quinisextum*, c. 82, in the *First Latin Nicaenum* was known to Anastasius, since the entire *First Latin Nicaenum* was before his eyes when he produced his second translation of the *Acta* of II Nicaea. The faulty *relictus est* for παρελήφθη in that version (see above P, after B) does not occur in Anastasius' versions of c. 82. He reads instead *praeteriit* (Mansi XII.1080A) and *praecessit* (XII.1125A), respectively, two readings which hardly render the meaning of the Greek verb. His translations obviously represent an adaptation of the text to John the Baptist's role as precursor of Jesus. Such liberties taken by Anastasius when dealing with the test of c. 82 can be observed in his version C.b1–2 (above) which renders the original Κατὰ τὸν ἀνθρώπινον χαρακτῆρα καὶ ἐν ταῖς εἰκόσιν ἀπὸ τοῦ νῦν as follows:

C.b1: . . . secundum humanitatem etiam in iconis ex hoc pro veteri agno;
C.b2: . . . secundum humanitatem, characterem et imaginem hominis;

while the *First Latin Nicaenum* translates literally (see above, section P, text B.b): . . . secundum humanam figuram et in imaginibus a nunc.

The same version of the *Quinisextum*, c. 82, is independently cited in the *Hadrianum* I.35 (p. 32.11) and II.19 (p. 51.3).

The internal investigation of the various versions of c. 82 does not seem to offer evidence that would testify that the version in the *First Latin Nicaenum* and that in Hadrian's *JE* 2449 are identical. This conclusion is supported by certain specific historical aspects of the *Trullianum* which will be discussed below.

At II Nicaea, *actio* IV, the *Quinisextum* c. 82 was read publicly, once ἀπὸ χάρτου (*ex charta*), and again ἐν βίβλῳ (*in codice*), according to Mansi XIII.40D, 41C. Tarasius replied to the doubts of those ignorant people who, as he says, questioned the fact that c. 82 actually belongs to the canons of the Sixth Ecumenical Council. In his reply, Tarasius briefly outlines the historical connection between the Sixth Ecumenical Council of 680–681 and the *Trullianum* of 692. A similar sketch on the same subject is contained in Tarasius' refutation of the iconoclastic definition (*horos*) of 754 in *actio* VI (Mansi XIII.219f.). These facts indicate that Hadrian I became familiar with c. 82 also through the *Acta* of the *Nicaenum*, and for this reason endorsed c. 82 and the Sixth Ecumenical Council in the *Hadrianum* I.35 (p. 32, 6f.) of about 791. But this recognition is of little help to the problem under consideration, since Hadrian had already endorsed c. 82 when he quoted it affirmatively in *JE* 2449 of the year 785 after Tarasius' earlier *Synodica*—this means almost three years before he had received a copy of the Greek *Acta* of II Nicaea. The acknowledgment by Hadrian I of this canon of the *Quinisextum*, which as a whole was never sanctioned by Rome, has a precedent, for example, in the recognition by Constantine (708–715) of another decision of the *Trullianum*, referred to in Section P. The fact that a patriarch of Constantinople advocated image-worship for which even he found synodal proof in c. 82 of the *Trullianum* greatly astonished Hadrian I, because for decades "New Rome" had been the center of iconoclasm. This is the true reason why Hadrian in *JE* 2449 calls Tarasius' quotation of c. 82 in his *Synodica* a miracle most worthy of praise and adulation (miraculum laude et veneratione dignissimum). In the Greek translation of *JE* 2449, read after the Latin original of *JE* 2449 at II Nicaea during *actio* II (Mansi XII.1077–1084), the Byzantine translator quite significantly keeps Hadrian's enthusiasm about Tarasius' action in check by reducing Hadrian's superlative in the *miraculum . . . dignissimum* to a mere positive statement (Mansi XII.1079A): Θαῦμα αἰνέσεως καὶ περιπτύξεως ἄξιον.

The satisfaction voiced by Hadrian I in Tarasius' positive attitude toward image-worship, at a time when iconoclasm still was the accepted official policy at Byzantium, may well indicate that Hadrian was in 785 unfamiliar with the *Trullianum*, c. 82, as a proof of image-worship. The draftsman in Hadrian's *scrinium* who compiled a collection of patristic testimonia of image-worship which were inserted in *JE* 2448 must have known that John of Damascus, ultimately the source of some of those χρήσεις, had already listed the *Quinisextum* c. 82, in *De imaginibus, oratio III* (*PG* 94.1417D–1420A). This was actually the authority followed by Tarasius when he quoted canon 82 in his *Synodica* (Grumel, *Reg.* 351) as a proof of image-worship. Tarasius' introductory words to his citation of c. 82 require special attention (see the texts listed above under A. a–b and B. a–b).

The identity of Tarasius' introduction to his quotation of c. 82 in his *Inthronistica* to the Eastern patriarchs (A. a), and in the Byzantine translation of Hadrian's *Synodica* (*JE* 2449), addressed to Tarasius (A. b), is obvious. The Byzantine translator of *JE* 2449 does not retranslate the Latin version of Tarasius' introduction here quoted by Hadrian. Instead the translator cited the Introduction directly from the Greek *Synodica* of Tarasius that had been sent to Hadrian and was available to the translator of *JE* 2449 in the form of a copy kept in the patriarchal archives at Constantinople. The discrepancy between the Latin original in *JE* 2449 (B. b) and its Greek version in the *Acta* of II Nicaea is immediately evident. While Tarasius refers (A. a; B. a) to the Sixth Ecumenical Synod including the *Trullianum*, Hadrian (B. b) refers to the acceptance of the first six universal councils. If Anastasius' version (B. b) does offer the original wording of *JE* 2449, then Hadrian must have changed the text of Tarasius' introduction, because the *Trullianum* of 692 was as a whole never recognized by Rome, while the Eastern Church considered it as part of the *Acta* of the Sixth Ecumenical Council of 680–681. On the other hand, one cannot suppress the suspicion that Anastasius himself may have changed the original Latin version, especially so because we repeatedly saw him doing this in *JE* 2448. But these and other problems can be answered only by the future critical editions of the Greek and Latin *Acta* of the Sixth and Seventh Ecumenical Councils. On the manuscripts of II Nicaea see Chapter V.

R. Severianus of Gabala, *De legislatore.*—A passage from the homily *De legislatore* is repeatedly cited in the Greek *Acta* of II Nicaea, but always ascribed to John Chrysostom. Since one or two particular sentences from the same text occur in the *Capitulare adversus Synodum*, the *LC*, the *Hadrianum*, and the *Libellus Synodalis* of the Paris Synod of 825, the text deserves special attention. Compare the following quotations:

a. *LC* II.3 (p. 64.28f.) cites in the chapter heading Ps. 72.20: "Domine, in civitate tua imaginem illorum ad nihilum rediges."
b. *Hadrianum* I.42 (p. 34.31f.): The *Capitulare adversus Synodum* asks "Quomodo intellegendum est: 'Domine, in civitate tua imaginem eorum ad nihilum rediges'" (Ps. 72.20).

c. *LC* III.20 (p. 143.29–31) reads: "... verba Iohannis Chrysostomi et dicente: 'Vidi angelum in imagine persequentem barbarorum multitudinem.'" It is obvious that the texts a, b, and c render the same version that is inserted in the *First Latin Nicaenum* as quoted also in:

d. *Hadrianum* I.42 (p. 34f.), *In actione quarta:* "... Iohannis Crisostomus ... dicens: "Ego et cerae profusa dilexi scriptura pietatis repleta. Vidi enim angelum imaginem persequentem multitudo barbarorum; [vidi conculcatas barbarorum]^e tribus et David vere dicente: 'Domine, in civitate tua imagines eorum ad nichilum rediges'" (Ps. 72.20).

^{e} Supplemented according to Mansi XIII.299D3.

The pertinent Greek original of Severianus of Gabala, *De legislatore*, *PG* 56.407, with the variants of Mansi XIII.9A and John of Damascus, *De imaginibus, oratio III*, reads as follows:

Ἐγὼ καὶ τὴν κηρόχυτον γραφὴν¹ ἠγάπησα εὐσεβείας πεπληρωμένην.
S.1. Εἶδον² ἐν εἰκόνι ἄγγελον ἐλαύνοντα³ νέφη⁴ βαρβάρων,
S.2. εἶδον πατούμενα βαρβάρων φῦλα, καὶ τὸν Δαυὶδ ἀληθεύοντα
S.3. "Κύριε, ἐν τῇ πόλει σου τὴν εἰκόνα αὐτῶν ἐξουδενώσεις" (Ps. 72.20).

¹ *ἠγ. γρ.* Mansi XIII.9A; also John of Damascus, *De imaginibus oratio, PG* 94.1313B.
² *εἶδον γὰρ ἄγγελον ἐν M*; *J* 1313B, 1400C.
³ om. *J* 1400C, who reads ἐν εἰκόνι, στίφη βαρβάρων διώκοντα
⁴ *β.ν. M*; στίφη *J* 1313B.

The excerpt from Severian's *De legislatore* is repeatedly referred to, and cited in, the *Greek Nicaenum* by various speakers: the first sentence (S.1) in Mansi XII.1019B and XIII.324C, the entire passage in addition to Mansi XIII.9A, also in 299CD. Possibly one of the earliest occurrences is to be found in the letter of Gregory II sent to Germanus of Constantinople (*JE* 2181) which is inserted in the *Greek Nicaenum* (Mansi XIII.93C).⁹¹ The first sentence (S.1) reads in the translation of the *First Latin Nicaenum*, cited in the *Libellus Synodalis* of 825 (*LS*, p. 509.4f.): "Ego et cerae perfusae

⁹¹ See Jean Gouillard, "Aux origines de l'iconoclasme: Le témoignage de Grégoire III," *Travaux et mémoires* III (Paris, 1968), 276–303, and Erich Caspar, "Papst Gregor II. und der Bilderstreit," *Zeitschrift für Kirchengeschichte* 52 (1933), 29–89.

dilexi picturam pietate repletam." The fragment from Severian's homily was mentioned and utilized often at II Nicaea; it occurs twice among the testimonia of image-worship in John of Damascus, *De imaginibus, oratio III*, and it was looked upon as a quotation from a writing by John Chrysostomos. This fact naturally accounts for the parallels between textual variants to be found in Mansi XIII.9A and in the fragment's transmission in *De imaginibus*, as listed above. As a matter of fact, it now seems to be quite probable that John of Damascus inserted the fragment among his testimonia of image-worship, because it was used as such authoritatively in the earlier *JE* 2181. John of Damascus' version of the excerpt from *De legis-latore*, and not the treatise itself, was the actual source for the quotation's appearance in the *Acta* of II Nicaea. Thus a question previously raised by von den Steinen (see above, section M, note 76) concerning the differences between the fragment's second sentence (above, S.2) in the wording of the *Nicaenum* and in the original text of the treatise can be satisfactorily answered. The differences properly traced by von den Steinen to the *Nicaenum* are explained by the fact that the pseudo-Chrysostomean passage, that is, Severianus of Gabala, *De legislatore*,[92] is quoted in the second-hand transmission of John of Damascus, and not directly after the original treatise. This becomes obvious on the basis of the variants to the text S listed above: the *Hadrianum*'s *enim*, which does not occur in the original, is found in the *Nicaenum* and in John of Damascus' γάρ; also word sequences which deviate from the original are easily traceable to the *Nicaenum* and its source, the excerpt from John of Damascus. I therefore question the correctness of the thesis put forth by Paul van den Ven, "La patristique et l'hagiographie au Concile de Nicée de 787," *Byzantion* 25–27 (1955–57), 336 and 360, according to which the testimonia of image-worship by John of Damascus were not utilized by the synodal assembly of II Nicaea in 787 (cf. above, Chapter II at note 20).

The investigation of the Latin quotations from Greek *patres* in the *LC* refutes Bastgen's belief that these testimonia are retranslated into the Latin of the *First Latin Nicaenum* from the Greek transla-

---

[92] Zellinger, *Studien zu Severian von Gabala*, 61 n. 2, does not deal with the passages in the *LC*. On *De legislatore* see J. A. de Aldama, *Repertorium pseudochrysostomicum*, No. 490.

tion of *JE* 2448, which had been inserted into the Greek synodal
protocols of II Nicaea, 787, and that the *LC* retains *ineptias transla-
tionis actorum concilii antiquae.*[93] In reality, the patristic texts are
inserted into the context of the *LC* in the original Latin version in
which they initially occur in *JE* 2448, which had been inserted into
the *Latin Nicaenum* in its authentic form. Thus the often-repeated
assumption that Anastasius Bibliothecarius[94] in his translation of the
synodal *Acta* of II Nicaea preserves the genuine version of *JE* 2448
is not at all borne out by the available evidence. It is obvious that
Anastasius frequently rewrites the Latin versions of those testimonia following the abbreviated and otherwise adulterated Greek
version[95] of *JE* 2448 that had been inserted into the synodal protocols of II Nicaea, *actio* II. Anastasius therefore occasionally
falsified the genuine text of *JE* 2448, although he supplemented[96]
the long Latin section of the *Synodica* which had been deleted in a
falsified Byzantine MS, s. IX, of the Greek synodal protocols of II
Nicaea, 787, on which he based his own Latin translation dedicated
in 873 to John VIII. Textual differences are obviously noticeable
not only between the alleged original Latin text of *JE* 2448 and
its abridged and otherwise falsified Byzantine-Greek version in the
Greek Nicaenum, but also between the supposedly genuine text of the
Synodica and its occasionally falsified sections in the Latin version
preserved in Anastasius' second Latin translation of II Nicaea.
The abbreviated Greek version omits the long Latin section of the
Latin original of *JE* 2448 dealing with Hadrian I's claim to papal
authority over Illyricum, Calabria, and Sicily which had been
transferred in 732–733 to the jurisdiction of the patriarchate of

---

[93] See *LC*, 74 n. *a*, 78f. notes *d*.

[94] Cf., e.g., Wilhelm Levison, *Aus Rheinischer und Fränkischer Frühzeit* (Düsseldorf,
1948), 434 n. 6; Ostrogorsky (below, n. 95), 75; Anastos (below, n. 97), 24.

[95] Cf. Georg Ostrogorsky, "Rom und Byzanz im Kampf um die Bilderverehrung,"
Seminarium Kondakovianum 6 (Prag, 1933), 73ff.

[96] Mansi XII.1073A–1076D, after the copy of *JE* 2448 which Anastasius found
in the papal *scrinium*. The section 1074D1, *Ipse enim Tarasius*—1075B6 *tribuere
nequivimus*, is preserved in a Greek translation in Photius' falsified Greek version
of *Epistola* 208 by John VIII, ed. Erich Caspar, *MHG, Epistolae* 7 (Karolini Aevi 5;
Berlin, 1928), 178. The section, Mansi XII.1075A2 *et quod dicere pudet*—1075B3
repente transire, is an unacknowledged, anonymous citation from Gregory the Great's
Registrum IX, 215 ed. Ludo Moritz Hartmann, *MGH, Epistolae* 2 (Berlin, 1899),
202.18–26, and line 34, and may be added to Caspar's edition of *Epist.* 208.
Cf. also Chapter I, D.

Constantinople.[97] New investigations indeed prove that the abbreviated and falsified Greek version of Hadrian's *Synodica* contained
in MSS of the synodal protocols of II Nicaea is in all probability a
product of the Photian controversy, and not of the Seventh Ecumenical Council of 787.

The new Latin and Greek source material made known in the
present study must show the extent and the scope of research, philological, literary, and historical, that is required in order to improve
Bastgen's recension of the *LC*. Much of the palaeographical work
done by Bastgen will remain unchanged, but in detail, a large
number of minor, and very many larger, changes—which correct
misreadings and wrongly identified Bible citations, and present
newly discovered Latin and Greek patristic sources—will have to
be recorded, all of which should contribute to a better understanding
of the context and of the genesis of the treatise. The new edition
should include also all the instances, palaeographical or philological
and literary, which reveal traces of the first redaction. The Tironian
notes in the *LC*,[98] omitted by Bastgen, should be added at their
proper places within the context of the treatise, and so also should
the passages in the Greek *Acta* of II Nicaea, which are referred to
on the basis of the lost *First Latin Nicaenum* of ca. 788 in the chapter headings of the *LC* and in the context of individual chapters.
Bastgen's references are mostly to the translation of 873 by Anastasius Bibliothecarius, a version that was composed almost one
hundred years after the lost *Latin Nicaenum*, whose method of translation was severely criticized by Anastasius. A modern edition of the

---

[97] Cf. M. V. Anastos, "The Transfer of Illyricum, Calabria, and Sicily to the
Jurisdiction of the Patriarchate of Constantinople in 732/33," in *Silloge Bizantina
in onore di Silvio Giuseppe Mercati* (Studi Bizantini e Neoellenici 9; Rome, 1957),
14–31.

[98] Heinrich Fichtenau, "Karl der Grosse und das Kaisertum," *MIOEG* 61
(1953), 276–287, has successfully proved that Charlemagne was not the author
of these Tironian notes, which were otherwise used in the Carolingian chancellery;
see Georges Tessier, *Diplomatique royale française* (Paris, 1962), 100f. Fichtenau's
new interpretation (p. 284) of the notes—which do not represent Charlemagne's
opinion, but an evaluation of the correct usage made in the *LC* of patristic materials—is borne out in two instances dealt with in the present study, Sections A
and D, above. In both instances the note reads *optime* (see *Neues Archiv* 49, 1931,
211f.), and both approve corrections which had been made in the first redaction
of the *LC*! This fact should convince Gert Haendler, *Geschichte des Frühmittelalters
und der Germanenmission* (Göttingen, 1961), 46 n. 37, that Fichtenau's new interpretation is indeed correct. See Chapter XIII.

Libri Carolini will substantiate the fact that this treatise is the work
of one of the most critical and independent minds among the scholars
in Charlemagne's entourage during the last decade of the eighth
century, and the outstanding accomplishment of the Carolingian
Renaissance. Theodulph of Orléans was probably endowed with
some of the qualities that enabled the author of the *LC* to write
this treatise, but no evidence is available to identify him as the
auctor of the *LC*. The notion that Theodulph was the author of the
LC has been carried for a few decades by von den Steinen's reputation, although he never proved it. He drew some encouragement
for his thesis also from the observation[99] that *LC* III.3 (111.8–112.2)
is a literal excerpt from Vigilius of Thapsus, *Contra Arianos* II.13–14
(*PL* 62.176–8), assuming that "the silent copying of Vigilius points
to a Spanish author," namely Theodulph, who in *De spiritu sancto*
(*PL* 105.273A–C) quotes Vigilius, *Contra Eutychetem* I.10 (*PL*
62.100D–101A). But von den Steinen's assumption concerning the
LC's allegedly direct quotation of Vigilius was mistaken from the
very beginning, since the *LC* does not quote any "Spanish author,"
but from a non-Spanish Pseudo-Vigilius, *Contra Arianos Dialogus*,
which represents an abridged Carolingian excerpt-version of Vigilius, *Adversus Arrianos* (*PL* 62.180–238), a fact known to Gerhard
Ficker[100] long ago. Certainly, the presence of Pseudo-Vigilian excerpts in the *LC*, and of genuine Vigilian texts in one of Theodulph's
treatises in no way speaks for Theodulph's authorship of the *Libri*

---

[99] *Neues Archiv* 49 (1932), 231 n. 2; Theodulph of Orléans' alleged authorship
of the treatise (Haendler, *op. cit.*, 58 and 60 n. 59) should not be mentioned any
longer. Arthur Allgeier, "Psalmenzitate und die Frage nach der Herkunft der
Libri Carolini," *Historisches Jahrbuch der Görresgesellschaft* 46 (1926), 333–353, overlooked the important fact that the citations from the Psalms in the *LC* as a rule
are second-hand quotations, which were inserted by the author of the *LC* into his
treatise when he was using other writers and works, and for this very reason the
origin of such second-hand quotations from some specific version of the *Psalter*
does not guide us to the unknown author of the *LC*. In connection with this study
it became obvious to the present writer that von den Steinen's thesis in *QF*, p. 21
and n. 4, concerning the *Neuübertragung* of quotations from the Psalms by the
translator of the *Greek Nicaenum* of 787 must be renounced, because the fifteen
quotations from the Psalms cited in the *LC* in the version of the *Psalterium Romanum*
are mostly identical with the version cited in Cassiodorus, *Expos. in Ps.*, who is
extensively used and anonymously cited by the author of the *LC*.

[100] *Studien zu Vigilius von Thapsus* (Leipzig, 1897), 25–42. The *Clavis patrum
latinorum* does not list Pseudo-Vigilius, *Contra Arianos Dialogus* (*PL* 62.155–180) in
its concordance of *PL* 62 on p. 598; see also *PL, Supplementum* III.4 (Paris, 1966),
1257.

Carolini! One could never maintain that Alcuin is the author of the *LC* solely because he is quoting Vigilius. And Alcuin cites not just one Vigilian treatise but two in his antiadoptionist writings.[101] Bastgen saw Alcuin as the author of the *LC*, but the evidence he offered in support of his contention seemed unconvincing to the present writer, who at the time assumed that Alcuin was only the final editor of the treatise. In the meantime, my preparation of a modern critical edition of the *LC* has brought to light a great deal of unknown evidence which points convincingly to Alcuin as the actual author of the *Libri Carolini*. There is, for instance, the identical logical terminology in Alcuin's writings and in the *LC*, as pointed out in section F of Chapter IV. *LC* I.1 contains quotations (above, E) which are indeed drawn from Alcuin's edition of the *Categoriae decem*, dedicated to his royal friend. The *LC*'s extensive acquaintance with Ambrosiaster's works, as shown in Chapter VI, has its counterpart in Alcuin's thoroughgoing familiarity with Ambrosiaster's *Quaestiones*.[102] The edition of the *Libri Carolini*, *in statu nascendi*, will hopefully show Alcuin's authorship of the work, which he wrote for Charlemagne.

---

[101] Alcuin, *Adversus Elipandum* IV.9 (*PL* 101.292C–D), quotes Vigilius of Thapsus, *Contra Eutychetem* II.7 (*PL* 62.108B–C), and *Adv. Elip.* I.3 (*PL* 101.244C–D), Alcuin cites Vigilius, *Contra Felicianum Arianum de unitate trinitatis* c. 6 (*PL* 42.1161a). The latter text is also cited by Alcuin, *Adversus Felicem* VI.6 (*PL* 101.206C–D), and Alcuin, *ibid.*, col. 207A–D contains other excerpts from Vigilius, *Contra Felicianum* cc. 10, 11, 14, 8 (in this sequence), *PL* 42.1164f., 1169, 1163.

[102] See the remark in my review in the *Journal of English and Germanic Philology* 68 (1969), 159.

CHAPTER V

The Textual History of a Greek Ambrose Text: *Libri Carolini* II.15*

The *Libri Carolini* accuses the synodal assembly of II Nicaea, 787, of having falsified a statement by Ambrose of Milan in such a manner that it favored their own error of image-worship, "ut illorum errori faveret."[1] On the surface, the author of the *Libri Carolini* offers in II.15 a nearly perfect specimen of textual criticism by comparing the original Ambrose text with the allegedly falsified version to be found in the first Latin translation of the Greek *Acta* of II Nicaea. He cites the genuine Ambrose passage in *LC* II.15 (p. 75.2–4):

A.

a. "Numquid, cum et divinitatem eius adoramus et carnem, Christum dividimus?"

b. "Numquid, cum in eo imaginem Dei crucemque veneramur, dividimus eum?"

---

* The author is indebted to the Bibliothèque Nationale (Paris) and to the Bibliotheca Vaticana (Rome) for providing him with photostats from the following MSS referred to in the present chapter: *Vaticanus Lat.* 1329; Vat. Reg. lat. 1046; Vat. graec. 660, 834, 1181; Vat. Ottobon. graec. 27; Paris, B.N. lat. 17339. There is not sufficient evidence available to assume that Ambrose, *De incarnat. dom. sacramento*, was ever translated into Greek as a whole. The question is left undecided by E. Dekkers, "Les traductions grecques des écrits patristiques latins," *Sacris Erudiri* 5 (1953), 201f.

[1] Ed. Hubert Bastgen, 74.18–19, Bk. II.15; the second part of the Ambrose text A.b, cited above, appears also in the discussion of the adoptionist heresy: Paulinus of Aquileia, *Contra Felicem Urgellitanum* III.21, *PL* 99 (Paris, 1851), 455A9–11, cites Ambrose, *De incarnationis dominicae sacramento* 7.75, 126–127, ed. Otto Faller (*CSEL* 79; Vienna, 1964), 262.

The falsified *sententia* of Ambrose reads as follows (p. 75.5–7):

B.

a. "Numquidne, quando et deitatem et carnem eius adoramus, dividimus Christum?"

b. "aut, quando in ipso et dei imaginem et crucem adoramus, dividimus eum?"

Bastgen identified the first text with Ambrose, *De incarnationis dominicae sacramento*, c. 7 (*PL* 16; Paris, 1880), 873B. The passage is identical with Chapter 7.75, 125–127, in the modern critical edition by Otto Faller (*CSEL* 79; Vienna, 1964), 262. The author of the *LC* criticizes in the best philological fashion the differences noticeable between the original and the version he found inserted in the first Latin translation of the Greek *Acta* of II Nicaea. He charges the synodal assembly with the falsification of Ambrose's original text as to *ordine, sensu verbisque* (p. 74.18–19)[2]—as to its occurrence in one of Ambrose's works, and as to its meaning and wording. He states that the text quoted does not occur, as those people at Nicaea dream ("ut illi somniant": p. 74.20), "in libro tertio, capitulo nono," but *in libro nono*. He could arrive at Book 9 because he quotes from all of Ambrose's nine dogmatic treatises destined for Emperor Gratian, namely, the five books of *De fide*, the three books of *De spiritu sancto*, and the single book of the treatise *De incarnationis dominicae sacramento*, dealt with in *LC* II.15.[3] The latter Ambrose treatise is also referred to as *Liber Nonus* in the *Incipit* and *Explicit* of some Ambrose MSS of the ninth century. Thus two codices of Ambrose's *De spiritu sancto* (*CSEL* 79; Vienna, 1964; p. 222, app. crit.) offer: "Explicit Liber Octabus [sic], Incipit Liber Nonus" (Casinensis KK4, saec. ix in.); "Explicit De Spiritu Liber VIII Incipit Liber VIIII De Incarnatione" (*Vaticanus Latinus* 267, saec. ix/x). Some MSS of the latter treatise read as follows: "Incipit liber nonus" (*CSEL* 79, p. 225); "Incipit Liber VIIII De incarnatione." The same MSS read correspondingly at the very end: "Explicit . . . Liber Nonus." It is obvious that the author of

[2] A similar criticism appears in *LC* I.23 (p. 52.7): " . . . et sensu et verbis cohaereant ut unum sine alio vix intelligi possit."

[3] Ambrose, *De fide*, ed. Otto Faller (*CSEL* 78; Vienna, 1962), is quoted in *LC* I.4 (p. 17), I.7 (p. 22), II.16 (p. 76); *De spiritu sancto*, ed. Faller (*CSEL* 79; 1964), in *LC* II.5 (p. 67).

the *LC* who quotes from all three of Ambrose's treatises was fully aware of the fact that the manuscript transmission counted the three works as one coherent work of nine books.

The meaning of the Ambrose text is altered, and turned from a negation into a confirmation, as the *LC* states, by the change of Ambrose's *Numquid* (p. 74.22; 75.2) to *Numquidne* (pp. 74.23; 75.5).

The wording of the original is changed *in sequenti commate* (p. 74.27; in text A.b., above); where Ambrose puts *veneramur*, II Nicaea reads *adoramus* (above B.b; p. 74.27, 75.7).

While the *LC*'s textual criticism is certainly valid, its assumption that the changes made in Ambrose's original wording and meaning originated with the synodal assembly of II Nicaea is mistaken, and the repeated reference to the latter's participants in the form of the pejorative *illi* (pp. 74.18.20.23.27; 75.1) is unjustified. For those textual changes were not made at II Nicaea, since the *LC*'s Ambrose text criticized in II.15 is directly derived from Hadrian I's *Synodica* of 785 (*JE* 2448),[4] as Bastgen properly stated (p. 74 n. 2). This fact means that the *LC*'s criticism applies to the version of the Ambrose passage in *JE* 2448, which was accessible to the author of the *LC* in the original Latin version inserted in the *First Latin Nicaenum* of about 788 of the Greek *Acta* of II Nicaea. A transmission of the Ambrose text quoted from *JE* 2448 is also preserved in the *Libellus Synodalis* of the Paris Synod of 825.[5] The misconception of the *LC*'s author as to *ordine* with reference to the origin of the Ambrose text is quite obvious. Since the chapter headings of the *LC*, as a rule, refer to very definite passages drawn from the Latin version of the *Acta* of II Nicaea, the numerical reference of *LC* II.15 (p. 74.10–13) hardly refers directly to any of the works of Ambrose, but perhaps to the occurrence of the Ambrose text within the context of the lost *First Latin Nicaenum*? The chapter heading openly criticizes the members of II Nicaea who are accused of adopting untruthfully and badly, to their own erroneous concept of image-worship, a *sententia* of Ambrose, which they unjustly appropriate (*usurpent*) "ex libro tertio, capitulo nono" (p. 74.11–12). Contrary to the assumption and criticisms of the author of the *LC*, this numerical reference does not at all originate with II Nicaea,

[4] See Chapter I.
[5] Ed. Albert Werminghoff, *MGH, Conc.* 2.2 (Aevi Karolini 1.2; Hannover, Leipzig, 1908), 513.

but is a quotation of an Ambrose testimonium in the patristic catena of Hadrian I's *Synodica* of 785 (*JE* 2448), which is referred to in *LC* II.15 and quoted *in toto* in the context of the same chapter (p. 75.5–7).

Compare the chapter heading of *LC* II.15 (p. 74.10–13) with this Ambrose text of *JE* 2448, a papal letter inserted in the *Acta* of II Nicaea, *actio* II, Mansi XII.1068E10–1069A2. This text (C) is edited here on the basis of the *Synodica JE* 2448, as inserted in the second Latin version of the Greek *Acta* of II Nicaea, translated by Anastasius Bibliothecarius. I have used the following codices of his Latin version of 873 and indirect transmissions:

L—Vaticanus lat. 1329, s.x, fol. 23v, lines 5–9;

P—Paris, B.N. lat. 17339, s.x, fol. 33r, col. a, lines 20–27;

R—Vaticanus Reginensis lat. 1046, s.x, fol. 31r, col. a, lines 20–27.

LS—An indirect transmission of the Ambrose testimonium of *JE* 2448 is inserted in the *Libellus Synodalis* of the Frankish Paris Synod of 825, ed. *MGH, Conc.* 2.2 (Aevi Karolini 1.2; Hannover, Leipzig, 1908), 513.19–21.

Gaudenzi—Another indirect transmission of the Ambrose testimonium is to be found in *JE* 2448, inserted in the *Vita Hadriani II*, ed. A. Gaudenzi in *Bulletino dell' Istituto storico italiano* 36 (1916), 305.

C. "Item beati Ambrosii (Mediolanensis episcopi *add. LS*) ad Gratianum imperatorem, ex libro tertio, capitulo nono:"

a. "Numquidne^c quando et deitatem et carnem eius^d adoramus, dividimus Christum?"

b. "aut quando in ipso et Dei imaginem et crucem adoramus,^{e} dividimus eum? Absit^f"

c. LPR; *Numquidne, LS* in MS P, p. 513.20; also Gaudenzi, p. 305.2; and in *LC* II.15, p. 74.23, 75.5; Numquidnam, Mansi XII. 1068E12.

d. LPR, *LS*, Gaudenzi, *LC* II.15, pp. 74.24, 75.6; *om.* Mansi XII.1068E13.

e. LPR, *LS*, Gaudenzi, *LC* II.15, pp. 74.27, 75.7; Mansi.

f. LPR, *LS*, Gaudenzi, Mansi XII.1069A2; *om. LC* II.15.

The *LC* reading *Numquidne*, as against *Numquidnam* of Mansi, is confirmed as the correct variant by the direct transmission of the Ambrose testimonium in the MSS, as well as by the indirect transmission of the *Vita Hadriani II*, and the still older transmission of the *Libellus Synodalis* of the Paris Synod of 825. Also the *LC* reading *d* is verified by the direct and the indirect transmission of the Ambrose text. Finally, adoramus (*e*) occurs in all the MSS, as well as in Mansi XII.1069A. The *LC* criticizes (p. 74.27–8) its Ambrose text by saying "ubi ille (*scil.* Ambrose) posuit *veneramur* [above, text A.b.], illi [*scil.* II Nicaea] *adoramus* posuisse deteguntur." This is a valid criticism as far as *JE* 2448 is concerned, but an incorrect one as far as concerns the synodal assembly of II Nicaea, as we now clearly recognize. The substitution of *adoramus* for Ambrose's *veneramur* is the result of the consistency shown by a translator, when he translated προσκυνοῦμεν in the Greek Ambrose text (below D.71a and b) with *adoramus*, in both instances. The same translator's *Numquidne* (instead of the correct *Numquid*) is severely dealt with and rejected as a falsification of the original text in the *LC*, since it changes Ambrose's meaning by the addition of the *particula* "ne" (*LC*, p. 74.24–6). The manuscript transmission of *JE* 2448, whether direct or indirect, plainly proves that the *LC* unjustly charged II Nicaea with the falsification of the genuine Ambrose text. Some of its readings led me to the origin of the Ambrose testimonium in Hadrian's *Synodica*: *et carnem eius* — τὴν σάρκα αὐτοῦ, and *Absit—Mὴ γένοιτο*, at the very end. Both suggested to me the probability that the *LC*'s so-called falsified Ambrose passage may well represent the Latin translation of some Greek version of the Ambrose testimonium. This is indeed the case.

The Ambrose text in *JE* 2448 (above, C) represents the Latin version of the Greek Ambrose testimonium for image-worship listed by John of Damascus, *De imaginibus, oratio III* (*PG* 94.1405B):[6]

D. Ἀμβροσίου ἐπισκόπου Μεδιολάνων, πρὸς Γρατιανὸν τὸν βασιλέα, περὶ τῆς ἐνσάρκου οἰκονομίας τοῦ Θεοῦ Λόγου.

(71): Θεὸς πρὸ τῆς σαρκός, καὶ Θεὸς ἐν σαρκί. (75): Ἀλλὰ φόβος, φησί, μὴ δύο ἡγεμονικά, ἢ σοφίαν διττὴν ἀπονέμοντες χριστῷ, μερίζειν δόξωμεν Χριστόν.

(a) Ἆρα οὖν, μὴ ὁπότε καὶ τὴν θεότητα αὐτοῦ καὶ τὴν σάρκα προσκυνοῦμεν, μερίζομεν τὸν Χριστόν

(b) ἢ, ὅτε ἐν τῷ αὐτῷ, καὶ τὴν τοῦ Θεοῦ εἰκόνα καὶ τὸν σταυρὸν προσκυνοῦμεν, διαιροῦμεν αὐτόν; Μὴ γένοιτο.

---

[6] John of Damascus' Greek version of the Ambrose text is found also in the florilegium in Paris, B.N. gr. 1115, according to Theodor Schermann, *Die Geschichte der dogmatischen Florilegien* (*TU*, N.F. 13.1; Leipzig, 1905), 75.

The preceding text renders Ambrose, *De incarnationis dominicae sacramento*, cc. 71 and 75, pp. 260.90 and 262.122–127 (*PL* 16.872A, 873B):

E. c. 71: " . . . Deus igitur ante carnem, Deus in carne . . . ";

  c. 75: "Sed verendum est, inquit, ne si duos principales sensus aut geminam sapientiam Christo tribuimus, Christum dividamus?" Next follows the text cited above under A. *a.–b.*, "Numquid—dividimus eum?"

The comparison of the texts E and D with the Latin version C makes it clear that it is the Greek Ambrose text quoted by John of Damascus whose Latin version appears in the patristic collection of Χρήσεις in *JE* 2448. D is therefore also the ultimate source— by way of *JE* 2448—of the Latin Ambrose cited in *LC* II.15 (above under B), and accounts for all the charges of falsification heaped by the author of the *LC* on the participants of II Nicaea.

There is finally the Byzantine version of the Latin Ambrose testimonium of *JE* 2448 which was publicly read at II Nicaea, during the second session of the assembly, after the reading of the original Latin version of the *Synodica*. The method of translation employed by the translator of the document becomes obvious, if Anastasius Bibliothecarius' version C (see above) is compared with the corresponding Byzantine translation:

F. *Καὶ ἕτερον πάλιν τοῦ μακαρίου 'Αμβροσίου πρὸς Γρατιανὸν τὸν βασιλέα, ἐκ τοῦ τρίτου βιβλίου, κεφαλαίου ἐννάτου·*

(a) *Τί γάρ; μή ποτε καὶ τὴν θεότητα καὶ τὴν σάρκα αὐτοῦ προσκυνοῦντες, μερίζομεν τὸν Χριστόν;*

(b) *ἢ ὅτε ἐν αὐτῷ τὴν θείαν εἰκόνα καὶ τὸν σταυρὸν προσκυνοῦμεν, μερίζομεν αὐτόν; Μὴ γένοιτο!* (Mansi XII.1067C9–D2).

In the MSS of the Greek *Acta* of II Nicaea, 787, we are offered the same text as printed by Mansi: Vaticanus Ottobon. gr. 27, fol. 30v, lines 13–18 (saec. xvi); Vat. gr. 660, fol. 241r, lines 12–16 (saec. xvi); Vat. gr. 834 (olim 553), fol. 284r, lines 24–28 (saec. xvi); Vat. gr. 1181 (olim 867), fol. 42v, lines 13–19. Only the latter MS reads in F (b) *ὅταν*, instead of *ὅτε*, which appears in all the other MSS collated. As a whole, the Byzantine version F reads like a literal translation of C, but at the same time approaches very closely the version D by John of Damascus, which may or may not have been known to the Byzantine translator. The latter's reading in F (a) seems to confirm the word *Numquidne* in C. a (above), and not Mansi's lone *Numquidnam*.

The ultimate origin of the Ambrose text within the Ambrosian corpus of the nine dogmatic treatises written for Emperor Gratian was conjecturally determined by the author of the *LC*. By a mere chance, the reference in C to "ex libro tertio, capitulo nono" coincides in part with the fact that the quoted text is from the ninth dogmatic *liber* of Ambrose. In the context of *LC* II.15 the author of the *LC* does not mention "*ex* libro tertio, capitulo nono" as he does in the chapter heading (p. 74.11), but he says "*in* libro tertio, capitulo nono," and then arrives at the conclusion that the Ambrose text is found "in libro nono" (p. 74.21–22). His criticism as to *ordine*, based on his conjecture, seems to be mistaken, since C is, as we saw, the Latin version of the Greek Ambrose text D. In this respect, one could be inclined to agree with the "ex libro tertio, capitulo nono," and then conclude that John of Damascus, *De imaginibus, oratio III* (D), corresponds to the reference. There is, however, no indication on the basis of the extant text of John's treatise in the edition of Migne, *Patrologia Graeca*, vol. 94, that the Greek Ambrose text is also to be found in "capitulo nono." The present writer therefore prefers to assume that "ex libro tertio, capitulo nono" does not indicate a reference to the fact of the occurrence of the Ambrose text in the ninth dogmatic treatise of Ambrose, as the author of the *LC* believed, together with Hubert Bastgen, Theodor Schermann, and Giovanni Cardinal Mercati.[7] Nor do I believe that it refers to the other fact shown in the present study, that C is the Latin version of the Greek Ambrose testimonium listed in *De imaginibus, oratio III*, by John of Damascus. I prefer to assume that "ex libro tertio, capitulo nono" refers to a manuscript of certain synodal *Acta* in which the Ambrose text in

[7] See the references listed by Bastgen, *LC*, p. 74 n. 3; and Mercati, *Opere Minori*, I (*Studi e Testi* 76; 1937), 148. Mercati, "Stephani Bostreni nova de sacris imaginibus fragmenta e libro deperdito Κατὰ 'Ιουδαίων," *Opere Minori*, I, 202–206, publishes a fragment from Stephen's lost apologetic work after the Ambrosianus A 84, s.xii–xiii, without realizing that this fragment is nothing but a stray transmission of the Greek version of the Latin Stephen of Bostra quotation in *JE* 2448 (cf. above n. 4); see Mansi, XII.1069A6–1072B1 and XII.1067D5–1070D12. H. Savon, "Quelques remarques sur la chronologie des oeuvres de Saint Ambrose," *Studia Patristica*, X, ed. F. L. Cross (*TU*, 107; Berlin, 1970), 156–160, does not deal with the dogmatic treatises dedicated to Emperor Gratian.

JE 2448 appeared within a patristic catena of testimonia of image-worship which had culled the Ambrose testimonium from the collections by John of Damascus. Wolfram von den Steinen indeed thought that the patristic testimonia in *JE* 2448 are largely (*grossenteils*) based on the lost *Acta* of the Lateran Council of 769, which dealt with the problem of image-worship.[8] These *Acta* contained a collection of testimonia of image-worship originally attached to the *Acta* of the Roman Synod of 731. We do not know for certain that the *Synodica* by Theodore of Jerusalem, with its appended patristic testimonia of image-worship, sent to Paul I, was subsequently inserted in a Latin version into the *Acta* of the Lateran Council of 769, in which Carolingian theologians participated.[9]

Certain aspects of the very complicated composition of the *Libri Carolini* became evident also through the investigation of the textual history of the Greek Ambrose text in *LC* II.15 and *JE* 2448. Another problem is posed by the fact that the chapter heading of *LC* II.15 has no equivalent in the earlier Frankish *Capitulare adversus Synodum* (*scil.* II Nicaea, 787), sent by Charlemagne to Hadrian I, who replied by means of the so-called *Hadrianum* (*JE* 2483).[10] Von den Steinen assumes that *LC* II.15 was inserted into the autograph of the *LC*, that is in *Vaticanus Latinus 7207*, probably after the arrival at the Frankish court of the *Hadrianum* (during 791), and that the *LC*'s quotation of the genuine Ambrose text (above, A) is traceable to the citation of the original Ambrose passage in the *Hadrianum* II.20 (ed. Karl Hampe, p. 52.35–37).[11] The latter offers Hadrian I's answer to a chapter heading in the *Capitulare adversus Synodum* whose text is taken, like that of *LC* II.28, from a passage *in actione septima* of the *First Latin Nicaenum* of 787, while the Greek Ambrose text in *LC* II.15 is derived from *JE* 2448 *in actione secunda*. There is indeed no equivalent to the Greek Ambrose text in *LC* II.15 to be found in the *Hadrianum*. But von den Steinen's surmise as to the alleged insertion of *LC* II.15 into the manuscript of the *LC*, after the arrival in about 791 of the *Hadrianum* at the Frankish court, is not at all required if we are to understand the occurrence of the genuine Ambrose text (above, A) in the *LC* (p. 75.2–4).

---

[8] "Entstehungsgeschichte der *Libri Carolini*," *QF* 21 (1929–30), 28, 50.

[9] Cf. Chapter IV, nn. 73–74.

[10] On the interrelationship of the three writings involved see my remarks at the beginning of Chapter III.

[11] "Entstehungsgeschichte," 62.

We recall that the author of the *LC* misinterpreted "ex libro tertio, capitulo nono" to mean *in libro nono*, namely, book nine of the nine dogmatic treatises written by Ambrose for Emperor Gratian. He could make this seemingly convincing conjecture only because he was familiar with all nine books, and because he quotes in the *LC* from Ambrose, *De fide* I–V, and from *De spiritu sancto* I–III. In addition, the single book of *De incarnationis dominicae sacramento* was naturally before his eyes when he made his computation *in libro nono* (*LC*, p. 74.20–21). He culled from this treatise the genuine Ambrose text cited by him in *LC* II.15 (p. 75.2–4). He did not need the *Hadrianum* II.20, which cites the same Ambrose passage, in order to copy from it the genuine Ambrose text, as von den Steinen argues. These reasons refute von den Steinen's assumption that *LC* II.15 was inserted into the *LC* after the arrival of the *Hadrianum* at the Frankish court. *LC* II.15 undoubtedly belongs to the first redaction of the work; it is by no means an insertion in the *LC* made on account of the *Hadrianum* II.20.

Ambrosii verba retro versa e translatione Graeca, as cited and discussed in *LC* II.15, can now be added to the Greek Ambrose texts dealt with by Agostino Pertusi.[12] The retranslation into Latin of Greek versions of Ambrose texts is not as unusual a feature as one might at first sight think. Eduard Schwartz pointed to Ambrose, *De inc. dom. sacr.*, c. 50 (*PG* 16.831), cited by Theodoretus, *Eranistes* 3.243–4.[13] Other Greek texts from the same Ambrose treatise are found in the Greek *Acta* of the councils of Ephesus (431), Chalcedon (451), and II Constantinople (553).[14]

The textual history of the Greek Ambrose text in *LC* II.15 can be summarized as follows. A Latin version of the Greek Ambrose passage in John of Damascus, *De imaginibus, oratio III*, was inserted in a collection of patristic testimonia of image-worship that belonged to the *Acta* of the Lateran Council of 769. This Greek-Latin Ambrose testimonium was subsequently inserted, together with other testimonia of the same synodal source, in the patristic catena of testimonia of image-worship contained in Hadrian I's *Synodica* of 785

---

[12] "Le antiche traduzioni greche delle opere di S. Ambrogio," *Aevum* 18 (1944), 184–207; cf. M. Adriaen in *Corpus Christianorum*, ser. lat. XIV.4 (1957), viiif.

[13] *PG* 83.297A; Eduard Schwartz, *Publizistische Sammlungen zum Acacianischen Schisma*, Abh. Bayer. Akad. der Wiss., NF. 10; München, 1934, 104 to paragraph 55.

[14] Now conveniently listed by Otto Faller, *S. Ambrosii opera*, IX (*CSEL* 79; Vienna, 1964), 299.

(*JE* 2448), addressed to the Byzantine Emperors Constantine VI and Irene. The papal letter *JE* 2448 in turn was inserted, in its original Latin version, including the Greek-Latin Ambrose testimonium, in the Greek *Acta* of II Nicaea, 787, as well as in their first Latin translation of about 788. A copy of the latter was sent by Hadrian I to Charlemagne before 791. The author of the *Libri Carolini* II.15 found the allegedly falsified Ambrose text in Charlemagne's copy of the *First Latin Nicaenum*.

The familiarity of the *LC* with Ambrose's nine dogmatic treatises was mentioned in the preceding section of the present study. *De fide* is quoted in *LC* I.4, I.7, and II.16; *De spiritu sancto* in *LC* II.5, and *De incarnationis dominicae sacramento* in *LC* II.15. The impact of Ambrose's *De fide* on the author of the *LC* is even greater than is indicated by Bastgen. There is, for instance, *LC* II.16 (p. 75) "o inpudens dementia! o improvida vecordia," modeled on *De fide* 1.7.5 (p. 23.41f.): "O inprovida amentia, o inpudens pervicacia." Ambrose is furthermore the *LC*'s source of the primary part of a rhetorical device concerning the validity of the testimony of biblical figures reiterated again and again in the treatise. Thus Ambrose, *De fide* I.6.43 (ed. Otto Faller, *CSEL* 78 [1962], 18), suggests: "*Sed nolo argumento* credas, sancte imperator, et nostrae disputationi. *Scripturas interrogemus, interrogemus apostolos, interrogemus prophetas, interrogemus Christum.* Quid multa, *patrem interrogemus.* . . ."[15] And *LC* III.26 (p. 159.25) correspondingly counsels reliance not only on argumentation, but also on the scriptural text and on the interrogation of the words of sundry biblical authorities: "*Sed* ne forte nostris solummodo *argumentationibus* hoc videamur edicere, recurramus ad divinas *Scripturas! Interrogemus* legislatorem! Dicat, utrum . . ? Dicat, qualiter . . ! Dic, oro, sancte Moyses, dic . . . !" The traces of Ambrose's *Interrogemus* are frequently noticeable in the *LC*'s exposition. Compare the following instances:

a. *LC* II.28 (p. 90.9f.): "*Interrogemus* igitur doctorem gentium [cf. 1 Tim. 2.7],
   interrogemus egregium praedicatorem,
   dicat nobis, utrum . . ?; Dicat etiam, utrum . . . [p. 90.12];
   Dicat etiam, utrum . . . " (p. 90.14f.).

---

[15] Cf. also Ambrose, *De fide* 1.11.68 (p. 29.3): "aut testimoniis aut argumentis collige veritatem"; 1.11.70 (p. 30.18): "Superest, ut et argumentis veritas colligatur . . . Argumentare tamen, heretice, ut voles."

b. *LC* III.2 (p. 109.12f.): "Accedamus ad Apostolum,
veniamus ad *vas electionis* [Acts 9.15],
interrogemus egregium praedicatorem!"

c. *LC* III.13 (p. 128.16):
"*Interrogemus* ergo apostolum!
Dicat egregius praedicator,
dicat *vas electionis*, utrum. . . ."

d. *LC* IV.25 (p. 224.14f.): ". . . interrogetur vir sapientissimus
[*scil.* Augustinus] . . . ; dicat, utrum. . . . ;" etc., etc.

It cannot be doubted that Ambrose's precedent provided the *LC*
with the rhetorical device concerning the testimony of Old and
New Testament authorities, be it Moses (*LC* III.26; p. 159.25),
Solomon (II.9; 70.10), Isaiah (III.14; 132.30), Daniel (I.4; 18.3),
or the apostles Paul (*LC* III.2; p. 109.2), Matthew (IV.5; 183.19),
and John (I.16; 38.29). The same method was extended by the
author of the *LC* to patristic authors such as Ambrose (*LC* II.16;
p. 75.40) and Augustine (I.9–27.12; II.15–75; IV.25–224.4).
Bernhard Bischoff's contention, reported in *Speculum* 40 (1965), 235
n. 123, that the pseudo-Augustinian homily *Contra Judaeos, paganos
et Arianos*, often ascribed to Quodvultdeus,[16] fathered the rhetorical
device used in the *LC* is sufficiently contradicted by the results of
the preceding and the following investigations. The coincidence
between *LC* I.16 (p. 38.29) "Dic, rogo, sancte Iohannes, . . . si
nosti," and *Contra Iudaeos* c. xii (*PL* 42.1124), "Dic, sancte Daniel,
dic de Christo, quod nosti," only indicates the application of a
similar rhetorical school method of the *artes liberales* by two different
authors, but hardly any interdependence between them! Ann
Freeman[17] cites Bischoff's untenable contention and admonishes us
somewhat sternly: "We should take note of the fact that Daniel's
oration in self-defense, supplied by the *LC*'s author [in I.9, p. 28.8–
30], is notable for the freedom with which Biblical materials are
adapted," and in note 126 she specifies that "Daniel's speech contains more than two hundred words of which fewer than fifty are
italicized by Bastgen as belonging to the Biblical text." There is
no truth in anything she says here concerning *LC* I.9, since she is
doubtless not acquainted with the sources of the chapter which

[16] Manlius Simonetti has now shown that the author was an anonymous writer
of the fifth century living in Africa; see Berthold Altaner, *Kleine patristische Schriften*
(Berlin, 1967), 84.
[17] "Further Studies in the *Libri Carolini*," *Speculum* 40 (1965), 235.

were also unknown to Bastgen. The secondary rhetorical device, "*Dic, sancte* . . . ," is by no means alone at work in the chapter, nor does Daniel's speech contain only the words of the *LC*'s author. At least two writings account for the occurrence in the *LC* of the rhetorical device as well as for Daniel's oration, namely, a) Leontius, sermo v, *Christianorum responsum adversum Iudaeos et de imaginibus sanctorum*, cited in the *First Latin Nicaenum* of the Greek *Acta* of II Nicaea, 787 (Mansi XIII.43–54),[18] and b) Jerome, *Commentary on Daniel*, the newly discovered source of Daniel's speech.[19]

(a). Leontius' homily (Mansi XIII.43–54) is, like Hadrian I's *Synodica* of 785 (*JE* 2448), a text which provides the author of the *LC* with numerous texts used as chapter headings, discussed and refuted in the *LC*, especially in *LC* I, chapters 9, 12–14, 21; II, chs. 5, 6, 9; III, chs. 25, 27, 28; and IV, ch. 26.[20] The intimate knowledge which the author of the *LC* evidently possessed of Leontius' sermon should make it clear that it impressed on the *LC* the application of the rhetorical device ("Dic, . . . ") under consideration. For we read repeatedly in Leontius' homily:

Mansi XIII.45D1 : *Εἰπέ μοι, σὺ ὁ νομίζων χειροποίητον μηδέν,*
        XIII.46C13: Dic ergo mihi tu qui opinaris nihil manu-
                factum;
Mansi XIII.48B1 : *εἰπέ μοι, οὐ φρίσσεις,*
        XIII.47A14: dic mihi, non horrescis?
Mansi XIII.48C7–8: *πόσαι, εἰπέ μοι, ἐπισκιάσεις,*
        XIII.47C7: Quot, dic mihi, visitationes;
Mansi XIII.48D5: *εἰπέ μοι, πῶς ἐσμεν εἰδωλολάτραι,*
        XIII.47D5: Dic mihi, quomodo sumus idolatrae;
Mansi XIII.48D11–12: *εἰπέ μοι, ἡ γῆ καὶ τὰ ὄρη,*
        XIII.47D12: Dic mihi, terra et montes;

[18] In the Latin version by Anastasius Bibliothecarius of the Greek *Acta* of II Nicaea, 787. On Leontius see Paul van den Ven, "La patristique et l'hagiographie au Concile de Nicée de 787," *Byzantion* 25–27 (1955–57), 353 no. 46, to whose list of fragments of Leontius' homily should be added the fragments of the now lost Latin translation of the Greek *Acta* of II Nicaea of ca. 788, preserved in the *Libellus Synodalis* of the Paris Synod of 825, ed. by A. Werminghoff, *MGH, Conc.* 2.2 513.30–514.38.

[19] Jerome, *Commentariorum in Danielem*, ed. Fr. Glorie, *CCL* 75A (1964).

[20] See the synopsis by von den Steinen, "Entstehungsgeschichte," 48, and Bastgen's notes to the chapter headings.

Mansi XIII.52A3: εἰπέ μοι, θαυματουργεῖν,
 XIII.50E11–12: Dic mihi, mira facere;
Mansi XIII.52B10: εἰπέ μοι, ἀπολογήσασθαι αὐτῷ,
 XIII.51B6: dic mihi, respondere illi.

The Latin version is in all instances a verbatim translation of Leontius' original Greek questions.

(b). Jerome's *Commentary on Daniel* is extensively used in the *LC*'s fictitious oration of Daniel. Compare the following texts:

Jerome, *Commentariorum in Danielem*, Prologus, ed. Fr. Glorie, *CCL* 75A (1964), 772.13f.:	*Libri Carolini*, I.9, ed. Bastgen, p. 28.8–30, *passim*:
... sed ea quae a *propheta* [*scil.* Daniel] dicta sunt nostris disserere, id est, Christianis, illud in praefatione commoneo, nullum prophetarum tam *aperte dixisse de* Christo. *Non* enim *solum scribit eum esse venturum, quod est commune cum ceteris, sed quo tempore venturus sit docet et reges per ordinem digerit et annos enumerat ac manifestissima signa praenuntiat.*	Dic ergo tu, dic sancte Danihel, dic *vir desideriorum*, dic scrutator archanorum, dic indagator scripturarum, dic *propheta* qui de redemptore mundi in eo *apertius ceteris dixisse* probaris, *quia non solum scribis eum esse venturum, quod est tibi commune cum ceteris, sed, quo tempore venturus sit, doces et reges per ordinem digeris et annos enumeras ac manifestissima signa praenuntias, dic*, utrum Nabuchodonosor, ut illi garriunt, adoraveris?
(p. 795,423): ob signorum magnitudinem;	(p. 28.19): *ob signorum magnitudinem.*
(p. 806,693): Ananiam, Azariam, Misael;	(p. 28.21): *Ananiam, Azariam et Misaelem* ...
(p. 831,276): Felix conversatio;	(p. 28.25): Nam cum tam *felicem* quondam habuerim *conversationem* ...
(p. 833,331): invidia; (p. 834,340): accusare propter invidiam;	(p. 28.26f.): ... quibus *accusari* possem, *ab invidis*, et non in alio, ... *accusatus* fuerim ...
(p. 835,373): *ad lacum leonum perrexit;*	(p. 28.27f.): ... et in lacum leonum proiectus.

It is obvious that the contents and the literary form of Daniel's alleged oration in the *LC* are indebted to Jerome's comments as well as to the references in the chapter heading of *LC* I.9 (p. 26.11– 16), which in turn question three passages contained in two documents inserted in the *Acta* of II Nicaea, namely, in Mansi XIII. 46E, 54B, and 406D–E. The first two references are to texts in Leontius' homily, the third is to a passage in a letter addressed by Tarasius to the Byzantine Emperors Constantine VI and his mother Irene. Tarasius' epistle (Mansi XIII.404E–405A2; Latin version 403E and 406A1–3) has left traces also within the context of *LC* I.9: examples of *acyrologia* (pp. 27.36–28.2), the employment of improper terms, concerning various words improperly used at II Nicaea for *adorare*. "ipsi ponunt," says the author of the *LC* (p. 27.37) about the members attending the council, " 'habere' et 'salutare' et 'osculari' et 'venerari' pro 'adorare' "; in addition they consent to the employment of this habit by others: "et ab aliis positum accipiant." Also Leontius, at the beginning of his homily (Mansi XIII.43), discusses the differences between *adorare, salutare, osculari*, and *venerari*. Since Mansi's Latin version of the *Acta* of II Nicaea represents Anastasius Bibliothecarius' translation of 873 of the Greek *Acta*, but not the first Latin version of ca. 788 actually used by the author of the *LC*, it should be instructive to compare Anastasius' version with the pertinent Latin fragments of the version of ca. 788 of Leontius' homily which luckily are preserved in the *Libellus Synodalis* of the Paris Synod of 825 (*LS*).[21]

Compare the following three texts:

a) Leontius' Greek original of his homily, Mansi XIII.44D11–E2;
b) its first Latin translation of ca. 788, preserved in *LS* p. 514.8–12;
c) Anastasius' version of 873, Mansi XIII.43D10–E4.

    I. a. *καὶ ὥσπερ ὁ κέλευσιν βασιλέως δεξάμενος, καὶ ἀσπασάμενος τὴν σφραγῖδα;*

          b. Et sicut qui iussionem imperatoris suscipiens et *osculatus* est signum,

          c. Et sicut is qui iussionem imperatoris suscepit, et *salutavit* sigillum,

---

[21] See n. 18, above.

II. a. οὐ τὸν πηλὸν ἐτίμησεν, ἢ τὸν χάρτην, ἢ τὸν μόλυβδον;
  b. non lutum *honorat*, aut chartam, aut plumbum;
  c. non lutum *adoravit*, aut chartam, aut plumbum;

III. a. ἀλλὰ τῷ βασιλεῖ τὴν προσκύνησιν καὶ τὸ σέβας ἀπένειμεν . . . ;
  b. sed imperatori *salutem et venerationem* reddidit;
  c. sed imperatori *adorationem et cultum* impendit.

IV. a. (44E2) οὐ φύσιν τοῦ ξύλου τιμῶμεν;
  b. (p. 514.11) non naturam ligni *veneramur*;
  c. (43E1) non naturam ligni *adoramus*,

V. a. (44E5f.) . . . ἀσπαζόμεθα καὶ προσκυνοῦμεν;
  b. (514.11f.) . . . *osculamur et adoramus* et cetera;
  c. (43E3–4) . . . *salutamus et adoramus*.

The comparison of the Greek original with its two Latin versions shows that the first Latin version of the *Nicaenum* contains in the fragment from Leontius' homily the terms employed for *adorare* (save *habere*) criticized by the author of the *LC*. And the comparison of the first Latin translation with the one by Anastasius exemplifies the degree to which the latter's Latin version follows the one of about 788. Rather remarkable is the fact that Anastasius' translation changes, with the exception of *adoramus* (in item 5, below), all the translations of the first Latin version's key terms concerning image-worship. The comparison of the translated Greek words is quite illustrative in this respect:

1. Leontius: ἀσπασάμενος—first Latin version: *osculatus est*—Anastasius: *salutavit*; and correspondingly the remaining instances:
2. ἐτίμησεν—*honorat*—*adoravit*;
3. προσκύνησιν καὶ τὸ σέβας—*salutem et venerationem*—*adorationem et cultum*;
4. τιμῶμεν—*veneramur*—*adoramus*;
5. ἀσπαζόμεθα καὶ προσκυνοῦμεν—*osculamur et adoramus*—*salutamus et adoramus*.

Indeed there is consistency in Anastasius' method of translation, since ἀσπασάμενος (in 1) and ἀσπαζόμεθα (in 5) are translated uniformly: *salutavit* and *salutamus*. The same is to be observed in his translation of ἐτίμησεν (2) and τιμῶμεν (4) as *adoravit* and *adoramus*. Correspondingly he translated προσκύνησιν (3) and προσκυνοῦμεν (5) with *adorationem* and *adoramus*. We notice that

Anastasius translates τιμάω (4) and προσκυνέω as *adorare* and *adoratio*, and that he uses instead of the *First Latin Nicaenum's venerationem* (3) and *veneramur* (4) the replacement: *cultum* and again *adoramus*. It is clear that Anastasius avoids the terms *veneratio* and *venerari*, which are acceptable in the first Latin version, while Anastasius shows a preference for *adorare*.

The results of the preceding analysis can be tested in an instance which offers a quotation from another section of Leontius' homily. The chapter heading of *LC* III.27 (p. 161.17) reads: "Veneramur et adoramus sicut locum dei." Bastgen (p. 161 n. 1) refers to Anastasius' translation in Mansi XIII.46A12: "colimus et adoramus ut locum dei." Leontius reads (Mansi XIII.46A12): σεβόμεθα καὶ προσκυνοῦμεν ὡς τόπον Θεοῦ. The citation from Leontius' homily in *LC* III.27 renders the text of the *First Latin Nicaenum*, and therefore σεβόμεθα becomes *veneramur*, in conformity with the translation of τὸ σέβας (above, under 3) as *venerationem*. Anastasius, as we have learned, avoids the latter term, and therefore substitutes *colimus* for *veneramur*, as he also does in the example listed above, under 3. That he likewise consistently translates προσκυνοῦμεν with *adoramus* we have seen previously, when analyzing the first example from Leontius' homily.[22]

The author of *LC* I.9 borrowed from Jerome's commentary not only when writing that particular chapter, but also elsewhere in his work. Bastgen properly indicates the *LC*'s indebtedness to Jerome for II.19 (p. 77f.), while the author of the *LC* openly lists Jerome as his source in III.15 (p. 134.25–38). I refer to a newly found instance in I.10 (p. 29.28–29): "Tertium [*scil.* officium] quod typum gerebat nostri Mediatoris . . . quem et Danihel *lapidem abscisum* dicit *de monte sine manibus praecidentium* [cf. Dan. 2.34], *absque coitu et humano* videlicet *semine ex utero virginali* genitum; . . ." This passage renders Jerome, *Comm. in Dan.* (I.2.45), 795.408–10: "*Abscisus est lapis*—Dominus atque Salvator—*sine manibus* [Dan. 2.45], id est absque coitu et humano semine de utero virginali." This borrowing makes clear the manner employed by the author of the *LC* when dealing with Bible quotations supplemented by him. Jerome's version reads "abscisus est lapis sine manibus"; the *LC* version, which reappears in *LC* III.25 (p. 157.9f.), is fuller:

[22] Mansi XIII.44D10–E2, above.

"lapidem abscisum . . . de monte sine manibus *praecidentium*."
Isidore of Seville, *De fide catholica* (*PL* 83.470A), and the Mozarabic
Antiphonary of the Cathedral of León offer Dan. 2.34–35 with
the reading *praecidentium*.[23] The author of *LC* I.10 may well have
supplemented Jerome's version of Dan. 2.34–35 on the basis of
Isidore's version.

The same passage from Jerome's commentary cited in *LC* III.15
(p. 134) is listed among the testimonia of image-worship in the
Libellus Synodalis of the Paris Synod of 825 (p. 491.3–8, no. XXII).
The compilers of the *Libellus* certainly used the *LC*. The comparison
of the *LC*'s quotation from Jerome's commentary with the same
Jerome text cited in the *Libellus* proves that the original *Explicit*
of the Jerome text in *LC* III.15 (p. 134.38), *servis dei non convenit*,
is written in the *Vaticanus Latinus 7207* on an erasure. This means
that a corrector restored the original Jerome text at the very end
of the *LC* quotation, since the first redaction of the *LC* text offered
a wording of the Hieronymian *Explicit* which differed from the
original. The corrector may have been identical with the author
of the *LC*, or else with a scribe of the Vatican codex.

I have dealt at length and in depth with Jerome's commentary as
the basic source of *LC* I.9, I.10, and III.15, by taking into account,
especially for I.9 and II.15, the pertinent Greek sources,[24] in order
to show the very involved complexity of the *LC*'s literary genesis;
its authorship can by no means be determined solely by the external
similarity between Bible quotations occurring in the *LC* and in
other writings.

[23] *Antifonario Visigótico Mozárabe de la Catedral de León*, ed. Louis Brou and José
Vives (Barcelona, Madrid, 1959), 91, fol. 70v16. Isidore's version is identical with
that of the antiphonary. On the exegesis of the testimonia in *LC* I.10 (p. 29f.)
see, for example, L. W. Barnard, "The Testimonium concerning the Stone in the
New Testament and in the Epistle of Barnabas," *Studia Patristica*, III, ed. F. L.
Cross (*TU*, 88; Berlin, 1964), 306–313, to which may be added Wallach, "The
Origin of Testimonia Biblica in Early Christian Literature," *Review of Religion* 8
(1943), 130–136.
[24] To *LC* II.11 (p. 71.31–33), on Onias and his Temple in Egypt, see also
Jerome, *Comm. in Dan.* III.14b, 908f., which seems to be the actual source of the
passage.

CHAPTER VI

Ambrosiaster and the *Libri Carolini*

The discovery of many hitherto unknown literary sources used in the *Libri Carolini* is discussed throughout the present studies. The presence of one of these sources, the pseudo-Augustinian *Categoriae decem*,[1] re-edited by Alcuin, and dedicated to Charlemagne, strengthens Bastgen's and my belief that Alcuin was the author of the *LC*. The frequent occurrence of numerous conditional, and of some categorical, syllogisms in the *LC*'s logical, exegetical, theological, and grammatical discussions again points to Alcuin, who compiled an *ars dialectica* and taught the art as one of the subjects in the curriculum of the *artes liberales*. On the other hand, modern studies of various transmissions of the fifth-century florilegium *De divinis scripturis*, known in the list of *Vetus Latina* manuscripts under the symbol *m*, should discourage any attempt at constructing a connection between Theodulph and the author of the *LC* on the grounds that both authors happen to be familiar with some of the biblical texts of the florilegium.[2] The extensive influence on the *LC*, however, of Ambrosiaster's *Quaestiones Veteris et Novi Testamenti CXXVII* (hereinafter referred to as Souter)[3] and of the *Commentarius in*

---

[1] See Chapter IV, item M.

[2] See on the transmission and textual history of this florilegium Ernst Nellessen, *Untersuchungen zur altlateinischen Ueberlieferung des ersten Thessalonicherbriefes* (Bonner Bibl. Beiträge 22; Bonn, 1965), 138–141. The Bible MSS of Theodulph of Orléans, written a few decades after the composition of the *LC*, contain appended excerpts from *m*. Three other MS transmissions of *m*, discovered by D. de Bruyne, are described by Nellessen.

[3] Ed. Alexander Souter, *CSEL* 50 (Wien, Leipzig, 1908).

Epistulas Paulinas[4] is deserving of a special treatment,[5] especially in view of the additional fact that Alcuin was familiar with Ambrosiaster's commentaries and used them in some of his writings.

Hubert Bastgen recognized in *LC* IV.27 (p. 226.32–43)[6] the citation from Ambrosiaster's *quaestio* 27 (pp. 55.11–56.1, Souter). The MS of the *Quaestiones* which the author of the *LC* had before his eyes was in all likelihood not ascribed to *Augustinus*, as are other MSS on which Souter based his edition. I deduce this fact from the *LC*'s reference (pp. 226.43–227.2) at the end of the excerpt from *quaestio* 27 according to which not only *Augustinus*, but also other *doctores*, expressed views different from Ambrosiaster's opinion whether Saul "cum diabolo futurus erat" (p. 226.42): "quamquam et a beato Augustino et ab aliis doctoribus diversa de hac re opinentur et liber Ecclesiasticus [*Ecclus.* 46.23] ad laudem Samuhelis refert eo quod mortuus prophetarit." Bastgen (p. 227 n. 1) refers for the reference to Augustine, *De diversis quaestionibus ad Simplicianum* II, *quaestio* 3, whereas the *LC* undoubtedly has in mind Augustine's *De octo Dulcitii quaestionibus* VI.5 (*PL* 40.165): " . . . quando inveni in libro Ecclesiastico (46.23), ubi patres laudantur ex ordine, ipsum

---

[4] *Ambrosiastri qui dicitur Commentarius in Epistulas Paulinas* I: *In Epistulam ad Romanos*, ed. H. I. Vogels (*CSEL* 81.1; Wien, 1966); II: *In Epistulas ad Corinthios*, ed. Vogels, *CSEL* 81.2 (Wien, 1968); III: *In Epistulas ad Galatas, ad Efesios, ad Filippenses, ad Colosenses, ad Thesalonicenses, ad Timotheum, ad Titum, ad Filemonem*, ed. Vogels (*CSEL* 81.3; Wien, 1969). I am aware of the strictures concerning v.81.3 expressed by H. J. Frede in Kurt Aland, *Die alten Uebersetzungen des Neuen Testaments, die Kirchenväterzitate und Lektionare* (Berlin, New York, 1972), 471f. For the Ambrosiaster text referred to in item E and in *DA* 29 (1973), 201, compare Werner Affeldt, *Die weltliche Gewalt in der Paulus-Exegese* (Göttingen, 1969), 53–85.

[5] On Ambrosiaster see A. Stuiber's article in *Jahrbuch für Antike und Christentum* 13 (1970), 119–123; also Michaela Zelzer, "Zur Sprache des Ambrosiaster," *Wiener Studien* 83 (1970), 196–213. On the MSS of the commentary on the Pauline Epistles see H. J. Vogels, *Die Ueberlieferung des Ambrosiasterkommentars zu den Paulinischen Briefen*, Nachrichten der Akademie der Wiss. in Göttingen (philo.-hist. Klasse, 1959, No. 7), 107–142, and *CSEL* 81.1 (1966), VII–LVI; on those of the *Quaestiones* see Alexander Souter in *CSEL* 50 (1908), *Prolegomena*, pp. vii–xxxv, and various studies by Caelestinus Martini; also G. C. Martini, "Le recensioni delle 'Quaestiones Veteris et Novi Testamenti' dell'Ambrosiaster," *Ricerche di storia religiosa* I (1954), 40–62.

[6] *LC* IV.27 (p. 226.20–23) contains a quotation (not identified) from Jerome, *Adversus Vigilantium*, c. 5 (*PL* 23; Paris, 1845), 343A: "Quis enim, o insanum caput, aliquando martyres adoravit." The same passage is cited in the *Libellus Synodalis* of the Paris Synod of 825, *MGH, Conc.* 2, 496.25ff. (Epitome, p. 546.27), and also alluded to in *LC* III.14 (p. 155.15–16).

Samuelem sic fuisse laudatum ut prophetasse etiam mortuus diceretur." This is also the text of the testimonium of image-worship cited by the compilers of the *Libellus Synodalis* of the Paris Synod of 825, who included numerous texts referred to in the *LC* in their own compilation of testimonia.[7]

All the traces, subsequently listed under A–H, of Ambrosiaster's *Quaestiones*, occur in the context of the *LC* without the slightest direct indication of their true origin.

A. The definition of *deus* and the enumeration of the divine attributes in *LC* III.14 (p. 131.31–38) together with the introductory remark on man's incapacity to recognize the divine, follow *quaestio* I, 1–2 (p. 13 Souter).[8] Compare:

Ambrosiaster, *Quaestio* I.1–2:

Quid est Deus?—Deus hoc est quod *nulla attingit opinio. plus est* enim *quam quicquid dici poterit aut cogitari* . . . aspiciunt, quid deus sit opinione, non definitione; . . . Igitur *est* deus, sicut hominibus videtur, *spiritus natura simplex, lux inaccessibilis, invisibilis, inaestimabilis, infinitus, perfectus, nullius egens, aeternus, inmortalis* omni modo, *a quo omnia initium consecuta sunt; venerandus, diligendus, metuendus, extra quem nihil est, immo in quo sunt omnia quaequae sunt sursum, deorsum, summa et ima; omnipotens, omnitenens, vere in omnibus dives, quia nihil est,* quod non eius sit; bonus, iustus, misericors: . . .

Libri Carolini III.14:

Quomodo ergo Deus . . . *nulla potest adtingere opinio,* nulla complecti definitio, quoniam *plus est quam quicquid dici aut cogitari potest? Est* enim *spiritus natura simplex, lux inaccessibilis, invisibilis, infinitus, perfectus, nullius egens, aeternus, inmortalis*—et revera inmoratlis, cui omnia vivunt, *a quo omnia initium consequuta sunt*—*venerandus, diligendus, metuendus, extra quem nihil est, immo in quo sunt omnia quaequae sunt sursum deorsumve, summa et ima, omnipotens, omnia tenens* [Ambrosiaster MS B: *omnia tenens*], *vere in omnibus dives, quia nihil est,* ubi non sit, nec aliquis ei locus absens est [*ubi*—*est* on erasure in MS V] . . .

The first redaction of the *LC*, erased by a corrector, from *ubi* to *est*, read in all probability with Ambrosiaster, *quod* to *misericors*.

---

[7] Cf. *MGH*, Conc. 2.2 (Aevi Karolini 1.2; 1908), 515.35–516.10.

[8] Caelestinus Martini, *Ambrosiaster: De auctore, operibus, theologia* (Spicilegium pontificii Aethenaei Antoniani, 4; Rome, 1944), 35, shows that Ambrosiaster follows Novatianus, *De trinitate* 2 (*PL* 3.948), concerning man's incapacity to recognize the divine.

There may well be a connection between the corrector's words and the correction in *LC* III.19 (p. 165.37) "Deus enim nusquam absens est," also written on an erasure.[9]

B. *LC* III.16 (p. 137.13–20) discusses the reasons why Joseph prevented the *veneratio* of his *ossa—post obitum—*by expressing the wish that his *cineres* be removed from Egypt *ad terram repromissionis* (Hebr. 11.9). The basis of the argumentation is provided by Ambrosiaster, *quaestio* 25 (p. 51.19–52.11, Souter): "Ut quid Ioseph post prophetiam addiurat filios Israhel ut, cum a deo liberarentur, cineres eius de Aegypto transferrent?" The borrowings from Ambrosiaster are indicated in *LC* III.16 (p. 137.13–20) by italics:

Hinc est, quod beatus *Ioseph post prophetiam ossa sua* cum adiuratione *filiis Israhel ad terram repromissionis*[10] venturis secum deferenda percenset, ne, dum Aegyptii memores essent illius sive *administrationis, qua in magna aegestate Aegyptum gubernaverat,* eius ossibus inutilem exhiberent venerationem, et, qui erat *in Dei creatoris devotione* firmatus et *a vana superstitione Aegyptiorum* omnino alienus, eo propensius suam ostenderet sanctitatem, quo et vivens humiliter et recte Deo servierit et post obitum cineribus suis inconpetens obsequium exhiberi recusaverit.

C. Bastgen refers for *LC* III.25 (pp. 156.30–157.1) "Numquidnam quia Dominus de rubo in igne Moysi loquutus est, ideo rubi adorandi sunt?" to Isidore of Seville, *Quaestiones in Vetus Test.* But the *LC*'s actual source is Ambrosiaster, *quaestio* 42 (p. 69.5–19, Souter): "Cur angelus missus loqui ad Moysen in igne et rubo apparuit in monte?" This *quaestio* has left numerous literal and paraphrased traces in the *LC* text which easily become evident if the latter is compared with its source. Souter does not offer for *quaestio* 42 the version in the collection of *CL Quaestiones, PL* 35.2239 (a), *ex*

---

[9] Ernst Dümmler, *MGH, Epistolae* 5 (Karolini Aevi 3; Berlin, 1899), 616.41–44, published a text from MS. Würzburg, M. p. th. fol. 56, s,IX, "Augustinus dixit: Deus est, sicut hominibus videtur . . . bonus, misericors, iustus," which is from Ambrosiaster, *quaestio* I.2 (p. 13.17–19, 21–24), *passim.* Preceding this stray piece, p. 616.31–37, Dümmler prints an unidentified excerpt from Augustine, *De trinitate* 5.1,2 (*PL* 42; Paris, 1845), 912, lines 11–16, where the divine attributes are identified with Aristotelian categories. These two identifications may be added to the description of the Würzburg MS by Bernhard Bischoff and Josef Hofmann, *Libri Sancti Kyliani* (Würzburg, 1952), 127f., no. 107.

[10] Cf. *LC* III.24 (p. 154.34f.): *Ioseph . . . ossa sua filiis Israhel ad terram repromissionis* vehenda praecepit (cf. Hebr. 11.9).

MSS secundi generis. This version is obviously based on the text of Souter's chapter 42, and there is no evidence that it is used in the *LC*, regardless of some parallelisms with the *LC* text. See below Chapter IX, G.

D. Ambrosiaster, *quaestio* 16 (p. 42.6–20, Souter), "Quare angelus, qui in via occidere volebat Moysen, circumcisione infantis pacatus est?" is the source of *LC* III.25 (p. 157.1–5 Bastgen): "Numquid quia circumcisione acutissimo lapide facta legislator tremendi iudicis et mortis interitum evasit, lapides adorandi sunt?" The borrowings from Ambrosiaster are printed in italics: "Merito enim legislator *angelum in se* tam *infestum vidit,* quia *habitans in* terra *Madian filium circumcidere neglexit,* et qui *Dei Abrahe nuntius erat, signum fidei* [Rom. 4.11] *Abrahae* in filio *non ferebat, in quo gloriari Iudaeos sciebat."* Bastgen (p. 157.4d) states that *fidei* is written on an erasure and that three additional letters are erased in the *LC* manuscript *V,* the *Vaticanus Latinus 7207.* We now recognize on the basis of the underlying text that Ambrosiaster's original *iustitiae* in the first redaction of the *LC* was erased by a corrector and that *fidei* was substituted for it. Since the author of the *LC* was familiar not only with Ambrosiaster's *Quaestiones,* but also with the latter's *Commentary on Romans,* it may well be that he changed Ambrosiaster's *iustitiae* to *fidei,* because he accepted the exegesis *ad Rom.* 4.13 (ed. H. I. Vogels, *CSEL* 81.1, Wien, 1966), p. 136.24f., concerning Abraham: "non ergo merito servatae legis Abraham heres factus est mundi, sed *fidei."*

E. *LC* III.29 (p. 166.30–38 Bastgen) proclaims that emperors and kings must be honored (honorandi) by their subjects. "Si enim honorandi minime essent, nequaquam *David,* vir sanctus, *Saulem postquam Deus ab eo recesserat, 'Christum Domini'* [1. Reg. 26.9] *vocaret"* says the *LC* following the title of Ambrosiaster, *quaestio* 35 (p. 63.6–8): "Qua ratione David Saul postquam Deus ab eo recessit, *Christum Domini* vocat et defert ei?" The entire answer in the *LC* is taken from Ambrosiaster (p. 63.9–16). I have dealt in detail with the pertinent corrections of this passage in Chapter IX. H. Eugen Ewig, "Zum christlichen Königsgedanken im Frühmittelalter," in *Das Königtum: Mainauvorträge 1954 (Vorträge und Forschungen,* III; Lindau, Konstanz), p. 59 n. 235, was the first to recognize the use of Ambrosiaster, *quaestio* 35, in *LC* III.29. He overlooked, however, the highly interesting fact that the author of the *LC*, a theologian who was close to Charlemagne, nevertheless, quite significantly deemed it advisable to omit (*LC*, p. 166.35, between *decrevit* and *Quamdiu*) from the Ambrosiaster text, otherwise quoted almost verbatim, the words (*quaestio* 35, p. 63.12–13) "dei enim imaginem habet rex, sicut et episcopus Christi." The author of the *LC* was evidently reluctant to ascribe to a king any divine kinship! See my expanded argument in *DA* 29 (1973), 201.

F. *LC* IV.7 (p. 187.2–7) refers to the first commandment written on the second tablet, namely, "Honora . . . patrem tuum et matrem tuam," called in Eph. 6.2 *mandatum primum*. The reference renders the opinion of Ambrosiaster, *quaestio* 7.2 (p. 31.18–23, Souter): " . . . quo modo esset primum, nisi in secunda tabula ab ipso coepisset? 'in promissione' autem ideo dixit, *quia statim subiecit*: 'ut sis longaevus super terram et bene tibi sit'" (Eph. 6.3). The *LC* (p. 187.4–7) reads accordingly: " . . . in ea videlicet promissione, *qua statim subiecit*: 'ut sis longevus super terram et bene tibi sit'" (Eph. 6.3).

The sequence of the Bible quotations in *LC* IV.7 (p. 187.2–29), with the exception of Eph. 6.2–3 (p. 187.5–7) that renders Ambrosiaster's text, follows the florilegium *De divinis scripturis*, c. XX (*CSEL* 12; 1887), 386.5ff., as was pointed out by Bastgen in his *Addenda* (*LC*, p. 230b). However, the Bible quotation, p. 187.19–20, does not render Eph. 6.1, but *Col.* 3.20 (see *m*, p. 388.2–3). The text of Prov. 20.20 (p. 187.26–28), "Qui maledicit patri suo et matri, extinguetur lucerna eius in mediis tenebris," represents in all probability the second redaction of the *LC*. This means that it was written on erasure in the lost part of the *codex authenticus* of the *LC*, the *Vaticanus Latinus 7207*. The original text of the first redaction probably read with *De divinis scripturis*, c. XX (p. 389.3), "Maledictis patri aut matri extinguetur lumen, pupillae autem oculorum eius videbunt tenebras" (Prov. 20.20; 20.10 in the Greek sequence), since the author of the *LC* cited from a MS of *m* which resembled the codices MC of the florilegium, as D. de Bruyne concluded ("La composition des Libri Carolini," *Revue Bénédictine* 44 [1932], 232).

G. *LC* IV.13 (p. 194.14–15) reads: "Est autem creator Deus, *ex quo omnia*, *per quem omnia* [cf. 1 Cor. 8.6], in quo omnia, dicente Apostolo [Rom. 11.36]: 'quoniam ex ipso et per ipsum et in ipso sunt omnia,'" and follows the exegesis of Ambrosiaster, *Quaestio* 122.27 (p. 374, Souter): "Quem modum custodiens apostolus Paulus [1 Cor. 8.6]: 'unus, inquit, deus pater, *ex quo omnia*, et nos in ipso, et unus . . . *per quem omnia*, et nos per ipsum,' ut primus gradus sit, *ex quo* sunt *omnia*, secundus, *per quem omnia*, tertius, in quo omnia. et quia nullus ex his degener est, in unitate dei significati sunt dicente apostolo [Rom. 11.36]: '*quoniam ex ipso et per ipsum et in ipso sunt omnia*,' ipsi gloria."

It is obvious that the *LC* renders Ambrosiaster's interpretations and also adopts his third gradus "in quo omnia." In addition, the *LC*'s "creator deus" may well be a conscious reference to Ambrosiaster *ad Rom.* 11.36 (p. 390.22 Vogels): " . . . quia enim omnium creator est deus."

H. *LC* IV.24 (p. 222.39) contains a reference to the Nicene creed, "de eo dicitur: Natum, non factum," which is tied up with Rom. 1.3, "Qui factus est ei ex semine David." The latter verse is connected with Prov. 9.1, "Sapientia edificavit sibi domum," a text which appears also in the title of Ambrosiaster's *quaestio* 52 from which *LC* IV.24 draws, as we shall see, a longer passage dealing with the trinity. Also *quaestio* 54 (p. 99.18) discusses, like the *LC*, the formula *non factus, sed natus* in connection with Rom. 1.3.

Quaestio 52 (p. 98.19–26, Souter) is inserted verbatim without the slightest indication of its origin into *LC* IV.24 (p. 223.6–12):

Nam *si effectu Spiritus sancti factum est corpus, quod et domum dici arbitramur, quare ad personam Christi relatum est, quaeri* potest. *Factum Filii factum Patris est, quia utriusque una virtus est. Simili modo etiam factum Spiritus sancti factum Filii Dei est propter naturae et voluntatis unitatem. Sive enim Pater faciat sive Filius sive Spiritus sanctus, Trinitas est quae operatur; et quicquid tres fecerint, Dei unius est operatio.* Potest etiam et ecclesia domus Christi accipi, quam aedificavit sibi sanguine suo. . . .

The *LC*'s concluding statement from *Potest* to *suo* is taken from the beginning of Ambrosiaster's *quaestio* (p. 98.14–16):

Quaestio ista gemina ratione debet intellegi. primum enim *domus Christi ecclesia* est, *quam aedificavit sibi sanguine suo.* deinde *potest.* . . .

Bastgen (*LC*, p. 223 n. 1) refers for the unified *operatio* of the *opera trinitatis* to sermons by Augustine and to similar, if not identical, formulations in the works of Alcuin (which can be easily supplemented). Bastgen has properly seen the basic Augustinian origin of these texts (cf. *De trinitate* I.5, *PL* 42.824, and XV.23, 43–44, *PL* 42.1090–1091). But the use made in *LC* IV.24 of Ambrosiaster's *quaestio* and of the *Dialogus quaestionum LXV* has escaped his attention.

I have shown in Chapter IV, D that the *Dialogus quaest. LXV* is anonymously cited in *LC* III.3 and III.26[11] I now add the following newly found instance in *LC* IV.24. Compare

Dialogue quaest. LXV, *quaestio* 6 (*PL* 40; Paris, 1865), 736:

Si una substantia est patris et filii et spiritus sancti, quomodo filius sine patre et spiritu sancto suscepit carnem?
Resp. Neque persona patris neque spiritus sancti, *sed sola filii persona suscepit carnem.* . . . Ita pater et filius et spiritus sanctus cum sint una substantia, *tota trinitas operata est* hominem quem non tota trinitas assumpsit, *sed sola filii persona,*[12]

and *LC* IV.24 (p. 223.5–6):

Tota enim *trinitas operata est* in incarnatione Domini, *sed sola filii persona suscepit carnem.*

The comparison of the preceding texts clearly shows that the concept of the sole incarnation of the son's person is hardly copied directly from the Augustinian source, but more likely derived from the pseudo-Augustinian *Dialogus*. The use made of the identical doctrine in Alcuin's treatment of the trinity and in that of the *LC*, together with the *LC*'s and Alcuin's familiarity with Ambrosiaster's works, may be counted as contributing, partial evidence for the correctness of the assumption of Alcuin's authorship of the *Libri Carolini*.[13]

---

[11] Cf. Chapter IV, D.

[12] Cf. Pseudo-Augustine, *De trinitate et unitate dei*, c.2 (*PL* 42.1196, lines 7–15), which borrows from the *Dialogus*, c. 6; cf. also Alcuin, *De fide s. trin.* (*PL* 101.57D–58A), and *De trin. ad Fredegisum, Quaestiones* 28, *quaestio* 24 (*PL* 101.62C). See Augustinus, *serm.* 213.6 (*PL* 38.1063), suggested by Bastgen, and *Contra serm. Arianorum* 4 (*PL* 42.686), Fulgentius of Ruspe, *PL* 65.696B and 462B.

[13] See Alexander Souter, in his edition of Ambrosiaster, *Quaestiones* (*CSEL* 50; Wien, Leipzig, 1908), on Alcuin's familiarity with the *Quaestiones*, which is greater than indicated by Souter. Cf. Chapter XIV n. 6.

I. Traces of Ambrosiaster's exegesis from his *Commentarius in Epistulam ad Romanos*[14] occurring in the *LC* together with quotations from Ambrosiaster's *Quaestiones* have been pointed out previously for *LC* III.25 (D) and IV.13 (G). *LC* I.1 contains longer excerpts from the *Commentarius ad Romanos*.

1. Bastgen, *LC* I.1 (p. 9.25–26) emends the *LC* text and reads: et Apostolus [Rom. 8.17], *Si tamen compatiamur ut et conglorificemur,* id est: simul glorificemur. But Ambrosiaster *ad Rom.* 8.17 (p. 276.5) reads like the *LC* text *Si tamen conpatiamur ut et simul glorificemur,* and Bastgen's variants *e* and *f* belong in the context of the *LC*; Bastgen's emendations are not necessary. The *LC* reads with Ambrosiaster as follows: et Apostolus [Rom. 8.17]: *Si tamen conpatiamur ut et simul glorificemur,* id est conglorificemur." The same passage from Ambrosiaster *ad Rom.* 8.17 (p. 276.5–10) appears in *LC* I.1 (p. 11.1–4): "Conpatiamur enim Christo. . . . *carnem* nostram *crucifigimus, id est mundum, cum vitiis et concupiscentiis* (Gal. 5.24), et morimur mundo et *conmorimur Christo.* . . . " Bastgen states in note *a* that after *Christo* "sequitur locus unius linea rasus" in the *Vaticanus Latinus 7207* of the *LC*. The erased text of the first redaction reads in all likelihood with Ambrosiaster *ad Rom.* 6.3 (p. 190.24–25) " . . . *conmorimur Christo* ‹hoc est in morte eius baptizamur›." The *LC*'s interpretation of *Gal.* 5.24 "carnem nostram crucifigimus, id est mundum, . . . " renders Ambrosiaster's exegesis in the commentary *ad Galatas* 5.24 (*CSEL* 81.3; Wien, 1969), 61.3, " . . . *carnem, id est mundum.*"

2. *LC* I.1 (p. 11.4–8) follows the exegesis (in italics) of Ambrosiaster *ad Rom.* 6.4 (p. 192.4–6 and 17–21 Vogels):

" 'Consepulti enim sumus cum illo per baptismum in mortem, ut quemadmodum Christus resurrexit a mortuis per virtutem patris, ita et nos in novitate vitae ambulemus,' [Rom. 6.4], et sic *baptizati consepulti sumus* ei, *ut de cetero hanc vitam sequamur, in qua Christus resurrexit. Baptismum resurrectionis pignus est et imago, ut iam in preceptis Christi manentes ad praeterita denuo non revolvamur.*"

3. *LC* I.1 (p. 11.8–11) follows again Ambrosiaster *ad Rom.* 6.5 (p. 192.29–p. 194.1–7), and more specifically the recension β (or γ) of the commentary *ad Rom.*:

---

[14] See n. 4 above.

Convivificamur autem et consurgimus ei, *si similitudini mortis eius* sumus
conplantati id est si in baptismo omnia vitia
  β *deponentes in novam vitam translati*
de caetero non peccemus. Similitudo enim mortis similem praestavit resurrectionem.

The reading *deponentes in novam vitam translati* indicates that the
author of the *LC* used a MS of Ambrosiaster's *ad Romanos* that
belonged either to the second or to the third recension of the commentary. Also the interpretation of 1. Ioh. 3.2 in *LC* I.1 (p. 12.3–7)
" . . . ut 'dum apparuerit quod erimus,' id est *immortales* et *gloriosi,*
in quo 'similes ei erimus,' " may well render Ambrosiaster *ad Rom.*
6.5 (p. 194.7–10), " . . . quod in epistula sua Iohannes apostolus
memorat dicens: *scimus enim, quia cum apparuerit, similes illi (ei) erimus*
(1. Ioh. 3.2), hoc est *immortalem* et *gloriosum* resurgere. . . ."

K. *LC* II.16 (p. 75.13) opens the discussion with the quotation of
John 1.18 with which Ambrosiaster *ad Col.* 1.15 concludes his
interpretation.[15] *LC* II.16 (p. 75.15–17) reads: "Qui si invisibilis
est, immo quia invisibilis est, necesse est, ut incorporeus sit; et si
incorporeus est, necesse est, ut corporaliter pingi non possit. Igitur,
si invisibilis est et incorporeus, prorsus corporalibus materiis *pingi
non potest,*" following Ambrosiaster *ad Col.* 1.15, ed. H. I. Vogels
(*CSEL* 81.3; Wien, 1969), 170.23–26: "*Qui est imago dei invisibilis.*
1. invisibilis dei imago visibilis esse non potest, alioquin nec imago;
quod enim invisible est, *pingi non potest*; nec enim visibilis potest
invisibilem videre."

L. Appendix: *Ambrosiaster and the Libellus Synodalis of the Paris Synod
of 825.* The compilers of the *Libellus Synodalis* of the Paris Synod
of 825 list among their testimonia for image-worship some passages
from Ambrosiaster's *quaestio* 114, *Adversus paganos,* under the name
of Augustinus, *in libro quaestionum Veteris et Novi Testamenti*:[16]

---

[15] This was first pointed out by the present writer in "The Unknown Author of
the *Libri Carolini*: Patristic Exegesis, Mozarabic Antiphons, and the *Vetus Latina,*"
in *Didascaliae: Studies in Honor of Anselm M. Albareda,* ed. Sesto Prete (New York,
1961), 492.

[16] On the importance of the *Libellus Synodalis* for *LC* studies see Chapters I and
IV. I have not made a point of recording numerous minor passages in the *LC*
that indicate the author's acquaintance with Ambrosiaster. Cf., e.g., *LC* I.9
(p. 27.5), the reference to *Apoc.* (19.10) 22.9, and Ambrosiaster, *quaestio* 91.6
(p. 156.8 Souter); or *LC* II.30 (p. 93.10) and Ambrosiaster, *ad Rom.* 5.15 (p. 168.7
Vogels): "Moyses autem . . . *scribendo* manifestavit"; and other references.

1. *Libellus Synodalis*, Paris Synod, 825, ed. Albert Werminghoff, *MGH, Conc.* 2.2, (Aevi Karolini 1.2; Hannover, Leipzig, 1908), no. 28, p. 492.5–8 (in the *Epitome*, p. 543.8–11), *"Christiani, inquit, utpote pauperes . . . ad salutem;"*—Ambrosiaster, *quaestio* 114.9 (p. 307.12–15, Souter). Werminghoff identified this text in the *Addenda*, p. 1013, with the *quaestio* in *PL* 35.2215–16 (in *PL* 35; ed. Paris, 1841, 2343).

2. *Libellus Synodalis*, no. 51 (p. 497.3–8): *"Inrationabile*, inquit, *vulgus . . . aeternum est;*—Ambrosiaster, *quaestio* 114.29 (p. 316.8–15, Souter); no. 51 (p. 497.9–11) *"Quod colunt (pagani) . . . nos creatorem"*;—Ambrosiaster, *quaestio* 114.29 (p. 316.16–19, Souter); *"Factus ergo homo . . . hoc exegit"*;—Ambrosiaster, *quaestio* 114.30 (p. 316.22–23).

3. *Libellus Synodalis*, no. 57 (p. 498.21–32), renders Ambrosiaster ad 1. Cor. 8.1 and 13, ed. H. I. Vogels, *CSEL* 81.2 (1968), 92.1–7, 96.7–13. The *Libellus* variants are identical with those of the former Corbie codex Ambianensis (Amiens) 87 from about 800. Other variants of the Ambianensis are also identical with readings in *Libellus Synodalis*, no. 35 (p. 493.23–29), which cites Ambrosiaster *ad Rom.* 1.22, p. 42.22–30, 45.1–4.

The *Libri Carolini*'s eighth-century testimonia of Ambrosiaster's *Quaestiones* seemingly are older than the oldest ninth-century MSS of the collection used by Souter. The testimonia of the commentary *ad Romanos* belong either to the second or the third recension of the exegetical work. That the author of the *LC* could not have taken his relevant texts from the first recension is obvious on account of the special reading listed as being characteristic of the second recension (above, I.3), which does not occur in the first recension. I list two instances which indicate that the author of the *LC* was also acquainted with Ambrosiaster's comments *ad Galatas* (I, 1) and *ad Colosenses* (K). Chronologically, the *LC*'s testimonia from the last decade of the eighth century stand within the textual transmission of the *Commentarius in Epistulas Paulinas* approximately between the two MSS of the third recension, the Casinensis 15, s.VII inc., and the Ambianensis (Amiens) 87 of about 800 (from Corbie), and the oldest MS of the second recension, the Trevirensis, Bibl. municip. 122, s.VIII/IX (cf. Vogels, *CSEL* 81.1; p. XL). It is clear that the *LC*'s author used the *Quaestiones* and the Commentary

on the Pauline Epistles side by side. We notice this scholarly
approach in item D (above), where he seems to correct a passage
from *quaestio* 16 after his interpretation recorded for *ad Romanos*
4.13. He uses the same method in G (above) and thereby explains
a text from *quaestio* 122.27 with the help of the commentary *ad
Romanos* 11.36. In another instance (I, at the end), he interprets
1. *Ioh.* 3.2 with the aid of Ambrosiaster's comments *ad Rom.* 6.5.
There is finally the interesting distribution of the *LC* chapters in
which Ambrosiaster's works are used. By far the majority of those
texts are drawn from the *Quaestiones*, a much smaller number from
the *Commentarius in Epistulas Paulinas*, and at that mostly from
ad Romanos. The *Libri Carolini* uses Ambrosiaster's texts from the
first to the next to the last chapter, namely, from *LC* I.1 (see section I,
above) to *LC* IV.27 (see above, Introduction), *passim*. This fact is
stressed here because it is an important one from among others
that speak for only a single author of the *Libri Carolini*.[17]

[17] A German translation of the present original English version of Chapter VI
appeared under the title "Ambrosiaster und die Libri Carolini," in *DA* 29 (1973),
197–205.

CHAPTER VII

Actus Silvestri, Libri Carolini, and the *Constantine Donation*: The Solution of a Pseudo-Problem

The *Libri Carolini* II.13 (Bastgen, p. 73f.) cites and discusses the narration in the *Actus Silvestri* dealing with the images of the apostles Peter and Paul which Sylvester had shown to Emperor Constantine the Great. Excerpts from the same section of the Sylvester legend are incorporated in paragraphs 7–8 of the *Constitutum Constantini*.[1] The same text from the *Actus* that underlies *LC* II.13 as well as the section inserted in the text of the *Constantine Donation* is quoted in Hadrian I's *Synodica* of October 26, 785 (*JE* 2448), Mansi XII.1057D–1060C, addressed to the Byzantine Emperors Constantine VI and his mother Irene. In recent years, the question of the interdependence between the *Actus*, the *Libri Carolini*, and the *Constitutum* has been discussed with energy and perseverance by Wolfgang Gericke[2] and by Horst Fuhrmann.[3] But the specific points raised by both scholars seem to be the result of a very particular misinterpretation of certain texts, while some of the problems stated never actually existed in reality, as we shall see subsequently.

---

[1] Ed. Horst Fuhrmann, *Das Constitutum Constantini (Konstantinische Schenkung): Text.* Fontes iuris Germanici antiqui in usum scholarum X (Hannover, 1968), 69–74; for the Sylvester legend see R. J. Loenertz, "Actus Sylvestri: Genèse d'une légende," *Revue d'histoire ecclésiastique* 70 (1975), 426–439. See further, N. Huyghebaert, "La donation de Constantin ramenée à ses véritables proportions," *Revue d'histoire ecclésiastique* 71 (1976), 45–69.

[2] Gericke, "Das Constitutum Constantini und die Silvester-Legende," *ZSRG*, Kan. Abt. 44 (1958), 342–350; and the counterreply against H. Fuhrmann (see below, n. 3) by Gericke, "Konstantinische Schenkung und Silvesterlegende in neuer Sicht: Entgegnung und Weiterführung," *ZSRG*, Kan. Abt. 47 (1961), 293–304.

[3] Fuhrmann, "Konstantinische Schenkung und Silvesterlegende in neuer Sicht," *DA* 15 (1959), 523–540, Fuhrmann, "Konstantinische Schenkung und abendländisches Kaisertum," *DA* 22 (1966), 121.

The argument put forth by Gericke with regard to the *Actus Silvestri* as used in the *Libri Carolini* runs as follows:[4]

(a) *LC* II.13 (p. 73.12–13) reads: ... ut idem imperator *quos in somnis viderat*, eorum vultus *in picture fucis cognosceret*. This text obviously relies on the wording of the

(b) version A of the *Actus Silvestri*: Quam imperator aspiciens, ingenti clamore coepit dicere, ipsos esse *quos viderat*. The section in the *LC* (above, a) after *viderat*, that is, "eorum vultus in picturę fucis cognosceret," follows, according to Gericke, the

(c) *Actus* version B1 which reads: "Quorum vultus in visione conspexi." Gericke furthermore postulates[5] a relationship of the *LC* text with a passage in

(d) the *Constitutum Constantini* c. 8, 117–118 (Fuhrmann, p. 73): " ... et eorum, quos in somno videram figuratos in ipsis imaginibus cognovissem vultus." Gericke believes that "the *Constitutum* is somehow related to the *LC* not only on account of the phrase *eorum vultus*, but also on account of *in somno videram*, and because of the verb *cognoscere* which is common to both." Fuhrmann[6] rejects Gericke's opinion "that the *LC* quite clearly adopts the B-version [of the *Actus Silvestri*]," and concludes against Gericke that B2 is that version of the legend that is farthest removed from the *LC*. In his argument, Fuhrmann singles out the *LC* phrase *in picturę fucis* (p. 72.12–13), which provides, as will be shown afterward, one of the keys that enable us to relegate the alleged relationship between *LC* and the *Constantine Donation* to the sphere of a pseudo-problem that never existed.

Some of Gericke's and Fuhrmann's arguments lean heavily on earlier statements made by Wilhelm Levison[7] on the *Actus Silvestri*,

---

[4] *ZSRG*, Kan. Abt. 44 (1958), 346.

[5] *Ibid.*, p. 348; the division of the sources in the *Const. Const.* suggested by Gericke has no bearing on my argument.

[6] Fuhrmann, "Silvesterlegende," p. 534f.

[7] "Konstantinische Schenkung und Silvester-Legende," *Miscellanea Francesco Ehrle* II (Studi e Testi 38; Rome, 1924), reprinted in Levison, *Aus Rheinischer und Fränkischer Frühzeit* (Düsseldorf, 1948), 390ff., especially pp. 395, 397, 435, 459, 473. (The references are always to the reprinted study.) W. Ohnsorge, "Das Constitutum Constantini und seine Entstehung," in *Konstantinopel und der Okzident* (1966), 95, criticizes Levison, and, p. 107 n. 40a, questions on good grounds, as does also Fuhrmann in his edition, p. 10f., the validity of Schafer Williams, "The Oldest Text of the Constitutum Constantini," *Traditio* 20 (1964), 448ff.

the *LC*, and the *Constitutum Constantini*. Levison[8] assigned the excerpt
from the *Actus* in the patristic catena of *JE* 2448 to the version A of
Sylvester's *vita*, and then assumed the independent use made of the
version A by the author of *LC* II.13 (Bastgen, p. 73.12). He therefore
mistakenly postulated for the author of the *LC direct* acquaintance,
at first hand, with the *Actus Silvestri*, thus overlooking the undeniable
fact, properly indicated by Bastgen for the *LC* (p. 73 n. 1) that the
LC derives its knowledge of the A version of the *vita* from Hadrian I's
Synodica of 785 (*JE* 2448). Levison furthermore assumed the existence of another independent transmission of the same excerpt of
version A in the *Libellus Synodalis* of the Paris Synod of 825.[9] But
contrary to Levison's assumptions, the compiler of the *Libellus* never
used the *Actus* independently, on his own, because his excerpt from
the A version of the *Actus* also is directly derived from *JE* 2448.
This *Synodica* of 785 served as one of the sources for the Paris collection
of testimonia of image-worship, as the compilers of the *Libellus
Synodalis* of the Paris Synod of 825 openly state in their Introduction.[10] They found *JE* 2448 inserted in *actio* II of the (now lost)
First Latin Nicaenum (of about 788) of the Greek *Acta* of II Nicaea,
787, that was then still available. Levison[11] furthermore suggested
a solution to the question as to how one might explain, notwithstanding the proximity of *LC* II.13 to the A version of the *Actus
Silvestri*, that the *LC* still contains a few words more than does the
original A version of the Silvester text. The words in *LC* II.13
(p. 73.12–13), namely, *in somnis, vultus, cognosceret*, cannot be regarded "als vorlagefrei Füllsel," says Levison, because they appear
in a similar form in the wake of an expanded A recension also in the
Constantine Donation, paragraph 8.114–119 (Fuhrmann, p. 73f.):
(Constantine requests pictures of the apostles Peter and Paul) "ut
ex pictura disceremus, hos esse quos revelatio docuerat . . . Quas
dum aspicerem et eorum quos in somno videram figuratos in ipsis
imaginibus cognovissem, . . . confessus sum, eos esse quos in somno
videram." Levison then concluded that one might be inclined in
this case to assume a lacuna (*einen Ausfall*) in the texts of the A
version known to him, since the words under consideration are
otherwise transmitted in the strongly deviating B1 version of the

[8] Levison, *Frühzeit*, p. 434f.
[9] Ed. A. Werminghoff (*MGH, Conc.* 2; Aevi Karolini 1.2, 1908), 485, 536f.
[10] Ibid., p. 481.
[11] Levison, *Frühzeit*, p. 459, and Fuhrmann, "Silvesterlegende," p. 535.

Actus. But the origin of the *LC* words in the *Libri Carolini* singled out by Levison does not at all allow for his postulated connection with the passage in the *Constantine Donation*, since the words in question originated beyond doubt with the author of the *LC* and are elements of his personal style, as will be shown in the following section.

The chapter heading of *LC* II.13 (p. 72f.) refers, as is properly indicated by Hubert Bastgen, to a section in the *Actus Silvestri* cited in *JE* 2448,[12] which tells of the images of the apostles Peter and Paul shown by Sylvester to Constantine the Great. Bastgen does not point out the fact that a trace of the *Actus* is also noticeable within the context of the chapter. Compare *LC* II.13 (p. 73.12f.):
" . . . sed ut idem *imperator, quos* in somnis *viderat*, eorum vultus in pictur̨e fucis cognosceret," with *Actus Silvestri*, as cited in *JE* 2448, Mansi XII.1060C 1–9, and following *JE* 2448 in the *Libellus Synodalis* of the Paris Synod of 825 (*MGH, Conc.* 2: Aevi Karolini I.2; 1908), 485.28–33:
" . . . interrogare coepit augustus, utrumnam istos [*Mansi adds* apostolos] haberet aliqua imago impressos, ut ex pictura disceret hos esse quos revelatio docuisset [*Mansi* docuerat].
. . . imaginem quam *imperator* aspiciens, ingenti clamore coepit dicere, ipsos esse *quos viderat*, . . . "

The author of the *LC* questions the validity of the Constantine story in the *Liber actuum beati Silvestri* (p. 73.28) as a proof of image-worship: "non tamen ad ea quae in questionem veniunt, adfirmanda plene idoneus [*scil.* Liber . . .]" (p. 73.30).[13] Nowhere in this chapter, nor anywhere else in the treatise, does the author of the *LC* betray any first-hand acquaintance with the *Actus* going beyond the contents of the excerpt from the *Actus* inserted in Hadrian I's *Synodica* of 785 (*JE* 2448). The boastful remark in the *Libri Carolini* that the *Actus* is read *a pluribus catholicis* (p. 73.29), is no more than a literary reflection made by the author of the *Libri Carolini* on the

----

[12] Cf. above, Chapter II, section B. In addition to the parallels between *JE* 2448 and the text of the *Constitutum Constantini* which are traceable to the identical passages in the *Actus Silvestri* independently used in both documents, Hadrian I's *Synodica* of 785 has in common with the *Constitutum* also some diplomatic phraseology customarily used in papal documents issued by the *scrinium* during the rule of Hadrian I and his predecessors.

[13] The same phrase is used again in relation to the *Decretum Gelasianum* in *LC* IV.10 (p. 189.37–38): " . . . a beato Gelasio . . . non sunt . . . quia ad ea quae in quaestionem veniunt adprobanda."

basis of the *Decretum Gelasianum*, where he read concerning the *Liber actuum beati Silvestri:* "*a multis* tamen in urbe Roma *catholicis* legi cognovimus."[14]

It is necessary to recall at this juncture that of the scholars in the entourage of Charlemagne, Alcuin indeed possessed a first-hand knowledge of the version A of the *Actus*.[15] He quotes in his *Epistle* 245, addressed to Charlemagne,[16] the information drawn from the *Actus Silvestri* concerning a law decreed by Constantine on the fifth day after his baptism.

The previously mentioned conjecture made by Wilhelm Levison concerning the alleged loss of a passage within the version A1 of the *Actus* then at his disposal, which might have explained the "additional words" in *LC* II.13 (p. 73.12–13), namely, *in somnis, vultus, cognosceret,* that go beyond the underlying source (and allegedly are reminiscent of a passage in the *Constitutum Constantini*) is without any basis. We recall that the words *imperator quos viderat* occur in the underlying excerpt from the A version of the *Actus* cited in *JE* 2448. All of Levison's allegedly additional words used in the *LC* clearly belong to the personal style of the *LC*'s author who, in *LC* III.26 (p. 161.13), when dealing with dreams, says: " . . . dum quis quid se *in somnis vidisse cognoscit*." Compare furthermore *LC* I.12 (p. 31.37): "Qualiter ergo beatus Iacob tunicam filii non osculatus fuisse aut oculis imposuisse, sed *vidisse* tantum et *cognovisse* credatur." This leaves, as far as Levison's thesis is concerned, the occurrence of the word *vultus*, and as far as Fuhrmann is concerned, the phrase *in pictur̦e fucis.* Both instances are expressions of the personal style of the *LC*'s author, used by him elsewhere in his treatise.

In the *LC* the meaning of *vultus* is repeatedly discussed. *LC* I.23 (p. 51.3) deals at length with the meaning of *vultus* in Ps. 4.7 and 26.8, and concludes: "nil ad manufactarum imaginum vultus

---

[14] See H. Bastgen, "Das Bilderkapitular Karls des Grossen (libri Carolini) und das sogennante Decretum Gelasianum," *NA* 41 (1919), 683. The assumption of Heinz Loewe, "Von Theoderich d. Gr. zu Karl d. Gr.," *DA* 9 (1952), 359 n. 26, that *LC* II.13 proves the popularity of the *Actus Silvestri*, neglects the indicated secondhand nature of the reference.

[15] Cf. Wallach, *Alcuin and Charlemagne* (Cornell Studies in Classical Philology 32; 2nd ed. New York, London, 1968), p. 130 n. 8.

[16] Ed. E. Dümmler (*MGH, Epistolae* 4; Karolini Aevi 2; Berlin, 1895), 396.13. In addition Alcuin was also familiar with the *Constitutum Silvestri*; see Chapter XVI. I add that Aldhelm, *De virginitate*, ed. R. Ehwald (*MGH, Auctores Antiquissimi* 15, 1919), 257–260, already knew the *Actus Silvestri*.

pertinet." *LC* I.24 (p. 52.25) discusses Ps. 44.13, and arrives at the conclusion that the term *vultus* of the biblical text cannot be understood "de quodam manufacto vultu." These three quotations from the Psalms, which are cited in the *LC* as chapter headings, are in reality derived from *JE* 2448 (Mansi XII.1065C) where they are followed by a statement dealing with the *vultus dei* that serves as chapter heading of *LC* II.16 (p. 75f.).[17] The actual meaning of *vultus*, as understood in *LC* II.13 (p. 73.12) of the images of the Apostles seen by Constantine *in somnis*, is quite obviously a genuine contribution of the author of the *LC* going beyond the underlying text from the *Actus Silvestri*, and not at all indebted to any other version of the *vita*. This assumption finds some support in the *LC*'s interpretation according to which Sylvester urged Constantine, *qui visibilium cultor erat*—he means, in other words, a pagan—to see with the help of visible things the invisible ones (per visibilia ad invisibilia provocaret, p. 73.19). This formulation reflects what the author of the *LC* had read in *JE* 2448 (Mansi XII.1061C): the *sacrae imagines* are permanently honored *in universo mundo*, so that the human mind is drawn *per visibilem vultum* to the invisible majesty of the divinity.[18] It must be evident by now that Levison's so-called "additional words" in the *LC* exposition are manifestations of the personal style of the *LC*'s author. The same origin can be shown for the remaining phrase *in picturę fucis* (*LC* II.13; p. 73.10), especially singled out by Horst Fuhrmann.[19]

Fuhrmann argued that Constantine's recognition of the figures which he saw in his dream occurred to the emperor *in picturę fucis*. He assumed this expression to be the reflection of the preceding term *pictura* in the A version of the *Actus* (see above). This would seem a sufficiently reasonable assumption, if only the same expression did not occur in *LC* III.18 (p. 141.1–3): "Cum ergo isti pene

[17] This chapter contains a reference to an unknown writing by Augustine which has not been identified until now: B. Altaner, *Kleine patristische Schriften* (1967); 94f. See above, the testimonium D in *JE* 2448, Chapter II.

[18] The same text from *JE* 2448 is quite significantly inserted in a broader context in the *Hadrianum* II.25 (p. 56.11), ed. K. Hampe (*MGH, Epistolae* 5; Karolini Aevi 3, 1899).

[19] "Silvesterlegende," p. 535 and n. 47. Fuhrmann, in *DA* 30 (1975), 556, assumes that *LC* II.16 (p. 76.10), a quotation from Ambrose, *De fide* I.7, offers "dieselbe Phrase." This assumption is not borne out by the text he has cited whose phraseology has no relation to the "personal style" of the *LC* author's *in picturę fucis* in *LC* II.13 and III.18 referred to.

omnem auxilii sui spem in imaginibus defigant, non mediocriter a sancta et universali dissentiunt ecclesia, quae spem auxilii sui non *in picturę fucis*, non in manufactis artificum operibus. . . . " Quite significantly, *fucis* in this text is written *in loco raso*: it is the first of nineteen words written on an erasure. This text is clearly visible on the facsimile of fol. 158a of the *Vaticanus Latinus 7207* (Plate IV) referred to below in Chapter VIII at n. 6. Since chapter 13, in all probability, was inserted into Book II of the *LC after* the arrival at the Frankish court of the *Hadrianum* (*JE* 2483), that is some time during 791,[20] it is hardly possible to determine whether the instance that produced in *LC* III.18 the writing of *fucis* and eighteen additional words on an erasure (after the deletion of the original first version of the text), coincides with the insertion of *LC* II.13 and its *in picturę fucis* (p. 73.10f.), or to determine which of the two occurrences of *in picturę fucis* precedes the other.

In order to round out the possible connection of the text under discussion with other documents, a word must be said about the *Actus Silvestri* and *JE* 2483, the *Hadrianum*, repeatedly mentioned above. Bastgen (p. 73 n. 1) properly states that the chapter heading of *LC* II.13 does not have a corresponding text in the *Hadrianum*, as is the case for numerous other chapter headings of the treatise. *JE* 2448 introduces the excerpt from the *Actus Silvestri* after the lemma (Mansi XII.1057D6–9): "In ipsis enim exordiis Christianorum, cum ad fidem converteretur pius imperator Constantinus, sic legitur. . . . " The *Hadrianum* I.53 uses the same words, "In ipsis enim exordiis cristianorum, cum ad fidem converteretur imperator Constantinus,"[21] in order to introduce a paraphrase of the text in the *Actus Silvestri* relating the attendance of the Empress Helena at Pope Silvester's disputation with Jews.[22] Her presence is mentioned

---

[20] See W. von den Steinen, "Entstehungsgeschichte der Libri Carolini," *QF* 21 (1929–30), 61.

[21] See n. 18, ed. K. Hampe, p. 39.26f.; Hampe overlooked the identical lemma in *JE* 2448 and 2483. The lemma in *JE* 2483 should have been printed in italics.

[22] Cf. A. Ehrhardt, "Constantine, Rome and Rabbis," *Bulletin of the John Rylands Library Manchester* 42 (1959), 288–312. Chapter VII is referred to by Horst Fuhrmann, *Einfluss und Verbreitung der pseudoisidorischen Fälschungen* II (Schriften der *MGH*, 24.2; Stuttgart, 1973), 387 n. 78; cf. also Fuhrmann, "Das frühmittelalterliche Papsttum und die Konstantinische Schenkung," in: *I problemi dell' Occidente nel secolo VIII* (Settimane di studio del centro italiano di studi sull' alto medioevo XX; Spoleto, 1973), 285 n. 62. On the secondhand nature of the reference to the *Actus Silvestri* in the *LC* II.13 see above n. 14.

in *JE* 2483 as a precedent in order to justify the uncanonical participation of a woman—Empress Irene—in the activities of II Nicaea, 787.

The relationship between the *Libri Carolini* and the excerpt from the *Actus Silvestri* inserted among the testimonia of image-worship in Hadrian I's *Synodica* of 785 (*JE* 2448) may be summarized as follows:

JE 2448 cites Constantine's conversion episode in the A version of the *Actus Silvestri*. *LC* II.13 neither refers to, nor quotes from, the *Actus Silvestri* directly, but depends entirely on the excerpt in Hadrian's *Synodica*. The latter was accessible to the author of the *LC* in its Latin original that had been inserted into the first Latin translation of the Greek *Acta* of II Nicaea produced by a Roman ecclesiastic probably during 788. There is no direct or any indirect relationship between the *LC* and the *Constitutum Constantini*, paragraphs 7–8, which uses the same section of the *Actus Silvestri* as does *JE* 2448, the source of *LC* II.13. Some similarities in phraseology between the *Constantine Donation* and the *LC* are readily understandable on the basis of the same source used in both writings, and the identical subject matter dealt with, namely, the dream of Constantine.

PART THREE

Theodulph of Orléans' Alleged Authorship of the *Libri Carolini*: On Fictions and Facts

The view that Theodulph of Orléans is the author of the *Libri Carolini* was convincingly disproved by Donatien de Bruyne in 1932[1] when he revealed the fallacies in Arthur Allgeier's study of 1926 on the Mozarabic origin of quotations from the Psalms occurring in the *LC*.[2] Though Wolfram von den Steinen[3] adopted the view of Theodulph's authorship of the *LC* in the wake of Allgeier's disproved suggestion, he himself never offered his own proof, as he had promised to do.[4] His long-held assumption that a silent borrowing in *LC* III.3 (pp. 111.7−112.2) from one of Pseudo-Vigilius of Thapsus' treatises presumably lends support to his thesis of a Visigothic authorship of the *LC* lacked from the very beginning any factual basis, as I have pointed out toward the end of Chapter IV at note 100. In 1957, Ann Freeman renewed von den Steinen's thesis,[5] listing twenty Bible quotations from the four books of the *LC* for whose formulations certain Mozarabic antiphonary texts were cited as underlying sources: ten examples are listed for *LC* I,

---

[1] Donatien de Bruyne, "La composition des Libri Carolini," *Revue Bénédictine* 44 (1932), 227–234.

[2] Arthur Allgeier, "Psalmenzitate und die Frage nach der Herkunft der Libri Carolini," *Historisches Jahrbuch der Görresgesellschaft* 46 (1926), 333–353; cf. the note in the *Revue d'histoire ecclésiastique* 23 (1927), 148f.

[3] "Entstehungsgeschichte der Libri Carolini," *QF* 21 (1929–30), 1–93; "Karl der Grosse und die Libri Carolini," *Neues Archiv* 49 (1932), 207–280. On the disproof of von den Steinen's thesis see below Chapter XIII and Fichtenau, cited in Chapter XVI n. 6.

[4] Cf. M. Cappuyns in *Bulletin de théologie ancienne et médiévale* 2 (1933–36), 265.

[5] "Theodulf of Orléans and the Libri Carolini," *Speculum* 32 (1957), 663–705.

three for II, six for III, and one for IV. The present writer stated in 1959 that Freeman's view is untenable,[6] and in 1961 published a refutation under the title "The Unknown Author of the *Libri Carolini*: Patristic Exegesis, Mozarabic Antiphons, and the *Vetus Latina*."[7] In 1965, Freeman replied to my study in *Didascaliae* with her "Further Studies in the *Libri Carolini*,"[8] which is discussed below in Chapters X, XI, XII. The opinions of A. E. Mayer, Heinrich Fichtenau, M. Cappuyns, and Heinrich Weisweiler concerning the controversy are listed in my book *Alcuin and Charlemagne* (2nd amended printing).[9] Merely because the *LC* seems to contain a few so-called "Spanish Symptoms" in the form of some Bible texts whose identical version also appears in a certain Mozarabic service book one can hardly maintain that Theodulph is the author of the *LC*. Most of the so-called Mozarabic Bible texts are, in any event, of non-Mozarabic origin, or else occur not only in the Mozarabic rite, but also in the Frankish rite, as will be shown in detail below in Chapters X and XI. The few "Spanish Symptoms"[10] actually visible in the context of the *LC* are not sufficient evidence for the belief that the author of the *LC* was a Visigoth, and therefore Theodulph of Orléans.[11] Their occurrence in the *Vaticanus Latinus 7207*, which is written throughout in the Caroline minuscule by four scribes who use Visigothic abbreviation signs and some Visigothic spellings, is easily understandable historically, but does not speak for a Visigothic author at work.

Visigothic Spain contributed to the South of the Frankish kingdom during the eighth and ninth centuries its manuscripts and its Visigothic scribes, as it had done before the Arabic invasion.[12] We

---

[6] *Alcuin and Charlemagne: Studies in Carolingian History and Literature* (Cornell Studies in Classical Philology, 32; Ithaca, N.Y., 1959), 170 n. 50; amended reprint (New York, London, 1968), 170 n. 50.

[7] In *Didascaliae: Studies in Honor of Anselm M. Albareda*, ed. Sesto Preto (New York, 1961), 469–515; see Georges Mathon in *Bulletin de théologie ancienne et médiévale* 10 (1966), 152f. no. 450.

[8] *Speculum* 40 (1965), 223–286.

[9] New York and London, 1968, p. 177.

[10] On these "Symptoms" see Louis Brou, *Hispania Sacra* 7 (1954), 27–45; Leo Eizenhöfer, *Sacris Erudiri* 4 (1952), 27; and Klaus Gamber, *Sacris Erudiri* 12 (1961), 28.

[11] About Theodulph see below Chapter XII.

[12] Cf. Emile Lesne, *Histoire de la propriété ecclésiastique en France* vol. IV: *Les livres, scriptoria et bibliothèques* (Lille, 1938), 72–75, who cites numerous manuscripts.

know, for instance, of Visigothic scribes who during the ninth
century corrected and supplemented a damaged half-uncial manuscript from the seventh century of Origen's *Homilies* in the library
of the Visigoth Leidrad of Lyon, the codex Lugdunensis 443.[13] The
settlements of the Visigothic population in the Frankish provinces
of Aquitania and Septimania, at times belonging to the Visigothic
kingdom of Spain, account for the presence of a variety of Mozarabic
service books in these regions, whose remnants are coming to light
more and more, as Louis Brou has shown.[14] Witnesses of such a
Visigothic background and influence in the South of the Frankish
kingdom are, for instance, Alban Dold's manuscript called a
"Schabcodex";[15] the palimpsest fragments of a *Liber Commicus* of
the codex Paris, B.N. lat. 2269, investigated by Anscari M. Mundó;[16]
the Spanish litanies adapted in Septimania during the eighth and
ninth centuries, now published by Michel Huglo,[17] and others.[18]
The few "Spanish Symptoms" in the *LC*, perhaps as few as five
instances (see at the end of Chapter XI, V, g), may be looked
upon as peripheral manifestations of the wider Visigothic cultural
background surviving in Charlemagne's kingdom. On Visigothic
background see the opinion of Bonifatius Fischer referred to at the
end of section E of Chapter X, that of Bernhard Bischoff listed in
Chapter X, E at note 16, and that of E. A. Lowe, as quoted in
Chapter XI, section A.

New paleographical studies of the *Vaticanus* of the *LC* undertaken
by the present writer in connection with the preparation of the future

[13] Cf. W. A. Baehrens, *Ueberlieferung und Textgeschichte der lateinisch erhaltenen
Origineshomilien zum Alten Testament* (*TU* 42.1; Leipzig, 1916), 10–14; E. A. Lowe,
Codices Lugdunenses Antiquissimi (Lyons, 1924), 37.

[14] "Le IVe livre d'Esdras dans la liturgie hispanique et le graduel Roman *Locus
iste* de la Messe de la Dédicace," *Sacris Erudiri* 9 (1957), 104–107.

[15] *Das Sakramentar im Schabkodex M 12 der Bibliotheca Ambrosiana* (Texte und
Arbeiten 1.43; Beuron, 1952).

[16] "El Commicus Palimpsest Paris lat. 2269: amb notes sobre litúrgia i manuscrits
visigòtics a Septimània i Catalunya," in *Liturgica: Cardinali I. A. Schuster in Memoriam*
I (Scripta et Documenta 7; Montserrat, 1956), 151–175.

[17] "Les *Preces* des Graduels Aquitains empruntées à la Liturgie Hispanique,"
Hispania Sacra 8 (1955), 361–383.

[18] Listed by Jorge M. Pinell, "Boletín de Liturgia Hispano-Visigótica, 1949–
1956," *Hispania Sacra* 9 (1956), 405–428; cf. in addition Pinell, "Los textos de la
antigua liturgia hispánica—fuentes para su estudio," in *Estudios sobre la liturgia
mozárabe*, ed. Juan Francisco Rivera Recio (Toledo, 1965), 109–164.

critical edition of the work[19] deal with the origins of the codex in Chapters VIII, IX, and XIII. The discovery of numerous unknown sources used by the author of the *LC* without any indication of their actual provenance[20] is recorded not only in the preceding Chapters I–VII, but also throughout the Chapters VIII–XIV. These new materials determine decisively the genesis of the *LC*'s textual transmission through the *Vaticanus Lat. 7207*, and thus enable us to comprehend in greater detail and depth the role of the codex as the archetype of the *Libri Carolini*. These critical results go beyond Bastgen's recension of the *LC* text, and as such contribute not only to the negation of von den Steinen's notion that Theodulph of Orléans was the author of the work, but in addition also to the negation of von den Steinen's thesis that the *Vaticanus'* marginalia transcribed in Tironian notes represent Charlemagne's personal comments on certain passages in the *LC*. In the meantime von den Steinen himself has abandoned this view, which Heinrich Fichtenau had convincingly refuted independently on valid grounds, as is shown in detail below in Chapter XIII.

---

[19] I have not dealt with the initials of the Vatican codex, which should be investigated by a historian of medieval art. Bastgen, *Neues Archiv* 37 (1912), 50, mentions Haseloff's opinion concerning the straight Merovingian character of the initials. See below Epilogue to Part III.

[20] Previously listed newly discovered sources are listed in Wallach, *The Classical Tradition* (1966), 498 n. 101, and also in the first publication of Chapters I–VII.

CHAPTER VIII

The *Vaticanus Latinus 7207* and Paleographical Problems

The *Vaticanus Latinus 7207* (*V*) served as the basis of Hubert Bastgen's critical edition of the *Libri Carolini*.[1] His *apparatus criticus* naturally lists the many scribal corrections, erasures, and deletions of *V* and records in the margin of his edition, from p. 9.5 to p. 169.22,[2] the foliation fol. 3–fol. 192 of the Vatican codex. Von den Steinen refers to the fact that Bastgen[3] in *Neues Archiv* 37 (1911/12), 483f., lists erasures in the text of *V* for *LC* I.9, I.17, II.31, and III.21, which are not recorded in Bastgen's edition. Freeman[4] believed that *V* was in need of a new paleographical investigation because Bastgen "did not undertake" it; she states in *Speculum* 40 (1965), 205 n. 10, that "Bastgen treats it in two pages, *Neues Archiv* 37 (1912), 48 49, containing much misinformation, especially on MS hands." But Bastgen[5] deals in *Neues Archiv* 37 (1912), 29–34, with the *LC*'s only completely preserved manuscript, namely, Paris, Bibliothèque de l'Arsenal lat. 663 (subsequently always referred to as "A"); he proved on pp. 34–38 that A is a copy of *V* written when the *Vaticanus* was still unimpaired, and Bastgen's pp. 38–51 are entitled by him "Der Codex der Bibl. Vaticana 7207." In all these sections, variant

---

[1] *MGH, Legum Sectio III: Conc. 2*, Supplementum (Hannover, Leipzig, 1924).

[2] "Entstehungsgeschichte der *Libri Carolini*," 21 (1929–30), 5 n. 1.

[3] "Das Capitulare Karls d. Gr. über die Bilder oder die sogenannten Libri Carolini," III, *Neues Archiv* 37 (1912), paragraph 9, pp. 475ff.

[4] "Further Studies in the *Libri Carolini*," *Speculum* 40 (1965), 203–286.

[5] See title above in n. 3.

readings of *V* and many of its characteristics and peculiarities are discussed, often in their basic relationship to A. Freeman follows Bastgen closely when she says in her "Palaeographical Problems in Vaticanus Latinus 7207," *Speculum* 40 (1965), 218, "ten lines are cancelled on f. 163v (so Bastgen, p. 145h) and nine on fol. 189–190 (so Bastgen, p. 167f.). An enormous hole interrupts the text on fol. 158." This hole is not mentioned by Bastgen. Upon inquiry, I was informed through the good offices of the Rev. Sac. Alfonso Stickler, S.D.B., Prefect of the Biblioteca Apostolica Vaticana, that the hole is neither enormous nor does it interrupt the text of the *LC*; he states: " . . . un foro, il quale, però, non è enorme, nè interrompe il testo."[6] The attached facsimiles of fol. 158 *a* and *b* of *V*, Plates IV–V, generously supplied by the Vatican Library, show a small, oval-shaped hole and a text of the *LC* which is not interrupted by it. This means that the hole existed in the parchment before a scribe wrote on it the text of the *LC*, f. 158, *recto* and *verso*. Freeman's description of *V* culminates in a Diagram. Comparison of this Diagram with Bastgen's *Tabelle* of the gatherings and missing leaves is self-explanatory. Compare:

Bastgen, *Neues Archiv* 37 (1912), 32–33:   Freeman, *Speculum* 40 (1965), 206:

	Cod. Vat. 7207			Gathering Marked	No. of Folia	Contains Fol.	Scribe
Lagen	Seiten	Blätter					
	fehlt			(i lost)			
I							
II	10			ii	8	3–10	
III	11–18	8		iii	8	11–18	
IV	19–26	8		iv	8	19–26	
V	27–34	8	I	v	8	27–34	Hand 1
VI	35–42	8		vi	8	35–42	
VII	43–50	8		vii	8	43–50	
VIII	51–58	8		viii	8	51–58	

[6] I am indebted to the Biblioteca Apostolica Vaticana through the good offices of its Prefect, Rev. Alfonso Stickler, for the following information kindly communicated to me under the date of September 21, 1973, together with photographs (Plates IV and V) of fol. 158 *a* and *b*: " . . . il f. 158 del Vat. lat. 7207 ha realmente un foro, il quale, però, non è enorme, nè interrompe il testo, poichè si è prodotto per naturale lacerazione durante la preparazione della pergamena ed è, pertanto, preesistente allo scritto."

Bastgen, *Neues Archiv* 37 (1912), 32–33 :   Freeman, *Speculum* 40 (1965), 206:

Cod. Vat. 7207		
Lagen	Seiten	Blätter
IX	59–65	8¹
X	66–73	8
XI	74–81	8
XII (I)	82–89	8
XIII (II)	90–95	6
XIV (III)	96–100	6²
XV (IV)	101–108	8
XVI (V)	109–116	3
XVII (VI)	117–124	8
XVIII (VII)	125–132	8
XIX (VIII)	133–140	8
XX (IX)	141–146	6
XXI (X)	147–154	8
XXII (XI)	155–162	8
XXIII (XII)	163–170	8
XXIV (I)	171–178	8
XXV (II)	179–186	8
XXVI (III)	187–192	6*

	Gathering Marked	No. of Folia	Contains Fol.	Scribe
II	ix	7	59–65	}Hand 1
	x	8	66–73	}Hand 2
	xi	8	74–81	}Hand 3
	?			
	i	8	82–89	
	ii	6	90–95	>Hand 4
	iii	5	96–100	
	iv	8	101–108	
III	v	8	109–116	}Hand 1
	vi	8	117–124	
	vii	8	125–132	
	viii	8	133–140	}Hand 4
	ix	6	141–146	
	x	8	147–154	
	xi	8	155–162	
	xii	8	163–170	>Hand 1
	i	8	171–178	
	ii	8	179–186	
	iii	6	187–192	

¹ Ein Blatt ist ausgeschnitten.
² Auch von dieser Lage ist ein Blatt ausgeschnitten.
* [L.W.'s addition: Cf. Bastgen's edition of the *LC*, p. 169.25, fol. 192r.]

[I have omitted the last column of the Diagram, referring to the initials in *V*—L.W.]

The first and the last item in this Diagram are incorrectly listed. Folios 3–10 of the second gathering of *V* are ascribed to the hand of the first scribe, but the first page of f.3 is written on erasures in a gothic minuscule, saec. XIII. Bastgen, *Neues Archiv* 37 (1912), 48–49, properly recognized this fact; he lists it in his edition of *LC*, p. 9 note *a*. The same circumstances apply to the last item in the Diagram: also fol. 191v and fol. 192r (p. 169.25 errorem, Bastgen) are written on erasures in the same gothic minuscule, saec. XIII, as is stated by Bastgen, and further recorded in his edition, p. 169 note *a*. Both items mark the mutilation of *V* which resulted, on the one hand, in the loss of the Preface to the *LC*, of the table of contents of *LC* I, and of part of *LC* I.1 (up to p. 9.5, Bastgen), on the other hand, in the loss of *LC* IV (pp. 169.28–228.11), including the last five words of *LC* III.31 (p. 169.25–26), and the "Explicit Liber

Tertius." Freeman fails to record the important fact that in the seventeenth quaternion of *V*, between folia 117 and 118, two original folia are excised, as Bastgen reports in his edition, p. 106 note *a*. The present writer referred to those two excised original leaves in *V* in *Alcuin and Charlemagne* (1959), 173.

Paleographical and source-critical improvements to Bastgen's edition have been contributed by von den Steinen and de Bruyne and by the present writer throughout this volume. Freeman offers in *Speculum* 40 (1965), 287–289, a list of "apparent" emendations to Bastgen's edition, whose actual nature is discussed in this chapter's last section D below. But the literary genesis of the *LC* is much more complicated than Freeman has realized. Only when the underlying sources of the *LC* text are fully perceived can a firm coordination be established between those sources and a paleographical analysis of the Vatican codex. I give three examples of this.

A. In the ninth quaternion, fol. 59–65 in *V*, one folium of its eight original leaves is missing, a fact already noticed by Bastgen, *Neues Archiv* 37 (1912), 33 n. 1: "Ein Blatt ist ausgeschnitten." Freeman, *Speculum* 40 (1965), 208f., assumes a compression of materials in *LC* I.29 (pp. 57–59), necessitated by the excision of the missing second half of fol. 61 (between fol. 63–64). She cannot find a break in the context of the *LC* because there is none, as we shall see in a moment. She states that the ninth gathering contains a long passage on fol. 62 and 63 "which is apparently uncorrected," although Bastgen records for p. 57 the corrections *d–g*, and for p. 58 the corrections *a–e*. In addition she conjectures that this passage with its elaborate allegory was inserted "into the heart of the quire" by "editors," and does not belong to the *LC*'s original text, but to a second edition of the *LC*. But these assumptions are disproved by the discovery that the source underlying *LC* I.29 (pp. 57–59) is Origen, *In Exodum, homilia IX, De tabernaculo*, especially IX.3–4, *passim*.[7] The corrections in *V*, on fol. 62–63, listed by Bastgen, are now easily explained on the basis of Origen's text. That the corrector of the *LC* endeavors to restore in the *LC* Origen's anonymously cited words is shown below in Chapter IX, C–C2.

---

[7] Ed. W. A. Baehrens, *Homilien zum Hexateuch in Rufins Uebersetzung: Origenes Werke* VI (*GCS*; Leipzig, 1920), 240–243, *passim*.

Also the statement in *Speculum* 40 (1965), 209, that fol. 64 launches into "videlicet sancti praedicatores (*LC* I.29, p. 57.7–12) with which the chapter resumes and concludes" is nullified by the underlying source, namely, Origen, *In Ex. homilia* IX.4 (p. 243.16–22, *passim*, Baehrens). Since the passage (p. 57.13–18) following the former in *LC* I.29 also is derived from Origen's *homilia* (p. 243.22–29, *passim*), Origen turns out to be the source of *LC* I.29 for almost half of fol. 64r. Freeman's assumption that the bifolium 62–63 was inserted into the ninth gathering in order to replace original materials discarded by "editors" and that it represents "a second version" of the *LC* is not borne out by the source underlying *LC* I.29, which, in addition to fol. 62–63, also covers part of the text of fol. 64r, and therefore voids all her conjectures. This fact proves that paleographical assumptions can by no means be used for the drawing of conclusions concerning the nature of a writing's context. Origen's homilies were well known to the author of the *LC* and were used in other chapters of the work. We recall that Origen, *In Ex. homilia* XIII.3 (pp. 274.21–275.7, *passim*) is cited verbatim in *LC* I.17 (p. 40.15–21),[8] and that Donatien de Bruyne pointed to Origen, *In Ex. homilia* XIII.2 (pp. 270f.) for *LC* I.16 (p. 39.13–23, *passim*).[9] The name of Origen is nowhere mentioned in the *LC* because the *Decretum Gelasianum*,[10] which provided the author of the work with a list of canonically approved and disapproved writings, rejects Origen, and only a few of his works were deemed acceptable upon Jerome's recommendation. This circumstance may explain the reason why the words from *Et* to *cum* in *LC* I.29 (p. 57.13–14), "Et idcirco in plerisque Scripturae sanctae locis, cum domus dei legitur . . . ," are written *in loco raso* (Bastgen, p. 57.42a): the words replace in all probability an original reference to Origen's homily, which is extensively quoted in *LC* I.29.

B. What is said about quaternion XI with its eight folia, namely, 74–81, containing the last section of *LC* II.5, and *LC* II.6 up to the first part of *LC* II.16 (Bastgen, p. 75.35), again fails to coordinate the *LC* context written on these sixteen pages of *V* with the literary

---

[8] So Wallach, *The Classical Tradition* (1966), 498 n. 101.

[9] "La composition des *Libri Carolini*," *Revue Bénédictine* 44 (1932), 229.

[10] Ernst von Dobschütz, ed., *Das Decretum Gelasianum* (*TU* 38.4; Leipzig, 1912), 280.

genesis of the *LC*. Freeman states: "We should take special note of the relationship of the contents of this quire (XI) to Hadrian I's *responsio* (*JE* 2483). Of its eleven chapters, four are not treated by Hadrian and presumably were not seen by him until the final, finished version of the *LC* came, with an episcopal delegation to Rome" (*Speculum* 40, 1965, 210f.). These four chapters are *LC* II.11, 13, 15, 16[11]; she also refers to *LC* II.17, which appears in the next gathering XII, which in *V* is numbered "I." Her following remark that "Hadrian might have enlightened them, had this capitulum been placed before him in the preliminary list," that is, in the so-called *Capitulare adversus Synodum*, cited in *JE* 2483, presupposes that Hadrian I is ready to criticize his own texts, since the four *LC* chapters are quoted in the *LC* after Hadrian I's *Synodica* of 785 (*JE* 2448), as I shall show subsequently. It is rather clear that the four *LC* chapters "are not treated" by Hadrian in *JE* 2483 (of about 791), not because he did not see them "until the final finished version of the *LC*" arrived at Rome, but because Hadrian himself in *JE* 2448 of 785 had already cited these four texts in support of image-worship.

1. *LC* II.11 (p. 71.27–30), "Erit altare Domini in medio terrae Egypti" (Isa. 19.19). Bastgen, p. 71 n. 2, properly refers to *JE* 2448, addressed to the Byzantine emperors, Mansi XII.1065B7–8, as the source of Isa. 19.19. This text is not discussed in the *Hadrianum* (*JE* 2483), and therefore presumably did not occur in the *Capitulare adversus Synodum*, whose *capitula* are otherwise cited in *JE* 2483.

2. *LC* II.13 (p. 72.40–73.2), concerning Pope Sylvester and Constantine the Great. The text is not cited in the *Hadrianum* because it did not occur in the *Capitulare adversus Synodum* (subsequently

---

[11] These facts can be easily established by following Bastgen's notes in his edition of the *LC*, and by a quick glance at von den Steinen's *Tabelle I* (p. 48), who corrected Bastgen's verifications of texts cited from the *First Latin Nicaenum* in the chapter headings of the *LC*. Von den Steinen's survey can be supplemented and corrected in some instances. I have shown in Chapter IV, H, and n. 43 that *LC* III.31 does not refer to Mansi XIII.194, but to XIII.62A, and that *Hadrianum* I.14 is to be found not *in actione quinta*, but *in actione quarta*. *LC* I.18 (p. 42.41–45), cites *JE* 2448, Mansi XII.1065A6–10 (and not Mansi XIII.167, as Bastgen assumed), and the *Hadrianum* I.26 (p. 27.29) identifies the origin of this text "in predictis sacris conciliis," that is, in the *Acta* of the Lateran Council of 769. Von den Steinen's *Tabelle* can be adjusted accordingly.

referred to as *CAS*). Bastgen, p. 73 n. 1, correctly refers as source to *JE* 2448, Mansi XII.1057D–1060C. See in detail Chapter VII above.

3. *LC* II.15 (p. 74.10–13), concerning a "falsified" Ambrose text. The text is not cited in the *Hadrianum* because it does not occur in the *CAS*. Bastgen, p. 74 n. 2, correctly refers to its source in *JE* 2448, Mansi XII.1068E–1069A2. On the unsolved textual problem see now Chapter V, above.

4. *LC* II.16 (p. 75.10–12), concerning an untraced *sententia* of Augustine. The text is not listed in the *Hadrianum* because it was not listed in the *CAS*. Bastgen correctly lists as source (p. 75 n. 2) *JE* 2448, Mansi XII.1065C. On the Augustinus text see Chapter II, D above, and the discussion under 2, to *LC* II.13. See also the treatment of *LC* II.16 under Chapter XI, B. I add here: although the middle of *LC* II.16 (fol. 81v in *V*), Bastgen, p. 75.34, marks the end of the eleventh quaternion, there is not any break in the context of the *LC*. Freeman's conjecture (p. 209 to Book II) that "at this point an entire gathering may be missing" is hardly correct. Further, Bastgen in *Neues Archiv* 37 (1912), 49, already correctly observed that twice the counting of the gatherings begins with a first quaternion, at *V* fol. 82 with the twelfth, and at fol. 171, with the twenty-fourth gathering, while the first quaternion (with the Preface and the *LC* text, Bastgen, pp. 1–9, 5a mutabilis) is missing in *V*.

5. The fifth chapter "not treated by Hadrian" (p. 210 n. 19) is *LC* II.17 (p. 76.35–37) on fol. 83r of *V*, belonging to the twelfth quaternion, which is marked as gathering I, as Bastgen noticed long ago in *Neues Archiv* 37 (1912), 33. The chapter deals with two testimonia by Gregory of Nyssa, both of them derived from Hadrian's *JE* 2448, though not directly dealt with in the *Hadrianum*, since they obviously did not appear in the *CAS*. I have investigated the Greek and Latin transmissions of both texts in Chapter IV, I and K. Unknown to Freeman, the first Gregory testimonium, cited in *JE* 2448, Mansi XII.1065C–D, is indeed referred to in the context of the *Hadrianum* I.37 (p. 33.9), as I pointed out in Chapter IV, section I. It is cited in *JE* 2483 after the *First Latin Nicaenum*, and it reads: "Sanctus Cyrillus Alexandrinus et sanctus Gregorius Nisenus uno tenore in istoria Abrahae pro sacris imaginibus veneratione dixerunt." This is a translation of the following passage in the

Greek *Acta* of II Nicaea, Mansi XIII.13A: . . . Κυρίλλος <u>σύμφωνα</u> τῷ ἁγίῳ Γρηγορίῳ τῷ Νύσσης λέγει.

The preceding verifications of the sources in the *LC* chapters II.11, 13, 15, 16, 17 should make it clear that Hadrian I could hardly question in the *Hadrianum* (*JE* 2483) the texts he had cited in *JE* 2448 of 785, which in their turn were cited in the *LC* chapters. All this should answer the question why some of Hadrian's texts cited in the *LC* after *JE* 2448 do not occur in the *Hadrianum*, which provides his reply to the earlier (and now lost) Frankish *Capitulare adversus Synodum*, whose *capitula* are preserved in the chapter headings of *JE* 2483.[12] Hadrian I could not very well begin to doubt about 791 the very texts he had cited in 785 in support of image-worship. This also is the reason why Freeman[13] could not find the text of *LC* I.29, "Domine, dilexi decorem domus tue" (Ps. 25.8), "among the topics to which the pope [Hadrian I] replied [in the *Hadrianum*]." Since this Bible text is quoted from Hadrian's *Synodica* of 785 (*JE* 2448), Mansi XII.1065C1–2, "Domine dilexi decorem domus tuae, et locum tabernaculi gloriae tuae" (Ps. 25.8), Hadrian hardly could have criticized in the *Hadrianum* a text cited by himself in favor of image-worship. Freeman does not ask, in connection with the five chapter headings, why some texts cited by Hadrian, which are identical with those cited in *JE* 2448, are indeed treated in the *Hadrianum*. Such is the case, for instance, in *LC* II.14, not dealt with, although its text appears on fol. 80 of the eleventh gathering that she discusses.

The principle that explains the diversified treatment accorded to Hadrian's texts cited in the *LC* is to be found in the fact that the *Hadrianum* (*JE* 2483) preferably deals with those Hadrian texts that are ultimately derived from the lost *Acta* of the Lateran Council

---

[12] I refer to the characterization of these documents at the beginning of Chapter III, above; for *JE* 2448 see Chapters I and II.

[13] *Speculum* 40 (1965), 208 n. 14, where she speaks of the *Hadrianum* (*JE* 2483) as a papal reply to "a preliminary version of the *LC*," and states that it is "extant in several collections," which is incorrect. We have only Codex Vaticanus lat. 3827, s. X, on which Karl Hampe based his edition in *MGH, Epistolae* 5, 5–57. The other two MSS are late copies of the Vaticanus, and therefore are of no help; also the fragments of the B.M. Add. 8873, s. XII, contribute nothing to alleviate the bad transmission of the Vaticanus.

of 769, in which Frankish ecclesiastics had participated.[14] This fact can be shown, for example, also for *LC* II.14, and other chapter headings.

LC II.14 (p. 73f., Bastgen) on fol. 80 of *V* concerns a *sententia* by Athanasius of Alexandria which is cited after Hadrian's *Synodica* of 785, *JE* 2448, Mansi XII.1068D–E (see Chapter IV, N, above).

The *Hadrianum* I.34 (p. 31.31) tells us that this *sententia* is mentioned among other *sententiae* of Athanasius "in sacris conciliis predictorum predecessorum sanctissimorum pontificum." This means that the *LC*'s Athanasius text is ultimately, through the intermediary of *JE* 2448, derived from the *Acta* of the Lateran Council of 769, into whose synodal protocol those of the Roman Synod of 731 had been inserted (see Karl Hampe in his edition of the *Hadrianum*, p. 15 nn. 15 and 16). The *Hadrianum* I.34 refers to the *Acta* of the Lateran Council of 769, in which also other *sententiae* of Athanasius are cited.

In the same fashion and for the same reasons Hadrian's two pseudo-Chrysostomian texts in *JE* 2448 are cited in *LC* II.19 (p. 77), also the two texts from Cyril of Alexandria's lost *Commentary on Matthew* in *LC* II.20 (p. 79). Both doublets are treated in the *Hadrianum* because their texts in *JE* 2448 and *JE* 2483 are ultimately drawn from the lost *Acta* of the Lateran Council of 769.[15] The identical fragment from the *Acta* of the latter synod is quoted by Hadrian's redactor of *JE* 2448 without any indication of its origin in Mansi XII.1064E4–1065A13, while the redactor of the *Hadrianum* I.26 (pp. 27.30–28.1 Hampe) correctly cited the source of his texts in "sacris conciliis predecessorum meorum sanctissimorum pontificum," as I have shown in Chapter I, E, above. The same text from the *Acta* of 769 is cited in the chapter heading of *LC* I.18 (pp. 42.14–43.2) after *JE* 2448, Mansi XII.1065A6–10, while Bastgen mistakenly refers to Mansi XIII.167, as does also von den Steinen (*QF*, p. 48), whose *Tabelle* should be corrected as follows: "*LC* I.18—*Hadrianum* I.26—*Nicaenum*, actio II—Mansi XII.1065."

Freeman's further discussion (p. 211f.) of fol. 88v–89v, and her conclusions go, as I believe, too far, because the origins of the

---

[14] See Albert Werminghoff, in *MGH*, *Conc.* 2 (Aevi Karolini 1; Hannover, Leipzig, 1906–8), 74–92, who collected the fragments of the lost *Acta* of the Lateran Council of 769.

[15] Cf. in detail Chapter II, above, at the very end of the chapter.

chapter headings of *LC* II.23 and II.24 and the differences between their transmission and that of the *Hadrianum* I.50 (p. 37) were, as Freeman notes, properly worked out and correctly discussed by von den Steinen (*QF*, p. 62f.). The latter records Bastgen's earlier treatment in *Neues Archiv* 37 (1912), 484, concerning the splitting of the chapter headings in the *Capitulare adversus Synodum*. Freeman's discussion adds nothing save the insertion into the *Hadrianum* I.50 (p. 37) of the three words *Romanae urbis antestitis* (her p. 212, line 7). It is not true that "the *capitulum* now appearing as [LC] II.23 is quoted by Hadrian as follows,"[16] since the *Hadrianum* does not contain these three words. An editorial practice similar to the splitting of chapter headings in *LC* II.23–24, occurs, for example, toward the end of MS *V*. There a neat editorial deletion and splitting occurs on fol. 189v, in *LC* III.30 (Bastgen, p. 167). The text of the first redaction of the *LC* on p. 167, lines 37–42, is deleted in *V*, and the *LC* author's reference to this section, namely, "ut haec quae praemisimus" (p. 167.42–43), is properly removed by the author of the *LC*, since these words had lost their meaning within the context of the *LC*. Some words from the context of the deleted section are then used by the author of the *LC* for the formation of the next chapter heading, *LC* III.31 (pp. 167.34–35, 168.1–4), whose text is also listed among the *capitula* of the *Capitulare adversus Synodum*, since it appears in the *Hadrianum* I.14 (p. 20f.). But *LC* III.31 does not refer to Mansi XIII.194, in the *Acta* of II Nicaea, as Bastgen, p. 168 n. 1, records, but to a forged iconoclastic text of John Moschus, *Pratum spirituale*, c. 45, Mansi XIII.60D–61B, read during *actio* IV of the council, as I have shown in Chapter IV, H above.

C. Freeman's assumption that the chapter headings of the *LC* took their subject matter "directly from Scripture" reveals a grave misunderstanding of the *LC*'s literary genesis. Calvin had long ago recognized that the biblical texts in the *LC* are derived from the synodal *Acta* of II Nicaea of 787. Some of those *LC* texts are inserted by him into the Geneva edition of 1550 of his *Institutio christianae religionis* I, cap. XI, 14–16 (*Opera selecta* III, ed. P. Barth and Guilelmus Niesel, edit. sec. emendata; München, 1957, 101–105).

---

[16] See Karl Hampe, *MGH, Epistolae* 5 (Karolini Aevi 3; Berlin, 1899), 37.

He excerpted them from Jean du Tillet's *editio princeps* of the *LC* which was published in 1549.

a. Freeman mentions (p. 214) "this excursus of Scripture which extends from *LC* I.7 through *LC* II.12," and then states that "of the chapters whose subject matter is taken directly from Scripture, almost half concerned themselves with the Psalms." But contrary to her assumption, none of the *LC*'s 120 chapter headings takes its text "directly from Scripture." Von den Steinen's *Tabelle I* in *Quellen und Forschungen* 21 (1929–30), p. 48, lists for about 100 of those headings the respective passages quoted from, or referring to, the *Acta* of II Nicaea in Mansi XII–XIII, following and supplementing the identifications offered by Bastgen in his *LC* edition. The origin of some of the remaining headings can be easily ascertained. There is, for example, *LC* III.12 (p. 125.3–4), "Quod magna ex parte consuetudinem et patientiam abiecerint in non continendo os suum et inordinate loquendo," whose origin is readily determined on the basis of Bastgen's comments. It evidently mirrors the chapter headings of the fifth-century biblical florilegium *De divinis scripturis* (*CSEL* XII; 1887), ch. 35, "De mansuetudine"; ch. 36, "De patientia"; ch. 51, "De continentia oris." The *Decretum Gelasianum* provides the text for *LC* I.6, an Augustinian writing the one for *LC* I.8. Gregory I's *Registrum* supplies the contents of the heading of *LC* II.23. A text similar to the heading for *LC* II.24, which is paralleled neither by the lost *Capitulare adversus Synodum* nor by the *Hadrianum* (*JE* 2483), appears nevertheless in the *First Latin Nicaenum*, as is evident from Bastgen's seven references to the *Acta* of II Nicaea.

Other chapter headings are dealt with elsewhere in the present work. For *LC* I.18 see Chapter II, section U; for *LC* III.2, which is not identified in von den Steinen's tabulation, compare above Chapter I,D.

b. The many occurrences in the *Acta* of II Nicaea of Basil of Caesarea's often-repeated *sententia* which in *LC* III.6 appears also as a chapter heading are recorded in Chapter IV, section L. All the scriptural passages occurring in the *LC*'s chapter headings are secondhand quotations, or even thirdhand quotations. The latter type is represented by those scriptural quotations which are derived from Hadrian I's *Synodica* of 785 (*JE* 2448), such as the following cited from Mansi XII.1065C: *LC* I.23 citing Ps. 4.7 and Ps. 26.8; *LC* I.24 citing Ps. 44.13; *LC* I.29 citing Ps. 25.8; and *LC* II.11 citing Isa. 19.19 from Mansi XII.1065B7–8. Thirdhand scriptural quotations in the chapter headings of the *LC* are also those texts cited from Leontius' *sermo* v, inserted into the *Acta* of II Nicaea (Mansi XIII.43–54),[17] namely, in *LC* I.9—Gen. 23.7 and *Exod.* 18.7; I.12—cf. Gen. 37.33; I.13—Gen. 47.31;[18] I.14—cf. Gen. 47.10; I.21—*Ios.* 4.7; II.5—Ps. 98.5; II.6—Ps. 98.9; II.9—cf. 3. Reg. 7.29. The largest number of secondhand scriptural quotations in the context of the *LC* is accounted for by those drawn from the pseudo-Augustinian *Liber de divinis scripturis*, ed. Fr. Weihrich (*CSEL* 12; Vienna, 1887), a discovery made by Donatien de Bruyne,[19] and adopted by Hubert Bastgen in his edition of 1924. Numerous other secondhand scriptural texts were inserted into the context of the *LC* in the form of passages drawn from Cassiodorus' *Expositio Psalmorum*, from the writings of Origen, Augustine, Ambrose, Jerome, Ambrosiaster,[20] Isidore of Seville, and the Venerable Bede.

c. The pseudo-Augustinian rhetorical style which, in *Speculum* 40 (1965), 235–237, is ascribed to *LC* II.30, the longest chapter of the *LC* (pp. 92–100), covering an entire gathering and two folia of the following quaternion in *V*, fol. 101–113v, represents a very definite literary influence adopted by the author of the *LC* on the basis of his thoroughgoing acquaintance with Ambrose's nine dogmatic treatises dedicated to Emperor Gratian, as I have shown in Chapter V. The characterization of *LC* II.30 presented in *Speculum* 40, p. 215, is untenable. We are told, "with this new gathering [IV] begins a new chapter (II.30) and new series . . . of *sententiae*, quoted from

[17] See the third part of Chapter V, above.

[18] See my correction of Bastgen's text in Chapter III, C, above. Also the reference to *JE* 2448, Mansi XII.1064B–C.

[19] "La composition des Libri Carolini," *Revue Bénédictine* 44 (1932), 227, who says with some resignation, "Bastgen promit . . . de me remercier dans sa préface. . . . Quant à la préface, elle ne parle pas de mon petit service." De Bruyne also disproved Arthur Allgeier's mistaken assumption ("Psalmenzitate und die Frage nach der Herkunft der Libri Carolini," *Historisches Jahrbuch der Görresgesellschaft* 46 [1926], 333–353), that the *LC* used Mozarabic Psalter texts, by calling attention—as it seems in vain—to the *De divinis scripturis* as the *LC*'s source of alleged "Mozarabic" Bible quotations! See Ernst Nellessen cited in Chapter VI n. 2 and Walter Thiele referred to in Chapter XII n. 2.

[20] See Chapter VI, above.

the prelates of the council." But the chapter heading of *LC* II.30 is not a *sententia*, nor is it quoted from the council's prelates. Bastgen (p. 92 n. 3) assigns the text to Mansi XIII.19 in the *Acta* of II Nicaea. But *LC* II.30 (p. 92.15–17), "Contra eos qui dicunt: 'Sicut divinae Scripture libros, ita imagines ob memoriam venerationis habemus nostre fidei puritatem observantes,'" is not quoted from Mansi XIII.19, but from Hadrian I's *Synodica* of 785 (*JE* 2448), which had been inserted in 787 into the synodal *Acta* of II Nicaea, *in actione secunda*, Mansi XII.1061D11–14: "Et sicut divinae Scripturae libros ipsas imagines ob memoriam venerationis habemus nostrae fidei puritatem observantes." Von den Steinen (*QF* 21 [1929–30], 48) corrected Bastgen's mistaken reference a few decades ago!

d. The cross-reference in *LC* I.29 (p. 58.31–32, Bastgen), fol. 63r in *V*, "de quibus superius in quodam capitulo disputatum est," cannot refer to *LC* I.19 and I.20, as is suggested in *Speculum* 40 (1965), 209 n. 17, because Bastgen's reference to *LC* I.15, p. 34.13 is quite correct, as is the one for *LC* I.20 (pp. 47.29f.), "sicut iam in superiore capitulo (i.e., *LC* I.15, p. 36.10 [and 35.33 f.]) exsequuti sumus." The cross-reference *"ut diximus"* in *LC* I.20 (p. 48.32), fol. 51r, however, is not by the author of the *LC*, and does not refer to *LC* I.15, but to *LC* I.20 (p. 47.1), since Bede, *De templo Salomonis* I, 1448,[21] anonymously cited in *LC* I.20, reads as follows: " . . . utrumque enim cherub, *ut diximus*, et angelos *videlicet* [this is the unknown, erased word recorded by Bastgen, p. 48.43c: *7 litt. erasae in V*] et testamenta designant." The original two and one-third lines erased in *V* (Bastgen, p. 48.43d) can be restored after the underlying source, that is, after Bede, *De templo* I, 1448ff., "confestim . . . unde apte subditur" (3. *Reg.* 6.29). The restoration of the erased text of *LC* I.20 with the help of Bede's *De templo Salomonis* is mentioned in *Speculum* 40 (1965), 281 n. 300. For more on Herbert Schade's discovery concerning Bede and the *LC* see below in Chapter XII, E, 2.

[21] Ed. David Hurst, in *Bedae Venerabilis Opera II, 2A, CCL* 119A (1969). Hurst's reference (p. 181) to Bede, *De templo Salomonis* I, 1355, for *LC* I.20 is inaccurate. We must read I, 1342ff. for *LC* I.20 (pp. 46.26ff.–48.32), plus the two and one-third lines erased at the very end of *LC* I.20 which now can be restored. Altogether overlooked by Hurst is *LC* I.20, p. 47.1–5, the definition of *cherubim* derived from *De templo* I, 1269ff., which should be listed among the testimonia. See, furthermore, below Chapters IX n. 11 and XII n. 47.

The conclusions arrived at with regard to the production of *V* as outlined in *Speculum* 40 (1965), 221–222, cannot stand critical analysis. There is no proof in the codex supporting the assumptions that the writing of *V* was "accompanied by almost continuous discussion," and that it is "a palace product, the work of royal scribes." The detailed philological analysis I shall give in Chapter IX, A–H, clearly indicates the philological origin of the corrections in *V*. The same analysis also contradicts the final assumption made by Freeman without any supporting evidence that it was decided in some still unknown scriptorium that "the MS. now known as Vaticanus lat. 7207 should not be presented to Pope Hadrian in Rome." To be sure, we know that Hincmar of Reims reports about a codex of the *LC* sent by Charlemagne to Rome (*PL* 126.360),[22] which certainly was not identical with the *Vaticanus*. In 1934 the paleographer E. A. Lowe (*CLA* I No. 52) knew little about the origin of *V*; he stated briefly that it was written "probably north of the Alps." By 1955 he had hardly changed his mind concerning the provenance of the codex when he told Freeman that he still felt *V* to have come from "one of the better German monasteries" (see below Chapter IX n. 2).

D. Since the apparent "Emendations to the *MGH* text" of the *LC* in *Speculum* 40 (1965), 287–289, are mentioned at the very beginning of the present chapter, the indicated reservation requires the discussion of a number of shortcomings which are connected with these emendations. The faulty paleographical description of a fragment from a lost Corbie manuscript of the *LC* of the ninth century is corrected below, p. 202, in connection with the treatment of the manuscript transmission of the *LC*. The list of "emendations" does not present actual emendations which depend on decisions involving a choice between various manuscript readings that are based on philological deliberations concerning grammar, syntax, and textual contents. We are told that the emendations consist of "errors of transcription" occurring in Bastgen's edition which resulted from the collation of his text with the two manuscripts *V* and *A*, which are the basis of his text. But the list of these errors does not show any evidence of the compiler's critical approach concerning the *LC* text's *recensio*, its *emendatio*, and the *eliminatio codicum descriptorum*

---

[22] Cf. *Speculum* 32 (1957), 664f.; 40 (1965), 205.

after the generally accepted system of Paul Maas's *Textual Criticism* (tr. by B. Flower; Oxford, 1958).

The readings of A listed in *Speculum* 40 (1965), 287–289, from *LC*, p. 11.46 to p. 168.27, should have been omitted, because A was copied from the archetype of the *LC*, MS *V*, when the latter was still unimpaired, and all these A readings are basically preserved in *V*. Only those A readings should have been listed that are preserved for those parts of *V* that are no longer extant, that means the readings of *A* for *LC*, p. 2.23 to p. 9.3, and those for *LC*, pp. 169.35 to 226.11. In addition, these "emendations" naturally appear for the most part in earlier printed editions of the *LC* that render the text of the MS A, such as the editions by Melchior Goldast von Haiminsfeld (Frankfurt, 1608 and 1615), which are basically reprints of Jean du Tillet's *editio princeps* of 1549. Goldast's text of the *LC* is reprinted in Migne, *PL* 98 (Paris, 1851). I have listed below in the sections 5 and 11 the occurrences of some of those readings in Migne's edition that are identical with emendations offered in *Speculum* 40 (1965) as allegedly new emendations.

The merely paleographical origin of the listings in *Speculum* does not turn them automatically into accomplished "emendations." This can be achieved only through their text-critical investigation which must be conducted in conjunction with Bastgen's recension of the *LC* text in order to determine whether they can be accepted into the context of the *LC* as truly new emendations. In other words, the veracity of those new readings must be tested and supplemented, if it should become necessary. To be certain, a number of probable readings not listed or else wrongly listed by Bastgen are introduced from the MSS; but simultaneously a number of new but false readings crop up. Some of the latter will be subsequently discussed together with certain doubtful ascriptions of emendations which are presented as new, although Bastgen has provided the identical emendations in 1924 in his own *Emendanda et Addenda* on p. 231 of his edition of the *LC* which are preceded on pp. 229–230 by a set of other *Addenda* concerning sources used by the author of the *LC* and many stylistic parallels between the writings of Alcuin and the text of the treatise. These facts will be illustrated here by a few selected examples (1–11).

1. Bastgen, in his *apparatus criticus*, *LC*, p. 56.44, states in note *f* that the word *et* in *LC* I.28 (p. 56.25) is missing in *V* and A, and that he

supplemented it: "deest VA; *supplevi.*" But contrary to Bastgen's assumption MS *V*, f. 60b, line 5 from below, indeed reads "et."

Speculum 40 (1965), 288 to *LC*, p. 56.44 now suggests that note *f* should read "deest A." It is indeed true that *A* does not read *et*, but the fact itself is quite irrelevant for the recension of the *LC* text, because in accordance with the universally accepted text-critical methodology concerning the elimination of MSS and their readings whose archetype is available, the information that A does not offer the reading *et* must be disregarded. It is indeed "worthless"—if I may follow Paul Maas's generally accepted terminology—as a witness for the recension of the *LC* text.

2. *Speculum* 40 (1965), 287 to *LC*, p. 7.38, suggests that Bastgen's reading *est* in the chapter heading of *LC* I.23 should be omitted, presumably because A, fol. 7v, indeed omits this *est*. We remind ourselves at this point that the *LC* text in *V* is not preserved up to Bastgen's p. 9.23. But the chapter heading of *LC* I.23 (p. 50.42) certainly contains the reading *est*, which appears in a text cited in the *LC* from Hadrian I's *Synodica* of 785, *JE* 2448, inserted into the *Acta* of II Nicaea, 787, Mansi XII.1065C9. All this means that Bastgen's insertion of *est* at *LC* 7.38 is well justified on the grounds of its occurrence in *V*, fol. 54a (*LC* I.23, p. 50.42) and cannot be omitted as suggested in *Speculum*.

3. Bastgen, *LC* II.4 (p. 66.15) reads "loquutionis," and at 66.18–19 "loquutionum." His note c claims for both spellings "qu corr. e c V." But this is not correct because *V*, fol. 71b, second line from below, reads "loqutionis," spelled with one *u*, and a scribe who is hardly identical with the one who wrote the *LC* text *ad locum* put suprascript above the middle between *qu* a very tiny *c*. In contrast to this correction, *V*, fol. 72a, line 5, spells "loquutionum," as printed by Bastgen. The suggestion made in *Speculum* 40 (1965), 288, to read "c. corr. e qu V," is incorrect, since the correction does not apply to *LC*, p. 66.18–19.

4. *Speculum* 40 (1965), 287, suggests for the chapter heading of *LC* I.15 (p. 7.12) the reading "testimonii" instead of Bastgen's "testamenti," because A, fol. 7r, reads "testimonii." But this emendation is incorrect, because in the context of the *LC* the chapter heading of *LC* I.15 (p. 34.33) reads "testamenti," the reading offered in *V*, fol. 34, line 4. This is also the word, correctly

copied in A, fol. 37v, for *LC*, p. 34.33. The true reading of *LC*, p. 7.12, is certainly "testamenti," as correctly listed by Bastgen, because this is the reading in *V*, the archetype of A.

5a. A, fol. 181v, Ch. 16, line 4, reads for *LC*, p. 171.31, "sine oratione sacra fatur a nobis," as listed in *Speculum*, p. 289. The insertion of "sacra" in A corresponds to its source in the Greek *Acta* of II Nicaea, Mansi XIII.269D9, cited by Bastgen, *LC* IV.16 (p. 202.41): χωρὶς εὐχῆς ἱερᾶς.

5b. *LC* IV.22 (p. 172.11) reads "subversione turbulenta," but A, f. 182r, line 3 from below, reads "subversionem turbulentam," as listed in *Speculum*, p. 289. The correct reading occurs already in *PL* 98.1231D10–11 as well as at Bastgen's *LC* IV.22 (p. 215.11). The accusative correctly renders the passage in the Greek *Acta* of II Nicaea, Mansi XIII.401D7, cited by Bastgen, p. 215.45: ἀνατροπὴν θολεράν. The Latin version of this text in Mansi XIII.402D8, "subversione turbulenta," represents the translation of those *Acta* by Anastasius Bibliothecarius from the year 873, but not the version of the *First Latin Nicaenum* of ca. 788, which is cited here and through-out the *LC*, as well as in other Carolingian documents (see above, Chapter I).

5c. *Speculum*, p. 289, reads for *LC*, p. 172.21, "participo" and not "participio." The correct reading of A, fol. 182v, line 12, appears already in *PL* 98.1233D6, also in *LC* IV.23, p. 217.6. The source of the passage, the Greek *Acta* of II Nicaea, is cited by Bastgen, p. 217.

5d. *Speculum*, p. 289, suggests on the basis of A, f. 185r, line 1, for *LC*, p. 174.30, the reading "quod idem Johannes." The same reading "idem" is found in the lost *Capitulare adversus Synodum* cited in the *Hadrianum* II.4 (*JE* 2483), ed. Karl Hampe, *MGH, Epistolae* 5 (Karolini Aevi 3; Berlin, 1899), 43.28. *LC* and *Hadrianum* are citing here the same passage from the *First Latin Nicaenum*, referred to above in section 5b.

5e. For *LC*, p. 180.4, *Speculum*, p. 289, suggests the reading "alia" instead of "talia," because A, f. 191r, line 18, reads "quoddicitalia" without separating spaces between the three words. But this sug-gestion is hardly acceptable. A should be read instead "quod dicit talia"; *PL* 98.1191C12 indeed offers "talia." The source of the passage, the Greek *Acta* of II Nicaea, Mansi XIII.161B4, cited in the *LC* IV.5, p. 180.34, unmistakenly reads τοιαῦτα, and therefore

Bastgen's "talia," p. 180.4, cited verbatim from a quotation of the *First Latin Nicaenum* (see above section 5b), represents the *LC*'s original reading.

6. Bastgen, *LC*, p. 7.45 n. b, states that *et* in 7.22, in the list of the chapter headings for *LC*, Book I, is missing in A; but this is not true, since A, fol. 7v, line 4, reads *et horum*. This fact seems to be the reason why *Speculum* 40 (1965), 287, suggests the deletion of Bastgen's note b. But beyond this merely paleographical evidence, additional proof for the correctness of the reading *et* is available that is based directly upon the transmission of the archetype *V*, and for this reason carries greater weight than the evidence provided by A.

LC I.17 (p. 40.3) reads *et eorum* in *V*, fol. 40b; therefore the *et* in the list of the chapter headings of *LC*, Book I, at p. 7.22 is certainly the correct reading. The authenticity of *et* is supported by other textual transmissions which are independent from *V*, and therefore enable us to test the *LC* readings of *V* and A.

The text of the chapter heading of *LC* I.17 (pp. 39.43–40.4), in which the *et* occurs, is quoted from the *Epistola* of the Patriarch Germanus of Constantinople, addressed to Thomas of Claudiopolis. This letter is a Greek document whose original was inserted into the Greek *Acta* of II Nicaea, 787, Mansi XIII.113E–116A; its Latin translation appears in the Latin translation of the *Acta*, Mansi XIII.114E–115A. This passage reads χαì (116A1), and correspondingly "et" horum (115A4).

The identical text from the *Epistola* of Germanus, which was cited in *LC* I.17 from the *First Latin Nicaenum*, was quoted also in the now lost *Capitulare adversus Synodum* from which the text is cited in the *Hadrianum* II.10 (*JE* 2483), ed. Karl Hampe, *MGH*, *Epistolae* 5 (Karolini Aevi 3; Berlin, 1899), 46.6; also this text reads *et horum*.

The preceding documentation for the reading under consideration has been offered in such a detailed manner for the purpose of supplementing the meager paleographical evidence of A. Numerous other readings listed as "emendations" which are drawn from A will be tested and supplemented with the help of the same philological, text-critical method. This approach requires the indispensable utilization of available Greek texts cited in the protocols of the Greek *Acta* of II Nicaea, 787, that are the sources of many of the texts cited in chapter headings of the *LC*. The importance of the Greek sources which are used in their Latin translations for the recension of the *LC* has been shown in Chapters III and IV and throughout the present volume.

7. *Speculum* 40 (1965), 287, offers for *LC* I.20 (p. 47.3) the emendation "factae angelica" in place of Bastgen's reading "facta, evangelica ministeria." The listing of the reading "evangelica" in A is superfluous, since *V*, the source of A, is extant. The original "facte angelica" in A, fol. 53, line 1, was changed by a corrector who wrote "eu" between the two words, and also altered "facte" to read "facta."

V, fol. 48b, line 1, reads "cherubim quae in oraculo erant factae, angelica ministeria." The correctness of this reading can be tested, since the passage belongs to a literal quotation in *LC* I.20 (p. 47.1–5) drawn from Bede, *De templo Salominis* I.1269–1273, ed. David Hurst (*CCL* 119A, 1969), 178. This means that the correct reading is indeed "factae, angelica ministeria" and not "factae angelica," as proposed in *Speculum*.

A larger number of emendations could be presented for *LC* I.20 (pp. 46.26–48.32), because these pages represent an anonymous insertion of Bede, *De templo Salomonis* I.1342–1450 (*op. cit.* pp. 180–183). I mention just one of these emendations involving haplography, the omission of one line through oversight, an error which is found elsewhere in Bastgen's edition, as will be shown afterward (see sections 9 and 11 below).

LC I.20 (p. 47.33) reads "quia per viros misericordie unctione spiritus sancti inlustratos." This is a quotation from Bede, *De templo Salomonis* I.1393–1394, p. 182, which reads: "quia per viros misericordiae [quorum pietates non defuerunt (Ecclus. 44.10) viros] unctione spiritus sancti inlustratos." Bastgen reads with *V*, fol. 49b, line 6 from below: "per viros misericordie unctione spiritus sancti inlustratos." This could indicate that the error of omitting the *LC* text from "quorum" to "viros" is a haplography that must be charged to Bastgen's account, although the error might have originated with the scribe of *V*, or else even with the scribe of the Bede text.

8. Some emendations which are listed in *Speculum* 40 (1965), 287–289, as new corrections of the *LC* text, are listed by Hubert Bastgen among his numerous *Addenda* which he attached to his edition of 1924 on pp. 229–231. Compare the following instances.

a. *Speculum*, p. 288, suggests for *LC*, p. 56.43, the deletion of Bastgen's note a. The contents of this note are indeed incorrect, and Bastgen, p. 231, col. b, line 4 from below, suggested the elimination of the note.
b. *Speculum*, p. 288 to *LC*, p. 134.17, proposes the reading "concilio" instead of "consilio." Bastgen, p. 230, refers to the source of the text, the pseudo-Augustinian *De divinis scripturis* 18, ed. Franciscus Weihrich, *CSEL* 12 (Wien, 1887), 383.2, which suggests "concilio."
c. *Speculum*, p. 288 to *LC*, p. 126.37, reads for Ephes. 4.1 "Obsecro ergo vos ego." Bastgen, p. 230, refers for this correct reading to *De divinis scripturis* 35, p. 462.9.
d. *Speculum*, p. 288 to *LC*, p. 52.39, lists the correction "Dominus deus tuus" which is listed by Bastgen, p. 231, line 20, with the misprint "tum" for "tuus."

9. *Speculum*, p. 288, suggests for *LC* II.25 (p. 84.16) the insertion of the line "permisissent nequaquam ideo imagines adorari" after the word "adorari." Bastgen has listed this correction among his "Emendanda et Addenda," p. 231, lines 25–27. One glance at *V*, fol. 91a, provides the solution: the lines 12, 13, 14 end with the same word "adorari," and Bastgen mistakenly omitted line 14 by providing a well-nigh classical example of that error of textual omission that is called haplography. Compare *V*, fol. 91a, lines 11–15:

(11)   .... ve
(12) sanus est qui dicere audeat eos imagines adora
(13) ri instituisse presertim qui etsi se adorari
(14) [permisissent nequaquam ideo imagines adora
(15) ri] deberent ....

The lacuna in Bastgen's text of *LC*, p. 84.16, after "adorari" in *V*, line 13, occurred when Bastgen's eyes strayed from the last word "adorari" in line 13 to the same word at the end of line 14. *Speculum*, p. 288, reports that the omitted line in Bastgen's edition does not occur in A. But this information must be disregarded and has no bearing on the recension of the *LC* text, since *V*, the source of *A*, is available.

10. In connection with the preceding text in *LC* II.25 (p. 84.16) a strange case of omission must be recorded. Bastgen reads p. 84.8 "inhibita salva oratione [read correctly: adoratione] qua nos mutuo salutantes adoramus, solius dei adoratio instituitur." In *V*, fol. 90b,

the words from "salva adoratione" to "adoramus" are written in small Caroline minuscule in the left margin, with the tiny insertion sign *hd* (hoc deest) suprascript between "inhibita" and "solius"; *hp* (hoc ponas) introduces the *LC* text supplied *in margine*. Bastgen did not list in his *apparatus criticus* the marginal correction of the *LC* text, although his recension contains the text in question. A, fol. 92r, line 6, correctly copied the insertion into the context of the *LC*.

11. Haplography, the specific error of omission committed by a scribe when transcribing or reading the text of a manuscript, previously dealt with in sections 7 and 9, accounts for three missing lines in Bastgen's recension of the *LC*, Book IV, which is missing in *V*, but preserved in A. *Speculum* 40 (1965), 289, lists these lines for *LC* IV.1, pp. 174.3 and 174.25, and for IV.5, p. 181.34.

At the outset, it must be stated that the three missing lines are extant already in the *LC* edition by Melchior Goldast von Haiminsfeld (Frankfurt, 1608), which was reprinted in Migne, *PL* 98 (Paris, 1851), and ultimately renders the *LC* text preserved in A. Compare for *LC* IV.1 (p. 174.3) A, fol. 184r, lines 15–16, and *PL* 98.1184D1–2; correspondingly for *LC* IV.1 (p. 174.25) see A, fol. 184v, line 9 from below, and *PL* 98.1185B8–9; and for *LC* IV.5 (p. 181.34) see A, fol. 192r, line 4 from below, and *PL* 98.1193B3.

The following text will show for one of these *LC* passages the genesis of the error of omission and at the same time provide the possibility of testing the correctness of the restored *LC* text damaged by haplography.

Compare *LC* IV.1 (p. 174.2–6, Bastgen) in the transmission of the text in A, fol. 184r, lines 13–21:

(13)   *Nam si* tale menda
(14) cium proferre, ut ille fassus est, peccatum non est; Inli
(15) cita quaequae perpetrare nullum peccatum est: [*et si* In
(16) licita quaeque perpetrare nullum peccatum est] sanctarum script
(17) turarum vigor, quae utique ab inlicitis abstinere cen
(18) sent, fatescere credendus est. *Non autem* sanctarum
(19) scripturarum vigor, quae ab Inlicitis quibusque abstine
(20) re censent, fatescere credendus est. *Est igitur*
(21) tale mendacium proferre peccatum.

This instance shows clearly the obvious origin of Bastgen's error of omission of the *LC* text bracketed in lines 15–16. His eyes strayed from the "peccatum est" in 15 to the "peccatum est" in line 16.

The transcription further enables us to confirm the correctness of the restoration of the missing line on the basis of the syllogistic reasoning contained in the text.

The importance of the syllogistic type of argumentation employed throughout the four books of the *LC* has been investigated in Chapter IV, sections E, E1, and F. The hypothetical argument developed in the *LC* text goes through the successive stages of proposition, probation, and final conclusion. The various logical steps are clearly indicated by the conditional structure which is arranged after the obvious syllogistic scheme of *Nam si* (line 13), *et si* (15), *non autem* (18), and the functor *Est igitur* (20). The identical logical structure that appears in the preceding hypothetical syllogism is used elsewhere in the *LC*, for instance, in *LC* III.26 (p. 159.9–13): *Quoniam si, Et si, non autem, igitur est*. The syllogism most often used in the *LC* seems to be structured somewhat after the second modus of the hypothetical syllogism, "si est . . . est . . . non est autem . . . non est . . . igitur." The logical sequence of the hypothetical syllogism in the *Libri Carolini* is most frequently arranged after the formula *Nam si, Et si, Non autem, Non igitur* (see, for instance, *LC* I.24, p. 52.29–33; III.2, p. 109.1–5; III.28, p. 165.8–13; IV.24, p. 222.4–7).

It should have become obvious on the basis of the preceding diversified philological treatment that also the textual criticism of the *Libri Carolini* must go beyond the merely technical paleographical listing of readings, and use what A. E. Housman once called "the application of thought" for the proper understanding of the complicated text of a difficult historical work from the age of Charlemagne.[23] I shall offer in the following chapter for the first time my classification of scribal corrections in the *Vaticanus Latinus 7207*.

[23] See A. E. Housman, *Selected Prose*, ed. John Carter (Cambridge, England, 1961), 131–150.

CHAPTER IX

The Origins, Corrections, and Tironian Notes of the *Vaticanus Latinus 7207*

Von den Steinen (*QF* 21, [1929–30], 88f.) assumed that the *Vaticanus Latinus 7207* might have been deposited at some Frankish *Pfalz, in palatio*, presumably at Aix-la-Chapelle. Freeman (*Speculum* 40 [1965], 278) believes that the manuscript is firmly associated with the Frankish court of Charlemagne. But neither von den Steinen nor Freeman ever proved their contentions. A copy of the *LC* had been certainly deposited somewhere at the court, be it in its library or in its Scriptorium, or even in the Capella of the Carolingians, since the *LC* was an official state paper. The existence of such a codex of the *LC* at the Frankish court is indeed verified by Hincmar of Reims, who saw there a "sizeable volume" of the *LC* when he visited the court. Hincmar, in one of his treatises,[1]

---

[1] Hincmar of Reims, *PL* 126.360A–B, refers to the Synod of Frankfurt, 794, and to this synod's rejection of image-worship, decreed by II Nicaea, 787. On the occasion of a visit to the Frankish Court, he saw a MS of the *LC* which appeared to him as "a sizable volume," "non modicum volumen quod in palatio adolescentulus legi, ab codem imperatore Romano est per quosdam episcopos missum. In cuius voluminis quarto libro [in *LC* IV.28] haec de universali nomine scripta sunt."

On Carolingian archives see H. Fichtenau, "Archive der Karolingerzeit." *Mitteilungen des oesterreichischen Staatsarchivs* 25 (1972), 15–24. Heinz Loewe, "Hinkmar von Reims und der Apocrisiar," *Festschrift für Hermann Heimpel* 3 (Göttingen, 1972), 201f., believes that Hincmar may have seen and read a MS of the *LC* as early as 822 when he belonged to the entourage of his teacher, the archicapellanus Hilduin of St. Denis.

Bastgen, *Neues Archiv* 37 (1912), 468 n. 5, apparently assumed that the last section in *LC* IV.28 (p. 228.6 Universitas namque . . . ,) is omitted in Hincmar's quotation; however, Hincmar transferred the section to the very beginning of his excerpt in *PL* 126.360!

quotes from *LC* IV.28 (pp. 227.20–228.8, Bastgen). But the *Vaticanus* did not originate at the court of Charlemagne. E. A. Lowe concluded only that the codex may have come from north of the Alps.[2] Freeman, in attempting to associate *V* with the Frankish court and its Scriptorium, states flatly that the manuscript's "scribes were trained, as Bischoff has found, in the court scriptorium. One of their hands appears also in a lectionary related to the Ada-School." But this is to take as an ascertained fact what Bernhard Bischoff puts forth only as a hypothesis. Bischoff[3] assumes—he says "wie ich glaube"—that one of the hands that wrote certain sections in the Carolingian *Evangelistar* (now in the private MS collection of Dr. Ludwig at Aix-la-Chapelle), which was certainly not written at the Carolingian court, is somehow reminiscent of the script of the second hand in *V*. Says he: "Ihre Formen, und wie ich glaube, auch der spezifische Duktus, sind in der Schrift der zweiten Hand des Orginalkodex der Libri Carolini, Vat. lat. 7207 (fol. 66r–73v) wiederzuerkennen." Bischoff continues his evaluation of the Aachen MS by stating: "If the scribe [of the second hand of *V*] wrote the *LC* in the year 791 at the Court, together with other [scribes], he then worked on the *Evangelistar* in another scriptorium, in which his better schooling granted him a distinct superiority."[4] If we compare Bischoff's opinion with Freeman's report, we see immediately that she has expanded Bischoff's theory, but has added nothing to confirm it. While Bischoff speaks of one of the hands in the Aachen MS and assumes that he recognizes a resemblance between this one hand and the second hand of the *Vaticanus*, Freeman ascribes to Bischoff what he never stated, namely, that the scribes of the *Vaticanus* were trained in the Carolingian Court Scriptorium. In *Aachener Kunstblätter* 32 (1966), 53, as a confirmation of his view cited in translation above ("Wenn der Schreiber zusammen mit anderen die Libri Carolini im Jahre 791 am Hofe schrieb . . ."), Bischoff refers to Freeman's interpretation of his opinion, and to her own unsupported statement referred to at the beginning of the

---

[2] *Codices Latini Antiquiores* I (Oxford, 1934), 16 no. 52.

[3] "Eine karolingische Prachthandschrift in Aachener Privatbesitz," *Aachener Kunstblätter* 32 (1966), 46–53, here p. 50. Freeman, *Speculum* 40 (1965), 219f. and n. 41, refers to Bischoff's Paris lecture on the subject during 1963. I assume that the content of his article is—*mutatis mutandis*—by and large identical with his lecture.

[4] Bischoff, *loc. cit.*

present discussion. Naturally, such circular reasoning based on individual conjectures and obvious misinterpretations is inconclusive and incorrect. Bischoff's reference (p. 53 nn. 9 and 12) to Freeman's article (*Speculum* 40, 1965) does not confirm his own view that hand two of *V* may have been involved in the writing of part of the *Evangelistar*, which may have originated in the wider sphere of the Frankish court's influence. All these conclusions, which are tied up with some conditional "ifs," do not represent facts. Nobody has provided evidence that *V* originated at the Carolingian court, notwithstanding Bischoff's further remark[5] that *V* was written, according to Freeman, for Hadrian I at the Court Scriptorium, but not presented to him on account of the corrections made in the codex. Also this description and ascription is nowhere verified. She mentions in *Speculum* 40 (1965), 220, the possibility that *V* is a product of the Carolingian Scriptorium, and on p. 221 presents her conjecture as a fact.

Freeman's belief (p. 279) concerning the Tironian notes in the margins of the *Vaticanus* still follows von den Steinen's abandoned thesis that these notes render the personal opinions of Charlemagne on certain passages in the *LC*. But in 1953, Heinrich Fichtenau[6] convincingly disproved von den Steinen's notion. These Tironian marginalia (see below, Chapter XIII), whose author remains unknown, represent evaluations of the use made of patristic materials in the context of the work. Fichtenau's interpretation of these notes is certainly confirmed by the critical results of the present investigations.[7] Compare the following items A–H, which will repeatedly provide reasonable explanations for corrections in the text of the *LC* resulting from some corrector's collation of the *LC*'s source with the text excerpted by the author of the *LC*.

A. The Tironian note for *optime*, written next to the words *Hanc quidam doctorum* (see von den Steinen, *Neues Archiv* 49 [1932], 211) in *LC* III.6 (Bastgen, p. 117.29) could well refer to these words, of which the last two are written on an erasure. The note might indicate somebody's approval of the fact that the name of *Victorinus*

---

[5] In "Die Hofbibliothek Karls des Grossen," in *Karl der Grosse* II: *Das geistige Leben* (Düsseldorf, 1965), 56f.

[6] "Karl der Grosse und das Kaisertum," *MIOEG* 61 (1953), 276–287; now also available as a book; see below Chapter XVI n. 6.

[7] See Chapter IV n. 98, above.

Petavionensis was erased, and the anonymous *quidam doctorum* substituted for it, as the present writer has shown.[8] The note *optime*
would thus recognize the correctness of the name's replacement by
the anonymous reference to *quidam doctorum*, because Victorinus'
writings are designated as *apocrypha* in the *Decretum Gelasianum*, which
provided the author of the *LC* with lists of canonically approved
and not approved writings.

B. The Tironian note for *optime* is written next to the words *Corporale
igitur* (genus) *est* (*Neues Archiv* 49 [1932], 211) in *LC* III.26 (Bastgen,
p. 160.37). After *igitur* (p. 160.37), the *Vaticanus*, f. 182, has an
erasure of four letters, according to Bastgen, p. 160.43, probably
indicating the erasure of the word *genus*, and *optime* could mean the
confirmation of this erasure. In addition, I believe, *optime* could
express approval of the erasure of the deleted remark (p. 160.36d)
"ut ait scs Augustinus" by some reader of the MS, who knew that
the passage is not excerpted from a genuine Augustinian text but
from Pseudo-Augustinus, *Dialogus quaestionum LXV, quaestio* 63, as
has been shown by the present writer.[9]

C. There are two Tironian notes next to passages in *LC* I.29, whose
newly found source, unknown to Bastgen, is Origen, *In Exodum,
homilia IX*, ed. W. A. Baehrens, *Origenes Werke* VI (*GCS*; Leipzig,
1920), 234–244, *passim*.[10] This discovery enables us to see the author
of the *LC* and a corrector at work on the text of the chapter. The
corrector restores in most instances the text of Origen cited in the
context of the *LC*, as we shall see.

C.1. The note for *sapienter* stands next to the words "idcirco in
plerisque scripturae sanctae locis" (cf. *Neues Archiv* 49 [1932], 210)
in *LC* I.29 (p. 57.13–14). Since these words are written on an
erasure, it may well be that the Tironian note means to indicate
approval of the erasure of the first text and of its replacement by
the words written *in loco raso*. The erased words may have consisted
of a reference to Origen's homily, the newly discovered source of
LC I.29; see more below, C.2.

---

[8] See Chapter IV, A.
[9] In Chapter IV, D.
[10] Cf. Wallach, *The Classical Tradition*: 498 n. 101, and above Chapter VIII, A.

C.2. The Tironian note for *tota mire* is written on the same level with the words *viscera misericordiae* in *LC* I.29 (p. 57.36). We read as follows (p. 57.34–39):

His materiis eius sacerdotes induantur iuxta David vocem qui ait [Ps. 131.9]: *Sacerdotes tui induantur iustitia.*[f] Quos et Paulus his verbis hortatur cum dicit [Col. 3.12]: *Induite vos viscera misericordiae.* Habent etiam eius sacerdotes alia nobiliora indumenta quae idem *vas electionis* [Acts 9.15] designat cum dicit: *Induite vos Dominum Iesum Christum, et carnis curam ne feceritis in*[g] *concupiscentiis vestris.*[g]

This section in *LC* I.29 cites, without indication of its actual source, Origen, *In Ex.*, *homilia*, p. 240.12–21:

Istae sint interim materiae ex quibus omne tabernaculum construatur, induantur sacerdotes, ornetur et pontifex. Quorum indumenta quae sint vel qualia, in alio loco propheta pronuntiat et dicit [Ps. 131.9] *Sacerdotes tui induantur iustitiam*; sunt ergo ista omnia indumenta iustitiae. Et iterum Paulus Apostolus dicit [Col. 3.12]: *Induite vos viscera misericordiae*; sunt ergo et indumenta misericordiae. Sed et alia nihilominus idem Apostolus indumenta nobiliora designat cum dicit [Rom. 13.14]; *Induite vos Dominum Iesum Christum, et carnis curam ne feceritis ad concupiscentias.* Ista ergo sunt indumenta, quibus ornatur ecclesia.

The note *tota mire* expresses astonishment at the words "viscera misericordiae" in Col. 3.12, which like all the other Bible texts in the quoted *LC* passage are copied verbatim from Origen. One can hardly assume that the author of the *LC* himself marveled at these *viscera*, since he was familiar with Origen's explanation (p. 240.17, cited above): "sunt ergo et *indumenta* misericordiae." I therefore believe that some reader of the *LC* is responsible for the note.

The newly discovered patristic source of *LC* I.29 enables us to account for the occurrence of the two corrections in the notes *f* and *g* in Bastgen's *apparatus criticus*. Bastgen, p. 57*f*, reads as follows: "iustitia) a *corr. ex* am V." In the light of Origen, the underlying source of the *LC*, we notice that *iustitiam* is Origen's reading (p. 240.15, Baehrens). This reading was changed by a correction in all probability because the Vulgate reading of Ps. 131.9 is *iustitia*. Bastgen, p. 57*g*, indicates that the end of Rom. 13.14 in Origen's version (p. 240.19–20), *ad concupiscentias*, in the first redaction of the *LC* text was erased, and "in concupiscentiis vestris" was written by a corrector *in loco raso*. Otherwise the corrector of *LC* I.29 clearly betrays the fact that he endeavors to restore the original text of

Origen in the excerpts of the *LC*. Accordingly, *LC* I.29 (p. 58.15) and note *a, qui ex*, in "qui expectant," is written on an erasure because Origen, p. 241.28, indeed reads "qui expectant." This means that Origen's reading was intentionally restored in the *LC* text by a Carolingian corrector. Bastgen remarks in note *e* to *LC*, p. 58.42 that in " . . . quod rationale^e dicitur quaterno lapidum ordine distinctum quo^e," the text between *e–e* is written on an erasure. This clearly proves that the same corrector of *LC* I.29 restored the original text of Origen's homily (p. 243.3, Baehrens): "quod rati (onale dici potest . . . quaterno lapidum ordine distinctum; sed . . . " I finally state in this context that Origen, p. 241.11, provides the missing word *dilatatur* in *LC*, p. 58, line 3, note *a*, where Bastgen records a *rasura* of ten letters in the manuscript: "sequitur rasura 10 litt. in V."

D. A Tironian note for *optime* is written in *LC* I.20 (p. 47.7) on the same level with *sanctos etiam homines* (see *Neues Archiv* 49 [1932], 208). This note comments ultimately on a passage in Bede's *De templo Salomonis*, c. 13, *PL* 91.765D,[11] (see Chapter XII, E, on "Alleged Evidence at Germigny-des-Prés") and seems to be just the affirmative expression of some reader. Von den Steinen, *Neues Archiv* 49 (1932), 254 n. 1, refers for the discussion of a passage in *LC* I.20 to Bede, *De templo Salomonis*, c. 9 (*PL* 91.756C), but did not notice that two-thirds of the chapter render the text of Bede's treatise, probably not directly but after a transmission of the treatise appended to, or inserted into, some medieval Bible commentary.

E. The Tironian note next to *induti sunt arietes* in *LC* III.18 (p. 141.17) reads *eximie* (*Neues Archiv* 49 [1932], 212). The words commented upon belong to Ps. 64.12–14. The latter and other Bible quotations on p. 141.7–32 are drawn from Pseudo-Augustine, *De scripturis divinis*, ed. F. Weihrich, *CSEL* 12 (1887), 659.6, as is pointed out by Bastgen in his Addenda, p. 230. The first quotation, Joel 3.18 (p. 141.7–8) with the Explicit . . . *et colles fluent lac*, is followed, according to Bastgen note *b*, by an erasure of five letters (5 litt. erasae sunt V). I can see after *lac* in *V*, f. 158v, line 5, not five, but just three erased letters, namely, "tem." Thus Ioel 3.18 in the

---

[11] Ed. David Hurst in *CCL* 119A (1969), 181; on this edition see Chapter VIII n. 21 and Chapter XII n. 47.

first redaction of the *LC* reads " . . . et colles fluent *lactem*," in accordance with *m*, p. 660.5 . . . *lactem*. D. de Bruyne, *Revue Bénédictine* 44 (1932), 231, arrived at the same conclusion without looking at *V*.

F. A Tironian note for *syllogistice* is written on the same level with the words *tria distinguenda sunt* (*scil.* imago, similitudo, aequalitas) in *LC* I.8 (p. 25.13), according to von den Steinen, *Neues Archiv* 49 (1932), 209. The note refers, as he says (p. 240), to the *LC*'s statement:

> Omne quod imago est, similitudo est,
> non tamen omne quod similitudo, imago est.

But unknown to Bastgen and von den Steinen, this is a reference to Augustine, *Quaestiones in Heptateuchum* V.4, from the *Quaestiones Deuteronomii* on Deut. 4.16 (ed. J. Fraipont, *CCL* 33 [1958]), 274:

> Omnis imago etiam similitudo est,
> non omnis similitudo etiam imago est.[12]

Since the *LC* uses in the same context of the discussion of *imago* and *similitudo* the paragraphs 104 and 110 of the pseudo-Augustinian *Categoriae decem* in the edition of Alcuin, as has been shown elsewhere,[13] there can be certainly no doubt that the Tironian *syllogistice* has a purely logical meaning, that it indeed characterizes the *LC*'s argument, and that it cannot be anything else but a mere scribal comment referring to the contents of *LC* I.8. See below the last page of Chapter XIII.

G. The Tironian note for *vere* (*Neues Archiv* 49 [1932], 212) is written on the same level with *Numquidnam quia Dominus* in *LC* III.25 (p. 156.30). Bastgen refers for the passage (p. 156.30–36) to a similar one in Isidore of Seville's *Quaestiones in Vetus Test.* But the *LC* text is closer to, and derived from, Isidore's source, namely, Ambrosiaster, *Quaestiones Veteris et Novi Testamenti CXXVII*, ed. Alexander Souter (*CSEL* 50; 1908), *quaestio* 42 (p. 69): "Cur angelus missus loqui ad Moysen in igne et rubo apparuit in monte?"[14] The *vere* seems to confirm in our instance the negative question in *LC* III.25 (p. 156.30), "Dominus de rubo in igne Moysi loquutus est,

---

[12] In ed. J. Zycha, *CSEL* 28.2 (1895), 371.
[13] See Chapter IV, E.
[14] See in detail Chapter VI, C, above.

ideo rubi adorandi sunt," which is implicitly denied by the author of the treatise. One can hardly assume that the author of the *LC* remarked *vere* in this instance. But a scribe who read the text whose source was unknown to him is more likely to have uttered this *vere* with its doubtful connotation.

H. The editorial nature of corrections made in the *codex authenticus* of the *LC* is plainly established in instances in which the often hitherto unknown underlying sources of a chapter have been found, as is the case in the section heads C2, D, E, F, and G. The recognition of the purely scribal characteristics of the corrections is of importance, since it definitely voids the assumption of some scholars who still mistakenly believe that those corrections resulted from the oral discussions of Carolingian theologians about the problems taken up in the individual chapters of the *Libri Carolini*.

A good example of the scholarly method of the author of the *LC*, which plainly denies any such assumption concerning the origins of corrections in the *LC* allegedly resulting from oral discussions of Carolingian theologians, is provided, for example, in *LC* III.29 (p. 166.30–38). The *LC* purports to exemplify the honor subjects owe to emperors and kings according to scriptural texts: "Quia ergo imperatores et reges sint a subditis honorandi, quibusdam divinae scripturae exemplis potest adprobari." Unknown to Bastgen, the *LC* conducts the proof of its assertion by citing—without any indication of its actual source—from Ambrosiaster's *quaestio* 35: "Qua ratione David Saul, postquam Deus ab eo recessit, Christum Domini vocat et defert ei?"[15] This fact provides us with an interesting insight into the thinking of the *LC*'s author as well as of the *LC*'s literary method. At the same time it offers the proper explanation for all the corrections listed by Bastgen, p. 166.30–38, but not explained by him. The notes *f*, *g*, *h*, *i*, listed by Bastgen in the *apparatus criticus* to p. 166.34–38, can now be properly understood.

Bastgen, p. 166.34, *dignitate*, according to *f*, is written on an erasure; the erased word was *traditione*, according to Ambrosiaster, *Quaestiones, quaestio* 35 (p. 63.10, Souter).
Bastgen, p. 166.35, *inpertiendum*, according to *g*, is written *in margine* by a corrector; the word is not to be found in the underlying

[15] Ambrosiaster, *Quaestiones Veteris et Novi Testamenti CXXVII*, ed. Alexander Souter (*CSEL* 50; 1908), 63.6–16; see also Chapter VI, E.

text, p. 63.11–12, and for this reason, seems to be an addition made by the corrector.

Bastgen, p. 166.36, *dignitate*, according to *h*, is written on an erasure; the erased word was *traditione*, according to Ambrosiaster, *Quaestiones, quaestio* 35, p. 63.13.

Bastgen, p. 166.38, *potestas*, according to *i*, is written on an erasure. This indicates that a corrector restored Ambrosiaster's original reading *potestas* in Rom. 13.1 (p. 63.16, Souter).

Quite illuminating is the omission by the *LC*'s author of Ambrosiaster's short sentence (p. 63.12–13) "dei enim imaginem habet rex, sicut et episcopus" from the passage, otherwise copied verbatim from Ambrosiaster's *quaestio*. This short sentence contradicts the thesis of the *LC* according to which the sentence "Pater iussit imaginem Christi adorare sicut imperatorem" (p. 166.19), presupposes, "ut imago Christi eminentiorem in tali ratione locum teneret," (p. 166.26f.). The *adorare* in *LC*, p. 166.19d, written by a corrector above the line, is contradicted by the remark in the *LC*, p. 166.27–28: "Non ergo Pater imaginem Christi quoquam legitur aut depingere aut *adorare* aut honorare iussisse." This contradiction may indicate that the corrector of the passage was hardly identical with the *LC*'s author who otherwise anonymously inserted the text from Ambrosiaster's *quaestio* at the end of *LC* III.29.

I. A persistently repeated, though clearly mistaken notion, assumes that the *LC* is a collective work by Charlemagne's theologians who wrote against the Council of II Nicaea of 787.[16] But the work is certainly by one author, who, to be sure, was not Theodulph of Orléans. Some of the evidence that speaks for Alcuin's sole authorship of the *LC* is referred to, for example, at the end of Chapter IV, and in the sections D–F of the same chapter. The uniformity of style in the *LC* has been indicated very often in Bastgen's edition, and his proof can be supplemented in many details of which I shall

---

[16] Hubert Schrade, *Malerei des Mittelalters I: Vor- und Frühromanische Malerei* (Köln, 1958), 300 n. 13, states: "I am not convinced that the *LC* are the work of one person, and therefore I speak [especially, pp. 114–117] of the Carolingian theologians of the *Libri*, without investigating the question of authorship any more closely." Herbert Schade on "Images" in *Sacramentum Mundi: An Encyclopedia of Theology*, ed. Karl Rahner *et al.*, III (Freiburg i. Br., 1958), 105, says: "The theologians of Charlemagne wrote against this council [*scil.* II Nicaea of 787] in the *Libri Carolini*."

give an example subsequently. That the *LC* is written by one author alone is furthermore assured by the fact that its main sources are used uniformly throughout the work, be it Cassiodorus, *Expositio in Psalmos*, the pseudo-Augustinian biblical florilegium *De divinis scripturis*, Ambrosiaster's *Quaestiones* and his Commentary *ad Romanos*, the nine books of dogmatic treatises dedicated by Ambrose to Emperor Gratian,[17] the *Decretum Gelasianum*, homilies by Origen, certain writings by Augustine, and others. All of these appear as basic sources, which are often only anonymously cited, some from the first to the next to the last chapter of the *Libri Carolini*.

I conclude this section with an analysis of the interdependence between *LC* III.15 (pp. 133–136) and III.29 (pp. 165–166) which has not been properly recognized by Bastgen. The *LC* author's references in III.29 (pp. 165.27 and 166.40) to earlier discussions of the same subject matter do not refer only, as Bastgen believes (pp. 165 n. 3 and 166 n. 2), to *LC* II.19 (pp. 77f.), but also to *LC* III.15, which has a number of expressions and phrases in common with *LC* III.29.

LC III.29 (p. 165.25–26) from "exemplo *imperialium imaginum . . . sanctorum omnium*" refers to, and cites verbatim from, the chapter heading of III.15 (p. 133.7–12), "Si enim *imperiales effigies . . . sanctorum omnium*." The reference to the words *beati Hieronymi* (III.29, p. 165.28) is to Jerome's *Commentarii in Danielem*, cited in III.15 (p. 134.26–38). In addition, a number of identical phrases appear in the discussions of both chapters. I list the following selection of phrases:

LC III.29 (p. 165.28) *exempla sumere*;
III.15 (p. 133.27) *exempla sumere*;
III.29 (p. 166.5f.) imagini Dei *qui inlocalis est*, adsimilare, *profanum est*;
III.15 (p. 135.12) In tabulis ergo Deum *qui inlocalis . . . est*, adorare velle . . .
        profanum est;
III.29 (p. 166.5f.) qui *a re inlicita rem inlicitam* conroborare affectat;
III.15 (p. 133.33) et *a re inlicita res inlicita* stabiliri paretur; etc.

K. Heinrich Fichtenau, p. 286 (see above n. 6), came to the conclusion that we do not know who the author of the Tironian notes was, and that the underlying marginalia could not have originated

---

[17] Cf. Chapter V, above.

with the *LC*'s author. I now believe that certain groups of corrections in the *codex authenticus*, the *Vaticanus Lat. 7207* of the *LC*, can be recognized on the basis of the preceding selection of items A–I. I have arrived at the following classification of corrections in the codex.

a. First-degree corrections possibly made by the author of the *LC* on doctrinal grounds.—There are corrections in the MS of the type described in item A which take their justification from the canonically approved and not approved writings listed in the *Decretum Gelasianum.* The latter's impact on the text of the *LC* has been investigated by Hubert Bastgen,[18] who in this connection dealt with numerous corrections caused by the direct influence of the *Decretum*, which is openly accepted as a norm for the *LC* in I.6 (Bastgen, p. 20). Thus the correction in item A, namely, *quidam doctorum* in *LC* III.6 (p. 117.29), perfectly corresponds to the *LC*'s request in *LC* I.6 (p. 20.8) "... nec *aliorum doctorum* nisi eorum qui a Gelasio ... suscepti sunt," and it is furthermore parallel in letter and spirit to *LC* III.30 (p. 167.19) "... *eorum doctorum.* ... " These correspondences make it quite likely that the author of the *LC* himself may have urged the correction in *LC* III.6 when revising his work. I should like to designate corrections of this type as first-degree corrections.

b. Second-degree corrections made by the author of the *LC* on the basis of factual grounds.—Item B may be designated as a second-degree correction because an initially mistaken ascription of the pseudo-Augustinian text to Augustine proper, and the subsequent deletion of the words "ut ait s̄c̄s Augustinus" presupposes on the corrector's part the factual knowledge that the text cited is drawn from the pseudo-Augustinian treatise *Dialogus quaestionum LXV.* Since this is a much less well-known writing than any genuine work of Augustine, I am inclined to assume that the author himself may well be responsible for the factual correction in the form of the deletion of the four words.

c. Third-degree corrections made by the author of the *LC* based on the collation of the *LC* text with its underlying source.—The two

---

[18] "Das Bilderkapitulare Karls des Gr. (libri Carolini) und das sogenannte *Decretum Gelasianum,*" *Neues Archiv* 41 (1917–19), 682–690.

items C.1 and C.2 (above) contain corrections based on the collation of the *LC* text, which is anonymously quoted from a homily
by Origen, *In Exodum, homilia IX* with its underlying source. Corrections of this type resulted in the restoration by a corrector of
passages of Origin's text cited in the *LC*. Since the corrector's
knowledge of the anonymously cited source underlying the *LC* text
is a prerequisite for such a collation of the *LC* with the corresponding
Origen passage, I am inclined to believe that the corrections originated with the author of the *LC*, although a learned corrector, other
than the author, may have been able to undertake such a collation,
all the more because Origen's homilies were widely read during
the eighth century.[19]

d. Editorial corrections and changes made by the *LC*'s author in an
anonymously cited patristic author.—A good example for this type
of correction is provided by item H concerning editorial changes
presumably made by the author of the *LC* himself. We plainly
notice that the traces of his re-editing of the passage from Ambrosiaster's *quaestio* 35, consist of (1) the omission of a sentence in
Ambrosiaster's context, in order to avoid a contradiction between
it and the theory expounded in the *LC*, (2) the substitution of
dignitate in two instances for the word *traditione*, and (3) the restoration by the corrector of Ambrosiaster's reading *potestas* in the *LC*
quotation of Rom. 13.1.

e. Editorial corrections of an older transmission of a patristic text
by a corrector other than the author of the *LC*, and not necessarily

---

[19] See the description of the Origen MSS by W. A. Baehrens, *Ueberlieferung
und Textgeschichte der lateinisch erhaltenen Origeneshomilien zum Alten Testament* (*TU*
42.1; Leipzig, 1916), 76, who assumes that Bede's Pentateuch Commentary
(*PL* 91.189ff.)—which, after all, is not by Bede, according to M. L. W. Laistner,
Harvard Theological Review 46 (1953), 33—when using Rufinus' translation of
Origen's *homilies* . . . renders Origen "in ganz freier Form." But this assessment is
incorrect, since Bede, *In Ex.*, c. 27 (*PL* 91.324C), from *Moraliter quoque potest* to
col. 325B2–3, *florida severitas disciplinae*, renders verbatim Rufinus' version of
Origen, *In Ex.*, *homilia IX.4*, ed. Baehrens, *Origenes Werke* VI (*GCS*; Leipzig, 1920),
240.22–242.21, *passim. LC* I.29 is not derived from this Bede text, but directly
from Origen, as I pointed out for the first time in *The Classical Tradition*, 498
n. 101. See also the Origen codex Lyons 443, s.VI–VII, retraced in parts, and
supplemented, during the ninth century, by Visigothic scribes. Cf. E. A. Lowe,
Codices Lugdunenses Antiquissimi (Lyons, 1924), 37, plate 18.

contemporary with him.—An instance of this type of correction in the *Vaticanus Lat. 7207* may be found, for example, in *LC* I.7 (Bastgen, pp. 23.12–24.32), a long quotation from Augustine, *De diversis quaestionibus 83*, c. 51 (*PL* 40.32–34). The identical text appears in Eugippius, *Excerpta ex operibus S. Augustini*, ed. Pius Knöll (*CSEL* 9.1; Wien, 1885), no. 328, pp. 1041.8–1044.13. It seems that the author of the *LC* cited the old text in Eugippius' *Excerpta*, and that a Carolingian corrector, who may or may not have been contemporary with the *LC*'s author, corrected this old Augustine transmission after another, presumably younger transmission of the treatise. This resulted in Bastgen's notes (p. 23*a–f*, p. 24*a–d*), all of which can now be properly understood, since we know the origin of the *LC*'s text. The nature of the corrections will become clear, as will the fact that some corrections proposed by Bastgen are not at all necessary, because the *LC* follows Eugippius' older MS transmission of the Augustinian text. Compare the following readings in the Vatican MS with Eugippius' transmission of the text:

Bastgen, *LC* I.6 (p. 23.16–17): (Quis enim) dubitat[a]; the first two words are missing in the *Vaticanus*. Bastgen supplements them after the text of Augustine's writing. Eugippius, p. 1041.13–14, likewise reads *Quis enim*.

Bastgen, p. 23.21 reads: et ipse est[b] interior, and lists in the *apparatus criticus* under *b* the word *etiam*, omitted by Bastgen on the basis of the printed Augustine text used by him. But Eugippius, p. 1041.20, offers the same *etiam*, which therefore cannot be omitted from the text cited in the *LC* that parallels the older transmission of the Augustine text offered by Eugippius. The *etiam* in the *Vaticanus* (V) also occurs in the Arsenal MS (A) of the *LC*, as listed in Bastgen's *apparatus*.[20]

Bastgen, p. 23.22: An[c] secundum corpus, MS *V* offers *ac*, also one MS of Eugippius, p. 1041 in *app. crit.* to line 20.

Bastgen, p. 23.28*d*: Bastgen reads *qui* with the printed Augustine text, while *V* has *quae*; Eugippius, 1042f, *qui*.

Bastgen, p. 23.35 reads: "summe et prime[f] vivit," and states in *f* that *prime* in *V* is "*corr. ex primitus.*" Eugippius, p. 1042.15, already reads "summe et primitus vivit." *V* thus used in its first redaction the correct reading of the older transmission of the Augustine text. The correction in *V* belongs in the *apparatus criticus*, and the *primitus* in the context of the *LC* text.

Bastgen, p. 24.12: cetera corpora animalium factum[a] iure videri potest; *V* reads *facta iure*, a reading also offered by Eugippius, p. 1043.14.

Bastgen, p. 24.13: non corpus solum[b] homo exterior; *V* reads solus, Eugippius, p. 1043.16 solum.

Bastgen, p. 24.25: qui finxit spiritum hominis[c]; according to Bastgen, *hominis* is "*corr. ex* omnibus" in *V*; Eugippius, p. 1044.3, indeed reads *omnibus* in *Prov. 24.12.

The corrections in the Augustine text listed in the *LC*, p. 23*a*, *b*, *c*, and *f*, and p. 24*a*, *b*, and *c*, evidently belong to the older text transmission represented also in Eugippius' *Excerpta*. The primary variants of the first redaction of the *LC* text in *V* should have appeared in the context of Bastgen's edition, and not in the *apparatus criticus*. But Bastgen did not use the text transmission of Eugippius.

Parallel transmissions between Augustinus texts cited in the *LC* and by Eugippius can be observed elsewhere in the *LC*. There is, for example, the reading *ministeria* in *V* (for misteria) in *LC* I.14 (p. 36.10*c*) in an excerpt from Augustine, *Quaestiones in Heptateuchum* II, c. 105 (*CSEL* 28). Eugippius, *Excerpta*, no. 113, p. 394.3, also has the variant *ministeria* in two MSS.[21]

The preceding section K, *a–e*, dealing with various categories of scribal correction in *V*, negates Freeman's statement in *Speculum* 40, p. 203, referred to at the very beginning of her "Palaeographical Problems" of the *Vaticanus*: "The Vatican manuscript of the *Libri Carolini* demonstrates, in page after page heavily scored by correction, the lively interplay of argument that accompanied its composition." But our investigations show that the corrections in *V* can hardly have resulted from any oral argument between Carolingian theologians and the author of the *LC*. They are indeed the result of editorial and scribal changes made (1) by the author of the *LC*, and (2) by some Carolingian corrector or by correctors, some of whom may well be identical with some of the four scribes who wrote the codex. Uniformity of style and argument is observable

---

[21] On the importance of Eugippius' transmission of Augustinian texts see Chapter IV, B, n. 12.

throughout the four books of the *LC*, as is uniformity in the use
made of patristic and dialectical sources underlying the work. This
speaks for the correctness of the conclusion that the *LC* is indeed
the work of a single author, and certainly not at all the collective
product of oral arguments exchanged between theologians and the
LC's author who discussed disputed topics they found in the *First
Latin Nicaenum* of the Greek *Acta* of II Nicaea. To be sure,
Carolingian theologians undoubtedly discussed with the *LC*'s
author some of the objections against image-worship voiced at the
Frankfurt Synod of 794, and certainly also between 791, when the
main part of the *LC* was composed and 794, when image-worship
was rejected by the synodal assembly. The chapter headings presumably inserted into the first recension of the *LC* text after the
arrival during 791 at the Frankish court of Hadrian I's answer
(*JE* 2483) to the earlier Frankish *Capitulare adversus Synodum* have
been investigated by von den Steinen.[22] But none of the scribal
corrections involving a corrector's collation of the patristic source
underlying the context of the *LC* can be presented as the end result
of any debate carried on between the author of the *LC* and any
other Carolingian theologian, since they plainly represent philological corrections (see above, the sections A–H, and the subsections
a–e of K). Only some larger corrections involving the deletion of
longer text passages in the first redaction of the *LC* could perhaps
indicate some external impact exerted by discussions between the
author of the *LC* and some other theologians, especially in cases
involving doctrinal matters, though it cannot be proved with certainty, not even for one single instance. *LC* III.3 (Bastgen, pp. 110–
113), for example, deals with a doctrinal matter concerning the
creed, which may well have been discussed by the *LC* author with
some of his colleagues, although it cannot be proved. The author of
the *LC* could have undertaken all these corrections in the chapter—
without any doubt—on his own! It contains a long section deleted
from the first redaction of the *LC* (p. 113.28 *f*—line 47). In addition, a scribal revision *in loco raso* replaces the text cited from
Augustine's *De trinitate*, first quoted by the author (p. 112.32*i*–35*i*),
with the rewritten Augustinian formulation offered by Isidore of

---

[22] "Entstehungsgeschichte der Libri Carolini," *QF* 21 (1929–30), 1–93; I have
shown in Chapter V, above, that *LC* II.15 cannot be an insertion into the context
of the *LC*; it is an original part of the first redaction.

Seville, *Etymologiae* 7.4.4, as I have shown in detail in Chapter III,
B.[23]

I conclude the present critical evaluation of the *Vaticanus* with a
survey of the manuscript transmission of the *LC* as far as it can be
reconstructed.

The *Vaticanus* was written by four scribes, certainly under the
supervision of the *LC*'s author. They copied the author's manuscript
of the *Libri Carolini*, which presumably consisted of loose leaves
and/or loose gatherings of parchment (*LC*). One codex, a clean
copy of the work, without the corrections and deletions now to be
found in *V*, was sent by Charlemagne to Pope Hadrian I (H), as
Hincmar of Reims reports (*PL* 126.360). Another MS of the same
type existed either at the Frankish court or among the documents
deposited with the Carolingian Capella, since the *LC* was the official
Frankish rejection of image-worship, decreed by II Nicaea of 787
(O). This MS O may have been the *LC* manuscript called by
Hincmar of Reims "non modicum volumen," a sizable codex, that
he had seen as a young man (adulescentulus) somewhere at the
Frankish court when he was visiting there. Corbie possessed a large
folio MS of the *LC* (C), of which one folium with the text of *LC* I,
cc. 12–13 (Bastgen, pp. 31.31–33.5) survives as flyleaf of Paris,
B.N. lat. 12125, fol. 157. Bernhard Bischoff, who discovered this
fragment, as reported in *Speculum* 40 (1965), 218f., assigns this
Corbie MS to the middle of the ninth century. Freeman's description of the *LC* fragment in *Speculum* 40 (1965), 287, misreads f. 157v,
line 11, "Item virgae Ioseph . . . " as the beginning of *LC* I.13
(p. 32.25, Bastgen). But the "Jtem" consists of the last syllable of
"summita(*tem*" in the erased line 10, while the elongated "J,"
which reaches to line 10 above, and to line 12 below, represents
the initially elongated "J" of "*J*)llud" at the actual beginning of
LC I.13 (p. 32.25): "*J*)llud sane quod dicunt Iacob etiam summita
(*tem* virgae Ioseph . . . . " The *LC* text from "llud . . . . summita"
in line 10 is erased. Freeman further misreads "iob" as a "variant"
for "Iacob" (p. 31.38, Bastgen), whereas it is actually an abbreviation of "Iacob" in the form of a contraction.

---

[23] Cf. Augustine, *De trinitate* XV.26.47–27.48, ed. W. J. Mountain and F. Glorie,
CCL 50A (1968), 529.113–115, and 529.1–4, who overlook my identifications in
LC III.3, pp. 112.32–35 and 113.18–20, as first listed in *Didascaliae*, pp. 478f.,
and also in Chapter III, B, above.

Bischoff now assigns to Hincmar of Reims the codex of the Bibliothèque de l'Arsenal lat. 663 (A),[24] for whom it was written about 850–860. This is the only extant completely preserved MS of the *LC*, and a copy of *V* when *V* was still unimpaired. Hitherto, A had been assigned to the year 825, when the Synod of Paris used a MS of the *LC* (P), from which testimonia of image-worship were copied and inserted into the *Libellus Synodalis* of the Paris Synod of 825. We must assume that the MSS H, O, and P naturally descend from *V*, the *LC*'s archetype, when it was still complete. The folio-sized fragment of C may well point to the probability that other large-sized MSS, larger than *V* and its copy A, had been produced at one time for the official recipients of H, O, and P. The textual transmission of the *LC* can be summarized as follows in a tentative stemma, in which the nonextant MSS are put in parentheses:

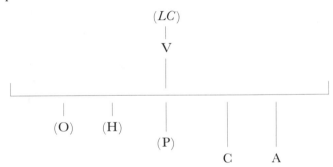

Von den Steinen (*QF*, p. 89 n. 2) identified H or its copy with a MS of the *LC* that was in the possession of the Vatican from 1481 to 1559, according to Giovanni Cardinal Mercati, "Per la storia del codice Vaticano dei libri Carolini," *Bessarione* 37 (1921), 112–119 (reprinted: *Opere minori* IV, *Studi e Testi* 79; 1937). This still lost MS, which is not identical with *V*, appears in registers saec. XVI edited by Maria Bertola, *I due primi registri di prestito della Biblioteca apostolica vaticana: codici vaticani latini 3964, 3966* (Codices e Vaticanis selecti 27; Città del Vaticano, 1942), 100 and n. 3, in an entry from May 26, 1522.

[24] See Bischoff in *Karl der Grosse: Werk und Wirkung* (Aachen, 1965, Zehnte Ausstellung unter den Auspizien des Europarates), no. 346. I am indebted to the Bibliothèque Nationale of Paris for sending me a good photostat of the *LC* folium from Corbie in codex Paris, B.N. 12125, fol. 157.

The existence of a MS P which originated at Tours, is not entirely impossible, if we recall that Fridugis, Alcuin's pupil, and in 804 his successor as abbot of Tours, was in 825 the *archicancellarius* (819–832) of Louis the Pious (see Georges Tessier, *Diplomatique royale française* [Paris, 1962], 44). As the head of the Frankish chancellery he was in all probability involved in the preparations of the Paris Synod of 825, and certainly also familiar with Tironian notes, whose occurrence in *V* could thus be connected with the quick reproduction of a MS copy of the *LC* for the use of the synodal assembly and the compilers of its *Libellus Synodalis*. Carl Erdmann, as reported by Wolfram von den Steinen (*Neues Archiv* 49 [1932], 213), once asked whether the erasures of the marginalia in *V* and their rendering in Tironian notes may not have been indeed intended as a help for scribes before they hastily produced a copy of *V*? Tours with its large scriptorium could have quickly recruited a larger number of scribes who could have copied rapidly the quires of our hypothetical MS P.

Bischoff's ascription of A to Hincmar reminds me of the only extant MS of the *Libellus Synodalis* of the Paris Synod of 825, codex Paris, B.N. lat. 1597A, which, as synodal *Libellus*, may have been ultimately connected with P, which was used by the compilers of the *Libellus* as a source for some of their testimonia of image-worship. It is not without interest to find that 1597A contains on fol. 11v to 103 not only the text of the *Libellus*, but on the pages from 11v to 107v (to be sure: *passim*) also a Tironian lexicon which was edited by Paul Legendre, *Un manuel tironien du Xe siècle publié d'après le manuscrit 1597A de la Bibliothèque Nationale* (Paris, 1905). Albert Werminghoff, *MGH, Conc.* 2.2 (Aevi Karolini 1.2; 1908), 1013, ascribes the Paris MS to the ninth century; that it was written between 882 and 900 is assumed by F. M. Carey, "The Scriptorium of Reims during the Archbishopric of Hincmar," in *Classical and Mediaeval Studies in Honor of E. K. Rand*, ed. L. W. Jones (New York, 1938), 58. It is not possible to ascertain at present whether there does exist an interconnection between the unique MS of the *Libellus* and the Tironian Lexicon (both written at St. Remy de Reims), and the Tironian notes in *V* and the production of A for Hincmar at Reims. The Berlin codex Lat. F. 626, fol. 34v–51v, probably written soon after 1100, offers the only other MS of the *Libellus Synodalis Parisiensis* of 825, a transmission unknown to Werminghoff.

But Wilhelm A. Eckhardt, "Zur Ueberlieferung des Pariser Konzils von 825," *Zeitschrift für Kirchengeschichte* 65 (1953–54), 126–128, shows that many variants of the Berlin codex, now deposited in the University Library at Tübingen, are identical with the Paris MS 1597A. The Berlin codex is copied from the Paris manuscript. The uniqueness of the Paris codex as the source of the Berlin MS remains unchallenged.

The involved philological problems connected with the *Vaticanus Lat. 7207* as the archetype of the *Libri Carolini* are here illustrated by two examples from *LC* II.29 and III.29.

I. Erasure and correction in the *Libri Carolini* II c. 29.—*LC* II.29 (p. 91.18–19, Bastgen) reads as follows: "Quod presumptive et indocte eas Tarasius cum *sequacibus* suis sacratis *vasis* aequiperare non formidet." *Sequacibus* is written on erasure, and *vasis* is corrected from an original *vasibus*. The former is certainly a substitute for an original *complicibus*, since the so-called *Capitulare adversus Synodum*, cited in the *Hadrianum* I.39 (p. 33.29–30, Hampe), offers a not corrected parallel text to *LC* II.29 with the readings *complicibus* and *vasibus*. The *Hadrianum* I.39 (pp. 33.28 and 33.15, Hampe) refers to a text *in actione sexta* of the synodal *Acta* of II Nicaea of 787, and also *LC* II.29 may well refer to the identical passage, in Mansi XIII.270E8–11: "Nam et sacra diversa vasa habentes, haec salutamus et amplectimur, et sanctitatem quandam percipere ab eis speramus." This is from the Latin version of the Greek *Acta* translated by Anastasius Bibliothecarius by 873. The corresponding text in the earlier (now lost) Latin translation from about 788 is preserved in the fragmentary citation of the *Hadrianum* I.39 (p. 33.31–34): "Pro hoc in synodo dictum est a Tharasio patriarcha Constantinopolitano: Quia et sacra diversa vasa habentes, has osculamus et amplectimus, et sanctificationem quandam accipere ab eis speramus." The same Tarasius text of the *Hadrianum* I.39 is cited independently in a longer context in the chapter heading of *LC* IV.16 (pp. 202.17 and 171.36–37) as well as in the chapter's context (p. 205.8–9) after the *First Latin Nicaenum* of ca. 788: "Nam et sacra diversa vasa habentes has osculamur et amplectimur et sanctificationem quandam speramus." The relationship between Anastasius' second Latin version of this passage in the Greek *Acta* of II Nicaea to that of the *First Latin Nicaenum* of 788 of the same

Greek passage corresponds to the principle of Anastasius' translation method investigated in Chapter V at n. 21. Again we notice Anastasius' consistency when translating the ἀσπαζόμεθα of the synodal text with *salutamus*, while the 788 version has *osculamus*. We notice in this connection that the *Hadrianum* I.39 (p. 34.1–3) cites verbatim a statement from the iconoclastic *horos* of the Synod of Hiereia of 754, a fact overlooked in Hampe's edition, since the three lines should have been printed in italics. Compare the following three texts *a*, *b*, and *c*:

a. Hadrianum I.39 (p. 34.1–3, Hampe):

neque orationem sacram sanctificantem eam, ut ex hoc ad sanctam a communi transferatur, sed manet communis et inhonorata, sicut operavit eam pictor;

b. Greek *Acta* of II Nicaea, 787, *actio* VI, Mansi XIII.268B–C and also 269C–D, from the *horos* of the iconoclastic Synod of Hiereia, 754:

οὔτε εὐχὴν ἱερὰν ἁγιάζουσαν αὐτήν, ἵν᾽ ἐκ τούτου πρὸς τὸ ἅγιον ἐκ τοῦ κοινοῦ μετενεχθῇ. ἀλλὰ μένει κοινὴ καὶ ἄτιμος, ὡς ἀπήρτισεν αὐτὴν ὁ ζωγράφος.

c. Anastasius Bibliothecarius, translation of the *Acta* of II Nicaea, Mansi XIII.267C2–6, and again 270C–D:

neque orationem sacram sanctificantem illud, ut ex hoc ad sanctitatem ex eo [sanctificationem ab eo col. 270] quod commune est, transferatur: sed manet commune et inhonoratum, sicuti patravit hoc pictor [ac inhonorandum quem admodum, hoc pictor effecit col. 270].

The differences between the translations in *a* and *c* of the identical Greek text *b* indicate how closely Anastasius in 873 followed the first translation of 788. It seems that the author of the *LC* II.29 (above) was certainly aware of the distinctions between the more neutral meaning of *sequacibus*, and the *complicibus* in the *Hadrianum* I.39. The latter's more criminal meaning may have been the reason why he replaced it with the less pejorative term, all the more because he differentiated in *LC* III.14 (p. 155.15–16) between Jerome's *Vigilantius eiusque sequacibus* and *Simon Mago eiusque complicibus*.

II. The meaning of two erasures in the *Libri Carolini* III.29.—Two erasures in the *Vaticanus Latinus 7207* at *LC* III.29 (p. 166.34 and

36) in an anonymously cited text drawn from Ambrosiaster's *quaestio* 35 may well have a very specific meaning. The author of the *LC* lists the biblical Saul as a *rex*, and therefore also changed Ambrosiaster's original *traditione* (p. 166.34) to *dignitate*. He postulates that this royal *dignitas* is respected by the king's subjects not for its own sake but *propter ordinem*, since the king's authority is based, according to Ambrosiaster's opinion, *in officio ordinis regalis*. It is probably on this ground that Ambrosiaster's second occurrence of *traditione* (p. 166.36 *h*) is replaced in the *Vaticanus* again by the word *dignitate*, which is written *in loco raso*. The *LC* does not outline the status of an *imperator*, but describes that of a *rex* whose Frankish *dignitas* was certainly familiar to the author of the *LC*. This preference presumably accorded to the Frankish king is strongly reminiscent of Alcuin's well-known statements concerning the three *personae* who until now have occupied the highest positions in life, as he states in his *Epistola* 174 of June 799, addressed to Charlemagne. Those three are the pope who "vicario munere" occupies the *sedes Petri*, the *imperialis dignitas* of the Byzantine emperor at Constantinople, and finally the *regalis dignitas* of the *rex Francorum*. The latter, according to Alcuin, is more sublime in relation to *ceteris praefatis dignitatibus*, and more excellent and outstanding in wisdom, *sapientia clariorem*. F. L. Ganshof pointed out in 1949 that Charlemagne's superiority as the Frankish *rex* in Alcuin's *Epistola* 174 is traceable to the historical fact that the imperial *dignitas* at Byzantium had been infringed upon by a woman's incumbency, namely, the Empress Irene. I suggest that a similar, if not the identical, reason and meaning may be seen in the preference ascribed to the king's office in *LC* III.29 (p. 166.30–38), all the more because *LC* III.13 (p. 127.25–26) deals with the uncanonical status of Irene at II Nicaea of 787: "Quia mulier in synodo docere non debet, sicut Herena in eorum synodo fecisse legitur." The author of the *LC* (p. 127.37–38), following Isidore of Seville, *Etymologiae* 9.7.27, argues that woman customarily obeys man (viro concedi solere) in three aspects: "causa prolis, causa adiutorii, causa incontinentiae." But absolutely nowhere, *nusquam penitus*, do we read that woman helps man *causa vero docendi* (p. 128.24). Otherwise, Empress Irene is somewhat ridiculed in the *LC* (p. 127.35–36). She is referred to as "an unmarried woman of advanced age" when the *LC* speaks of "feminas innuptas quamvis *provectae* sint *aetatis*, propter ipsam animi

levitatem in tutela consistere debere." Bastgen has not noticed that
the *LC* is citing Isidore of Seville, *Etymologiae* 9.7.30: " ... et
veteres voluerunt feminas innuptas, quamvis *perfectae aetatis* essent,
propter ipsam animi levitatem in tutela consistere." Isidore's "mar-
riageable age" (perfectae aetatis) is altered by the author of the *LC*
rather sarcastically to the "advanced age" (provectae . . . aetatis)
of the widowed Irene. There can be little doubt that the intimate
acquaintance of the *LC*'s author with Ambrosiaster's *Quaestiones*
only strengthened his traditional opinion concerning the status of
women. He read at the end of *quaestio* 45 that a *mulier* can neither
teach nor be a legal witness, "neque fidem dicere nec iudicare,"
and therefore she cannot rule: "quanto magis imperare"!

A play on words similar in sound, but different in meaning (as in
the just-mentioned instance involving Empress Irene), is employed
in *LC* III.2 (p. 110.3–5) and I.20 (46.37–39) with reference to the
Patriarch Tarasius of Constantinople, who chaired the Council of
II Nicaea, 787; it is explained above in Chapter I, item D, at
note 43.

illo non donantur Quibus de proprie caritas nun
cupatur uel quia naturaliter eos a quibus proce
dit coniungit & seunum cum eis esse ostendit Uel
quia in nobis id agit ut in dō maneamus & ipse in nobis
Vnde & in domini dī nihil maius est caritate & nullum
est maius donum dī quam spr̄s s̄c̄s ipse est & gratia
Quae quia non meritis nostris sed diuina uoluntate
gratis datur Inde gratia nuncupatur Sicut autem
unicum dī uerbu proprie uocamus nomme sapientie cūsit
uniuersaliter & spr̄s s̄c̄s & pater ipse sapientia ita spr̄s s̄c̄s
proprie nuncupatur uocabulo caritatis cūsit & pater & filius
uniuersaliter caritas est qui spr̄s patris ad cuius dilectio quiati
[...] non enim uos estis qui loquimini sed spr̄s patris uestri
qui loquitur in uobis Est & spr̄s filii paulo ad ter
tante quia Quisquis autem spiritum xp̄i non habet
hic non est eius Xc per hoc spr̄s amborum dicitur

quia ex patre & filio procedens unius probatur
esse substantiae & naturae Quis ingenitur di
ceretur duo patres profiterentur Si genitur du
filii inconuenienter dicerentur Sed quia nec pater
est nec filius Ideo nec ingenitus nec genitus sed ab
utroque procedens dicitur Pater enim solus non
est de alio Ideo solus appellatur Ingenitus non
quidem in scripturis sed in consuetudine disputa
tantium & de re tanta sermonem qualem ualu
erint ad presentium siue futurorum profectum
proferentium Filius solus de patre est natus Ideo
solus dicitur genitus Spr̄s s̄c̄s solus de patre & filio

procedit. Ideo solus amborum nuncupatur sps
procedit enim ex utroque non nascendo ut ali
eatur filius dici potest

Dicetur autem filius patris & filii si quod absor
ret ab omnium fidelium sensibus eum ambo genu
issent. Non igitur ab utroque est genitus sed pro
cedit ab utroque amborum spr. A patre illum
autem procedere dns noster ihs xps discipulos
docuit dicens Cum autem venerit inquit paracli
tus quem ego mittam vobis a patre spm veritatis
qui a patre procedit Ille testimonium perhibebit
de me. Et rursum ipse dei hominum mediator
dns ihs xps post resurrectionem suam ut osten
deret a se procedere spm scm sicut & a patre insuf
flans in discipulos suos ait Accipite spm scm
Qui nisi ab eo procederet nequaquam eum insuf
flans discipulis daret Unus ergo est spr patris
& filii unus ut supra memoravimus amborum spr
Quod si quis quaeret quomodo filius a patre nas
cendo procedit Spr vero scs procedendo non nasci
tur Aut quare non uterque sint filii cum uterque
a patre procedant Aut quare non & spr scs dicatur
ingenitus sicut pater Aut quomodo ab utroque pro
cedat . . . Aut quare filius dicat . . . sicut
habet pater vitam in semetipso sic dedit et filio vita
habere in semetipso . . . quia antea sine vita idem
filius & vita est & hanc a patre dante susceperit
Aut quomodo pater . . . numquam sine filio
et tamen pater genuit filium . . . Aut quomodo

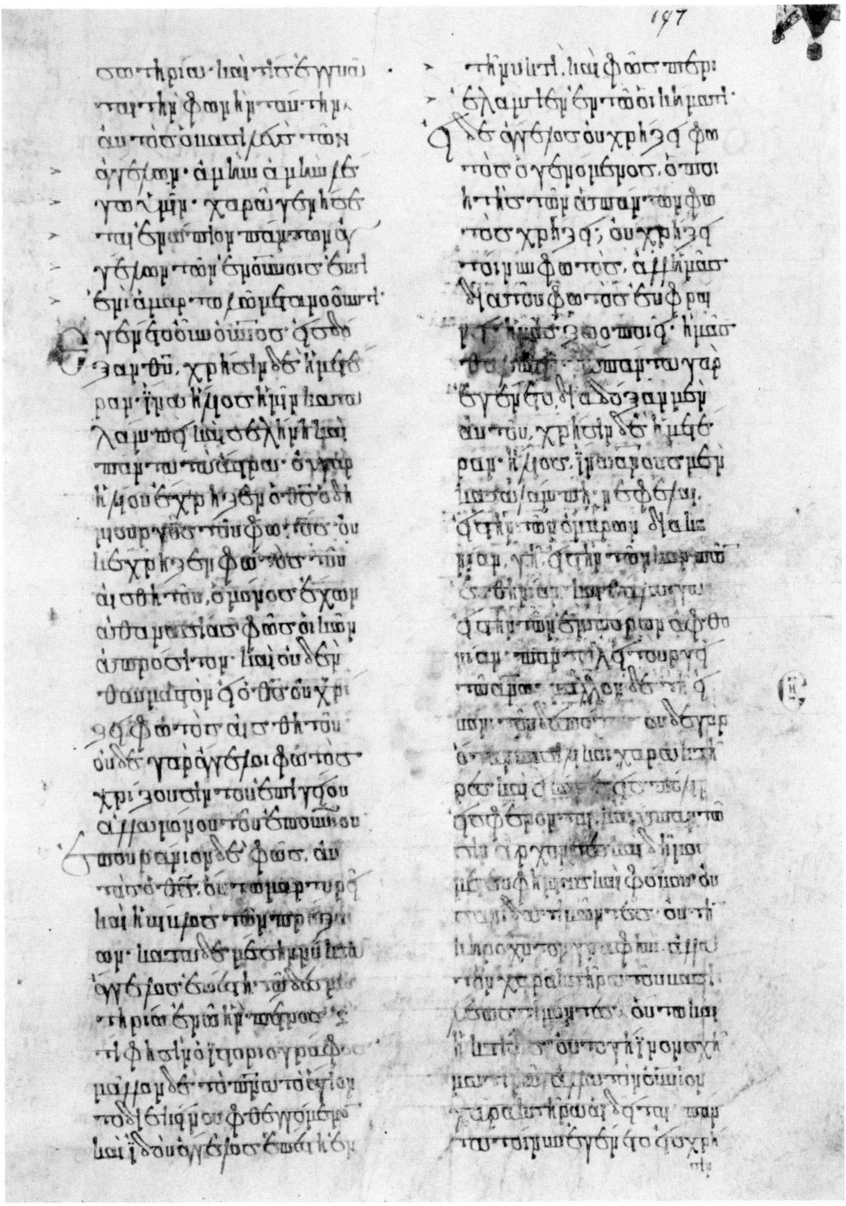

Plate III. Vaticanus Ottobonianus Graecus 85, fol. 197r

no illor enim qualiter aut contrarie ih
ruine auc dog marizant contra seas ima
ginef alienor catholice ecclesie depucap
& praedico &heraicos adnuncio

Cum eutimiuf sardensis eps constantino
constantiae cypri epo pene par sit Incon
fessione noneft ambiguum parem eor habere
fidem parem que adepturos r&ributionem si
si emendatio In utro illorum praecesserit
Exto to enim corde uterque se confite uif sus
cipere Imaginef cumsummo honore &amplec
tibili adoratione O demens epoqum con
fessio Olnsana praesulum praedicatio ecclesia
catholica uocepraesulum Incarnationis xpi
mysterium sesusefpisccongratulans dño dicet
suscepimus dr misericordiam tuam Inmedio
templitui &isti dicunt suscipimus &adoramus
Imaginef caterua credentium xpim quieft pax
noftra quisfecit utraque unum apostolos siue
xpostolicos uiros suscipere pr ecatur dicens
Suf cipiant montes pacem populitui &isti di
cunt suscipimus Imaginef adoratione ampletti
bili Cum ergo isti pene omnem auxiliisui spe
In imaginibus defigant nonmediocriter a sca
&uniuersali dissentiunt ecclesia quaespem
auxiliisui non Inpicture sucis nonlnmanufacus
artificium operibus sed Indo omnium creatoredesigt Quae
habe& ad iutorereptor &apostolicos uirosquipro eaquotidi e
dnm interpellant &suscep tium dono scisssss

desuper nr̄ sedibus Imbrem scī praedicationis
utpote altiora Inecclesia loca fidelibus plebibus
siue rectoribus diffundunt secundum iohel uati
cinium dicentis &erit Inilla die distillabunt mon
tes dulcedinem &colles fluent lac   quod &iam
his uerbis ezechiel Intonat dicens. uestri autem
montes israhel facient uiam &fructum uestrum
quemuos manducabitis populus meus quia uia &
quis fructus quamquam xpr̄ dr̄r Intellegatur quide
montibus israhel processit Apatri archis uideli
cæt hominem adsu in eos potest &iam dulcedo
    praedicationis uideri &nouo testamento con
    paginata Intellegi quaediffunditur perhumili
um fidelium mentes &Incredulorum corda ad
credendum &adfructum afferendum mollificat
&rectorum sensus aeternae spei retributione
laetificat eorque iustitia Indui &cum subiectis plebi
bus dō ymnum canere exortatur Inpl&ur que
illud prophǽticum campi tui replebuntur ubesta
te pinguescent fines deserti &exultatione colles
accingentur Indutisunt arietes ouium &conual
les abundabunt frumento &enim clamabunt
& ymnum dicent leuat enim oculos suos adeos
cum dicit leuaui oculos meos admontes undeue
ni& auxilium mihi . Nonenim ait leuaui oculos
meos adres Insensatas   uocab his adiutorium ad
ipiceret sedleuaui oculos meos admontes Adeos
uidelicæt montes super quos ecclesia xp̄i fundata
est dicente proph &a fundamenta eius Inmon

Plate V. Vaticanus Latinus 7207, fol. 158b

Auditum sit k̄mi &diuulgatum e̅ p̄ multa loca qualiter
homines mali aduersusme insurrexer & debilitare
uoluerunt. & miserunt sup me g̅rauia crimina
propt quam causam audiendam iste clementissimus
ac serenissimus domnus rex Carolus unacu sacer
dotibus & optimatibus suis istam po . . . . ad urbē
quam obrem ego leo pontifex sc̄e romane ecc̄e
a nemine iudicatus neq: coactus sedspontanea mee
uoluntate purifico & purgo me in conspectu
uestro coram dō & angelis eius qui conscientiam
meam nouit & beato p&ro principe apostoloru̅
incuius basilica consistimus quia istas criminosas
& sceleratas res quas illi mihi obiciunt nec per
pṣ . . . . ui nec pp̄ parere iussi. testis mihi e̅ dn̄ in
cuius iudicium uenturi sumus & incuius conspectu
consistimus. & hoc propt sus praiones tollendas
mea spontanea uoluntate facio nonquasi in
canonibus inuentum sit aut quasi ego hanc con
suetudinem aut decretum in sc̄a ecc̄a successo
ribus meis necnon & fratribus & coepis̄ nostris
inponam .

pater
noster

A A ab oriente obgata antiquitus a regina e(ius)
nomen finxit imperio: haec inter uaq; p
orbis est disposita. Ab oriente ab occasu sol
maris americ(us) ab oziano q; mare terre
no coniungitur A septentrione pluuialem
denieq; cingitur; h. b& primu paradisi ostio
rum dilicias; qui omni genere pomoru circu
septus g. emin. t; hab& &iam uitae ligru
Inter medias; p. onest aestus; &eq; frigus
sincere temperies; fons manat in depennis
fluit&; in riuolis; post peccatu includusus
est primi hominis; & circum septus e. d;
rompheaq; ignita ita pene usq; ad caelos
iun&aquae incendia angelorum est uallatus
cherubin presidia; India habe.
lenta patria gentes plurimas; qua e&u
magna oppida; Insula quo; probana
heli fantes nuricat; Auro argen
fecundia; atq; pluras gemmulas; Biril
los &cr solitos adamantes; carbunculos
leoni&e & margaritas unionespullula

q; ni. De ill. & putant

CHAPTER X

Valid and Invalid Argumentation ·
concerning "Spanish Symptoms"

The reviewer for a leading liturgical journal expressed his doubt concerning Freeman's article in *Speculum* 32 (1957) with regard to the validity of her argumentation.[1] He suggested that further investigations are required in order to find out "ob die Beweisführung ganz stichhaltig ist." His doubt is certainly justified. In my Section A, below, her approach to Bible texts that do not fit her thesis is dealt with. The actual meaning of an important study by Donatien de Bruyne is shown in B. A few strangely incorrect references to the present writer's opinions are listed in C. Section D proves that the *Clavis Melitonis* was not one of the *LC*'s sources, as had been assumed mistakenly by von den Steinen, by Freeman, and by the present writer. The degree of liturgical similarity between the Mozarabic Antiphonary of León and the Frankish Antiphonary of Compiègne is investigated and otherwise tested in Section E.

A1. The specific approach used by Freeman in *Speculum* 32 (1957) when dealing with biblical texts in the *LC* was rejected in the study which I published in *Didascaliae* (1961). The same approach reappears in *Speculum* 40 (1965), where she states that the Vulgate texts printed in her first study were supplied from the Clementine version of the Vulgate. She maintains in *Speculum* 40 (1965), 252 n. 177, that one of her readings, that I had called "erroneous," is that of the Clementine Vulgate. Since there were three Clementina texts during the last years of the sixteenth century, her reference

---

[1] *Archiv für Liturgiewissenschaft* 8 (1963), 219 no. 337; I assume that A. E. Mayer, the editor of this journal, expressed this judgment.

remains vague, for she never tells which one she has used. She justifies her choice in *Speculum* 40, p. 234 n. 117, by saying that it was "for consistency's sake" and that she took no liberties with the Bible text. But in *Speculum* 32 (1957), 679, she nevertheless omitted verse 28 from *Prov.* 8.22–31, as she states in *Speculum* 40 (1965), 241 n. 149: "This Vulgate passage [Prov. 8.22–31], as printed in *Speculum* 32, 679 omitted v. 28. . . ." The procedure of altering texts through the omission of words is inadmissable,[2] historically and philologically. The same approach is applied by her to Ecclus. 24.7 in *LC* III.14 (p. 131.4). "This citation," she says in *Speculum* 40 (1965), 243.3, "was not listed in *Speculum* 32 (1957), 679 because it contains no specifically Spanish variant. . . ." But Ecclus. 24.7 presumably was omitted by her from the text of the *LC* because it is not cited in the Mozarabic Antiphonary of León. Its omission creates a closer conformity between the Bible texts in the *LC* and in the *AL*, and leads to the assumption of a "Spanish Symptom" in the *LC* where there is none.

A2. I stated in *Didascaliae*, p. 501, that the words *egredietur et* are omitted from the Vulgate text of John 10.9. Freeman says in *Speculum* 40 (1965), 257 N, that these words were omitted by her because "the Vulgate texts printed in *Speculum* 32 (1957) were supplied from the Clementine version; it was the Clementine editors who omitted the words *egredietur et* from John 10.9." Naturally, the comparison between the sixteenth-century text of a Clementina and *LC* Bible texts from the eighth century is meaningless. We expect a comparison between the *LC*'s biblical text and the critical NT edition of Jerome's Vulgate by Wordsworth and White. Bastgen, *LC* III.17 (p. 140.1), reads in John 10.9 *et regredietur*, and remarks that *et* is written in *V* on erasure. He does not mention that the *r* of *regredietur* is written in *V*, fol. 157r, either on an erasure (as I believe), or else perhaps added by a corrector in a different ink. This means that the wording of John 10.9 in the first redaction of the *LC* was not at all identical with the version in *AL*. With this

---

[2] Von den Steinen, *QF* 21 (1929–30), 52 n. 1, calls the similar procedure used in the *Hadrianum* (*JE* 2483): "Zitatverfälschung durch blosses Auslassen." Elizabeth Dahlhaus-Berg, *Nova Antiquitas et Antiqua Novitas* (Köln, Wien, 1975), 175, 178, justifiably dares to question some practices encountered by her in Freeman's article in *Speculum* 40 (1965), which she obviously finds objectionable.

fact, we lose another of the alleged "Spanish Symptoms" of the *LC* (see below, Chapter XI, N).

B. The real meaning of de Bruyne's article in *Revue Bénédictine* 44 (1932), 227–234.[3]—Certain ideas concerning Theodulph of Orléans' alleged authorship of the *Libri Carolini* are read by Freeman, *Speculum* 40 (1965), 223–224, into de Bruyne's statements when we are told that the latter "points out the pitfalls of an unsophisticated approach toward the liturgical texts of the period, and demonstrated that certain citations ascribed by Allgeier (*Hist. Jahrbuch* 46, 1926, 352) to the Mozarabic Psalter, actually came from the Pseudo-Augustinian *Liber de divinis scripturis*; de Bruyne concluded (*RB* 44,227): 'celles-là au moins ne pouvaient pas démontrer la thèse nouvelle.'" The new thesis of Allgeier was not at all the assumption of Theodulph's authorship of the *LC*, as Freeman conjectures, but Allgeier's mistaken assumption of the occurrence of quotations from the Mozarabic Psalter in the *LC*, disproved by de Bruyne. Allgeier's new thesis is mentioned a second time by de Bruyne, when he reports on his conversation with Allgeier, who told him about his alleged discovery that the Mozarabic Psalter had been utilized by the author of the *LC*, a discovery Allgeier believed to be "un argument décisif contre l'attribution de ces livres à Alcuin" (*Revue Bénédictine* 44, 228). This, then—that is, the alleged utilization of the Mozarabic Psalter by the author of the *LC*—was the new thesis referred to by de Bruyne, to which he refers again on p. 228 as "la réfutation que nous devons faire de la thèse d'Allgeier." To be sure, Mozarabic Psalters are liturgical texts too, but nevertheless Freeman's contention that de Bruyne speaks of "liturgical texts" is as mistaken as is her assumption that "de Bruyne did not suggest that no relationship would ever be found between *LC* citations and liturgical sources." Contrary to her understanding of de Bruyne's point of view, de Bruyne indeed correctly assumed that he had disproved Allgeier's wrong notion that Alcuin could not have been the author of the *LC*. For this very reason also Allgeier's thesis of Theodulph's authorship of the *LC* had been demolished. In 1947, F. L. Ganshof stated in "La révision de la Bible par Alcuin," reprinted in translation in Ganshof's *The Carolingians and the Frankish Monarchy* (Ithaca,

[3] D. de Bruyne, "La composition des Libri Carolini," *Revue Bénédictine* 44 (1932), 227–234.

N.Y., 1971), 39 n. 39, that Allgeier's arguments against Alcuin's authorship of the *LC* "have been demolished by D. de Bruyne." Reports on de Bruyne's study of 1932 in scholarly journals confirm Ganshof's and the present writer's interpretation of his article,[4] and not Freeman's. The article was in the eyes of its author a contribution to "Biblical literature," and for this reason Cyrille Lambot's announcement of it appeared in a section entitled "Littérature biblique" which was supervised by de Bruyne himself: "Etude sur les citations scripturaires des L.C. Contrairement à ce qu'affirmait M. Allgeier . . . elles proviennent en grande partie du *Liber de divinis scripturis.* . . ."[5]

C1. A selection of some strange and incorrect references must be mentioned here. Freeman says in *Speculum* 40 (1965), 270 n. 244: "In this reference to "noster Gregorius" there is an indication of Alcuin's hand in the Frankish letter that has not been noticed by Mr. Wallach." She then refers to Edmund Bishop "cited by Wallach, *Alcuin and Charlemagne*, p. 159. . . ." But on the very page (n. 33) of my book to which she refers, I say: "Edmund Bishop, *Liturgica Historica* (Oxford, 1918), 171 sees the hand of Alcuin in the reference to 'noster vero Gregorius' . . . following the example of Bede in referring to Gregory I as 'noster Gregorius.'" A similar strange reference to my book is discussed in Chapter XII, G below, another in Chapter XI, N.

C2. The statement in *Speculum* 40, 273 n. 263, that by dating Helisachar's letter to the year 814 in *Didascaliae* I "apparently" misinterpreted a footnote by Ernst Dümmler, is incorrect. I refer in *Didascaliae*, 510 n. 72, also to Heinz Loewe, *Deutschlands Geschichtsquellen im Mittelalter: Die Karolinger III* (Weimar, 1957), 305 n. 48, who lists as *terminus ante quem non* for Helisachar's letter the year 814, and thus properly adjusts Dümmler's date.

[4] Cf. M. Cappuyns in *Bulletin de théologie ancienne et médiévale* 2 (1933–36), 264, no. 481; H. N. in *Revue d'histoire ecclésiastique* 29 (1933), 197; David Amand in *Revue Bénédictine* 55 (1943–44), 178.

[5] See *Bulletin d'ancienne littérature chretiénne latine*, ed. Donatien de Bruyne and Cyrille Lambot, 2 (1929–38), 148f., no. 519. The reliability of Dom de Bruyne's studies on the pseudo-Augustinian *Liber de divinis scripturis*, one of the *LC*'s main sources of biblical texts, is acknowledged by Walter Thiele, *Die lateinischen Texte des I. Petrusbriefs* (Freiburg i.Br., 1965), 67.

C3. *Speculum* 40 (1965), 285 n. 231, reports that a passage in *LC* III.3 (Bastgen, p. 113.18–20) is taken from Augustine, *De trinitate*. But I said in *Didascaliae*, p. 479, which appeared in 1961, that *LC* III.3 (p. 113.18–20) is taken from Augustine, *De trin.* XV.27,48 (*PL* 42.1095, 21–24). See also above Chapter III, B.

C4. *Speculum* 40 (1965), 251, states that the conflation of 2 Cor. 3.18 with 2 Cor. 4.2 is not available in the *Liber de divinis scripturis* and as proof Freeman refers in her note 72 to *CSEL* 12.222. But this is a reference to Augustine's *Speculum*, and not to the pseudo-Augustinian *De divinis scripturis*. The latter, edited by F. Weihrich, *CESL* 12, pp. 375.11–376.3, indeed offers the conflation, as Weihrich records: "II Cor. 3.18 et II Cor. 4.1–2."

D. The *Clavis Melitonis* and the *Libri Carolini*.—Wolfram von den Steinen reiterated in 1954, as reported in *Speculum* 32 (1957), 694 n. 131, his opinion that the *Libri Carolini* used the *Clavis Melitonis (CM)*, a glossary of biblical words and concepts based on Latin Fathers with corresponding scriptural quotations, first edited by J. B. Pitra, *Spicilegium Solesmense* II–III (Paris, 1855), and later re-edited by Pitra, *Analecta Sacra Spicilegio Solesmensi parata* II (Paris, 1884), on the basis of the Codex Claromontanus, a ninth-century MS from Orléans, now Vaticanus Barberini lat. 492.[6] In *Didascaliae* (pp. 497 H, 503 P, 501 N, 504 R) I adopted von den Steinen's view, but herewith withdraw my endorsement of the *CM* as a source used by the author of the *LC* as assumed by von den Steinen and Freeman. Both believed that the *LC* used the *CM* because Theodulph's Bible MSS contain excerpts from the *CM*, although neither of them ever mentioned the fact that Theodulph's Bible MSS originated a few decades after the composition of the *LC*. The remarks in *Speculum* 40 (1965), 257, do not take into account the fact that von den Steinen, *Neues Archiv* 49 (1932), 254 n. 1,

---

[6] Cf. Adolf Harnack, *Die Ueberlieferung der griechischen Apologeten des zweiten Jahrhunderts* (*TU* I.1–2; Leipzig, 1883), 275f., also Harnack, *Geschichte der altchristlichen Litteratur bis Eusebius* I (Leipzig, 1893), 254, section 5. Harnack ascribes the Claromontanus not to the ninth, but to the tenth century. See D. Rottmann, "Ein letztes Wort über den Clavis Melitonis," *Theologische Quartalschrift* 78 (Tübingen, 1898), 614–629. Cf. J. Quasten, *Patrology* I (Utrecht, Brussels, 1960), 248, and the reference to Pitra, *Analecta Sacra* II (Paris, 1884).

already referred to the 1884 edition of the *CM*. I no longer share his assumption that the *LC* used the *CM* for the following reasons.

In *Neues Archiv* 49 (1932), 254 n. 1, von den Steinen mentions the peculiar exegesis of walls as allegories for saints mentioned in *LC* I.20 (p. 47.6–7). In this context, he refers to Pitra, *Spicilegium Solesmense* II (Paris, 1855), lxxvii no. 509: "muri: munimenta scripturarum, vel prophetae, aut sancti." Although von den Steinen indeed mentions Pitra, *Analecta Sacra* II (1884), 67 nn. 53–55, he does not refer to the identical allegory for *sancti* to *muri* in *CM* 9, in Codex Claromontanus, *Analecta Sacra* II, p. 64 n. 6. But he was also unaware of the fact that the allegory of the *CM* is derived from Eucherius of Lyons, *Formulae* 9, ed. Carl Wotke (*CSEL* 31; 1894), 55.3: "Muri: munimenta scripturae divinae vel prophetae aut sancti." Since the author of the *LC* was certainly familiar with Eucherius' *Instructiones*,[7] one might assume that he also could have known the *Formulae* of Eucherius. But such an assumption as well as the alleged acquaintance with the *CM* are untenable. The reason is quite simple: the *LC* passage I.20 (Bastgen, p. 47.6–7) does not at all render words written by the author of the *LC*. It belongs—unknown to von den Steinen and Bastgen—to a lengthy section, not identified by Bastgen, from Bede's *De templo Salomonis*, which appears as an appendix to some medieval Bible commentaries, as is pointed out below in Chapter XII, E, dealing with "Evidence at Germigny-des-Prés." In 1932, von den Steinen was not aware of the fact that the passage under consideration renders the text of Bede, and for this reason he could suggest the *LC*'s familiarity with the *Clavis Melitonis*, for which there is now no evidence available.

The assumption stated in *Speculum* 32 (1957), 695, that the use of the *CM* may be suspected again in *LC* I.16 (Bastgen, p. 38f.) and also in *LC* I.29 (pp. 55–59) is disproved by my findings recorded in *The Classical Tradition* (Ithaca, N.Y., 1966), 498 n. 101, where I list the dependence of the *LC* I.17 (p. 40) on Origen, *In Exodum, homilia 13*, ed. W. A. Baehrens (*Origenes Werke* VI [GCS], Leipzig, 1920), 274f., and of the *LC* I.29 on Origen, *In Exodum, homilia 9* (Baehrens, pp. 234–244, *passim*). For *LC* I.16 see Chapters VIII, A

---

[7] Bastgen refers for *LC* IV.18 (p. 208.10–13) to Gregory's *Hom. in Ez.*, but the direct source of the passage is Eucherius, *Instructiones* I: *De Ezechiele*, ed. Carl Wotke (*CSEL* 31; 1894), 87.

and IX, C–C2. The *Clavis Melitonis* evidently is not one of the sources of the *Libri Carolini*.

E. The Mozarabic Antiphonary of León and the Frankish Antiphonary of Compiègne.—After the Visigothic Antiphonary of León (*AL*) had been brought into connection with the *LC* in *Speculum* 32 (1957), the importance of the Carolingian Antiphonary of Compiègne (*AC*), the codex Paris, B.N. lat. 17436, was called to Freeman's attention (*Speculum* 40 [1965], 271f.), although this service book has been published long ago in *PL* 78 as *Liber Responsalis*. *AC* is an antiphonary for the Mass and the Office whose text undoubtedly was similar to the antiphonary used by the generation of the *LC*, including Alcuin and Theodulph.[8] The antiphons and other liturgical texts for the Office reflect in both books the core of identical texts inherited by Latin liturgies from an ultimately common origin. They may be compared with one another because, despite the structural differences of the various rites which they represent, they nevertheless contain common characteristics and in particular possess a really considerable number of "pièces de chant identiques, où presque identiques, quant aux textes et aux sources littéraires."[9] In addition, notwithstanding all apparent differences, there exists between the two repertoires, from the textual point of view, "un air de famille incontestable," neglected by Freeman, and for this reason alone, her treatment, based on outmoded liturgical considerations, cannot stand critical examination. Some of the *AL* texts adduced by her as alleged sources of the *LC* also occur in the *AC*, as I shall show subsequently.

The date of the *AL* has been severely questioned by scholars, but Freeman fails to report sufficiently on the various opinions. Agustín Millares Carlo, "Manuscritos visigóticos: Notas bibliográficas,"

---

[8] Cf. Cyrille Vogel, *Introduction aux sources de l'histoire du culte chrétien au Moyen Age* (Spoleto, 1966), 331f.; on other MSS related to MS Compiègne see the edition of the antiphonary by Hesbert, cited below, n. 12. B. Fischer, *Verzeichnis der Sigel* (Vetus Latina I.1; 1963), 180, says of *Brev. Goth.*, on good grounds, "Es wird nur einiges angeführt."

[9] Louis Brou, "L'antiphonaire wisigothique et l'antiphonaire grégorien au début du VIIIe siècle," *Anuario Musical* 5 (Barcelona, 1951), 7; see also José Janini, "Sacramentorum Prefationes y liturgia visigótica," *Hispania Sacra* 17 (1964), especially section IV on "Expresiones romanas imitadas en la liturgia visigótica," pp. 160–163.

Hispania Sacra 14 (1961), 362f., no. 35, dates *AL* "mediados del siglo X," while M. Férotin ascribed it to the seventh century. But now M. C. Díaz y Díaz, *Index scriptorum latinorum medii aevi Hispanorum* I (Salamanca, 1958), no. 638, p. 155, says "potius X antiquiores non arbitror," and Dekkers-Gaar, *Clavis patrum latinorum* (2nd ed.; 1961), no. 1943, agree with him: "merito recentiorem *(scil.* text.) aestimat." Dom Serrano, one of the co-editors of the Benedictine *AL* edition of Silos (1928), denies Férotin's assumption that *AL* is a witness of the Mozarabic liturgy of the seventh century (F. Cabrol, *DACL* 12 [1936], 409). And Bernhard Bischoff, *Mittelalterliche Studien* II (Stuttgart, 1967), 300, ascribed the MS of *AL* to "ca. 1067." Origin, date, and provenence of *AL* are highly controversial,[10] but still Freeman's characterization of *AL* is somewhat arbitrary when she states *(Speculum* 40, 272) that the Antiphonary of Compiègne *(AC)* derives "its formulae not only from Scripture, but also from patristic and hagiographical sources absent altogether in *AL*." The latter view concerning *AL* is manifestly incorrect, as one look at the Index of the *Hagiographica* in *AL* in the edition by Louis Brou and José Vives (Barcelona, Madrid, 1959), 621—used by Freeman—will prove. Vives wrote a special study on the hagiographical sources of *AL*: "Fuentes hagiográficas del Antifonario de León," *Archivos Leoneses* 8 (1954), 288–299.

While Freeman acknowledges that "the *LC* were written well within the orbit of antiphonaries like *AC*," she continues, "but when the author quotes a text used in both rites (that is in *AL* and *AC*), his citation follows *AL*." But her general conclusion is clearly contradicted by the texts themselves. Compare, for example, the following text. *LC* III.14 (p. 131.3–6) reads: " . . . dicens: 'Ego in altissimis habitavi et thronus meus in columna nubis' [Ecclus. 24.7]; et iterum 'Girum caeli circuivi sola et in fluctibus maris ambulavi, et in omnem gentem et in omnem populum primatum tenui' " (Ecclus. 24.8–10).

Of these two biblical texts, Ecclus. 24.7 does not occur at all in *AL* (see above, section A.1). This is the actual reason why its

---

[10] See the discussion by Clyde Waring Brockett, *Antiphons, Responsories and Other Chants of the Mozarabic Rite* (Brooklyn, N.Y., 1968), 69–90; see also Higinio Angles, "Die Rolle Spaniens in der mittelalterlichen Musikgeschichte," *Gesammelte Aufsätze zur Kulturgeschichte Spaniens* 19 (Münster, 1962), 5–13.

occurrence in the *LC* is not mentioned in *Speculum* 32 (1957), 679, and why this omission is finally mentioned in *Speculum* 40 (1965), 243.1. Of Ecclus. 24.8–10 she says (*Speculum* 32, 679, 689) that "only the first half of the antiphon" is given in the León MS, but its full form may be found in the so-called *Breviarium Gothicum* (*PL* 86.1296): "Gyrum caeli circuivi sola et in fluctibus maris ambulavi, et in omnem terram et in omni populo primatum habui."

In truth, *AL*, f. 105 (pp. 148f.), reads as follows: "Girum celi circuibi sola alleluia et in fluctibus maris ambulabi alleluia," and Freeman supplemented in 1957 the text of Ecclus. 24.7 (cited in the *LC* but missing in *AL*) after the notorious *Breviarium Gothicum*, reconstructed and published in 1502 at Toledo by Cardinal Ximénès, and republished by Cardinal Lorenzana at Madrid in 1775, whose text is reprinted in Migne, *PL* 86 (Paris, 1862). In *Speculum* 40 (1965), 242, she reprints a text cited in *Speculum* 32 (1957), 680, drawn from *PL* 86.1296. She refers to this text as "*AL* (supplemented by *BG*)," without any closer reference for the reader, who naturally does not know that he is confronted by a text fabricated in the sixteenth century. This text of the Mozarabic Missal and Breviary is in fact correctly characterized by Freeman as "an *artificial* fabrication"[11] (see further, Chapter XI, Introduction). Her attempt to find the *LC* versions of Ecclus. 24.7–10 in *AL* comes to naught because the Frankish *AC* offers texts that are identical with those of the *LC*. Freeman herself lists them in *Speculum* 40 (1965), 272 n. 258, without realizing that the *AC* texts cited by her nullify her ascription of the *LC*'s quotations of Ecclus. 24.7–10 to the Visigothic

---

[11] Louis Brou, "Etudes sur le missel et le bréviaire 'Mozarabes' imprimé," *Hispania Sacra* XI (1958), 368; Brou says that Ortiz himself composed a large part of "l'Office des Morts." See furthermore Brou, "Deux mauvaises lectures du Chanoine Ortiz dans l'édition du Bréviaire de Ximénès: 'Lauda, Capitula,'" *Miscelánea en homenaje a Monsenor Higinio Anglès* I (1961), referred to in *Speculum* 40 (1965), 228, n. 97. Marius Férotin, *Le Liber mozarabicus sacramentorum et les manuscrits Mozarabes* (Paris, 1912), lviii, says: "Le Brév. Moz. imprimé en 1502 ... ne représente pas la liturgie wisig. dans sa pureté première." J. M. Martín Patino, "El Breviarium Mozárabe de Ortiz: Su valor documental para la historia del oficio catedralicio hispánico," *Miscelánea Comillas* 40 (Universidad Pontificia Comillas; Santander, 1963), 205–297, intends to reassess the historical foundations of Ortiz' work, apparently without always succeeding in his endeavor; cf. Don M. Randel, "Responsorial Psalmody in the Mozarabic Rite," *Etudes grégoriennes* 10 (1969), 116, n. 60.

liturgy. Accordingly, we read in *AC*, among *Responsoria* (*PL* 78.833B*):[12]

Resp. Gyrum coeli circuivi sola, et in fluctibus maris ambulavi. In omni
    gente et in omni populo primatum tenui . . . ˙
Vers. Ego in altissimis inhabitavi, et thronus meus in columna nubis.

It is obvious that this combination of Ecclus. 24.7–10 in *AC*
(also cited by Freeman in *Speculum* 40, 1965, 272 n. 258) forms a
much more exact parallel to the corresponding *LC* texts than the
Mozarabic texts which are incomplete and lack Ecclus. 24.7 altogether. For *AC* and Ecclus. 24.7–10 see Hesbert, *CAO* IV (Rome,
1970), no. 6793, p. 199, and below, Chapter XI, C, D, L.

Another example for the largely identical texts of John 15.16
in *AL* and *AC* can be pointed out for the item *O* in *Speculum* 40
(1965), 259f., with regard to the non-Vulgate reading *plurimum*.
LC IV.20 (p. 211.7) reads: "Ego elegi vos, ut fructum plurimum
afferatis, et fructus vester maneat in aeternum." *AL* 217r4 (p. 363)
offers: "Ego elegi vos, dicit dominus, ut fructum plurimum afferatis,
et fructus vester maneat in aeternum." But also *AC, PL* 78.821B1–2
(Hesbert, *CAO* I, p. 350; III, no. 2609 and 3940), reads *et fructum
plurimum afferatis.* The occurrence in *AC* of a specific reading that
parallels the one in *AL* (and in the *LC*) leads me to repeat what I
said in 1961 (in *Didascaliae*, p. 501): "On the basis of this one passage
from Bk. IV of the *LC*, an alleged quotation of John 15.16 after a
Mozarabic antiphon, Freeman (p. 689: *Speculum* 32, 1957) maintains
that this Book also of the *LC* (pp. 169–228 in Bastgen's edition) is
'the work of a Spanish ecclesiastic'! For this contention there is no
evidence whatever."

It may be illustrative to offer an example of the textual similarities
between *AL* and *AC* which are ultimately based on some common
foundation. I have selected for such a test case the description in
the *Vita Alcuini* of liturgical texts used by the Saxon shortly before
his demise, as we are told by his biographer. This anonymous
author wrote about the year 830 after reports he had received

---

[12] For the *Compendiensis* see also R.-J. Hesbert, ed., *Corpus Antiphonalium Officii I:
Manuscripti "Cursus Romanus"* (Rome, 1963), 130 (p. 383); both texts are found
as antiphons in other MSS related to *AC* in *CAO II: Manuscripti "Cursus Monasticus"*
(Rome, 1965), 102.11 (p. 507); and *CAO III: Invitatoria et Antiphonae* (Rome,
1968), nos. 2576 and 2986.

from Alcuin's Anglo-Saxon pupil Sigulf. The list of the chant texts used by Alcuin will enable us to exemplify the textual proximity between the two types of antiphonaries dealt with in this section. We recall that *AL* originated, according to Bernhard Bischoff, about 1067, while the *Compendiensis* (*AC*), which offers an antiphonary of the Roman Mass and of the Office, was written between 860 and 880.[13] The texts in *AC* and *AL* corresponding to those quoted by Alcuin are concurrently referred to, though I do not always indicate whether the text appears also as an antiphon, as a responsorium, or as a mere verse. I furthermore call the reader's attention to the fact that Louis Brou once compared texts in *AL* with the Antiphonary of Hartker, a MS related to our *AC*.[14]

Compare the texts cited in the *Vita Alcuini*, c. 14, ed. W. Wattenbach, *Monumenta Alcuiniana* (Berlin, 1873), 30f. (also ed. W. Arndt, *MGH, Scriptores* XV.1, p. 186) with *AL* and *AC* (and/or related MSS):

1. [Alcuinus] Vespertinum siquidem pro se agens officium . . . hymnum sanctae Mariae evangelicum cum hac *antiphona* decantabat:
2. *O clavis David . . . mortis*; see this antiphon in the *Liber Responsalis*, PL 78.732D–733A1; cf. in *CAO* I, 16a (p. 28); *CAO* II, for example, 7.2 (pp. 40f.), 8.2 (pp. 44f.); 16 (pp. 56f.); *CAO* III, 4010 (p. 366). This antiphon, which appears in *AC* and in related MSS, does not occur in *AL* or in any of the preserved fragmentary MSS of the Mozarabic antiphonary related to *AL*.
3. dicens post orationem dominicam hos versus: *Quemadmodum cervus desiderat ad fontes aquarum*, [Ps. 41.2]; see this *versus* in *AC*, R.-J. Hesbert, *Antiphonale Missarum Sextuplex* (Bruxelles, 1935), 79b (pp. 98f.); cf. also *AL*, f. 175.10 (p. 285), f. 109v.2 (p. 154), and f. 119.16 (p. 174).
4. *Quam dilecta tabernacula tua, domine virtutum* [Ps. 83.2]; see in MSS related to *AC* in *CAO* II, 114.5a (p. 584); *CAO* II, 120.4b (p. 649); also in *AL*, f. 264v.4 (p. 439), and f. 267v.4 (p. 443).
5. *Beati qui habitant in domo tua* etc. [Ps. 83.5]; see this text in MSS related to *AC* in *CAO* II, 114.5a (p. 584), and 120.4b (p. 649), *CAO* III, 1590 (p. 71); also in *AL*, f. 247.14 (p. 414), f. 263.12 (p. 438), f. 265.2 (p. 440).
6. *Ad te levavi oculos meos* [Ps. 122.1]; see Hesbert, *AMS* 53 (p. 69); cf. *CAO* I.127a (p. 373); cf. also *AL*, f. 124.2 (p. 184), "ANT. Ad te lebamus oculos nostros;" the same text f. 126.12 (p. 188); 204v.13 (p. 340); 255v.2 (p. 425); 275.15 (p. 456).

[13] See *CAO* I (Rome, 1963), xvii.
[14] Cf. *Ephemerides Liturgicae* 52 (1938), 249, and compare pp. 242, 251.

7. *Unam petii a Domino* [Ps. 26.4]; See *AC* in Hesbert, *AMS* 39a (pp. 5of.) and *AMS* 177 (pp. 176f.), in MSS related to *AC*; also in *AL*, f. 104.14 (p. 147) . . . unam peti a domino . . . ; and f. 282v.6 (p. 468).

8. Domine, locavi animam meam [cf. Ps. 24.1], et reliqua huiusmodi, in the *Vita Alcuini* requires the obvious emendation "[Ad te] Domine, l [ev]avi animam meam," according to *AC* in *PL* 78.66oB, and in *CAO* I.14 (p. 22), "ANT. Ad te Domine levavi animam [meam]," and in related MSS: *CAO* II.8a (p. 41), II.14 and 15a (pp. 50–51), and Hesbert, *AMS* Ia (pp. 2–3) in related MSS; also in *AL*, f.114.4 (p. 163), "ANT. Ad te domine levabi anima[m] mea[m]," and f. 282v.1 (p. 468).

The preceding investigation shows that of the liturgical texts ascribed in the *Vita Alcuini* to Alcuin,[15] six occur in *AC* (and MSS related to it) as well as in *AL*. Only the antiphon (no. 2) is not to be found among the texts of *AL*. The proximity of the textual transmissions of the identical passages in two antiphonary types so far apart in time, place, and rite is quite illuminating, but not altogether too startling because of their ultimate common antiphonal heritage. It would be nonsensical to say that Alcuin was as close to Mozarabic liturgical habits as he was to Frankish customs. I list below in Chapter XI, under the letter U, another example for which *AC* and *AL* offer texts that are identical with that of the *LC*. The predominance claimed by Freeman for *AL* in the case of the identity of the *LC* with *AL* and *AC* is without *textual* foundation. Her sweeping generalization (*Speculum* 40 [1965], 272) according to which the *LC*'s Bible citations "follow *AL*" when the author [of the *LC*] quotes a text used in "the Gregorian and Mozarabic rites" is incorrect. The assumption that *AL*'s "distinctive formulae were not replaced from his mind in maturity by those of the Gregorian chant, [that] his memory remained faithful to the liturgical usage of his youth" is without basis, since the author of the *LC* does not cite Scripture by memory. This is, for example, refuted in detail in the investigation of item H, below, in Chapter XI.

The probative value of the unique occurrence of some biblical quotations in the Mozarabic liturgy and in the context of the *LC*

---

[15] Hariuf's *Vita Angilberti* reports that Alcuin wrote *antiphonae*, *responsoria*, and *hymns* concerning St. Richarius; cf. Friedrich Wiegand, *Die Stellung des apostolischen Symbols im Kirchlichen Leben des Mittelalters* (Leipzig, 1899), 294. See also Pierre Hadot, "Les hymnes de Victorinus et les hymnes *Adesto* et *Miserere* d'Alcuin," *Archives d'histoire doctrinale et littéraire du moyen âge* 35 (1960), 7–16.

for the origin and the author of the *LC* is hardly of importance, since such reasoning does not take into account that modern research has shown that Mozarabic liturgical materials and texts were used in Southern Gaul, in the Frankish provinces of Aquitania and Septimania. This recognition meets the alternative suggested by Bonifatius Fischer (*Speculum* 40 [1965], 286, n. 335) concerning the surmised occurrence of some fragments from the Visigothic liturgy in the *LC*. In view of the problem of source criticism involved he took into consideration the possibility that "perhaps some antiphons or such like were also used in Southern Gaul." This is indeed the case, as several recent studies have shown.[16] But traces and stray pieces of Mozarabic liturgical versions of a few biblical passages, even if found in the *LC*, by no means prove Theodulph's alleged authorship of the *Libri Carolini*.

[16] See the studies by Brou, Huglo, Dold, and Mundó cited in Part Three, Introduction, above, nn. 14, 15, 16. On the Visigothic impact on the Frankish territory to the south of the river Loire up to the Pyrenees and in Septimania see also Bernhard Bischoff, "Panorama der Handschriftenüberlieferung aus der Zeit Karls des Grossen," in *Karl der Grosse* II (Düsseldorf, 1965), 241f.

CHAPTER XI

On "Spanish Symptoms" in the *Libri Carolini*

The following items A–T deal with Bible quotations of the *Libri Carolini* that appear or do not appear in the same versions in the Antiphonary of the Cathedral of León (and in related MSS) or in the Frankish Antiphonary of Compiègne (and related MSS), or in neither of these two antiphonaries, but in some other text or writing. The non-Mozarabic origin of a few alleged Mozarabic Bible texts supposedly used by Theodulph of Orléans is proved under U and V. The letter numbering in Freeman's article in *Speculum* 40 (1965), 227–266, A–T, follows my discussion in *Didascaliae* (1961), 486–507, A–T. The references in the subsequent sections always refer to both treatments of Bible quotations in the *LC*. For the sake of brevity, I shall omit for the most part references to the *Clavis Melitonis* whose florilegium of biblical quotations was not used in the *LC*, as I have shown in Chapter X, D. I shall furthermore for the most part abstain from referring to marginal identifications of biblical texts in *AL*, the Antiphonary of León, repeatedly mentioned by Freeman, because they do not constitute a characteristic of *AL*, as she assumed, but an isolated regional peculiarity, as I can point out on the basis of the manuscript evidence in Chapter XII, A: the Mozarabic antiphonary did not list *in margine* the identifications of its biblical texts. Nor do I always list the continuous attempts made at strengthening the Theodulphian argument by references to *OV*, the *Oracional Visigótico*, edited by José Vives (Barcelona, 1946), and to *BG*, the *Breviarium Gothicum*, published in 1502 in Toledo by Ximénès, republished by Lorenzana at Madrid in 1775, and finally reprinted in *PL* 86 (Paris, 1862). The probative value of references to *OV* is rather limited because *OV* offers as a rule only the *Incipit* of the biblical text and not the entire liturgical quotation. And the late origin of *BG* does not warrant the use of its modern text when we deal with the *LC*'s biblical quotations from the eighth century because of the uncertain origin of *BG*'s biblical texts. We must keep in mind that Freeman herself quite properly calls *BG* "an artificial fabrication" in *Speculum* 32 (1957), 681. On the present state of research concerning *BG* see the studies cited in Chapter X, E, at notes 8 and 11.

Alleged or Genuine "Spanish Symptoms" A–T

A. Wallach, *Didascaliae*, 486–490; *Speculum* 40 (1965), 227–233; *LC* III.14 (Bastgen, p. 133.1–2): *Exod. 15.11, and *LC* II.6 (p. 68.40–42): *Exod. 15.17–18.—The assumption that *Exod. 15.11, "*honorificus* in sanctis," is typical of the Mozarabic liturgy may be true, but whether the *LC*'s *honorificus* is due to any direct Mozarabic influence remains doubtful. The same text of the *Vetus Latina* version of Exod. 15.17–18 as in *LC* II.6 also occurs in the MS of St. Catherine's Monastery on Mount Sinai, Slavonicus 5, f. 83, which is not of Mozarabic origin. I prefer E. A. Lowe's reasonable suggestion that "it may not be necessary to invoke a Spanish explanation for every Visigothic Symptom. It seems not only possible but likely that a number of what we call Visigothic Symptoms were actually common to both Spain and Latin Africa. And I would not be surprised if it were as true of liturgical texts as it may be of palaeographical features. That only the evidence from Spain survives may be reasonably explained by the fortunes of history."[1]

Freeman tries to find a Mozarabic source for the *Vetus Latina* version of *Exod. 15.17–18, "Introduc et planta eos," in *LC* II.6 (p. 68.40). I had called attention in 1961 to the fact that the *LC* reading occurs "uniquely" in the *Canticum Exodi* attached to the famous Greek-Latin Verona Psalter, Biblioteca Capitolare I, saec. VI. Freeman maintains that the reading is not unique, not only because it also occurs in the Mount Sinai MS, saec. IX (which, by the way, became known only in 1964), but also because "Introduc

---

[1] E. A. Lowe, "Two Other Unknown Liturgical Fragments on Mount Sinai," *Scriptorium* 19 (1965), 21; texts in *Revue Bénédictine* 74 (1964), 254–289.

et planta" (*Speculum* 40 [1965], 233, lines 1–2) is in addition found in Mozarabic sources. But this assumption is philologically incorrect since the text under consideration is not "Introduc et planta," but "Introduc et planta *eos*" (*Exod. 15.17–18, LXX). Naturally, the object *eos* of the entire phrase belongs to the *Vetus Latina* version of the original Greek text. Further, *AL*, fol. 296.4 (p. 491) does not offer "Introduc et planta," but "Induc et planta *nos*," and *AL*, fol. 34.2 (p. 24), reads ". . . planta *eum*." The *AL* texts certainly are not identical with the *LC* text.

In connection with the present section A, MS Toledo 35.1 is ascribed to the second half of the tenth century. The assumption that I am unaware of the fact that the *LC*'s citation has an exact counterpart in a ninth-century Toledo MS is mistaken because the MS is incorrectly dated. In 1961, Agustín Millares Carlo gave the new designation of the MS in question and dated "Madrid, Bibl. Nacional Vitr. 5.1 (10001)–Siglos IX–X."[2] In 1965, Anscari M. Mundo, after a renewed comprehensive study of all Toledo MSS, assigned Toledo 35.1 (Madrid, B.N. 10001) to the middle of the eleventh century.[3]

The nature of the "Canticles" as such, mentioned by Freeman in the context of the passages from the *Canticum Exodi*, has been misjudged in *Speculum* 40 (1965), 231 n. 110, where we find it stated that "Canticles [are] appended to the seventh century Lectionary of Luxeuil." In fact, neither this lectionary nor any other lectionary has "Canticles . . . appended." Only the *Psalter* has biblical *Cantica* "appended" at the very end. The *Canticum Exodi*, taken as a liturgical unit or genre, that is, Old Latin *Exod. 15.1–19, or 1–21, is neither preserved by, nor appended to, the *Lectionnaire de Luxeuil*. But the Old Latin text of *Exod. 15.1–19 (or 1–21) is indeed preserved in the lectionary's *lectio* VII of the twelve Lessons listed, as c. 41, *In Vigiliis Paschae*,[4] however, not as *Canticum Exodi*. *Lectio* VII consists of *Exod. 13.18–15.21; the preceding Lesson VI contains Exod. 12.1–50; Lesson VIII is made up of Ezechiel 37.1–14. I also refer in this connection to the Old Latin text of the *Canticum*

[2] "Manuscritos visigóticos: Notas bibliográficas," *Hispania Sacra* 14 (1961), no. 84, pp. 379–381.

[3] "La datación de los códices litúrgicos visigóticos Toledanos," *Hispania Sacra* 18 (1965), 14, 20.

[4] Pierre Salmon, *Le Lectionnaire de Luxeuil* (Collectanea biblica latina 7; Rome, 1944), 105; Introduction, p. cxii.

Exodi occurring in Jerome's Vulgate.[5] Thus the text of the **Canticum Exodi* could have been accessible to the author of the *LC* not only in the form of the *Canticle* appended to the Latin *Psalter*, but also through the Old Latin text of some lectionary known to him.

B. Wallach, *Didascaliae*, 490; *Speculum* 40 (1965), 233–238; *LC* II.16 (p. 75.22–25): Col. 1.12–15.—Freeman assumes that the beginning of the Vulgate text is corrected after a Mozarabic antiphon in *AL*, f. 192 (pp. 317f.), which, however, offers but Col. 1.12–14, omitting the decisive text of Col. 1.15, "qui est imago dei invisibilis." I gave in *Didascaliae*, pp. 490–493, my interpretation of the corrections made in the text of Col. 1.12–15. The quotation occurs with others in the context of a rhetorical device frequently employed in the *LC*. It appears in the guise of pretended colloquies carried on, or fictitious orations delivered by, apostles, prophets, and church fathers. This device concerning the validity of the testimony of biblical and patristic figures is assigned to its alleged source, namely, Quodvultdeus, *Contra Judaeos, paganos et Arianos*, following an untenable suggestion made by Bernhard Bischoff, as reported in *Speculum* 40, 235 n. 123. But I have shown that Ambrose's suggestions "Interrogemus apostolos, interrogemus prophetas, interrogemus Christum" (*De fide* I.6.43, ed. Otto Faller, *CSEL* 78 [1962], p. 18) fathered the *LC*'s often-used rhetorical device.[6] We read accordingly in *LC* II.16 (p. 75.20f.): "Interrogemus ergo egregium praedicatorem" (also in *LC* II.28, p. 90.9; III.2, p. 109.12–13; and so on), and the apostle is asked to explain "quid sit imago dei," a question which is also posed in the untraced Augustine text that serves as the chapter heading of *LC* II.16 (p. 75.11–12): "Quid est imago dei, nisi vultus Dei, in quo signatus est populus Dei."[7] The *LC* answers the question by means of a pretended consultation of Augustine and Ambrose concerning the problem "quid sit imago Dei." Ambrose is asked rhetorically by the author of the *LC* to defend Augustine's position: "Dic itaque etiam tu, sanctissime Ambrosi, quid de hac imagine sentire te constet. Defende beatum Augustinum . . . " (*LC*, p. 75.40). He finally states (*LC*, p. 76.5f.), on the basis of the suggestions referred to above, "Hoc ergo modo cum prophetis et apostolis Augustino meo, immo vero Dei cultori,

---

[5] See *Biblia Sacra: Libros Exodi et Levitici*, ed. Henri Quentin (Rome, 1929), 154.
[6] See Chapter V.
[7] Dealt with in Chapter II, D.

tutelam conferre curabo," and therefore he ultimately quotes in *LC* II.16 (p. 76.6–18) from Ambrose's *De fide* I.7.

The preceding discussion and analysis of the *LC*'s literary method is required in order to show the ultimate origin of the text of Col. I.12–15 in *LC* II.16, which cannot be primarily derived from the Mozarabic antiphon that offers a version of Col. I.12–14, omitting v. 15, "qui est imago dei invisibilis," the most important part of the text discussed in the chapter. Col. 1.15 is actually answered in the *LC* by the source underlying the *LC* text (p. 75.13–19), "pingi non potest," namely, Ambrosiaster on Col. 1.15, "Qui est imago dei invisibilis": invisibilis dei imago visibilis esse non potest, alioquin nec imago; quod enim invisible est, *pingi non potest*; nec enim visibilis potest invisibilem videre."[8] Since we have seen in Chapter V that the *LC*'s rhetorical device in *LC* II.16 and throughout the entire work had been suggested to the author of the *LC* because of his extensive knowledge of Ambrose's *De fide*, whom he cites verbatim in the same chapter (p. 76.6–18), it should be readily understandable that he answers the question "quid sit imago dei" (*LC* II.16, p. 75.21) by relying on an answer[9] also provided by Ambrose, *Exameron* 6.7,41: " . . . sed quid [so MS S] sit imago dei audi dicentem: 'qui eripuit nos,' inquit, 'de potestate tenebrarum et transtulit in regnum fili claritatis suae, in quo habemus redemptionem et remissionem peccatorum, qui est imago dei invisibilis et primogenitus universae creaturae.' "[10] The *LC*'s author may well have used this Ambrose text whose Bible quotation he supplemented after the Vulgate of Col. 1.12–15; for this reason he read in Col. 1.14 *dilectionis*, and not *claritatis* with Ambrose. The facsimile of MS V, fol. 81v, of *LC* II.16 (published as Plate II, Fig. B), between pages 674 and 675 in *Speculum* 32 (1957), shows no corrections for Col. 1.14–15, from *eripuit* to *invisibilis*. Only Col. 1.12–13, from *Gratias* to the second *qui*[a] contains corrections which I explained in *Didascaliae*, p. 491, on the basis of the probability that the *LC* author read ad Col. in a text written *per cola et commata*, and that he read twice *quia* instead of *qui* because he had also Col. 1.16 in

---

[8] Ambrosiaster, *Ambrosiastri qui dicitur Commentarius in Epistulas Paulinas*, ed. H. I. Vogels (*CSEL* 81.3; Wien, 1969), to Col. 1.15,1, p. 170.23–27.

[9] *LC*, p. 75.40: "Dic itaque etiam tu, sanctissime Ambrosi, quid de hae imagine sentire te constet."

[10] Ambrose, *Exameron* VI.7.41, ed. Carl Schenkl (*CSEL* 32; Wien, 1896), 232.9, 14.

mind: "*quia* in ipso condita sunt." The corrector tried afterward
to restore the original Vulgate version by the erasure of the "*a*" in
quia, occurring twice, and otherwise supplemented the missing verses
of the Bible text. He really did not need a Mozarabic liturgical
text in order to achieve this great feat. Freeman's assumption
(*Speculum* 32 [1957], 690) that Frankish correctors "altered an unfamiliar Mozarabic formula . . . by changing *Gratias agamus* to
gratias agentes . . . " is superfluous because *Gratias agamus* was to the
learned author of the *LC* by no means "an unfamiliar Mozarabic
formula" but a very well-known liturgical Frankish formula from
the beginning of the Canon of the Roman Mass which he certainly
knew by heart, namely, "*Gratias agamus* domino deo nostro."[11] In
addition, the author of the *LC* quotes—again extemporaneously—
from the normal *praefatio* of the Canon of the Roman Mass in *LC*
IV.2 (p. 175.22–26):[12] " . . . *dignum et iustum aequumque et salutare*
dicit esse, ut *nos ei semper et ubique gratias agamus, per quem* ineffabilem
Patris *maiestatem* . . . ," and also in *LC* II.27 (p. 87, Bastgen).

I will add here briefly a correction concerning the contents of
LC I.9 (p. 28.8–30), dealing with Daniel's fictitious speech. The
present writer has shown in Chapter V, above, that Jerome's *Commentarii in Danielem* is the hitherto unknown source of Daniel's
oration. See pages 135–136.

C, D, L. Wallach, *Didascaliae*, 493–495; 499–500; *Speculum* 40
(1965), 238–244; *LC* III.14 (p. 131.1–8): Prov. 8.25–27.30; Ecclus.
24.7, 24.8–10, 24.22, 24.6; Prov. 8.17, 9.35 (8.35).—*LC* III.14
(pp. 130.35–131.9) contains eight biblical quotations. Freeman
maintains (p. 243) that seven of them "display a long chain of
sapientia texts each of whose links has its counterpart in the Mozarabic liturgy." But this is incorrect, as the following critical discussion of the individual quotations I–VIII will show.

The *LC*'s author desires to explain the meaning of *consilium Dei*
mentioned in the chapter heading of III.14 (p. 130.2). He explains
it with the aid of the *Sapientia Dei* of 1 Cor. 1.24 (pp. 130.35–131.1)
by stating: "Est enim *sapientia dei* Patris quae ei consempiterna est
et quę dicit: . . . . " The following combination of *sapientia* texts

---

[11] See Bernard Botte, *Le Canon de la messe romaine* (Textes et Etudes Liturgiques 2;
Louvain, 1935), I.6 (p. 30).

[12] *Ibid.*, p. 30, *Praefatio* ii.

from Proverbia 8 and Ecclesiasticus 24 (see below, sections I–VII) are cited as examples of the *sapientia dei*. Of these, Ecclus. 24 is entitled in the Septuagint as well as in the Vulgate, Σοφίας αἴνεσις and *Sapientiae laus*, respectively.[13] I add that the *Laus patrum* of Ecclus. 44 is referred to in *LC* IV.18 (pp. 207.34, 208.28) and the *Laus Ezechiae* (4. Reg. 18.3–7) in *LC* I.18 (p. 43.29). The seven *Wisdom* texts in *LC* III.14 (p. 131.1–8) are subsequently discussed in the sequence in which they are cited.

I. *LC* III.14 (p. 131.1–3) Prov. 8.25–27, 29: "Ante colles ego parturiebar, Adhuc terram non fecerat, quando parabat caelos, aderam illi; dum vallaret mari terminum et legem poneret aquis, ego cum illo eram."

a. Freeman believes that the *LC* renders the identical quotation occurring in the Mozarabic Antiphonary of the Cathedral of León,[14] fol. 69vⅠⅠ (p. 90), that it "repeats in unbroken sequence the classic statement of this theme in the Advent liturgy of Spain" (*Speculum* 40 [1965], 275), and that it is an antiphon for Matins on Christmas Day (pp. 239, 241). But the antiphon is incompletely cited by her, since the *Versus* connected with it in *AL* (p. 90) is omitted; it reads: "VR. Audi popule meus et loquar. . . . tibi. Quando."

b. I suggested in *Didascaliae* (p. 493f.) as the origin of "Ante colles . . ." its occurrence in Elipand of Toledo's *Epistle* defending adoptionism, written for the Spanish episcopate, and addressed to the Frankish assembly meeting at Frankfurt in 794.[15] This letter is not preserved, as Freeman (p. 239) believes, "in the acts of the Frankish Synod of 794." For one, the synodal *Acta* of 794 are lost, and only a final summarizing protocol is preserved and edited by Albert Werminghoff. The latter published in *MGH, Conc.* 2, Elipand's letter together with others of sundry provenance as a dossier of documents which undoubtedly were discussed, like the *LC*, during the sessions of the synod held at Frankfurt in 794. But all these documents were at no time "preserved" in the Acts of that synod. Her further polemics against my suggestion that the author

---

[13] See *Sapientia Iesu Filii Sirach*, ed. Joseph Ziegler (Septuaginta XII.2; Göttingen, 1965), 236, and *Liber Hiesu Filii Sirach* (Biblia Sacra XII; Rome, 1964), 249.

[14] Louis Brou and José Vives, *Antifonario visigótico Mozárabe de la Catedral de León* (Monumenta Hispaniae Sacra, ser. liturgica, vol. V.1; Barcelona, Madrid, 1959).

[15] Ed. Albert Werminghoff, *MGH, Conc.* 2 (Aevi Karolini 1; Berlin, 1906), 114.

of the *LC* could have found our text in Elipand's epistle do not present my actual opinion concerning the origins of the *LC* as described in *Didascaliae*, pp. 474f. (see above, Chapter III), because I assume that in addition to the production of its first and main version during 791, supplementary chapters were inserted into the context of the *LC* also between 791 and 794, before the contents of the *LC* were discussed by the synodal assembly of 794.

The allegation (*Speculum* 40, 240) that "Ante colles ego parturiebar" is found on f. 146, on one of the outer leaves of *V*, "untouched by the corrector's hand," is mistaken because Bastgen lists in his *apparatus criticus* for f. 146r the corrections *c–d* (see p. 130.36–37), and on p. 131.41 the correction *a*. Fol. 146v has a long erasure, listed by Bastgen among his Addenda, p. 230, col. 2: "131.11–17 in loco raso." The text of this correction is drawn, almost verbatim, from Cassiodorus, *Expositio in Ps.* 32.11, ed. M. Adriaen, *CCL* 97 (Turnhout, 1958), 288, lines 208–223, as is properly stated by Bastgen, p. 131 n. 1.

The further assumption that Alcuin's Frankish *Epistola Synodica*, which reads "Ante colles ego parturiebar, *et cetera*," has avoided Elipand's liturgical text "Ante colles ego parturiebar," is hardly correct because Alcuin's Vulgate version is identical with Elipand's version. In addition, Elipand's version can by no means be looked upon as an exclusively Mozarabic version because of its occurrence in the non-Mozarabic item *d*, listed below.

c. The Mozarabic origin of the *LC* version of Prov. 8.25–27.30 is not proved by the fact that the *Incipit* of the antiphon *Ante colles ego parturiebar* also occurs in the *Verona Orationale* (*OV* 288) from the early eighth century.

OV 288 offers only the *Incipit* of the antiphon *Ante colles ego parturiebar*, and nothing else of the antiphon text. Since this *Incipit* is identical with the *Incipit* of Prov. 8.25 in Jerome's Vulgate, *OV* does not at all provide support for any allegedly exclusive Mozarabic origin of the *LC* text *Ante colles . . . ego eram*. Of course, everybody knows that antiphons are often referred to by means of their *Incipits* alone. But in the case of a critical investigation of the characteristic wording of an entire antiphon text, the probative value of the antiphon's *Incipit* is no substitute for the rest of the antiphonal text. This rule applies to *OV* 288, as well as to all references to the same

Mozarabic work: they prove nothing for the entire text of any antiphon.

d. The fact that the text under consideration cannot be of Mozarabic origin is further proved by its occurrence among the fragments of a Latin non-Mozarabic antiphonary, written in North Africa, and preserved in the Greek MS 567, f. 3v, of St. Catherine's Monastery on Mount Sinai, saec. X ex., recently published by E. A. Lowe:[16]

> Ante colles ego parturiebar ad(h)uc te
> rra non feceram quando celos prepara
> berat dum ballaret mari terminos
> et legem poneret aquas ego eram.

This text again disproves the assumption of any unique Mozarabic origin of the antiphon text in question. Lowe's studies referred to above are cited in *Speculum* 40 (1965), 230f., and in n. 107.

e. The omission of v. 28 from Prov. 8.22–31 has been mentioned in Chapter X, section A1. The unacknowledged omission of words otherwise contained in biblical texts naturally creates a parallelism between the *LC* text and its alleged Mozarabic equivalent, when in reality no parallel exists.

II. *LC* III.14 (p. 131.4): "Ego in altissimis habitavi, thronus meus in columna nubis" (Ecclus. 24.7). This text was omitted by Freeman, as I have shown in Chapter X, A1, because it does not occur in the Mozarabic antiphonary *AL*, and therefore contradicts the view that all the Bible texts in *LC* III.14 have their source in the Mozarabic liturgy.[17] Ecclus. 24.7 occurs, however, in the Frankish Antiphonary of Compiègne, as I have shown in Chapter X, E.

III. *LC* III.14 (p. 131.4–6): "et iterum: Girum caeli circuivi sola et in fluctibus maris ambulavi, in omnem gentem et in omnem populum primatum tenui" (Ecclus. 24.8–10). This text as well as the preceding one in II, above, occurs in the Frankish Antiphonary of Compiègne; that both texts cannot be derived from *AL* is shown

---

[16] "Two New Latin Liturgical Fragments on Mount Sinai," *Revue Bénédictine* 74 (1964), 261, texts 14–17; cf. also Lowe, "Two Other Unknown Latin Liturgical Fragments on Mount Sinai," *Scriptorium* 19 (1965), 3–29, on the paleography of those fragments. See the quoted text in E. A. Lowe, *Palaeographical Papers, 1907–1965*, ed. Ludwig Bieler (Oxford, 1972), 528.14–17.

[17] On the nature of this approach see von den Steinen, above, Chapter X, A1.

in Chapter X, E. As a matter of fact, none of the texts cited in sections I, II, and III can be of Mozarabic origin.

IV.–VII. *LC* III.14 (p. 131.6–8): "et iterum: Ego quasi terebyntus expandi ramos meos (Ecclus. 24.22). Ego feci, ut oriretur lucifer in caelo (Ecclus. 24.6). Ego omnes qui me amant diligo (OL Prov. 8.17 LXX). Exitus enim mei exitus vitae sunt" (OL Prov. 8.35 LXX). These texts IV–VII appear also in *AL*, the Mozarabic León Antiphonary, f. 107 (p. 151), as Freeman recognized for the first time. Brou and Vives, the editors of *AL*, do not identify these four texts. Bastgen and Freeman refer for VI to the Vulgate version of Prov. 8.17. Text VII was identified by Bastgen as the Old Latin version of Prov. 8.35; he indicated this origin by the addition of the asterisk in the margin. According to *Speculum* 32 (1957), 680, Prov. 8.35 (Exitus . . .) "cannot be located in the Vulgate"; it is characterized as being "typical of the small group of Mozarabic liturgical texts which are inspired by Scripture, but clearly independent of it." But the *LC* text *Exitus . . .* is by no means a Mozarabic text. I showed for VII in *Didascaliae*, pp. 499f., its Old Latin origin as a verbatim translation of Prov. 8.35 LXX: αἱ γὰρ ἔξοδοί μου ἔξοδοι ζωῆς. Bastgen's reference (p. 131.7) is correctly to Prov. 8.35. For the Old Latin literal translation of Prov. 8.17 (above VI), I referred to the underlying Septuagint text: ἐγὼ τοὺς ἐμὲ φιλοῦντας ἀγαπῶ. Freeman does not record the occurrence of Old Latin Prov. 8.35 LXX in *LC* III.12 (p. 126.13): " . . . secundum magistrae nostrae, sapientiae, vocem *exitus nostri exitus vitae sunt*" (Prov. 8.35 LXX). The identification of **Prov. 8.17 as an Old Latin version offered in the *LC* and in *AL*, is not listed by Sabatier; for **Prov. 8.35 see Pierre Sabatier, *Bibliorum sacrorum Latinae versiones seu Vetus Italica* II (Paris, 1751), 311.[18]

The sequence of the four Bible texts in *LC* III.14 (p. 131.6–8) is indeed identical with the sequence of the same four texts in *AL*, fol. 107 (p. 151).[19] But I must caution against a possible optical

---

[18] See also *Liber de divinis scripturis*, ed. F. Weihrich (*CSEL* XII; Wien, 1879), 471.12: "omnia custodia serva cor tuum: ex his enim exitus sunt vitae," for which Weihrich refers to Prov. 4.23; I should like to add a reference to Prov. 8.35. For Ecclus. 24.6 (above, text V) see Weihrich, p. 303.9: "Ego in caelis feci ut oriretur lumen indeficiens."

[19] I do not discuss the occurrence of the sequence in *BG*, the *Breviarium Gothicum*, characterized by Freeman, *Speculum* 32 (1957), 681, as a modern fabrication; cf. also Bonifatius Fischer on the *BG*, above Chapter X n. 8.

illusion concerning a too hasty assessment of the degree of identity observable between the two sets of *LC* and *AL* texts as printed in *Speculum* 40 (1965), 242, because the *AL* sequence is cited out of context, so that the reader who does not look at the two texts in their larger printed context assumes that he sees total identity of textual congruity. As it stands, almost half of the chant text of *AL*, which begins with the four cited biblical texts (comprising twenty-six words) is thus omitted. The omitted text of twenty-three words, immediately following text VII (*Prov. 8.35), reads in *AL*, f. 107 (p. 151): "transite ad me omnes qui me concupiscitis et a generationibus meis implemini [Ecclus. 24.19] quia spes mea est alleluia [cf. Ecclus. 24.25] et supra mella dulcis est a e u ia [Ecclus. 24.27]."

The degree of congruity between the two sequences of four biblical texts in the *LC* and in *AL* is reduced to still greater insignificance if the two sets of chants listed in *AL*, f. 107 (p. 151), namely, "Dominus mici dat linguam" (I), and "Petibi deo meo sapientiam . . . " (II), preceding set III, "Ego quasi terebinctus expandi . . . et supra mella dulcis est a e u ia," should form one coherent set of chants. In that case, the two and a half printed lines of our four Bible texts in *A*'s chant III are preceded by the six and a half lines of chants I and II, and followed by the remaining two and a half lines of chant III. The relation of our four Bible texts' portion in chant III to the entire text unit of chants I–III would then be two and a half lines of eleven and a half printed lines, or a little less than one-fifth of the entire chant unit I–III. This is the actual degree of congruity between the four Bible texts and their equivalent in the *AL* chants.

It is obvious that the *LC* cited the Bible texts in question from a written source, and not by "memory." The *LC* joins the biblical quotations I–VII in *LC* III.14 by the connective expression *et iterum* (p. 131.4 and 6): Ecclus. 24.7; *et iterum*: Ecclus. 24.8–10; *et iterum*: Ecclus. 24.22; Ecclus. 24.6; Old Latin Prov. 8.17, LXX; Old Latin Prov. 8.35, LXX.

Et iterum is otherwise used in the *LC* in instances that show that the author of the *LC* quotes texts from a written source. The following examples will suffice to prove this point.

LC IV.5 (p. 180) contains a number of literal quotations from the now lost first Latin version of ca. 788 of the Greek *Acta* of II Nicaea of 787, a copy of which had been sent by Hadrian I to Charlemagne. This Latin version of II Nicaea was undoubtedly

kept either in the court Library or else in the Royal Capella that
served as Charlemagne's chancellery. The author of the *LC* introduces the texts he excerpted by means of the connectives *et iterum*
(p. 180.4 and 8) and *et post pauca* (p. 180.7 and 12), partly in conformity with an old, established custom of synodal diplomatics.[20]

LC I.29 (p. 58.1–2) reads: Et iterum: *beatos dicit eos qui memoria
tenent mandata eius, ut faciant ea*. Bastgen refers to Ps. 102.18. The
source of *LC* I.29, unknown to him, is Origen, *In Exodum, homilia*
9.4: . . . . et bibliotheca efficitur librorum dei, quia et propter *beatos
dicit eos qui memoria tenent mandata eius, ut faciant ea* (cf. Ps. 105(106).3
and Ezech. 37.24ff.).[21] It is clear that the author of the *LC* introduces his excerpt from Origen's homily by the connective *Et iterum*.

The *LC*'s author thus consistently uses *et iterum* when introducing
quotations from other writings into his own exposition. We saw this
procedure when he is quoting on his own from the first Latin version of the Greek *Acta* of II Nicaea, when he is citing from one of
Origin's homilies translated by Rufinus, and when he is quoting a
unique sequence of Bible texts perhaps from some antiphonal service
book. The rather insignificant degree of congruity existing between
the *LC* and *AL* texts openly contradicts the assumption of a Mozarabic source used by the *LC* in this instance.

E. Wallach, *Didascaliae*, 495; *Speculum* 40 (1965), 245–248; *LC* I.12
(p. 32.10): 1 Pet. 2.24.—There are certainly some similarities
between *AL* and our text, but not enough to say with certainty that
our author quotes from an exclusively Visigothic version. Regardless of any congruence between both texts, *LC* indeed has in contrast to *AL* the distinct liturgism *a malis liberati*, and also reads for
ὡς *velut*, not *sicut*. These two distinctive features set off the *LC* text
sufficiently from any dependence upon a Mozarabic source.

F. Wallach, *Didascaliae*, 496; *Speculum* 40 (1965), 248–250; *LC* I.10
(p. 30.13) and *LC* I.16 (p. 38.28): Acts 10.38, 40–41.—Acts 10.38–
41 is referred to, but the fact is not mentioned that the larger part
of Acts 10.38 as well as all of Acts 10.39 does not occur in the *LC*
text. We hear at first of the *LC*'s "non-consecutive quotation" of

---

[20] See Chapter IV under N, section D.

[21] Ed. W. A. Baehrens, *Origenes Werke* VI (GCS; Leipzig, 1920), 242.18–19; see
Wallach, *The Classical Tradition* (Ithaca, N.Y., 1966), 498 n. 101.

Acts 10.38–41, and then Acts 10.38, as it appears in *LC* I.10 (p. 30.13) in the Old Latin version is cited: "Iesum Nazarenum quem unxit Deus spiritu sancto et virtute." Then this so-called "non-consecutive quotation" is assumed to be "continued in *LC* I.16" (p. 38.28–29) in Acts 10.40–41:

> Hunc Deus suscitavit post diem tertium
> et dedit illum manifestum fieri, non omni populo.

It is hard to see how one can be sure that Acts 10.40–41 is "continued" in *LC* I.16 after the quotation of Acts 10.38a in *LC* I.10. But since neither the larger part of Acts 10.38, nor the whole of Acts 10.39, occurs in the *LC*, the statement that the *LC* texts are "an exact repetition of Acts (10.38–41) common to all the Mozarabic MSS cited in *Speculum* 32 (1957), 684," is hardly correct. The *Liber Commicus*[22] has the complete text of Acts 10.38–41, including Acts 10.38, *hic perambulabat*, to Acts 10.39, *suspendentes in ligno*, while *AL*, f. 197v (p. 327), offers only Acts 10.38a, and of 10.39 only the end "quem . . . in ligno." The statement concerning the identity of the texts of Acts in the *LC* and in "all Mozarabic MSS"[23] is contradicted by the MSS themselves (see below).

Faustinus, *De trinitate sive de fide contra Arianos* (*PL* 13.71C) offers Acts 10.38 in the same Old Latin version as does the *LC*: "Jesum Nazarenum quem unxit Deus spiritu sancto et virtute." The same is true of *Incerti auctoris Liber de trinitate*, ed. J. Fraipont (*CCL* 90; 1961): "Iesum Nazarenum quem unxit Deus spiritu sancto." Alcuin in one of his antiadoptionist treatises (*PL* 101.284D) cites Acts 10.38 in the discussion of an Augustinian text in a manner that presupposes that the Old Latin version underlies his quotation: " . . . unxit eum Deus spiritu sancto et virtute." The assumption (p. 249) that "an exact repetition of the *Acts* text common to all the Mozarabic MSS" is cited in *Speculum* 32 (1957), 684, is incorrect because only two Mozarabic MSS contain the text of Acts 10.38–41, and none of the others:

---

[22] *Liber Commicus* II, ed. Justo Pérez de Urbel and Atilano González y Ruiz-Zorrilla (Monumenta Hispaniae Sacra, ser. liturgica III; Madrid, 1955), 401.

[23] And their alleged prototype in the eighth-century palimpsest from León, edited by Bonifatius Fischer, "Ein neuer Zeuge zum westlichen Text der Apostelgeschichte," in *Biblical and Patristic Studies in Memory of Robert Pierce Casey*, ed. J. N. Birdsall and R. N. Thomson (Freiburg i.Br., 1963), 58 to Acts 10.38.

1. BM6, f. 95 (s. X–XI) does not offer the text cited there at the end of Acts 10.38.40–41; only the *Incipit* of Acts 10.38 appears in Marius Férotin, *Le Liber mozarabicus sacramentorum et les manuscrits mozarabes* (Paris, 1912), col. 856, as Psallendum: "Ihesum Nazarenum quem unxit."

2. *OV* 989 (s. VII–VIII), the *Oracional Visigótico* ed. José Vives (MHS, ser. liturgica I; Barcelona, 1946), 320, has the Responsorium "Iesum Nazarenum quem unxit Deus," that is, the first words of Acts 10.38, and nothing from Acts 10.39–41.

3. Codex Toledo 35.4, ed. Férotin, *op. cit.*, col. 702, now dated ca. 1192–1208, by A. M. Mundó, *Hispania Sacra* 18 (1965), 21, reads as Responsorium "Ihesum Nazarenum," the first two words of Acts 10.38 (which are also identical with the beginning of Acts 2.22), and nothing else, it seems.

4. *BG* 1122, the *Breviarium Gothicum*, published in 1502 by Cardinal Ximénès, is a modern reconstruction that should not be counted among the Mozarabic MSS for the reasons repeatedly stated in the present investigation.

5. ML (Morin 215), that is, the *Liber Commicus*, now available in a modern edition (cited above in note 22) offers Acts 10.38 and 40–41 in a lectionary in II.401.19 and 23f. But this lectionary cannot be looked upon any longer as an exclusively Mozarabic service book, since MSS of the work were evidently also available in the southern part of Charlemagne's realm, that is, in Aquitania and Septimania. Thus Anscari M. Mundó assigns the provenance of a Commicus palimpsest, Paris, B.N. lat. 2269,[24] written about the year 800, to the *Gallia Narbonensis*, and tentatively to the city of Carcassonne.

The preceding *Incipits* in Mozarabic MSS of Acts 10.38 have scant probative value for the occurrence of the desired Old Latin text of Acts 10.38–41. The examples plainly show that the assumption of the identity of "the *LC* citation [of Acts 10.38, 40–41] . . . with those of the Mozarabic MSS (p. 249)" is not borne out by the available evidence. On the exegesis of Acts 10.38 see François Bovon, *De vocatione gentium: Histoire de l'interprétation d'Act. 10.1–11.18* (Tübingen, 1967), 224–246.

G. Wallach, *Didascaliae*, 496f.; *Speculum* 40 (1965), 250–251; *LC* I.15 (p. 37.14): 2 Cor. 3.18–4.2.—I have listed in Chapter X, C4, the treatment accorded to this text. *OV*, the *Oracional Visigótico* (*OV* 1119; p. 361, ed. José Vives; Barcelona, 1946), is hardly a

---

[24] Mundó, "El Commicus palimsest," in *Liturgica: Cardinali I. A. Schuster in memoriam* I (Scripta et Documenta 7; Montserrat, 1956), 151–247.

reliable witness, since it contains only the *Incipit* "Nos omnes revelata facie" and nothing else of the text under consideration. A palimpsest fragment of the *Liber Commicus*, written in the South of the Frankish kingdom about 800 "in Gallia Narbonensi, fortisan in ipsa urbe Carcassonensi," contains the text of 2 Cor. 3.14–4.6; see Anscari M. Mundó, in *Liturgica: Cardinali I. A. Schuster in memoriam* I (Scripta et Documenta 7; Montserrat, 1956), 247.

H. Wallach, *Didascaliae*, 497; *Speculum* 40 (1965), 251–253; *LC* I.17 (p. 42.33): Heb. 11.33–34, *vel cetera quae sequuntur.*—Freeman concludes (p. 253) that the present writer "does not point to any patristic or other source presenting *Hebrews* 11.33–34 in the abbreviated Vulgate version common to both *LC* and Mozarabic MSS." Her assumption of an interdependence between these is out of the question for sundry reasons. She renews her earlier quotation of the *LC* text, although I quietly corrected in *Didascaliae*, p. 497, her first incomplete citation in *Speculum* 32 (1957), 685, when I cited *LC* I.17 (p. 42.30–35) by adding the *LC*'s concluding remarks—always omitted by her—which in the *LC* are appended to the text of Heb. 11.33–34, namely, "vel cetera quae sequuntur" (p. 42.35). This means that the *LC* has at least also Hebrews 11.35 in mind. Heb. 11.13 and Heb. 11.33–34ff. are contrasted in *LC* I.17 (p. 42.30–35):

Exitum ergo conversationis . . . . demonstrat Apostolus, cum dicit: Sancti *omnes iuxta fidem defuncti sunt non acceptis repromissionibus, sed a longe aspicientes et salutantes et confidentes, quia peregrini et hospites sunt super terram* [Heb. 11.13], sive cum dicit: Sancti *per fidem vicerunt regna, operati sunt iustitiam, adepti sunt repromissiones, exstinxerunt impetum ignis, convaluerunt de infirmitate, fortes facti sunt in bello* [Heb. 11.33–34], vel cetera, quae sequuntur [Heb. 11.35].

It is obvious that the *Sancti* connected with Heb. 11.33 in *LC*, p. 42.33, which are substituted for the *qui* of the Vulgate text, are here not just a liturgical reminiscence of the *LC* author referring to the beginning of a pericope in a lectionary. The *LC*'s *Sancti* belong to the argument of *LC* I.17, which discusses the "exitum conversationis sanctorum virorum" (p. 40.2–3; cf. especially p. 41.14, p. 42.13, 17, 29–30), and clearly compares Heb. 11.13 with Heb. 11.33–34 "and ff.," or, as the *LC* puts it: "vel cetera quae sequuntur."

    LC III.17 (p. 140.11–12) again reads: sancti *per fidem vicerunt regna* (Heb. 11.33), et sancti *omnes iuxta fidem defuncti sunt* (Heb. 11.13).

The latter formation seems to be identical with the beginning of the pericope in a Visigothic lectionary, the *Liber Commicus*.[25] But the occurrence of traces from Mozarabic service books in the non-Mozarabic liturgy and in Frankish writings which originated in the southern Frankish, formerly Visigothic, provinces of Aquitania and Septimania, is by now a fact proved by Anscari M. Mundó[26] and by Michel Huglo.[27] Louis Brou pointed this out a few years ago.[28] The explanations given for missing parts in the *LC* citation of Heb. 11.33–34 and in its alleged Mozarabic source, *AL* f. 94v (p. 132) are not convincing. The Frankish origin of *Heb.* 11.33–34 in the *LC* might have become obvious from the fact, mentioned in *Speculum* 40 (1965), 272 n. 258, that the *LC* was written within the orbit of the Antiphonary of Compiègne, codex Paris, B.N. lat. 17436, saec. IX, whose text is published in *PL* 78 as *Liber Responsalis*. This Frankish antiphonary[29] abbreviates Heb. 11.33–34, like the Mozarabic *AL*, in a fashion similar to the abbreviated text in *LC* I.17. Compare the following three versions of Heb. 11.33–34:

LC I.17 (p. 42.33–35):	*Liber Responsalis, PL* 78.822D (Hesbert, *CAO* I.123b):	*AL*, fol. 94v (p. 132):
Sancti per fidem vicerunt regna, operati sunt iustitiam, adepti sunt repromissiones, exstinxerunt impetum ignis, convaluerunt de infirmitate, fortes facti sunt in bello, vel cetera quae sequuntur.	Omnes sancti p. f. v. r., operati sunt iustitiam; adepti sunt promissiones, obturaverunt ora leonum, et fortes f. s. i. b., Effugerunt aciem gladii, convaluerunt d. i., Et fortes (f. s. i. b.).	Sancti qui p. f. v. r., operati s. iustitiam, adepti s. repr., extinxerunt i. i., fugaberunt a. g., fortes f. s. i. b. Steterunt contra hostes et de inimicis se vindicaberunt. For(tes).

[25] See also *Epistula ad Hebraeos*, ed. H. F. D. Sparks (Oxford, 1941), 746, app. crit. to Heb. 11.13 (in Wordsworth-White's NT).

[26] "El Commicus palimpsest Paris lat. 2269: amb notes sobre litúrgia i manuscrits visigòtics a Septimània i Catalunya," in *Liturgica: Cardinali I. A. Schuster in memoriam* I (Scripta et Documenta 7; Montserrat, 1956), 151–247.

[27] "Les *Preces* des graduels aquitains empruntées à la liturgic hispanique," *Hispania Sacra* 8 (1955), 361–383.

[28] Louis Brou, "Le IVe livre d'Esdras dans la liturgie hispanique et le Roman *Locus iste* de la Messe de la Dédicace," *Sacris Erudiri* 9 (1957), 106f.

[29] Now edited with related MSS by R.-J. Hesbert and Renato Prévost, *Corpus Antiphonalium Officii I: Manuscripti "Cursus Romanus"* (Rome, 1963), 123b (p. 354), also *CAO II: Manuscripti "Cursus Monasticus"* (Rome, 1965), 1236 (p. 668).

Unabridged Vulgate versions of Heb. 11.33–34 occur in various lectionaries. For instance, in the Mozarabic *Liber Commicus*,[30] in Alcuin's Lectionary,[31] in a Carolingian *Comes*, saec. 8 fin.,[32] from Upper Italy, in the *Lectionnaire de Luxeuil*,[33] and in others. There can be little doubt that *LC* I.17 does not cite Hebrews after any Mozarabic text.

I. Wallach, *Didascaliae*, 497; *Speculum* 40 (1965), 253f.; *LC* I.28 (p. 56.36): Deut. 32.40–41.—The same version of the quotation appears as a *versus* in *AL*, fol. 159v, 9 (p. 258). Since the text is somehow connected with the Old Latin *Canticum Deuteronomii*, it may well be one of the *LC*'s indirect "Spanish Symptoms," especially because the canticle seems to be of Spanish origin, as Heinrich Schneider, *Die altlateinischen Biblischen Cantica* (Texte und Arbeiten I, 29–30; Beuron, 1928, 166ff.) reports, and as such is also often found in Carolingian compilations.

J. Wallach, *Didascaliae*, 498f.; *Speculum* 40 (1965), 254; *LC* II.3 (p. 64.38): *Isa. 60.20,

> Non enim in occasum tibi veniet sol
> et luna tibi non deficiet in aeternum tempus.

A closer parallelism between the two Old Latin texts in the *LC* and in the *AL* is effected through the omission in Cassiodorus' quotation (*PL* 70.911A) of the last part of *Isa. 60.20, namely, "erit enim tibi dominus deus lumen aeternum," since Cassiodorus' version does not end with *deficiet*, as Freeman cites it. Cassiodorus' version of Isa. 60.20 continues with "erit enim tibi dominus deus lumen aeternum," as I printed it in *Didascaliae*, p. 499. She alters not only the text of Cassiodorus' version, but also that of *AL*, fol. 88v15 (p. 121), when she says that "a less literal version is the one preserved in *AL* and other Mozarabic MSS":

> . . . non enim in occasu tibi veniet sol
> et luna tibi non deficiet in aeternum tempus,

---

[30] *Liber Commicus*, ed. Justo Pérez de Urbel and Atilano González y Ruiz Zorrilla I–II (Madrid, 1950 and 1955), 51, 456, 477, 479.

[31] See André Wilmart, "Le Lectionnaire d'Alcuin," *Ephemerides Liturgicae* 51 (1937), 125, no. 23: Heb. 11.33–39; Wilmart assumes that Alcuin's work coincided with his arrival in France in 781.

[32] Described by Robert Amiet, "Un comes carolingien inédit de la Haute-Italie," *Ephemerides Liturgicae* 73 (1959), 344, no. 55: Heb. 11.33–39.

[33] Pierre Salmon, *Le Lectionnaire de Luxeuil* (Rome, 1944), 81, 185f.

because she omits the Old Latin ending of *Isa. 60.20, cited at the end of the *AL* text, namely, "sed erit tibi dominus in luce aeterna." Thus two texts are altered by the mere omission of words belonging to these two texts. Nor does she notice that *AL*, f. 88v15 (p. 121) puts the ending of *Isa. 60.20 also at the beginning of its chant III: "Iherusalem erit tibi dominus lux eterna et deus honor tuus / non enim. . . ." The reasons for all those omissions may be found in the endeavor to produce a greater parallelism between the *LC* and the *AL* texts than there exists in reality. *AL* can hardly be the *LC*'s source.

K. Wallach, *Didascaliae*, 499; *Speculum* 40 (1965), 255; *LC* II.30 (p. 93.19): *Exod. 24.7.—The fact that the Old Latin origin of Exod. 24.7 is evident in the *LC* text, in Augustine's quotation, and in *AL*, f. 160v (p. 260), is obvious. The author of the *LC* knew Augustine's *Quaestiones in Heptateuchum*, which he repeatedly cites elsewhere in his work (for example, p. 31.5; 32f.). The assumption that the *LC*'s argument was better served by the liturgical version is certainly without any basis in fact.

L. See above, under the section C, D, L.

M. Wallach, *Didascaliae*, 500f.; *Speculum* 40 (1965), 255–257; *LC* I.25 (p. 54.24): cf. Isa. 61.7–8.—A "Spanish Symptom." The text "Laetitia sempiterna erit electis meis, dum dedero opera eorum in veritate" may be called a real "Spanish Symptom" in the context of the *LC*. It is written in the *Vaticanus Latinus 7207* on the last line of f. 58r, and on the first line of f. 58v (Bastgen, p. 54.24–25). It also occurs in *AL*, f. 250r (p. 417). In connection with the present section, Freeman refers to Heinrich Schneider, *Die altlateinischen Biblischen Cantica*, to whom I had referred previously in *Didascaliae* (1961), 501 n. 56. On the fate of my reference to Schneider see below, section N.

N. Wallach, *Didascaliae*, 501; *Speculum* 40 (1965), 257f.; *LC* III.17 (p. 140.1): John 10.9.—The text of John 10.9 cannot be derived from a Mozarabic antiphon for the reasons stated in Chapter X, A2, and what has been said of the *Clavis Melitonis* in connection with N is now irrelevant, since the *CM* is not one of the *LC*'s sources, as the present writer shows in Chapter X, D.

Another strange reference of the type listed in Chapter X, C1 is associated with section N. In *Speculum* 40 (1965), 256, Freeman quotes my remark in *Didascaliae*, p. 500f. on the Mozarabic *Psalter*, but omits from my statement my note 56 on p. 501, where I cite Heinrich Schneider (referred to above in section M), p. 134f. This reference naturally meant to explain the well-known substitution of the Vulgate text for the Old Latin version in such contexts as described by Schneider on p. 134. She mentions the phenomenon (p. 256 n. 191) and adds, "See the remark of H. Schneider in n. 232 below." In this note on p. 267, she cites the same German text of Schneider, p. 134, that I recorded in my note 56 in *Didascaliae*, p. 501, and although she refers to my note 56, she states, for reasons unknown to me: "Although he refers repeatedly to Schneider's work (in notes 36, 37, 53, 56), this allusion to OL antiphons escaped Mr. W. . . . "

O. Wallach, *Didascaliae*, 501f.; *Speculum* 40 (1965), 259–260; *LC* IV.20 (p. 211.9): John 15.16.—I have shown in Chapter X, E, that the Mozarabic Antiphonary of León and the Frankish Antiphonary of Compiègne offer the same reading *et fructum plurimum afferatis*, a fact that does not speak for an exclusive Mozarabic influence.

P. Wallach, *Didascaliae*, 502f.; *Speculum* 40 (1965), 260; *LC* I.10 (p. 29.31): 1 Pet. 2.6 supplemented with *fundamentis* and *probatum* from Isa. 28.16 Vulgate.—The *AL* antiphon has nothing to do with the *LC* text. The explanation I gave in *Didascaliae*, pp. 502f., shows that the LXX of Isa. 28.16 represents the *in eo* of the *LC* quotation. This Old Latin *in eo* is changed in its citation in 1 Pet. 2.6 to *in eum*. A corrector of the *Vaticanus Latinus 7207* changed *in eo* to *in eum*. The *in eo* in the *LC* is original with the Old Latin *LC* quotation, and neither copied nor borrowed from the *in eo* in *AL*, which on its own offers the same Old Latin variant *in eo*. Freeman's remarks and the present writer's remarks concerning the *Clavis Melitonis* as a source of the *LC* must be voided, since this *florilegium* is not used in the *LC*, as I have shown in Chapter X, D. Also her assumption that the Mozarabic antiphon is marked "In Esaya" in the margin of the Antiphonary of León must be abandoned in connection with our critical discussion because the identifications of biblical passages in *AL* represent a regional peculiarity of the MS, but hardly a general characteristic of the Mozarabic antiphonary as such, as is shown in Chapter XII, A, on the basis of the antiphonary's manuscript transmission.

Q. Wallach, *Didascaliae*, 503f.; *Speculum* 40 (1965), 261; *LC* I.10 (p. 29.36): Zach. 3.8–9.—There is no connection between this text and the *Clavis Melitonis* because the *Clavis* is not a source of the *LC*, as I have shown in Chapter X, D. The text of an antiphon is indeed identical with the *LC* version, save for *AL*'s *dicit dominus*. I would be inclined to speak of a "Spanish Symptom" in the *LC*, if only the two versions of Zach. 3.8–9, as cited by Jerome in his *Commentary on Zach.* (*PL* 25.1438C–D), were not available; both contain basically our text with the exception of *in eo*, which has certainly an Old Latin origin, as I discussed in the case of P (above) in *Didascaliae*, pp. 502f.

R. Wallach, *Didascaliae*, 504; *Speculum* 40 (1965), 262; *LC* III.13 (p. 129.38): Zach. 6.12.—The assumption of any connection of this text with the *Clavis Melitonis* as advocated by Freeman and the present writer must be dismissed for the reasons stated under the preceding item Q. Freeman's additional belief that *AL*, fol. 36v (p. 28), "*Ecce veniet* vir cuius oriens nomen eius" (incompletely cited by her because she omitted the nine words: " . . . ante eum orietur iustitia et ipse erit salus populi"), is the *LC*'s source is contradicted by the *cuius*, missing in the *LC* text. Zach. 6.12 Vg reads: "Ecce vir oriens est nomen eius." The beginning *Ecce veniet* . . . in the *LC* text is a feature of the Frankish Antiphonary of Compiègne and related MSS,[34] and as such sufficiently explains the *veniet* in the *LC*'s citation. Neither the *Clavis Melitonis* nor the Mozarabic antiphonary text is necessary to explain the addition of *veniet* to the Vulgate text of Zach. 6.12. The quotation in the *LC* belongs to a long section written on erasure in MS *V*, fol. 145, as is evident from Bastgen's edition, p. 129.29–42 and line 44, while the reference in *Speculum* 40 (1965), 217 n. 35, contributes nothing new: it repeats what can be exactly read from Bastgen's edition and his *apparatus criticus* without looking at the *Vaticanus*, f. 145.

[34] Cf. R.-J. Hesbert, *Corpus Antiphonalium Officii* III (Rome, 1968), nos. 2548–2552; cf. no. 1071 among the *Invitatoria*, also IV (Rome, 1970), nos. 6612–6613.

S. Wallach, *Didascaliae*, 504f.; *Speculum* 40 (1965), 263f.; *LC* I.12
(p. 32.13): and *LC* III.11 (p. 124.31): Col. 1.24.—The *LC* reads
"Paulo adtestante qui ait" and "ille qui dicebat": "Gaudeo in
passionibus meis quia expleo ea quae desunt passionum Christi in
carne mea propter corpus eius, quod est ecclesia." Contrary to
Freeman's statement, this text of Col. 1.24 does not occur in all
Mozarabic MSS. Marius Férotin, *Le Liber moz. sacramentorum et les
manuscrits mozarabes* (Paris, 1912), col. 809, offers for Col. 1.24
nothing but the *Incipit*, "Gaudeo in passionibus," which is also the
Incipit of the Vulgate. But his MS B.M. 30844, fol. 73, indeed
offers a version of Col. 1.24 that is identical with the *LC* text, as
Professor Don Randel (Cornell University) kindly informs me. The
Explicit of Col. 1.24, as printed by Freeman for *AL*—namely, " . . .
quod est ex Ihesu"—does not occur in *AL*, f. 74.12 (p. 97, ed. Brou
and Vives; Barcelona, Madrid, 1959). Nor does the text of Col.
1.24 occur in *OV* (see *Speculum* 32 [1957], 684, no. 4). The *Oracional
Visigótico*, ed. José Vives (Barcelona, 1956), 109, no. 327, offers
nothing but the *Incipit* "Gaudeo in passionibus meis." All this
means that only B.M. Add. 30844, fol. 73, saec. XI, and *AL*,
fol. 74, whose MS was written about the year 1067, offer parallel
versions to the *LC*'s text of Col. 1.24, which originated about 791.
Our text may be counted for the time being among the "Spanish
Symptoms" of the *LC*. See also *Epistula ad Col.*, ed. H. J. Frede
(*Vetus Latina* 24.2; Beuron, 1970), 378.

T. Wallach, *Didascaliae*, 504f.; *Speculum* 40 (1965), 264f.; *LC* I.16
(p. 39.25–26) and *LC* I.1 (p. 9.23–24): two "Spanish Symptoms."—
1. *LC* I.16 (pp. 39.25f.) offers, *dicente scriptura*, the formula: Sapientia Dei super lapides pretiosos est, habitatio eius in vasis aureis.
The same text is listed by Louis Brou and José Vives among the
(not identified) formulae of *AL*, f. 292 v. 10 (p. 485), where the
text is found as a responsorium, while Freeman refers to it as an
antiphon. The *LC* text only looks to be completely parallel with
the *AL* text, because the longer *AL* text is quoted by her in an
abbreviated fashion:

    RS.: Sapientia dei super lapides pretiosos, alleluia!
           habitatio eius in vasa aurea, alleluia!
           prudentia sua de thesauro invisibili procedet, alleluia,
           alleluia, alleluia!
    VR.: Deus sapientia fundabit terram stabilibit caelos. Pru[dentia].

She omits the two "alleluia" in the first two lines[35] and the entire text portion from *prudentia* to *Pru[dentia]*. This naturally means that the *LC* text is but partly parallel with the *AL* passage. The *Incipit* "Sapientia dei super" appears as a responsorium in Toledo, Cathedral Archive, codex 35.4, fol. 133, now dated 1192–1208, by A. M. Mundó, *Hispania Sacra* 18 (1965), 21. Férotin, *Le Liber moz. sacr.*, col. 715, prints an abbreviated *initium*. The formula appears to me like a combination of *Sapientia dei* from 1 Cor. 1.24, with the *Sapientia* of Ecclus. 50.1: "*Quasi vas auri* solidum, ornatum omni *lapide pretioso.*" The *AL* text, printed above (from *Sapientia* to *Pru[dentia]*) is preserved not only in Toledo 35.4, but also in MS. Silos 6, f. 126 (B.M. Add. 30845). The occurrence of the formula in the *Breviarium Gothicum* proves nothing, since the *BG* is, as Freeman admits, "an artificial fabrication" (*Speculum* 32 [1957], 681).

2. *LC* I.1 (p. 9.23f.) offers a text similar to the one just discussed: Congregatur omnis ecclesia Israhel, et conveniat ad diem festum. The *LC* explains the meaning of these two texts by stating: "id est, simul in gregem glomeretur, simul veniat." The same formula appears as an antiphon in *AL*, fol. 189, 6 (p. 311), which is, however, incompletely cited by Freeman. It reads:

A. Congregetur omnis eclesia Israhel et conveniant ad diem festum alleluia quia hodie sancta sunt domino deo vestro alleluia alleluia., a(ll)e(l)uia. VR. Exaltent.

Bastgen refers for the *LC* text to Lev. 8.3 and Dan. 3.2 as probable sources. But I assume that the first part offers more likely a special version of 2. Reg. 7.11 (2 Sam. 17.11): "Congregetur ad te universus Israhel,"[36] since *ad te universus* has the same number of six syllables as *omnis ecclesia*, above. The latter version may well be some Old Latin version derived from 2 Sam. 17.11: συναγόμενος συναχθήσεται ἐπὶ σὲ πᾶς Ἰσραὴλ.[37] The insertion of two Mozarabic formulae into the *LC* may be traceable to the fact that the author of the *LC* perhaps recognized the partial proximity of the formulaic framework of a Mozarabic antiphonary text, especially of the words "et conveniant ad diem festum," to that of the Frankish Antiphonary of

---

[35] All "alleluia" belong to the chant text and are listed as such by R.-J. Hesbert, *Corpus Antiphonalium Officii III*, nos. 1325–1338.

[36] See *Biblia Sacra* (edited by the Benedictines of St. Jerome; Rome, 1944), 315.

[37] Cf. *The Old Testament in Greek* II, ed. Brooke and McLean (Cambridge, 1927), 164.

Compiègne with regard to the *Paschal Officium*. Compare, for example, *AL*, f. 189 (p. 311) : in the "Officium in dominico de Octabas Pasche" and *AC*, ed. R.–J. Hesbert, *Antiphonale Missarum Sextuplex* (Bruxelles, 1935), f. 87 (p. 107) : "Dominica octabas Pasche."

Alleged "Spanish Symptoms" in
Theodulph's De ordine baptismi

U. Wallach, *Didascaliae*, 505; *Speculum* 40 (1965), 265; Theodulph of Orléans: Old Latin Cant. cant. 4.10.—Theodulph, *De ordine baptismi*, *PL* 105.228, cites Cant. cant. 4.10, "et odor vestimentorum tuorum super omnia aromata," with the Old Latin variant "vestimentorum," while the Vulgate reads *unguentorum*. I explained in *Didascaliae*, p. 505, the philological origin of the Old Latin reading.

Freeman thinks of "an antiphon honoring female saints" as Theodulph's possible source. However, even the Carolingian Antiphonary of Compiègne, the *Liber Responsalis*, *PL* 78.778B, offers the responsorium: "et odor vestimentorum eius super omnia aromata." Also Ambrose, *De virginibus* I.7, *PL* 16 (Paris, 1845), 199D, cites Cant. cant. 4.10 in the version "odor vestimentorum tuorum super omnia aromata." There is naturally no reason for the assumption that Theodulph took the citation from any Mozarabic service book. I refer to Donatien de Bruyne, "Les anciennes versions Latines du Cantique des Cantiques," *Revue Bénédictine* 38 (1926), 101 : "et odor vestimentorum tuorum super omnia aromata."

V. Wallach, *Didascaliae*, 506; *Speculum* 40 (1965), 265f.; Theodulph: Rom. 6.3.—Theodulph of Orléans, *De ordine baptismi*, *PL* 105.224, cites Rom. 6.3 with the non-Vulgate insertion *fratres*: "An ignoratis, fratres, quia." Freeman assumes the Mozarabic origin of the variant because the *Liber Commicus* offers it too. She states that the reading is absent from "Carolingian Bibles, including the ones produced by Theodulph himself." In order to disprove the Mozarabic origin of *fratres* inserted in Rom. 6.3, I list the following occurrences:

a. Donatien de Bruyne, *Les Fragments de Freising* (Collectanea Biblica latina 5; Rome, 1921), 1 : "An ignoratis, fratres, quia. . . . ";
b. H. J. Vogels, *Untersuchungen zum Text der Paulinischen Briefe* (Bonner Biblische Beiträge 9; Bonn, 1955), 19: "An ignoratis, fratres, quia," in Ambrosiaster's third edition of his commentary

on Rom., according to MS Amiens 87, saec. VIII–IX; cf. also Vogels, *Das Corpus Paulinum des Ambrosiaster* (Bonner Biblische Beiträge 13; Bonn, 1957), 41;

c. Alcuin, *Epistula* 137, from about 798, ed. Ernst Dümmler, *MGH, Epistolae* 4 (Karolini Aevi 2; Berlin, 1895), 213.3, offers Rom. 6.3, "An ignoratis, fratres, quia . . . " in an excerpt from Leo the Great, *Epistola de baptismo*;

d. The Pseudo-Augustinian *Liber de divinis scripturis*, c. 103, ed. F. Weihrich (*CSEL* 12; Wien, 1887), 627.5, cites Rom. 6.3, "An ignoratis, fratres, quod . . . ";

e. The Frankish Council of Paris, held in 829, c. 6, *MGH, Conc.* 2 (Aevi Karolini 1.2; Hannover, Leipzig, 1908), 614.11, reads: "An ignoratis, fratres, quia. . . . "

It is quite obvious that the reading *fratres* in Rom. 6.3 is by no means of distinctly Mozarabic origin.

f. I add a third text from Theodulph's treatise for which Freeman (*Speculum* 32 [1957], 689) unjustifiably assumes Mozarabic origin. *De ordine baptismi* (*PL* 105.233) cites Dan. 3.92, "et aspectus quarti similis filio dei"; the Vulgate reads *species quarti*. Pseudo-Vigilius, *Contra Varimadum* 1.51, ed. B. Schwank (*CCL* 90; 1961), 62.2, reads: "et aspectus quarti similis est filio dei." The same version of Dan. 3.92 occurs in the Pseudo-Augustinian *Sermo contra Judaeos, Arianos et paganos* XV, *PL* 42.1126, which is inserted in Paulus Diaconus, *Homiliarium*, *PL* 95.1473D. Also the *Chrysostomus Latinus*, sermo 2 (extra collectiones) in Migne, *PL, Supplementum* IV (Paris, 1968), 840, cites Dan. 3.92 in the version " . . . *et aspectus quarti similis est filio dei.*"

g. 1 Pet. 2.9, "*Vos estis* genus electum, regale sacerdotium" (the Vulgate reads "Vos autem genus") in Theodulph's treatise (*PL* 105.235B) represents, according to Freeman (*Speculum* 32 [1957], 689), a Mozarabic antiphon. But some MSS of Alcuin, *Epistola* 17 from 793 (*MGH, Epistolae* 4, p. 47.8) read "*Vos estis* genus electum, regale sacerdotium," and so forth. I add that the Frankish Antiphonary of Compiègne and related MSS contain some antiphons with the *Incipit* "*Vos estis* . . . " (cf. R.-J. Hesbert, *Corpus Antiphonalium Officii* III [Rome, 1968], nos. 5497–5499).

Of the twenty "Spanish Symptoms" (see above, Part III, Introduction at n. 5) allegedly found by Freeman in the *LC*, not more than five seem to survive our critical scrutiny, namely, the items I, M, S, and T (bis), certainly not enough to justify any claim to a Visigothic authorship of Charlemagne's *Libri Carolini*.

The most recent advocate of Theodulphian authorship seems to be Elisabeth Dahlhaus-Berg, *Nova Antiquitas et Antiqua Novitas: Typologische Exegese und isidorianisches Geschichtsbild bei Theodulf von Orléans* (Kölner Historische Abhandlungen 23; Köln, Wien, 1975). The Latin title of this book is culled from the *LC* II.27 (p. 88.45 Bastgen). It allegedly represents (p. 36) the Visigoth's "Geschichtsinterpretation" . . . "von Analogien durchwaltet." This is a surprising misinterpretation of a plain figure of speech because the phrase in question is a mere verbal ornament and as such a figure of style which in rhetorical doctrine is called *commutatio* or *antimetabole*. One of the figure's best-known school examples has been Ovid, *Ars amatoria* 2,24: "Semibovemque virum et semivirumque bovem."

The *LC* uses the antimetabole *nova antiquitas et antiqua novitas* in a merely formal fashion as part of a comparison. *LC* II.27 (p. 88.37–38) states that the eucharist, "illud sacramentum dominici corporis et sanguinis" stands apart (distat) from the "imagines depictae arte pictorum." The eucharist "confirmat *nova antiquitas et antiqua novitas*," while "has (*scil.* the imagines) plerumque corrumpit *cariosa vetustas*." The latter expression is a quotation, not recognized by Bastgen, drawn from Prudentius, *Cathemerinon* X, 141, ed. I. Bergmann (*CSEL* 61; Wien, 1926), 62.

The antimetabole is used repeatedly by the author of the *LC* in a formal fashion within various contexts. Compare, for example, the following instances:

LC I.14 (p. 33.39) . . . ut nec *sequentia praecendentibus* nec *praecendentia* convenire videantur *sequentibus*;

LC I.17 (p. 40.10–11) . . . si quis dicat *argenteum aurum* vel *aureum argentum*;

LC I.19 (p. 45.26–27) . . . converso ordine *praestantioribus deteriora deterioribus praestantiora* dentur; etc., etc.

Alcuin, the actual author of the *LC*, very frequently employs the antimetabole in his writings, as the present writer has shown in *Alcuin and Charlemagne* (p. 160), for *eterna beatitudo et beata eternitas*.

Franz Brunhölzl recently expressed the view that there is no evidence available to prove Theodulph of Orléans' alleged authorship of the *Libri Carolini*. He lists in his *Geschichte der lateinischen Literatur des Mittelalters* I (München, 1975), 550, the studies published in *Speculum* 1957, 1965, 1971, which call for Theodulph's authorship, and some of the present writer's papers which deny the fiction of Theodulph's authorship. Brunhölzl makes it perfectly clear (p. 290) that Theodulph's alleged authorship of the *LC* remains unproved, "nach Lage der Dinge," as he puts it, "until a hitherto unknown or overlooked witness appears." *Sapienti sat*!

CHAPTER XII

Philological and Historical Evidence Disproving Theodulph of Orléans' Alleged Authorship

The attempt to prove Theodulph's authorship of the *Libri Carolini* (*Speculum* 40 [1965], 266–286) includes some untenable statements about the literary composition of the *LC* and its liturgical sources, which are dealt with in the following sections A–G.[1] The assumptions (A) that some of the *LC*'s biblical texts are cited by "memory" and that the Mozarabic antiphonary identifies its biblical texts through marginal notations in the manuscripts can be easily disproved on the basis of the surviving manuscripts. The opinion that Theodulph of Orléans was the "only" Visigoth in Charlemagne's entourage is refuted on definitive historical grounds in section B, while at the same time Benedict of Aniane's and Alcuin's acquaintance with the Mozarabic liturgy is put into proper relief. The non-Spanish Septimanian origin of Theodulph and the dependence of his non-Spanish biblical manuscripts on Italian codices is shown

---

[1] The statements concerning Theodulph and the *LC* made by Eugen Ewig in *Handbuch der Kirchengeschichte* III, 1, ed. Hubert Jedin (Herder, 1966), 92, are not at all supported by historical evidence; his conclusion that *LC* authorship had been "definitely clarified" in 1965 was obviously premature. See also the very end of Chapter XI.

in C. Evidence in Alcuin's correspondence brought in connection with the *LC* allegedly for the first time (D) turns out to have been used some decades ago by Hubert Bastgen and Wolfram von den Steinen. The absence of any iconographic connection between the famous apse-mosaic in Theodulph's little oratorium and the *LC*'s concepts of art concerning image-worship is shown in section E. Some literary evidence (in F) seen in the style of the *LC* that seems to be paralleled in that of Theodulph clearly appears to be the result of the independent use made by the author of the *LC*, as well as by Theodulph, of the same theological tradition concerning the doctrine of baptism that is traceable ultimately to Rufinus of Aquileia's *Expositio symboli*. Finally, the relationship of Alcuin to the *LC* is critically discussed in the last section, G.

A. Since I have not spoken in *Didascaliae*, pp. 470–515, of "the antiquity of liturgical texts preserved . . . in Mozarabic chant," as Freeman (p. 267) says, I certainly cannot have denied their antiquity. I stated (p. 507) that biblical quotations in the *LC* derived from Mozarabic antiphons could never have possessed the argumentative validity which the *LC* needed when questioning the *Acta* of II Nicaea "contra cuius errores ideo scribere conpulsi sumus" (*LC*, *Praefatio*, p. 5.4). The method employed by the *LC*'s author when he discussed with fellow theologians his refutation of texts excerpted from the synodal *Acta* of 787, the passages of which are cited or referred to in the chapter headings of the *LC*, indeed required the verification of all *LC* citations of patristic texts, derived from the *acta* of councils, in existing manuscripts that were available in the nearest libraries. This requirement certainly excludes the insertion of biblical citations in the *LC* for which the author allegedly drew on his memory. An instance of the described synodal procedure concerning the *ad oculos* verification of textual testimonia in manuscripts accessible to a synodal assembly is discussed above in Chapter IV, H. Freeman's assertion that the author of the *LC* cites Scripture by memory is easily disproved.

The scriptural passages occurring in the chapter headings of the *LC* are for the most part second- and third-hand quotations drawn from the first Latin version of about 788 of the Greek *Acta* of II Nicaea of 787, as has been shown in Chapter VIII, section C.

Numerous biblical texts of the *LC* are cited verbatim and without direct indication of their source from the fifth-century Pseudo-Augustinian *De divinis scripturis*,[2] including *LC* citations from the Psalms, to which Allgeier ascribed Mozarabic origin, a mistake that contributed to the rise of the much-cherished fiction of Theodulph of Orléans' authorship of the *LC*. Many other instances prove that the author of the *LC* did not cite biblical texts by memory. *LC* I.29 copies biblical texts verbatim from one of Origen's homilies, as I have shown in Chapter VIII, section A, and in Chapter IX, C2. *LC* II.31 cites Pope Anastasius' *Epistola* addressed to the Byzantine Emperor Anastasius (*JK* 744). Bastgen did not notice that also Rom. 14.7–13 in the same chapter (p. 101.39–44) is cited in the same version that occurs in the papal letter, and not by memory. The only texts with a biblical background that are cited in the *LC* by memory or by heart, extemporaneously, are phrases from the very beginning (see Chapter XI, B), and from the context, of the Canon of the Roman Mass in *LC* II.27, and also from the Canon's normal *praefatio* in *LC* IV.2. Otherwise Freeman's view received some support from her assertion in *Speculum* 40 (1965), 268 n. 235, of "marginal identifications" of scriptural texts in the Mozarabic antiphonary.

It is true that *AL*'s facsimile edition of 1953 by Louis Brou and José Vives offers throughout the MS identifications of the antiphonary's biblical quotations, to be sure not always correctly. Some parallels between biblical texts in *AL* and in the *LC* could be found quite readily with the aid of the scriptural Index in the first edition of *AL* by the Benedictines of Silos (León, 1928),[3] since the facsimile edition of *AL* had been published in 1953 without an Index; one was ultimately supplied by the text edition of *AL* in 1959. She

---

[2] The present status of research (cf. Ch. VI n. 2) dealing with this florilegium of Bible texts referred to as *m*, is summarized also by Walter Thiele, *Die lateinischen Texte des 1. Petrusbriefes* (Freiburg i. Br., 1965), 66–69. Cf. Arthur Allgeier, "Psalmenzitate und die Frage nach der Herkunft der *Libri Carolini*," *Historisches Jahrbuch der Görresgesellschaft* 46 (1926), and Donatien de Bruyne, "La composition des *Libri Carolini*," *Revue Bénédictine* 44 (1932), 227–234.

[3] *Antiphonarium Mozarabicum de la Catedral de León*, editado por los PP. Benedictinos de Silos (León, 1928), not listed by Freeman in the bibliography of texts in *Speculum* 32 (1957), 682f. She naturally used it together with *AL*'s facsimile edition *Antifonario Visigótico Mozárabe de la Catedral de León* (Monumenta Hispaniae Sacra, Ser. liturgica V,2; Madrid, 1953). The text edition by Brou and Vives of 1959 has abundant indices.

maintains in *Speculum* 40 (1965), 226 (to n. 86), that "Mozarabic antiphonaries have the unique distinction of identifying their sources in marginal notations, and the sources of antiphons are always 'in Esaya,' 'in Exodo,' etc." In note 86 she refers for this incorrect view to a remark made by Louis Brou when speaking about his facsimile edition of *AL* in 1953. But Brou's statement, "C'est là une disposition propre à certains antiphonaires purs mozarabes," is contradicted by the Antiphonary of San Juan de la Peña, also described by Brou: "Mais nos fragments . . . trahissent aucune préoccupation de cette sorte. . . ."[4] The study of the preserved MS fragments of Mozarabic antiphonaries proves clearly that Mozarabic antiphonaries as such did not identify their own scriptural quotations, as Louis Brou and Freeman believed.[5] There are no identifications of biblical texts in MS Additional 11695 (—A. Sil.II) of the British Museum, saec. XI (first half),[6] in the Mozarabic antiphonary (A. Peña) of the Monastery of San Juan de la Peña, saec. X (second half),[7] or in the Paris fragments (A. Sil. I) of the

[4] Louis Brou, "Fragments d'un Antiphonaire Mozarabe du monastère de San Juan de la Peña," *Hispania Sacra* 5 (1952), 64, no. 10, promised to publish fragments of an antiphonary "ayant aussi les références bibliques." This seems to be two folia of an antiphonary at Madrid, Biblioteca Nacional, MS. 11556, published by Brou as facsimiles VI and VII in *Anuario Musical* 7 (1952), between pp. 64 and 65. Don Michael Randel of Cornell University kindly called my attention to this fragment in 1969.

[5] Listed by Klaus Gamber, *Codices liturgici latini antiquiores* (Freiburg, 1963), 64–66; Brou's further promise to edit the fragments of two antiphonaries of Silos was partly fulfilled (Gamber, no. 381), while the other Silos fragment (Gamber, no. 383) was published by M. S. Gros, "Les fragments Parisiens de l'antiphonaire de Silos," *Revue Bénédictine* 74 (1964), 324–333. I could not find evidence for the systematic verification of Bible quotations (with the exception of *AL*) in the descriptions of MSS and facsimiles mentioned by Clyde Waring Brockett, Jr., *Antiphons, Responsories and Other Chants of the Mozarabic Rite* (Institute of Mediaeval Music: Brooklyn, N.Y., 1968) and by Don M. Randel, *The Responsorial Psalm Tones for the Mozarabic Office* (Princeton Studies in Music, 3; Princeton, N.J., 1969). I am indebted to H. E. Samuel (Yale University Library) for calling my attention to those books. I am very grateful to Don M. Randel, chairman of the Department of Music at Cornell University, for discussing with me (during two summer semesters) many aspects of the Mozarabic liturgy and for verifying for me numerous Mozarabic liturgical texts in his large microfilm collection of manuscripts, some time before the publication of his book *An Index to the Chant of the Mozarabic Rite* (Princeton Studies in Music, 6; Princeton, N.J., 1973).

[6] Louis Brou, "Un antiphonaire Mozarabe de Silos d'après les fragments du British Museum (MS. Add. 11695, fol. 1r-4v)," *Hispania Sacra* 5 (1952), 341–366.

[7] Louis Brou, "Fragments d'un antiphonaire Mozarabe du Monastère de San Juan de la Peña," *Hispania Sacra* 5 (1952), 35–65.

Antiphonary of Silos, B.N. nouv. acqu. lat. 2199, saec. IX–X.[8]
Such identifications in the León antiphonary (*AL*) and in the fragment, codex Madrid, B.N. 11556, are not features characteristic of
the Mozarabic antiphonary, but only a regional peculiarity. M. S.
Gros states that A. Sil. I in all probability belongs to the type of
Mozarabic antiphonary used in Septimania and in the territory
of the Tarraconensia. Any direct connection of *LC* texts with *AL*
is naturally out of question, since Mozarabic texts belonging to an
antiphonal tradition different from that of *AL* were evidently available in the Frankish, formerly Visigothic, provinces of Septimania
and Aquitania.

In order to support her view concerning the marginal identification of scriptural texts in Mozarabic antiphonaries, Freeman in
Speculum 40 (1965), 268 n. 235, states that Gerd Haendler[9] has
shown that the "primary appeal of Charlemagne's theologians was
always to the authority of the Scriptures; only later, under Louis
the Pious, did patristic authority predominate. . . . " But Herbert
Schade, in a very competent critical review of Haendler's book,
has proved convincingly that of a "farflung subordination of the
Holy Writ under the authority of the Church Fathers" in the appeal
to scriptural and patristic authority under Charlemagne and Louis
the Pious as advocated by Haendler "kann hier nicht die Rede
sein."[10] Contrary to Freeman's view (p. 203 n. 1), Haendler has not
established the theological orientation of the Carolingian age.

B. Visigoths from Septimania and Alcuin's knowledge of the Mozarabic liturgy (*Speculum* 40 [1965], 269–274).—Charlemagne's
capitularies and other historical sources of the Carolingian age
always stress the Frankish preference for the Roman liturgical rite,
as is pointed out below in my Epilogue (Chapter XIV). The
Roman rite was certainly also known to persons of Visigothic origin
who lived within the territory of the Frankish kingdom; some of
them were at the same time also familiar with elements of the
Mozarabic liturgy. I have mentioned the monastic reformer Benedict of Aniane and Helisachar, the later chancellor of Louis the

[8] M. S. Gros, see n. 5 above.

[9] Gert Haendler, *Epochen karolingischer Theologie: Eine Untersuchung über die karolingischen Gutachten zum byzantinischen Bilderstreit* (Berlin, 1958), 109ff.

[10] See Schade's important review of Haendler's book in *Theologische Literatur-
zeitung* 84 (1959), 440.

Pious (*Didascaliae*, p. 509), in order to question the mistaken assumption that Theodulph was the "only" Visigoth in Charlemagne's entourage. The argument that Benedict and Helisachar "achieved positions of influence at [the Frankish] court only in the time of Louis the Pious" (*Speculum* 40, p. 272) is contradicted by the historical evidence.

The Septimanian Visigoth Witiza, son of a count of Maguelone, was as a youth Pepin's and Charlemagne's cupbearer.[11] He withdrew from worldly pursuits in 774, and Charlemagne's esteem for the Benedictine monk Benedict of Aniane was so great that the Frankish king left him a free hand to the exclusion of everybody else, in his extensive missionary activities in Aquitania. My mention of Benedict as a prominent Visigoth of Theodulph's generation is countered by the contention that no "Mozarabic influence" (*Speculum* 40, 273) is noticeable in his writings; but such a conclusion, even if it should be correct, in no way affects his basic Visigothic origin, nor does it support Theodulph's alleged authorship of the *LC*. The importance of Benedict of Aniane cannot be questioned. Jean Deshusses[12] now ascribes to him the authorship of the *Supplement* to the *Gregorian Sacramentary*[13] connected with it through the famous Preface *Hucusque*. The strong influence of the Mozarabic liturgy noticeable in the *Supplement*, of which Alcuin has been considered the author since the days of Bäumer and Edmund Bishop, led Deshusses to the reassignment of the *Supplement's* authorship, and in this he has received the approval of liturgists[14] such as Antoine Chavasse, C. Coebergh, Odilo Heiming, and the disapproval of Klaus Gamber. The present writer shares Gamber's opinion in this instance because Benedict's authorship of the *Supplement* cannot be maintained without the support of some convincing factual philological proof. It seems to me that the new thesis does not pay sufficient attention to the close friendship between Alcuin and Benedict. We know about this friendship from the *Vita Alcuini*, c. 14

[11] Heinrich Fichtenau, *The Carolingian Empire: The Age of Charlemagne*, tr. by Peter Munz (Oxford, 1957), 184.

[12] "Le 'Supplément' au sacramentaire grégorien: Alcuin ou Benoît d'Aniane?" *Archiv für Liturgiewissenschaft* 9, 1 (1965), 48–71; cf. H. Barré and J. Deshusses, "A la recherche du Missel d'Alcuin," *Ephemerides Liturgicae* 82 (1968), 1–44.

[13] Ed. Jean Deshusses, *Le Sacramentaire Grégorien: Ses principales formes d'après les plus anciens manuscrits* (Spicilegium Friburgense 16; Fribourg, 1971).

[14] See *Ephemerides Liturgicae* 82 (1968), 8 n. 17.

(*MGH, Scriptores* XV.1 p. 192), and from Ardo's *Vita Benedicti*, c. 24
(*ibid.* p. 210) which states that their collected *epistolae* filled an entire
codex: "in unum unus conficeretur libellus." In addition the letters
of Alcuin indicate that Alcuin consulted Benedict repeatedly as an
expert in the adoptionist controversy.[15]

It seems that Louis Brou thought little of Alcuin's familiarity with
the Mozarabic rite.[16] But his opinion is sufficiently contradicted by
the fact that about twenty-five years later Deshusses judges the
Mozarabic contents in Alcuin's *Supplement* to the *Gregorian Sacramentary* to be of such a nature and of such weight that he proposes
the Visigoth Benedict of Aniane instead of Alcuin as the author of
the *Supplement*,[17] although Freeman has searched in vain for traces
of the Mozarabic liturgy in Benedict's writings.[18] His *Munimenta
fidei*, compiled after 800, and now edited by Jean Leclercq,[19] seem
to be unknown to her. The text of the *octavus tomus*, from *Primo
quidem* to *noster interior homo* (pp. 36.9–37.4), represents an anonymous quotation from Pseudo-Ambrose, *De dignitate conditionis
humanae*, c. 2 (*PL* 17; Paris, 1879), 1105B–1106B,[20] which is not
identified by Leclercq. The identical text portion from *De dignitate*
is quoted verbatim in the *LC* I.7 (pp. 22.21–23.6), where it is
ascribed to Ambrose of Milan. Naturally, it is inadmissible to con-
strue on the basis of the occurrence of the identical excerpts from
the same writing in Benedict's *Munimenta* and in the *LC* any relationship between these works and their respective authors. After all,
De dignitate was used not only by Benedict and by the author of the
LC, but also by other Carolingian authors, such as for example,

[15] Cf. E. Dümmler, *MGH, Epistolae* 4 (Berlin, 1895), Alcuin's *Letters*, 56, 57,
302; also 200, 201, 206, 207, and especially also *Epistle* 184.

[16] Louis Brou, "L'orthodoxie de la liturgie mozarabe," *Hispania Sacra* 2 (1940),
464.

[17] In *Speculum* 40 (1965), 274, line 2, we are told that "Alcuin's *Hucusque* Preface"
is placed "in the Gregorian Sacramentary." But this is impossible, since *Hucusque*
is not placed "in" the Sacramentary, but at its very end, as an introduction to
Alcuin's Supplement of prayer texts which are appended to the text of the service
book.

[18] This is a point as yet not investigated by Jean Deshusses. If such traces should
be largely missing in the writings of Benedict, the new thesis of Benedict's proposed authorship of the Supplement will be still further weakened.

[19] In *Analecta monastica*, première série (Studia Anselmiana, 20; Rome, 1948),
36–37.

[20] The same treatise also appears as a pseudo-Augustinian tract under the title
Tractatus de creatione primi hominis, PL 40 (Paris, 1845), 1213–1214.

Alcuin's pupil Wizo,[21] also called Candidus, and perhaps even by the patriarch Paulinus of Aquileia.

It is hardly an accidental coincidence that the identical passages from *De dignitate* which are verbatim listed in the *LC* I.7 (pp. 22.21– 23.11) occur also in Alcuin's *Dicta*, *PL* 100.566B–567A7, and 567B5–568A2. Wilhelm Heil in *Karl der Grosse* II: *Das Geistige Leben* (Düsseldorf, 1965), 150–151, recognized this fact.

Alcuin's *Dicta* on Genesis I.26 (*PL* 100.565–568) is made up of the first part and the end of *De dignitate*.[22] The pseudo-Alcuinian *Disputatio puerorum per interrogationes et responsiones* (*PL* 101.1101B– 1102D) also quotes extensively from *De dignitate*.[23] Alcuin's and the *LC*'s familiarity with *De dignitate* represent yet one more instance supporting Alcuin's authorship of the *LC*. Also the *Liber de salutaribus documentis*, cc. 2–3 (*PL* 140.1047–1048), occasionally ascribed to Paulinus of Aquileia, seems to quote from our treatise, which is also inserted into the pseudo-Augustinian *De spiritu et anima* (*PL* 40.805– 806).

We must finally mention that Freeman's reliance on Edmund Bishop's liturgical studies remains unsatisfactory, especially because C. Coebergh[24] and Antoine Chavasse[25] have shown some grave mistakes and fallacies in Bishop's older liturgical studies.

[21] See Heinz Loewe, "Zur Geschichte Wizos," *DA* 6 (1943), 363–372, for Alcuin, Candidus, and others; also Michael Schmaus, *Die psychologische Trinitätslehre des Hl. Augustinus* (Münsterische Beitrage zur Theologie, 11; Münster i. W., 1927), 30f. and n. 4, who earlier than Loewe disentangled the various interdependences. Henri de Lavalette, "Candide, théologien méconnu de la vision béatifique du Christ," *Recherches de science religieuse* 49 (1961), 426–429, is unfamiliar with Loewe's article and the sources mentioned in our treatment. Also P. Glorieux, *Pour révaloriser Migne* (Lille, 1952), 54f., can variously be supplemented according to the present exposition.

[22] On the *Dicta Albini* see Wilhelm Heil, "Der Adoptionismus, Alkuin und Spanien," in *Karl der Grosse* II: *Das Geistige Leben* (Düsseldorf, 1966), 150.

[23] Stephan Otto, *Die Funktion des Bildbegriffes in der Theologie des 12. Jahrhunderts* (Münster i. W., 1963), 26–28 nn. 6–13, cites this text in Pseudo-Alcuin's *Disputatio* throughout without realizing that it is derived from *De dignitate* and not from Alcuin. His assumption, p. 26 n. 2, that Alcuin copied from Godescalc d'Orbais is false, since Godescalc copied from Alcuin.

[24] "Sacramentaire léonien et liturgie mozarabe," in *Miscellanea liturgica in honorem L. Cuniberti Mohlberg* II (Bibliotheca Ephemerides liturgicae 23; Rome, 1949), 295–304.

[25] *Le Sacramentaire Gélasien (Vaticanus Reginensis 316): Sacramentaire presbytérial en usage dans les titres romains du VIIe siècle* (Bibliothèque de Theologie IV, 1; Paris, 1958), 62f. For Freeman's notions on the Mozarabic and Frankish antiphonaries as described in *Speculum* 40 (1965), 271–272, I refer to Chapter X, E, above.

C. Theodulph of Orléans' origins.—I pointed out in *Didascaliae*, pp. 508f., that the Septimanian origins of Theodulph cannot be questioned. Samuel Berger, E. A. Lowe, Hans Liebeschütz, and others claim Septimanian provenance for him. Even Madame May Vieillard-Troiekouroff speaks of him as "issue de la Septimaine visigothique plutôt que de l'Espagne proprement."[26] Others such as Charles Cuissard, Ernst Dümmler, Max Manitius, and Albert Hauck prefer Spain. Freeman (*Speculum* 40, 274–278) selects what favors her contention, and omits what contradicts it. Thus she fails to report that Max Manitius[27] and E. S. Duckett expressly (and correctly) state that Theodulph was neither a disciple of, nor a teacher at, the court school, and though he may have been as a bishop repeatedly at Charlemagne's court, he was not as close to the Frankish king as were Alcuin and other ecclesiastics of the age. Wolfram von den Steinen concludes that Theodulph's poems addressed to Charlemagne are "written from a clearly discernible distance" (aus deutlicher Distanz geschrieben).[28] All the poems referred to here and there by Freeman have been consistently used by everybody who has written about Theodulph. They contain no new information; on the contrary, Freeman's statement (*Speculum* 40 [1965], 276) that she used "a line less often cited" from a poem by Theodulph addressed to Charlemagne, namely, "Annuit is mihi qui sum immensis casibus exul," is questionable. This verse is cited by everybody, from Charles Cuissard in 1892 to Dietrich Schaller in 1960.[29] Her attempt (*Speculum* 40, 276–277) to connect Theodulph with the tradition of Spanish Bible MSS comes to nothing. There is some similarity in the sequence of biblical books according to the Old-Spanish order after the example of Isidore of Seville, *Ety-*

[26] "Tables de canons et stucs Carolingiens" in *Stucchi e mosaici alto medioevali* (Atti dell'ottavo Congresso di studi sull'arte dell'alto Medioevo I; Milano, 1962), 154f.; her assumptions that Theodulph was one of Charlemagne's principal councillors and the author of the *LC* are incorrect.

[27] Manitius, *Geschichte der lateinischen Literatur des Mittelalters* I (München, 1911), 537ff.; Duckett, *Alcuin: Friend of Charlemagne* (New York, 1951), 105; Hauck, *Kirchengeschichte Deutschlands* II (Leipzig, 1912; 3rd and 4th eds.), 169.

[28] "Karl und die Dichter," in *Karl der Grosse II: Das Geistige Leben*, 82. Otherwise von den Steinen still speaks (p. 80) of Theodulph's "spanische Vulgata Überlieferung" allegedly preserved in Theodulph's Bible MSS, a notion disproved by Bonifatius Fischer; see below, n. 30.

[29] "Die karolingischen Figurengedichte des Cod. Bern. 212," in *Medium Aevum Vivum: Festschrift für Walther Bulst*, ed. H. R. Jauss and D. Schaller (Heidelberg, 1960), 38; cf. Charles Cuissard, *Theodulfe, évêque d'Orléans* (Orléans, 1892), 57 n. 3.

mologiae IV.1.1–19, adopted by Theodulph, "whose Bibles are similarly related to Spanish tradition in their ornament." Her reference to Bonifatius Fischer's "Bibelausgaben des frühen Mittelalters" is misleading,[30] since the results of Fischer's investigation do not show any Spanish influence, and therefore contradict her assertion of Theodulph's genuine Spanish origin. Fischer's exposition leaves not the slightest doubt that Theodulph's Bible text is not indebted to Spanish MSS and texts, but relies almost entirely on manuscripts of Italian provenance. He even complains that the notion of Theodulph's alleged Spanish Bible text seems to be "unausrottbar," that is, "ineradicable."[31] Fischer says of Theodulph: "Th. took the biblical interpolations [in his biblical MSS] not from Spanish, but from Italian sources.... One prefers to assume for Theodulph the use of Spanish sources or one even designates his text as being of Spanish origin.... But not a single one of Theodulph's interpolations is of Spanish origin.... One must assume an Italian model [Vorlage] not only for the original text of Theodulph, but also for its further development."[32] Fischer speaks elsewhere, in a somewhat vague and summary fashion, of an elusive "Geist" noticeable in Theodulph and in the *LC*,[33] but

[30] "Bibelausgaben des frühen Mittelalters," in *La Bibbia nell'alto medioevo* (Settimane di studio del centro italiano di studi sull'alto medioevo X; Spoleto, 1963), 593–596. Fischer, p. 595, states that Theodulph "even takes recourse to the Hebrew Bible text and 'dares' (*wagt es*) to have St. Jerome corrected through a converted Jew." I assume that Fischer has in mind E. Porter, "Corrections from the Hebrew in the Theodulfian MSS of the Bible," *Biblica* 5 (1924), 233–258, who, however, nowhere mentions Fischer's "converted Jew." Fischer's conjecture may be connected with the *Hebraeus quidam* of Hrabanus Maurus, referred to by Fischer (p. 179 n. 37 see below, n. 33). On Maurus see Bernhard Blumenkranz, *Les auteurs chrétiens latins du moyen âge sur les juifs et le judaïsme* (Paris, La Haye, 1963), 174ff.–193 no. 163 b; see my note on "Moses ben Kalonymos und Paschasius Radbertus?," *Monatsschrift für Geschichte und Wissenschaft des Judentums* 77 (1933), 462f.

[31] Von den Steinen in *Karl der Grosse* II: *Das Geistige Leben*, 80, disregarded Fischer's decisive studies and therefore speaks of Theodulph's "Spanische Vulgataüberlieferung."

[32] Fischer (see above, n. 30), 529; cf. p. 595: [Theodulph] "procures MSS, predominantly from Italy"; cf. also pp. 534f. n. 50. Raphael Loewe, "The Medieval History of the Latin Vulgate," in *The Cambridge History of the Bible* II, ed. G. W. H. Lampe (Cambridge, 1969), 129, states, "The Legend of the Spanish parentage of Theodulf's Bible texts dies hard," and (p. 167) that Theodulph's Bible text is fundamentally of Italian origin.

[33] See Bonifatius Fischer, "Bibeltext und Bibelreform unter Karl dem Grossen," in *Karl der Grosse* II: *Das Geistige Leben*, 160, 176, 178.

nowhere does he mention "principles," as Freeman states in *Speculum* 40, 277, "adopted by Theodulph in his Biblical studies, determining the attitude toward Biblical tradition of the *LC*."

The picture painted of Theodulph's circumstances in his youth (*Speculum* 40, 278) seems to be too optimistic, since we know nothing of Theodulph's beginning and early career. There is not evidence available to show that he was the scion of a "good" Visigothic Spanish family, nor that he was "already in orders," as Freeman believes. We know, however, that he was "married," as Albert Hauck says,[34] and that he was a father, since one of his poems is addressed to a daughter called "Gisla."[35]

D. Alleged evidence in Alcuin's letters?—Freeman (*Speculum* 40 [1965], pp. 279–280) speaks of evidence for the year 798 "in the letters of Alcuin which has never been considered in connection with the *LC*. . . . In 798 it was an adoptionist work by Felix of Urgel that, like the Acta Concilii of II Nicaea, inspired official response." There is no evidence available for this emphatic opinion. Alcuin's letters, together with the texts referred to, are not cited by Freeman for the first time. They were listed by Hubert Bastgen in 1912, and by Wolfram von den Steinen in 1932.

Bastgen, "Das Capitulare Karls d. Gr. über die Bilder oder die sogenannten Libri Carolini," says: "No small proof for Alcuin's authorship [of the *LC*] is offered by the manner he employed when composing the books against the adoptionist doctrine of the Spanish bishop Felix of Urgel. . . ."[36]

---

[34] *Kirchengeschichte Deutschlands* II, 170; Hauck assumes that Gisla was not the only child of Theodulph. Von den Steinen in *Karl der Grosse* II, 81, recognizes Gisla's existence but ponders the possibility that she might have been a "geistliche Tochter." The latter station is also ascribed to her by Bonifatius Fischer, in *Karl der Grosse* II, 177 n. 31, I think unjustly. Why should Theodulph ascribe to a "spiritual" daughter the name "Gisla"?

[35] Charles Witke, *Latin Satire: The Structure of Persuasion* (Leiden, 1970), deals (pp. 168–199) with "Theodulf of Orléans and the Carolingian Renaissance." But his interpretations of Theodulph's poetry, especially of his *Paraenesis ad iudices*, is rather one-sided, since he does not take into account the patristic learning of Theodulph nor the legal procedures of the Carolingian age with which Theodulph naturally was quite familiar as an occasional royal *missus*. Cf. also P. M. Acari, "Un goto critico delle legislazioni barbariche," *Archivio storico italiano* 110 (1952), 3–37.

[36] *Neues Archiv* 37 (1912), 524–528.

Von den Steinen, "Karl der Grosse und die Libri Carolini," refers to " . . . several passages in Alcuin's epistolary. . . . I quote [says von den Steinen] *MG, Epp.* 4.233.27f.: ut sciam vel quo nomine scribo vel cui adsignetur [was he thinking that the writing should perhaps appear, like the *LC*, in the name of Charlemagne?!] (dachte er, dass die Schrift vielleicht, wie die *LC*, unter Karls Namen erscheinen solle?!)."[37] This reference is repeated by Freeman, *Speculum* 40 (1965), p. 279 and in notes 288 and 289, who follows von den Steinen's parenthetical and plainly tentative interpretation, the lack of probability of which von den Steinen himself sufficiently indicated by his exclamation mark that follows his own question mark! The context of the citation within Alcuin's *Epistola* 145 (pp. 233.27–234.10, Dümmler) makes it clear that Alcuin's inquiry addressed to Charlemagne "ut sciam vel quo nomine scribo vel cui adsignetur" (p. 234.8–9, Dümmler) does not refer to the name of a person in whose name Alcuin is writing, but rather to the title of Alcuin's "aliud opus" (p. 233.27) against adoptionism "in statu nascendi," or as Alcuin puts it, "not yet born" (necdum natum). He awaits Charlemagne's pleasure concerning the work's title (in nomine libelli: twice on p. 233.28 and 233.30, Dümmler). The expression "cui adsignetur" can only mean to whom the "aliud opus" is to be addressed, that is, either to Elipand of Toledo or Felix of Urgel, these two "contra adoptionis in Christo adsertores" (p. 233.38), who doubtlessly are meant in this context of Alcuin's letter.

There is no evidence in Alcuin's letters for Theodulph's authorship of the *LC*. Wilhelm Heil is justified when he summarizes the discussion on the never-proved connection between Alcuin's certain and Theodulph's alleged participation in the adoptionist controversy by stating that "Theodulph's participation in the controversy remains an unproved hypothesis; all proof for a literary participation on Theodulph's part is lacking."[38] Bernhard Bischoff, interpreting Alcuin's *Epistola* 145, concludes that Alcuin's anti-adoptionist writing, about which Alcuin had asked Charlemagne's opinion, did not receive a special dedication: "Eine Widmung, für

[37] *Neues Archiv* 49 (1932), 217.
[38] Wilhelm Heil, "Der Adoptionismus, Alkuin und Spanien," in *Karl der Grosse* II: *Das Geistige Leben*, 107.

die Alkuin ebenfalls nach einem etwaigen Wunsch Karls gefragt
hatte, hat die Schrift nicht erhalten."[39]

E. Alleged evidence at Germigny-des-Prés.—The famous apse-
mosaic in Theodulph's oratorium is looked upon by Freeman
(*Speculum* 40 [1965], 280–282) as proof supporting Theodulph's
alleged authorship of the *LC*. She says that its "unique and otherwise inexplicable iconography may now be understood as an ad
litteram illustration of a remarkable passage in the *LC*" (*Speculum*,
40, 223). I questioned her earlier documentation in *Didascaliae*,
pp. 512f., by expressing my agreement with Herbert Schade's conclusion that "an immediate influence of the *LC* and its doctrines
on [the] production of a work of [Carolingian] art does not seem
to exist."[40] She modestly counters my reference to Schade's reliable
study and final conclusion by saying that Schade's "study went to
press, however, before *Speculum*, xxxii [1957: that is her article]
appeared" (*Speculum* 40 [1965], 280, after n. 298). But Schade's
opinion has been confirmed by competent historians of medieval
art, as I shall show.

1. I stated in *Didascaliae*, p. 512, that Freeman's contention (*Speculum* 32 [1957], 699–702) of a causal connection between (a) the
description in *LC* I.15 and I.20 of the ark and the cherubim in
Moses' Tabernacle and in Solomon's Temple, and (b) the mosaic
depicting the ark and the cherubim preserved in Theodulph's
oratorium is without foundation. The excerpts cited by her (p. 700)
are said to offer the *LC*'s own "more precise description" and the
LC's "argument." But those excerpts are nothing but an unhis-
torical and arbitrary conflation of the description of the cherubim
offered in 2.Par. 3.10–13 and 3.*Reg.* 6.23–28. The same passages
are quite understandably also the source of the artist who decorated
Theodulph's apse. This artist's pictorial conflation of the biblical
passages has nothing to do with the textual conflation of the same

---

[39] Bischoff, "Aus Alkuins Erdentagen," *Medievalia et Humanistica* 14 (1962), 33;
reprinted in Bischoff, *Mittelalterliche Studien* II (Stuttgart, 1967), 15.
[40] "Die *Libri Carolini* und ihre Stellung zum Bild," *Zeitschrift für katholische Theologie* 79 (1957), 77.

biblical passages in the *LC*. The *LC*'s conflationary symbolism of ark and cherubim is not unique, for it certainly appears in patristic exegesis, for instance, in Augustine (see *LC* I.15, pp. 35f.), Gregory the Great, and Isidore of Seville. The author of the *LC* surely was familiar with the patristic tradition as well as with patristic sources. *LC* I.15 indeed indicates his dependence on Augustine's *Quaestiones in Heptateuchum* by two long quotations (pp. 36.4–18 and 36.26–37.4, Bastgen). Freeman misconstrues (*Speculum* 32, 700) the text of *LC* I.20 (pp. 47–48, Bastgen) when she says that "in the course of the *LC*'s analysis of their symbolic significance an even more precise description is given . . . : "Alas enim ad invicem super arcam extendunt . . . " and so forth. The *LC* neither offers its own "analysis" nor its own "description" because the passages cited from the *LC* present a conflation of biblical texts dealing with the ark and the cherubim. 3.*Reg.* 6.24 is cited in *LC* I.20 (p. 47.40f.): *Quinque cubitorum ala cherub una et quinque cubitorum cherub altera* (not acknowledged by Bastgen, p. 47.40); and p. 48.14–15: *Alae . . . se invicem contingebant*, which Freeman cites as the *LC*'s own "analysis" and "description," is a quotation of 3.*Reg.* 6.27. She assumes that *LC* I.20 (p. 46.29–30) reports that there were "in tabernaculo duo cherubim, in templo vero quatuor," because, according to her, the apse-mosaic in Theodulph's oratorium has four cherubim. This to her is contributing evidence that Theodulph is the author of the *LC*, a work written about a decade—if not more—before Theodulph began to build his little church, 799–818. Moreover, André Grabar, a noted art historian, sees in the apse-mosaic but two cherubim and two angelic figures who guard the ark of the covenant.[41] The important part of Theodulph's mosaic is *not* represented by the cherubim, but by the ark of the covenant, the *arca dei* or the *arca testamenti*.[42] No connection can be construed between the mosaic—however it is interpreted—and the basic ideas of the *LC* on images, and on the ark of the covenant and the cherubim, in particular; Hubert Schrade, in an illuminating investigation, has proved this

---

[41] André Grabar, "Mosaics and Mural Painting," in *Early Medieval Painting from the Fourth to the Eleventh Century* (The Great Centuries of Painting . . . directed by Albert Skira; 1957), 69f.

[42] See Peter Bloch, "Das Apsismosaik von Germigny-des-Prés: Karl der Grosse und der Alte Bund," in *Karl der Grosse* III: *Karolingische Kunst*, ed. Wolfgang Braunfels and Hermann Schnitzler (Düsseldorf, 1965), 234–261.

fact.[43] Theodulph cannot have derived from the *LC* any encouragement for the production of the ark of the covenant in his mosaic
because *LC* I.15 and II.26 brand the man-made image of the
divinely created ark of the covenant as manifestations of *great absurdity* and *great insanity*: "quantę sint absurditatis quantęque de-
mentiae illi qui ... " (*LC* I.15; p. 34.39) and similarly (II.26;
p. 85.29): "Magnę absurditatis, immo temeritatis est arcae testamenti Domini imagines coęquare conari." Says Schrade: "What
actually did Theodulph of Orléans do at Germigny-des-Prés? 'Er
hat aus einem Gotteswerk Menschenwerk, aus einem Mysterium
ein Bild gemacht.' Those who dare to equate pictures with the ark
of the covenant are insane." According to the concept of images
held by the author of the *LC*, Theodulph could never have allowed
the production of the mosaic presenting the divinely created ark of
the covenant in the form of an image fashioned by the hand of
man. It is therefore quite clear that Theodulph, when embellishing
his chapel, could not have followed the *LC*'s philosophy on images.
The man-made depiction of the ark in the mosaic is contrary to
the doctrine of the *LC*. Freeman's statement (p. 280) regarding the
influence exercised by the *LC*'s concept of art on the mosaic cannot
be verified. Madame May Vieillard-Troiekouroff's pronounce-
ment that "the decorations of Theodulf's Bibles and his church at
Germigny are true reflections of the philosophy of the *Libri Carolini*"
is rather illusory.[44]

2. The *LC*'s treatment of the ark of the covenant and the cherubim
(I.20, pp. 46.26–48.32) is identical with the text of Bede, *De templo*

[43] Hubert Schrade, "Zum Kuppelmosaik der Pfalzkapelle und zum Theoderich-
Denkmal in Aachen," *Aachener Kunstblätter*, 30 (Düsseldorf, 1965), 25–37, especially
p. 28, where Theodulph is referred to by some unknown *Druckfehlerteufel* as
"Theodor." Bonifatius Fischer in *Karl der Grosse* II: *Das Geistige Leben*, 181 n. 37a,
believes that H. Schnitzler and H. Schrade do not interpret certain relevant texts
with the necessary caution in their controversy in *Aachener Kunstblätter* 29 (1964),
17–44, and 30 (1965), 25–37. I agree with Schnitzler's and Schrade's reasonable
interpretations, but not with Stephen Gero's ideas on Carolingian art in the
Greek Orthodox Theological Review 18 (1973), 18ff., and 31f. nn. 93 and 106. Contrary to Gero's belief, I am convinced of H. Schade's reliable investigation entitled
"Die *Libri Carolini* und ihre Stellung zum Bild," *Zeitschrift für katholische Theologie*
79 (1957).

[44] May Vieillard-Troiekouroff, "A propos de Germigny-des-Prés," *Cahiers
archéologiques* 13 (1962), 267f.; also "Tables des canons et stucs carolingiens: Le
décor architectural et aniconique des Bibles de Théodulphe et celui de l'église de
Germigny-des-Prés," in *Atti dell'ottavo congresso di studi sull'arte dell'alto medioevo* I:
Lo Stucco-Il Mosaico; Studi vari (Milano, 1962), 154–178.

Salomonis c. 13 (*PL* 91.764–767D). Herbert Schade pointed this out for the first time to Peter Bloch, who then published this discovery in 1965.[45] Freeman (*Speculum* 40 [1965], 281), too, points to Bede as the source allegedly copied by the author of the *LC* (cf. also n. 48, below). But the fact of Schade's discovery of the *LC*'s source negates a close connection between the *LC*'s "quattuor cherubim" (I.20, p. 46.30) and the alleged four cherubim in Theodulph's apse-mosaic.[46] One could now even assume that Theodulph of Orléans may have been directly familiar with Bede's treatise, which was not directly quoted in the *LC*. There is some evidence available to show that the Bede text in *LC* I.20 is not derived from Bede's treatise but from another work which contained *De templo Salomonis*.[47]

The *LC* I.20 offers two unique variants in its Bede text for which no equivalents seem to be extant in the *De templo Salomonis*, edited in Migne, *PL* 91. Compare

LC I.20: alios duos *multo* maiores (scil. cherubim) (p. 46.28);

post incarnationem (p. 46.33);

Bede, *De templo Salomonis*, c. 13: alios duos maiores (*PL* 91.765C8);

per incarnationem (*PL* 91.765D1).

The two distinctive variants *multo* and *post* are to be found also in the following four Bible commentaries, all of which insert Bede's work into their context, including c. 13:

Claudius of Turin, *Commentarii in Libros Regum* 3.15:

alios duos *multo* maiores (scil. cherubim)

(*PL* 50.1126A9–10),

post incarnationem (*PL* 50.1126A15);

---

[45] See above, n. 42, Bloch, p. 261 n. 101.

[46] André Grabar speaks of "two" cherubim and "two" angelic figures, and I agree with this interpretation. Freeman sees four "cherubim" in Theodulph's apsis because the Bede text cited in the *LC* speaks of four cherubim. I found four also in Isidore of Seville, *Quaest. in Exod.* c. 46, *PL* 83.511B.

[47] David Hurst published in *CCL* 119A (1969) an edition of Bede, *De templo Salomonis*, which, in contrast to *PL* 91, contains the same unique variants that I found in the *LC* and in texts of Bede's treatise attached to the listed medieval commentaries (but not in the edition in *PL* 91). Since Hurst does not report on the nature of his edition and obviously did not take into account the indirect transmission of Bede's treatise attached to the medieval commentaries I have listed, I have changed nothing in my treatment. If it should turn out later that Hurst's text actually renders Bede's original text, then my conclusion that the anonymously cited Bede text in *LC* I.20 belongs to the indirect text transmission of the Bede treatise attached to some ninth-century medieval commentaries will have to be abandoned. Cf. Chapter VIII n. 21, Ch. IX n. 11.

Hrabanus Maurus, *Comm. in Libros IV Regum*:
　　alios duos *multo* maiores (scil. cherubim)

　　　　　　　　　　　　　　　　　(*PL* 109.155C11);

　　post incarnationem (*PL* 109.155D4);
Hrabanus Maurus, *Comm. in Paralipomena* 3:
　　alios duos *multo* maiores (scil. cherubim) (*PL* 109.430D1);
　　post incarnationem (*PL* 109.430D9);
Angelomus of Luxeuil, *Enarrationes in Libros Regum* 3:
　　alios duos *multo* maiores (scil. cherubim) (*PL* 115.427B),
　　post incarnationem (*PL* 115.427B14).

The occurrence of the two *LC* variants in the four Bible commentaries permits us to assign the *LC*'s Bede text to the same indirect transmission of *De templo Salomonis* that is attached to the works of Claudius, Hrabanus Maurus, and Angelomus. M. L. W. Laistner pointed in 1953 to the insertion of Bede's treatise in those commentaries without overlooking the possibility of a direct or indirect relationship between the four works.[48] We furthermore stress the recognition that the insertion of Bede's treatise into Claudius' commentary and the insertion of Bede's c. 13 into *LC* I.20 constitute for the first time a connection—even if tenuous— between the text of the *LC* and the fiercely iconoclastic Spanish bishop of Turin, appointed by Charlemagne.

The Bede text in *LC* I.20 comprises slightly more than two-thirds of the entire chapter. As an insertion into the chapter's context it may be looked upon as partial confirmation of von den Steinen's tentative argument (in: *QF* 21 [1929–30], 61) that *LC* I.19 and I.20 were inserted into the *LC* because of the forceful reply in the *Hadrianum* I.12 to the points made in the *Capitulare adversus Synodum*,[49] which are also dealt with in *LC* I.16 (pp. 37–39): not only the biblical Beseleel, "but also the Ark of the Covenant and the Temple

---

[48] M. L. W. Laistner, "Some Early Mediaeval Commentaries on the Old Testament," *Harvard Theological Review* 46 (1953), 37, 46. Paulino Bellet, "Claudio de Turín, autor de los comentarios *In genesim et regum* del'Pseudo Euquerio," *Estudios Bíblicos* 9 (Madrid, 1950), 209–223, proved that the commentaries on Genesis and Kings going under the name of Pseudo-Eucherius are in reality the commentary by Claudius of Turin with the addition of Bede, *De templo Salomonis*. Freeman, *Speculum* 40 (1965), 281, cites the second Hrabanus commentary, listed above, without realizing the implications it involves for our problem.

[49] On the relationship between the *LC* and the *Capitulare adversus Synodum* see the stemma in Chapter I, above.

with the Cherubim" are called *firmissima exempla*.[50] Schade's initial discovery and the historical foundation given to it by our recognition that the *LC*'s Bede text belongs to the indirect transmission
of Bede's treatise inserted into the mentioned biblical commentaries indeed strengthen the validity of von den Steinen's initial
assumption as to the secondary origin of *LC* I.20. We must further
recognize in connection with *LC* I.16 the illusory quality of any
assumption of an actual influence exercised by the *LC*'s doctrines
of images on contemporary Carolingian pictorial art. According
to Exod. 35.30ff., Beseleel is divinely endowed as an artist: "a
domino sit electus et spiritu sapientiae et intelligentiae et scientiae
repletus" (*LC* I.16, p. 37.38–39). The exegetical comments of the
LC's author make it plain that he does not ascribe such a divine
endowment to human artists who acquire their artistic skill through
practice and experience, as he states repeatedly. The biblical
Beseleel is therefore interpreted symbolically as a "figura Christi"
(p. 38.40), and not, as in Exodus, as the originator of human
artistic activities. The slight influence on Carolingian life of such
an exegesis may be seen in the fact that Alcuin's pupil Einhard,
a close confidant of Charlemagne whose biography he wrote in the
830's, carried among his friends at the Frankish court the surname
Beseleel,[51] because he was engaged in artistic activities of an architectural nature of which some traces seem to have come to light in
recent years.[52]

F. Alleged evidence for Theodulph's authorship in *LC* style?—The
very examples listed by Freeman in *Speculum* 40 (1965), 282–283,
as proof for the identity of style between the *LC* and Theodulph

[50] See *Hadrianum*, ed. Karl Hampe, *MGH, Epistolae* 5 (Karolini Aevi 3; Berlin,
1899), 19, 10.
[51] Hubert Schrade, *Malerei des Mittelalters I: Vor- und Frühromanische Malerei*
(Köln, 1958), 141–142, writes convincingly on *LC* I.16, Beseleel, and Einhard,
though his belief that the *LC* was written by more than one author is contradicted
by the uniformity in the use of the sources observable in the composition of the
work.
[52] Cf. the studies by Blaise de Montesquiou-Fézensac, "L'arc de triomphe
d'Einhardus," *Cahiers archéologiques* 4 (1949), 79–103, and 8 (1956), 147–174; also
"L'arc de triomphe d'Eginhard," in *Karolingische und Ottonische Kunst*, ed. B. Bischoff
(Baden-Baden, 1957), 49ff. Like F. L. Ganshof, I am not yet sufficiently convinced
of Einhard's authorship of that arch of triumph.

contradict, as a rule, her own mistaken conclusions. The discussion of a few examples should be sufficient.

The occurrences of *ambrosia* and *nectar* in connection with the mention of baptism in the *LC* and in texts cited by Theodulph in *De ordine baptismi* prove nothing regarding the authorship of the *LC*. The reader is not told that *De ordine baptismi* was compiled by Theodulph no earlier than the year 812, while the *LC* originated about 791. In addition, Theodulph draws heavily on the traditional sources for baptismal matters, offered by Isidore of Seville. *Ambrosia* and *nectar* became literary clichés during Carolingian times, originally indicating the food and drink of the pagan Greek and Roman gods. As such both were naturally familiar to medieval writers who studied the Roman authors in the cursus of the *artes liberales*. Both terms belong to the style of the Carolingian age, and neither to the writer of the *LC* nor to Theodulph's style alone.[53]

The same is true of the "pallia . . . decorata variis coloribus fucata" in *LC* IV.9 (p. 189.4–5). These are hardly characteristic of the style of Theodulph, who speaks in *Ad judices* of "varie fucata colore pallia." We read, for instance, in a poem by Aethilwald (*MGH, AA* XV; Berlin, 1919), 532: "viridi, fulvo, floreo | *Fucata* atque blaveo | ut peplorum per *pallia* | Pulchra pandunt ornamina." Ruricus, *Epist. lib.* 2.15 (*CSEL* 21 [1891], 394), speaks of a *pictor* who painted (depingit) "parietes variis colorum fucis multimoda arte." Similar expressions are known to me from the treatises by Ambrose written for Emperor Gratian (for example, *CSEL* 78, [1962], 50). Origen, some of whose homilies are extensively cited in the *LC*, says, for instance, *In Exod.*, *homilia* 6.1 (Baehrens 6, *GCS* [Berlin, 1920], 197): "Ista colorum fucus est, et cera tabulis sensu carentibus superposita."

In saying of the following example, "Even more impressive is the coincidence of phraseology with regard to the creed of [Theodulph's] *De ordine baptismi*" and the *LC* III.6, Freeman, *Speculum* 40, 282,

---

[53] On *ambrosia* and *nectar* see *Thesaurus linguae latinae* I.1867f., s.v.; for example, Prudentius, *Cath.* 3.21–25; *In Symm.* 1.276; Servius to Virgil, *Aen.* 1.403, 12.419; Jerome, *Comm. in Esaiam* 10, 33.13–19, ed. M. Adriaen (*CCL* 73; 1963), 416.59–61: "Panis ei dabitur, et aquae eius fideles sunt quae gentilium fabulae in ambrosia et nectare intelligunt" (cf. also *PL* 24; Paris, 1845, 367C). See further W. H. Roscher, *Ausführliches Lexikon der griechischen und römischen Mythologie* I,1 (Leipzig, 1884–86), 280–283; A. B. Cook, *Zeus: A Study in Ancient Religion* III,1 (Cambridge, 1940), 496f.

clearly misinterprets the origin of the *LC* text. Compare

(*a*) Theodulph of Orléans, *De ordine baptismi* (*PL* 105.226D):

> *Discessuri* enim *ab invicem normam* futurae praedicationis in commune statuerunt;

(*b*) *LC* III.6 (pp. 117.16f.):

> Hanc apostoli in conlatione fidei quam *ab invicem discessuri* quasi quandam credulitatis et *praedicationis normam statuerunt*.

Freeman omits from Theodulph's text the two words "in commune" preceding "statuerunt," which certainly belong to the original wording. By omitting the two words she achieves a complete parallelism between the two texts, and it looks for a moment as if the same author has written both texts.[54] But this is certainly an illusion: neither Theodulph nor the author of the *LC* wrote the basic text underlying the two texts. The coincidence in wording does not indicate identity in style. It is simply explained by the fact that the author of the *LC* and Theodulph, in dealing with the doctrine of baptism, are using the same explanation of the creed that, by the Carolingian age, had become a generally accepted element of theological tradition, as it occurs, for instance, already in:

(*c*) Isidore of Seville, *De ecclesiasticis officiis* 2.23.2 (*PL* 83.816A):[55]

> *Discessuri itaque ab invicem normam prius sibi futurae praedicationis in commune constituunt.*

(*d*) Isidore's source is Rufinus, *Expositio symboli* 2.7–8, ed. Manlius Simonetti (*CCL* 20; 1961), 134:

> *Discessuri itaque ab invicem normam prius futurae sibi praedicationis in commune constituunt.*

Rufinus' *discessuri* formula became through Isidore's transmission a text universally accepted and adopted during the ninth century. A circular letter by Charlemagne addressed, sometime during the years 809 to 812, to ecclesiastics of his empire, requested their opinions on baptismal procedures. About ten contemporary answers

---

[54] See other examples concerning inadmissable omissions listed in Chapters X, A 1–2, E; XI, A; C, D, L; F; H; J; R; T.

[55] Cf. H. Leclercq, "Symbole," in *DACL* 15 (Paris, 1953), 1756–1778, especially 1759; A. C. Lawson, "The Sources of the *De ecclesiasticis officiis* of S. Isidore of Seville," *Revue Bénédictine* 50 (1938), 30 n. 3.

are known, of which some can be attributed to leading Carolingians: letters and treatises sent to Charlemagne by Odilbert of Milan, Magnus of Sens, Leidrad of Lyons, Jesse of Amiens, and the Patriarch Maxentius of Aquileia.[56] Theodulph of Orléans' pertinent letter is addressed to Archbishop Magnus of Sens, but by no means to Charlemagne directly, since the emperor never asked Theodulph to submit his personal opinion on the subject.

The *discessuri* formula of Rufinus and Isidore, or parts of it, are clearly noticeable in some of these documents. Compare, for instance, the following texts:

(*e*) Maxentius of Aquileia, *Collectanea de antiquis ritibus baptismi* (*PL* 106.55B11):

> *Discessuri* itaque ab invicem normam prius sibi futurae praedicationis in communi constituunt;

(*f*) Leidrad of Lyons, *Liber de sacramento baptismi* (*PL* 99.859D2):

> *Discessuri* enim apostoli . . . ; [after Isidore, *Etymologiae* 6.19.57];

(*g*) Jesse of Amiens, *Epistola de baptismo* (*PL* 105.789A12):

> *Discessuri* apostoli . . . ; [after Isidore, *Etym.* 6.19.57]:

(*h*) For the seventh century see Hildefons of Toledo, *De cognitione baptismi* 32 (*PL* 96.126A):

> . . . corporaliter *ab invicem discessuri* . . . ;

(*i*) For the ninth century compare Hrabanus Maurus, *De institutione clericorum* 2.56, ed. Alois Knoepfler (München, 1900), 170:

> *Discessuri* itaque ab invicem normam prius sibi futurae praedicationis in communi constituerunt.

It is evident that Freeman has not offered parallels between the style of the *LC*'s author and that of Theodulph, but two passages in two writings that are based on the same source. Bastgen refers for *LC* III.6 (p. 117.16–17) in note 3 correctly to the *LC*'s source,[57]

---

[56] Cf. Cyrille Vogel, *Introduction aux sources de l'histoire du culte chrétien au moyen âge* (Spoleto, 1966), 11f.; and the texts ed. Ernst Dümmler, *MGH, Epistolae* 4 (Karolini Aevi 2; Berlin, 1895), 533ff., nos. 24–28.

[57] *LC* III.6, Bastgen, p. 117.18, refers for *verbum abbreviatum faciet Dominus super terram* to Isa. 10.23, but the *LC* actually cites the apostolic version of Isa. 10.22f., that is Rom. 9.28.

namely, to "Rufini Symbol. ap., c.2" in the older edition by Migne, *PL* 21.337. Rufinus is used in the same *LC* chapter, p. 118.22–29. The citations of Job 19.25–27 and 14.7–12 follow Rufinus' precedent quoting Job 19.25–26 and 14.7–10, though the *LC* text renders the version of the Vulgate while Rufinus offers his texts in a *Vetus Latina*.

It is not without interest to add that a Carolingian florilegium on the symbolism of baptismal ceremonies whose manuscript, according to André Wilmart,[58] comes from one of Alcuin's "fiefs," cites

(*j*) the *Discessuri* formula:

> Discessuri enim ab invicem apostoli normam sibi futurae praedica-tionis in commune statuerunt.

It is worthwhile to record the fact that this version, like the *LC*'s version, above under *b*, reads *apostoli* and *statuerunt*.

To summarize, there is no evidence available in *LC* style that connects Theodulph with the *Libri Carolini*.

G. Alcuin and the *Libri Carolini*.—Freeman refers to the characteristic "Alcuinisms" which I had pointed out in my book *Alcuin and Charlemagne*, p. 171. I refer to the fact that Alcuin, especially in two antiadoptionist documents composed by him for Charlemagne and for the Frankish episcopate, assembled at the Frankfurt Synod of 794, uses some topics that are also employed in the *LC* when questioning image-worship. The use made of the identical topics in the rejection of two subjects as far apart as adoptionism is from image-worship is surely valid proof that we are dealing not only with topics that are characteristic of the Carolingian age, but also that these topics constituted a part of Alcuin's personal style. Freeman, *Speculum* 40, 284 n. 321, assumes that Bastgen, *Neues Archiv* 37 (1912), 516–519, had "pointed out virtually all those parallels between *LC* and Alcuinian thought." The present writer refers in *Alcuin and Charlemagne* (1959), 171 n. 52, to Bastgen, "Der Verfasser des Capitulare über die Bilder," *Neues Archiv* 37 (1912), 491–533, and also offers, pp. 147–177, as is stated in his Preface, p. 4, new evidence beyond the evidence earlier listed by Bastgen. This new

---

[58] André Wilmart, "Un florilège carolingien sur le symbolisme des cérémonies du baptême," *Analecta Reginensia* (Studi e Testi 59; Rome, 1933), 168 n. 7.

link between Alcuin and the *LC* is provided by Alcuin's authorship of Charlemagne's letter addressed to Elipand of Toledo and the Frankish *Synodica* sent to the Spanish episcopate in 794. The identification of Alcuin as the author of both documents has found the approval of several scholars, including that of Bernhard Bischoff.[59] The characterization of the *Vaticanus Latinus 7207* as a working copy which allegedly presents a permanent record of the labors of its "editors" is disproved by the present writer's studies of the *Vaticanus* in Chapters VIII–XI, which always indicate that the *LC* was composed by one individual writer,[60] and not by several editors.[61] The uniformity in style and logical argumentation is the same throughout the four books of the *LC*, and the same sources are repeatedly used in an identical fashion from the *Praefatio* and from the first to the last chapter of the work. Heinrich Fichtenau proved that the Tironian notes transcribing marginalia in the *Vaticanus* do not constitute traces of Charlemagne's opinion on certain passages in the archetype of the *LC*, as Wolfram von den Steinen believed.[62] I believe that Fichtenau's interpretation of the marginalia finds additional confirmation through the discovery of important new sources used in the *LC*.[63]

I have outlined the genesis of the *LC* at the beginning of Chapter III. But Freeman (p. 284 in *Speculum* 40) states that I concede that "the *LC*'s first and main version dates from 790–791, and Alcuin was absent in England during those years." This argument is best answered by Bastgen's older laconic retort to such a point of view (*Neues Archiv* 37 [1912], 531 n. 1), as if Alcuin could not have worked also in England " . . . als ob Alkuin nicht auch in England hätte arbeiten können." Besides, I stated in *Didascaliae* (1961), 475, that the *LC* dates from 791, and not as she says from "790–791," and that additions to the context of the work may have been made between 791 and 794. Probable changes and additions are listed

---

[59] Bernhard Bischoff, "Aus Alkuins Erdentagen," *Medievalia et Humanistica* 14 (1962), 34 n. 32; also in Bischoff's *Mittelalterliche Studien* II (Stuttgart, 1967), 15 n. 32. Compare Goethe's "Erdetagen" in *Faust* II.11583.

[60] As Hubert Bastgen and the present writer believe.

[61] As Freeman, Herbert Schade, and Hubert Schrade (above n. 51 and Chapter IX n. 16) assume.

[62] "Karl der Grosse und das Kaisertum," *MIOEG* 61 (1953), 276–287; see further, above, n. 48 in Chapter IX.

[63] Cf. Chapter IV and throughout the present volume.

by von den Steinen in his "Entstehungsgeschichte," pp. 60–65. The
often-mentioned uniformity in style and source materials used from
the first to the last chapter of the *Libri Carolini* requires a theological
author whose extensive learning, biblical and patristic, literary and
dialectical, parallels the humanism of the Anglo-Saxon Alcuin in
many details which have been pointed out, again and again, in the
present investigations. On these grounds one can no longer accept
the view, mentioned by Freeman (*Speculum* 40 [1965], 285), which
still assumes that "a warning against theological innovations was
expressed by the king [*scil.* Charlemagne] himself." But this
warning against *vocum novitates* is not the king's, but from Paul,
1 Tim. 6.20: "O Timothee, depositum custodi, devitans *vocum
novitates* et oppositiones falsi nominis scientiae, quam quidem promit-
tentes, circa fidem exciderunt." This is a biblical injunction widely
cited in the discussions on image-worship (see *LC, Praefatio*, p. 4.40;
III.2, p. 125.6; etc.) and on adoptionism whose terminology is
partly indebted to that of the literature on the anti-Arian controversy. The latter is represented in *LC* III.3 by the Pseudo-Vigilian
treatise *Contra Arianos dialogus*,[64] and by Ambrose's nine dogmatic
treatises dedicated to Emperor Gratian.[65]

[64] Gerhard Ficker, *Studien zu Vigilius von Thapsus* (Leipzig, 1897), 22ff., and see
Chapter IV at n. 100.

[65] See above Chapter XI n. 6, and also Chapter V.

CHAPTER XIII

The Marginalia of the
Vaticanus Latinus 7207

Wolfram von den Steinen, in a famous study entitled "Karl der Grosse und die Libri Carolini: Die Tironischen Randnoten zum Codex Authenticus," maintained that the marginalia in the *Vaticanus Latinus 7207*, which were subsequently transcribed into Tironian notes, represent Charlemagne's own personal comments on certain passages in the *Libri Carolini*.[1] Von den Steinen's thesis was successfully questioned for the first time by Arthur Mentz, "Die Tironischen Noten: Eine Geschichte der römischen Kurzschrift,"[2] who doubted whether von den Steinen's interpretation of the notes could be maintained any longer in view of new, improved readings of some of these Tironian notes. In 1953, Heinrich Fichtenau proved, in part II of his study "Karl der Grosse und das Kaisertum,"[3] that von den Steinen's thesis is indeed "unbegründet," unfounded. I provided additional proof, if any was necessary, in a study published in 1966.[4] Von den Steinen himself, in a letter written in 1954, which has been made public recently in the Introduction to the republication of Fichtenau's study,[5] told Fichtenau: "You will allow me a kind of attachment to a hypothesis whose advocate I once had made myself. . . . You undo the train [of my arguments], fine. . . . "

In the face of von den Steinen's disavowal of his own thesis, and in spite of Fichtenau's convincing rebuttal of an untenable thesis,

---

[1] *Neues Archiv* 49 (1932), 207–280.

[2] Archiv\für Urkundenforschung 17 (1942), 261–263.

[3] *MIOEG* 61 (1953), 276–287.

[4] Wallach, *The Classical Tradition* (1966), 496 n. 99, and now above, Chapter IV n. 98.

[5] *Karl der Grosse und das Kaisertum* (Darmstadt, 1971), viiif.

Freeman upholds the fiction of Charlemagne's authorship of the marginalia in the *Vaticanus*.[6]

Bernhard Bischoff informed Freeman in 1963 that the Tironian notes in *V* "were invariably accompanied by marginal erasures of some length, and this suggested to him that the original notations had been made in minuscule" (*Speculum* 46 [1971], 598). But this information was not unknown by 1963. To the contrary, it was known a few decades earlier, at least to von den Steinen, to Carl Erdmann, Gerhard Laehr, Rudolf von Heckel, Arthur Mentz, Heinrich Fichtenau, Guilio Battelli, Alessandro Pratesi, and to the present writer.

Fichtenau, for instance, stated in 1953 that the Tironian notes in *V* are written on erasures, on which, here and there, with the help of the ultraviolet light of the "Quarzlampe" "... der in Minuskel geschriebene Text zutage tritt."[7] His assumption that the note for "mire" is not connected with an erased note must be abandoned, since Battelli once wrote him about some "asperita a destra della nota," as Fichtenau informed me some time ago. In 1931, von den Steinen reported that Carl Erdmann had noticed that "the notes are found throughout [durchweg] [the manuscript] on, or next to, an erasure of several centimetres in length" (dass die Noten durchweg auf oder neben einer mehreren Zentimeter langen Rasur stehen).[8] Erdmann assumed as reason for this rewriting the fact that the original marginalia written in ordinary Caroline minuscule script were afterward replaced by the inconspicuous Tironian notes. He took into account for the use of the Tironian notes the possibility that the replacement of the marginalia was a measure to prepare the archetype of the *LC* to be copied by a scribe or scribes. Erdmann

---

[6] "Further Studies in the Libri Carolini, III: The Marginal Notes in Vaticanus Latinus 7207," *Speculum* 46 (1971), 597–607; that the Tironian Notes replace original marginalia written in Caroline minuscule was reported in 1932 by Carl Erdmann, as stated by Wolfram von den Steinen, in *Neues Archiv* 49 (1932), 213. Bischoff in *Lexicon Tironianum* (Osnabrück, Otto Zeller, 1965), a reprint of U. F. Kopp, *Palaeographia Critica* II (Mannheim, 1817), lists in a postscript, p. iii, A. Mentz, *Die Tironischen Noten* (Berlin, 1942). The latter discusses on pp. 261–263 the Tir. Noten of *Vat. Lat. 7207*, and at the same time Mentz refers on p. 262 to von den Steinen's study in *Neues Archiv* 49 (1932). The use made of Tir. Noten at Tours, also during the time of Alcuin, is discussed by E. A. Lowe, *CLA* VI, xxviiif., and referred to by Bischoff, "Aus Alkuins Erdentagen," *Medievalia et Humanistica* 14 (1962), 32 n. 16.

[7] *MIOEG* 61 (1953), 282.

[8] *Neues Archiv* 49 (1932), 213.

also noticed in addition, as von den Steinen reports (p. 213), that
"also other marginal notes are occasionally found together with the
traces of the lost Tironian notes." While all this represents the state
of research known since 1931, Freeman concluded in *Speculum* 46
(1971), 603, that "up to now von den Steinen and others have told
us that *virtually* [her italics: L. W.] all the *LC*'s marginal notes were
accompanied by erasures, but the ultraviolet lamp now demonstrates
that it is true without exception of *all* the notes. There is not a
single one in the appended list that does not stand beside an erasure
of appropriate length." But this is by no means a new discovery,
because Carl Erdmann had already recognized in 1931 that all of
the *LC*'s marginal notes are accompanied "durchweg," that is,
throughout *V*, by Tironian notes (see above at n. 8). With regard
to the number of marginalia which have left only erasures in the
Vatican MS, but otherwise no readable trace of the erased text,
Freeman states (p. 601) that "the MS. has at least 31 notes . . . by
which von den Steinen's list of 80 Tironian notes may be increased
to 111. . . ." This is a miscalculation. Von den Steinen once
counted eighty Tironian notes, including fragments of such notes,
but he lists in addition in *Neues Archiv* 49 (1932), 213 note 2, ten
marginal erasures in *V* which indicate the *quondam* presence of
Tironian notes. Four of those ten additional marginalia listed by
von den Steinen are not recorded, as it seems, in Freeman's tabulation (see below), while six of them are listed in her Diagram without
special acknowledgment. Von den Steinen himself reports, in *Neues
Archiv* 49 (1932), 215, that there are certainly eighty Tironian notes
in the *Vaticanus*, but originally there had been more than one
hundred, " . . . und nun sind es sicher 80, wahrscheinlich über 100
gewesen." Nor does Freeman acknowledge the fact that the *bene*
on f. 101v in *V* is reported by Fichtenau in *MIOEG* 61 (1953),
282 n. 34, communicated to him by Giulio Battelli and Alessandro
Pratesi. She conjectures a few times that in connection with erasures
of marginal notes, the corresponding Tironian transcription most
frequently occurring possibly reads *bene* (p. 604), a conjecture that
is supported by the observation that "the scribe's *bene* may reflect
nothing more than Charlemagne's nod." Her listing of erasures
occurring in *V* contributes hardly a single new reading. She supplements in her tabulation in *Speculum* 46 (1971), 608–612, the earlier
Tabelle published by von den Steinen in *Neues Archiv* 49 (1932),
209–212, by the following means:

1. by the substitution of seven new readings of Tironian notes supplied by Arthur Mentz, *Archiv für Urkundenforschung* 17 (1942), 261–263, and by the adoption of one reading reported by Fichtenau (see above). She does not indicate her indebtedness in her tabulation in the same manner von den Steinen indicated his own indebtedness to others by listing the first letter of their names in his tabulation;

2. by the addition of six marginal erasures to her list as traces of lost Tironian notes, previously enumerated by von den Steinen in *Neues Archiv* 49 (1932), 213 n. 2, but not listed in his tabulation;

3. by the addition of some marginal erasures as traces of lost Tironian notes or partly lost notes, whose corresponding Caroline minuscule texts have left ink traces, as she believes, on the opposite pages *in margine*, since the scribe apparently was in a hurry for various reasons and did not use an ink blotter. Some of these inkblots are visible to the naked eye or under ultraviolet light. Her contribution to the subject matter under consideration will become obvious after comparison of the following two tabulations:

I

W. von den Steinen, *Neues Archiv* 49 (1932), 209: "Liste der tironischen Noten am Rande des Vatic. lat. 7207":

LC: Kapitel	MG. Conc. II Suppl. Seite	Note und Deuter	Nächststehende Textworte	Cod. V fol.	Vgl. unten Seite
			remansit		
12	*32* 4	*Fragment*	mulceatur. Ioseph	*30′ m*	*274*
			namque		
14	*33* 35	bene *E*	sed benedixisse	*32′ u*	*265*
			legatur		
17	*41* 2	*Fragment:* catholice? *M*	et inutiles synodos male	*41′ m*	*268*
19	*45* 12/13	rationabiliter *EH*	caelorum	*46′ u*	*275*
			conceditur. in illo		
20	*47* 7	optime *T*	sanctos etiam	*49 m*	*254 (275)*
			homines		
21	*49* 13	bene *E*	si vero tipice	*51′ u*	*275*
24a	*52* 24	acute *T*	omnes divites plebis	*56 o*	*270, 265*
24b	*53* 33	bene? *H*	a quorum	*57′ o*	*275*
			ornamentorum		
25	*54* 19	eleganter *T*	ad matutinum	*58 m*	*275*
			laetitia		

Erasures *in margine*, which represent traces of marginalia, are listed by von den Steinen, *Neues Archiv* 49 (1932), 213 n. 2, for:

LC I.15—p. 35.6	I.23—p. 51.8
I.16—p. 37.36–38	I.29—p. 59.23
I.17—p. 42.5	II.21—p. 80.30–31
I.18—p. 43.40	II.29—p. 91.33
I.22—p. 50.32–33	II.30—p. 95.38

II

Ann Freeman, *Speculum* 46 (1971), 609: "The Marginal Notes of Vaticanus Lat. 7207":

bene	32^v	33, 35–36	I 14	sed benedixisse legatur superius
_____?_____	37^v	37, 36–38	I 16	tamen utcumque testimonia proferre temp/tant Quia ergo beseleel ad faciendum opus
catholice**	41^v	41, 2	I 17	et inutiles synodos male et ipsi adorant et ali(os)
_____?_____	44^v	43, 15–16	I 18	oportet filium hominis Quem videlicet dum/sedula mente internis oculis aspicimus ma(lignorum)
_____?_____	45	43, 40–41	I 18	amorem imaginibus luminaria accendunt/easque adorant hoc modo beatus hieronimus
rationabiliter*	46^v	45, 12–13	I 19†	isto vita aeterna regnumque caelorum conceditur/In illo promittitur terra quae lacte et melle
optime*	49	47, 6–7	I 20†	(oracu)li parietes extendunt cum sanctos etiam homines
bene	51^v	49, 11–13	I 21	positi isticque sumus diu permansuri/Si vero tipice quid isti lapides praefigura(verint)
_____?_____	53^v	50, 32–33	I 22	quae imaginibus aniliter fit adorationi quae/sanctissimo regi per prophetam fiebat aequipera(re)
_____?_____	54	50, 40	I 22	Non igitur aequalis est adoratio quae illi a
acute*	56	52, 24	I 24†	tuum deprecabuntur omnes divites
bene	57^v	53, 32–33	I 24†	(indubitan)ter ostenditur a quibus sensibus et a quorum/ornamentorum insignibus quam expertes
eleganter*	58	54, 19	I 25	matutinum laetitia Vesperum scilicet

Freeman inserts in II the marginalia listed by von den Steinen, *Neues Archiv* 49 (1932), 213 n. 2, for *LC* I.16, 18, 22, 29; II.21, 30. She overlooked the marginalia and their traces listed by von den Steinen for *LC* I.15, 17, 23, and II.29.

The capital letters listed after the individual Tironian note in *Tabelle* I refer to the scholars who first deciphered the note: E—Carl Erdmann; H—Rudolf von Heckel; M—Arthur Mentz; T—Michael Tangl. One asterisk in II indicates traces of a marginal note in *V* visible in the margin of the opposite folium; two asterisks indicate that the traces are visible to the naked eye; daggers are added to the chapter heading in the *LC* if the heading does not occur in the *Hadrianum* (*JE* 2483) of about 791. This reason for the addition of daggers is superfluous, since no connection whatsoever exists between the marginalia and the chapter headings, considering the merely book-technical significance of the notes, that is the actual reason why these marginalia were rewritten and presented in the form of Tironian notes.

Freeman does not record in her tabulation the fact that the marginal notes she has listed in II for *LC* I.16, I.18, and I.22 are listed by von den Steinen in *Neues Archiv* 49 (1932), 213 n. 2, and not in his tabulation. Freeman also overlooked marginal erasures which indicate lost marginalia in *LC* I.15 (p. 35.6, Bastgen), I.17 (p. 42.5), I.23 (p. 51.8), II.29 (p. 91.33), all of them listed by von den Steinen, p. 213 note 2. On the other hand, the marginal notes listed by her for *LC* I.29, II.21, and II.30 are already recorded by von den Steinen.

Fichtenau quite properly surmised in 1953 (*MIOEG* 61, p. 285) that new discoveries of notes with the aid of ultraviolet light are hardly probable. "To be sure," he said, "one is not going to indulge in great expectations." The present writer arrived at the same conclusion after his studies of *V* during 1960 at the Vatican Library and after the investigation of a photograph of the *Vaticanus Latinus 7207* a few years later.

The thesis put forth by Bernhard Bischoff concerning the origin and purpose of the Tironian notes, as reported by Freeman, remains unconvincing to me, inasmuch as it contradicts the characteristic usage made of Tironian notes during the Carolingian age and is based on sundry assumptions none of which has been verified or can be verified in any way. We are told in *Speculum* 46 (1971), 598, that the original marginal notes in *V* were made in hasty script that disfigured the MS, and for that reason they were replaced by tiny Tironian notes. This beautification was "probably" undertaken when the MS was prepared "for deposit in the palace archives." Bischoff assumed that such an undertaking presupposes that the marginalia were the comments of an important person, "most probably the king himself," and he added that "if anyone should object that the Tironian system was known in that age to very few, so that the notes preserved would be limited in their usefulness, one could reply that the royal chancery would always include scribes trained in Tironian notation, and hence able to interpret, for official use, the official comments inscribed in the *LC*'s margins."

Bischoff's reference to the "usefulness" of the Tironian notes reminded me of a sententious remark customarily made a few decades ago by Johannes Haller, a medievalist at the University of Tübingen. When speaking of falsified or forged charters he used to say, "Man fälscht nicht auf Vorrat," one does not forge documents for the sake of building up a stockpile. He wanted to stress the fact that very definite, practical reasons are always connected with the production of forged documents. A similar realistic approach must be applied, to be sure *mutatis mutandis*, to the transcription in Tironian notes of marginalia in *V*, written, like the MS itself, in the Caroline minuscule. The basic usefulness of the Tironian notes in *V* is of decisive importance for the understanding of their purpose in relation to the codex itself. The transcription of marginal notes in the *Vaticanus* in the form of Tironian notes must fulfill a very practical purpose connected with the book technical nature of the manuscript which obviously is the archetype of the *Libri Carolini*. The scribe of the Tironian notes in *V* must have been aware and certain of at least two facts: a) that the numerous marginal notes in the MS do not constitute corrections of the *LC*'s context, and b) that they therefore do not belong in the context of the *LC*. He may have arrived at these conclusions because the marginal notes contain no reference signs to specific passages within the context of the *LC*, or because the scribe of the Tironian notes knew how to distinguish between a marginal note in *V* that referred to the context and contents of the *LC* and notes that constituted only comments on certain passages and sections of the *LC*. Some verification of these deliberations may be found in the following marginal note in *V*.

LC III.26 (p. 161.11g, Bastgen), in MS *V*, fol. 182r, contains the following remark *in margine*: "Hic interponendum de quinque generibus visionum iuxta Theodosium Macrobium," a reference to Macrobius, *Commentarii in somnium Scipionis* I.3, ed. I. Willis (*BSGRT*, 1963). I have shown in Chapter IV at note 16 that this remark originated with the author of the *LC*, since the text of a passage in the excerpt from the Pseudo-Augustinian *Dialogus quaestionum LXV*, cited in *LC* III.26, had been changed after Macrobius I.5.9. The marginal note cited above is neither erased in *V* nor is it transcribed in Tironian notes, although it was undoubtedly before the eyes of the scribe or notary who produced the Tironian notes in *V*. The note itself belongs to the editorial directives of the *LC*'s author, but was not followed up by a corrector. It belongs to the type of editorial corrections made by the *LC*'s author as listed in Chapter IX, K. The scribe of the *LC* MS A, the Paris codex of the Bibliothèque de l'Arsenal lat. 663, fol. 171v, lines 7–6 from below, inserts the marginal note in *V*, f. 182r, *Hic interponendum . . . Macrobium* (see above) into the context of *LC* III.26 (p. 161.11), and thus mistakenly assumes that the note belongs in the context of the *LC*. Since none of the words of any other marginal note in *V* seem to have been inserted elsewhere in the *LC* text of A, I am inclined to conclude that A was copied from *V* (when it was still unimpaired) after all the marginal notes in *V* had been transcribed into Tironian notes. This then would mean that the practical purpose of the transcription of the marginal notes into Tironian notes must be seen in the preparation of *V* for scribal copying when copies of the *LC* text were needed.

Historically attested situations that required the production of new MSS of the *LC* text occurred in connection with the Paris Synod of 825 and a few decades afterward when A was copied for Hincmar of Reims. The inconspicuous-looking small Tironian notes in *V* may indeed represent an endeavor to avoid the possibility that marginal notes written in Caroline minuscule might be looked upon by scribes as corrections of the *LC* text and mistakenly inserted into its context by a scribe while copying *V*. This seems to me the most realistic book-technical purpose for the production and appearance of the Tironian notes in the *Vaticanus* of the *LC*. Carl Erdmann, as reported by von den Steinen, *Neues Archiv* 49 (1932), 213, took into consideration such an explanation of the Tironian notes. In the light of the practical usage of Tironian notes in Charlemagne's chancery and the most likely purpose of such notes in *V*, which was certainly connected with the scribal production of new MSS of the *LC* text, Bischoff's conclusion (cited above) that the replacement of the original marginal notes in *V* through Tironian notes would hardly have occurred "unless the notes recorded were the comments of an important person, most probably the king himself," cannot command much credibility. There is not the slightest proof available for the assumption of any royal origin of the marginal notes. Why should one surmise that Charlemagne himself pronounced judgments on passages of a work whose *Incipit* presents it to the reader anyway as the *opus . . . viri Caroli*? The king's name is properly spelled with a capital C, in accordance with the custom followed in Charlemagne's charters issued by the chancery before 800. The *C* of *Carolus* in the *intitulatio* of extant diplomata was spelled as *K* only in documents of the imperial period after 800.[9] The actual author of the *Libri Carolini* was probably known to some of Charlemagne's contemporaries. Other contemporaries, overawed by the success of the Frankish king, may well have accepted Charlemagne's authorship of the *LC*. In either case, the ascription of simple and often laconic marginal notes in *V* to the king does not make much sense. The same may be said of Freeman's attempt to establish a connection between the marginalia in *V* and Charlemagne's trusted friend and adviser Alcuin. In a postscript attached to *Speculum* 46 (1971), 607, she says she has made a discovery in Alcuin's *Epistle* 172, addressed to Charlemagne, that has been overlooked by everyone who has ever used this letter. She can hardly be unaware that Bastgen and others, namely, Michael Tangl, *Neues Archiv* 36 (1911), 754 n. 1, and von den Steinen, *Neues Archiv* 49 (1932), 217, have used the same letter when describing Alcuin's habit of submitting his antiadoptionist treatises to the Frankish king for his alleged approval and correction. But Alcuin's procedure is no more than the rhetorical expression of the *captatio benevolentiae* in his relationship with the Frankish king as one of his friends and councillors. As far as Alcuin is concerned, this habit of his was largely an element of rhetorical modesty expressed in written form. The present writer has described and analyzed in Chapter III of his book *Alcuin and Charlemagne* (amended 2d edition; London, New York, 1968) the most important rhetorical topoi used by Alcuin in his correspondence with regard to Charlemagne, such as "The absolute wisdom of the ruler," and the authority lent to

[9] Mühlbacher, *MGH, Diplomata Karolinorum* I (Hannover, 1906), 77.

an author's work written upon the actual or alleged request of a person of higher station and substance. In this connection Alcuin's *Epistola* 172 (p. 284.23, Dümmler) is cited: Alcuin assures the king that the writer's work could hardly have found a more competent judge than Charlemagne: "Nam auctoritas praecipientis oboedientis industriam defendere debet." Alcuin knew that his anti-adoptionist treatises submitted to the Frankish king for approval and correction were read by some of Charlemagne's theological advisers in the king's entourage, if necessary, and not by Charlemagne himself. He certainly was aware of the fact that theological and educational opinions expressed in Charlemagne's letters were those expressed by theological councillors at the Frankish court. Heinrich Fichtenau showed this fact, for example, for Alcuin's *Epistles* 143 and 145, addressed to Charlemagne, and for Charlemagne's reply, addressed to Alcuin, *Epistle* 144. "When Alcuin . . . wanted to flatter Charles, he questioned him about a complicated problem of the Christian Calendar. Charles's authoritative reply [*Ep.* 144] to this letter [*Ep.* 143] did not prevent Alcuin, whose vanity was hurt, from tactlessly exposing the king. He wrote back [*Ep.* 145] that the clergy of the royal palace were the real authors of the reply (i.e., Charlemagne's letter, *Ep.* 144, addressed to Alcuin) and that the opinion they had given had betrayed their ignorance."[10]

Freeman disregards the rhetorical contents in Alcuin's *Epistle* 172, addressed to Charlemagne. She seems to assume that everyone who ever used this letter has overlooked a passage in it in which Alcuin confirms that "his little treatise against Felix of Urgel" (*Speculum* 46 [1971], 607) had been returned to him by Charlemagne. At the same time Alcuin complains—in the vein of the *captatio benevolentiae*— of not having received from the king annotations to passages in his antiadoptionist work that are presented *non docte* or *non catholice*.[11] Alcuin says: "Minus tamen quiddam fecistis, quam plenum postulasset caritatis officium, quod sensus *non docte* prolatos *vel catholice* exaratos similiter noluistis notare. . . . " Freeman mistranslates and

---

[10] Fichtenau, *The Carolingian Empire*, tr. by Peter Munz (Oxford, 1957), 29; in Fichtenau, *Das karolingische Imperium: Soziale und geistige Problematik eines Grossreiches* (Zürich, 1949), 38f.

[11] See Ernst Dümmler, *MGH, Epistolae* 4 (Karolini Aevi 2; Berlin, 1895), 284 n. 2 and 282 n. 3.

therefore misinterprets this passage and says: "If he looked in vain for *docte* and *catholice* as notes to his work against Felix, Alcuin must have had established precedents in mind." But Alcuin did not look for *docte* and *catholice* annotations in his work against Felix just because *docte* and *catholice* appear a few times among the Tironian notes of the *Vaticanus*. Wilhelm Heil[12] understands the passage correctly when he says, "Some *errata* [in Felix of Urgel's treatise] had been annotated for the purpose of correction, while other *errata* with '*sensus non docte* prolatos vel [*non*] *catholice* exaratos' had not been annotated for correction." Alcuin naturally knows well that these corrections are not the work of Charlemagne, but the work of theological advisers. He mentions them at the very end of *Epistle* 172 where they are called *palatini pueri* (p. 285.22, Dümmler), whom Alcuin sees under the guidance of Charlemagne's royal *auctoritas*: "ut elegantissime proferant quicquid vestri sensus lucidissima dictaverit eloquentia." The identification of Alcuin's *Libellus* (previously mentioned) with his "little treatise against Felix of Urgel," entitled *Contra haeresin Felicis*, is mistaken. In reality, Alcuin's "largest" antiadoptionist treatise, *Adversus Felicem libri septem* (*PL* 101.119–230), is referred to in *Epistle* 172. This fact was pointed out almost a century ago by Hermann Grössler, *Die Ausrottung des Adoptianismus im Reiche Karls des Grossen* (Programm des Königlichen Gymnasiums zu Eisleben, 1879), and again recently by Wilhelm Heil, who corrects Ernst Dümmler's mistaken reference to Alcuin's smallest antiadoptionist treatise instead of to his largest apologetic work.[13]

The present writer believes with Heinrich Fichtenau that the marginalia of the *Vaticanus* are not connected in any way with Charlemagne. Their erasure and subsequent transcription in Tironian notes occurred when the codex was prepared for the production of another copy of the *Libri Carolini*. What we have learned by now about the nature of the marginalia permits us to state with reasonable certainty that they do not possess any primary textual significance for the recension of the text of the *LC*. They contain value judgments in the form of various expressions (a) concerning the categorization of subject matter, and (b) concerning expressions

---

[12] *Alkuinstudien I: Zur Chronologie und Bedeutung des Adoptianismusstreites* (Düsseldorf, 1970), 31.

[13] Heil, *op. cit.*, pp. 28ff., 69.

of stronger or weaker approval and appreciation, as becomes evident
from the study of all the individual marginalia as well as of von den
Steinen's summary list in *Neues Archiv* 49 (1932), 209–213, supplemented on the basis of new readings offered by Arthur Mentz,
previously mentioned.

The first type of marginalia refers to specific disciplines of learning
in the curriculum of the *artes liberales*. Marginalia such as "scho-
lastice, syllogistice, rationabiliter, prudenter, sapienter" are indicative of "ars dialectica." Theological approval is certainly expressed
in "ecclesiastice" and in "catholice," the latter of which occurs in
four marginalia. I assume that those marginalia in *V* which appear
opposite passages within individual *LC* chapters fit the thesis concerning their actual origin which I shall propose toward the end of
the present chapter. We recall that some marginalia stand at the
first lines of *LC* chapters. The note for *placite*, f. 94v, for instance,
stands *in margine* on the same level with the first line of *LC* II.27.
Freeman accordingly argues (p. 601) that this note—and presumably other similarly located notes in *V*—represent "a considered
judgment on the chapter as a whole." But this is hardly a valid
conclusion, because one does not expect to find such "a considered
judgment" on a whole *LC* chapter opposite to the *opening* line (or
lines) of *LC* chapters, but more realistically and convincingly at the
very end of chapters.[14] Her assertion (p. 602 n. 15) that the scribe's
notes in *V* "sometimes . . . refer to whole chapters" is without any
basis in fact. We must now ask, as we did earlier with regard to the
Tironian notes, what the purpose was for the writing of those marginalia. We must understand their presence in the *Vaticanus* in the
light of their purpose and significance. Do we know of similar
marginalia or of paleographical procedures consisting of single notes
or marks that connote judgments concerning passages in the context of a literary writing? Several instances immediately come to
mind, of which we may mention a few.

There are the collections of *notae* edited by August Reifferscheid[15]
and the *notae* listed by Isidore of Seville, *Etymologiae* I.21–25.

---

[14] Heinrich Fichtenau (Vienna) in a recent letter to me kindly called my attention to this fact.
[15] In *C. Suetoni Tranquilli . . . Reliquiae* (Leipzig, 1860), 137–141. Robert Devreesse, *Introduction à l'étude des manuscrits grecs* (Paris, 1954), 81–82; Rudolf Pfeiffer,
History of Classical Scholarship (Oxford, 1968), on marginal sigla and marks, pp. 178,
174ff., 218–220.

The Prefaces to Bede's commentaries on Luke and Mark report that Bede listed his sources by signs in the margins of his manuscripts. E. J. Sutcliffe and M. L. W. Laistner describe extant codices of Bede's works in which such marginalia are preserved.[16]

Cassiodorus in the *Institutiones* I.26–27, *De notis affigendis*, and *De schematibus ac disciplinis*, ed. R. A. B. Mynors (Oxford, 1937), 67–68, speaks of red-colored *notae* to be added to the codex *in margine* as *indices* for the reader's convenience. Cassiodorus' *Expositio Psalmorum*, edited by A. Adriaen,[17] offers an application of Cassiodorus' own editorial technique. It contains at the very beginning the following set of *notae* and symbols which are placed in the margins of the Vivarium recension of his *Commentary*:

Diuersas notas more maiorum certis locis aestimauimus affigendas. Has cum explanationibus suis subter adiunximus, ut quidquid lector uoluerit inquirere per similitudines earum sine aliqua difficultate debeat inuenire.

	—hoc in idiomatis, id est propriis locutionibus legis diuinae.
	—hoc in dogmatibus ualde necessariis.
	—hoc in definitionibus.
$\overline{\text{SCHE}}$	hoc in schematibus.
$\overline{\text{ET}}$	hoc in ethymologiis.
	—hoc in interpretatione nominum.
$\overline{\text{RT}}$	hoc in arte rhetorica.
$\overline{\text{TOP}}$	hoc in topicis.
$\overline{\text{SYL}}$	hoc in syllogismis.
$\overline{\text{AR}}$	hoc in arithmetica.
$\overline{\text{GEO}}$	hoc in geometrica.
	—hoc in musica.
	—hoc in astronomia.

The symbols for 1–3, 6, 12, and 13, have been omitted for technical reasons, but Cassiodorus' descriptions of their respective meanings have been retained.

Cassiodorus' marginalia, which obviously depend also on older symbols used by pagan commentators on pagan texts, are not text-critical remarks, but refer the reader to rhetorical figures, to disciplines of the seven *artes liberales*, and to their specific subjects.

---

[16] Sutcliffe, *Biblica* 7 (1926), 428–439; Laistner, "Source-Marks in Bede Manuscripts," *The Journal of Theological Studies* 34 (1933), 350–355; see also the brilliant paper by Fred C. Robinson, "Syntactical Glosses in Latin Manuscripts of Anglo-Saxon Provenance," *Speculum* 48 (1973), 443–475.

[17] *CCL* 97 and 98 (1958); see the *Notae* in vol. 97, p. 2. Laistner, *Thought and Letters in Western Europe* (London, Ithaca, 1957), 102, points out that the commentary was widely known by the eighth century.

Cassiodorus' procedure concerning the "notas . . . certis locis . . . affigendas" is presented by him as a *mos maiorum* whose traces also appear, as we recall, in his *Institutiones* I c. 26, *De notis affigendis*. The Roman jurist obviously continued with this formulation the style and the tradition of an established legal custom. His proposed *notae affigendae* seem to mirror an administrative procedure employed in official reports on postclassical Roman trial proceedings. The identical terminology appears, for instance, in the edition by the Roman notary Marcellus *memoralis* of the *Gesta collationis Carthaginiensis* from the year 411 (*PL* 11).[18] The trial in question dealt with quarrels between Donatists and Catholics and was held in the Thermae Gargilianae of Carthage with the Roman imperial official Marcellinus presiding as judge. A Marcellus, who was one of this judge's legal aids, wrote in the introductory epistle to the edition of the *Gesta* (*PL* 11.1231B): "Quidquid . . . sedula breviatione succinxi consequenter *affigens* etiam per ordinem *notas* calculantibus familiares, ut inquirentis intentio *indicem* secuta brevitatem, ad id quod deprehendere velit in paginis actionis, non absque commoditate compendii, numeris ducibus directa perveniat."

I now assume that the many marginalia in Cassiodorus' *Expositio Psalmorum*, a commentary that is often cited anonymously in the *LC*, had some bearing on the origin of the marginalia in the *Vaticanus Latinus 7207*, the archetype of the *Libri Carolini*. Although Bastgen verified many borrowings from Cassiodorus' commentary to be found in the *LC*, some have remained unknown to him. Thus Cassiodorus' *Praefatio* 17 (*CCL* 97; 1958), 23.9–15, *passim*, is anonymously cited and paraphrased at the very beginning of the *LC*'s *Praefatio*, p. 1, lines 16–18, and other passages are drawn from the commentary throughout the *LC* up to Book IV.4, a fact which— together with other similar instances—speaks for our belief that the *LC* was written by a single author. This author of the *LC* was intimately familiar with Cassiodorus' exegetical work, as is especially obvious from the extensive borrowings listed by Bastgen for *LC* II.30, the longest chapter of the work (pp. 94–100). The many testimonia found in the *LC* may be added to the extant five MSS of the commentary from the eighth century, of which Durham,

---

[18] Cf. now Serge Lancel, *Actes de la Conférence de Carthage en 411* II (Paris, 1972), 418.24; a recension of the *Gesta* by Augustine is his *Breviculus Collationis cum Donatistis*, *CSEL* 53 (1910), 39–92. *Gesta* and *Breviculus* are reedited by S. Lancel, *CCL* 149A (1974).

Cathedral B.II.33, is the oldest complete MS. These MSS and fourteen others (saec. viii–ix and s.ix) represent the Carolingian transmission of Cassiodorus' large work. The unknown Carolingian scribe who wrote the original marginalia that accompany the text of the *LC* in the *Vaticanus* was in all probability familiar with Cassiodorus' *notae* and the symbols that accompany his *Expositio Psalmorum*. The latter work was widely used during the Carolingian age. The large number of Carolingian MSS of the commentary and its numerous listings in medieval library catalogues vouch for its popularity.[19] It is on these historical grounds that some unknown scribe may have been encouraged to add his own personal remarks in the form of quite simple marginalia to certain passages of the *LC* in the *Vaticanus*. There is, for instance, Cassiodorus' note *SYL*, meaning *hoc in syllogismis*, and our scribe's *syllogistice*, which he wrote, as Arthur Mentz stated, "silbentachygraphisch . . . mit einem Strich darüber" (see note 2, above). The meaning of the "chresimon, hoc in dogmatibus valde necessariis" may have inspired our scribe to list *catholice* four times, and once *ecclesiastice*. Such a not unlikely formal connection of the original marginalia in the *Vaticanus Latinus 7207* of the *Libri Carolini* with Cassiodorus' marginalia may be the answer to the question concerning the origin of the marginalia in the archetype of the *LC*. They may well represent—*mutatis mutandis*—such an adaptation by some unknown scribe, who was experienced in *ars rhetorica* and in *ars dialectica*, and therefore through his *syllogistice*, for instance, properly understood the Augustinian text and the application of the *Categoriae decem* in *LC* I.8 (Chapter IX, F). His particular *nota* may have been inspired also by his possible knowledge of Marius Victorinus, *Explanationes* 2.48 (ed. C. Halm, [Leipzig, 1863], p. 279,24) who remarks "id est *syllogistice* tractare" when commenting on Cicero, *De inventione* 49.142 (ed. Eduard Stroebel, *BSGRT* [Leipzig, 1915], 140 b): ". . . aut ex scripto non scriptum aliquid inducere per ratiocinationem."

---

[19] See M. Adriaen's Introduction, *CCL* 97, pp. v–vii; cf. Ursula Hahner, *Cassidors Psalmenkommentar: Sprachliche Untersuchungen* (München, 1973), 9–11, on the manuscript transmission. On Adriaen's edition see V. Bulhart in *Revue Bénédictine* 70 (1960), 639–641, and J. W. Halporn in the *Festschrift for Marcel Richard* (to appear). See the important investigations by Reinhard Schlieben, *Christliche Theologie und Philologie in der Spätantike: Die schulwissenschaftlichen Methoden der Psalmenexegese Cassiodors* (Berlin, New York, 1974).

CHAPTER XIV

Alcuin as the Author of the *Libri Carolini*: Epilogue to Part III

A few "Spanish Symptoms" in the *Libri Carolini* do not establish the Visigoth Theodulph of Orléans as the author of the work which represents the official Frankish state paper against the Byzantine worship of images decreed by II Nicaea in 787. The notion that *LC* I.20 provides an explanation of that strange mosaic in the apsis of Theodulph's oratorium at Germigny-des-Prés, which was built quite a number of years *after* the composition of the *Libri Carolini*, seems to be based on a lack of acquaintance with the work's conception of images. Theodulph hardly can have derived any encouragement from the *LC* for the production of the ark of the covenant in his mosaic, because *LC* I.15 and II.26 label the man-made image of the divinely created ark as manifestations of "great absurdity and great insanity" (see above, Chapter XII, E). In addition, the avowed Frankish preference for the Roman *ordo psallendi* expressed in *LC* I.6 (p. 21, Bastgen) obviates the view that any Visigothic author, who presumably was well experienced in the Mozarabic liturgical rite, wrote an official royal Frankish document extolling the Roman rite. Such a view is strongly contradicted by the intentional Romanization of the Frankish liturgy during the eighth century adhered to by the Frankish king Pippin and his son Charlemagne.[1] The latter's *Admonitio generalis*, c. 80, of about 789,

---

[1] Cf. Cyrille Vogel, *Introduction aux sources de l'histoire du culte chrétien au moyen âge* (Spoleto, 1966), 119, for the texts cited subsequently.

recommends the use of the *cantus Romanus*, while the *Epistola generalis* of 786–800 recalls, like *LC* I.6, Pippin's predilection for the *traditio Romana* in liturgical matters.

At present I cherish the hope that a historian of medieval art will investigate the Merovingian characteristics of the initials in the Vatican codex of the *Libri Carolini* (cf. Part III n. 19). I furthermore hope that a historian of the Latin liturgy is going to deal with the liturgical elements to be found in the work beyond those of the *formulae* from the Canon of the Roman Mass listed in Bastgen's edition. Nobody seems to have noticed that *LC* II.27 offers in an excerpt from the *Canon missae* a reading that is characteristic of the Ambrosian rite.[2] The occurrence of *gloriosissimae* in "et in caelos gloriosissime ascensionis" (p. 87.21), as against the version in the Roman rite X.79 (B. Botte, p. 40) "et in caelos gloriosae ascensionis," must be stressed. Also *LC* III.14 (p. 132.18–20) may well contain in its formulation, which renders the *Praefatio* of the Roman rite, another trace of the Ambrosian rite. The *LC* reads " . . . *quem cherubim et seraphim*, sublimes virtutes, . . . " like the Ambrosian rite " . . . *quem cherubim et seraphim* socia exultatione concelebrant,"[3] while the Roman rite reads "virtutes ac beata seraphim exultatione concelebrant." Keeping in mind the dictum of Horace (*Epist.* I.2.16), "Iliacos intra muros peccatur et extra," I close with the warning that notwithstanding the newly discovered traces of the Ambrosian rite in the *Libri Carolini*, I really do not believe that the author of the work was an Italian and that he hailed from Milan. Nor do I believe that Angilbert, Charlemagne's son-in-law, wrote the *LC* "vers l'an 790," as A. Jundt has stated.[4] Emile Amann assumed that the Anglo-Saxon Alcuin was the principal author of the work.[5] But the literary and historical evidence discussed in the

[2] Cf. Bernard Botte, *Le Canon de la Messe Romaine* (Textes et études liturgiques 2; Louvain, 1935), 40; and Hans Lietzmann, *Messe und Herrenmahl* (reprint: Berlin, 1955), 59 n. 3. See also André Wilmart, "Une exposition de la Messe Ambrosienne," *Jahrbuch für Liturgiewissenschaft* 2 (1922), 57, on "in caelos gloriosissimae ascensionis." I have not seen P. Borella, "Il 'Canon Missae' Ambrosiano," *Ambrosius* 30 (1954), cited by Alban Dold and Leo Eizenhöfer, *Das Irische Palimpsest Sakramentar in CLM 14429* (Texte und Arbeiten 53–54; Beuron, 1964), 17.

[3] See the text ed. Paul Lejay, *DACL* I (Paris, 1907), 1407.

[4] A. Jundt, s.v. *Carolins: Les livres Carolins*, in *La Grande Encyclopédie* IX (Paris, 1889–90), 497.

[5] *L'époque carolingienne* (Paris, 1947), 125.

present volume indeed allows but one single author. I believe that Alcuin's authorship of the *Libri Carolini* cannot be questioned.

The attribution of the *LC* to Alcuin has been advocated previously by Hubert Bastgen in his *LC* studies and in his *MGH* edition, also by Philipp Jaffé and Ernst Dümmler, the editors of Alcuin's letters and poems; others have expressed doubts. But the internal evidence to be found in the text of the *LC* supports Alcuin's authorship, since it is firmly grounded on identical subject matter occurring in the *LC* and in Alcuin's writings or else on documents composed by Alcuin for Charlemagne and for the Frankish episcopate.

Alcuin's *Dialectica* and his recension of the Pseudo-Augustinian *Categoriae decem*, of which the latter was dedicated to his royal friend, are anonymously quoted in the *LC* (see Chapter IV, E and E 1). The *Categoriae* is cited in the *LC* I.1, I.8, and IV.23. The *Dialectica*, c. XI, is the source underlying a passage in the *LC* II.31. The same chapter of the logical textbook has left some traces in the passage quoted in the *LC* I.1, just mentioned. The very extensive use made in the *LC* of syllogisms, categorical, hypothetical, and rhetorical (see Chapter IV, E and E 1), represents, I believe, the most numerous occurrence of syllogisms to be found in a literary work written between the age of Boethius and the time of Abelard (1079–1142). It is understandable on the basis of Alcuin's well-attested teaching of the disciplines of the trivium: the teacher of rhetoric and dialectics applied to the writing of the *LC* the logical skill he had acquired as a *magister*. Also the occurrence of certain patristic writers anonymously cited in the *LC* and in Alcuin's works support the attribution to Alcuin. Thus the exegetical writings of Ambrosiaster, which are anonymously quoted by Alcuin, are cited in the same fashion in the *LC*, from *LC* I.1 to *LC* IV.27, as I have shown in Chapter VI. The same may be said for the *LC* and Alcuin as to the newly discovered Origen texts which are anonymously quoted in *LC* I.17 and I.29 (Chapters VIII, A; IX, C–C2).[6] More than a unique coincidence is the fact that Alcuin in his little treatise "Dicta" on Genesis 1.26 and the *LC* I.7 quote sections from

---

[6] I have pointed out some of Alcuin's anonymous quotations from Origen's homilies in my review of J. D. A. Ogilvy, *Books Known to the English, 597–1066* (Cambridge, Mass., 1967), in *Journal of English and Germanic Philology* 68 (1969), 160.

the same Pseudo-Ambrosian (or Pseudo-Augustinian) writing *De
dignitate conditionis humanae*.[7] Also the newly discovered text from
Hilarius of Poitiers in the *Praefatio* of the *LC* II (Chapter IV, E1)
corresponds to Alcuin's thoroughgoing familiarity with Hilarius'
De trinitate, which is one of the patristic writings most often cited
in Alcuin's apologetic treatises and letters.

The description of the relationship between the ten Aristotelian
praedicamenta and the divine attributes as presented in the *LC* III.27
(Chapter IV, at the end of section F) was repeated by Alcuin as
the true author of the *LC* in Alcuin's dogmatic work *De fide sanctae
et individuae trinitatis*. The confrontation of the same categories with
the identical biblical quotations thus reappears in Alcuin's treatise,
which he dedicated to Charlemagne as emperor almost a decade
after the initial composition of the *LC* for the Frankish king.

Alcuin's authorship of the *LC* is in several aspects in close conformity with other well-documented official activities of the Anglo-
Saxon scholar in Charlemagne's service during the two last decades
of the eighth century. This work of Alcuin as the author and editor
of official Carolingian documents has been investigated in the
Chapters IX–XI of my book *Alcuin and Charlemagne*.

Alcuin's authorship of some of Charlemagne's letters sent to contemporaries and of various documents has been recognized. There
is, for instance, Charlemagne's famous letter of 796 to Pope Leo III,
that has been designated by Louis Halphen as a product of Alcuin's
pen. The epitaph of Hadrian I (772–795) at Rome, in which
Charlemagne is named as the author, was in reality composed by
Alcuin. The Anglo-Saxon's ideas on education are certainly utilized
in Charlemagne's mandate *De litteris colendis* addressed to Baugulf
of Fulda. Friedrich-Carl Scheibe has convincingly shown Alcuin's
coauthorship for three of Charlemagne's letters that are transmitted
within the Corpus of Alcuin's *Epistolae*; he furthermore successfully
proved Alcuin's coauthorship of Charlemagne's *Admonitio generalis*,
one of the larger educational capitularies.

---

[7] See above Chapter XII, B, where I show for the first time that Benedict of
Aniane in his *Munimenta fidei* and the *LC* I.7 cite the identical text passage from
De dignitate. This discovery proves that the latter tract is older than Benedict and
the *LC*; it further confirms the assumption just made by Franz Brunhölzl, *Geschichte
der lateinischen Literatur des Mittelalters* I (München, 1975), 288, concerning the earlier
origin of the interesting tractate.

The present writer could show a few years ago[8] that Alcuin is the author of two important political documents consisting of a Frankish *synodica* and of a parallel letter of Charlemagne sent to Spain from the Frankfurt Synod of 794. This letter's sober historical attitude toward the Constantine tradition, expressed in a document composed by Alcuin, is paralleled by a similar attitude in the *LC* II.13, as was observed by Eugen Ewig, "Das Bild Constantins des Grossen in den ersten Jahrhunderten des abendländischen Mittelalters," in *Das byzantinische Herrscherbild* (Darmstadt, 1975), ed. Herbert Hunger, pp. 176–177 (reprinted from *Historisches Jahrbuch der Görresgesellschaft* 75 [1956], 1–46).

Three apologetic treatises against the Spanish heresy of adoptionism propagated by Felix of Urgel and Elipand of Toledo were written by Alcuin before the year 800, certainly with Charlemagne's approval. His arguments in these documents are based not only on patristic writings, but also and especially on excerpts from the *acta* of ecumenical councils and of territorial synods of various countries.[9] At that time Alcuin had become the recognized authority among "the imperialist clerics" surrounding the Frankish king—to use Ganshof's formulation—[10] who sought his legal advice in matters concerning the papacy (as we well know from Alcuin's own letters), and surely also in their endeavors to see imperial dignity bestowed on Charlemagne. No other theologian of Charlemagne's age has displayed in his writings Alcuin's wide knowledge and acquaintance with the *acta* of ecumenical councils as well as with the *acta* of Frankish, Spanish, Italian, and Lateran synods, whose texts are profusely cited in Alcuin's antiadoptionist works and letters. One of the MSS that contain the *Acta* of Ephesus, 431, Paris, B.N. 1572, from Alcuin's abbey at Tours, that was actually used by him, was first recognized by Emile Amann, while Ludwig Ott proved the use made by Alcuin in detail in his antiadoptionist

---

[8] Wallach, *Alcuin and Charlemagne* (1959 and 1968), Part III, Chapter IX; B. Bischoff in *Medievalia et Humanistica* 14 (1962), 34, has stated his agreement; also Eugen Ewig in *Handbuch der Kirchengeschichte* III, 1, ed. Hubert Jedin (Freiburg, 1966), 96; Wilhelm Heil, *Alkuinstudien* I (Düsseldorf, 1970), 57 n. 323; and others.

[9] See below Chapter XVI, toward the end, where Alcuin's special competence in synodal *acta* has been outlined.

[10] F. L. Ganshof, *The Imperial Coronation of Charlemagne: Theories and Facts* (Glasgow, 1949), reprinted in Ganshof, *The Carolingians and the Frankish Monarchy: Studies in Carolingian History* (Ithaca, 1971), 46f.

writings, a fact ultimately supplemented and paleographically confirmed by Bernhard Bischoff.[11] Alcuin's special expertness in synodal *acta*[12] was certainly responsible for his influence on his contemporaries who managed the historical events preceding Charlemagne's recognition as emperor on Christmas Day of the year 800 (see below Chapter XVI). His familiarity with synodal *acta* as legal and historical documents must have been known as an integral part of his scholarly reputation; it may have manifested itself already about ten years earlier when he studied the Latin translation of the Greek *Acta* of II Nicaea, 787, a somewhat faulty version produced by an unknown Roman ecclesiastic at Rome. A copy of this *First Latin Nicaenum* sent by Hadrian I to Charlemagne provided Alcuin with those texts drawn from the *Acta* of II Nicaea which were afterward critically discussed by him in the *Libri Carolini* (see above Part II, Introduction, and Chapter III). Shortly afterward Alcuin composed two official Frankish documents that testify again to his special competence *in synodicis* and thus provide further important internal arguments for the attribution of the *LC*'s authorship to him.

The Frankish *Synodica* of the Frankfurt Synod, 794, was written by Alcuin during the time the synod was in session, together with a letter of Charlemagne, addressed to Elipand of Toledo (see above n. 8). The synodal assembly of Frankfurt, in which Alcuin participated as the representative of the Frankish king, rejected not only the heresy of adoptionism, but simultaneously also the worship of images decreed by II Nicaea, 787, certainly on the basis of the *Libri Carolini*. The preserved Capitulary condemns in c. 2 the identity of the adoration of images and of the trinity proclaimed in the First Latin translation of the Greek *Acta* of II Nicaea, whose formulation is also rejected in the *LC* III.17. The proximity of the synodal theory in those two Alcuinian documents to the synodal theory of the *LC* IV.28 has been recognized and analyzed by the present writer a few years ago.[13] Quite remarkably the same presuppositions on the correct method of theology are employed by

[11] See below in Chapter XVI, nn. 35–36, the references to Amann, Ott, and Bischoff.

[12] I have provided additional evidence for this fact in my review, cited above in n. 6.

[13] See Wallach, *Traditio* 11 (1953), 143–149; *Alcuin and Charlemagne*, 169–177.

Alcuin for the rejection of image-worship in the *LC* and for his refutation of adoptionism in the *Synodica* and the *Epistle* of 794. The topics that are identical in all three documents are listed in detail in *Traditio* IX (1953), 145, and in *Alcuin and Charlemagne*, 171. There exist, rather significantly, verbatim parallels in Charlemagne's Credo at the end of his *Epistle* to Spain and in the discussions on the belief in the trinity in the *filioque* chapter of the *LC* III.3. The references to the synodal theory in the two documents sound as if they presuppose the similar ones in the *LC*. The respective parallels in the *Synodica* of 794, in Charlemagne's *Epistle*, and in the *LC* IV.28 are so obvious in the three texts printed in *Alcuin and Charlemagne*, 171–172, that the fact itself points to a common originator, namely, Alcuin. He could have said with the *LC* IV.13 (p. 198.34): "sex tantummodo nos sanctis universalibus synodis et localibus conciliis . . . contenti simus," that renders the decision of canon I of the Greek *Acta* of II Nicaea, Mansi XIII.417E6–8.

The source-critical and paleographical investigations of the *Vaticanus Latinus 7207*, the archetype of the *Libri Carolini*, have established the work's uniformity of style and diction.[14] New discoveries of a variety of hitherto unknown sources used in the composition of the *LC* indicate quite clearly that the many corrections in the codex are not the result of discussions allegedly conducted between the author of the work and some of Charlemagne's court theologians, as has been occasionally assumed. On the contrary, the corrections in the *Vaticanus* are of a purely scribal origin (see Chapter IX). Some of them represent the editorial labors of the *LC* author himself when he was proofreading his four books. Thus, certain corrections resulted from the author's own collations of texts, cited by him anonymously, with the MS of the writing excerpted by him. Such collations, which may have been delegated to a scribe who worked under the author's direct supervision, can be shown conclusively, for instance, in the case of corrections of longer, anonymously cited passages from one of Origen's homilies in *LC* I.29 (see Chapter VIII, A and Chapter IX, C–C2) and also for the anonymous citations from the works of Ambrosiaster to be found from the first to the next to the last chapter of the *Libri Carolini*, a fact that speaks for only a single author of the work,

---

[14] Additional evidence for this fact will be presented elsewhere; see above Chapter IV, E 1.

namely, Alcuin (cf. Chapter VI). Other corrections of the *Vaticanus* originated with some unknown scribe who collated a younger manuscript transmission with an older text recension of a patristic author cited in the *LC*. An example of this type of correction occurs in *LC* I.7 (see Chapter IX, K e), where a text from Augustine, *De diversis questionibus 83*, c. 51, cited after Eugippius' older excerpt recension of Augustine's works, has been corrected on the basis of a certainly younger MS transmission of Augustine's treatise.

It was at all times rather obvious to me that a reasonable paleographical study of the *Vaticanus* could be undertaken only if such a study is simultaneously coordinated with a constant critical investigation of the text of the *LC* transmitted by the codex. The lack of such a coordination in studies dealing with Theodulph's alleged authorship of the *Libri Carolini* necessarily led to unacceptable conclusions that had to be disproved in detail and as a whole. In this connection it became paramount to reassess objectively the work properly done by Hubert Bastgen in his *LC* studies and in his *MGH* edition (see, e.g., Chapter VIII), and by Wolfram von den Steinen in his famous investigations (see, e.g., Chapter XIII).

PART FOUR

Charlemagne and Pope Leo III: On Forgery and Historical Truth

An "oath" was sworn by Pope Leo III at St. Peter's on December 23 of the year 800 before a synodal assembly at which Charlemagne presided; it occupies a central place among the events that culminated, only two days later, in the recognition of the Frankish king as *imperator*. The document customarily known as the text of this "oath" was edited in 1899 by Karl Hampe,[1] and in 1906 by Albert Werminghoff,[2] who followed his predecessor *ad verbum usque*, as he says. The apparatus of both editions establishes the insertion of a slightly re-edited oath in the *Decretum* of Burchard of Worms. Ivo of Chartres and, in an apologetic treatise, Gerhoh of Reichersberg, follow Burchard without major changes. The variants listed by Hampe and Werminghoff indicate that they both distinguished between the basic text of the oath in the oldest, ninth-century MS, Würzburg M. p. theol. fol. 46 (and its descendants, the Monacenses 6241 and 27246, saec. x–xi), and the oath's transmission by Burchard and the above-named authors who depend on Burchard. And Hampe[3] assigns the twelfth-century Vaticanus 1348 to the Burchard tradition, when he says that its readings largely correspond with Burchard's ("paene omnibus conveniunt Burchardi Wormat.

---

[1] *MGH, Epistolae* 5 (Karolini Aevi 3; Berlin, 1899), no. 6 pp. 63f.
[2] *MGH, Conc.* 2.1 (Aevi Karolini 1.1; Hannover, Leipzig, 1906), No. 26 pp. 226f.
[3] *MGH, Epistolae* 5.63.15–19.

decret. . . . "). Both scholars are fully conversant with the textual history of the document; they reprint in the notes the abbreviated version of the oath in Gratian's *Decretum*, and the text in a Roman *ordo* which represents a version rewritten in accordance with certain concepts of Roman law.[4] The Burchard tradition has been discussed in a recent study.[5] Some of the changes made by Burchard in the original text of the oath are readily understandable. The variant *in . . . conspectu*, instead of *in . . . basilica*, probably resulted from a scribal dittography because the same expression occurs in the oath of purgation in the lines preceding and following the correct reading. The variant *adversum*, instead of *adversus*, is an emendation of the original text. Burchard evidently recognized the resemblance between the original reading, "*qualiter homines mali adversus me insurrexerunt*" and Ps. 53.5 "*quoniam alieni insurrexerunt adversum me.*"[6]

The document that passes for Leo's oath of purgation has acquired special significance through its adoption by various sources of canon law. But an investigation of the "oath" within its particular historical setting convinces me that the text of this oath does not render the original words of the pope. It now turns out that the document known for centuries as the oath of purgation of Pope Leo III is not a source of canon law, but, as I believe, one of its products. If we emancipate ourselves from the various theories of the imperial

---

[4] See *infamasse* (p. 227.24); "Cuius rei *cognoscendae* gratia," (p. 227.25) for the Carolingian formula "propter quam *causam audiendam.*" The concluding statement (p. 227.32)," sed ut certius iniquis vos suspicionibus liberem," parallels the concluding statement of the Burchard tradition (p. 227.15) of the forged oath: "sed ut melius a vobis abscidatis rebelles cogitationes." The occurrence of *infamia* and the concluding statement in the Roman *ordo* link this version with the source of the forged oath of purgation, quoted below, Chapter XV, after n. 20, in section II: "sed me a praefata infamia et suspitione liberando." On the significance of Roman law in these documents see below Chapter XV n. 13, and Chapter XVI notes 24, 25, 40.

[5] Howard Adelson and Robert Baker, "The Oath of Purgation of Pope Leo III in 800," *Traditio* 8 (1952), 35–80, especially 39–46. The readings of Ivo's *Panormia* in the Basel edition of 1499 are added there to show the influence of the Burchard tradition but do not supply new information as compared with Werminghoff's apparatus. Read p. 42 variant 30, and p. 43 Table 2 variant 30: *ecclesi* (not *ecclesie*) M 1, and Werminghoff, p. 227.8 *ecclesia*. There is no difference between Werminghoff's text and the one given by Adelson and Baker.

[6] *MGH, Conc.* 2.1.226.26 and 227.4. The interpretation of Burchard's variants by Adelson and Baker, *op. cit.*, 79, reads too much into Burchard's text.

coronation of Charlemagne,[7] we shall arrive at this conclusion.[8] I can only agree with Fichtenau's observation that in the sphere of Carolingian history it is indeed dangerous to assume that one can rely on critical studies of fifty or even twenty years ago without re-examining or supplementing their results.[9]

[7] See F. L. Ganshof, *The Imperial Coronation of Charlemagne: Theories and Facts* (Glasgow University Publications 79; 1949).

[8] Cf. also Karl Heldmann, *Das Kaisertum Karls des Grossen: Theorien und Wirklichkeit* (Quellen und Studien zur Verfassungsgeschichte des deutschen Reiches in Mittelalter und Neuzeit 6.2; Weimar, 1928); Alfons Reck, *Das "Staatskirchentum" Karls des Grossen in der deutschsprachigen Forschung seit 1870* (Dissertation Freiburg-Switzerland, 1948).

[9] Heinrich Fichtenau, "Karl der Grosse und das Kaisertum," *MIOEG* 61 (1953), 258.

CHAPTER XV

The Genuine and the Forged
Oath of Pope Leo III

On April 25, 799, high papal officials,[1] relatives of the late Pope Hadrian I, instigated a revolt against Leo III with the support of the Roman nobility. He was mistreated, although without suffering serious injury, and finally escaped from the rebels, who had imprisoned him in a monastery. Winichis, duke of Spoleto, and Wirundus, who were acting as the representatives of Charlemagne at Rome, liberated the pontiff and led him away in safety. From Spoleto, Leo and some followers traveled to the Frankish king, the *Patricius Romanorum*, then camping at Paderborn, where they arrived toward the end of August. Charlemagne and his counselors weighed the grievances of Leo and the accusations leveled against him, which his Roman opponents had in the meantime submitted to the Frankish king. Charlemagne decided to re-establish the pope in Rome, and, in October 799, had Leo escorted back to the Papal State. On November 29/30, Leo arrived at Rome under the protection of Frankish *missi*. A little later, during the first week of December, a judicial inquisition was conducted by the royal representatives; this lasted for more than a week. The charges of Leo's accusers were investigated, but the ringleaders Paschalis and Campalus were unable to justify their complaints. Thereupon the *missi* returned the conspirators to Charlemagne as his prisoners.

The nature of the inquisitory activities of the ten royal *missi* is still a matter of speculation. They have been characterized as an "Untersuchungskommission,"[2] as a "preliminary investigation,"[3]

---

[1] On the sequence of events see Philipp Jaffé, *Regesta Pontificum Romanorum* I (2nd ed. Leipzig, 1885), 308–310; Boehmer-Mühlbacher, *Regesta Imperii* I (2nd ed. Innsbruck, 1908), Nos. 369a–370a; Johannes Haller, *Das Papsttum* II (Basel, 1951), 16–19; Emile Amann, *L'Epoque carolingienne* (Hist. de l'Eglise ed. Fliche-Martin 6; Paris, 1937), 155–160. See also Harald Zimmermann, "Papstabsetzungen des Mittelalters I: Die Zeit der Karolinger," *MIOEG* 69 (1961), 27–34.

[2] Erich Caspar, "Das Papsttum unter fränkischer Herrschaft," *Zeitschrift für Kirchengeschichte* 54 (1935), 225.

[3] Willibald M. Plöchl, *Geschichte des Kirchenrechts* I (Wien, München, 1953), 283.

and as "a judicial investigation."[4] The last phrase seems to characterize their activities best. Their judicial nature is guaranteed by the terminology used in the *Liber Pontificalis* in the description of the events that took place. The author of the *Vita Leonis* uses terms peculiar to the Carolingian court charter, the *placitum*. Thus we read that the *missi* are residing (*resedentes*) in Leo's Triclinium and are investigating (*inquirentes*) the enemies of the pope, but could prove "nothing" against Leo (*nihil habuerunt adversus eum quod dicerent*). The word *resederemus* commonly appears at the very beginning of Charlemagne's *placita*.[5] The term *inquirentes*, referring to judicial investigations of Charlemagne's *missi*, occurs, for instance, in the *placitum* for St. Vincenzo on the Volturno (*DK* 159: *MGH*, *Dipl.* Karol. 1.216.37): "*missos* nostros . . . ibidem directos habuimus, per quos omnem causam *inquirentes* omnem veritatem exinde cognovimus." The concluding remark, which renders the outcome of the investigation, "nihil habuerunt *adversus eum quod dicerent*," is—*mutatis mutandis*—reminiscent of similar phrases in the formulaic parts of the *placita*. Compare, for example, *Formulae Salicae Merkelianae*[6] Nos. 27 and 28: "Repetebat adversus eum, dum dicerent, eo quod. . . . "

   The occurrence of some of the terminology characteristic of the Carolingian *placitum* in the report on the judicial court action of Charlemagne's *missi* in December 799 at Rome can only mean that Leo's biographer in all likelihood had before him the official *placitum* drawn up by the *Königsgericht* at the close of the proceedings. It is obvious that this court possessed a so-called *mandatum ad inquirendum et referendum*,[7] but not also a *mandatum ad definiendum*; that is, it was empowered to investigate and to report to Charlemagne, but not empowered to pass a final sentence. The latter was reserved for a synod, which acted upon it, as we shall see, with Charlemagne presiding, in December 800. Gregorovius,[8] who considered the

---

   [4] Ludo Moritz Hartmann, *Geschichte Italiens im Mittelalter* II.2 (Gotha, 1903), 341.
   [5] See *MGH, Diplomata Karolinorum*, ed. E. Mühlbacher (Hannover, 1906), e.g., *DK* 63, 128, 110, 138, 148, 196.
   [6] *MGH, Formulae Merowingici et Karolini aevi*, ed. Karl Zeumer (Hannover, 1882), 251.20; 252.3.
   [7] See, for instance, Heinrich Brunner and Claudius Freiherr von Schwerin, *Deutsche Rechtsgeschichte* II (2nd ed. München, Leipzig, 1928), 690.
   [8] Ferdinand Gregorovius, *Geschichte der Stadt Rom im Mittelalter* II (2nd ed.; Stuttgart, 1869), 478. It seems that Gregorovius interchanges the meetings of December 799 and of December 800, mentioned above.

court action we have analyzed to be the most important trial conducted at Rome in centuries, long ago deplored the loss of its official *placitum.* "Even a small fragment," he says, "would be of the greatest historical value." Such a fragment, I believe, is preserved in the narrative of the *Liber Pontificalis.*

The difficulties of Leo were not solved by turning over his accusers to the custody of Charlemagne. The king's personal intervention at Rome was necessary. He entered the city on November 24, 800, and on the first of December he presided, in the presence of the pope, over a synodal meeting composed of clerics and Frankish and Roman nobles. The accusations against Leo were the main topic of discussion. We deduce this also from Charlemagne's charter for Arezzo of March 4, 801, where his sojourn at Rome "pro quibusdam causis sancte dei ecclesie ac domni Leonis pape" is mentioned (*DK* 196, p. 264.8). The assembly upholds the principle of papal immunity, "prima sedes a nemine iudicatur," a doctrine especially established by some popes of the fifth century.[9] This was also evidence of Alcuin's influence on Charlemagne,[10] for Alcuin had already in August 799 advocated the application of the doctrine to the case in a famous letter to his friend Arno of Salzburg; Arno, like Riculf of Mayence and Theodulph of Orléans, participated in the sessions of the synod. Leo's case was under deliberation for three weeks; then he declared: "I follow in the steps of my pontifical predecessors, and am willing to clear myself of such false charges as have been wickedly kindled over me."[11] The words spoken by him before the synod on December 23 are preserved in the *Liber Pontificalis*:

Quia de istis criminibus falsis, quibus super me inposuerunt Romani, qui inique me persecuti sunt, *scientiam non habeo,* nec talia egisse me cognosco.

Since I have no knowledge of those false crimes which the Romans, who unjustly persecuted me, have laid on me, I do not acknowledge that I have committed such crimes.

[9] Cf. H. E. Feine, *Kirchliche Rechtsgeschichte* (5th ed. Köln, Wien, 1972), 336; Walter Ullmann, *The Growth of Papal Government in the Middle Ages* (London, 1970), 117f.

[10] See the handy collections of relevant passages from Alcuin's letters in Heinrich Dannenbauer, *Die Quellen zur Geschichte der Kaiserkrönung Karls des Grossen* (Lietzmann's Kleine Texte no. 161; Berlin, 1931); and Kurt Reindel, *Die Kaiserkrönung Karls des Grossen* (Historische Texte: Mittelalter, ed. Arno Borst and Josef Fleckenstein, 4; Göttingen, 1970).

[11] Louis Duchesne, *Liber Pontificalis* II (Paris, 1892), 7. See below p. 333.

These are the actual words of Leo's genuine oath through which he denied the charges of his enemies—not the long document hitherto looked upon as his "oath of purgation"! Their authenticity is supported by a formulaic parallel in the Acts of the Roman Synod of 769, which tried the deposed Constantinus II as a usurper of the papal see. The incumbent Stephen IV (III), when questioned during the *prima actio* of the synodal proceedings about his knowledge of certain activities of the accused, declared:[12] "Ego *de* hac causa *nullam habeo scientiam quia . . .* "

It now seems that the author of Leo's biography had access not only to the *placitum* of the judicial investigation conducted by Frankish *missi* in December of 799, but also to the Acts of the synodal meeting that was held in Rome a year later. He must have taken Leo's statement of innocence from these Acts. This version of Leo's oath deserves more credence than the document that until now has passed for Leo's oath of purgation. For the *formula* used by Leo in 800, "quia de . . . scientiam non habeo," and in 769 by Pope Stephen IV (III), "de . . . nullam habeo scientiam quia," is a statement of innocence and not an "oath of purgation." And while in the case of criminal accusation Roman law does not know of an oath[13] voluntarily tendered by the accused, or even imposed on him by a judge, the oath of purgation is peculiar to Germanic law.[14] The reinterpretation during the ninth century of Leo's genuine oath in conjunction with the historical develop-

---

[12] *MGH, Conc.* 2.1.82.10–1. We are investigating here only the formula of Leo's oath, not the formalities surrounding the oath. Adelson and Baker, *op. cit.*, 66f., suggest as a precedent for these formalities those that accompanied the oath of Pope Pelagius I (556–561), the words of which are not preserved. The parallels between the descriptions in *Liber Pontificalis* I.303 (Pelagius I) and II.7 (Leo III)— arrival of the pontiff at St. Peter's, his holding of a copy of the Gospels, and his ascent to the *ambo*—are, however, devoid of actual historical significance; they are merely literary parallels, the author of the *Vita Leonis* having copied from the *Vita* of Pelagius.

[13] On the various oaths in Roman law see Artur Steinwenter, "Iusiurandum," Pauly and Wissowa, *Real-Encyclopädie* 19.1, ed. Wilhelm Kroll (Stuttgart, 1917), 1257–1260; Theodor Mommsen, *Römisches Strafrecht* (Leipzig, 1899), 436ff.; especially F. L. Ganshof, "Contribution à l'étude de l'application du droit romain et des capitulaires dans la monarchie franque sous les Carolingiens," *Studi in onore di Edoardo Volterra* III (Milano, 1969), and H. E. Feine, "Vom Fortleben des römischen Rechts der Kirche," *ZSRG*, Kan. Abt. 73 (1956), 1–24.

[14] Richard Schröder and Eberhard von Künssberg, *Lehrbuch der deutschen Rechtsgeschichte* (7th ed. Berlin, Leipzig, 1932), 378, 394, 410, 414, and Löning n. 45 below.

ment of the *purgatio canonica* evidently produced the forged oath of purgation surreptitiously ascribed to the pope.

Where shall we find the origin of the forged oath of purgation? In order to answer this question, we here print the text, and add an English translation. The Roman numerals I–VI in the left margin indicate the individual parts of the forgery. Quotations from, and possible imitations of, the Vulgate are listed in the notes *a–h*.

Würzburg Universitätsbibliothek, M. p. th. f. 46, fol. 149r (Cf. *MGH, Conc.* 2.1.226f.); see Plate VI:

I   Auditum, fratres karissimi, et divulgatum*ᵃ* est per multa loca, qualiter homines mali*ᵇ* adversus me insurrexerunt*ᶜ* et debilitare voluerunt et miserunt super me*ᵈ* gravia crimina.

II   Propter quam causam audiendam iste clementissimus ac serenissimus domnus rex Carolus una cum sacerdotibus et optimatibus suis istam pervenit ad urbem.

III   Quam ob rem ego, Leo, pontifex sanctae Romanae ecclesiae, a nemine iudicatus neque coactus, sed spontanea mea voluntate purifico et purgo me in conspectu vestro*ᵉ* coram Deo*ᶠ* et angelis eius, qui conscientiam meam novit, et beato Petro principe apostolorum, in cuius basilica consistimus,

IV   quia istas criminosas et sceleratas res*ᵍ* quas illi mihi obiciunt, nec perpetravi*ᵍ* nec perpetrare iussi.

V   Testis*ʰ* mihi est Deus, in cuius iudicium venturi sumus et in cuius conspectu consistimus.

VI   Et hoc propter suspitiones tollendas mea spontanea voluntate facio; non quasi in canonibus inventum sit, aut quasi ego hanc consuetudinem aut decretum in sancta ecclesia successoribus meis necnon et fratribus et coepiscopis nostris inponam.

    ᵃ Gen. 45.16 Auditum est et celebri sermone vulgatum; cf. Rom. 16.19 vestra enim obedientia in omnem locum divulgata est; 2. Macc. 4.39 divulgata fama, congregata est multitudo adversum Lysimachum.

    ᵇ 2 Tim. 3.13 mali autem homines . . . proficient in pejus.

    ᶜ Ps. 53.5 quoniam alieni insurrexerunt adversum me; Ps. 26.12 quoniam insurrexerunt in me testes iniqui; Ps. 85.14 iniqui insurrexerunt super me.

    ᵈ Cf. Ps. 85.14 in note *c*.

    ᵉ Cf. Gen. 50.4 (and often) in conspectu vestro.

    ᶠ 2 Cor. 4.2 ad omnem conscientiam hominum coram Deo.

    ᵍ Deut. 17.5 virum ac mulierem qui rem sceleratissimam perpetrarunt; Gen. 34.7 eo quod (Sichem) . . . violata filia Jacob, rem illicitam perpetrasset.

    ʰ Rom. 1.9 testis enim mihi est Deus, cui servio; Phil. 1.8 testis enim mihi est Deus, quomodo cupiam. . . .

Translation:

I   It is well known, dearest Brethren, and publicly discussed throughout many regions, how evil men have risen up against me and wished to cripple me and have brought serious charges against me.

II For the purpose of investigating the case, the most merciful and most illustrious Lord, King Charles, together with his priests and nobles, has come to this city.

III Wherefore I, Leo, pontiff of the Holy Roman Church, being neither judged nor coerced by any man, but of my own free will, in your presence vindicate myself and declare my innocence, [a] before God who knows my conscience, and before His angels, and before St. Peter, the prince of the Apostles, in whose Basilica we are assembled,

IV For I have neither committed, nor ordered the perpetration of these criminal and villainous deeds of which those [evil men] accuse me.

V   My witness is God, whose judgment we must undergo, and in whose presence we are assembled.

VI And this I do of my own free will for the sake of removing suspicions. It is not as though [this procedure] is found in the canons [of the Church], nor as though I should impose it, whether as custom or as decree, either on my successors in the Holy Church, or on our brethren and fellow bishops.

[a] For this meaning of *purgare* see "Purgat innocentem probat" in a glossary, *Corpus Glossariorum Latinorum* 4, ed. G. Goetz (Leipzig, 1889), 152.37; the gloss renders *Dig.* 48.1.5: "Is qui reus factus est purgare se debet . . . constitutionibus enim observatur, ut . . . innocentia [proof of innocence] reus purgetur."

This document, if looked upon as an oath, makes a strange impression, even in a formal view. It is redundant and lacks the concision expected in the wording of an oath. Parts I and II have informative connotation; III offers assurances that the person giving the oath is doing so without any coercion, while IV contains the assertory element of an oath, disclaiming that he has committed any crime. This latter part is strengthened in V by the invoking of God as witness and judge of man. In VI the purpose of the oath is given as the removal of the suspicions of guilt directed against the person who swears. At the same time the audience, to which the oath is addressed, receives express assurances that the present oath is not found in canon law; and although it thus establishes a precedent, it is not supposed to be considered as a source of law, nor to be used in the future.

As far as I know, there exists no other early medieval oath, whether assertory or promissory, even remotely comparable to this strange piece. If the contents of this oath are related to its purported historical setting, one again arrives at contradictions.

We remember that Leo gave an oath before a synodal assembly which he attended and which for three weeks debated the charges leveled against him. This audience heard the pope's oath and did not have to be told, with Part I, about the rumors, the attack made on Leo, and the accusations. Nor was there any need to let the assembly know, in Part II, that Charlemagne and his entourage had come to Rome in order to conduct a judicial meeting and investigation. Parts I and II are therefore hardly in consonance with the actual requirements of the historical situation. The same is true of the repeated assurances in Part III concerning the voluntary nature of the oath. It is not a historical fact that Leo was not forced by anyone, as we know from Alcuin's letters and the *Annales Laureshamenses* ad a. 800. The substance of the oath actually sworn by Leo, according to the *Liber Pontificalis*, is offered in Part IV, which denies direct or indirect involvement on his part in criminal actions. What Part VI maintains is impossible from the historical point of view, no matter how one judges it. Why should it be necessary for Leo to tell the assembly, which was by then well informed of the issues involved in the entire controversy, the obvious purpose of the oath? And why should he in this connection reiterate its "voluntary" nature, an assertion made in both a negative and a positive fashion in Part III? Part VI in an actually spoken oath is unthinkable. Leo's audience, partly composed of Frankish and Roman laymen, was not interested to hear from him that his oath had no precedent in canon law and that it would not be adopted in the future into this body of law. Leo himself would have lessened the stringency of his oath if he had included all these assurances and promises. Furthermore, there is the contradiction between the report of the *Liber Pontificalis* that he intends to vindicate himself after the example of his predecessors and, here in Part VI, the flat denial that a precedent for his oath occurs in the earlier law of the church. Finally, the entire oath as here presented would have been a profound humiliation of the pope, imposed on him by a meeting presided over by a layman.

Some points in the preceding analysis have not escaped the attention of historians. While Kleinclausz calls the oath a triumph of the pope over the ambuscades of his enemies, and Calmette[15] mistakenly judges it a procedure conforming "aux usages du temps," Duchesne[16] saw in the oath a "certaine dose d'humiliation." The most cogent criticism is advanced by Louis Halphen,[17] who points to the contradictory nature of the declarations contained in the oath, the strong reservations concerning the procedure of the oath as such, and generally characterized it as a "rude obligation" imposed on the pope by the master of the West.

A hint as to the origins of the fabrication is furnished by its own MS transmission. The Salzburg provenience of the ninth-century MS Würzburg M. p. theol. fol. 46,[18] which represents the oldest transmission of the text from which the others stem, directly or indirectly, is now advocated by Bernhard Bischoff (see below). But Caspar's statement[19] that Leo turned over to Charlemagne a copy of the oath is a mere invention, since we know that the text of the oath is not independently transmitted in several German MSS, as he believes. Equally arbitrary is the theory that infers a relationship between Arno of Salzburg and the oldest transmission of the forged oath, because at Rome, Arno personally heard Leo's oath, and because the Würzburg MS was, as it seems, in Salzburg during the ninth and tenth centuries.[20]

Any connection of the oath with Charlemagne and Arno of Salzburg is contradicted by the sources which the forger used when concocting the document:

a. the forged letter of Pope Sixtus III, *Ad Episcopos Orientales*, in *Decretales Pseudo-Isidorianae*, ed. Paul Hinschius (Leipzig, 1863), 561–565, *JK* 397;

b. the *Vita* of Leo III in the *Liber Pontificalis* II.6–7; and probably

---

[15] Arthur Kleinclausz, *Alcuin* (Paris, 1948), 259; Joseph Calmette, *Charlemagne* (Paris, 1945), 126.

[16] L. Duchesne, *Les premiers temps de l'état pontifical* (2nd ed. Paris, 1904), 175.

[17] Louis Halphen, *Charlemagne et l'empire carolingien* (Paris, 1949), 127f.

[18] Cf. Anton Chroust, *Monumenta Palaeographica* (München, 1901), Abt. I 1 Lief. 5, T. 5.

[19] *Op. cit.* (above n. 2), 229.

[20] Cf. B. Bischoff and J. Hofmann, *Libri Sancti Kyliani* (Würzburg, 1952), 109, and Adelson and Baker, *op. cit.*, 48f.

c. the *Annales Laureshamenses* ad a. 800, *MGH*, *Scriptores* 1.37–38. Let us consider these sources in their order.

a. The dependence of the forged oath on Sixtus' letter is best illustrated if we confront the texts. Compare:

Sixtus, *Ad Episcopos Orientales,* ed. Hinschius, pp. 562f.:

I. Quod ergo mandastis, ut scriberem vobis *qualiter* iurgium contra me suscitatum sit, id est a quo, ut vestro amminiculo pelleretur et causa mea firmaretur, scitote *me criminari* a quodam Basso et iniuste persequi.

II. Quod audiens *Valentinianus* augustus, nostra auctoritate *synodum congregari iussit* et facto concilio cum magna examinatione satisfaciens omnibus, . . . *suspitionem tamen fugiens coram* omnibus me *purgavi, me scilicet a suspitione et emulatione liberans, sed non aliis qui noluerint aut sponte hoc non elegerint, faciendum formam exemplumque dans,* . . . [p. 563]. Ista omnia postposui *non aliis,* ut paulo superius prelibatum est, *exemplum dando, sed me a praefata infamia et suspitione liberando. . . .*

III. His ita de me peractis, quia contra voluntatem omnium episcoporum qui nobiscum erant, propter humilitatem sensus mei *nullo compulsus iuditio aut vi passus, sed sponte eligens, non formam,* ut iam dictum est, *aliis dando, sed me purificando feci,* in aliis tamen episcopis competens adhibenda est de talibus medella vulneribus, ne immatura curandi facilitas mortifera capitis peste nihil possit, sed. . . .

Leo's forged oath of purgation, see above, p. 303:

I. Auditum, fratres karissimi, et divulgatum est per multa loca, *qualiter* homines mali adversus me insurrexerunt et debilitare voluerunt et miserunt super *me gravia crimina.*

II. Propter *quam causam audiendam* iste clementissimus ac serenissimus domnus rex *Carolus* una cum sacerdotibus et optimatibus suis *istam pervenit ad urbem.*

VI. Et hoc *propter suspitiones tollendas mea spontanea voluntate facio; non quasi* in canonibus inventum est, aut quasi ego *hanc consuetudinem aut* decretum in sancta ecclesia *successoribus meis necnon fratribus et coepiscopis nostris inponam.*

III. Quam ob rem ego, Leo, pontifex sanctae Romanae ecclesiae, *a nemine iudicatus neque coactus, sed spontanea mea voluntate purifico et purgo* me in conspectu vestro coram Deo et angelis eius.

The parallels between *S*(*ixtus*') letter and *L*(*eo*'s) alleged oath are obvious. Sixtus or Xystus (432–440) is accused of certain crimes by one Bassus, and unjustly persecuted (*S*.I); "homines mali" do the same to Leo III (*L*.I). The Emperor Valentinianus hears of this, and convokes a synod in order to examine the accusations (*S*.II); Charlemagne does the same for Leo (*L*.II). Sixtus submits to an investigation in order to prove his innocence, though he could have chosen other means (*S*.II); Leo follows suit by forcibly stressing his voluntary participation in the case (*L*.III). Sixtus accepts the procedure in order to remove suspicions, but does not want to establish a historical precedent for anyone else (*S*.II–III); Leo subscribes to exactly the same motives (*L*.VI).

b. The forger's familiarity with Leo's *Vita* in the *L*(*iber*) *P*(*ontificalis* II), which cannot have originated before the death of the pope in 816,[21] may be seen in the narrative of events and persons that are identical with events and persons mentioned in the text of the oath. Part IV corresponds with the genuine oath actually given by Leo (*LP* p. 7). The expression *super me* in *L*.I appears in *LP* 7.12 and 16. For the epitheta of Charlemagne in II, *clementissimus et serenissimus domnus rex*, see *LP* 6.9 and 13. The king's entourage, including *sacerdotes seu optimates* (*LP* 7.6), who attended the synodal meeting of December 800, reappear in *L*.II, *cum sacerdotibus et optimatibus*. "[Sedes apostolica] . . . *a nemine iudicatur*" (*LP* 7.10) parallels "pontifex sanctae Romanae ecclesiae, *a nemine iudicatus*," in *L*.III. Though some of these terms are also found in other documents of the Carolingian age, their occurrence in the forgery in the same context as in the *Vita* shows that the writer actually had the *Liber Pontificalis* before his eyes. Had this not been the case, he might have used other expressions as epitheta for Charlemagne and also for the members of his entourage.

c. Finally there is the statement in Part I that the attackers of Leo wished to cripple him, *debilitare voluerunt*. While many sources[22] report that Leo actually suffered the full Byzantine punishment of blinding and cutting out the tongue, the *Annales Laureshamenses*[23]

[21] Cf. Léon Levillain, "Le couronnement impérial de Charlemagne," *Revue d'histoire de l'Eglise de France* 18 (1932), 15.

[22] See the survey of the sources by S. Abel and B. Simson, *Jahrbücher des fränkischen Reiches unter Karl dem Grossen* 2 (Leipzig, 1883), 583–587.

[23] *MGH, Scriptores* 1 (1826), 37, ad annum 799.

alone report that the Romans wished to blind him, *voluerunt eruere oculos eius.* This unique parallel between oath and annals may possibly indicate that in addition the forger was familiar with the *Annales,* which stress the feigned voluntary nature of the oath: "spontanea voluntate se purificare debuisset."

The doctrine of the jurisdictional immunity of the pope, relentlessly upheld in the oath, makes it certain that the author of the forgery is an ecclesiastic. He seems to possess some acquaintance with official Frankish documents and possibly also with the *formulae* used in their composition. The fact that we can notice more or less close resemblances in diction between the oath and such documents[24] lends some support to this assumption, as can be shown in a few instances.

The listing of groups of persons who came with Charlemagne to Rome, " . . . *una cum* sacerdotibus et optimatibus" (in Part II), conforms to the identical formula in Carolingian charters and capitularies. The wording of the purpose of their coming, "propter quam *causam audiendam*" (in II) is characteristic of the *placita* and of immunity charters in combinations such as *causas audire* and *ad causas audiendas.* The formulation of the allegedly voluntary performance of the oath is parallel to a certain degree to some *formulae* to be found in Frankish collections[25] of the eighth century. Compare III: "a nemine iudicatus *neque coactus, sed spontanea mea voluntate,*" and

Cartae Senonicae 2.186.7: "Idcirco, nulli coagentis imperium, *nec* a iudiciaria potestate *coactus, sed mea* propria et *spontanea voluntate* arbitrium";
Formulae Salicae Merkelianae 9.234.34: " . . . quem *ego nullo cogente, sed spontanea voluntate* fieri vel firmare rogavi";
Formulae Turonenses 10.140–141: "quam *ego mea voluntate spontanea* fieri . . . rogavi."

A significant parallel to Part III occurs in the capitulary of the Synod of Frankfurt of 794, c. 9.[26] Bishop Petrus of Verdun, accused of treason, standing before the synod, like the Leo of the forgery (III), *coram Deo et angelis eius,* and in the presence of Charlemagne,

---

[24] See the Indices of *MGH, Conc.* (above, Introduction to Part Four, n. 2); *MGH, Dipl. Kar.* (above n. 5); *MGH, Formulae* (above n. 6); and *MGH, Capitularia Regum Francorum* 2 (1897), 587, s.v. *causa.*
[25] For the following quotations see *MGH, Formulae,* above n. 6.
[26] *MGH, Conc.* 2.1 (above, Introduction to Part Four, n. 2), 167.15–27.

is asked to clear himself with the aid of two or three oath-helpers. Since he cannot find anyone ready to serve in this capacity, one of his serfs, whom he frees for this specific purpose, submits himself to an ordeal, *ad iudicium Dei*. This procedure is chosen, as the capitulary expressly says: "*neque* per regis ordinationem, *neque* per sanctae synodi censuram, *sed spontanea voluntate*." The sentence " . . . istas . . . res . . . nec perpetravi nec perpetrare iussi," in IV, might be compared to a title on judicial procedure in an Italian Capitulary of Pippin (782–796),[27] where we read: 'et ipse . . . negaverit quod malum ipsum *nec* ipse *nec* homines ipsius perpetrassent."

The Frankish elements in the forged oath can hardly be questioned. We may next investigate its probable aim.

The letter of Sixtus III and the forged oath of purgation are open partisan expressions of the doctrine of the pope's jurisdictional immunity from judgment, "prima sedes a nemine iudicatur." The letter cannot depend on the oath, since the contents of the letter are fuller, and its source is available: the *Gesta purgationis* of Pope Sixtus III (432–440),[28] a literary product dating from the time of the conflict[29] between Symmachus (498–514) and the antipope Laurentius (498–ca. 505).

We remember that the unique position of the pope—his exemption from human judgment—was one of the keystones of the Symmachian controversy. It was a slogan of Symmachus' fight against his enemies, who had accused him of immorality and the squandering of church property. Judged by a synod in the presence of Theodoric the Great, Symmachus was rehabilitated at Rome in the year 501, while simultaneously the doctrine of the pope's judicial exception was confirmed. In the *Gesta purgationis* of Sixtus III, the events of Symmachus' struggle were read backward into the earlier history of the papacy. In the *Gesta*, Sixtus III is accused, like Symmachus after him, of *stuprum*.[30] He is tried before the Emperor Valentinian and the Roman Senate, and himself requests the *probatio*

---

[27] *MGH, Capitularia* 1.1 (1881), no. 91, pp. 192.4–193.1.

[28] See Mansi V., 1061–1068; *ibid.*, Sixtus' letter (*JK* 397), col. 1054–1056. Adelson and Baker, *op. cit.*, 73, maintain that any influence of the *Gesta* on the "oath of purgation" must be discounted.

[29] Erich Caspar, *Geschichte des Papsttums von den Anfängen bis zur Höhe der Weltherrschaft* 2 (Tübingen, 1933), 107–110; Johannes Haller, *Das Papsttum* I (Basel, 1950), 238–240, and 534f.

[30] Mansi V.1063B.

of his accusers. But the former consul Maximus, in this case the parallel to Symmachus' trusted follower Faustus, states, "non licet enim adversus pontificem dare sententiam." Like Symmachus, Sixtus answers: "Quoniam in meo arbitrio est iudicare et iniudicare, tamen meo non abscondatur veritas." Though Valentinian then asks the accuser Bassus to bring forth his charges, he tells Maximus that he agrees with his earlier opinion: "justa fuit postulatio tua." Thereupon the emperor rises and asks Sixtus to judge himself, "et dedit in arbitrio . . . iudicare iudicium suum." On the following day, the accusers of Sixtus are found guilty, since they could not prove their charges of *stuprum*. This situation is illustrated by the reference to the woman *in adulterio deprehensa* in John 8.3–7, who, according to the law of Moses, should have been stoned, but instead was brought by Pharisees before Jesus, whose final judgment was (John 8.7): "Si quis ex vobis sine peccato est, injiciat super *illam* lapidem." Sixtus judged himself—"per haec verba evangelii (John 8.7) iudicat sedem suam"—but he substituted *istam*, referring to *sedes*, for the *illam* of the Vulgate.

The obvious parallels between this story—which is the ultimate source of Sixtus' letter[31]—and Leo's forged oath may be gleaned from our analysis of the relationship between this letter and the oath, presented above. In this context, it is of some importance to know that the *Gesta purgationis* of Sixtus was probably known to Alcuin, whose correspondence supplies vital information about the events that led to the genuine oath of Leo III. In the famous letter No. 179 to Arno of Salzburg of August 799, Alcuin lists among the charges leveled against Leo by his accusers "crimina adulterii et periurii," and finally states that he would have rejected these accusations with the words: "Qui sine peccato est vestrum, primus in

[31] Hinschius, *op. cit.*, 562f., does not list this source of the forgery nor other sources of the forged letter of Sixtus; but cf. p. 563: "hi qui non sunt bone conversationis—admittantur," and *Capitula Angilramni* 13 (Hinschius, p. 761); "hi qui in aliquibus criminibus—accusandi' = *Cap. Angilr.* 14; "Si quis ergo iuratus—non ut reus criminis teneatur" = *Interpretatio of Cod. Theod.* 9.1.5 (*Breviarium Alaricianum* 9.1.3). As far as we can learn from Fr. Maassen, "Pseudoisidor-Studien," *Sb. Akad. Wien* 108–109 (1884–85), especially 109 (1885), 811, the Sixtus letter does not seem to be contained in the *Hispana of Autun*. Schafer Williams confirmed in a letter of November 25, 1956, that neither the Vaticanus lat. 1341 (Hispana Augustodunensis) nor the Vindob. lat. 411 (Hisp. Gallica corrupta) contains the Sixtus letter. See on both MSS Schafer Williams, *Codices Pseudo-Isidoriani* (Monumenta iuris canonici, ser. C: Subsidia, 3; New York, 1971), 117.

illum lapidem mittat." This is a reference to the same citation from
the Bible quoted by Sixtus in the *Gesta*, as we have shown above;
Alcuin changes *illam* of the Vulgate, referring to the adulterous
woman, to *illum*, referring to Leo. Since Alcuin in this letter seems
to be influenced by a literary source, the letter does not provide[32]
evidence of his belief in Leo's guilt, though the Saxon changed his
mind in the fall of 799.

Several of the apologetic writings of the Symmachian controversy
were evidently read during the ninth century. The *Gesta Polychronii*,
in which Sixtus III again appears, was known, for example, to
Pope Nicholas I. In a letter of September 25, 865, addressed to the
Byzantine Emperor Michael III, the *Gesta* is cited as evidence
for the judicial exemption of the bishop of Rome.[33]

Thus far the investigation reveals the direct literary dependence
of the forged oath on the fictitious letter of Sixtus III contained in
the *Pseudo-Isidorian Decretals*,[34] which originated during the ninth
century. In addition, the oath is indirectly a ninth-century descen-
dant of the propaganda literature of the Symmachian controversy.

Sixtus' letter is published by Hinschius after the MS Paris int.
suppl. latin. 840 (today Par. lat. 9629), from the third quarter of
the ninth century. Hincmar of Laon,[35] nephew of Hincmar of
Reims, inserted the letter in a collection of excerpts from Pseudo-
Isidore.

The Pseudo-Isidorian background of the forged oath finally
enables us to suggest a feasible interpretation of the last section of
the forgery. Why does the forger make Leo tell his imagined audience not only that the oath does not establish a historical precedent
for future popes (*successoribus meis*), but also that it has no legal
validity for his brethren and fellow bishops (*fratribus et coepiscopis
nostris*)? The explanation is to be found in the exalted position of

[32] As is assumed by Albert Hauck, *Kirchengeschichte Deutschlands* II (3rd and 4th
eds. Leipzig, 1912), 105, n.; Caspar, *Zeitschrift für Kirchengeschichte* 54 (1935), 223f.
and n. 33, pointed this out, and also Alcuin's probable acquaintance with the *Gesta
purgationis* of Sixtus.

[33] Ed. Ernst Perels, *MGH*, *Epistolae* 6 (*Karolini Aevi* 4; Berlin, 1925), 464f.;
JE 2682.

[34] See on the Paris MS. Schafer Williams, *Codices Pseudo-Isidoriani*, 45f.; on the
Excerpta by Hincmar of Laon cf. *ibid.*, pp. 89f.; also Horst Fuhrmann, *Einfluss und
Verbreitung der pseudoisidorischen Fälschungen* (Schriften der *MGH*, 24.1; Stuttgart,
1972), 172, 176.

[35] *PL* 124.1015–1018.

the bishop and the immunity requested for him in the *False De-cretals*. Bishops, we are told, are appointed by God, and endowed by Him with the power to judge man, while they themselves cannot be judged by human beings:[36] "summi sacerdotes, id est episcopi, a Deo sunt iudicandi, non ab hominibus." Besides, bishops are "gods" given to man by God, and it is not proper that gods be judged by man: "Deus vos constituit sacerdotes et potestatem vobis dedit de nobis quoque iudicandi. Et ideo nos a vobis recte iudica-mur, vos autem non potestis ab hominibus iudicari. . . . Vos etenim nobis a Deo datis estis dii. Conveniens non est ut homo iudicet deos."[37] This theory of episcopal supremacy is shared with Pseudo-Isidore by Benedictus Levita 1.315, both forgeries probably re-peating the identical statement of c. 2 in the *petitio* of the Frankish episcopate submitted to Louis the Pious in August 829, at the Synod of Paris. The famous passage on the divinity of the bishops is taken from the alleged *Oratio ad Sanctos* of Constantine the Great addressed to the episcopate assembled at the First Ecumenical Council of Nicaea, 325.

It seems probable that the forger of Leo's oath of purgation had a two-fold aim. The historical fact of Leo's oath was not to be considered as a precedent for future popes, nor was it to be taken as a precedent for bishops and clergy of lower rank, who apparently at one time aspired to a similar jurisdictional exception as the pope. If this was supposed to be the aim of the forgery, then it could not have originated directly among the followers and sympathizers of the deposed Archbishop Ebo of Reims, to whose circles the *False Decretals* was at times ascribed.[38] It could, however, have originated among the opponents of this group, led by Hincmar of Reims, who at times used the *Decretals* for his own purposes though he had recognized it as a forgery.

A prominent place in the historical development of the canonical oath of purgation can no longer be assigned to the forged oath of

[36] Ed. Hinschius, 76.

[37] Cf. Hinschius, 248, c. 11, and in the middle of p. 256; for the occurrence in the *Acts* of the Synod of Paris see *MGH, Capitularia* 2 (1897), 35f.; on the entire theory here described see Walter Ullmann, *The Growth of Papal Government* (above, n. 9), 39, 131, 181, 187. The text from "Deus . . . deos" is drawn verbatim from Rufinus, *Historia eccl.* I.2, *PL* 21.468B.

[38] Cf. for instance Johannes Haller, *Nikolaus I. und Pseudoisidor* (Stuttgart, 1936), 156.

Leo III. It is possible that Leo's genuine oath served as a precedent that enabled Pope Paschalis I to refute in 823 before a synod at Rome the suspicions leveled against him with respect to his alleged conspiracy in a murder case.[39] But even at that time an oath of purgation resorted to by members of the clergy was an issue as unsettled as later during the time of Pseudo-Isidore. Neither during the centuries preceding Leo's oath of 800 nor during the ninth century was purgation by oath a clearly established mode of trial for the clergy. Recent research,[40] however, reading the later growth of the canonical oath of purgation backward into earlier times, ascribed to Leo's forged oath a place in that development which it assumed only after Burchard of Worms, at about the year 1023,[41] had inserted the forgery into his *Decretum*. Obviously, the early history of the *purgatio canonica* must be investigated anew, and also in connection with its occurrences in the Eastern Church.[42] Like Burchard, the master forgers of the *False Decretals* undoubtedly would have included the forged oath in their collection, had it been available to them. The genuine oath, which actually jeopardized the doctrine of papal immunity, must have appeared in the eyes of his Frankish contemporaries as a humiliation of the pope and a scandal of major proportions. The profound impression the genuine oath made on the imagination of the generations after 800 may be seen in the traces it has left in Benedictus Levita's *False Capitularies*, which contains forged documents artificially tied up with Leo III and the canonical purgation. These fictions—which finally culminated in Leo's forged oath of purgation—are motivated by an astonishment similar to that which generated the wild rumor that the pontiff had been blinded and his tongue cut out. Most of the historical sources of the age credulously record as a fact the application of this Byzantine form of punishment and that Leo miraculously experienced a restoration of sight and speech. Some sober minds, however, were not taken in by the rumors and the miracle. Alcuin, writing to Charlemagne, mentions the *mirabilis*

---

[39] See *JE* I, p. 320.

[40] *Traditio* 8 (1952), 53ff., see above Introduction to Part Four, n. 5.

[41] When he made his collection, as argued by F. Pelster, in *Miscellanea Giovanni Mercati* 2 (Rome, 1946), 157ff.

[42] Artur Steinwenter, "Der antike kirchliche Rechtsgang und seine Quellen," *ZSRG*, Kan. Abt. 23 (1934), 58–61, calls attention to instances of the *purgatio canonica* in the Eastern Church during the fourth and fifth centuries.

sanitas of the apostolic shepherd.[43] The keen-minded Theodulph
of Orléans, who was present when Leo gave the oath, marvels at
the restoration of the pope's sight, and rather facetiously deliberates
whether to be more astonished about this miracle or about the other
miracle, namely, that Leo did not lose his eyesight completely.[44]

The popular legend that centered on the figure of Leo III is
apparent in Benedictus Levita's *False Capitularies*, in connection
with the problem of the purgation of Frankish ecclesiastics. While
the original form of Leo's oath consists in his denial of having
committed any crime, popular Frankish imagination, being familiar
with the customary Germanic *Reinigungseid*,[45] naturally visualized
Leo's in the forms of the Germanic oath of purgation. A brief
investigation of the growth of the *purgatio canonica* in the Empire of
Charlemagne, in conjunction with the influence of Germanic law[46]
on this very institution, will be helpful in illustrating some of the
issues here considered.

The Frankish Synod[47] held in 794 at Frankfurt imposed (c. 9) an
oath on Bishop Petrus of Verdun, accused of high treason. He was
to prove his innocence with the support of two or three oath-
helpers[48] or of the archbishop of his province. Since the defendant
could not secure any support, the purgation by oath was not accessible to him. His innocence had to be proved with the help of a
Germanic ordeal, which was undergone on his behalf by one of
his serfs freed by him for this purpose. The ordeal proved the
innocence of Petrus, and subsequently he regained his former honor
and Charlemagne's favor.

In another case that was debated by the assembly, the same
Synod of 794 did not, as one might have expected, suggest an oath
of purgation. The assembly stated (c. 39) that it did not know how

---

[43] *MGH, Epistolae* 4 (*Karolini Aevi* 2; Berlin, 1895), No. 178, p. 295.

[44] *MGH, Poetae* 1.523 no. 32 vv. 23–24: " . . . est tamen in dubio, hinc mirer an
inde magis."

[45] Cf. Richard Löning, *Der Reinigungseid bet Ungerichtsklagen im deutschen Mittelalter*
(Heidelberg, 1880).

[46] See Paul Hinschius, *Das Kirchenrecht der Katholiken und Protestanten* 4 (Berlin,
1888), 773, 840; and in Albert Hauck's *Realenzyklopädie für protestantische Theologie*
(3rd ed.), 6.595; also Edgar Loening, *Geschichte des deutschen Kirchenrechts* 2 (Strassburg, 1878), 503.

[47] *MGH, Conc.* 2.1.167, 170.

[48] Cf. Conrad Cosack, *Die Eidhelfer des Beklagten nach ältestem deutschem Recht* (Stuttgart, 1885).

to deal with a *presbyter* accused of a crime denied by him, in the event that the crime could not be proved by the plaintiff ("Et si forte negare voluerit, et accusator conprobationem dare non potuerit"). Thereupon it was decreed that such cases must be submitted for decision to a synod of the Frankish national church.

The dilemma of the Frankfurt Synod in the last-named case could have been caused by a reluctance to impose an oath on a cleric, since the giving of oaths was doctrinally forbidden on the basis of Matt. 5.33–37 and James 5.12. Ecclesiastics are to give an oath only in matters concerning their faith; otherwise they may not swear on their own initiative, nor may an oath be expected of them. This opinion, which appears in the *prima actio* of the Council of Chalcedon, 451,[49] is inserted in a Pseudo-Isidorian decretal ascribed to Pope Cornelius (251–253), and reappears in the *Corpus Iuris Canonici*, Decr. Grat. C.2 q.5 c.1.

The progressive Germanization of the genuine oath of Leo III is evident from the alleged connection of this pope with the unsettled problem of the *purgatio canonica* in Benedictus Levita's *False Capitularies*,[50] which originated not before April 21, 847, and consists of Carolingian capitularies; some of these are genuine, many falsified, and most forged.

Benedictus Levita, 1.35, is undecided what ought to be done with criminal priests ("presbiteris criminosis"), who deny the charges against them, and whose guilt cannot be proved ("unde adprobatio non est, et semper negant"). We are told that this case and the dilemma it caused had been discussed previously, but until now a definitive decision has not been made ("sed non ad liquidum actenus definitum"). The reference to former discussions of the case under consideration might well be to cap. 39 of the Frankfurt Capitulary of 794, whose contents confirm the contention of Benedict. Emil

---

[49] Eduard Schwartz, *ACO*, II.iii.1, 136 cap. 570; cf. Hinschius, *Decretales Pseudo-Isidorianae*, 173. On the prohibition in late classical times see Erwin Seidl, *Der Eid im römisch-ägyptischen Provinzialrecht* II (Münchener Beiträge zur Papyrusforschung und antiken Rechtsgeschichte 24; 1935), 36–43. Cf. further *Codex Justinianus* 1.3.25.1b (ed. Paul Krüger; Berlin, 1900), a.456: " . . . quia ecclesiasticis regulis et canone a beatissimis episcopis antiquitus instituto clerici iurare prohibentur"; also the Edict of Emperor Henry III, April, 3, 1047, *De iuramentis clericorum*, *MGH*, *Constitutiones et acta publica* I, ed. Ludwig Weiland (Hannover, 1893), no. 50, pp. 96f., forbidding the oath to ecclesiastics: " . . . set suis idoneis advocatis hoc officium liceat delegare."

[50] *MGH*, *Leges* 2.2 (Hannover, Leipzig, 1837), 48.

Seckel was on the right track when he assumed that the forger relied for 1.35 also on some genuine source.[51] In order to resolve the mentioned dilemma, Pope Leo III is allegedly consulted, and his instructions result in Charlemagne's forged capitulary, Bened. 1.36 *De sacerdotum purgatione*. Accordingly, the often-discussed question of the canonical purgation of a *sacerdos* is decided as follows:

If a *sacerdos* is accused of a crime by a person who has in accordance with canon law the right to make the accusation, the accuser should verify his accusations (*adprobare*) with the proper number of truthful and good witnesses as required by law; should the priest be found guilty, he is to be sentenced canonically. But if the charges against the *sacerdos* cannot be proved by the accuser ("Si vero . . . adprobare ipse accusator minime poterit"), and the *sacerdos* himself remains untrustworthy to his superior ("suspiciosus aut incredibilis suo episcopo") and also to other persons of his environment, the following provision is made: the accused priest must give an oath of purgation with three, five, or seven trustworthy and neighboring priests as oath-helpers, after the example of Pope Leo III, who had for his purgation the assistance of twelve presbyters;[52] the priest clears himself publicly with an oath on the Four Gospels.

The Germanization of Leo's original oath is completed in this forged capitulary: his alleged oath of purgation was supported by twelve oath-helpers. These helpers were "presbyters" according to some MSS of the *False Capitularies*. Hincmar of Reims, who inserts Bened. 1.36 in his treatise *De presbyteris criminosis de quibus approbatio non est*,[53] writes: " . . . exemplo Leonis papae qui duodecim *episcopos* in sua purgatione habuit." Benedictus Levita's motivation for the oath of purgation requested of the priest is " . . . ne . . . in . . . *suspicione* remaneat," that is, the same motive also mentioned in the last section of the forged oath: "propter *suspitiones* tollendas."

The role ascribed by Benedict to Leo III in 1.35–36 is again referred to in the context of 1.370: "Ut presbiteri criminosi ad

---

[51] Emil Seckel, "Studien zu Benedictus Levita," in *Neues Archiv* 29 (1904), 283 n. 4, and 31 (1906), 70f., shows that the beginning of Ben. 1.35 is derived "aus echter Quelle" and that the rest and 1.36 are "Fälschungen Benedicts." Adelson and Baker, *op. cit.*, 50 n. 57, mention Seckel's findings only for the second, not the first chapter.

[52] See *MGH, Leges* 2.2.48 variant *f*: "qui duodecim presbiteros in sua purgatione habuit."

[53] c. 3; *PL* 125.1094C.

synodum venientes in medio collocentur." The entirely forged[54] capitulary in 3.281, *De purgatione sacerdotum*, pretends to supplement 1.35–36 (1.370) by quoting from the letter of 726 by Pope Gregory II to Boniface[55] the passage "De presbitero vero vel quilibet sacerdos a populo accusatus." The same letter of Gregory II on the oath of purgation to be given by an ecclesiastic if witnesses cannot prove his guilt ("si certi non fuerint testes") is twice referred to in 852 by Hincmar of Reims in the *Capitula presbyteris data*, cc. 23 and 24.[56]

The procedure suggested by Benedict in the forged capitulary 1.36 is actually identical with the provisions *De excusatione prespiterorum et diaconorum* in c. 8 of the Synod of Mayence, held on October 3, 852.[57] A priest who endangers his reputation so that he becomes suspect of bad behavior ("mala de se suspicari permiserit") is first admonished by his bishop if the charge of his accusers is not proved by them (" . . . et certi accusatores criminis eius defuerint"). But if there are plaintiffs who can prove his crime, then the defendant has to clear himself with the help of seven men[58] of his own rank. In the case of a deacon, three persons are required.

The same c. 8 of the Synod of 852 is partly quoted by Gratian and, *in toto*, by Ivo of Chartres as an alleged title from the Acts of the Synod of Agde, 506.[59] An expanded version of Mayence c. 8[60] in two MSS expressly links the *purgatio canonica* with Leo III; it is presented as the supposititious c. 10 of the *Concilium Ilerdense* of 524 in Burchard of Worms and Ivo.[61]

The forged oath of Leo III and its Pseudo-Isidorian source, dealt with in our sections *a–c*, would well fit at this juncture into the development of the disputed *purgatio canonica*, especially so if we remember that the oath rejects the idea that Leo's purgation might be considered as a precedent to be imitated by future popes, bishops, and "fratres."

---

[54] Seckel, "Studien zu Benedictus Levita," *Neues Archiv* 40 (1916), 48–50, and in the continuation by Seckel and J. Juncker, in *ZSRG*, Kan. Abt. 23 (1934), 271–277.

[55] *MGH, Epistolae* 5.276.

[56] *PL* 125.784D–785A.

[57] *MGH, Capitularia* 2 (1897), 188.

[58] So the *codd. Monacenses*, also Benedict, Burchard of Worms, Gratian.

[59] Mansi VIII.338C–D, not mentioned *MGH, Capit.* 2.188.

[60] Published *MGH, Capit.* 2.188, note **.

[61] Mansi, VIII.616C–E.

There is finally c. 16, *De purgatione episcoporum*, of the Synod of Hohenaltheim,[62] held on September 20, 916, which follows Benedict's 1.36 and his phrase "exemplum Sancti Leonis papae qui supra IIII evangelia iurans coram populo se purgavit."

Another instance of the Germanization of Leo's original oath may be observed in the statement of some *ordines* of the Germanic ordeal by cold water, to the effect that this *iudicium aquae frigidae* was established by Leo and Charlemagne. The assumption of von Schwerin[63] that the Frankish king and the pope used this *purgatio vulgaris* at Rome during the events of the year 800 is hardly convincing.[64] The relation between Leo and the *ordines* of the ordeal seems to be another literary expression of the legendary rumors about the pope's "oath of purgation" having taken place in the forms of the Germanic *Reinigungseid*.

Our study shows that by the middle of the ninth century the oath of purgation was not as yet an established institution of canon law. The assumption of Plöchl[65] that it had developed "um die Wende des 9. Jahrhunderts" under the influence of the Germanic *Volksrechte* into a strictly canonical means of evidence is plainly contradicted by the historical material here discussed.

Had the forged "oath of purgation" ascribed to Leo III actually existed before the middle of the ninth century, it might have been quoted during this period, since we have from the same century a number of references, in a variety of sources, to the historical fact of Leo's oath. But it was not once quoted. Does not this absence of quotations indicate that the "oath of purgation" was then either not extant, or not available, let us say, to Benedictus Levita and Pseudo-Isidore, both of whom used in their works an enormous number of genuine, forged, and falsified texts, as Emil Seckel and

---

[62] *MGH, Constitutiones et acta publica* 1, ed. L. Weiland (Hannover, 1893), 622; cf. Manfred Hellmann, "Die Synode von Hohenaltheim," *Historisches Jahrbuch der Görresgesellschaft* 73 (1954), 142. Horst Fuhrmann, "Die pseudoisidorischen Fälschungen und die Synode von Hohenaltheim," *Zeitschrift für bayerische Landesgeschichte* 20 (1957), 136–151, rejects Hellmann's thesis of the Pseudo-Isidorian influence on the synodal *Acta* as an expression of episcopal self-assertion.

[63] Claudius Frh. von Schwerin, *Rituale für Gottesurteile* (Sb. Akad. Heidelberg, 1932–33, 3. Abh.), 43 48.

[64] Also H. Nottarp, *Gottesurteile* I (Bamberg, 1949), 226f.; Charlotte Leitmaier, *Die Kirche und die Gottesurteile* (Wien, 1953), 17f.

[65] *Geschichte des Kirchenrechts* I, 382f.

Paul Hinschius[66] have shown? Somewhere there might well have been, presumably in the *False Decretals*, a place for Leo's oath. It could have been used by Benedict and Pseudo-Isidore at their own discretion in the same arbitrary fashion as they used other texts. Continuing the argument, one might further ask why the text of the "oath" was not once cited at the time of the deep involvement of the Frankish episcopate in the wars between the sons of Louis the Pious and their descendants, or in the controversies centering on Ebo of Reims, or during the famous trials of Rothad of Soissons and Wolfhad of Reims and Bourges? Why does the forceful and learned Hincmar of Reims use Benedict's forged capitulary 1.36, when developing the principle of canonical purgation in one of his treatises, and not Leo's alleged oath of purgation? Why does Hincmar of Laon (858–871) include in his collection of excerpts from the *False Decretals* the very document that became the source of Leo's forged oath of purgation, but not the oath itself? The Synod of Hohenaltheim in 916 knows of the historical fact of Leo's oath from Benedict. The Monk of St. Gall does not seem to quote from the oath of purgation, but from the genuine oath when he says that Leo swore: "Sic in die magni iudicii sim particeps evangelii, sicut immunis sum criminis falso mihi ab istis obiecti" (*PL* 98.1387B). A Roman continuation of Paul the Deacon's *History of the Lombards* repeats Leo's genuine oath and not the forged oath of purgation.[67]

The preceding argument *e silentio* may be looked upon—naturally with all the reservations customary in such a case—as additional proof that the extant "oath of purgation" of Leo is a forgery which originated during the second half of the ninth century.

While internal evidence reveals that the oath is a forgery, a paleographical investigation of its oldest MS transmission in M. p. theol. fol. 46, of the Würzburg Universitätsbibliothek, should provide additional evidence. Pertz, Hampe, and Werminghoff only state that the oath is transmitted in a MS of the ninth century. An investigation of the forged oath within the context of the MS will lead to a better dating. The following synopsis of the Würzburg MS renders the results of Bresslau's minute study of its contents.[68]

---

[66] Cf. Schafer Williams, "The Pseudo-Isidorian Problem Today," *Speculum* 29 (1954), 702–707, and the studies by Williams and Fuhrmann, cited above in n. 34.

[67] *MGH, Scriptores rerum Langobardicarum* (Hannover, 1888), 202.

[68] Harry Bresslau, *Die ältere Salzburger Annalistik* (Abh. Akad. Berlin 1923, No. 2), 10–17, 36, 40. See E. A. Lowe, *CLA* 9 (Oxford, 1959), No. 1413, and pp. 49, 68.

M. p. theol. fol. 46, Würzburg Universitätsbibliothek:

A.   fol. 1r Computing table.
B.   fol. 1v–21r Bede, *Cyclus paschalis magnus*, 532–1063:
    a. fol. 1v–16r, years 532–816;
    b. fol. 16v, years 817–835;
(Bx: One quire of 2 sheets [8 pages] missing between fol. 16v and 17r);
    c. fol. 17r, years 969–987;
    d. fol. 17r–21r, years 988–1063.
B².   *Annales Juvavenses maiores*, in the margin fol. 1v–21r, dealing with Frankish and Bavarian history, 725–825.
C.   fol. 21v–22r Computing table and notes.
D.   fol. 22v *Annales Juvavenses minores*, 742–905.
E.   fol. 23r–144v Bede, *Liber maior de temporibus*:
    a. Written by first hand: fol. 23r–58v;
                 second hand: fol. 59r–97v;
(Ex: One quaternio missing after fol. 89v, Bede cc. 52, 54, 58);
                 third hand: fol. 98r–144v.
F.   fol. 145v–148v Computing tables.
Ga. fol. 149r *Sacramentum quod Leo papa iuravit*; see Plate VI.
Gb. fol. 149v *De globo mundi et coniecture orbis versus*; see Plate VII.
H.   Additions by later hands on the following folia:
    a. fol. 6, verses: "Inventor rutili dux bone luminis," saec. xi;
    b. fol. 19, formula of magic spell: "Porcis in pane scribtum," saec. x/xi;
    c. fol. 20v and 21r, exorcism for difficult birth: "Maria genuit Christum," saec. x/xi;
    d. fol. 98r, prescription how to make a person intoxicated: "Ut alium inebriaris," saec. x/xi.
    e. f. 149r: perhaps a *Sphaera Pythagorae*.[69]

The script of the codex is by various hands of the ninth to the eleventh centuries. B is written by the same hand of the beginning of the ninth century that wrote Ea. In B² Bresslau and Baethgen distinguish ten or twelve distinct scribes of the first half of the ninth century. D is ascribed to the same period; it originated either during or after 816, or else was excerpted after 830. The three hands in E belong to the beginning of the ninth century, but there is no resemblance between the first and second hands, nor among the three hands and those of B². Several small pieces by different hands, saec. x–xi, are scattered throughout the MS. The oath (Ga) is not written

---

[69] Because of the wording in the circle, I am inclined to see in it a *Sphaera Pythagorae* as published by F. J. H. Jenkinson, *The Hisperica Famina* (Cambridge, 1908), after MSS of Corbie and Echternach.

by the scribe of F, though Bresslau believes that it was written by a hand contemporary with F.

Ga and Gb occupy respectively the recto and the verso of the last folium. The text of Gb is in a minuscule script. Its first three lines may be by the same hand that wrote the first portion of Ga (see further); the remaining lines are broader and wider than the script of the second division of the oath. Josef Hofmann, Staatsoberbibliothekar of the University Library of Würzburg,[70] believes that both hands belong to the same school and time. Bernhard Bischoff writes[71] that the script of Ga resembles the style of the Scriptorium of St. Amand as we know it from the handwriting of the scribe Lotharius (d. 829). The script of the oath, says Bischoff, is so pure as to suggest that it was written at St. Amand, if we assume that the Salzburg MS was sent there for the purpose of collation; or else Salzburg scribes trained at St. Amand wrote the oath.[72]

The comparison of Ga and Gb, Plates VI and VII, reveals similarities, and it is not impossible that both were written by the same scribe, but with the use of different pens and inks. Though no ruling marks are visible on fol. 149r and 149v, it cannot be altogether accidental that both texts are written in twenty-one lines (with the titles, twenty-two), whereas the text of Bede (E) is written throughout in twenty-five, and only occasionally in twenty-four, lines to the page. The twenty-one lines of Gb are written in a larger script and cover all of f. 149v. The scribe of the oath wrote the twenty-one lines of his forgery in small characters. After having written the forged document, the scribe seems to have added the title on top of 149r in smaller minuscules: "Sacramentum quod Leo Papa iuravit." The title of Gb is written in a larger majuscule: "DE GLOBO MUNDI ET CONIECTURE ORBIS UERSUS." Gb, Plate VII, consists of the first 21 of the 144 verses of the rhythmical poem "Versus de Asia et de universi mundi rota."[73]

[70] I am indebted to Dr. Hofmann for sending me photographs of fol. 149r and 149v, for permission to reproduce both pages, and for his letters of April 29 and May 24, 1955, with their valuable information.

[71] In a note to me dated May 3, 1955.

[72] Compare Plate VI, the facsimile of the oath (in *Traditio* 11 [1955], between pp. 58–59) with that of the handwriting of Lotharius reproduced by E. K. Rand, *The Earliest Book of Tours* (Cambridge, Mass., 1934), 69 and pl. 35.1, fol. 2r of the MS Paris B.N. lat. 2109, saec. ix. See n. 81 below.

[73] Ed. Karl Strecker, *MGH, Poetae* 4 (1923), 549ff., and by Dag Norberg, *La poésie latine rythmique du Haut Moyen Age* (Studia Latina Stockholmiensia 2; Stockholm, 1954), 82–86.

There is additional evidence to show that the scribe of Ga intended to imitate Gb. First, the unnecessary separation of three words in Ga, lines 5–6, 18–19, 19–20 (while there would have been sufficient space to complete these words in lines 5, 18, 19) was obviously resorted to in order to fill twenty-one lines. Second, Ga employs a mark of punctuation after the model of Gb. There are three different marks of punctuation in Gb to indicate the respective pauses after each of the three verses of a stanza. One of these marks, the *distinctio finitiva*, resembling a semicolon whose comma is not rounded but angular, is employed in verses 6, 9, 15, 21, for the long and final pause at the end of the stanza. The mark is used for the same purpose in the prose text of the oath in Ga, line 6 after *urbem*, and line 21 after *imponam*. The dot (not used in Gb) between *iussi* and *testis* (line 14) and between *consistimus* and *et* (16) stands in this context for a brief pause that is somewhat shorter than the pause denoted by our modern semicolon.

The forged oath is written in the ordinary Carolingian minuscule. The scribe used the customary ninth-century symbols for the abbreviation of letters, syllables, and words. See Plate VI:

-m. The final *m* ending a syllable is replaced by the suprascript stroke whether the word is at the end of the line (6, 10, 11) or not (1, 5).

-ter. The stroke above the letter *t* is employed for the final syllable *-ter* to shorten the word "propter" (4, 16).

-runt. *r*, with a raised horizontal stroke to the right is used for *-runt* in "insurrexerunt" (2).

per. *p* with a horizontal stroke through the shaft of the letter appears in "perpetravi" (14), in the final syllable of "super" (3), and in line 1 as a preposition.

et. The ligature of *e* with *t*, resembling the modern &, occurs twelve times (1, 2, 3, 6, 9, 10, 11, 13, 15, 16, and twice in line 20); in addition five times within words (11, and twice each in lines 14 and 19).

est. The abbreviation is *e* placed between two dots with a horizontal stroke above the letter (in 1 and 14).

neque. The suspension for *-que* is indicated by the double-dotted form, "neq:" (8).

Nomina sacra. The usual contractions are employed by the scribe: *deus*: "dō" 10; "ds" 14. *sancta*: "scā" 19; "scā" (probably "scae") 7. *ecclesia*: "eccla" (with stroke through the shaft of the *l*) 19, "ecclae" (the same, and with an open *a*) 7. *fratres*: "frs" 1. *karissimi*: "kmi" 1. *coepiscopis*: "coepis" 20.

The caudated *e* is once employed in *romane* (7). There are only two capitals in the text, the large initial *A* (1), and *C* in *Carolus* (5).

The letter *n* occurs at the beginning of the word in two forms: as *n* in *nemine* (8) and in a form resembling a small expanded capital *N* in *neque* (8). Accordingly, *nec* is spelled with *n* in 14, and with the capital-like form in line 13.

The character of the script differs as to size between lines 1–9 *voluntate*, and lines 9 *purifico*-21. The second portion, which shows a script broader and wider than that of the first, consists of three parts. Lines 9 *purifico*-17 *voluntate* were not written without interruption. The scribe paused after 13 *res* and 17 *voluntate* and then continued in the same lines with *quas* and *facio*, which are placed lower than the words preceding them. The writing of the oath is clearly carried out in four stages:

    a.   Lines 1 *Auditum*—9 *voluntate*;
    b1. Lines 9 *purifico*—13 *res*;
    b2. Lines 13 *quas*—17 *voluntate*;
    b3. Lines 17 *facio*—21 *imponam*.

The identical words at the end of part *a*, "spontanea mea voluntate," and of part *b2*, "mea spontanea voluntate," must be especially noted. The use of a different ink (see Josef Hofmann's discovery, mentioned below) in each of the two portions (*a* and *b*) as well as the varied size of the script of the oath are not recorded by Hampe and Werminghoff in their critical apparatus. But regardless of all these differences, the oath seems to be written by the same hand; identical words in both portions resemble one another rather closely. Compare, for instance, *ego* in lines 7 and 18, *spontanea* in 8 and 17, and the two forms of the letter *n* at the beginning of words in 8, 13, and 14. The letter *a* in 7 *ecclesiae*, and 8 *mea*, resembles two small, closely connected *c*'s whose upper parts do not touch each other. A similarly formed pre-Carolingian *a* reappears in the second portion only after the letter *r* in 10 *coram*, and in 14 *perpetravi, perpetrare*; in these three instances the *a* is closed at the top, as in 3 *gravia*, and not open, as in the two other occurrences in the first portion. For the same ligature of *r* with the closed form of *a* see also the title, "Sac*r*amentum quod Leo papa iu*r*auit." (Gb has this ligature in common with Ga in *paradisi* 6, *graminat* 8, *sincera* 10, and *pluras* 19; also the minuscule and majuscule forms of the initial *n*, for instance in *nomen* 3, *Neque* 9.)

The paleographical examination warrants the conclusion that the uniform elements in the various parts of the oath outweigh the noticeable differences. The problem now is how to date the oath, which, we remember, is transmitted on the last folium of a collective manuscript.

Earlier attempts at dating larger parts of the Würzburg MS do not stand up well under scrutiny, as, for example, when Jones[74] assumes that E originated in Salzburg between 792 and 807, because "in ch. 49 [of Bede, *De ratione temporum*] the *annus praesens* is 800, which is written over an erasure by the original scribe." Bresslau[75] had previously argued against the dating of E based on this change of the year 725 to 800, because Theodor Mommsen[76] showed an identical or similar change in two other MSS: in MS Leyden, Scaliger 28, saec. ix, from Flavigny, the *annus praesens* is not the original 725, but 800 in cc. 49, 54, 58, and 801 in cc. 52 and 58. The corresponding dates in the Paris codex, Nouv. acquis. 1615, saec. ix, from Fleury, characterized by Mommsen as "ein seltsamer Wechselbalg," are (confusingly enough) 825 for Bede in cc. 49, 52, 54, and 801, 798, and 830 corrected into 825, in c. 58. MS Paris is not derived from the Leyden codex, but both MSS are copied from the same source in which the pure text of Bede was corrected in such a fashion as to fit the year 800 or 801. Since the same correction appears in the Würzburg MS, this belongs to the same tradition as Paris and Leyden, and its *annus praesens* 800 cannot be used for the dating of the script. The Würzburg MS almost exactly "reproduces B in a somewhat more accurate form," that is, Berlin, Preussische Staatsbibliothek MS lat. 128 (formerly Phillipps 1831), from Verona (later transferred to Metz), saec. viii–ix, whose *annus praesens* is given for various parts of the codex as 793 (on fol. 117v) and 819 (fol. 134r).[77] Whether this Berlin MS and Vienna, Nationalbibliothek MS lat. 387,[78] written at Salzburg between 809 and 821 (probably in 818), and—according to Jones—also its presumable source, *Clm* 210 (from Salzburg, A.D. 818), offer similar conditions and changes as the MSS just listed, cannot be ascertained at present. It is certain that the *annus praesens* 800 of the Würzburg MS does not coincide with the writing of the main parts of the codex; its scribe in all likelihood may have found 800 also in the

[74] C. W. Jones, *Bedae Opera de temporibus* (Cambridge, Mass., 1943), 159, no. 103; 152, no. 42; 156, no. 74; 161.

[75] *Op. cit.* 12 n. 1.

[76] "Zur Weltchronik vom J. 741," *Neues Archiv* 22 (1897), 548–553.

[77] Valentin Rose, *Verzeichnis der lateinischen Handschriften* I (Berlin, 1893), 280ff.

[78] H. J. Hermann, *Die frühmittelalterlichen Handschriften des Abendlandes* (Leipzig, 1923), 145ff.

MS from which he copied, or after which he corrected, the text of Bede's treatise. It cannot be maintained any longer that the codex was written "about 800";[79] a later date would be more accurate. This means that the forged oath is hardly written "in an early ninth-century hand";[80] it must be assigned to a comparably later date.

Bernhard Bischoff informs me[81] that the first three hands of the MS are from the beginning of the ninth century. While the first hand shows an influence perhaps traceable to the scriptorium of St. Amand, the two other follow the older Salzburg tradition. E. A. Lowe, to whom I submitted a photograph of the oath (Plate VI), writes[82] that "fol. 149r may easily be of the second half of the ninth century—but probably not far past the middle of the century."

A comparison of the various hands of the MS was undertaken by Josef Hofmann.[83] Like Bresslau, Hofmann identifies the same hand (No. 1) in B and Ea, another hand (II) in Eb, a third in Ee, and a fourth in F. A and C are by the same scribe (VI), though it is not impossible that fol. 21v is actually by the first hand. D, written in a small script and somewhat careless manner with certain insular traces, is assigned to the first half of the ninth century. The hand (No. VII) that wrote D seems to appear among the several hands that wrote B^2. Hofmann finds that the hand (V in his analysis) that wrote the "oath of purgation," fol. 149r, might have written in larger characters some verses of fol. 149v; he then concludes that "the entire oath does not seem to have been written all at once." The facsimile does not clearly show that "the first eight lines[84] are written by a normal pen in a black-brown ink, the remaining lines by a more worn pen in a light-brown ink. The script of the last

---

[79] Josef Hofmann in Bischoff and Hofmann, *Libri Sancti Kyliani* (Würzburg, 1952), 109 n. 180.

[80] As is maintained by Adelson and Baker *op. cit.*, 39 n. 15.

[81] Cf. n. 71.—A product of the St. Amand and the Salzburg scriptoria is the *Codex Vindobonensis 795*, ed. Franz Unterkircher (Codices selecti phototypice impressi, 20; Graz, 1969).

[82] In a letter to me written on April 12, 1955; see above, n. 68.

[83] This paragraph renders the results of the investigations of Dr. Hofmann; see n. 70, above.

[84] In the first portion I include also the first word of line 9, *voluntate*, as previously pointed out in my analysis of the oath; the word is unmistakably written by the same hand that wrote the first eight lines. (L. W.)

section is slightly larger and broader, and might well be by another hand; but since its character does not vary much from that of the first section, the distinctions between these sections may be explained by assuming the use of different pens and inks by the same scribe. In any event, the hands of both sections are contemporary." Hofmann's date for the oath is "rather the middle (?) than the first half of the ninth century."

The paleographical datings of the oath, independently suggested by E. A. Lowe and Josef Hofmann, are in agreement, not only with each other, but also with the dating of the contents of the forgery derived from internal evidence—to wit, the middle of the ninth century.

The document hitherto known as the oath of purgation sworn by Leo III on December 23, 800, is a forgery of the middle of the ninth century. Its composition parallels a forged letter of Sixtus III in the *False Decretals*. The oath actually given by the pope is preserved in the *Liber Pontificalis*.[85]

---

[85] Heinrich Fichtenau, *MIOEG* 64 (1956), 380, expressed his agreement with my proof of the forgery; also Peter Munz, *The Origin of the Carolingian Empire* (Leicester, 1960), 42; Walter Ullmann, *The Growth of Papal Government in the Middle Ages* (3rd ed. London, 1970), 469f.; Robert Folz, *Le couronnement impérial de Charlemagne* (Trente journées qui on fait la France: 25 décembre 800; Paris, 1964), 164. Wilhelm Köhler (Harvard University, Fogg Museum), in a letter of July 3, 1956, wrote: " . . . Eine glänzende Untersuchung! . . . Ich halte—wie Hofmann und Lowe—die Datierung um 850 für richtig. . . . " Also Harald Zimmermann, "Papstabsetzungen des Mittelalters" (above n. 1), p. 34, expressed approval. P. E. Schramm, *Gesammelte Aufsätze zur Geschichte des Mittelalters* I (Stuttgart, 1968), 256 n. 118, reports on the contents of my Chapters XV and XVI (available to him in *Traditio* 11 [1955], and in *Harvard Theological Review* 49 [1956]) and states that I have shown that "[der]im *Liber Pontificalis* überlieferte Eid [Leos] als echt anzusehen ist, während die längere Fassung dagegen bereits die pseudo-isidor. Dekretalien voraussetzt." Robert Folz, *The Coronation of Charlemagne* (tr. by J. E. Anderson; London, 1974), 138, concludes that "L. Wallach has shown that the formula, as it has come down to us, is apocryphal, and we are reduced to the very brief wording in the *Liber Pontificalis*." Bernhard Bischoff, in a letter of October 22, 1956, addressed to me, wrote: " . . . Dass der ausführliche 'Eid' gefälscht ist, und zwar nach dem paläographischen Befund offenbar in der Salzburg—St. Amander Küche, haben Sie glänzend bewiesen." Eugen Ewig's report in *Handbuch der Kirchengeschichte* III, 1, ed. Hubert Jedin (Freiburg i. Br., 1966), 98, is incomplete. He mentions Loewe's opinion which is not substantiated by any historical evidence, and fails to record the views of Fichtenau (1956), Munz (1960), Zimmermann (1961), and Folz (1964), who, by 1966, had agreed with my proof of the forged oath of Leo III.

CHAPTER XVI

The Roman Synod of December 800 and the Alleged Trial of Leo III*

A Roman Synod convoked by Charlemagne met on December 1, 800, for the purpose of investigating the accusations leveled against Pope Leo III. In the presence of the pope, the Frankish king presided over an assembly composed of ecclesiastics and Frankish and Roman nobles, including members of the Frankish episcopate— Arno of Salzburg, Theodulph of Orléans, Riculf of Mayence, Aaron of Angorra, the Saxons Witto and Fredugis, Alcuin's confidants—and other persons of consequence. The eldest son of Charlemagne, Charles, who together with his sisters had accompanied his father to Rome, was another participant.[1]

The accounts contained in ecclesiastical and Frankish historical sources of the proceedings of the Roman Synod of December 800,[2] whose acts are not preserved, seem to be somewhat contradictory and confusing. Historians have repeatedly discussed and argued over the significance of these accounts. The problem is whether to accept the description of the events that took place at St. Peter's in the version of the *Liber Pontificalis* (*LP*), the *Annales regni Francorum* (*ArF*), the *Annales Laureshamenses* (*AnL*), or in some combination of these sources.

---

* This chapter contains substantive additions made to the paper originally published under the same title in the *Harvard Theological Review* 49 (1956), 123–142; see below, n. 6.

[1] Cf. Sigurd Abel and Bernhard Simson, *Jahrbücher des fränkischen Reiches unter Karl dem Grossen* II (Leipzig, 1883), 224–229.

[2] See the collections of sources by Heinrich Dannenbauer, *Die Quellen zur Geschichte der Kaiserkrönung Karls des Grossen* (Lietzmann's Kleine Texte No. 161; Berlin, 1931); Kurt Reindel, *Die Kaiserkrönung Karls des Grossen* (Historische Texte; Mittelalter, 4; Göttingen, 1970).

Louis Halphen[3] bases his reconstruction of the happenings on the *LP* and the *ArF*, while rejecting the report of the *AnL*, written under the influence of the Frankish court, as being partial to a one-sided Frankish interpretation. A similar opinion of the *AnL* is shared by Erich Caspar,[4] while F. L. Ganshof[5] rejects such an assessment of the historical value of the *AnL*. For even if the *AnL* should not be contemporary with the events of the year 800, having been written perhaps in 803, the *LP* and the *ArF* are chronologically—so Ganshof argues—even farther removed from these events than is the *AnL*. On these and other grounds Heinrich Fichtenau[6] now attempts the rehabilitation of the *AnL* as a primary source for the important happenings of the year 800. He shows that the author of the *AnL*—probably Richbod of Trèves and Lorsch—occasionally wrote in the style of the official Frankish court charter, the *placitum*; for the year 802, Richbod used the extant Frankish *Capitulare missorum generale* of 802, a fact known for a long time. Fichtenau believes that the author of the *AnL* ad a. 800–801 fashioned the text of the annals not only on the basis of his own familiarity with the formulaic phraseology of the Frankish *placitum*, but also on the basis of "official protocols" that were accessible to him for his report on the Roman Synod of December 800 and on the negotiations leading to the coronation of Charlemagne on December 25. This assumption is—according to its own originator—a "bold thesis which will never be confirmed in such a manner that the scholar who clings to previously conceived interpretations will not reject it." "But," he adds, "anyone who approaches these problems with a somewhat open mind will not deny the probability of such a thesis."

Several arguments present themselves for the existence of "official protocols" used by the author of the *AnL*. Had there actually

[3] *Etudes critiques sur l'histoire de Charlemagne* (Paris, 1921), 236–238.

[4] "Das Papsttum unter fränkischer Herrschaft," *Zeitschrift für Kirchengeschichte* 54 (1935), 259. See reprint above in Chapter I n. 8.

[5] *The Imperial Coronation of Charlemagne: Theories and Facts* (Glasgow University Publications 79; 1949), 22–23.

[6] "Karl der Grosse und das Kaisertum," *MIÖG* 61 (1953), 287–327. The present writer disagreed with Fichtenau's thesis in the first version of this chapter published in the *Harvard Theological Review* 49 (1956), 124f. Since then he has found evidence for Fichtenau's thesis, as reported by the latter in *MIOEG* 65 (1957), 218, and again in Fichtenau's republication of *Karl der Grosse und das Kaisertum: Mit einer Einleitung zum Nachdruck* (Wissenschaftliche Buchgemeinschaft; Darmstadt, 1971), p. x.

been such documents, these "protocols" and the *AnL* ought to show traces reminiscent of the style of the Acts of the Synod that was in session from December 1 to 23, if not until December 25, the day of Charlemagne's recognition as imperator. Traces of the phraseology of synodal acts are indeed noticeable in the *AnL* ad a. 800 and 801, whose author describes events connected with these synodal procedures in the formulaic language of the Carolingian *placitum* and of the *acta* and protocols of synodal assemblies. Fichtenau's vindication of the *AnL* as a primary historical source for the reconstruction of the events leading to the "coronation" of Charlemagne can well stand the test of a critical analysis, and the negative estimate of Louis Halphen, Heinrich Dannenbauer, and other historians of the *AnL* is indeed refuted by Fichtenau's convincing thesis.

One may conclude from Fichtenau's proof of the occurrence of elements of the Frankish *placitum* in the report of the *AnL* ad a. 800–801 that the presence of Charlemagne, the highest Frankish judge, was to the author of the annals proof of the judicial nature of the synodal proceedings. While it is true, as Hefele and Leclercq state,[7] that these Acts are not extant, it can be shown that the original Acts were used by the individual authors of the *AnL* and of the *Vita Leonis* of the *Liber Pontificalis*, whose report on the Roman Synod of December 800 is analyzed below, and divided into the sections I–XII. These twelve sections are constantly referred to in the following discussion, which supports Fichtenau's new thesis.

Compare the following parallels in the *AnL* and in the *LP*, which are evidently based on the protocols of the Roman Synod of December 800, whose meeting is described in both documents as follows:

AnL ad a. 800:

Et ibi (*scil.* at Rome) fecit (*scil.* Carolus) conventum maximum episcoporum seu abbatum cum presbyteris, diaconibus et comitibus seu reliquo christiano populo, . . . (see Reindel, no. 8, p. 27);

LP Vita Leonis, I:

. . . fecit (*scil.* Carolus) in eadem aecclesia (*scil.* in basilica beati Petri) congregare archiepiscopos seu episcopos, abbates et omni nobilitate Francorum atque synclitu Romanorum.

---

[7] Cf. Carl Josef von Hefele, *Conciliengeschichte* 3 (2nd ed. Freiburg i. Br., 1877), 739; Hefele and H. Leclercq, *Histoire des Conciles d'après les documents originaux*, III, part 2 (Paris, 1910), 1113–1116, speak of the "Roman Synod of the year 800."

After Leo III had made his public statement of innocence (see below, *LP* X), we read that papal *laudes* were intoned in his honor, as reported in *AnL* and *LP*:

AnL ad a. 800 (Reindel, p. 27):

Et ipso sacramento expleto, incipiebant illi sancti episcopi cum universo clero seu ipso principe Carlo cum devoto christiano populo ymnum *Te Deum laudamus, te Dominum confitemur*; quo perexpleto et ipse rex et universus populus fidelis cum eo *dabant laudem* Deo, ... ;

LP Vita Leonis, XI–XII:

Et hoc peractum, omnes archiepiscopi, episcopi et abbates et cunctus clerus, letania facta, *laudes dederunt* Deo ...

The intonation of the *Te Deum* by the synodal assembly after the public rehabilitation of Leo, as reported in the *AnL*, is not mentioned in the *LP*. The author of the latter's *Vita Leonis*, who must have been well acquainted with liturgical customs at Rome, may have seen a liturgical irregularity in the singing of the hymn, and for this reason did not mention the *Te Deum*. Amalarius of Metz, when questioning Romans about the rite concerning the singing of the hymn, reports as follows:[8] "Interrogavi si canerent per dominicas noctes *Te Deum laudamus*, responsum est: tantum in natalitiis pontificum *Te Deum laudamus* canimus." It may well be that the spontaneous enthusiasm of the synodal assembly intended to celebrate the rehabilitation of Leo as some kind of a *natale pontificis*, as reported in the *AnL*, but that at a later time the author of the *Vita Leonis* in the *LP* failed to mention the *lapsus liturgicus* committed on the spur of the moment.

The *AnL* contains additional important information concerning Leo III which is certainly based on the lost original synodal protocols. Leo was not tried by the judgment of the synod (non tamen per eorum iudicium), but he cleansed himself of the charges leveled against him of his own free will by his statement of innocence. Compare the *AnL* ad a. 800 (Reindel, p. 27): " ... ut si eius voluntas fuisset et ipse petisset, non tamen per eorum iudicium sed spontanea voluntate se purificare debuisset," and the sections IV and

---

[8] Amalarius, *Liber de ordine antiphonarii*, prol. 7, ed. I. M. Hanssens (Studi e Testi 140; Rome, 1950), 14. Heinrich Fichtenau, in a letter of October 4, 1956, kindly called my attention to Amalarius; see also n. 6, above. The specific historical incident of the *Te Deum* is not mentioned, as far as I can see, by Ernst H. Kantorowicz, *Laudes Regiae* (Berkeley and Los Angeles, 1946), Chapter IV.

V in the *LP* (see below), which seem to be based on the same original statement in the lost synodal *Gesta*, which are definitely used in the *Vita Leonis* of the *Liber Pontificalis*, as the subsequent analysis will show.

The *Vita* of Leo III, the longest biography in the *Liber Pontificalis*, cannot have originated before the death of Leo in 816.[9] This means that the author had to rely on written material and documents on which to base his narration. The numerous gifts and buildings dedicated, sponsored, or built by Leo, and listed by his biographer, bear out this conclusion. Huelsen[10] already observed the chronological order of many notices in the *Vita* referring to the activities of Leo. That the author of the *Vita* used the *placitum* of the Frankish "Königsgericht," which in December 799 investigated the accusations of Leo's enemies at Rome, has been shown in Chapter XV at note 5. The narrative in the *LP* of this Frankish court action of Carolingian *missi* is followed by a report of the Roman Synod of December 800, which is based, as we hope next to prove, on the original Acts of this synod. We here print this section, and—in order to facilitate reference—we add in the left margin the Roman numerals I–XII representing the individual parts.

Vita Leonis III, in *Liber Pontificalis* II, ed. Louis Duchesne (Paris, 1892), 7:

I   Qui post modicum tempus ipse *magnus rex*, dum in basilica beati Petri apostoli coniunxisset et cum magno honore susceptus fuisset, *fecit* in eadem aecclesia *congregare archiepiscopos seu episcopos, abbates et omni nobilitate Francorum atque synclitu Romanorum.*

IIa   Et *sedentes pariter* tam *magnus rex* quam *beatissimus pontifex*, fecerunt *resedere et sanctissimos archiepiscopos seu episcopos et abbates,*

IIb   *stantes reliquos sacerdotes seu optimates Francorum et Romanorum,*

III   ut crimina quae adversus almum pontificem dicta fuerant delimarent.

[9] Léon Levillain, "Le couronnement impérial de Charlemagne," *Revue d'histoire de l'Eglise de France* 18 (1932), 15. Wattenbach-Levison, *Deutschlands Geschichtsquellen im Mittelalter* IV (Weimar, 1963), 457, is sufficiently contradicted by the present investigation as well as by the agreements with it listed in Chapter XV n. 85. See also P. E. Schramm, *Gesammelte Aufsätze zur Geschichte des Mittelalters* I: *Kaiser, Könige und Päpste* (Stuttgart, 1968), 256 n. 118.
[10] Christian Huelsen, "Osservazioni sulla biografica di Leone III nel Liber pontificalis," *Rendiconti della pont. accad. rom. di arch.* I (1923), 107–119.

IV   Qui *universi* archiepiscopi seu *episcopi* et abbates unianimiter audientes *dixerunt*:

V   "Nos sedem apostolicam, *quae est capud omnium Dei ecclesiarum,* judicare non audemus. Nam ab ipsa nos omnes et vicario suo iudicamur; ipsa autem a nemine iudicatur, quemadmodum et antiquitus mos fuit. Sed sicut ipse summus pontifex censuerit, canonice obediemus."

VI   Venerabilis vero praesul inquit:
"Praedecessorum meorum pontificum vestigia sequor et de talibus falsis criminationibus quae super me nequiter exarserunt, me purificare paratus sum."

VII   Alia vero die, in eadem ecclesia beati Petri apostoli,

VIII   *omnes* generaliter *archiepiscopi* seu *episcopi* et *abbates et omnes Franci* qui in servitio eidem *magni regis* fuerunt, *et cuncti Romani* in eadem ecclesia beati Petri apostoli,

IX   in eorum praesentia amplectens prelatus venerabilis pontifex sancta Christi quattuor evvangelia coram omnibus ascendit in ambonem et sub iusiurando clara voce dixit:

X   "*Quia de* istis criminibus falsis, quibus super me imposuerunt Romani qui inique me persecuti sunt, *scientiam non habeo*, nec talia egisse me cognosco."

XI   Et hoc peractum, *omnes archiescopi, episcopi* et *abbates* et *cunctus clerus,*

XII   letania facta, laudes dederunt Deo atque Dei genetricis semperque virginis Mariae dominae nostrae et beato Petro apostolorum principi omniumque sanctorum Dei.

This text consists of a general Introduction (I), expressly stating that the *Concilium Romanum* (CR) of December 800 met upon the request of Charlemagne; it mentions the meeting place, the ecclesiastical participants in their hierarchical order, and the lay groups in attendance. Next follows the order of seating observed by the assembly during the sessions of the synod (II): after king and pope are seated *pariter*,[11] archbishops, bishops, and abbots (or presbyters) occupy their seats (IIa), while the lower hierarchy (deacons, *etc.*) and the laymen present stand during the synodal meetings and debates. The accusations leveled against Leo III by

[11] Karl Heldmann, *Das Kaisertum Karls des Grossen* (see Introduction to Part Four, n. 8), p. 101 n. 4, rejects the report of the *LP* IIa, according to which the pope was seated "pariter mit dem König," without realizing that pariter belongs to the style of the diplomatics of synodal procedures; it occurs also in the "ordo celebrandi concilii" referred to in the following n. 12.

his enemies are on the agenda of the synod (III). Parts IV–X contain three verbatim excerpts from the debates that ensued in the course of an unknown number of *actiones*. The synod closed (XI–XII) with litanies.

Offhand this report conforms to the basic provisions of the *ordo celebrandi concilii* set forth, for example, in c. 4 of the Acts of the Council of Toledo, 633.[12] Part II especially conforms to the rule that the upper hierarchy is seated during the discussions of the synod, while the lower ranks of the participants, from the deacons down to mere laymen in attendance, occupy only standing room. Compare the following regulations of the *ordo*:

. . . convenientes omnes *episcopi pariter* introeant et *resideant* . . . vocantur deinde *presbiteri* . . . post hoc ingrediantur *diaconi* . . . et *corona facta de sedibus episcoporum*, presbiteri a tergo eorum resideant. *Diacones* in conspectu episcoporum *stent*. Deinde ingrediantur *laici* qui electioni concilii interesse meruerunt. Ingrediantur quoque et *notarii*. . . .

The actual use made of such an *ordo* in the case of some Frankish synods can be shown. Paulinus of Aquileia[13] writes of the opening of the Synod of Frankfurt, 794, convoked by Charlemagne: "Quadam die *residentibus* cunctis in aula sacri palatii, *adsistentibus in modum coronae* . . . *diaconibus cunctoque clero*, sub praesentia praedicti principis" (scil. Charlemagne). Another application of the same provisions is preserved in Paulinus' report of the Synod of Friuli, 796–797: "Igitur *resedentibus cunctis ex more* in sedilibus praeparatis, *adsistente* vero circumquaque non modica fratrum consentanea turba in ecclesia. . . ."

The traces of the original Acts of the CR of December 800 preserved in the report of the *LP* can also be recognized by the

---

[12] Mansi X.617f. Cf. Hans Barion, *Das fränkisch-deutsche Synodalrecht des Frühmittelalters* (Kanonistische Studien und Texte, ed. A. M. Koeniger; Bonn, Köln, 1931), 55ff., on the synodal ordines, 76ff., on the seating order of the participants, 173ff., on the authority of synodal decisions, 253ff., on the Carolingian national synods. Cf. Rudolf von Heckel, "Der Ursprung des päpstlichen Registerwesens," *Archiv für Urkundenforschung* 1 (1908), especially pp. 398, 402, 404, on early synodal acts modeled on Roman "Gerichtsakten," and on the imitations of the *Gesta* of the Roman Senate in other synodal acts. Peter Classen, "Kaiserreskript und Königsurkunde," *Archiv für Diplomatik* 1 (1955), 86, questions this basic dependence, but the evidence is convincing to me.

[13] *MGH, Conc.* 2.1 (Aevi Karolini 1.1; Hannover, 1904), 131.3 (subsequently referred to as *Conc.* 1.1).

comparison of our text with the extant acts of Roman synods (and others), especially the Roman Synods of 769 and 798. Compare, for instance, the structure of our text with the beginnings of the *prima actio* of the CR of 769 (*Conc.* 1.1.80f.):

" . . . praesidente ter beatissimo et coangelico Stephano summo pontifice ... in venerabili basilica salvatoris ... (*considentibus*) etiam cum eo ... episcopis, id est ... " (An enumeration of archbishops, bishops, and presbyters follows. The last-mentioned presbyter is called Theodosius, and then we read, p. 81.16): "*adstante* etiam Anastasio archidiacono et cunctis religiosis Dei famulis ... atque proceribus ecclesiae et *cuncto clero*, optimatibus etiam miliciae seu cuncti exercitus et honestorum civium et cuncte generalitatis populo. . . . "

Parts I and II of our text are clearly parallel to this text, except that Charlemagne presided over the Synod of 800, while that of 769 was called together under the presidency of Pope Stephen IV (III).

The identical formula observed in the Acts of 769 and 800 is found also in the *Gesta* of Roman Synods held in the years 495, 531, 595, 600, and 745.[14] The scheme of the *exordium* in these synodal *Acta* is comprised of the names of the Roman consuls and/or emperors in office, the date and place of the meeting, the pope present and presiding (*residente* or *praesidente*), the bishops and presbyters in attendance (*consedentibus* or *residentibus*), the mention of the deacons (*adstantibus diaconibus*), and other clerics (*cuncto clero*). The same structure of the *exordium* is clearly preserved in the report of the *LP* which is derived from the original Acts of the Synod of December 800.

Beatissimus as papal attribute (in IIa) is traceable to the original Acts of the Synod of 800, which—like the Acts of the CR of 769— designated the pontiff with this *epitheton* in conformity with a custom usually observed in all synodal acts. See, for instance, the *prima actio* of the CR of 798, presided over by Leo III himself (*Conc.* 1.1.203.15): "Leo, sanctissimus ac ter *beatissimus* ... universalis papa." In this connection note that Charlemagne, the *magnus rex* (see I, IIa, VIII), is as such also referred to by Leo III in the same Acts of 798 (p. 203.21.33.37; 204.10). But the *magnus rex* appears

[14] Cf. von Heckel (above n. 12), p. 404, also the Acts of the Roman Synod of 826, *MGH, Capitularia* 1.1 (Hannover, 1883), No. 180 pp. 370f.

already in the acrostic of the dedicatory poem in the codex of the *Dionysio-Hadriana* presented by Hadrian I to Charlemagne in 774 (Duchesne, *LP* I.516).

The repetitious enumeration of the participants in Parts I, II, IV, VIII, XI by no means constitutes a special rhetorical emphasis; it is indicative of the style of synodal acts. Compare Part IV, "Qui *universi . . . episcopi . . . dixerunt*," with the CR of 769 (*Conc.* 1.1.83.11), "*Universi* venerabiles *episcopi dixerunt*"; also *Concilium Matisconense* of 585,[15] for instance, "*Universi episcopi dixerunt*." The phrase belongs to the technical expressions of synodal acts; see the many examples[16] in the Latin Acts of the Ecumenical Councils of Ephesus and Chalcedon.

The characterization of the apostolic see in V, "quae est *capud omnium Dei ecclesiarum*," is paralleled in the *prima actio* of the CR of 769 (*Conc.* 1.1.82.28), where the participants in the sessions of the synod are addressed as "membra (huius) sacrosanctae Romanae ecclesiae, que *capud* et principatum *omnium Dei ecclesiarum* existit." The phrase is further found in the *tertia actio* of the CR of 798 (*Conc.* 1.1.204–223), at which Leo III presided: "Venerantes procul dubio sanctae catholicae et apostolicae ecclesiae, quae est *caput ecclesiarum Dei*." The phrase frequently occurs in the acts of ecumenical councils; see *Gesta Chalcedone* (*ACO* II.iii.1 [1935] 40.5): "Beatissimi atque apostolici viri papae urbis Romae, quae est *caput omnium ecclesiarum*."

A significant parallel between the Acts of 800 and those of the CR of 769 occurs in Part X, which offers the genuine oath of innocence of Leo III by which he vindicated himself before the synod.[17] The formula used in the oath, "quia de . . . scientiam non habeo," also occurs in the statement of Pope Stephen IV (III) concerning his lack of knowledge of certain facts investigated during the *prima actio* of the CR of 769.

Our division of the *LP* text above into twelve parts helps us to recognize the formal structure of the original Acts of the CR of December 800 as preserved in the report of the *LP*. The vestiges that are typical of synodal acts are printed in italics, and those parts that may well constitute verbatim excerpts from the *actiones* of the synod are set off by indentation. In order to recognize the style of

---

[15] *MGH, Concilia Aevi Merovingici*, ed. F. Maassen (Hannover, 1893), 164.25.

[16] See Eduard Schwartz, *ACO* I.ii, II.ii.1–2, III.iii.1–3.

[17] See above Chapter XV, pp. 301–302.

the *Gesta* preserved in our text, we may compare it with some of the Latin versions of the *Gesta* of the Ecumenical Councils of Ephesus and Chalcedon,[18] and also with the Acts of the Roman Synods dealing with Symmachus from 499 to 502 during the reign of Theodoric the Great.

Since the report of the *LP* of the Roman Synod of December 800 is based on the lost acts of this assembly, it may be looked upon as an addition to Albert Werminghoff's *Concilia Aevi Karolini* 1.1 (1904) where it should be placed with No. 26, the forged oath of purgation, ascribed to Leo III.

The Synod of December 800, though held at Rome, was not a Roman synod in the usual meaning of the word because it had not been convoked by the incumbent pope; it met upon the command of Charlemagne, the head of the Frankish national church. Nor did the pope preside; the Frankish king held the chair. The basic Frankish character of the meeting is clearly noticeable in the report of the *LP*: the mention of the "magnus rex" seems to have preceded that of the "beatissimus pontifex" in the synodal Acts (see above); in like fashion the *Franci* are mentioned (in I, IIb, VIII) before the Roman nobility. Thus the synod was actually in origin and guidance a Frankish synod,[19] though the majority of the active participants doubtless was of non-Frankish provenience. We know that the synod was in session from December 1 to 23 or 25, but the number of *actiones* that were required to transact its order of business is unknown. The original synodal Acts with the signatures of the participants in the sessions would have been of the most decisive importance for the solution of several vexing questions. As it is, we must be satisfied with the use made of them in the report of the *LP*, which deserves equal consideration with the *Annales Laureshamenses* and the official *Annales regni Francorum* regarding the reconstruction of the historical events preceding the "coronation" of Charlemagne. Though the *Vita leonis* of the *LP* as a whole was not written before

---

[18] Cf. *ACO* I.iii.52,17ff., 99,1ff., 119f., etc.; II.ii.2.17,32ff., II.iii.1.27ff., 196ff.; on the Symmachian councils see ed. Theodor Mommsen, *MGH Auct. Ant.* XIII (Berlin, 1894), 399–455. The "Diplomatics" of synodal acts is still to be written. Von Heckel and Barion (see above, n. 12) have made a start.

[19] Erich Caspar, *Zeitschrift für Kirchengeschichte* 54 (1935), 226f., recognized this fact. The censures of Caspar's statement by Adelson-Baker, "The Oath of Purgation of Pope Leo III," *Traditio* 8 (1952), 61f., are disproved by our investigation, also their denial of the synod's judicial significance (pp. 62, 67).

816, the close resemblance of our report to the original Acts of the Synod of December 800 justifies the conclusion that the information which the report contains stands as close to the events at Rome as does the report of the *AnL*, written by Richbod of Trèves and Lorsch, and for this reason offers an official Roman picture in a fashion similar to the Frankish understanding of the events in the *Annales regni Francorum*. To sum up, Louis Halphen's original estimate of the primary position of the report of the *LP* for the reconstruction of events preceding the coronation is again confirmed by our findings, and Döllinger's condemnation[20] of the partiality of the *LP* must be somewhat restricted as far as concerns our report.

The report in the *LP* obviously contains a very small fragment of the original Acts of the synod that was in session for more than three weeks. Taking into consideration the controversial and complex main issue of its agenda, we may conclude that the original Acts together with the supporting documents, which were read before the assembly in the course of the debates, must have formed a few sizable volumes consisting of numerous documents. One of these documents read by a notary into the record during one of the earlier sessions of the proceedings undoubtedly was the Frankish *placitum* describing the investigation of the charges of Leo's accusers that had been conducted by Frankish *missi* in December 799 at Rome.[21] In addition the lost Acts must have contained depositions of the charges made against Leo, submitted by the attackers and the attacked; also statements by witnesses who testified for Leo; and in all probability also some of the letters by which Charlemagne summoned members of his episcopate to participate in the meeting. In order to gain some idea of the varied nature of this collection of documents included in the original Acts of the synod, one has only to look, for instance, at the scanty remnants of the lost *Acts* of the Synod of Frankfurt of June 794 (*Conc.* 1.1.110–171), consisting of a few supporting documents, that is, the letters of the accused Spanish party, of the incumbent pope, and of Charlemagne, the synodal report of the Frankish episcopate written by Alcuin,[22] the *Synodica* composed by Paulinus of Aquileia for the Italian episcopate, and the official Frankish capitulary, which summarizes the decisions

[20] Ignaz von Döllinger, "Das Kaisertum Karls des Grossen," *Münchner Historisches Jahrbuch* (1865), 332f.
[21] See above, pp. 299–301.
[22] Wallach, *Alcuin and Charlemagne*, 158–165.

of a Frankish Diet simultaneously held with the synodal meeting. The original protocols of the various synodal sessions are lost.

What we have thus far found warrants basing the reconstruction of the events preceding Charlemagne's coronation primarily on the report in the *LP*. In this process of reconstruction, the Frankish annals should serve only as secondary and supplementary sources, provided that their information fits—*mutatis mutandis*—into the procedural course of an accusatory trial conducted before a synodal meeting. That this may have been the *modus procedendi* of the Synod of December 800 may be assumed, since Eduard Schwartz[23] and Artur Steinwenter[24] have shown for earlier synods the reception by the church of the procedures of the Roman accusatory trial. If this recognition is applied to the Synod of 800, we must assume that it conducted at first a one-sided court action solely placed on the plaintiffs, who presented their accusations against Leo. These charges were the main topic of the synod which the pope attended, but not as a person formally on trial. We remember that at the opening he was seated with the Frankish king who officially presided over the meeting, as though it were a meeting of the national Frankish church. In accordance with Roman law, the proof of the accusations leveled against the pope rested with the plaintiffs.[25] The synod which was to investigate and to judge these charges denies its own competence in the case and declares unanimously (*LP*, above, section V):

"We do not dare to judge the Apostolic See which is the head of all the churches of God. For all of us are judged by it [*scil*. the Apostolic See] and its vicar; it [*scil*. the Apostolic See] however is judged by nobody as it is the custom from ancient times. But as the highest pontiff will have decided [in the case of the accusations leveled against himself] we shall obey canonically."

[23] *Der Prozess des Eutyches*, SB. Bayer. Akad. des Wiss. (1929), Heft 5, p. 66; R. Draguet, "La christologie d'Eutyches d'après les Actes du Synode de Flavien," *Byzantion* 6 (1931), 441, questions Schwartz's hypothesis concerning Florentius' opposition against Eutyches. Cf. further Plöchl, below n. 40, pp. 228f.
[24] "Der antike kirchliche Rechtsgang und seine Quellen," *ZSRG*, Kan. Abt. 23 (1934), 114.
[25] Cf. Steinwenter, *ibid*., p. 73; Rhaban Haacke in *Das Konzil von Chalkedon 2* (Würzburg, 1953), 96–98. Cf. *Digest* 22.3.2 "ei incumbit probatio qui dicit non qui negat." On Roman law in Frankish documents see F. L. Ganshof in *Ius Romanum Medii Aevi*, Pars I, 2 b cc alpha (Milano, 1969), 1–43, and *ibid*., beta, pp. 1–33.

The synodal assembly bases its refusal to sit in judgment over the pope on the principle of the jurisdictional immunity of the pontiff, "prima sedes a nemine iudicatur"[26]; simultaneously it suggests that Leo should be his own judge. The adoption of the older doctrine of the judicial exemption of the pope has been stressed in many treatments of the precoronation events. But scant attention has been paid to the second principle propounded, namely, that the pope himself should judge his own case (Sed sicut ipse summus pontifex censuerit, canonice obediemus).[27] Both principles applied by the synod are adaptations of doctrines developed by the apologetic literature that originated as an aftermath of the synodal trial of Pope Symmachus (498–514) in his conflict with the antipope Laurentius (498–ca. 505).[28] By inventing trials of popes preceding Symmachus, his age exercised pseudo-historical criticism on the outcome of the trial of Symmachus. These apocrypha are connected with the names of the popes Sylvester, Marcellinus, Liberius, and Sixtus III. Thus we read the first principle in the *Constitutum Silvestri*, c. 3 (*PL* 8.833D):[29]

Et non damnabitur praesul nisi septuaginta duobus, neque praesul summus a quoquam iudicabitur, quoniam his scriptum est: Non est discipulus super magistrum [Matt. 10.24]; and (*PL* 8.840D): Nemo enim judicabit primam sedem, quoniam omnes sedes a prima sede iustitiam desiderant temperari. Neque ab Augusto, neque ab omni clero, neque a regibus, neque a populo iudex judicabitur. . . . Et fixit canonem hunc Silvester episcopus in urbe Roma . . . .

In the Acts of the pseudo-Synod of Sinuessa (Mansi I.1257), which tried Pope Marcellinus (296–304), we read:

[26] Cf. A. Koeniger, "Prima sedes a nemine iudicatur," in *Festgabe für Albert Ehrhard* (Bonn, Leipzig, 1922), 273–300.

[27] The assumptions of Adelson and Baker, *Tradito* 8 (1952), 68, that "in the LP Leo is cited as making the suggestion" to swear "voluntarily" an oath, misinterpret this passage; nor did Leo undertake the task on his own as is stated on p. 75. The pope clearly followed a suggestion made by the synod. See F. L. Ganshof, *Histoire du Moyen Age* 1 (Paris, 1928), 455.

[28] See on this literature Erich Caspar, *Geschichte des Papsttums* 2 (Tübingen, 1933), 107–110.

[29] Walter Ullmann, "Cardinal Humbert and the Ecclesia Romana," *Studi Gregoriani* 4 (1952), 116f., on the *Constitutum Silvestri*. See also H. Mordek, "Dionysio-Hadriana und Vetus Gallica–historisch geordnetes und systematisches Kirchenrecht am Hofe Karls des Grossen," *ZSRG* 86, Kan. Abt. 55 (1969), 39–63.

Nemo enim unquam judicavit pontificem, nec praesul sacerdotem suum, quoniam prima sedes non iudicabitur a quoquam.

The second principle of the Synod of 800, namely, that the pope should be his own judge, also appears in the Synod of Sinuessa (Mansi I.1255A). Marcellinus is told: "Tuo ore judica causam tuam et non nostro judicio solve conditionem."

In the *Gesta purgationis* of Sixtus III (432–440) Emperor Valentinian III suggests that the pope himself ought to judge his own case (Mansi V.1063): "et dedit in arbitrio . . . iudicare iudicium suum."

The acceptance by the synod of these two basic principles is hardly accidental. It reveals the great influence wielded by the Saxon Alcuin on the course of the Roman events preceding the coronation. Before Charlemagne came to Rome on November 24, 800, he had visited Alcuin at Tours.[30] Shortly afterward Alcuin thanked the king for an invitation to come to Rome; the infirmities of old age prevented him from accepting.[31] Alcuin's ideas of Leo III and the Roman question were, however, well presented at the synod[32] by his friends Arno of Salzburg, Theodulph of Orléans, Riculf of Mayence, and the Saxons Witto and Fredugis. It might well be that the work of these men whom Ganshof calls "imperialist clerics" resulted in the acceptance by the synod of the principle of the judicial immunity of the pope. For this was the formula recommended by Alcuin for the solution of the embarrassing Roman problem. In the well-known letter 179 of August 799, he wrote to Arno of Salzburg:

Memini me legisse quondam, si rite recordor, *in canonibus beati Silvestri*, non minus septuaginta duobus pontificem accusandum esse et iudicio presentari; et ut illorum talis vita esset, ut potuissent contra talem auctoritatem stare. Insuper *et in aliis* legebam *canonibus* apostolicam sedem iudiciariam esse, non iudicandam.

Alcuin here refers to the same forged canonical sources that about sixteen months later formed the basis of the synodal refusal to judge Leo: the *Constitutum Silvestri* and the Synod of Sinuessa. Alcuin's leadership of the Frankish episcopate at the Synod of December 800

[30] Cf. Abel and Simson (above, n. 1), 211 n. 4.
[31] See Alcuin's *Epistle* 177.
[32] So also A. Kleinclausz, *Alcuin* (Paris, 1948), 258.

becomes evident in the influence of his friends who participated in the synodal decisions. This expression of Alcuin's personal influence on the events preceding the coronation is paralleled by the important role played by Alcuin in 794 at the Synod of Frankfurt— as the author[33] of the Frankish *Synodica* against the heresy of adoptionism, and as the author of Charlemagne's letter to the Spanish clergy informing them of the decisions of the assembly. Alcuin attached great importance to the "conventus" of December 800. In a letter to Arno of Salzburg (*Epistle* 218), who had attended the meeting, Alcuin eagerly requested information on the final decisions of "such a great and illustrious synod" dealing with the affairs of the church. He believed that the transactions of the gathering that was in session for such an extended period of time must have been of great significance to the Christian people.

The further development of the synodal proceedings according to the report of the *LP* finally implies that Leo declared his willingness to vindicate himself as some of his predecessors had done before him in the case of false accusations. He met the refusal of the synod to judge him by making a public statement of innocence (*LP* X): Leo III never gave an "oath" of purgation. The one ascribed to him since the ninth century is a forgery.

At this juncture, I should like to discuss a specific aspect of Alcuin's strong interest in the activities of the Roman Synod of December 800 which he expressed in letters to his friends who participated in the legal and synodal decisions concerning Leo III. In addition to his *Epistle* 218, previously mentioned, I refer to another one of those letters, probably from the end of the year 800, or from the beginning of 801, addressed to Riculf of Mayence, who was one of the pope's supporters at Rome. Accordingly, Alcuin, *Epistle* 212 (p. 353.5, Dümmler), writes to him, "quomodo stetisti cum domno apostolico." He openly voices his misgivings about the inertia among the Frankish participants at the Roman Synod when he says: "Besides, as I have heard . . . the very masters badly disagree among themselves" (insuper, sicut audivi . . . ipsos male inter se dissentire magistros, p. 353.24f.). Arno of Salzburg, Riculf of Mayence, and other Frankish participants at the synod must

---

[33] Cf. Wallach, *Alcuin and Charlemagne*, 147–165.

have responded to Alcuin's interest in the important events because they considered him to be the leading expert in matters of law, ecclesiastical as well as secular. His expertness in, and acquaintance with, the decisions of ecumenical and territorial synods, with the past and current legislation of royal courts, Frankish diets, and synods, is observable throughout his sundry writings.

Alcuin knew the *Acta* and canons of synods held during the sixth century at Orléans,[34] as well as the *Gesta* of the Sixth Ecumenical Council of III Constantinople, 680–681 (*PL* 101.92D). As the author of the *Libri Carolini*, he naturally was quite familiar with the first Latin translation of the Greek *Acta* of II Nicaea, 787, the so-called *First Latin Nicaenum* of about 788 (see above, Chapter III). During the last decade of the eighth century, Alcuin derived many patristic testimonia listed in some of his letters, and in his three apologetic treatises against the adoptionist heresies of Felix of Urgel and of Elipand of Toledo, from the Latin versions of the protocols of the third ecumenical council held at Ephesus in 431. Elipand is reminded by him of the council "celeberrimae auctoritatis" which assembled "in Ephesina civitate." He admonishes him "quod certissime eiusdem synodi litteras legentes agnoscere potestis," if only a small part of a rational being should have remained in him, "si aliqua in vobis rationalis creaturae particula remanserit" (*PL* 101.290C, 291C). Alcuin tells Elipand that the *Acta* of the numerous Visigothic Synods of Toledo, held during the sixth and seventh centuries, do not contain anything to support adoptionism: "venerabilium patrum in Toleto synodales ad nos pervenerunt sanctiones in quorum litteris nihil novi vel antiquis contrarium patribus, sed omnia catholico stylo perscripta agnovimus" (*PL* 101.266B; cf. 279D). Ludwig Ott has verified the bulk of the Greek patristic testimonia cited by Alcuin from the *Acta* of the Council of Ephesus, edited by Eduard Schwartz.[35] Paleographical traces of the use made by Alcuin himself of the pre-Carolingian codex Paris, B.N. 1572, from Tours, extensively used in his smallest and first antiadoptionist

---

[34] Cf. Wallach, *Alcuin and Charlemagne*, 129f. The following texts are from Alcuin, *Adversus Elipandum libri IV*, *PL* 101.231–300.

[35] Ludwig Ott, "Das Konzil von Ephesus (431) in der Theologie der Früh-Scholastik," in *Theologie in Geschichte und Gegenwart: Michael Schmaus zum 60. Geburtstag*, ed. Johann Auer and Hermann Volk (München, 1957), 279–308.

treatise, have been discovered by Bernhard Bischoff.[36] Alcuin certainly displays in his writings such a broad knowledge of synodal sources that none of his better-known Frankish contemporaries connected with the Roman Synod of December 800 can be compared with him. His familiarity with synodal collections must be stressed in this context of Leo's case because it constitutes the decisive justification for Alcuin's influence on his fellow theologians whom he counseled accordingly. Thus he really shared with them the responsibility of the decisions of the year 800. Alcuin's unique competence will be of help in the following treatment concerning the predecessors of Leo III after whose example he cleared himself of the accusations leveled against him.

Was Leo III thinking of the statement made by Pope Stephen IV (III) in 769 when he referred to predecessors after whose manner he declared his innocence? He might have thought of certain popes of whom the *Liber Pontificalis*[37] reports "purgation" (*purgatur*) as a means of denying criminal charges: Damasus I, Sixtus III, Symmachus, and Pelagius I. But in none of these cases do we know for certain that the "purgation" consisted in the swearing of an oath.

The case of Pelagius cannot be called a precedent for Leo's oath. The description of the rite used in this instance (*LP* I.303)—walking up to the ambo and carrying the Gospels—probably influenced the wording in the *Vita Leonis* (*LP* II.7). This merely literary connection does not warrant a conclusion on the nature of the statement made by Pelagius, who—to be sure—did not swear an oath.[38]

Nor can the trial of Symmachus in 501[39] be considered a precedent for Leo's case. Symmachus was tried by a synod in an accusatory

[36] "Aus Alkuins Erdentagen," *Medievalia et Humanistica* 14 (1962), 31–37; it is only fair to point out that Alcuin's connection with the *Turonensis* was stated for the first time by Emile Amann, "L'Adoptionisme espagnol du VIIIe siècle," *Revue des sciences religieuses* 16 (1936), 307, while Ott and Bischoff provided the detailed evidence. See Bischoff, *Mittelalteriche Studien* 2 (Stuttgart, 1967), 17, who added to n. 40 a reference to Ludwig Ott's study (above n. 35).

[37] Cf. *MGH, Gesta Pontificum*, ed. Theodor Mommsen (Berlin, 1898), Nos. 39, p. 84; 46, p. 96; 53, p. 121; for Pelagius I see Duchesne, *LP* I.303.

[38] Edgar Loening, *Das Kirchenrecht im Reiche der Merowinger* (Strassburg, 1878), 499 n. 1; the conclusions of Adelson and Baker, *Traditio* 8 (1952), 66f., based on the assumption that Pelagius swore an oath are untenable.

[39] Cf. Erich Caspar, "Das Verfahren gegen Leo III. Dezember 800," *Zeitschrift für Kirchengeschichte* 54 (1935), 255–257, who points out the distinctions between the trial of Symmachus and Leo's case.

trial with a *libellus accusatorius* properly listing the charges of his accusers. Leo, however, was never officially indicted *per accusationem*, nor was he officially tried by the synod. The acts of the trial of Symmachus may nevertheless be studied to advantage by the student interested in our problem, since they unfold the judicial machinery of a trial before a synod.

There never was a formal trial of Leo by the synod, nor an official indictment. His oath of innocence was given within the framework of a synodal meeting that conducted an accusatory trial[40] of his accusers. Nevertheless, the statement through which he cleared himself before the synodal assembly is not exactly an extrajudicial oath. His oath was a part of synodal transactions and therefore possessed judicial quality because the public proceedings of every synod have a judicial significance.[41] This basic nature of synodal decisions was not unknown to Charlemagne and his entourage: the capitularies incessantly demand their observation holding out severe punishment to transgressors. Though it is true that Leo's oath of innocence was not the result of a formal judicial decision, the judicial nature of the oath cannot be denied. At this point it might be helpful to remember that an oath has a greater authority than a judgment according to the *Digest* 12.2.2, ed. Paul Krueger and Theodor Mommsen, *Corpus iuris civilis* I (14th ed. Berlin, 1922), 194: "Iusiurandum speciem transactionis continet maioremque habet auctoritatem quam res iudicata."

The presence of Charlemagne, the highest Frankish judge, who had convoked the synod, and—though the pope was present— presided at the opening, again testifies to the judicial nature of the synodal proceedings. But this position then occupied by the Frankish king was not unusual. Already in 794 he had convoked the Synod of Frankfurt (simultaneously held with a Frankish Diet), which condemned the heresy of Spanish adoptionism, and the Byzantine worship of images, which had been decreed in 787 by the Seventh

[40] Cf. Willibald M. Plöchl, *Geschichte des Kirchenrechts* I (Wien, München, 1953), 228f.: "Im Gerichtsverfahren galt grundsätzlich der Akkusations-Prozess, ein Prinzip, das aus dem römischen Recht übernommen wurde. . . . Der Prozess selbst lehnte sich an das römisch-rechtliche Verfahren an . . . Der römisch-rechtliche Prozess wurde als das subsidiäre Recht im kirchlichen Gerichtsverfahren angesehen"; see also p. 381, and above nn. 23–26.

[41] Cf. *ibid.*, 1.134ff., 297–299; and Hans Erich Feine, *Kirchliche Rechtsgeschichte* (5th ed. Köln, Wien, 1972), 106ff.

Ecumenical Council held at Nicaea. At Frankfurt, Charlemagne presided, rather than the two papal legates of Pope Hadrian I who were present. Quite significantly, the king also participated in the debates of the synod which he opened. After the reading—upon royal request—of a letter by Elipand of Toledo concerning the adoptionist theories, Charlemagne rose from the *sella regia* and addressed the assembly at length (*prolixo sermone*) on the theological question.[42] Then Charlemagne actively participated in the synodal decisions which, for this reason, are introduced in the Frankfurt Capitulary (*Conc.*1.1 No.19G) cc. 4, 6, 7, 9, 10, 16, with the words "decreed by the Lord King and the Holy Synod," "definitum (or statutum) est a domno rege et sancta synodo." Charlemagne's participation in the decisions of the Frankfurt Synod plainly indicates the judicial character of its proceedings. We doubt that the Frankish king actually voted with the episcopate on the various issues under debate. He certainly had more than merely a vote at the meetings: his was the decisive voice, and the assembly complied with his wishes. Thus we read in the Capitulary of Frankfurt cc. 55–56: "Dixit enim domnus rex—omnis synodus consensit"; and "Commonuit [*scil.* Charlemagne] etiam—omnis namque synodus secundum ammonitionem domni regis consensit."

A similar procedure can be safely assumed for Charlemagne at the Roman Synod of December 800. At Rome, Charlemagne's position largely resembled that of Roman emperors[43] who not only claimed the exclusive right to convoke councils, but also participated in the debates of the meetings, although they did not vote with the assembled episcopate on the synodal decisions.

Charlemagne doubtless determined the proceedings and the course taken by the Synod of December 800, since we know that his relentless leadership imposed itself so strongly on the affairs

---

[42] *Conc.*1.1.131, quoted by Paulinus of Aquileia in the report he wrote against adoptionism in the name of the Italian episcopate assembled at Frankfurt: "Quid vobis videtur? Ab anno prorsus praeterito et ex quo coepit huius pestis insania tumescente perfidiae ulcu diffusius ebulisse, non parvus in his regionibus, licet in extremis finibus regni nostri, error inolevit, quem censura fidaei necesse est modis omnibus resecare." This is *the only extant literal fragment* of any of the many speeches delivered by Charlemagne.

[43] Cf. generally Francis Dvornik, "Emperors, Popes, and General Councils," *Dumbarton Oaks Papers* 6 (1951), 1–23; Hans Barion, *Das fränkisch-deutsche Synodalrecht des Frühmittelalters* (Bonn, Köln, 1931), *passim*.

of the church. This was true even in the case of those Frankish synods which he did not attend, yet whose Acts were submitted to him for approval and support.[44] How much more must he have exerted his will on a synod over which he personally presided! The prerogatives of Charlemagne as the head of his own national church were openly recognized and acknowledged by Frankish synods. The Synod of Tours, 813, for instance, could unabashedly express at the end of the official *Gesta* its willingness to submit the Acts to the approval of, and the possible changes suggested by, Charlemagne— "quomodo deinceps piissimo principi nostro de his agendum placebit" (*Conc.*1.1.293); the assembly openly states that it is ready to act in accordance with the king's nod and wish—"ad nutum et voluntatem eius parati sumus." A recent[45] portrait of Charlemagne in the service of the church neglects to state that Charlemagne unreservedly used and governed the institutions of the church for the advancement of his secular government.

The official Frankish report of the events in the *Annales regni Francorum* (*ArF*) and the narrative of the *Annales Laureshamenses* (*AnL*) are compatible with the present interpretation of the papal report. At the outset, neither of these sources speaks of a formal trial of Leo III by the Synod of December 800. Not the pope, but his accusers, stood before the synod which interrogated them about the criminal charges brought forth against the pontiff. In the course of this examination, which—in accordance with the custom observed in the proceedings of synods—was conducted in all likelihood by the leading metropolitan present, and not by Charlemagne,[46] the king recognized that the motive of the accusers was not justice, but envy or hatred of the pope (*AnL*: . . . cum cognovisset rex, quia non propter aliam justitiam sed per invidiam eum condemnare volebant, tunc . . .). Thus the evidence offered by the accusers against Leo was deemed insufficient. The accusers could not make their case, or as the official *ArF* puts it: "nullus probator criminum esse

---

[44] Cf. Karl Voigt, *Staat und Kirche von Konstantin dem Grossen bis zum Ende der Karolingerzeit* (Stuttgart, 1936), 321.

[45] Etienne Delaruelle, "Charlemagne et l'Eglise," *Revue d'histoire de l'Eglise de France* 39 (1953), 166–199.

[46] Adelson and Baker, *Traditio* 8 (1952), 62, maintain that Charlemagne himself "questioned" the assailants of the pope; none of the sources warrants this assumption which, in addition, is contradicted by the above-mentioned synodal procedures.

voluit."[47] At this juncture the synod decided to invoke the doctrine of the judicial exemption of the pope; simultaneously it suggested that it would abide by Leo's own decision of the case, or in other words: Leo was told to be his own judge. The same decision of the synod is reported in the *AnL*: "non tamen per eorum iudicium," and the pope agreed to vindicate himself before the synod after the example of earlier pontiffs. Contrary to the advice Alcuin (*Epistle* 179) had given to Arno of Salzburg, Leo at another session of the synod made a public statement of innocence (*LP* X, above, and Chapter XV).

This solution of the embarrassing problem meant a partial victory of Leo's enemies who had expected his resignation without an oath. Alcuin[48] had learned of their plans against Leo from the overtures they made to Charlemagne during August 799 when the king was at Paderborn. To achieve the deposition[49] of the pope they had openly charged him with adultery and perjury. These charges were supposed to elicit from Leo a very heavy oath for the purpose of clearing himself of falsely attributed crimes. Contrary to expectation, these "enviers" (aemulatores) of Leo—as Alcuin called them—did not succeed in gaining the support of Charlemagne in their conspiratorial machinations. During the investigation of their charges by the synod the Frankish king very acutely recognized that they were motivated by envy, not by justice.

The original Acts of the Roman Synod of December 800 were used in the *Liber Pontificalis* and in the *Annales Laureshamenses*. The report of the meeting in the *Vita Leonis* must be looked upon as a primary historical source for the reconstruction of the events preceding the recognition of Charlemagne as emperor on Christmas Day 800. Heinrich Fichtenau has convincingly named Richbod of Trèves and Lorsch as the author of the part of the *AnL* covering

---

[47] This argument reminds me of the *Acta purgationis Felicis episcopi Autumnitani*, ed. C. Ziwsa (*CSEL* 26; Vienna, 1893), 204.6: . . . Felicem . . . liberum esse . . . cum nemo in eum aliquid probare potuerit.

[48] *Epistle* 179, addressed to Arno of Salzburg.

[49] That the deposition of Leo was requested by his enemies is also known from the *Annales regni Francorum* ad a. 801 where we read of those who had deposed the pontiff in 800: "eos qui pontificem anno superiore deposuerint." See Zimmermann, above, Chapter XV n. 1.

the important years 800–801 for which the original manuscript, the Vindobonensis 515, is now available in a facsimile edition.[50] The accounts of the official Frankish and papal reports of the synod do not contradict one another. The synod investigated the charges of the accusers of Leo III, who was never indicted or tried by the assembly which he personally attended. Properly speaking, a public trial[51] of Leo never took place. The pope's condemnation by synodal decision was hardly intended by Charlemagne.[52] The synod suggested to the pontiff that he be his own judge. Thereupon Leo cleared himself by a public statement of innocence during a session of the synod on December 23; two days later Charlemagne was recognized[53] and acclaimed as emperor.

The momentous event that took place on Christmas Day of the year 800 is connected with another happening that occurred on the same day, if not during the same hour, though it is rarely mentioned by historians. I am thinking of the festive coronation and unction as *Rex Francorum* of Charlemagne's oldest son, Charles. We know of this event from Alcuin's congratulatory *Epistle* 217 (p. 360.38–39, Dümmler) of 801,[54] addressed to the twenty-eight-year-old Frankish heir, whose unction, connected with his coronation, is reported in

[50] Franz Unterkircher, *Das Wiener Fragment der Lorscher Annalen. . . . Codex Vindobonensis 515 der Oesterreichischen National-Bibliothek* (Codices Selecti, XV; Graz, 1967).

[51] Walter Ullmann, *The Growth of Papal Government in the Middle Ages* (London, 1970), 97 and 117f., still speaks of Leo's "trial," and maintains that Charlemagne sat in judgment over the pope. Neither of these contentions is borne out by the sources.

[52] So also Johannes Haller, *Das Papsttum* 2 (Basel, 1951) 18f.

[53] See Percy Ernst Schramm, "Die Anerkennung Karls des Grossen als Kaiser," *Historische Zeitschrift* 172 (1951), especially p. 488. F. L. Ganshof, *The Carolingians and the Frankish Monarchy: Studies in Carolingian History* (Ithaca, 1971), 52 n. 43, repeats his endorsement (see above n. 5) of the *Annales Laureshamenses* as a "most important source" of the events at Rome and in the Frankish kingdom.

[54] "Audivi [per] domnum apostolicum [= Leonem III.] regium nomen, domino exellentissimo David consentiente, cum corona regiae dignitatis vobis inpositum." Alcuin's *Epistola* 217 should be added to p. 59 of Kurt Reindel, *Die Kaiserkrönung Karls des Grossen* (Göttingen, 1970). Cf. *Einhardi Vita Karoli Magni*, ed. G. H. Pertz and Georg Waitz, ed. sexta cur. Oswald Holder-Egger (Hannover, 1911; reprint 1965). See Peter Classen, "Karl der Grosse und die Thronfolge im Frankenreich," *Festschrift für Hermann Heimpel* 3 (Göttingen, 1973), 109–134; Carlrichard Brühl, "Fränkischer Königsbrauch und das Problem der Festkrönungen," *Historische Zeitschrift* 194 (1962), 312–319.

the *Vita Leonis* of the *Liber Pontificalis* (Duchesne II.7). This fact, if considered together with Charlemagne's recognition as *imperator*, could well account for Einhard's famous report in the *Vita Karoli*, c. 28, concerning Charlemagne's reaction to the pope's participation in the making of the new emperor. The role of Leo III in the coronation of Charlemagne's son Charles was certainly agreed upon in advance by papal *and* Frankish officials, while part of the procedure of Charlemagne's recognition as imperator evidently depended on Leo's action, which Charlemagne somewhat resented, as Einhard has told us. Einhard's report represents more than the mere repetition of a literary expression of feigned modesty which is topically associated in historical sources with statements showing the proper *cunctatio* displayed by designated Roman emperors before they accepted the high office bestowed upon them.[55] Charlemagne's *cunctatio* must be understood as a historical fact, although it is expressed in terms of a literary convention.

It is only reasonable to assume that in addition to the prearranged coronation of Charlemagne's son Charles as "rex Francorum" by Leo III—to be sure, as Alcuin reports in *Epistola* 217, "domino excellentissimo David (= Charlemagne) consentiente"—Charlemagne's special recognition as imperator had also been arranged in advance by mutual agreement between king and pope. The procedural execution of the ceremonies connected with the act may well have contained some unforeseen element that annoyed Charlemagne. But Heinrich Fichtenau's reinterpretation of the report of the *Annales Lauvreshamenses* (*MIOEG* 61, 1953) has taught us that Charlemagne had not been caught unawares on Christmas Day of the year 800. The historically determined Byzantine background is quite obvious in the ceremonial aspects of Charlemagne's recognition as imperator. His coronation by Leo III and the acclamations of the assembly consisting of clerics, visiting Franks, and Romans were modeled after the Byzantine coronation ceremonies practiced by the Patriarch of Constantinople. Leo III's prostration before Charlemagne, corresponding to the patriarch's *proskynesis* before the Roman emperor, symbolized thus the homage rendered by a subject to his new emperor.

---

[55] Cf. Jean Béranger, *Recherches sur l'aspect idéologique du principat* (Schweizer Beiträge 6; 1953), 137ff. on "Le refus du pouvoir."

The actual recognition of the Frankish king as emperor hardly occurred *nesciente domno Karolo*. This fact can be substantiated, at least in part, also by the substantive donations and gifts made by Charlemagne, according to the *Liber Pontificalis* (Duchesne, II.7ff.)[56] to the Petrus Basilica and other Roman churches after Christmas Day of the year 800.[57]

There remains the much discussed but still unsolved question why Einhard in the *Vita Karoli*, c. 28, used the formulation "imperatoris et augusti nomen accepit" in order to designate Charlemagne's new status, and none of the other formulations occurring in sundry historical documents. In view of the acknowledged literary impact of Suetonius' *Lives of the Caesars* on Einhard's *Vita Karoli* it should not be surprising to discover that Einhard also in this case followed a literary model, namely, Vegetius' *Epitoma rei militaris* II.5, ed. Carl Lang (Leipzig, 1885), 38. Einhard seems to know Vegetius' description of the military oath (militiae sacramenta) requested of the Roman soldier, where he found the statement "Nam imperator cum augusti nomen accepit, . . . "[58]

Einhard's teacher Alcuin in his *Epistola* 257 from the year 802, addressed to Charlemagne, ascribes nothing less than omniscience to the Frankish king as emperor—to be sure, for a commendable purpose, namely, the good of his subjects. I have discussed the anonymous citation of the corresponding passage from the *Preface* of Vegetius, *Epitoma rei militaris* in *Alcuin and Charlemagne* (1959), 50.

---

[56] See, e.g., Josef Deér, "Der Kaiser und das Kreuz," *Jahrbuch des Römisch-Germanischen Zentralmuseums Mainz* 12 (1965), 170f.

[57] Carolingian studies published by the present writer since 1933 are listed by Percy E. Schramm, *Gesammelte Aufsätze zur Geschichte des Mittelalters* I (Stuttgart, 1968), 172, 198, 252, 256, 327f., 331f. On the "coronation" of Charlemagne see also the studies by Helmut Beumann, Arno Borst, Peter Classen, Josef Deér, and Walter Schlesinger conveniently reprinted by Gunter Wolf, *Zum Kaisertum Karls des Grossen: Beiträge und Aufsätze* (Wege der Forschung 38; Darmstadt, 1972).

[58] We read in the official Carolingian court annals, in the *Annales regni Francorum*, ed. G. H. Pertz and Friedrich Kurze (Hannover, 1895), 161.2–3, that Lotharius, the son of Emperor Louis the Pious, in 823 was crowned at Rome by Pope Paschalis I as *rex Francorum* "et regni coronam et imperatoris atque augusti nomen accepit." This statement contains the identical formulation used by Einhard, *Vita Karoli*, c. 28, for Charlemagne! We mention that Lotharius had been crowned by Louis the Pious in 817 at Aachen. The *Annales regni Francorum*, p. 146, report that Louis "filium suum primogenitum Hlotharium coronavit et nominis atque imperii sui socium sibi constituit, caeteros reges appelatos unum Aquitaniae, alterum Baioariae praefecit."

It is obvious that Alcuin expects to discover in Charlemagne, the new imperator and Augustus, the same ethical quality that Vegetius recommends to a Roman Octavianus Augustus.

Vegetius' formulation "augusti nomen accepit" was adopted by Einhard for Charlemagne because it corresponded to the thinking of the leading minds around Alcuin who ideologically and actively helped the Frankish king in the establishment of his imperial rule.

Bibliographies and General Index

A. Abbreviations
B. Text Editions Used
C. Select Bibliography
General Index

A. Abbreviations

AC	Antiphonary of Compiègne, *PL* 78, and in *CAO*.
ACO	*Acta Conciliorum Oecumenicorum* I–IV, rec. Eduard Schwartz. Berlin, Leipzig, 1914–40; IV, vol. I, ed. Johannes Straub. Berlin, 1971.
AL	*Antifonario Visigótico Mozárabe de la Catedral de León*, ed. Louis Brou and José Vives. (Monumenta Hispaniae Sacra, Serie Liturgica: Vol. V, 1.) Barcelona, Madrid, 1959.
Bastgen	See *LC*.
BG	*Breviarium Gothicum, PL* 86 (Paris, 1862).
BSGRT	*Bibliotheca script. graecorum et romanorum Teubneriana.*
CAG	*Commentaria in Aristotelem Graeca.*
CAO	*Corpus Antiphonalium Officii*, ed. R.-J. Hesbert, I–IV. Rome, 1963, 1965, 1968, 1970.
CCL	*Corpus Christianorum*, Series Latina. Turnhout, 1953ff.
CLA	See Lowe.
Clavis	*Clavis Patrum Latinorum*, ed. Eligius Dekkers and Aemilius Gaar. (Sacris Erudiri III, 2nd ed.) Brugge, The Hague, 1961.
Conc.	*Concilia.*
CSEL	*Corpus Scriptorum Ecclesiasticorum Latinorum.* Wien, 1866ff.
DA	*Deutsches Archiv für Erforschung des Mittelalters.*
DACL	*Dictionnaire d'Archéologie chrétienne et de Liturgie.* Paris, 1907ff.
Didascaliae	Luitpold Wallach, "The Unknown Author of the *Libri Carolini*: Patristic Exegesis, Mozarabic Antiphons, and the *Vetus Latina*," in: *Didascaliae: Studies in Honor of Anselm M. Albareda.* ed. Sesto Prete (New York, 1961), 469–515.
DK	*Diplomata Karolinorum*, see *MGH*.
Dölger, *Reg.*	Franz Dölger, *Regesten der Kaiserurkunden des oströmischen Reiches*. I. Teil*: Regesten von 565–1025*. München, Berlin, 1924.
GCS	*Griechische christliche Schriftsteller der ersten drei Jahrhunderte.* Berlin, 1897ff.
Grumel, *Reg.*	Venance Grumel, *Les Regestes des Actes du Patriarcat de Constantinople* I: *Les Actes des Patriarches*, Fasc. II: *Les Regestes de 715 à 1043*. Socii Assumptionistae Chalcedonenses, Chalcedon, 1936.

Hadrianum	Hadrian I's Epistle of c. 791, addressed to Charlemagne, ed. Karl Hampe, *MGH, Epistolae* 5 (Karolini Aevi 3; Berlin, 1899), 5–57.
Jaffé, *Reg.*	See following item:
JE, JK, JL	*Regesta Pontificum Romanorum*, ed. Philipp Jaffé; editio altera, supervised by Wilhelm Wattenbach, ed. S. Löwenfeld, F. Kaltenbrunner, and P. Ewald, I–II. Leipzig, 1885–88.
JE 2448	Hadrian I's *Synodica* of 785, ed. Mansi XII.1055–1076D.
JE 2483	See *Hadrianum*.
LC	*Libri Carolini sive Caroli Magni Capitulare de Imaginibus*, ed. Hubert Bastgen, *MGH, Legum Sectio III: Concilia 2*, Supplementum. Hannover, Leipzig, 1924.
Lowe	E. A. Lowe, ed., *Codices Latini Antiquiores* I–XI. Oxford, 1934–66; *Supplement*, 1971; vol. II, 2nd ed., 1972.
LP	*Liber Pontificalis Ecclesiae Romanae*, ed. Louis Duchesne. I–II. Paris, 1886–92; reprint I–II. Paris, 1955; III, ed. Cyrille Vogel. Paris, 1957.
LS	*Libellus Synodalis* of Paris Synod 825, ed. Albert Werminghoff, *MGH, Concilia* 2.2 (Aevi Karolini 1.2; Hannover, Leipzig, 1908), 473–551.
Mansi	I. D. Mansi, ed., *Sacrorum Conciliorum Nova et Amplissima Collectio* I–XVI. Florence, 1766–71; reprint, Paris, 1901–2.
MGH	*Monumenta Germaniae historica*:

Auctores Antiquissimi	*Formulae*
Capitularia	*Leges* (series in folio)
Concilia	*Legum* sectiones I–V
Constitutiones et acta publica	*Poetae*
Diplomata	*Scriptores* (series in folio)
Epistolae	

MIOEG	*Mitteilungen des Instituts für oesterreichische Geschichtsforschung.*
Neues Archiv	*Neues Archiv der Gesellschaft für ältere deutsche Geschichtskunde.*
Nicaea II	Greek *Acta* of II Nicaea, 787, ed. Mansi XII–XIII.
Nicaenum, First Latin	Lost Latin translation of c. 788 of Nicaea II; fragments preserved in *JE* 2483, *LC*, *LS*, and in *Second Latin Nicaenum*.
Nicaenum, Second Latin	Anastasius Bibliothecarius' Latin translation of Nicaea II of 873, ed. Mansi XII–XIII.
OV	*Oracional Visigótico*, ed. José Vives. (Monumenta Hispaniae Sacra, Serie Liturgica I.) Barcelona, 1946.
PG	*Patrologia graeca*, ed. J. P. Migne. Paris, 1857ff.
PL	*Patrologia latina*, ed. J. P. Migne. Paris, 1844ff.; *Supplementum* I–V, ed. Adalbert Hamman. Paris, 1958–74.
QF	*Quellen und Forschungen aus italienischen Archiven und Bibliotheken* 21 (1929–30).
SCBO	*Scriptorum classicorum bibliotheca Oxoniensis.*
TU	*Texte und Untersuchungen zur Geschichte der altchristlichen Literatur.* Leipzig, 1882ff.
ZSRG	*Zeitschrift der Savigny-Stiftung für Rechtsgeschichte.*

B. Text Editions Used

Note. The works of authors are listed alphabetically by title; works under categories are arranged chronologically as in *Acta, Biblia Sacra, Papal Diplomatic Documents*.

ACTA OF ECUMENICAL COUNCILS
  Ephesus 431, *ACO* I.
  Chalcedon 451, *ACO* II.
  III Constantinople 680–681, Mansi XI.195–922.
  Trullianum 692, Mansi X.921–1006.
  II Nicaea 787, Mansi XII.951–1154, XIII.1–485.
  IV Constantinople 869–870, Mansi XVI.1–208.
  Conciliorum oecumenicorum Decreta, ed. P. P. Ioannou. Freiburg, 1962.

ACTA OF OTHER COUNCILS
  Agde 506, Mansi VIII.319–346.
  Lateran 649, Mansi X.863–1184.
  Hiereia 754, Mansi XIII.208–235.
  Lateran 769, fragments: *MGH, Conc.* 2.1 (1904), 74–92.
  Frankfurt 794, *Capitulare*, pp. 165–171, dossier, pp. 110–165, no. 19, in *MGH, Conc.* 2.1 (Aevi Karolini I.1). Hannover, Leipzig. 1904–1906.
  Aachen, May-June 799, *MGH, Conc.* 2.1, pp. 220–225, no. 25.
  Roman, December 800, see our Chapters XV and XVI.
  Paris, 825, see Abbreviations: *LS*.
  Mayence, 852, *MGH, Capitularia* 2, 1897.

ACTUS SILVESTRI
  ed. Boninus Mombritius, *Sanctuarium seu Vitae Sanctorum* II.
  2nd ed., Paris, 1910.

ALCUIN
  Adv. Elipandum Libri IV, PL 101.230–300.
  Adv. Felicem Libri VII, PL 101.119–230.
  Adv. Felicem haeresin, PL 101.87–120.
  Comm. in Joannem, PL 100.665–1008.
  De dialectica, PL 101.951–976.
  De rhetorica et de virtutibus, ed. Carl Halm, in *Rhetores latini minores* (Leipzig, 1863), 523–550.

Epistolae, ed. Ernst Dümmler, *MGH, Epistolae* 4 (Karolini Aevi 2, Berlin, 1895);
additions *ibid.* 5 (Karolini Aevi 3; Berlin, 1899), 643–645; additional letters
belonging to the *Corpus Epistularum Alcuini* are listed by Wallach, *Alcuin and
Charlemagne*, (2nd ed., New York, London, 1968), 273–274.

Libri Carolini, see Abbreviations: *LC*.

Vita Alcuini, ed. Wilhelm Arndt, *MGH, Scriptores* XV.1 (Hannover, 1887),
182–197.

See: LITURGICAL SERVICE BOOKS, Lectionaries, s.v. Wilmart, and Sacramentaries,
s.v. Deshusses.

ALDHELM

De virginitate, ed. Rudolf Ehwald, *MGH, Auctores Antiquissimi* 15.1913–19.

AMALARIUS

Amalarii Episcopi Opera Liturgica I, ed. I. M. Hanssens. (Studi e Testi 138.)
Rome, 1948.

AMBROSIASTER

Ambrosiastri qui dicitur Commentarius in Epistulas Paulinas I–III, ed. H. I. Vogels,
CSEL 81.1–3, 1966–69.

Quaestiones Veteris et Novi Testamenti CXXVII, ed. Alexander Souter, *CSEL* 50,
1908.

AMBROSIUS

De fide ad Gratianum Augustum, ed. Otto Faller, *CSEL* 78, 1962.

De incarnationis dominicae sacramento, ed. O. Faller, *CSEL* 79, 1964.

De spiritu sancto libri tres, *ibid.*

AMMONIUS

In Porphyrii Isagogen, ed. Adolf Busse, *CAG* IV.3. Berlin, 1891.

ANASTASIUS BIBLIOTHECARIUS

Epistolae sive Praefationes, ed. Ernst Perels and Gerhard Laehr, *MGH, Epistolae* 7
(Karolini Aevi 5; Berlin, 1928), 395–442.

Translator in 873 of Greek *Acta* of II Nicaea, 787, Mansi XII–XIII.

Translator in 871 of Greek *Acta* of IV Constantinople, 869–870, Mansi XVI.1–
208.

ANNALES LAURESHAMENSES

ed. G. H. Pertz, *MGH, Scriptores* I (Hannover, 1826), 22–39.

ANNALES REGNI FRANCORUM

ed. G. H. Pertz, rec. F. Kurze. Hannover, 1895.

ANTIPHONARIES see LITURGICAL SERVICE BOOKS.

APRINGIUS

Tractatus in Apocalipsin, ed. P. A. C. Vega. El Escorial, 1940.

APULEIUS

Liber Peri Hermeneias, ed. Paul Thomas, in *Apulei Opera* III, *BSGRT*, 1908.

ARISTOTELES LATINUS see BOETHIUS.

ATHANASIUS OF ALEXANDRIA

De incarnatione verbi dei, *PG* 25.

AUGUSTINUS

Breviculus Collationis cum Donatistis, *CSEL* 53 (1910), 39–92.

Confessionnes, ed. Martin Skutella, *BSGRT*, Leipzig, 1934.

Contra sermonem Arianorum, PL 40.683–708.

De civitate dei, ed. Emanuel Hoffmann, *CSEL* 40.1–2, 1899–1900; ed. Dombart & Kalb, *CCL* 47–48, 1955.

De diversis quaestionibus ad Simplicianum, PL 40.101–148.

De diversis quaestionibus 83, PL 40.11–100.

De doctrina christiana, ed. W. M. Green, *CSEL* 80, 1963; ed. J. Martin, *CCL* 31, 1961.

De Genesi ad litteram, ed. Ioseph Zycha, *CSEL* 28.1, 1894.

De VIII Dulcitii quaestionibus, PL 40.147–170.

De trinitate, PL 42.819–1098; ed. W. J. Mountain and Franciscus Glorie, *CCL* 50 and 50A, 1968.

Principia dialecticae, ed. Wilhelm Crecelius. Elberfeld, 1857.

Quaestiones in Heptateuchum lib. VII, ed. Ioseph Zycha, *CSEL* 28.2, 1894; ed. J. Fraipont, *CCL* 33, 1958.

Retractationes libri duo, ed. Pius Knöll, *CSEL* 36, 1902.

Speculum quis ignorat, ed. Franciscus Weihrich, *CSEL* 12 (1887), 1–285.

PSEUDO-AUGUSTINUS

Categoriae decem (Anonymi Paraphrasis Themistiana), ed. Laurentius Minio-Paluello, in *Aristoteles Latinus* I.1–5 (Bruges, Paris, 1961), 129–175.

Dialogus quaestionum LXV, PL 40.733–752.

Liber de divinis scripturis, ed. F. Weihrich, *CSEL* 12 (1887), 287–725.

Liber XXI Sententiarum, PL 40.725–732.

BASIL THE GREAT

Apocryphal Epist. 360 to Emperor Julian, Mansi XIII.72–73; *PG* 32.

Sermo in XL martyres, PG 31.

BEATUS OF LIEBANA

In *Apocalipsin,* ed. H. A. Sanders. (Papers and Monographs of the American Academy in Rome 7.) 1930.

BEDE

De templo Salomonis, PL 91.735–805; ed. David Hurst, *CCL* 119A, 1969.

In Ioan. evang. Expositio, PL 92.

Opera de temporibus, ed. C. W. Jones. Cambridge, Mass., 1943.

BENEDICT OF ANIANE

Munimenta fidei, ed. Jean Leclerc, in *Analecta Monastica,* première serie. (Studia Anselmiana 20.) Rome, 1948.

BENEDICTUS LEVITA

Benedicti Capitularia, ed. F. H. Knust, *MGH, Legum* (in folio) II, pars altera (Hannover, 1837), 17–158.

Biblia Sacra

Note. The Hebrew, Greek, and Latin versions are listed here in the sequence OT, LXX, NT, Vetus Latina, Vulgate, Psalter, Clementina.

Biblia Hebraica, ed. Rudolph Kittel and Paul Kahle. 3rd ed., Stuttgart, 1937.

Septuaginta id est Vetus Testamentum iuxta LXX interpretes, ed. Alfred Rahlfs. 6th ed., I–II, Stuttgart, s.a.

Septuaginta: Vetus Testamentum Graecum auctoritate Societatis Litterarum Gottingensis editum:

I   *Genesis*, ed. J. W. Wevers, 1974.

XII.1   *Sapientia Salomonis*, ed. Joseph Ziegler, 1962.

XII.2   *Sapientia Iesu Filii Sirach*, ed. J. Ziegler, 1965.

XIV   *Isaias*, ed. J. Ziegler, 1939.

XVI.1   *Ezechiel*, ed. J. Ziegler, 1952.

XVI.2   *Susanna, Daniel, Bel et Draco*, ed. J. Ziegler, 1954.

Novum Testamentum Graece, ed. Eberhard Nestle. 25th ed., cur. Erwin Nestle and Kurt Aland. Stuttgart, 1962.

Novum Testamentum Graece, ed. B. F. Westcott and F. J. A. Hort. New York, 1935.

Petrus Sabatier, *Bibliorum sacrorum latinae versiones antiquae et Vetus Italica*. Paris, 1751.

Vetus Latina: Die Reste der altlateinischen Bibel, ed. Erzabtei Beuron: I.1, ed. Bonifatius Fischer. 2nd ed., Freiburg, 1963;

II, ed. B. Fischer, 1951–54; XXIV.2, ed. H. F. Frede, 1966–71; XXV, Introduction, ed. H. F. Frede, 1975–76;

XXVI.1, ed. Walter Thiele, 1956–69.

Itala: Das Neue Testament in Altlateinischer Überlieferung, ed. Adolf Jülicher, I–IV. Berlin, 1938–63.

Biblia Sacra iuxta Latinam Vulgatam versionem . . . cura et studio monachorum Abbatiae Pont. S. Hieronymi in Urbe O. S. B. edita, I (Genesis)–XIII (Liber Isaiae). Rome, 1926–69.

Novum Testamentum Latine sec. editionem Hieronymi, ed. J. Wordsworth and H. J. White *et al*. I–IV. Oxford, 1889–1954.

Robert Weber, ed., *Le Psautier romain et les anciens psautiers latins*. (Collectanea Biblica Latina X.) Rome, 1953.

Henri de Sainte-Marie, ed., *Sancti Hieronimi Psalterium iuxta Hebraeos*. (Coll. Bibl. Lat. XI.) Rome, 1954.

Th. A. Marazuela, ed., *Psalterium Visigothicum—Mozarabicum*. Madrid, 1957.

J. P. Gilson, ed., *Mozarabic Psalter*. (Henri Bradshaw Society 30.) London, 1905.

Biblia Sacra iuxta Vulgatam Clementinam . . . , denuo edd. . . . Professores fac. theol. Parisiensis . . . Declée, Romae, Tornaci, Parisiis, 1956.

G. Nolli and A. Vacarri, ed., *Biblica Sacra Vulgatae editionis iuxta Decretum PP. Clementis VIII*. I–III Vetus Test., IV Nov. Test. Graece et Latine, 1956.

BOETHIUS

Aristotelis Categoriae, translatio Boethii, ed. Laurentius Minio-Paluello, in *Aristoteles Latinus* I.1–5: *Categoriae vel Praedicamenta* (Bruges, Paris, 1961), 1–41.

Aristotelis Liber Periermenias, ed. L. Minio-Paluello, in *Aristoteles Latinus* II.1–2: *De interpretatione vel Periermenias* (Bruges, Paris, 1965), 1–38.

De differentiis topicis, PL 64.1173–1216.

In categorias Aristotelis libri IV, PL 64.159–294.

In librum Aristotelis Peri Hermeneias Commentarii. editio duplex, ed. Carl Meiser, I–II, *BSGRT*, 1877–80.

In Porphyrii Isagogen comment., editio duplex, ed. Samuel Brandt, *CSEL* 48, 1906.

Opuscula Sacra, ed. H. F. Stewart and E. K. Rand. (5th ed., Loeb Classical Library.) Cambridge, 1953.

Philosophiae Consolatio, ed. Ludwig Bieler, *CCL* 94, 1959; ed. Wilhelm Weinberger, *CSEL* 67, 1934.

Porphyrii Isagoge, translatio Boethii, ed. Laurentius Minio-Paluello, in *Aristoteles Latinus* I.6–7: *Categoriarum Supplementa* (Bruges, Paris, 1966), 1–31.

BREVIARIUM ALARICIANUM

Codex Theodosianus I.2, ed. Theodor Mommsen and P. M. Meyer. Berlin, 1895.

Lex Romana Visigothorum, ed. Gustav Haenel. Leipzig, 1849.

Max Conrat (Cohn), *Breviarium Alaricianum: Römisches Recht im Fränkischen Reich.* Leipzig, 1903.

CANON MISSAE ROMANAE

ed. Bernard Botte, *Le Canon de la Messe Romaine.* (Textes et études liturgiques 2.) Louvain, 1935.

CASSIODORUS

Expositio Psalmorum, ed. A. Adriaen, *CCL* 97–98, 1958.

Historia ecclesiastica Tripartita, rec. W. Jacob, ed. Rudolf Hanslik, *CSEL* 71, 1952.

Institutiones, ed. R. A. B. Mynors, *SCBO*, Oxford, 1937.

CHARLEMAGNE

Capitularia: MGH, Capitularia regum Francorum, ed. Alfred Boretius. *Legum Sectio II* 1. Hannover, 1883.

Diplomata: MGH, Diplomata Karolinorum I, ed. E. Mühlbacher. Hannover, 1906.

Epistolae: MGH, Epistolae Karolini Aevi 2 (Epistolae 4). Berlin, 1895; *MGH, Concilia aevi Karolini* 1. Hannover, Leipzig, 1906; *MGH, Epistolae Karolini Aevi* 3 (Epistolae 5). Berlin, 1899. See Abbreviations: *LC.*

CLAUDIUS OF TURIN

Commentarii in Libros Regum, *PL* 50.

CLAVIS MELITONIS

ed. J. B. Pitra, *Spicilegium Solesmense* II–III. Paris, 1855.

Analecta Sacra Spicilegio Solesmensi parata II. Paris, 1884.

CODEX CAROLINUS see PAPAL DIPLOMATIC DOCUMENTS.

CODEX JUSTINIANUS

see *Corpus Iuris Civilis*

COLLECTIONS OF HISTORICAL TEXTS

Heinz Dannenbauer, *Die Quellen zur Geschichte der Kaiserkrönung Karls des Grossen.* (Kleine Texte, ed. Hans Lietzmann, 161.) Berlin, 1931.

Hans-Jürgen Geischer, *Der byzantinische Bilderstreit.* (Texte zur Kirchen- und Theologiegeschichte, ed. Gerhard Ruhbach.) Gütersloh, 1968.

Herman Hennephof, *Textus Byzantinos ad Iconomachiam Pertinentes in usum academicum.* (Byzantina Neerlandica, series A, Textus, fasc. I.) Leiden, 1969.

Kurt Reindel, *Die Kaiserkrönung Karls des Grossen.* (Historische Texte: Mittelalter, ed. Arno Borst and Josef Fleckenstein, 4.) 2nd ed., Göttingen, 1970.

CONSTITUTUM CONSTANTINI

ed. Horst Fuhrmann. (*Text: Fontes iuris Germanici antiqui in usum scholarum* X.) Hannover, 1968.

CORPUS GLOSSARIORUM LATINORUM
rec. and ed. G. Loewe and Georg Goetz, I–VII, 1888–1923; reprint 1965.

CORPUS IURIS CANONICI
ed. E. A. Friedberg. Leipzig, 1879–81.

CORPUS IURIS CIVILIS, I: *Institutiones,* rec. Paul Krueger; *Digesta,* rec. Theodor Mommsen. 14th ed., ed. Paul Krueger. Berlin, 1922.

CYRIL OF ALEXANDRIA
Lost *Comm. on Matthew,* fragments, Mansi XII.1067B.
Matthäus-Kommentare aus der griechischen Kirche, ed. Joseph Reuss, *TU* 61, v. Reihe, Bd. 6. Berlin, 1957.
S. Patris Cyrilli . . . in XII Prophetas I, ed. P. E. Pusey. Oxford, 1868.

DECRETUM GELASIANUM
De libris recipiendis et non recipiendis, ed. Ernst von Dobschütz, *TU* 38.4. Leipzig, 1912.

DOXOGRAPHI GRAECI
ed. Hermann Diels. 3rd ed., Berlin, 1958.

EPIPHANIUS OF SALAMIS
Ancoratus und Panarion I–III, ed. Karl Holl, *GCS.* Leipzig, 1915, 1922–33.

ERMENRICH OF ELLWANGEN
Epistola ad Grimaldum, ed. Ernst Dümmler, *MGH, Epistolae* 2 (Karolini Aevi 3; Berlin, 1899), 534–579.

EUCHERIUS OF LYONS
Formulae and *Instructiones,* ed. Carl Wotke, *CSEL* 31, 1894.

EUGIPPIUS
Excerpta ex operibus S. Augustini, ed. Pius Knöll, *CSEL* 9.1, 1885.

EUSEBIUS OF CAESAREA
Die Kirchengeschichte, ed. Eduard Schwartz and Theodor Mommsen, in *Eusebius Werke* II.1–3, *GCS* 9.1–3. Berlin, 1903, 1908–9.
Die Praeparatio Evangelica I–II, ed. Karl Mras, in *Eusebius Werke* VIII, *GCS.* Berlin, 1954, 1956.

FAUSTINUS
De trinitate sive de fide contra Arianos, PL 13.37–80.

GESTA COLLATIONIS CARTHAGINIENSIS of 411
PL XI; ed. Serge Lancel, *Actes de la conférence de Carthage en 411,* I–II. (Sources Chrétiennes.) Paris, 1972.

GESTA PURGATIONIS of Sixtus III (432–440)
Mansi V.1061–1068.

GLOSSARIA LATINA IUSSU ACADEMIAE BRITANNICAE EDITA
ed. W. M. Lindsay. Paris, 1926.

GREGORY I see PAPAL DIPLOMATIC DOCUMENTS.

GREGORY OF NYSSA
Commentarius in Canticum Canticorum, ed. Hermann Langerbeck. Leiden, 1960.
De deitate filii et spiritus sancti et in Abraham, PG 46.

HIERONYMUS
Adversus Jovinianum, PL 23.211–338 (221–352).
Commentarii in Danielem, ed. Franciscus Glorie, *CCL* 75A, 1964.

Contra Vigilantium, PL 23.339–352 (353–368).

Epistulae I–III, ed. Isidor Hilberg, *CSEL* 54–56, 1910–18.

Liber quaestionum hebraicarum in Genesim, after Paul de Lagarde's edition of 1866, *CCL* 72, 1959.

HINCMAR OF REIMS

De presbyteris criminosis, PL 125.

Epistolae, pars prior, ed. Ernst Perels, *MGH, Epistolae* 7, fasc. I (Karolini Aevi 6, fasc. I; Berlin, 1939), 1–228.

ISIDORE OF SEVILLE

De differentiis rerum, PL 83.69–98.

De ecclesiasticis officiis, PL 83.737–826.

De fide catholica, PL 83.449–538.

De ortu et obitu patrum, PL 83.129–150.

Etymologiae sive Origines Libri XX, ed. W. M. Lindsay, *SCBO,* 1911.

Quaestiones in Vetus Test., PL 83.204–424.

Sententiae, PL 83.537–737.

JEROME see HIERONYMUS.

JEROME OF JERUSALEM

dialogue, fragment, Mansi XII.1072.

JESSE OF AMIENS

Epistola de baptismo, PL 105.781–793.

JOHANNIS VIII REGISTRUM see PAPAL DIPLOMATIC DOCUMENTS.

JOHN OF DAMASCUS

De imaginibus, oratio I–III, PG 94.

JOHN MOSCHUS

Pratum Spirituale, PG 87.

LECTIONARIES see LITURGICAL SERVICE BOOKS.

LEIDRAD OF LYONS

Liber de sacramento baptismi, PL 99.853–884.

LIBER DIURNUS ROMANORUM PONTIFICUM

ed. Th. von Sickel. Wien, 1884.

Gesamtausgabe, ed. Hans Foerster. Bern, 1958.

LITURGICAL SERVICE BOOKS

Antiphonaries:

Antiphonale missarum sextuplex, ed. R.-J. Hesbert. Bruxelles, 1935.

Corpus Antiphonalium Officii, see Abbreviations: *CAO.*

Frankish Antiphonary of Compiègne, see Abbreviations: *AC.*

Mozarabic Antiphonary of León, see Abbreviations: *AL.*

Antiphonarium Mozarabicum de la Catedral de León, editado por los *PP. Benedictinos de Silos.* León, 1928.

Antifonario Visigótico Mozárabe de la Catedral de León. (Monumenta Hispaniae Sacra, ser. liturgica V,2.) Madrid, 1953. (Facsim. edition of MS); text edition of 1959 see under Abbreviations: *AL.*

Lectionaries:

Liber Commicus I–II, ed. Justo Pérez de Urbel and Atilano González y Ruiz-Zorrilla. (Mon. Hisp. Sacra, ser. lit. II.) Madrid, 1950, 1955.

Le Lectionnaire de Luxeuil I–II, ed. D. P. Salmon. (Collectanea bibl. latina 7 and 9.) Rome, 1944, 1947.

André Wilmart, "Le Lectionnaire d'Alcuin," *Ephemerides liturgicae* 51 (1937), 137–197.

Sacramentaries:

Antoine Chavasse, *Le sacramentaire Gélasien (Vaticanus Reginensis 316).* (Bibliothèque de Theologie IV,1.) Paris, 1958.

Jean Deshusses, *Le Sacramentaire Grégorien: Ses principales formes d'après les plus anciens manuscrits.* (Spicilegium Friburgense 16.) Fribourg, Suisse, 1971.

Alban Dold and Leo Eizenhöfer, *Das Irische Palimpsest Sakramentar in CLM 14429.* (Texte und Arbeiten 53–54.) Beuron, 1964.

Alban Dold, *Das Sakramentar im Schabcodex M 12 Sup. der Bibliotheca Ambrosiana.* (Texte und Arbeiten I.43.) Beuron, 1952.

Marius Férotin, *Le Liber Mozarabicus Sacramentorum et les Manuscrits Mozarabes.* Paris, 1912.

MACROBIUS

Commentarii in somnium Scipionis, ed. Iacobus Willis, *BSGRT*, 1963.

MARTIANUS CAPELLA

ed. Adolf Dick, *BSGRT*, 1925; with addenda by Jean Préaux, 1969.

MAXENTIUS OF AQUILEIA

Collectanea antiquis ritibus baptismi, PL 106.

OPTATUS OF MILEVE

Opera, ed. Carl Ziwsa, *CSEL* 26, 1893.

ORIGEN

Homilien zum Hexateuch in Rufins Übersetzung, ed. W. A. Baehrens. (*Origenes Werke* VI and VII.2; *GCS*.) Leipzig, 1920–21.

Frederick Field, ed., *Origenis Hexaplorum quae supersunt* I–II. Oxford, 1875.

PAPAL DIPLOMATIC DOCUMENTS

Gregorii I papae Registrum Epistolarum, ed. Paul Ewald and L. M. Hartmann, *MGH, Epistolae* 1–2; Berlin, 1891–99; reprint 1957.

Codex Carolinus, ed. Wilhelm Gundlach, *MGH, Epistolae Merowingici et Karolini Aevi* 1 (Epistolae 3; Berlin, 1892), 469–657.

Hadrian I to Constantine VI and Irene, see Abbreviations: *JE* 2448.

Hadrian I to Tarasius of Constantinople, *JE* 2449, Mansi XII.1077C–1084D.

Hadrian I to Charlemagne see Abbreviations: *JE* 2483.

Nicholae I papae epistolae, ed. Ernst Perels, *MGH, Epistolae* 6 (Karolini Aevi 4; Berlin, 1925), 257–690.

Hadriani II Papae Epistolae, ed. Ernst Perels, *MGH, Epistolae* 6 (Karolini Aevi 4; Berlin, 1925), 691–765.

Johannis VIII Papae Registrum, ed. Erich Caspar, *MGH, Epistolae* 7 (Karolini Aevi 5; Berlin, 1928), 1–333.

Regesta Pontificum Romanorum, see Abbreviations: Jaffé, *Reg.*

PAULINUS OF AQUILEIA

Contra Felicem Urgellitanum, PL 99.

Liber de salutaribus documentis, PL 140.

PHILO OF ALEXANDRIA
Philonis Opera, ed. Paul Wendland and Leopold Cohn, II, IV. Berlin, 1897, 1902.

PHILO OF KARPASIA
Comment. on the Canticles, PG 40.

PHILOPONUS
In Aristotelis Categorias Comment., ed. Adolf Busse, *CAG* XIII. Berlin, 1898.

PORPHYRIUS
Isagoge, ed. Adolf Busse, *CAG*, IV.1. Berlin, 1887. See also BOETHIUS.

PSEUDEPIGRAPHORUM FRAGMENTA QUAE SUPERSUNT GRAECA
ed. A. M. Denis. Leiden, 1970.

PSEUDO-AUGUSTINUS follows AUGUSTINUS.

PSEUDO-VIGILIUS follows VIGILIUS.

REGESTA of the Emperors at Constantinople, see Abbreviations: Dölger, *Reg.*

REGESTA IMPERII
ed. J. F. Böhmer and E. Mühlbacher: *Die Regesten des Kaiserreiches unter den Karolingern, 751–918*. 2nd ed., Innsbruck, 1908.

REGESTA of the Patriarchs of Constantinople, see Abbreviations: Grumel, *Reg.*

REGESTA PONTIFICUM ROMANORUM see Abbreviations: Jaffé, *Reg.*

RUFINUS OF AQUILEIA
Expositio Symboli, ed. Manlius Simonetti, *CCL* 20, 1961; translator of Origen, *Homilies*, see above.

SACRAMENTARIES see LITURGICAL SERVICE BOOKS.

SEPTUAGINTA see BIBLIA SACRA.

SEVERIANUS OF GABALA
De legislatore, PG 56.
De sigillis librorum, PG 63.
In lavationem quintae feriae, ed. Antoine Wenger, *Revue des études byzantines* 25 (1967), 219–234.

STEPHEN OF BOSTRA
De imaginibus sanctorum, fragment, Mansi XII.1069.

SUETONIUS
Reliquiae, ed. August Reifferscheid, *BSGRT*, 1860.

TERTULLIAN
De anima, ed. J. H. Waszink. Amsterdam, 1947.

THEODULPH OF ORLÉANS
De ordine baptismi, PL 105.
De spiritu sancto, PL 105.

VETUS LATINA see BIBLIA SACRA.

VICTORINUS OF PETTAU
Commentarii in Apoc., *recensio Hieronymiana*, ed. Iohann Haussleiter, *CSEL* 49, 1916.

VIGILIUS OF THAPSUS
Adversus Eutychetem, PL 62.95–154.
Contra Arianos, Sabellianos, Photinianos dialogus, PL 62.179–238.
Contra Felicianum Arianum, PL 42.1157–1172.

PSEUDO-VIGILIUS
  Contra Arianos Dialogus, PL 62.155–180.
  Contra Varimadum, ed. Benedictus Schwank, *CCL* 90, 1961.
VITA ALCUINI
  ed. Wilhelm Arndt, *MGH*, *Scriptores* XV.1.
VITA BENEDICTI
  by Ardo, *MGH*, *Scriptores* XV.1.
VITA HADRIANI II
  ed. Augusto Gaudenzi, *Bulletino dell' Istituto storico Italiano* 36 (1916), 297–310.
VITA LEONIS III see Abbreviations: *LP*.
VULGATE see BIBLIA SACRA.

C. Select Bibliography

Note. The sequence in individual listings is determined by the publication date, but an author's major work may be listed first.

ABEL, SIGURD, and SIMSON, BERNHARD. *Jahrbücher des fränkischen Reiches unter Karl dem Grossen* I, 2nd ed., Leipzig, 1888; II, 1883; reprint, Berlin, 1969.

ACARI, P. M. "Un goto critico delle legislazioni barbariche," *Archivio storico italiano* 110 (1952), 3–37.

ADELSON, HOWARD, and BAKER, ROBERT. "The Oath of Purgation of Pope Leo III in 800," *Traditio* 8 (1952), 35–80.

AFFELDT, WERNER. *Die weltliche Gewalt in der Paulus-Exegese*. Göttingen, 1969.

ALAND, KURT. *Die alten Übersetzungen des Neuen Testaments, die Kirchenväterzitate und Lektionare*. Berlin, New York, 1972.

ALEXANDER, P. J. *The Patriarch Nikephorus of Constantinople*. Oxford, 1958.

———. "The Iconoclastic Council of St. Sophia (815) and Its Definition (Horos)," *Dumbarton Oaks Papers* 7 (1953), 35–66.

ALLGEIER, ARTHUR. "Psalmenzitate und die Frage nach der Herkunft der Libri Carolini," *Historisches Jahrbuch der Görresgesellschaft* 46 (1926), 333–353.

ALTANER, BERTHOLD. *Kleine patristische Schriften*, ed. G. Glockmann, *TU* 83; 1967.

AMANN, EMILE. *L'époque carolingienne*. Paris, 1947.

———. "L'Adoptianisme espagnol du VIIIe siècle," *Revue des sciences religieuses* 16 (1936), 281–317.

ANASTOS, M. V. "The Transfer of Illyricum, Calabria, and Sicily to the Jurisdiction of the Patriarchate of Constantinople," in *Silloge Bizantina in onore di Silvio Giuseppe Mercati* (Studi Bizantini e Neoellenici 9; Rome, 1957), 14–31.

ANGLES, HIGINIO. "Die Rolle Spaniens in der mittelalterlichen Musikgeschichte," in *Gesammelte Aufsätze zur Kulturgeschichte Spaniens* 19 (Münster, 1962), 5–13.

BAEHRENS, W. A. *Überlieferung und Textgeschichte der lateinisch erhaltenen Origineshomilien zum Alten Tetsament*, *TU* 42.1; Leipzig, 1916.

BARDY, GUSTAVE. "Sur les anciennes traductions latines de Saint Athanase," *Recherches de science religieuse* 34 (1971), 239–242.

BARNARD, L. W. "The Testimonium Concerning the Stone in the New Testament and in the Epistle of Barnabas," in *Studia Patristica* III, ed. F. L. Cross, *TU* 88 (Berlin, 1964), 306–313.

DÖLGER, FRANZ. *Byzanz und die europäische Staatenwelt.* Ettal, Bavaria, 1953.

DÖRRIES, HERMANN. *De spiritu sancto: Der Beitrag des Basilius zum Abschluss des trinitarischen Dogmas.* (Abh. der Akad. der Wiss. zu Göttingen; phil-hist. Klasse: Dritte Folge 39.) 1939.

DUCHESNE, LOUIS. *Les premiers temps de l'état pontifical.* 2nd ed., Paris, 1904.

DUCHROW, ULRICH. *Sprachverständnis und Biblisches Hören bei Augustin.* (Hermeneutische Untersuchungen 3.) Tübingen, 1965.

DÜRR, KARL. *The Propositional Logic of Boethius.* (Studies in Logic and the Foundations of Mathematics.) Amsterdam, 1951.

DVORNIK, FRANCIS. "Emperors, Popes, and General Councils," *Dumbarton Oaks Papers* 6 (1951), 1–23.

———. *The Photian Schism: History and Legend.* Cambridge, 1948.

ECKHARDT, WILHELM A. "Zur Überlieferung des Pariser Konzils von 825," *Zeitschrift für Kirchengeschichte* 65 (1953–54), 126–128.

EHRHARD, ALBERT. *Überlieferung und Bestand der hagiographischen und homiletischen Literatur der griechischen Kirche* I: *Die Ueberlieferung,* 3 vols, *TU* 50–52; Leipzig, 1937–52.

EHRHARDT, A. "Constantine, Rome and Rabbis," *Bulletin of the John Rylands Library Manchester* 42 (1959), 288–312.

EISSFELDT, OTTO. *The Old Testament. An Introduction.* Trans. by P. A. Ackroyd. New York, Evanston, 1965; reprint, 1966.

FEINE, HANS E. *Kirchliche Rechtsgeschichte.* 5th ed., Köln, Wien, 1972.

———. "Vom Fortleben des römischen Rechts der Kirche," *ZSRG, Kan. Abt.* 73 (1956), 1–24.

FICHTENAU, HEINRICH. *Das karolingische Imperium: Soziale und geistige Problematik eines Grossreiches.* Zürich, 1949.

———. "Karl der Grosse und das Kaisertum," *MIŒG* 61 (1953), 257–333.

———. *Arenga: Spätantike und Mittelalter im Spiegel von Urkundenformeln. MIOEG, Erg. Bd. 18.* Graz, Köln, 1957.

———. *The Carolingian Empire.* Trans. by Peter Munz. (Studies in Mediaeval History IX.) Oxford, 1957.

———. *The Carolingian Empire: The Age of Charlemagne.* Trans. by Peter Munz. New York, Evanston, 1964.

———. *Karl der Grosse und das Kaisertum. Mit einer Einleitung zum Nachdruck.* Wissenschaftliche Buchgemeinschaft. Darmstadt, 1971.

———. "Archive der Karolingerzeit," *Mitteilungen des oesterreichischen Staatsarchivs* 25 (1972), 15–24.

———. *Beiträge zur Mediävistik. Ausgewählte Aufsätze* I–II. Stuttgart, 1975–76.

———. "Bayerns älteste Urkunden," in *Gesellschaft. Kultur. Literatur: Beiträge Luitpold Wallach gewidmet,* ed. Karl Bosl (Monographien zur Geschichte des Mittelalters XI; Stuttgart, 1975), 179–189.

FICKER, GERHARD. *Studien zu Vigilius von Thapsus.* Leipzig, 1897.

FISCHER, BONIFATIUS. "Bibelausgaben des frühen Mittelalters," in *La Bibbia nell' alto medioevo* (Settimane di studio del centro italiano di studi sull' alto medioevo X; Spoleto, 1963), 519–600.

———. "Bibeltext und Bibelreform unter Karl dem Grossen," in *Karl der Grosse* II: *Das Geistige Leben* (Düsseldorf, 1965), 156–216.

——. *Vetus Latina*, see Text Editions Used: *Biblia Sacra*.

FOERSTER, HANS. *Abriss der lateinischen Paläographie*. 2nd ed., Stuttgart, 1963.

FOLZ, ROBERT. *The Coronation of Charlemagne, 25 December 800*. Trans. by J. E. Anderson. London, 1974.

——. *Le Couronnement impérial de Charlemagne*. (Trente journées qui ont fait la France: 25 décembre 800.) Paris, 1964.

FREEMAN, ANN. "Theodulf of Orléans and the Libri Carolini," *Speculum* 32 (1957), 665–705.

——. "Further Studies in the Libri Carolini I–II," *Speculum* 40 (1965), 203–289; "III," *Speculum* 46 (1971), 597–612.

FUHRMANN, HORST. *Einfluss und Verbreitung der pseudoisidorischen Fälschungen*. (Schriften der *MGH* 24.1–3.) Stuttgart, 1972–74.

——. "Konstantinische Schenkung und Silvesterlegende in neuer Sicht," *DA* 15 (1959), 523–540.

——. "Das frühmittelalterliche Papsttum und die Konstantinische Schenkung," in *I problemi dell' Occidente nel secolo VIII*. (Settimane di studio del Centro Italiano di studi sull' alto medioevo XX; Spoleto, 1973), 257–292.

FUNK, F. X. *Didascalia et Constitutiones Apostolorum* I–II. Paderborn, 1905.

——. *Kirchenrechtliche Abhandlungen und Untersuchungen* I–II. Paderborn, 1897.

GAMBER, KLAUS. *Codices liturgici latini antiquiores*. Freiburg, 1963.

GANSHOF, F. L. "La révision de la Bible par Alcuin," *Bibliothèque d'Humanisme et Renaissance* 9 (1947), 7–20.

——. *The Imperial Coronation of Charlemagne: Theories and Facts*. (Glasgow University Publications.) Glasgow, 1949.

——. *Ius Romanum Medii Aevi*, Pars I, 2 b cc alpha (Milano, 1969), 1–43, and *ibid*. beta, pp. 1–33.

——. "Contribution à l'étude de l'application du droit romain et des capitulaires dans la monarchie franque sous les Carolingiens," in *Studi in onore di Edoardo Volterra*. III. Milano, 1969.

——. *The Carolingians and the Frankish Monarchy: Studies in Carolingian History*. Trans. by Janet Sondheimer. Ithaca, N.Y., 1971.

——. "L'Empire Carolingien: Essence et Structure," in *Gesellschaft. Kultur. Literatur: Beiträge Luitpold Wallach gewidmet*, ed. Karl Bosl (Monographien zur Geschichte des Mittelalters XI; Stuttgart, 1975), 191–202.

GERICKE, WOLFGANG. "Das Constitutum Constantini und die Silvester-Legende," *ZSRG, Kan. Abt*. 44 (1958), 342–350.

——. "Konstantinische Schenkung und Silversterlegende in neuer Sicht: Entgegnung und Weiterführung," *ZSRG, Kan. Abt*. 47 (1961), 293–304.

GERO, STEPHEN. "The Libri Carolini and the Image-Controversy," *Greek Orthodox Theological Review* 18 (1973), 7–34.

GIRY, ARTHUR. *Manuel de diplomatique*. 2nd ed., Paris, 1925.

GOUILLARD, JEAN. "Aux origines de l'iconoclasme: Le témoignage de Grégoire III," in *Travaux et mémoires* III (Paris, 1968), 276–305.

GRABAR, ANDRÉ. *L'Empereur dans l'art Byzantin*. Paris, 1936.

——. "Les mosaiques de Germigny-des-Prés," *Cahiers archéologiques* 7 (1954), 171–183.

——. *L'Iconoclasme byzantin: Dossier archéologique*. Paris, 1957.

——. "Mosaics and Mural Painting," in *Early Medieval Painting from the Fourth to the Eleventh Century.* (The Great Centuries of Painting . . . directed by Albert Skira; 1957.)

GRABMANN, MARTIN. *Bearbeitungen und Auslegungen der aristotelischen Logik aus der Zeit von Peter Abaelard bis Petrus Hispanus.* (Abh. der Preuss. Akad. der Wiss., phil.-hist. Klasse) Berlin, 1937. No. 5.

GROS, M. S. "Les fragments Parisiens de l'antiphonaire de Silos," *Revue Bénédictine* 74 (1964), 324–333.

HADOT, PIERRE. "Un fragment du commentaire perdu de Boèce sur les catégories d'Aristote," *Archives d'histoire doctrinale et littéraire du Moyen Age* 34 (1959), 11–27.

HAENDLER, GERT. *Epochen karolingischer Theologie: Eine Untersuchung über die karolingischen Gutachten zum byzantinischen Bilderstreit.* Berlin, 1958.

HALLER, JOHANNES. *Das Papsttum: Idee und Wirklichkeit* I–V. Basel, 1951–53.

HALPHEN, LOUIS. *Charlemagne et l'Empire Carolingien.* Paris, 1949.

HAMPE, KARL. "Hadrians I. Vertheidigung der zweiten nicaenischen Synode gegen die Angriffe Karls des Grossen," *Neues Archiv* 21 (1896), 85–113.

HARNACK, ADOLF. *Geschichte der altchristlichen Litteratur bis Eusebius* I.1. Leipzig, 1893.

——. *Lehrbuch der Dogmengeschichte* II. 4th ed., Tübingen, 1909.

HARTMANN, LUDO M. *Geschichte Italiens im Mittelalter* I–IV. Leipzig, Gotha, 1897–1915.

HAUCK, ALBERT. *Kirchengeschichte Deutschlands* I. 4th ed., Leipzig, 1914; II, 3rd and 4th eds., Leipzig, 1912.

HEFELE, C. J. VON, and LECLERCQ, H. *Histoire des Conciles d'après les documents originaux* I–III. Paris, 1907–9.

HEIL, WILHELM. *Alkuinstudien* I. Düsseldorf, 1970.

HELDMANN, KARL. *Das Kaisertum Karls des Grossen: Theorien und Wirklichkeit.* Weimar, 1928.

HOFMANN, J. B., and SZANTYR, A. *Lateinische Syntax und Stilistik.* (Handb. der Altertumswissenschaft, vol. II of Abt. II, 2.) München, 1972.

HUELSEN, CHRISTIAN. "Osservazioni sulla biografica di Leone III nel Liber Pontificalis," *Rendiconti della pont. accad. rom. di arch.* 1 (1923), 107–119.

HUGLO, MICHEL. "Les *Preces* des graduels aquitains empruntées à la liturgie Hispanique," *Hispania Sacra* 8 (1955), 361–383.

ISAAC, JEAN. *Le Peri Hermeneias en Occident de Boèce à Saint Thomas.* Paris, 1953.

JANIN, R. "Rôle des commissaires impérieux Byzantines dans les Conciles," *Revue des études byzantines* 18 (1960), 97–108.

JUGIE, MARTIN. *Le schisme byzantin: Aperçu historique et doctrinal.* Paris, 1941.

KANTOROWICZ, ERNST H. *Laudes Regiae.* Berkeley, Los Angeles, 1946.

Karl der Grosse: Lebenswerk und Nachleben I–V, ed. Wolfgang Braunfels. Düsseldorf, 1965–68.

KERRIGAN, ALEXANDER. *St. Cyril of Alexandria: Interpreter of the Old Testament.* Rome, 1952.

LADNER, G. B. "The Concept of the Image in the Greek Fathers and the Byzantine Iconoclastic Controversy," *Dumbarton Oaks Papers* 7 (1953), 3–34.

LAISTNER, M. L. W. *Thought and Letters in Western Europe.* London, Ithaca, 1957.

LEONARDI, CLAUDIO. "Le glosse di Anastasio Bibliotecario," *Studi Medievali* ser. III, 8 (1967), 163–182.

LESNE, EMILE. *Histoire de la propriété ecclésiastique en France* IV: *Les Livres, Scriptoria et Bibliothèques.* Lille, 1938.

LEVILLAIN, LEON. "Le couronnement impérial de Charlemagne," *Revue d'histoire de l'Église de France* 18 (1932), 3–19.

LEVISON, WILHELM. *England and the Continent in the Eighth Century.* Oxford, 1946.

——. *Aus Rheinischer und Fränkischer Frühzeit.* Düsseldorf, 1948.

——. See WATTENBACH AND LEVISON below.

LINDHOLM, GUDRUN. *Studien zum mittellateinischen Prosarhythmus.* Stockholm, 1963.

LOENERTZ, R. J. "Actus Sylvestri: Genèse d'une légende," *Revue d'histoire ecclésiastique* 70 (1975), 426–439.

LOEWE, RAPHAEL. "The Medieval History of the Latin Vulgate," in *The Cambridge History of the Bible* II, ed. G. W. H. Lampe. Cambridge, 1969.

LOWE, E. A. *Palaeographical Papers 1907–1965* I–II, ed. Ludwig Bieler. Oxford, 1972.

——. *Codices Latini Antiquiores*, see Abbreviations: Lowe.

MAAS, PAUL. *Kleine Schriften*, ed. Wolfgang Buchwald. München, 1973.

——. *Textual Criticism.* Trans. by B. Flower. Oxford, 1958.

MANGO, CYRIL. *The Homilies of Photius.* Cambridge, 1958.

MANZ, GEORG. *Ausdrucksformen der lateinischen Liturgiesprache.* (Texte und Arbeiten I,1.) Beuron, 1941.

MARTIN, E. J. *A History of the Iconoclastic Controversy.* London, 1930.

MARTINI, G. C. "Le recensioni delle 'Quaestiones Veteris et Novi Testamenti' dell'Ambrosiaster," *Ricerche di storia religiosa* I (1954), 40–62.

MCNEILE, A. H. *An Introduction to the Study of the New Testament.* 2nd ed. by C. S. C. Williams. Oxford, 1953; reprint 1960.

MENTZ, ARTHUR. "Die Tironischen Noten: Eine Geschichte der römischen Kurzschrift," *Archiv für Urkundenforschung* 17 (1942), 261–263, on the *Vaticanus Latinus 7207.*

MERCATI, J. M. "Stephani Bostrani nova de sacris imaginibus fragmenta," in *Opere Minori* I (Studi e Testi 76; 1937), 202–206.

MEYER, H. B. "Zur Stellung Alkuins auf dem Frankfurter Konzil," *Zeitschrift für katholische Theologie* 81 (1959), 455–460.

MICHEL, ANTON. "Die Kaisermacht in der Ostkirche," *Ostkirchliche Studien* 5 (1956), 1–32.

MOMMSEN THEODOR. *Römisches Strafrecht.* Leipzig, 1899.

MORDEK, HUBERT. "Dionysio-Hadriana und Vetus Gallica-historisch geordnetes und systematisches Kirchenrecht am Hofe Karls des Grossen," *ZSRG, Kan. Abt.* 55 (1969), 39–63.

MUNDÓ, ANSCARI M. "La datación de los códices litúrgicos visigóticos Toledanos." *Hispania Sacra* 18 (1965), 1–25.

MUNZ, PETER. *The Origin of the Carolingian Empire.* Leicester, 1960.

NELLESSEN, ERNST. *Untersuchungen zur altlateinischen Überlieferung des ersten Thessalonicherbriefes.* (Bonner Bibl. Beiträge 22.) Bonn, 1965.

NOTTARP, HERMANN. *Gottesurteile* I. Bamberg, 1949.

OHNSORGE, WERNER. "Das Constitutum Constantini und seine Entstehung," in Ohnsorge, *Konstantinopel und der Okzident*. Darmstadt, 1966.

OSTROGORSKY, GEORG. "Rom und Byzanz im Kampf um die Bildverehrung," *Seminarium Kondakovianum* 6 (Prag, 1933), 73–87.

——. *Geschichte des byzantinischen Staates*. 2nd ed., München, 1952.

OTT, LUDWIG. "Das Konzil von Ephesus (431) in der Theologie der Frühscholastik," in *Theologie in Geschichte und Gegenwart: Michael Schmaus zum 60. Geburtstag*, ed. Johann Auer and Hermann Volk (München, 1957), 279–308.

OTTO, STEPHAN. *Die Funktion des Bildbegriffes in der Theologie des 12. Jahrhunderts*. Münster i. W., 1963.

PAOLI, CESARE, and G. C. Bascapè, *Diplomatica*. Firenze, 1963.

PATINO, J. M. MARTÍN. "El Breviarium Mozárabe de Ortiz," *Miscelánea Comillas* 40 (Universidad Pontificia Comillas; Santander, 1963), 205–297.

PATZIG, GÜNTHER. *Die Aristotelische Syllogistik*. (Abh. der Akad. der Wiss. in Göttingen; phil.-hist. Klasse: Dritte Folge, No. 42.) 1959.

PETIT, LOUIS. "Un texte de Saint Jean Chrysostome sur les images," *Echos d'Orient* 11 (1908), 80–81.

PINBORG, JAN. "Das Sprachdenken der Stoa und Augustins Dialektik," *Classica et Medievalia* 23 (1962), 148–177.

PINELL, JORGE M. "Los textos de la antigua liturgia hispánica–fuentes para su estudio," in *Estudios sobre la liturgia mozárabe*, ed. Juan Francisco Rivera Recio (Toledo, 1965), 109–164.

——. "Boletín de Liturgia Hispano-Visigótica, 1949–1956," *Hispania Sacra* 9 (1956), 405–428.

PLÖCHL, WILLIBALD M. *Geschichte des Kirchenrechts* I. Wien, München, 1953.

PRETE, SESTO, ed. *Didascaliae: Studies in Honor of Anselm M. Albareda*. New York, 1961.

RANDEL, DON M. *The Responsorial Psalm Tones for the Mozarabic Office*. (Princeton Studies in Music 3.) Princeton, N.J., 1969.

——. "Responsorial Psalmody in the Mozarabic Rite," *Etudes grégoriennes* 10 (1969), 87–116.

——. *An Index to the Chant of the Mozarabic Rite*. (Princeton Studies in Music 6.) Princeton, N.J., 1973.

ROSCHER, W. H. *Ausführliches Lexikon der griechischen und römischen Mythologie* I, 1. Leipzig, 1884–86.

SAVON, H. "Quelques remarques sur la chronologie des oeuvres de Saint Ambrose," *Studia Patristica* X, ed. F. L. Cross, *TU* 107 (Berlin, 1970), 156–160.

SCHADE, HERBERT. "Die Libri Carolini und ihre Stellung zum Bild," *Zeitschrift für katholische Theologie* 79 (1957), 69–78.

SCHALLER, DIETER. "Die karolingischen Figurengedichte des Cod. Bern. 212," in *Medium Aevum Vivum: Festschrift für Walther Bulst* (Heidelberg, 1960), 22–47.

——. "Philologische Untersuchungen zu den Gedichten Theodulfs von Orléans," *DA* 18 (1962), 13–91.

SCHEIBE, FRIEDRICH-KARL. "Alcuin und die *Admonitio Generalis*," *DA* 14 (1958), 221–229.

——. "Geschichtsbild, Zeitbewusstsein und Reformwille bei Alkuin," *Archiv für Kulturgeschichte* 41 (1959), 35–62.

SCHERMANN, THEODOR. *Die Geschichte der dogmatischen Florilegien vom V.–VIII. Jahrhundert, TU* NF. 13.1; 1904.

SCHMAUS, MICHAEL. *Die psychologische Trinitätslehre des Hl. Augustinus.* (Münsterische Beiträge zur Theologie XI.) Münster i. W., 1927.

SCHNEIDER, HEINRICH. *Die altlateinischen Biblischen Cantica.* (Texte und Arbeiten I, 29–30.) Beuron, 1928.

SCHNITZLER, HERMANN. "Das Kuppelmosaik der Aachener Pfalzkapelle," *Aachener Kunstblätter* 29 (Düsseldorf, 1964), 17–44.

SCHRADE, HUBERT. *Malerei des Mittelalters* I: *Vor- und Frühromanische Malerei.* Köln, 1958.

——. "Zum Kuppelmosaik der Pfalzkapelle und zum Theoderich-Denkmal in Aachen," *Aachener Kunstblätter* 30 (Düsseldorf, 1965), 25–37.

SCHRAMM, PERCY E. *Gesammelte Aufsätze zur Geschichte des Mittelalters* I: *Kaiser, Könige und Päpste.* Stuttgart, 1968.

——. ed., with Wolfgang Braunfels, of *Karl der Grosse* IV: *Das Nachleben.* Düsseldorf, 1967.

SCHRÖDER, RICHARD, and EBERHARD FRH. VON KÜNSSBERG. *Lehrbuch der deutschen Rechtsgeschichte.* 7th ed., Berlin, Leipzig, 1932.

SCHWARTZ, EDUARD. *Gesammelte Schriften* I–V. Berlin, 1938–63.

——. *Der sog. Sermo major de fide des Athanasius,* in SB. der Bayerischen Akad. der Wissenschaften, phil.-hist. Klasse. München, 1924.

——. *Aus den Akten des Konzils von Chalkedon,* (Abh. der Bayer. Akad. der Wiss., 32.2.) München, 1925.

——. *Der Prozess des Eutyches,* in SB. der Bayer. Akad. der Wiss., phil.-hist. Klasse. München, 1929.

——. "Zweisprachigkeit in den Konzilsakten," *Philologus* 88 (1933), 245–253.

——. *Publizistische Sammlungen zum Acacianischen Schisma.* (Abh. der Bayer. Akad. der Wiss. NF. 10.) München, 1934.

——. *ACO see Abbreviations.*

SIEGMUND, ALBERT. *Die Überlieferung der griechischen christlichen Literatur in der lateinischen Kirche.* München, Pasing, 1949.

SPEYER, WOLFGANG. *Die literarische Fälschung im heidnischen und christlichen Altertum.* München, 1971.

STEINACKER, HAROLD. "Die römische Kirche und die griechischen Sprachkenntnisse des Frühmittelalters," *MIOEG* 62 (1954), 28–66.

STEINWENTER, ARTUR. "Der antike kirchliche Rechtsgang und seine Quellen, *ZSRG, Kan. Abt.* 23 (1934), 58–61.

STICKLER, A. M. *Historia iuris canonici latini* I: *Historia fontium.* Turino, 1950.

STIERNON, DANIEL. "Autour de Constantinople IV (869–70)," *Revue des études byzantines* 25 (1967), 155–188.

SZÖVÉRFFY, JOSEF. *Weltliche Dichtungen des lateinischen Mittelalters. Ein Handbuch.* I: *Von den Anfängen bis zum Ende der Karolingerzeit.* Berlin, 1970.

TESSIER, GEORGES. *Diplomatique royale française.* Paris, 1962.

THIELE, WALTER. *Die lateinischen Texte des 1. Petrusbriefes.* Freiburg i. Br., 1965.

ULLMANN, WALTER. "Cardinal Humbert and the Ecclesia Romana," *Studi Gregoriani* IV (1952), 111–127.

——. *The Growth of Papal Government in the Middle Ages.* 3rd ed., London, 1970.

UNTERKIRCHER, FRANZ. *Das Wiener Fragment der Lorscher Annalen.* (Codices Selecti XV.) Graz, 1967.

VAN DEN VEN, PAUL. "La patristique et l'hagiographie au Concile de Nicée de 787," *Byzantion* 25–27 (1955–57), 325–362.

VIVES, JOSÉ. "Fuentes hagiograficos del Antifonario de León," *Archivos Leoneses* 8 (1954), 288–299.

——. See Abbreviations: *AL, OV.*

VOGEL, CYRILLE. *Introduction aux sources de l'histoire du culte chrétien au moyen âge.* Spoleto, 1966.

——. "La réforme liturgique sous Charlemagne," in *Karl der Grosse* II: *Das Geistige Leben* (Düsseldorf, 1965), 217–232.

VOGELS, H. J. *Untersuchungen zum Text der Paulinischen Briefe.* (Bonner Biblische Beiträge 9.) Bonn, 1955.

——. *Das Corpus Paulinum des Ambrosiaster.* (BBB 13.) Bonn, 1957.

——. "Die Überlieferung des Ambrosiasterkommentars zu den Paulinischen Briefen," in *Nachrichten der Akademie der Wiss. zu Göttingen,* phil.-hist. Klasse, 1959, no. 7, 107–142.

——. See Text Editions: AMBROSIASTER.

VON DEN STEINEN, WOLFRAM. "Entstehungsgeschichte der Libri Carolini," *QF* 21 (1929–30), 1–93.

——. "Karl der Grosse und die Libri Carolini: Die Tironischen Randnoten zum Codex Authenticus," *Neues Archiv* 49 (1932), 207–280 (the issue with von den Steinen's study appeared during May 1931).

——. "Der Neubeginn," in *Karl der Grosse* II: *Das Geistige Leben* (Düsseldorf, 1965), 9–27.

——. "Karl und die Dichter," *ibid.,* 63–94.

VON HECKEL, RUDOLF. "Das päpstliche und sicilianische Registerwesen," *Archiv für Urkundenforschung* 1 (1908), 371–511.

WALLACH, BARBARA P. *Lucretius and the Diatribe against the Fear of Death: De Rerum Natura III 830–1094.* (Mnemosyne, Supplementum quadragesimum.) Leiden, 1976.

——. "Bibliographie der Schriften von L. Wallach," in *Gesellschaft. Kultur. Literatur: Beiträge Luitpold Wallach gewidmet,* ed. Karl Bosl (Monographien zur Geschichte des Mittelalters, XI; Stuttgart, 1975), 279–289.

WALLACH, LUITPOLD. *Alcuin and Charlemagne: Studies in Carolingian History and Literature.* (Cornell Studies in Classical Philology 32.) Ithaca, N.Y.; Cornell University Press, 1959.

——. *Alcuin and Charlemagne.* Amended edition. New York and London; Johnson Reprint Corporation, 1968.

——. ed. *The Classical Tradition: Literary and Historical Studies in Honor of Harry Caplan.* Ithaca, N.Y.; Cornell University Press, 1966.*

——. Editor. *The Classical Tradition: Literary and Historical Studies in Honor of Harry Caplan.* Oxford University Press. London, 1967.

* The references to this work in the present volume are always to the American edition.

——. "Amicus amicis, inimicus inimicis," *Zeitschrift für Kirchengeschichte* 52 (1933), 614–615.

——. "Moses ben Kalonymos und Paschasius Radbertus?" *Monatsschrift für Geschichte und Wissenschaft des Judentums* 77 (1933), 462–463.

——. "The Origin of Testimonia Biblica in Early Christian Literature," *Review of Religion* 8 (1944), 130–136.

——. "Charlemagne's *De litteris colendis* and Alcuin: A Diplomatic-Historical Study," *Speculum* 26 (1951), 288–305; reprinted in *Alcuin and Charlemagne*, Chapter XI.

——. "Charlemagne and Alcuin: Diplomatic Studies in Carolingian Epistolography," *Traditio* 9 (1953), 127–154; reprinted in *Alcuin and Charlemagne*, Part III, Chapter IX.

——. "Charlemagne's *Libri Carolini* and Alcuin," *Traditio* 9 (1953), 143–149; reprinted in *Alcuin and Charlemagne*, Chapter IX, Part IV, pp. 169–177.

——. "Alcuin on Sophistry," *Classical Philology* 50 (1955), 259–261.

——. "The Genuine and the Forged Oath of Pope Leo III," *Traditio* 11 (1955), 37–63; reprinted with additions in the present volume as Chapter XV.

——. "The Roman Synod of December 800 and the Alleged Trial of Leo III," *Harvard Theological Review* 49 (1956), 123–142; reprinted with substantial additions in the present volume as Chapter XVI.

——. "A Manuscript of Tours with an Alcuinian Incipit," *Harvard Theological Review* 51 (1958), 255–261.

——. "The Unknown Author of the *Libri Carolini*: Patristic Exegesis, Mozarabic Antiphons, and the *Vetus Latina*," in *Didascaliae: Studies in Honor of Anselm M. Albareda*, ed. Sesto Prete (New York, 1961), 469–515; pp. 469–485 are reprinted in the present volume as Introduction to Part Two and as Chapter III; pp. 486–515 are dealt with in Chapter XI.

——. "The Greek and Latin Versions of II Nicaea and Hadrian I's *Synodica* of 785 (*JE* 2448)," *Traditio* 22 (1966), 103–125; reprinted in the present volume as Chapter I.

——. "The *Libri Carolini* and Patristics, Latin and Greek: Prolegomena to a Critical Edition," in *The Classical Tradition: Literary and Historical Studies in Honor of Harry Caplan*, ed. L. Wallach (Ithaca, N.Y., 1966), 451–498; reprinted in the present volume as Chapter IV with the newly added sections E1, F1, Q, and R.

——. "Ambrosii verba retro versa e translatione Graeca," *Harvard Theological Review* 65 (1972), 171–189; reprinted in the present volume as Chapter V.

——. "Ambrosiaster und die *Libri Carolini*," *DA* 29 (1973), 197–205; the English original of this German translation is published in the present volume as Chapter VI together with some additions.

——. "The Testimonia of Image-Worship in Hadrian I's Synodica of 785 (*JE* 2448)," in *Geschichte in der Gesellschaft: Festschrift für Karl Bosl*, ed. F. Prinz *et al.* (Stuttgart, 1974), 409–435; reprinted in the present volume as Chapters II and VII, and as section Q of Chapter IV.

——. Review of Arthur Kleinclausz, *Alcuin* (Annales de l'Université de Lyon, IIIe sér., Lettres, fasc. 15; Paris, 1948), in *Speculum* 24 (1949), 587–590, with remarks on the *Libri Carolini*.

——. Review of E. S. Duckett, *Alcuin, Friend of Charlemagne: His World and His Work* (New York, 1951), in *Speculum* 27 (1952), 102–106, with remarks on the *Libri Carolini*.

——. Review of Wilhelm Wattenbach and Wilhelm Levison, *Deutschlands Geschichtsquellen im Mittelalter;* II: *Die Karolinger vom Anfang des 8. Jahrhunderts bis zum Tode Karls des Grossen.* Bearbeitet von Wilhelm Levison und Heinz Löwe (Weimar, 1953), in *Speculum* 29 (1954), 820–825, with a discussion of the *Libri Carolini*.

——. Review of *Karl der Grosse: Lebenswerk und Nachleben* I–IV, ed. Wolfgang Braunfels *et al.* Düsseldorf, 1965–67, in *American Historical Review* 73 (1967), 115–116; 74 (1968), 132–133.

——. Review of J. D. A. Ogilvy, *Books Known to the English, 507–1066* (Cambridge, Mass. 1967), in *Journal of English and Germanic Philology* 68 (1969), 156–61.

——. " Charlemagne's Libri Carolini, critically edited with Introduction and Notes." (Prepared for future publication.)

——. "The Syllogisms of the Libri Carolini: Aristoteles Latinus and Alcuin." (Prepared for future publication.)

——. "A textual falsification in a lost Hilary Codex from Charlemagne's Court Library," in *Studies in Honor of Charles W. Jones.* (To appear in 1978.)

WATTENBACH [Wilhelm] and LEVISON, WILHELM. *Deutschlands Geschichtsquellen im Mittelalter: Vorzeit und Karolinger* I–V. Weimar, 1952–1973: I, ed. Wilhelm Levison, cur. Walther Holtzmann, 1952; II, ed. W. Levison and Heinz Loewe, 1953; III–V, ed. H. Loewe, 1957, 1963, 1973. I–III, reviewed by L. Wallach, *Speculum* 29 (1954), 131–137, 820–825, 34 (1959), 343–344.

WIEGAND, FRIEDRICH. *Die Stellung des apostolischen Symbols im kirchlichen Leben des Mittelalters.* Leipzig, 1899; reprint Aalen, 1972.

WILLIAMS, SCHAFER. *Codices Pseudo-Isidoriani.* (Monumenta iuris canonici, ser. C: Subsidia 3.) New York, 1971.

WILMART, ANDRÉ. "Un florilège carolingien sur le symbolisme des cérémonies du baptême," in *Analecta Reginensia* (Studi e Testi 59, Città del Vaticano; 1933), 153–179.

WITKE, CHARLES. *Latin Satire: The Structure of Persuasion.* Leiden, 1970.

WOLF, GUNTER. *Zum Kaisertum Karls des Grossen: Beiträge und Aufsätze.* (Wege der Forschung 38.) Darmstadt, 1972.

WOLFF, PHILIPPE. "L'Aquitaine et ses marges," in *Karl der Grosse* I: *Persönlichkeit und Geschichte* (Düsseldorf, 1965), 269–306.

ZELLINGER, JOHANNES. *Studien zu Severian von Gabala.* (Münsterische Beiträge zur Theologie 8.) Münster i. W., 1926.

ZELZER, MICHAELA. "Zur Sprache des Ambrosiaster," *Wiener Studien* 83 (1970), 196–213.

ZIMMERMANN, HARALD. "Papstabsetzungen des Mittelalters I: Die Zeit der Karolinger," *MIOEG* 69 (1961), 1–84.

——. "Valentin Ernst Löscher, das finstere Mittelalter und dessen Saeculum obscurum," in *Gesellschaft. Kultur. Literatur: Beiträge Luitpold Wallach gewidmet,* ed. Karl Bosl (Stuttgart, 1975), 259–277.

General Index

Note. Frequently cited proper names are listed selectively, but always judiciously. With a few exceptions, references to footnotes are noted by page number alone.

Diplomatic Studies in
Latin and Greek Documents
from the Carolingian Age

Designed by R. E. Rosenbaum.
Composed by Syntax International Pte. Ltd.
in 11 point Monophoto Baskerville 169, 2 points leaded,
with display lines in Monophoto Baskerville.
Printed offset by Vail-Ballou Press, Inc.
on Warren's Olde Style Wove, 60 pound basis.
Bound by Vail-Ballou Press in
Joanna Arrestox A book cloth,
with stamping in All Purpose Gold foil.
Illustrations printed by Art Craft of Ithaca, Inc.

Library of Congress Cataloging in Publication Data
(For library cataloging purposes only)

Wallach, Luitpold.
    Diplomatic studies in Latin and Greek documents from the Carolingian Age.

    Bibliography: p.
    Includes index.
        1. Council of Nicaea, 2d, 787,   2. Libri Carolini.
3. Idols and images—Worship.   4. Leo III, Saint, pope,
d. 816.   I. Title.
BX830787.W34   270.3   76-28027
ISBN 0-8014-1019-3